A Study of
FUTURE
WORLDS

PREFERRED WORLDS FOR THE 1990'S

Saul H. Mendlovitz, General Editor

On the Creation of a Just World Order
Preferred Worlds for the 1990's
edited by Saul H. Mendlovitz

Footsteps into the Future
Diagnosis of the Present World and a Design
for an Alternative
Rajni Kothari

A World Federation of Cultures
An African Perspective
Ali A. Mazrui

A Study of Future Worlds
Richard A. Falk

The True Worlds
A Transnational Perspective
Johan Galtung

A program of the World Order Models Project.
Sponsored by the Institute for World Order, Inc.
New York, New York.

A Study of
FUTURE
WORLDS

Richard A. Falk

THE FREE PRESS
A Division of Macmillan Publishing Co., Inc.
New York

The Free Press
A Division of Macmillan Publishing Co., Inc.
866 Third Avenue, New York, N.Y. 10022

Collier–Macmillan Canada Ltd.

Library of Congress Catalog Card Number: 74-10139

Printed in the United States of America

printing number
1 2 3 4 5 6 7 8 9 10

Library of Congress Cataloging in Publication Data

Falk, Richard A
  A Study of future worlds.

  (Preferred worlds for the 1990's series)
  Includes bibliographical references and index.
  1. International organization. 2. International relations. I. Title.
  JX1954.F25   341.2   74-10139
  ISBN 0-02-910060-7
  ISBN 0-02-910080-1(pbk.)

The publication of this volume has been made possible by collaboration among the following publishers:

The Free Press
A Division of Macmillan Publishing Co., Inc.
New York, N.Y.

Ghana Publishing Corporation
Accra, Ghana

North-Holland Publishing Company
Amsterdam, The Netherlands

Orient Longman Limited
New Delhi, India

The poem on page 415 is from Allen Ginsberg, "Howl," in *Howl & Other Poems*, San Francisco: City Lights, 1956, page 9. Copyright © 1956, 1959 by Allen Ginsberg. Reprinted by permission of CITY LIGHTS BOOKS.

So that my children

and your children

and all children

might live

in a future world

that is peaceful and fair

that is mindful

of nature

and that is hopeful

about the

material and spiritual

development

of humankind

CONTENTS

One
POINTS OF DEPARTURE

Two
TRENDS AND PATTERNS IN WORLD SOCIETY

Three
DESIGNING A NEW WORLD ORDER

Four
DESIGNING A PREFERRED WORLD POLITY

Five
THE TRANSITION PROCESS

Six
THE WORLD ECONOMY AS A WORLD ORDER DIMENSION:
SELECTED ASPECTS

Seven
AMERICA'S STAKE IN GLOBAL REFORM

LIST OF ILLUSTRATIONS

LIST OF TABLES

GENERAL INTRODUCTION

I

Scholars and intellectuals, like human beings in other walks of life, need to interpret and come to grips with the crises plaguing the contemporary global political and social system. Indeed their obligation to do so may be a particularly special and important one. They are, or are supposed to be, able to discern trends, detect signals warning us of emerging social problems, think seriously and critically about alternative solutions and possible future worlds, as well as recommend strategies for achieving those solutions and worlds. One would think that this somewhat crucial albeit relatively precious sector of the world's population, more than others, is capable of avoiding too firm an anchor in the particulars of what is. "Reality" may, for a number of reasons, constrain and overwhelm the thinking and imagination of those who have to struggle for daily existence. But surely professional thinkers and analysts have a mandate to look beyond the obvious, the immediate, and to see the possibilities open for reform and improvement.

For reasons that I suspect to be familiar to most of us, social scientists have yet to meet this challenge adequately. There is, initially, the bias in the social sciences against work that explicitly utilizes preferences and values as a way of defining problems to be investigated, and as a standard to be used for what will be considered an adequate solution to the problems. Research that deviates from the confines of a perspective that is viewed by its adherents as empirical and scientific is either dismissed as ideological or as being an exercise in wishful thinking. In this view, description is a proper social science concern, while prescription is not. Second, the same tradition's narrow sense of realism and empiricism operates quite decisively to inhibit futuristic thinking and orientation. If one wants maximum certainty and minimum speculation, concern with what prevails is preferable to what might or will be. If some social scientists manage to get over their reluctance to engage in futuristic thinking, their work generally confines itself to relatively simple extrapolations of current trends. The future then becomes a mere extension of the present, as though humanity has little or no ability to shape the future in preferred directions.

Two additional factors are also to blame for the lack of creative thinking about the contemporary world order system and its major crises—e.g., war, social injustice, widespread poverty, ecological imbalance, and alienation—as well as alternative systems more compatible with a humane and just world order. The crises are global in scope, yet most social scientists who pay attention to them are wedded to an analysis in which the nation–state system informs their definitions and solutions to global problems. At the same time it is becoming increasingly clear that most of the major problems confronting humankind defy national solutions and perspectives, and are generally aggravated, if not directly caused, by the imperatives of national sovereignty.

Finally, creative thinking about the globe, its crises, and future is hindered by an element which is inherent in the nature of social knowledge itself and the extent to which it is culture-bound and geographically circumscribed. Even the most sympathetic and globally-minded scholar can only perceive the world from a particular angle and perspective; his (or her) roots in a particular nation, race, or class help determine and shape the choice of the problems—and the proposed remedies to them—that concern that person. Certain cultural assumptions, values, and concerns may sensitize a person to some problems at the same time they cause the individual to neglect a number of different problems that other people in other places deem important. Or, the same global problem or phenomenon is frequently interpreted in different ways by observers from different cultures. Given the global dimensions of our major world order concerns, these truisms of the sociology of knowledge recommend in favor of transnational and cross-cultural perspectives being brought to bear upon the questions and problems that concern us. In short, it speaks against ethnocentric knowledge and research. While this point has long been well known, there has been much too little social science research carried out in this fashion. The work of other scholars may be available, but collaborative research across cultures and world views is yet to be widely practiced.

II

A Study of Future Worlds is one book in the series of volumes entitled *Preferred Worlds for the 1990's* resulting from a transnational research enterprise, the World Order Models Project. Because the World Order Models Project (WOMP) is likely to be the forerunner of many more such transnational and global enterprises, it seems appropriate to say something about its genesis, development, and future.

WOMP was initially conceived in response to pedagogical needs related to the study of the problem of the elimination of war as a human social institution. The individuals involved at the outset of this program brought to it a seriousness one associates with those individuals and groups who, between the eighteenth and nineteenth centuries, advocated and participated in the global movement to abolish slavery, or with those persons in this century who have been participating in the dismemberment of colonialism and imperialism.

To put the matter forthrightly, it was a conscious "political" act, based on a theory of social change which reasoned that most individuals in the globe, including political leadership, were encapsulated in a view of the world in which war, while perhaps unfortunate, was a necessary and permanent ingredient of human society. Thus the decision to enlist the energies of educational structures throughout the globe was partially based on the notion that the seriousness of the idea might be legitimated if the academic community throughout the world were to give it the status of a subject matter of discipline, or at least admit it was the kind of social problem which was amenable to rational analysis. Concomitantly and certainly as important as legitimation, was the possibility of enlisting the talent and skills of the academic community in the research and education necessary for a successful global peace movement.

And so it was in 1966 that we began to examine how to enroll volunteers so that our educational effort would merit serious attention by scholars and educators throughout the globe. WOMP emerged as an answer.

The notion which we began to pursue was that if we were to get outstanding scholars as well as thoughtful individuals throughout the globe to become involved in the problem of war prevention, it would be necessary that they contribute actively in the inquiry. We decided to invite groups of scholars in various parts of the world to direct nationally or regionally based inquiries into the problem of war prevention. We did not proceed very far in our recruitment of individuals for the project when it soon became clear that the subject matter would have to be expanded to include the related problems of economic well being and social justice, if we were to generate a world interest in this inquiry.

There were two reasons advanced for the inclusion of these problem areas. To begin with, there were many persons who argued that it was impossible to deal adequately with war prevention without taking into account poverty and social injustice; that as an empirical matter, these matters were so inextricably interwoven, they should be seen as part of the definition of the problem of war prevention. More importantly, however, it became increasingly clear that while peace, in the sense of the elimination of international violence, might have a very high priority with individuals in the industrialized sector of the globe, economic well being and social justice received a much higher rating in the Third World. When we discussed these three problems, war, poverty, and social injustice, as they persisted in national, regional, and global context, and proposed examining them in the light of the next three decades, with particular reference to the countervailing values of peace, economic well being and social justice, virtually all the scholars we approached agreed to participate in the project.

We held the first meeting of the World Order Models Project in New Delhi in February 1968. At that time five research groups had been organized, representing West Germany, Latin America, Japan, India, and North America. Groups representing Africa, the Soviet Union, and some Scandinavian scholars who preferred to present a non-territorial perspective, joined in subsequent years. More recently we benefited from the involvement in the project of a Chinese as well as a Middle Eastern scholar. One meeting was held with a group of economists organized by Jagdish Bhagwati of the Massachusetts Institute of Technology. This resulted in the first WOMP book, *Economics and World Order, From the 1970's to the 1990's* (Macmillan, 1972). A second book, *Africa and World Affairs* (The Third Press, 1973) edited by Ali Mazrui and Hasu Patel resulted from a conference organized by the African research group. All together, some nine meetings have been held in various parts of the world: India, Japan, East Africa, Western Europe, United States, and Latin America.

The results of nearly seven years of individual and collaborative work are only partially represented by this and the other WOMP volumes. We set out to create the basic instructional materials needed for a worldwide educational movement whose ultimate thrust would be global reform. No one is more aware than we are today of how many more and different materials still need to be created and disseminated. We set out to do normative social research that was at one and the same time oriented to the future, interdisciplinary, and focused on the design of social change actions, policies, and institutions. No one realizes more than the WOMP research groups how difficult it is to do this task with competence, combined with true imagination and intellectual power.

The project has fundamentally affected the personal and professional commitments of virtually everyone who participated in it. It is fair to say that what started out for almost all the participants as a short term and secondary interest has now become a lifetime scholarly and political vocation. At a meeting of the Directors of the World Order Models Project in Bogotá, Colombia, over the New Year period in 1974, the group decided to collaborate on a series of enterprises which they hope will continue to promote research, education, and a genuinely transnational social movement to realize the world order values of peace, economic well being, social justice, and ecological stability. The first of these ventures will be a transnational journal, *Alternatives,* of which Rajni Kothari will be editor, with a distinguished editorial board of some two dozen scholars throughout the globe.

Second, a number of the individuals associated with WOMP have assumed the responsibility for issuing an annual State of the Globe Message. This Message will attempt to evaluate local, regional, and global trends, rating the extent to which the world order values have been diminished or realized during the preceding year, and to make recommendations as to what ought to be done in the coming years. The State of the Globe Message, issued by a group of transnational scholars independent of any formal structures of authority, should be seen as complementary to the messages which are now coming from such formal sources.

Third, we have embarked upon a modest but significant research program for measuring world order indicators based on our values, which we hope will support the State of the Globe Message and provide alternative ways for social scientists to think about and measure the quality of social life. In addition, there will be a series of transnational seminars for scholars, public figures in all professions, expanded formal educational programming, and the beginning of a mass public education movement on a global basis. All of this programming has already begun in some form and we hope will involve constructive criticism, support, and participation by many people throughout the globe.

III

The world order images and change strategies presented in these WOMP books are strikingly diverse, reflecting the different methods, intellectual styles, and cultural/political backgrounds of their authors. Although we were able to agree on a way of stating world order problems, and establish a framework of value criteria for what we considered to be appropriate solutions, as well as devise a common methodology, it certainly would be premature to attempt to provide a consensus statement for these various manuscripts. There were, however, a set of guidelines which were stated with some precision early in the project; despite repeated critical examination and elaboration they have remained essentially intact. It seems appropriate to summarize these guidelines so that the volumes might be read and evaluated in their proper context.

WOMP was not principally a "utopian" undertaking, despite our refusal to succumb either to a complacent or a doomsday view of reality. Where our thinking is utopian, it advances what we call *relevant utopias*, that is, world order systems that make clear not only alternative worlds but the necessary transition steps to these worlds. In fact, each author was asked to attempt a diagnosis of the contemporary world order system, make prognostic statements based on that diagnosis, state his *preferred future* world order and advance coherent and viable *strategies of transition* that could bring that future into being. A stringent time frame, the 1990's, served to discipline and focus thought and proposals.

While easy to list, this set of steps impose severe demands on our methodological and creative capacity. It is probably fair to say that we discovered more methodological problems than we were able to solve to our satisfaction. Some of these problems are associated with how to do each of the steps, while others arise from trying to link different steps and to integrate the normative, descriptive, and theoretical modes of thought. In the end, most of the WOMP research groups chose to adopt the more traditional analytic interpretive style of research, rather than the more methodologically sophisticated behavioral science approach. The reasons for this choice varied from outright rejection of the presumed conservative biases of strictly data-based methods to pragmatic considerations of limited time and resources. In essence, we decided it was more important at this time to prepare full world order statements involving an integrated treatment of all the steps than it was to do a more rigorous investigation of only one or two of them.

While a full report on the methodological difficulties we faced shall have to await another occasion, it might be useful if I were to outline here the major problem areas and some questions that arose in the course of our investigation. Let me begin, however, by reiterating that we were able to agree that humanity faced four major problems: war, poverty, social injustice, and environmental decay. We saw these as social problems because we had values—peace, economic well being, social justice, and environmental stability—which, no matter how vaguely operationalized, we knew were not being realized in the real world. Our task then was to develop an analytic frame of reference that would provide us intellectual tools for coming to grips with these problems so as to realize world order values.

There was also general agreement that we should go beyond the nation–state system, at least in terms of the traditional categories applied to it, namely the political, military, economic, and ideological dimensions of foreign policy. Instead of asking how states manipulate their foreign policies along these four dimensions, or even, how they might move the present system to a world order value system, there was general agreement that we would have to use a much broader range of potential actors, including world institutions, transnational actors, international organization, functional activities, regional arrangements, the nation–state, subnational movements, local communities, and individuals. Even here, however, each of the groups placed different emphases, diagnostically, prognostically, and preferentially on the roles of this range of actors.

Second, far more effort than I anticipated was put into clarifying the values implied by these problems and into making some ordered value agenda from which operational strategies or policies could be formulated. Among the points to emerge from these efforts are:

1. The crucial importance of developing global social indicators or operational definitions of value goals.

2. The difficulty and necessity of preparing a set of decision rules for dealing with value conflicts.

3. The need for a unified approach to these problem/value areas and for more data and theory on the interrelationships among them.

4. The extent to which one's personal position on the value ques-

tions influences every other aspect of the world order research process.

5. The importance of maintaining a tension between some operational notions of "world interest" and the deeply-felt value agenda of one's particular social group and geographic region.

Third, a number of issues not associated with standard empirical research emerged because of our emphasis on constructing preferred worlds. In this connection it should be noted that the term *preferred world* came to have a relatively rigorous meaning. Building on the concept of relevant utopia previously stated a preferred world is an image of a reformed world stated in fairly precise behavioral detail, including a description of the transition process from the present to the new system. Since it is possible to depict a range of reformed systems and transition paths, a preferred world is the relevant utopia selected by a proponent because it is most likely to realize his or her value goals. Each of these issues that arose in this context requires separate examination, conceptual and methodological advances, and the testing of a variety of integrated research strategies before we will really be able to move systematically through the steps of world order research to preferred world statements that meet rigorous tests of workability and feasibility. To illustrate:

1. What are appropriate criteria for evaluating workability and feasibility and what are the appropriate testing procedures for each?

2. Notions of time and time horizons are critical to both feasibility and workability, yet both are far more complicated than the simple notion of years and decades. Assumptions about time seem to play a critical role in one's optimism or pessimism about the possibility of fundamental change. Also, time, as a key variable, is surprisingly easy to forget or discount when thinking about such things as value and attitude shifts, or reorientations in bureaucratic objectives and procedures.

3. Equally perplexing is the problem of adequately defining the relevant environment and its dynamics within which one's desired changes must take place. The tendency is to define the environment as the nation–state system itself, and to ascribe relatively little destabilizing or fundamental dynamics to it. As noted earlier, this can severely restrict creative thinking about alternative futures and transition processes. But it is not easy to come up with equally detailed and useful alternatives to the nation–state image, so rooted is it in our consciousness. To really examine this question is to open oneself to the most fundamental philosophical and methodological search.

4. On a more mundane level, the presentation of a preferred world in a way that is compelling and persuasive is far more difficult than it

might appear. Like good fiction or poetry, utopia writing is an art attempted by many but achieved by few. It involves crucial choices of style and form. For example, how much and what kind of behavioral detail should be used to describe the workings of the preferred world? What are the differences between revolutionary and reformist rhetoric, and, more importantly, what bearing does this answer have on concrete strategies and programs? How much attention is paid to immediate public issues and how are they made to relate to the preferred future, to explicate the method and perspective of the author?

Finally there was a set of issues which arose from my guidelines that each of the groups be as explicit as possible about the kinds of authority structure, about the formal constitutive order of the world community, that would be needed and preferred, both during the transition period, as well as at the end of this century. That is to say, there was a distinct weighting of institutional–constitutional issues and approaches in my original definition of our task.

I emphasized this approach despite the obvious dangers of formalism essentially for three reasons: first, an institutional approach requires a high degree of specificity and precision and focuses attention on procedures as well as principles; second, this approach leads readily to statements in the form of models with all that that implies for comparability across models and manipulation of parts within them; third, as a form of presentation, constitutional–institutional models can be easily, even powerfully, communicated.

In this connection I should like to acknowledge formally my debt to the book *World Peace Through World Law* (Harvard University Press, 1956, 1962, 1966) by Grenville Clark and Louis B. Sohn. My use of this book as an instructional model and as a source of research hypotheses leads me to conclude that many social scientists, as well as lay people, underestimate the extent to which formal constitutional models can lead to clarification of issues, and perhaps even more important, become a mobilizing instrument for social and political action. I remain convinced of the value of this way of thinking about world order, but the extent to which this view has been resisted, revised and ignored by the WOMP groups will be apparent in these volumes. Within this context, it should also be noted that the individual authors resolve the actors–levels–authority process questions differently. Some of the issues that surfaced during our discussions in this context included:

1. The extent to which an institutional or single actor-oriented conception of the world political system is useful either for understanding how the system is operating, how it might be made to change, or how it could or should operate. Such conceptions seemed to some to stul-

tify imaginative thinking about alternatives and to mask important change potentials in the current system.

2. In thinking about transition, some argued for the "primacy of the domestic factor," i.e., fundamental reform in national societies, particularly within the major countries, preceding global social change. Others argued for the primacy of the global agenda and the critical role of transnational functional and political movements and institutions. This debate identified two further issues needing more attention.

3. Which problems require policy making and review at what level of social organization from the individual to the global? How much centralization and decentralization was appropriate in various substantive arenas? What are the relevant criteria for deciding the appropriate level or mix of levels?

4. What are and what might be the linkages between these levels for purposes of analysis, policy making and practical implementation?

IV

Finally, I wish to state my own view as to the significance of these manuscripts. As I see it, it is necessary to accept seriously not only the rhetoric but the reality of the term "the global village." The fact that the overwhelming majority of humankind understands for the first time in history that human society encompasses the entire globe is a phenomenon equivalent to humankind's understanding that the globe is round rather than flat. This knowledge is having an enormously dramatic impact on the images and attitudes we have with regard to the authority structures of the international community, as well as those of our domestic societies. I should like to state here a conclusion, for which I will not fully argue, but which I believe needs to be articulated for an understanding of the significant global political processes that are now taking place.

It is my considered judgment that there is no longer a question of whether or not there will be world government by the year 2000. As I see it, the questions we should be addressing ourselves to are, how it will come into being—by cataclysm, drift, rational design—and whether it will be totalitarian, benign, or participatory (the probabilities being in that order).

Since the so-called "age of discovery" (a Eurocentric concept which sorely needs modification in this global community), three major historical processes, or if you will, revolutions, have propelled humankind toward global community, and now toward global governance. These processes are the ideological revolution of egalitarianism, the technological and scientific revolution and the closely allied economic–interdependent revolution. It might be noted in passing that of these three, the egalitarian revolution has been least appreciated in recent times, but in fact may account for much of the disorder, dislocation, and social tensions throughout the globe.

These three processes or revolutions have converged in such a fashion that five problems have emerged and been identified as global in nature. War, poverty, social injustice, ecological instability, and alienation or the identity crisis, are recognized as having a planetary scope. It is now generally understood by policy elites and observers of world community processes generally that these problems are closely interrelated and that "solutions" in one area affect the other four areas. Furthermore, despite gross inadequacies if not outright failure of the recent global conferences run by the United Nations around the issues of environment, economic order, food and population, it is now obvious that governance processes and structures will become increasingly a focus of international and global politics.

In short, I believe that global community has emerged and global governance is not far behind. To my mind, this book and the other volumes in the *Preferred Worlds for the 1990's* series is a contribution to the serious dialogue about what will be the normative basis and constitutive structure of the global community. We hope these volumes will contribute to creating the social processes needed for a peaceful and just world order.

September 1974

> Saul Mendlovitz
> Director, World Order
> Models Project

Special Acknowledgment

The Institute for World Order, Inc., would like to thank the Carnegie Endowment for International Peace and the Rockefeller Foundation for the financial support they gave to specific research within the World Order Models Project.

PREFACE

In *A Study of Future Worlds* I have attempted to evolve a comprehensive framework for studying global reform. My objective, in the first instance, is educational—to encourage disciplined inquiry into the future of international relations from an avowed and explicitly normative perspective. The book argues against a value-neutral approach to this subject matter as ethically misleading, politically irresponsible, and historically irrelevant. At the same time, I have tried to understand and present the state system as it operates and to avoid exercises in wishful thinking when considering prospects for global reform. Speculation about global reform has traditionally been marred by tendencies toward moralism and legalism. I believe that drastic types of global reform are both possible and necessary, but that their success depends upon our ability first to comprehend and then to institute a credible politics of transformation. Much of this book is an attempt to close this credibility gap.

My second objective is to move the domains of feeling and action closer to the domain of thought. We need, I believe, a new conception of knowledge that encompasses the processes of man's material, social, and spiritual development. We need better access to our feelings and better outlets for our informed interpretations. In more specific terms, we need a broadly based transnational movement for global reform that seeks both to influence public opinion and to encourage responsiveness from centers of power and wealth. Part of the purpose of this book is to provide an orientation toward feeling and action that can help individuals make up their own minds about the case for global reform.

The world setting is in a state of extraordinary flux. Occurrences which highlight the need for drastic world order reform have become daily fare for the media. Yet the basic challenge remains essentially constant: can we devise humane means to fashion a new system of world order from which a decent form of global society can evolve? Put differently, in this period when the state system is eroding and rapidly being superseded, can we facilitate the transition to a system of world order that is an improvement upon what now exists? What constitutes an improvement is itself a matter of controversy. We make our case for improvement by reference to the four world order values discussed in Chapter I. Even if that case is not persuasive, the more fundamental claim remains that we desperately require at this time "a great debate" on the future of world order. Its outcome in the United States and elsewhere may well mark a decisive moment in the history of our species and our planet.

ACKNOWLEDGMENTS

Over the years of work on this manuscript many people have been implicated in one way or another. Above all others, it is Saul Mendlovitz, as general director and inspirer of the World Order Models Project (WOMP), who influenced the process and the product. He persuaded me to work within the framework of normative futurism, to put aside other claims on my time, and to be mindful, if not altogether respectful, of the schedule of deadlines set for the project as a whole. The whole experience was made possible and plausible by Harry Hollins in his role as leader of the Institute for World Order.

And, really, the Institute for World Order as a whole deserves my deep gratitude. Its sponsorship of WOMP brought about an exciting series of collaborations. First and foremost, the meetings with the seven other research directors over the past five years have been the most valuable learning experience of my life. Second, the several workshops of younger American social scientists devoted to considering preliminary and partial versions of this manuscript gave me more feedback than I could assimilate, but did influence the outcome in major ways (e.g., Chapter VI on the world economy was added).

I wish to express particular thanks to the Sponsoring and Policy Review Committee of WOMP/USA for their assistance. This Committee of distinguished North Americans consisted of the following individuals:

Richard J. Barnet, C. Douglas Dillon, C. Clyde Ferguson, Jr., Frances FitzGerald, James M. Gavin, Arthur J. Goldberg, Mason W. Gross, Ivan L. Head, Theodore M. Hesburgh, George B. Kistiakowsky, Robert H. Knight, Harold D. Lasswell, Robert S. McNamara, Howard C.

Petersen, Edwin O. Reischauer, James W. Rouse, and John F. White. The Committee was chaired by Mr. Dillon for part of the period of the project and by Mr. Knight for the remainder.

With such a variety of backgrounds and viewpoints it is not surprising that meetings of the Committee produced stimulating discussions and provocative suggestions. The book reflects the consultative process that occurred, but at the same time there is no intention to suggest that the Committee or any of its members approve of all the positions taken or conclusions reached, or for that matter, even endorse the general approach taken here to the subject of global reform. Participation as a Committee member implies, really, no more than a willingness to associate oneself with the general endeavor of the World Order Models Project which is to develop educational materials concerned with the future of world order.

I was fortunate to have the benefit of Janet Lowenthal's acute editorial judgment, her energy and enthusiasm, and even her levity, during the final stages of a prolonged effort to domesticate an unwieldy manuscript. No acknowledgment, however ardent, could do justice to the full extent of her contributions, and I am most grateful.

Princeton University has in a variety of ways supported my role in WOMP. I want to thank, in particular, Marver Bernstein who while Dean of the Woodrow Wilson School joined with the Institute of World Order in sponsoring the United States Group in WOMP, made an early, important grant, and provided facilities for meetings of the Sponsoring and Policy Review Committee. I also am most grateful to the Center of International Studies, especially its Director, Cyril E. Black, for providing a stimulating and efficient atmosphere in which to carry on work of this kind. Indeed, under Professor Black's leadership, the Center has founded and evolved a major world order studies program of its own. Among those whose reactions to this work was especially helpful to me I would mention Fouad Ajami, Donald McNemar, and Beverly Woodward. As always, the secretaries of the Center, under the spirited guidance of Jean McDowall, typed the several drafts with customary skill and good spirits. I am especially grateful to June Traube, who has so graciously borne the main burden of my logistical mismanagement in recent years, for benefitting me with her wide range of secretarial and administrative talents.

Finally, my family was at all stages, for better or for worse, involved in this project. As before, my wife Florence has been a strong supporter, really a co-worker, who shares the concerns and the vision that underlie this book. More than in earlier scholarly work, the boundaries between feeling, knowing, and doing have grown blurred, happily so. As is evident in the dedication, my children Dimitri and Noah, so alive to the present and future, provided a continuous rationale for trying harder to build the case for global reform.

LIST OF ABBREVIATIONS

WOMP	World Order Models Project
WOMP/USA	World Order Models Project/United States Proposals
S_0	World Order System at present point of origin, i.e., 1974
S_1	World Order System composed of sovereign states
S_2	A sequel to the state system
$S_{2(WOMP)}$	A sequel to the state system which substantially realizes WOMP values
$S_{2(WOMP/USA)}$	That sequel to the state system deemed by the American group to be the most beneficial form of world order for the realization of WOMP values
$S_1 \longrightarrow S_2$	The process of transition from the state system to a subsequent world order system
t_1	The first stage of transition deemed to involve consciousness raising and consensus formation in relation to WOMP values
t_2	The second stage of transition to $S_{2(WOMP/USA)}$ involving mobilization to implement the consensus emergent from t_1
t_3	The third stage of transition to $S_{2(WOMP/USA)}$ involving the transformation of institutions and structures into a new world order system
WOMP values	V_1, V_2, V_3, and V_4
V_1	Minimization of violence
V_2	Maximization of social and economic well-being
V_3	Maximization of social and political justice (i.e., human rights)
V_4	Maximization of ecological quality (i.e., resource conservation and environmental protection)

Prescript

A NOTE IN ANTICIPATION

In his great prophetic essay "Democratic Vistas," Walt Whitman wrote:

> I say we had best look our times and
> lands searchingly in the face, like a
> physician diagnosing some deep disease.[1]

Such a diagnosis would lead nowhere unless coupled with health-restoring therapies, but diseases of the body politic on a worldwide scale are coming increasingly to be viewed as terminal. The argument of this book is that such despair is unfounded, because a new world order based on peace and justice is not only desirable and necessary but possible, although by no means probable.

In the chapters that follow, we seek to develop appropriate ways of thinking seriously (as opposed to sentimentally or cynically) about the political prospects of global society, and to put forward a set of proposals for accomplishing global reform within a period of several decades. We are convinced of the need for a global framework of thought which is both free of the outmoded stereotypes of statecraft, and yet mindful of the realities of power that now thwart even the most earnest conceptions of global reform. We feel more tentative about the *substance* of our proposals (outlined in Chapters IV and V), as distinguished from their *framework*.

To depict that which has never existed in human affairs and yet endow it with plausibility requires humility as well as political imagination. To quote Walt Whitman again,

> we presume to write, as it were, upon
> things that exist not, and travel by maps
> yet unmade, and a blank.[2]

1

We are overly accustomed to a world of sovereign states in which the best interests of humankind are entrusted to the calculations and wisdom of national governments. But many among us are now convinced that most governments today are, in the main, not disposed to act as the guardians of human well-being, although we do not yet know what to make of this startling reality. Perhaps the ecological strains of an overwrought planet will awaken the human race from a period of dangerous slumber. Perhaps, as people in rich countries shiver through winters with heating oil shortages and endure the inconvenience of the world energy emergency, they will understand that the need and the occasion cry out for a bold course of global reform. Perhaps it is encouraging that as popular a forum of sophisticated comment as *The New Yorker* magazine seems to share this conviction:

> There was a time when the notion of a world
> order was thought to be a utopian vision. We
> can see now that, in many respects, it is a
> hellish necessity. As for man's old dream of
> the world's becoming one, that, whether we
> like it or not, occurred years ago.[3]

While the affluent West is seeking to mitigate the dislocations arising from insufficient oil supplies, much of the rest of the world is more worried about the prospect of a deepening world food crisis. At present, the world food reserve is so low that even one bad harvest year could generate far more widespread hunger and a massive famine.[4]

One salient inference can be drawn: A world system composed of sovereign states cannot deal effectively or equitably with the problems facing humankind. Some form of global integration is needed to facilitate the shaping of policy and the sharing of resources. Without such integration, the difficulties of today seem destined to become the nightmares of tomorrow. But as matters now stand, the state system remains ascendant, and continues to control the instruments of violence as well as the existing procedures for peaceful change. Whether the issue is preventing nuclear war, maintaining world food or oil supplies, eliminating poverty and repression, or avoiding dangerous levels of air or water pollution, we most urgently require that which is most lacking, namely, the capacity and willingness of national governments to be enlightened, to think and act globally rather than nationally.

The German philosopher Arthur Schopenhauer, disturbed that his ideas had made so little impact in earlier editions, contended shortly before his death that "the true and the genuine would more easily obtain a footing in the world, were it not that those incapable of producing it were at the same time pledged not to let it gain ground." [5] Proposals for global reform seem faced with such a situation of unreasonable resistance.

Undoubtedly, many people sincerely believe that governments will somehow do what is necessary when the situation grows serious enough, or that the United Nations provides a satisfactory institutional nucleus for a new system of world order. Either confidence seems dangerously complacent. Many civilizations of the past have crumbled due to an inability to adapt their ways to some new challenge. Governments lack both the tools and the outlook to overcome a crisis based upon fragmented global authority and gross inequality among the peoples of the world. The United Nations is primarily a reflection of the state system, a useful instrument of intergovernmental diplomacy and a benign, if marginal, influence in many areas of international life; but the UN provides no realistic hope for substantially modifying the state system. Indeed, it is important to acknowledge the limited ability of the United Nations to deal with even the most flagrant abuses of the state system. A recent incident illustrates our concern. On December 3, 1973, the United Nations Educational, Scientific and Cultural Organization (UNESCO) summarily canceled its earlier agreement to provide facilities to Amnesty International, a highly respected nongovernmental organization, for a world conference on torture scheduled to be held in Paris a few days later. Why? Because an advance report for the conference implicated 63 UNESCO member states "in the practice of officially-sanctioned torture!" [6] If a UN agency cannot even *talk* about such extreme behavior as torture, then certainly it is unable to *act* effectively to overcome the more generic defects of the state system which are responsible for such grave problems as pervasive war, poverty, and repression.

This illuminating vignette represents more than merely an occasion on which to berate governments or their institutional creations such as UNESCO. Governments are part of the state system whose cardinal principle is the pursuit of state interests, and whose corollary principle is the mutual toleration of domestic political rule. Governing groups will tend to do what is necessary to sustain their own power, while friendly governments will rarely be moved to action, as distinct from rhetoric, if foreign atrocities are confined to alien territory. The most enlightened governments, including our own, turned their backs on Nazi terror to such an extent that they even refused asylum to most Jewish refugees.[7] But let an unfriendly elite accede to power in a state viewed as "vital," and the Marines (or their equivalent) will be dispatched to rectify the geopolitical wrong. Again, a sense of outrage or wonder is not the most appropriate emotion. Any student of international relations knows that the state system has been sustained by a series of governing groups in key states who have sought to maximize their power, wealth, and prestige at the expense of one another. To complain about such maximizing behavior is as irrelevant as complaining about the tendency of corporations to maximize profits or the tendency of bacteria to multiply within a host animal. We need to evolve a strategy of transformation and to rid ourselves of illusions about what we can expect from the existing world order system.

This orientation has guided our inquiry into the prospects for global reform. We understand that there are dangers and costs associated with global reform, especially for Americans who seem to have it so good under present arrangements of power and authority. But it is our conviction that the future, even for American patriots, lies in the embrace of a bold and cosmopolitan program of global reform, before it is too late. By patriots, we mean those fellow citizens who seek what is best for this, their land, and who are proud and respectful of the most hallowed national traditions on which this country was founded almost 200 years ago, in a great spiritual burst of revolutionary energy.

The imminence of the Bicentennial Year in 1976 creates a symbolic occasion for both a renewal and redefinition of American patriotism. Today, the cause of liberation cannot be limited in time and space to national frontiers, but must reach out to encompass the globe. Barrington Moore, Jr., points out that "a general opposition to human suffering constitutes a standpoint that both transcends and unites different cultures and historical epochs." [8] This standpoint provides a lodestar for the sort of global humanism that is needed as an ethical foundation for a new world order worth struggling to achieve.

Not every pattern of drastic global reform is to be encouraged. A new world order system based on the control of a few governments who retain their privileged positions, or one based on the profit-oriented globalism of the multinational corporation, is more to be feared than sought, consolidating much that is undesirable and further postponing what is most needed.

In the chapters that follow it is our intention to outline a world order system responsive to global humanism. We believe it can be achieved, that its pursuit is the highest priority for people everywhere, and that the shape of global reform is too important to leave in the hands of statesmen, generals, or businessmen.

REFERENCES

1. Walt Whitman, *Democratic Vistas and Other Papers,* London, Walter Scott, 1888, p. 11.

2. *Ibid.,* p. 37.

3. *The New Yorker,* Dec. 10, 1973, p. 38.

4. See Lester R. Brown, "The Next Crisis? Food," *Foreign Policy* 13:3–33 (1973–1974).

5. A. Schopenhauer, *The World as Will and Representation,* Indian Hills, Colo., Falcon's Wing Press, 1958, p. xxxvi.

6. See report in the *New York Times,* Dec. 4, 1973, p. 2.

7. This morbid story is fully told and documented in Arthur D. Morse, *While Six Million Died: A Chronicle of American Apathy,* New York, Random House, 1968.

8. Barrington Moore, Jr., *Reflections on the Causes of Human Misery and Upon Certain Proposals to Eliminate Them,* Boston, Beacon Press, 1972, p. 11.

Chapter One

POINTS OF DEPARTURE

SCOPE OF UNDERTAKING

This presentation of the World Order Models Project (WOMP/USA) sets forth a comprehensive set of proposals designed to strengthen world order by the end of this century. These proposals have been evolved within the collaborative framework of inquiry developed in the World Order Models Project, and focus upon the design of *relevant utopias* that could be realized by the 1990's. In this context, *utopia* denotes a positive model of world order, and a utopia is considered to be *relevant* if its presentation includes *transition* proposals and strategies to bring it into being. From an array of relevant utopias, a preference model is defined as that model which seems most promising on the basis of its desirability and attainability. It is highly likely that the content given to WOMP values, and their relative priority, might influence the selection of a preferred world from the array of relevant utopias. Also, the concept of transition (see Chapter IV) may have a bearing on notions of desirability and attainability. Thus, depending on such considerations, different WOMP groups—even assuming they agreed on the array of relevant utopias (not realistic) would not be likely to make the same choice of a preferred world. It may be possible at a more advanced stage of WOMP to achieve a substantial consensus as to both the *array* and *the preference model.** We depict the situation of hypothetical choice as follows:

---

* In depicting a preference model in Chapter IV we present both a sketch of the recommended structure and a series of building instructions. However, we have sought to avoid the impression of blueprinting a constitutional model of a new world order.

Array of relevant utopias as specified by WOMP values	A (Central Guidance)	B (World Government)	C (Condominium)	D (Regionalist)
Preference Model	WOMP/USA	A		
	WOMP/Lat. Am.	D		
	WOMP/India	D [1]		

[1] Resembling D, but with variations.

The preferred world of WOMP/USA has been modeled in light of several constraining conditions.

TIME

The time for realization is conceived to be the interval between 1974 and the decade 1990 (or the year 2000). Such a time interval places limits on the extent of change that can realistically be expected. The process of transformation involves a complex mixture of changes in attitude, values, behavior, and structure such that the cumulative outcome can be aptly identified as a different system of world order. Our focus is upon the sort of changes in political structure and authority patterns that are needed to realize WOMP values within the time interval available, but it should be understood that these modifications will be the outgrowth of more fundamental changes in prevailing modes of political consciousness. These more fundamental changes may be taking shape already in various sectors of public awareness and even governmental behavior, but their interpretation may be misleadingly associated with old forms of belief and action.

Some social and political movements seeking drastic change seem plausible only in retrospect. An account of revolutionary potential in Russia around 1910 would probably not have been sanguine about the chances for an effective uprising within the decade, whereas in retrospect the forces that led to revolution can be outlined fairly clearly, making the revolutionary outcome appear less than surprising. The same point is illustrated by an analysis of the prospects of anti-colonialism in

India or Indonesia in the 1930's or of Zionism in the same period. We are saying that preparations for drastic change may be largely latent until a sudden energy gives them relevance of a visible kind at a particular historical moment. We believe that such latent preparations for a new system of world order are part of the reality of the present context. Hence, mainstream judgments as to what is possible by the year 2000 are likely to be too conservative because they tend to overlook these latent preparations. The term *preparation* may be deceptive to the extent that it suggests deliberative acts aimed at a specific goal. World order preparations, in our use, refer to the combination of forces that are undermining or imperiling the structure of the present system and making the emergence of a new system more likely, perhaps even inevitable, by a certain time. As with undiagnosed termites demolishing a house, one might not have much warning of the proximity of collapse.

Having made something of an argument for the prospect of drastic changes in the world order system by the year 2000, we would emphasize that very little of our analysis is dependent on this kind of prognosis. As later chapters will make clear, our main concern is with depicting *a process of change* (the transition) and sketching the structural outlines of a new system of world order that substantially realizes WOMP' values (the preference model). These tasks do not depend for their validity on precise correlations with historical time periods.

We are living in a period of upheaval and transition. Many observers note the decay of old forms and traditional values under the impact of basic changes in the economic, social, and moral order. The adequacy of the sovereign state as a central organizing basis for post-industrial national societies seems increasingly questionable. The vulnerability of all societies to nuclear attack, however strong their military capability, illustrates the inability of states to solve the challenges of national security, although the drive to develop superior defense systems continues to divert unprecedented peacetime resources and energies to the creation of new weapons systems.[1] All societies are potentially vulnerable to the consequences of the mismanagement of basic ecological issues involving pollution, climate, and the maintenance of ocean quality. Whereas nuclear catastrophe can be caused by a human decision, implemented in a matter of minutes, ecological catastrophe may be brought about by cumulative developments that are virtually imperceptible, and whose danger points are not yet generally understood.[2] The interdependent aspects of modern industrial societies also make traditional statist modes of unilateral policy-making dangerously anachronistic in relation to the dynamics of the world economy. Finally, well-organized nongovernmental groups with highly motivated personnel can severely disrupt the structure of national well-being; in this regard, diplomat-kidnapping and aerial hijacking may be but a mild foretaste of things to come.

On all fronts, it is evident that national governments are unable to protect their populations from external events which they neither understand nor control. As matters now stand, the agencies of the United Nations are incapable of providing a world policy that could uphold the shared interests of all peoples in avoiding either nuclear or ecological catastrophe. The institutional basis of world order, which is largely concentrated on the state level, is ill-equipped to provide for the fundamental well-being of most national populations; nor does it inspire confidence for an improved capacity in the future.

This proposition applies to a certain extent to every state, but it is particularly applicable to the highly industrialized societies of the Northern Hemisphere, especially to the richest and most powerful among them—the United States and the Soviet Union. In the Afro–Asian context, the nation-building process is at a stage that continues to give the state mechanism a high degree of viability. This *objective* situation of institutional strain and obsolescence arising from the dominance of state sovereignty is perceived and appreciated by many people around the world, but generally only in a loose rhetorical way. Part of the purpose of WOMP/USA is to deepen the subjective appreciation of this reality and to provide a positive world order alternative more capable of meeting these emerging challenges.

The objective situation, while precarious, bears on the plausibility of the changes we project as attainable by the 1990's. We proceed on the assumption that we are living in a period of crisis and transition for the nation–state—a crisis which emerged after World War I and which will continue until the occurrence of a catastrophe that would confirm a dimly apprehended potential for drastic adjustment. In this spirit, we have a sense of openness about the future that has a double-edged quality, providing the basis for hope as well as anxiety. There is some possibility that world order can be strengthened in an unexpectedly rapid fashion, at a pace that would appear foolishly optimistic given the present setting. We are not *predicting* that such a positive adjustment will occur by or during the decade 1990, but only that the deepening crisis of world organization provides a reasonable ground for affirming the possibility.*

---

* To deal fully with the concept of the realistic possibility of a WOMP/USA preference model by the decade 1990, it might be helpful to write an imaginative scenario set in the

WOMP/USA VALUES

The model of a preferred world is specified in light of specific and explicit value preferences. These preferences are associated with the promotion and substantial realization of four central values: (1) The minimization of large-scale collective violence; (2) the maximization of social and economic well-being; (3) the realization of fundamental human rights and conditions of political justice; (4) the rehabilitation and maintenance of environmental quality, including the conservation of resources. To simplify reference, these four values are designated as V_1, V_2, V_3, and V_4, respectively, in the course of this book.*

In the following sections each value will be discussed in some detail to provide a more specific indication of the project's normative outlook and to enable a clearer understanding of what we mean by *a better system of world order*. We are also concerned with issues of validation—how to measure or otherwise assess progress in the pursuit of these values, and how to compare world order performance in different time periods.†

The Minimization of Large-Scale
Collective Violence (V_1)

In essence, we are identifying a better system of world order with a more peaceful one. The idea of peace has a number of different dimensions. It entails less reliance upon violence and war as a basis for national security and the resolution of conflict. Reduced reliance on the war system would seem to imply, in turn, the development of a credible set of substitute mechanisms. In particular, it would imply shifting away from a military concept of security toward a police (or at least a quasi-military) concept.‡ To achieve this, central institutions would

---

year 2002, with a historical account of the birth and realization of the new world system. This kind of world order "fiction" might be a healthy antidote to the mechanistic world order excesses of futurology and technological forecasting in which the future becomes a field of interesting trend lines constituted by measurable variables about which global data exist.

* This form of notation is part of a wider effort to develop a more disciplined approach to world order studies. See, especially, Chapters III–V.

† In WOMP/USA our emphasis on performance is conceived mainly in relation to WOMP values, although we are also concerned with conceiving of a transition process to our *preference model* (see Chapter IV) based on peaceful and voluntary action.

‡ A *military* concept of security is related to successful national participation in the war system, whereas a *police* concept of security is concerned with the discouragement and

have to be equipped with police capabilities while national institutions would be substantially deprived of military capabilities. Furthermore, since we are not so naive as to anticipate the disappearance of conflict or tensions, we foresee the need for a series of reliable and readily available settlement techniques that could take over the role presently filled by the war system. Such substitutions would involve the development of workable adjudicative and conciliatory mechanisms, with means to assure their implementation. Legislative and equity procedures should be highly sensitive to pleas for peaceful change of existing norms and distributions of rights and duties. This series of structural reforms would not be effective unless reinforced by an upsurge in the ethics of nonviolence and a belief that nonviolent approaches could be successfully used on a far wider range of conflict situations than is presently the case.*

Minimizing international violence would imply a substantial decrease, by say 75 percent, in two of the central indicators of the war sys-

---

detection of crime and the apprehension of suspected criminals. The war system involves an ongoing "legitimate" military rivalry and encourages governmental belief that force or its threat is at the basis of statecraft; peace treaties validate the outcome of war, regardless of responsibility for their initiation or the barbarous character of their prosecution. Of course, political crime is a domestic species of "war" and the phenomenon of civil war illuminates the interface between police and military approaches to security. When political crime occurs on a massive scale, involving the formation of countergovernmental armies and institutions, routine reliance on police capabilities tends to give way to a military, warlike approach. In the context of a disarmed world, the idea of a police approach to security will have to be carefully thought through in relation to a large number of contingencies. There is a danger that an insufficient police capability would encourage military adventurism by groups opposed to whatever status quo exists, whereas excessive police capability would encourage a repressive approach to diversity and dissent. As with other fundamental issues, there is no fully satisfying solution. At this state of sketching a preference model, sensitivity to the issue at stake is the most that can be expected. Also, the pervasive notion of checks and balances can be used to reconcile conflicting public order requirements. With respect to the role of violence in a new system of world order several factors will be important: the basic equity of the overall approach to well-being, the provision of procedures for peaceful change and peaceful settlement, and the rejection on normative grounds of violence-laden approaches to grievances and frustration. More careful work is needed on this set of issues.

* Certain analogies may be helpful to illustrate issues of ethics and efficacy, and their interrelations. Consider the following contexts: the American civil rights movement until the death of Martin Luther King; labor–management negotiations in the United States since World War II; India's struggle for national independence; Vietnam's struggle for national independence; the movement against racism in South Africa; the effort to protect rights of dissent in the Soviet Union.

tem's present role in international life: the number of battle deaths per year and per conflict; and the amount of money devoted to the national maintenance of war-fighting capabilities, computed both in absolute terms and as a proportion of GNP.

Certain supplemental indicators of war system activity would also help measure progress toward the minimization of large-scale, collective violence of an official or governmental character: *

A decline in the frequency of wars

A reduction in casualties (battle and civilian) per war

A reduction in the geographical scope of war and in the average duration of wars

A reduction in the incidence of threats of war and of "pre-war" crises

A reduction of "incidents" relying on the assertion of military capability, ranging from reprisals to "showing the flag" [3]

We emphasize the elimination of preparations for war and war threats, as well as the elimination of combat itself. Such emphasis is essential because the strategic arms race has, according to some analysts, actually been responsible for a sharp reduction in the prospect and incidence of large-scale warfare.[4] Mutual deterrence—in the sense of discouraging either principal rival to initiate war—increases the prospects for nuclear peace among the most powerful countries and reduces the likelihood of large-scale and general community wars of the World War I and II variety. Yet there are several reasons for regarding mutual deterrence as an unsatisfactory basis for a peaceful world:

1. The consequence of a failure of the deterrence system is likely to be a nuclear war of catastrophic proportions that includes the distinct possibility of only a very incomplete recovery.

2. The principal competitors, especially the United States and the Soviet Union, are necessarily seeking military capabilities that exceed the requirements of mutual deterrence; they also are pursuing weapons developments that look toward superiority in matters of of-

---

* The general role of violence in human affairs should also be taken into consideration. V_1 is directly concerned with the drastic reduction of official violence in external relations among states, but the prospects for V_1 depend on a general climate of increasing non-violence. Furthermore, the implications of V_1 in state-to-state relations are clearly applicable to people-to-people and people-to-government relations.

fense and defense. The reliability of mutual deterrence varies because its conditions are not inherently stable. They are susceptible to erosion by actual and perceived technological innovation, quantitative buildups in weaponry, changes in personnel or orientation of contending governments or their main allies. Furthermore, reliance on secrecy and intelligence estimates introduces an element of uncertainty as to the intentions, activities, and capabilities of the other side. The existence of bureaucratic and economic interests gives impetus to arms policy in each state and makes it more difficult to negotiate agreements in the area of arms control and disarmament. Opposing elites, with an interest in sustaining the forward momentum of the arms race, premise minimum security upon an analysis of "the worst possible case" and, therefore, claim a need for redundant weapons and weapons systems, and project a variety of "essential" military missions other than national defense strictly construed. The interaction of these opposing security requirements makes it appear necessary to keep several steps ahead to avoid falling one step behind.

The logic of an arms race is based on a symmetry of competing forces, but this is misleading if understood as descriptive of U.S./USSR arms competition. Herbert York, a former Defense Department official who at one time played a major role in weapons acquisition, has written that American "unilateral decisions have set the rate and scale of the individual steps in the strategic-arms race." [5] He attributes this asymmetry to the greater wealth and power of the United States, not to imperial aspirations or paranoid fears. [6] There are periodic efforts by American leaders to project unfavorable gaps in the future so as to justify increased arms spending in the present. Obviously, each of these allegations of emerging inferiority has to be assessed on its merits, but the record of governmental exaggeration in the past causes some degree of skepticism about alleged present needs.

As a feature of Soviet–American rivalry, the arms race has to be reassessed in light of the détente achieved during the Nixon years. It is worth observing that this détente has not led to any revived advocacy of large-scale disarmament. On the contrary, the shared objectives of the United States and the Soviet Union seem to involve making deterrence more stable and somewhat less expensive, while continuously augmenting the awesome military capabilities of each side. These capabilities appear to be important expressions of domestic relations of forces, and involve a shared Soviet–American belief that their own continuing prosperity, prestige, and authority in world affairs depend on widening the military gap between primary and secondary nuclear powers.

Additionally, in each case, governing authorities in the United States and the Soviet Union seem especially eager to maintain such a gap with respect to their respective "allies," a feature of the new world security milieu that cannot be formally admitted. This kind of tacit condominium is a reflection, in part, of changing ideological currents in world affairs (e.g., Sino–Soviet split, East–West détente) and, in part, of altered economic factors and calculations (especially the intensification of competition among those advanced industrial societies that rely on private ownership of productive facilities). Thus, Soviet–American arms policy must be reinterpreted in the light of these wider changes in the international setting.

In sum, then, nuclear deterrence is concerned with hegemony and condominium as well as with security, since security founded on this basis does not necessarily lead to increased stability, but involves dynamic competition that passes through various phases of greater and lesser stability, cost and uncertainty. The phrase "the delicate balance of terror" expresses this vulnerability of deterrence to technological innovation, intelligence operations, and political militancy.[7] The balance of terror also involves the maintenance of credible threats to kill millions of innocent and helpless hostages in foreign societies and to destroy vast centers of industry and culture for no positive reason. Beyond this, the fallout from any major nuclear exchange would inflict great damage on the population of additional bystander countries. Such a system of threats is totally inconsistent with the development of the values and attitudes appropriate for a world community in which men might eventually live in harmony on the planet. A threat is effective only if the other side is reasonably convinced that it will be carried out in the presence of certain provocations. However, unscrupulous or unstable leaders who do not care about the welfare of their own population or society might not be deterred or might misconstrue the threshold of provocation, and thereby bring about consequences dreadful for mankind. The stability of deterrence depends both on a government's concern for its population and on an adequate understanding of when a nuclear power is likely to exercise its nuclear option.

The role of nuclear weapons tends to be extended beyond defending the homeland from nuclear attack. The most obvious explicit illustration of *extended deterrence* involves the defense of Western Europe against a possible Soviet-led conventional attack. Another illustration is the role of Soviet nuclear superiority in deterring the People's Republic of China from adopting military approaches to their territorial dispute. At various times there has been speculation about American plans to use nuclear weapons in an Asian context. The direction of policy embodied in the Nixon Doctrine suggests that in the future there may be increased pressure to use or threaten the use of nuclear weapons to maintain Vietnam-type treaty commitments without losing American lives.

Nuclear deterrence * is also vulnerable to accidents, unauthorized use, and subversion. Although elaborate precautions apparently are taken by all nuclear powers to prevent an outbreak of unintended nuclear war, the fallibility of men and machines creates continuing risks. Such risks are likely to become greater as additional governments acquire nuclear weapons and as newer weapons systems are deployed in significant numbers by the U.S. and the USSR. However, SALT talks and détente are likely to have an offsetting effect by making Soviet–American relations far less crisis-prone.

The cost of arms competition is leading to the failure to meet other needs of civilian society and aggravates such problems as inflation. Military expenditures are, by and large, unproductive investments.† Seymour Melman has demonstrated that the size of the defense establishment injects a virulent parasite into the bloodstream of American society that not only depletes the industrial base of the economy, but also retards public response to desperate demands for social welfare.[8] America's failure to maintain the competitive quality of its machine tool industry, steel production, and mass transit systems, as compared to the modern economies of Europe and Japan, can be explained in large part by the enormous drain on resources and distortion of government priorities caused by the large military budget.

The mind-set of a government beholden to a military–industrial complex seems impervious to the changes needed to move toward a preferred world by the decade 1990. The resources and energies required for the arms race make it difficult to promote other social goals—the simultaneous pursuit of "guns and butter" does not seem possible, even for a country as rich as the United States. Furthermore, a

---

* This discussion of the deficiencies of nuclear deterrence should be understood as a special and extreme case of a more general indictment of the sort of deterrence thinking that is characteristic of the war system in pre-nuclear and non-nuclear settings. In certain settings the war system, on a small scale, might be appropriately regarded as an adequate or the best available basis for security, given such factors as the importance of diversity and change in human relations and given the absence of normative or institutional foundations for the administration of a truly global peace system.

† Although military research and development can have some positive side-effects: Boeing's 747 is evidently a technological spinoff from design work done to develop the military cargo plane, the C5A.

military approach to national security presupposes that the ideology of national sovereignty continues to be a valid basis of world order. But national sovereignty is linked to outmoded organizational images that associate wealth and power with the control over physical space.[9] This reaffirmation of sovereign prerogatives for nuclear states also places very firm limits upon the prospects for changing the structure of international society.

Thus, in summary, the reliance upon the military capabilities of governments for national security is too dangerous, too expensive, too degenerate, and too rigidifying to be tolerable in the nuclear age. The first and central priority of the movement for a preferred world is to make progress toward *diminishing the role of the war system in international life* and toward *dismantling the national security apparatus in the major states of the world.**

The Maximization of Social and Economic Well-Being (V₂)

At present it is estimated that more than half of the world's population is hungry and over two-thirds is malnourished. Starvation, disease, short life expectancy, poor housing, poor education, illiteracy, and generalized deprivation are the chronic lot of most people living in Asia, Africa, and Latin America. Famine conditions threaten or prevail in several heavily populated portions of the world. Such misery contrasts with the affluence of Europe and North America, where waste is abundant and, in order to sustain superfluous consumption, advertising must stimulate continuous demand for new products and styles. The organization of the world economic system, especially its division into an urban industrial sector and a rural agricultural sector, perpetuates dependency links between the affluence of rich societies and the poverty of poor societies.[10] Patterns of trade and investment, as well as the upper-class orientation of the elites in most poor countries, help preserve the highly inequitable distribution of the Gross Global Product (GGP).

Such a pattern of inequity also seems to be associated with recourse to collective violence, especially under modern conditions of global communication. Increasingly, deprivation is being experienced and in-

---

* It is a significant geopolitical fact of the period since World War II that the control of the war system has been concentrated in the nuclear superpowers, whereas its horrific by-products—death and destruction—have been concentrated in the Third World.

terpreted as a species of exploitation if not of actual violence.* This awareness of deprivation has a demonstrable link to the incidence of civil strife and to various forms of counter-governmental violence.[11]

Progress toward the goal of maximizing well-being can be appraised from two principal perspectives: (1) progress toward the satisfaction of elemental human needs and the elimination of poverty; (2) general improvement of the quality of life. We must be concerned with acutely deprived individuals (for example, the millions of hungry Americans) as well as with poor nations; most of our statistical measures are organized around national totals and per capita averages and thus tell us nothing specific about the actual living conditions of the poorest segments of the population. There are a number of ways to define poverty for both individuals and nations. Customary reliance on GNP accounts is quite misleading. They completely obscure distributive relationships, for instance. Thus, it is quite conceivable for a country to enjoy a steadily rising GNP, while the poorer sectors of its population are simultaneously experiencing a worsening of conditions. For example, there are grounds for believing that Brazil's "economic miracle" has benefited the top 2–20% of the population to varying degrees during the last decade, but that the situation of the bottom 70% of the population has deteriorated in almost every crucial respect. Among important indicators of economic achievement are the following: infant mortality rate, life expectancy, physicians per capita, average years of educational experience, income per capita, percentage of the unemployed, gross national product, rate of economic growth, and rate of demographic growth. Indicators are also needed to depict the situation and changes through time of various social strata of the population. For instance, it would be illuminating to know the protein intake per capita of the top 10%, the top 25%, the top 50%, and the bottom 25% of various societies; the number of physicians per capita; housing space; and so on. These stratified indicators would show over time the relative distribution of the benefits of annual increases in GNP, and would provide a powerful instrument for reform.

If a preferred world is to be realized, gross forms of deprivation will by definition have to be eliminated. But the level of human well-being by the year 2000 cannot be assessed by comparison with or imitation of

---

* Johan Galtung's stress on "structural violence" makes clear the contention that to deprive individuals of the instruments needed for self-realization is to practice violence against them. Governments that do not meet the needs of the citizenry for food, shelter, health, clothing, and education, but yet insist on submissiveness, are practicing violence against deprived sectors of their own populations.

the living standards and styles prevailing in Western Europe and North America. Indeed, concern for environmental quality and economic equity may require constraints on the growth of these economies during the period needed for equalization of living standards and for making technological adjustments to the biosphere. The final determination of acceptable biospheric adjustments involves a determination of the resources and carrying capacities of the planet. These determinations can in turn be grossly affected by technological innovation, especially with respect to energy costs and supplies, as well as by demographic policies pursued by principal governments. Ecological concerns can be divided into issues of pollution control and of resource conservation. A standard of living associated with *human needs* for a healthy, comfortable, and dignified life will have to be worked out in specific detail to assess realization of V_2. The sum total of "needs" may also vary with the climate, ideology, economic organization, and value structure of various societies. The wisdom of government policy in poor countries will also be an important determinant of whether economic growth contributes greatly to the realization of this value. At present, the absence of distribution statistics for income, goods or services makes it virtually impossible to calculate progress. Also, the extent of popular acceptance of the government, and its relations with neighboring countries, will determine the proportion of its annual budget devoted to maintaining domestic police or quasi-military capabilities and participation in the international war system.

The problems of world poverty are also relevant to the widespread quest for political autonomy. Charges of exploitation, intervention, and manipulation are often made when rich countries purport to give foreign aid to poor countries. To assess these charges it will be important to observe, in addition to the *volume and rate of transfer,* such factors as the *conditions of receipt, the balance between military and nonmilitary assistance, the association between ideological approval and the quantity of aid,* and *the rationale* of foreign aid.*

Greater reliance on multilateral and international channels of resource transfer would be desirable, as would graduated assessments levied upon national governments on the basis of their per capita income. Such assessments would tend to diminish the political character of aid transfers.

---

* Trends in foreign assistance can be evaluated from a WOMP perspective by reference to such indicators as ratio of military to nonmilitary aid, as a percentage of GNP of donor or recipient country, or as related to improved satisfaction of V_2 in the recipient society.

Reform of the trade and investment structure would also promote the objectives of V_2, if it enabled poorer and less industrial countries to participate more actively and positively in the operations of the world economy. Such reform would involve some upward adjustment of the terms of trade to favor producers of primary products; some regulatory framework to assure that multinational corporations and world money markets were operated in light of world and regional interests; subsidies for capital development; and regional cooperation. Progress along these lines would have to be measured by qualitative interpretation, although certain more operational indices could be developed. One useful index might involve ratios between GNP and GGP per capita for each country and region, but such a correlation would have to be complemented by a general scrutiny of trading policies and trends.

The intersection of socialist and nonsocialist economies in relation to V_2 is also a significant aspect of this problem. Should socialist countries be divided into advanced industrial and developing countries? Would socialist countries participate in the same way in an international assessment scheme? Should state trading companies be treated, for regulatory purposes, as multinational corporations? Will it be feasible or desirable to erode the boundaries between the socialist and nonsocialist sectors of international society in the years ahead? How does the special Japanese association of government and business fit into this scheme of analysis? What are the consequences of economic regionalism in Europe and elsewhere?

In the context of our proposals, progress toward the realization of V_2 depends on several principal lines of achievement:

The elimination of poverty

The reduction of disparities in per capita income *between* and *within* national societies

The reduction of economic patterns of exploitation and dependence

The reduction of "waste" and the allocation of increasing proportions of resources for beneficial purposes *

The notion of poverty may be too circumscribed unless it is associated with specific conceptions of life quality. Considerations of self-realization should take into account schools, housing, clothing, health and recreational facilities, foods, jobs, and general opportunities for

---

* The definition of *beneficial* is inevitably vague and controversial. In this book we associate beneficial use with satisfaction of WOMP values.

self-realization, including meaningful work. Relief from human misery would seem to require more than obtaining the necessities of life, although provision of these necessities is obviously an indispensable first step. It is important that social indicators be constructed to reflect these qualitative considerations.

The reduction of disparities between rich and poor societies, and between social classes within a given society, expresses the commitment to the idea of equality as one aspect of a system designed to secure the well-being of all people. Such a commitment can not be taken for granted. Criteria of relative merit of returns, based on the extent of social contributions, have normally been embodied in the political and economic ethics of most societies, and have reemerged in contemporary socialist societies despite ideological commitments to the contrary. Inequality of rewards seems to be an integral feature of almost every known complex society. The extent of inequality among groups or social classes and particularly among nations, regions, and ethnic units, is a major emphasis in most movements for radical change. Progress toward the moderation of inequality within and between national societies would also contribute positively to the realization of V_1 under most sets of conditions.

It is also important to take into consideration the amount of exploitation and dependence in any assessment of the circumstances and prospects for progress in relation to V_2. Exploitation has two dimensions: the subjective and the objective. *Subjective exploitation* involves the sense of being exploited, the perception that an unfavorable and unfair form of inequality underlies a relationship; *objective exploitation* involves the existence, whether perceived or not, of unfair or unfavorable forms of inequality.

It is evident that either dimension of exploitation can exist without the other and that both dimensions can exist together. From a political point of view, the subjective appreciation of exploitation is a necessary precondition for discontent and action in response, although it may not be a sufficient precondition.

The undesirability of objective types of exploitation forms part of the content of V_2. The identification of what is exploitative is to some extent an ethical and ideological question, but its relevance is obvious in relation to such central issues in the world economy as the conditions of foreign investment, the terms of world trade, relative standards of living, and the character of international pricing and monetary policies.

Dependence involves the obverse of exploitation, the susceptibility of a dependent sector of the world economy to exploitation by a dominant one. In addition, the dependent status entails a loss of control, an exclusion from the decision process, a denial or restriction of participation, and hence engenders "an inferiority complex" and an absence of self-respect.

Measures of exploitation and dependence are difficult to establish, given presently available data as well as the vagueness of the concepts themselves. There is a need to assess profit margins and flows, returns on capital and reinvestment policies, and degrees of participation in councils of authority and decision in relation to major international economic activities. Different expectations about participation and dependence exist in various parts of the world as a consequence of variations in ideology, economic system, political consciousness, information, and national and regional experience. At this point, it is important only to emphasize that V_2 is not a purely materialistic goal concerned solely with eliminating poverty and increasing living standards. The position of blacks in South Africa is *not*, in general, materially worse than in most other parts of Africa, but it is far worse when considerations of exploitation and dependence are taken into account. Some of these considerations overlap with matters of political justice that are embraced within V_3 (i.e., fundamental human rights for individuals and groups).

The dignity of work has to do, however, with living conditions prevailing in all countries. Problems of work force alienation associated with unsatisfying or degrading work often afflict even high-salaried employees in relatively rich nations. Recent experimental evidence in a factory for digital computers suggests, for instance, that even from the perspective of quality and productivity, it may be better to abandon assembly line methods of ultra-specialization and allow a worker the job satisfaction of putting together an entire product. With respect to providing all people with the necessities of life, job enhancement for individuals would be a major concern in an adequate system of global well-being.

In conclusion, it is difficult to delimit V_2 at the present time, for it pertains to both the satisfaction of widely shared minimal needs (i.e., elimination of poverty) and the pursuit of more divergent requirements of well-being based on variations of culture, ideology, climate, and expectation.[12]

The Realization of Fundamental Human Rights and of Conditions of Political Justice (V_3)

V_3 is difficult to specify in operational terms. The data are not available and, in any event, conditions of tolerance and dignity often depend on matters of quality rather than quantity. There are some crude operational measures, which could perhaps be illustrated by mapping and graphing techniques, to depict progress and regress with respect to V3: the number of colonial regimes, the number of regimes censured by some reputable organization for violations of human rights, the number of petitions delivered to the United Nations complaining about human rights violations, the number of instances of political prisoners as determined by such nongovernmental organizations as the International Commission of Jurists or Amnesty International, and the number of individuals classified as refugees or as stateless persons; comparable indicators of denials of human rights could be developed to assess regional standards and trends with respect to V3.

The main objective of V3 is to assure conditions for the realization of individual and group dignity within national societies. Related transnational concerns involving rights of mobility, emigration, and immigration are also very significant aspects of V3 as we comprehend it. One specific goal of a new world order system would be to remove travel and residence policy from the control of national governments. It would be desirable to set certain minimum supranational standards of right, and then to entrust local communities with the authority to control population size and degrees of contact with outsiders. We are seeking to reconcile values associated with mobility with those connected with individual and community autonomy. The complete process of reconciliation is a goal that falls outside the scope of WOMP objectives, being a more ambitious goal than V3. V3 seeks only to assure *minimal conditions*, rather than to establish *optimal* arrangements. The concerns of V3 emphasize the relevance of human rights issues on a domestic level for creating and maintaining a preference model of world order along the lines specified by WOMP/USA. We can clarify the nature of V3 by discussing some of its principal dimensions.

1. *The prevention of genocide.* A minimum obligation of national governments is to avoid taking steps to destroy any distinct national, ethnic, or religious group that lives within its midst. A government violates this obligation if it kills or punishes individuals merely because of their identity, or makes renunciation of that identity a condition of employment or access to educational institutions.* A

---

* The Genocide Convention of 1950 to which the U.S. Senate has not yet given its "advice and consent" defines genocide in Article 2 as follows:

In the present Convention, genocide means any of the following acts committed with intent to destroy, in whole or in part, a national, ethnic, racial or religious group, as such:

government has no right to destroy such group identity or to discriminate against members of a group, and should offer groups protection when they become the target of unofficial persecution (e.g., blacks vis-à-vis the Ku Klux Klan). Whether the idea of genocide should be extended to matters of ideological position is less clear: is it "genocide" to destroy "Communists" in a Western society, "capitalists" in a Communist society, or "imperialists" in a Third World society? What is clear is that the destruction of a group's tribal, racial, or religious identity is forbidden. A widely ratified Genocide Convention sets forth the basic rights and duties with respect to genocide. An assessment of the incidence and magnitude of violations of its terms, and the effectiveness of steps taken to rectify such violations, could give insight into whether genocide is disappearing from human affairs or, on the contrary, is becoming more widespread, as has been the case in the 1960's and early 1970's.

2. *The elimination of colonial regimes.* The persistence of several colonial regimes, most notably those of the Portuguese administration, flaunt the trend of recent international history and defy specific directives of the General Assembly of the United Nations. South Africa's administration of Namibia (South-West Africa), and Zimbabwe's (Rhodesia's) assertion of independence under minority rule present contemporary examples of a repressive foreign elite which governs in defiance of the well-being of the majority of the population.* An aspect of V_3 is to secure national independence for these societies and to eliminate all remaining colonial regimes. The refusal of Portugal to abandon its claims to colonial title over Angola and Mozambique has generated a long, expensive, and destructive "war

---

A) Killing members of the group;

B) Causing serious bodily or mental harm to members of the group;

C) Deliberately inflicting on the group conditions of life calculated to bring about its physical destruction in whole or in part;

D) Imposing measures intended to prevent births within the group;

E) Forcibly transferring children of the group to another group.

Obviously such a definition is broad and somewhat ambiguous; here genocide is clearly intended to be broader than intentional killing of a group. As a crime, elements of intent and overt act must both be present. As a concept, the important concern involves avoiding any calculated effort to destroy the basis of group existence or identity, however the group defines its own existence.

* The characterization of southern African elites as "foreign" involves the judgment that their central ethnic identification is not with the peoples of their society or region.

of liberation" in each of these countries. Support for such a war, because of V₃, may entail giving the anti-colonial struggle priority in these specific contexts over the effort to eliminate large-scale violence from international life (V₁). Of course, it would still be very important to promote liberation objectives by relying on nonviolent tactics to the extent possible, and, in any event, to minimize the violence that often accompanies the assertion of basic claims of national self-determination. India's invasion of the Portuguese enclave of Goa in 1962 resulted in an inconclusive debate in which the Asian, African, and socialist countries supported India's position, despite its conflict with the apparent obligations of the Charter to renounce force except for purposes of self-defense.

3. *The drastic modification of racist regimes.* The content of V₃ is also associated with the struggle against apartheid policy in South Africa, and with the related practice of suppression of African populations by whites in the countries of southern Africa. To some extent, this issue overlaps and complements the struggle against colonialism, except perhaps in relation to South Africa. But there are two distinct aspirations: first, the rights and status of national independence; second, the liberation of black majority populations from white minority rule and related discriminatory practices. V₃ is concerned with the promotion of fundamental human rights with respect to race relations, especially as these rights are defined by the explicit practices and policies of a government. In this respect, apartheid is presumed to be an extreme example of this aspect of V₃.

4. *The elimination of all forms of torture and cruelty.* Throughout human history official policy has been sustained, in part, by employing torture against opponents. At present, governments in all parts of the world continue to rely on torture to punish and discourage opposition.[13] A major test of progress toward V₃ would involve the reduction of the frequency, intensity, and geographic dispersion of official torture and cruelty. The effective renunciation of torture and cruelty, as a matter of behavior as well as rhetoric, would also contribute to the dynamics of self-determination and would seem to put the governing process on a more humane foundation. Of course, less use of terror and torture by opponents of governments would also be a contribution to V₃. It is true that a militant minority opposition to the governing process can be as disruptive of self-determination as can a repressive minority government.

5. *Related progress toward equality of treatment for different races, sexes, ages, religions, tribes, political groups.* In what would strike many as an overstatement, Zbigniew Brzezinski has written that "the nineteenth century can be said to represent the intellectual supremacy of the idea of liberty, but the twentieth century is witnessing the triumph of equality." [14] In effect, the earlier concern with securing certain inalienable rights of individual freedom has been supplanted by a focus on eliminating the grossest forms of social and economic inequality. Specific forms of discrimination against ethnic and religious groups and against women exist in many societies, and the elimination of these explicit types of discrimination represents a step toward the equality aspect of V_3. Some of the more subtle forms of discrimination of a *de facto* variety arise from unequal educational opportunities and experiences. Another fundamental abuse involves widespread suppression of women, including paying women less than men for the same job or in not compensating women at all for certain forms of labor (e.g., role as housewife). The idea of equality is associated mainly with the elimination of specific burdens, handicaps, and inequalities that seem to arise from such arbitrary factors as race, tribe, sex, or religion. Equality issues are also rising in relations between the city and the country, in terms of the ratio between public spending and revenue contributions (for proportion of the population). Issues of equality should be related to issues of minimal threshold. In the coming decade, more significant progress under V_3 may be made by eliminating the most severe forms of denial (and, hence, inequality) than by working across the board for equalization; that is, it may be qualitatively more important to equalize the bottom quartile of a population with the third quartile, than to equalize the third quartile with the second, or the second with the first. Indeed, if severe forms of denial are eliminated, the persistence of some other forms of inequality might even be compatible with V_3, although not those based on arbitrary factors of birth, color, sex, beliefs, or family background.

6. *The rights of self-expression and meaningful political participation.* A further aspect of V_3 concerns the conditions of political life in a domestic society: first, the rights of free expression; second, protection against arbitrary behavior by the government; third, the existence of political choices based on the possibilities of organizing a political opposition; fourth, the existence of procedures that encourage some kind of citizen participation in the formation of basic social and political policy.

Assessing progress and regress with respect to these issues requires the collection of considerable data, but it should be possible to develop some reasonably objective indicators:*

Number of political parties and differences among platforms

Number of newspapers and differences in editorial policy

Amount of public funds per capita spent on internal security, including general surveillance of citizenry

Formal rights of an individual as laid down in the legal code

Number of political trials per year and per capita

Proportion of political trials that result in acquittal of the defendants

Assessment of V3 will have to take account of variations in the scale of societies, in cultural and ideological orientation, and in the stages of social and political development. There are different ways to facilitate political participation and it would be undesirable to identify progress exclusively with movement toward the model of liberal democracy that has flourished in Western Europe and North America.

The Maintenance and Rehabilitation of Ecological Quality (Pollution and Resources) (V4)

The promotion of environmental quality is multi-faceted and complicated. Ecological quality as a world order value embraces both the containment of pollution and the conservation of resource stocks. A series of problem areas can be identified, each of which requires distinct forms of planning, judgment, and action:

Type A. Ecological disasters of a sudden, dramatic character, such as the breakup of a large oil tanker or the collision between a nuclear submarine and a merchant vessel.

Type B. The gradual deterioration of environmental quality by cumulative processes (e.g., buildup of CO_2 in the atmosphere or DDT in the oceans).

---

* Obviously, a society does not necessarily serve the concerns of V3 merely by having a larger number of political parties. The issue at stake is whether a meaningful opposition party can operate to enlist popular support and whether new opposition constituencies can organize around a new party structure. Excessive fragmentation may be a genuine impediment to meaningful competition for political control and, therefore, some constraints on party formation may be fully consistent with the realization of V3.

Type C. Various risks and injuries associated with the handling, storage, disposal, and generation of ultra-hazardous materials (e.g., nuclear explosions, ocean-dumping of nerve gas, storage vaults for radioactive wastes).

Type D. Infringements on the heritage of mankind as a consequence of deliberate policy or negligence with respect to the preservation of cultural or natural wonders (e.g., Abu Simbal, Murchison Falls) or with regard to the conservation of endangered animal species (e.g., blue whale).

Type E. Failures to conserve scarce resource stocks for the benefit of future generations or to satisfy the development requirements of poorer sectors of the world.

Type F. Use of scarce resources for unproductive, wasteful, and destructive purposes (e.g., arms spending, consumer advertising).

Type G. The control of environmental warfare and the prohibition of ecocide (e.g., herbicides, systematic plowing).

Type H. The control of weather modification capabilities and policy in times of peace and war.

There are several preliminary steps that should be taken to promote V₄:

The initiation of serious data collection to permit intelligent assessments of ecological issues

The establishment of early-warning systems and quick-reaction facilities and the development of expert knowledge to deal with environmental emergencies

The adoption of a Declaration of Ecological Quality to identify problem clusters Types A–H and to establish aspirational standards of behavior

The assessment of the environmental effects of DDT, the SST, nuclear testing, toxic waste disposals

The strengthening of norms, procedures, and institutional arrangements of international society with respect to environmental harm and the settlement of environmental disputes

The initiation of long-range forecasts of resource shortages, and of discussions of allocation and use policy with respect to such shortages.*

Improving information about ecological issues is itself a contribution to V₄, as better information can provide the awareness and knowledge

---

* There are two separate concerns here: (1) resource availability for future generations, i.e., *through time;* (2) resource availability for deprived societies or sectors of a given society, i.e., *through space.*

necessary for more direct action. A more concrete set of actions would involve taking steps to prevent Type A environmental damage and to develop facilities and know-how for response. In addition, monitoring and regulatory activities associated with Type B environmental damage would have to be assessed. Type C situations call particularly for some kind of international review procedures. Although it is difficult at this time to select critical indicators of environmental quality—for instance, incidence of oil tanker accidents or offshore blowouts, concentration of DDT or lead in the oceans, ozone balance, temperature or climate change—it will be necessary to isolate some such indicators of environmental quality in the years ahead to measure progress in relation to V_4. Type D issues require some sort of international mechanism that asserts global concern and gives hard-pressed governments an incentive to protect the heritage of mankind without inhibiting the satisfaction of fundamental human needs. Type E and F issues require information, intergovernmental coordination, and the development of ethical attitudes. Types G and H present problems of technological assessment in the first instance, but presuppose the evolution of effective behavioral standards in areas of relative novelty. A significant start on these issues was made at the 1972 Stockholm United Nations Conference on the Human Environment and its follow-up.

The boundaries of V_4 are controversial and indistinct. The maintenance of diversity with respect to the earth's habitat is itself a positive world order goal. Thus, even if DDT were not harmful to human health or marine ecology, its use would impose a serious environmental cost if it were responsible for the extinction of animal species such as the peregrine falcon. Of course, the preservation of an animal species has to be measured against the need for DDT (including cost comparisons with more degradable substitutes) in tropical countries, where danger of malaria exists and agricultural productivity must be increased. Environmental quality is not an absolute, nor is its relevance limited to considerations of material welfare. It incorporates intangible values of an aesthetic and spiritual character, and raises profound issues of an ethical sort, including human obligations to animals and nature, and the obligation of present generations to the future.

The specific elements of V_4 may have to be reformulated frequently during our period of inquiry, but it is clear that as a general *desideratum* ecological quality deserves high priority in a study of the future of world order. Ten years ago this would not have been the case, and the perception of V_4 as a critical world order value is not yet shared by many of the less industrial countries in the world society. (There are, of course, varying degrees of appreciation of other world order values as well; rich countries are less likely to support an emphasis on V2 than are the poor countries.) From the point of view of WOMP/USA, V4 is one of the principal world order values to be realized by drastic reforms of the existing world order system.

ADDITIONAL VALUES

The four primary values represent the main areas of international life where constructive responses are needed and where it is possible to overcome the most severe inadequacies in the present world order system: war, poverty, oppression, and ecological decay. WOMP values concentrate upon the prevention of catastrophe and the alleviation of misery rather than on the positive realization of human potentialities. Such an emphasis seems appropriate at present, given the dangers and costs of maintaining the competitive state system, and given the difficulty of securing changes in the structure of world order.* But an adequate vision of the future must also be informed by additional interrelated values that pertain to the quality of life. However, the promotion of these additional values will not be conceived as a world order task during the period of our concern, i.e., before the year 2000. Nor is it at all self-evident that promotion of these additional values should be regarded as a world order task in the future. It may be more beneficial to withhold from authority structures control or responsibility for the conditions and character of human fulfillment. The record of official morality does not encourage the view that governing groups should play an active role, but rather that their role should be tightly circumscribed so as to permit freedom to flourish. This is the position of classical liberalism, which seems to provide a highly relevant perspective on the proper limits of any governing process. Therefore, awareness of these additional values is quite different from any expectation that the world order system will or should take an active role in their promotion.

---

* It is also true that a consensus is more appropriately formed around the elimination of dangerous and destructive circumstances that menace life or deprive people of fundamental needs, than it is around some image of "the good life." Barrington Moore, in *Reflections on the Causes of Human Misery* (previously cited) effectively distinguishes between the unity of judgment about human misery and the diversity of judgment bearing on human fulfillment.

Some of these additional values include:

1. Securing the conditions of social life in each society that promote harmony, joy, and creativity

2. Eliminating coercive and manipulative approaches to the exercise of governmental authority at any level of social organization

3. Planning the physical milieu of human existence to reflect a concern with beauty and the maintenance of privacy and personal dignity

4. Conserving the diversity of nature and conceiving of ethics and politics as embracing the relations between men-and-nature as well as between men-and-men

5. Experimenting with different social and political for organizing human activities

6. Affirming the diversity of life-styles, political organizations, belief systems, and economic arrangements, provided only that their espousal and practice reflect a general pattern of adherence to the four WOMP values and a general orientation of humanistic toleration of others

7. Assuring a better appreciation of differences in male and female value perspectives and of their beneficial embodiment in various social circumstances

8. Assuring that advances in science and technology (for instance, genetic engineering and computer technology) are used for purposes consistent with the realization of primary and secondary values [16]

The relationship between WOMP and these additional world order values can be depicted in terms of rotating circles (see Figure 1–1). These circles will have different relations to one another through time and their interplay will increase with the evolution of political consciousness. A preference model of world order represents only the most formal statement of political arrangements needed to sustain life on earth in a beneficial fashion; the adequacy of a given system of world order ultimately depends on how it affects concrete conditions of existence at every level of human interaction. At the same time, the ordering system of authority should be given only certain kinds of tasks in the immediate future. These tasks have to do with the implementation of WOMP values and, to some extent, with the development of a world setting in which individuals and groups can realize their full potential for growth and happiness.

Figure 1-1. The Wheel of Values

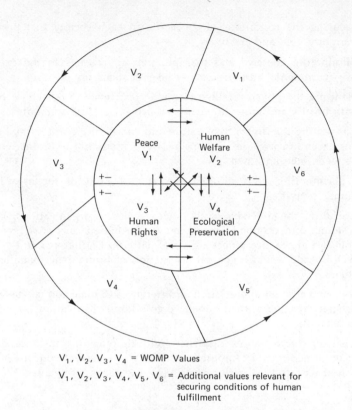

V₁, V₂, V₃, V₄ = WOMP Values

V₁, V₂, V₃, V₄, V₅, V₆ = Additional values relevant for
securing conditions of human
fulfillment

Note: These are rotating, superimposed value wheels; the inner circle contains WOMP values, as defined by WOMP/ USA, whereas the outer circle displays additional values. The arrows in the inner circle emphasize the six forms of interdependency among WOMP values that affect the cumulative prospects for world order reform; the plus and minus signs make clear that deterioration as well as progress may occur as a result of these value interactions.

VALUE INTERRELATIONSHIPS AND WEIGHTINGS

Figure 1–1 displays the interrelatedness of the value goals that give shape to our vision of an improved system of world order for the decade 1990, and thereafter. The interrelatedness of these values present decision-makers with many difficult choices. It may be unrealistic, for instance, to suppose that V_1 and V_3 are mutually consistent with respect to solving the problems of southern Africa within a reasonable period of time. Certain forms of bureaucratic socialism may serve the cause of V_2, but at the sacrifice of V_3 and V_4. There are many areas of conflict between minimizing ecological harm (V_4) and promoting material well-being (V_2). Each setting should be examined in light of all its major value consequences, and prevailing policy justified or repudiated by a reasoned assessment of its *net* effects.

Particular settings and personal outlooks will inevitably influence value weighting in situations of potential conflict among the four WOMP values.* Perhaps, at least, a strong presumption against irreversible damage can be developed as one guideline to policy decision. For instance, regardless of the extent of poverty and oppression within a nuclear superpower, on balance it would seem destructive of world order to risk "liberation" if the likely consequence is World War III. Similarly it would seem wrong to provoke ecological collapse even if motivated by V_2 policies. No values are absolute, including the prohibition on war, but certain situations of irreversible danger generate inherent restraints on conduct. In reinforcing these limitations on human discretion it might be desirable to develop categorical prohibitions, such as a prohibition on recourse to weapons of mass destruction under any circumstances. Such a prohibition would accord minimization of violence (V_1) a clear priority, in certain settings, over the promotion of political justice (V_3).†

To summarize, these four WOMP values are not absolute, and their interrelations must be considered in any context of decision. The weighting will inevitably reflect the perspective of the particular decision-makers, and their overall institutional and political orientation. There is no objective scale for weighting these value interrelationships. However, certain value denials involving massive and irreversible damage may be prohibited by categorical rule. A "liberation" movement may be able to build a plausible case within our normative framework for recourse to violence, but not in a situation of nuclear danger. Progress toward the preferred world can be measured by comparing the

---

* Indeed even within WOMP, the different interpretations of V_1, V_2, V_3, and V_4 and their relative weights illustrate the diversity of perception and priority that exists throughout the world. See other WOMP books for alternative descriptions of the four value perspectives.

† Such categorical guidelines create some problems of their own. For instance, an oppressive regime is given a maximum incentive to acquire weapons of mass destruction. By acquisition it will, in effect, secure immunity for its gross V_3 violations.

situation with respect to WOMP values at various points in time. A somewhat different calculus enters into the *making of concrete decisions* in a manner that is compatible with these values, and *assessing aggregate changes* with respect to the four values.

The world order content of a concrete decision depends on assessing relative impacts on V_1–V_4 and then shaping policy to maximize net positive impacts and minimize net negative impacts. The *aggregate* appraisal of a world order reform movement depends on measuring V_1–V_4 at various points in time according to agreed-upon indicators and then determining whether there has been overall progress between two or more points in time. An index number approach for each WOMP value is what we have in mind, with each index number being given equal weight. The approach can be illustrated in a purely hypothetical fashion:

t_0	t_1	t_1–t_0	t_2	t_1–t_2
$V_1 = 100$	$V_1 = 134$	$V_1 = +34$	$V_1 = 132$	$V_1 = -2$
$V_2 = 100$	$V_2 = 109$	$V_2 = +9$	$V_2 = 115$	$V_2 = +6$
$V_3 = 100$	$V_3 = 86$	$V_3 = -14$	$V_3 = 89$	$V_3 = +3$
$V_4 = 100$	$V_4 = 95$	$V_4 = -5$	$V_4 = 90$	$V_4 = -5$
V_1–$V_4 = 400$	V_1–$V_4 = 424$	t_0–$t_1 = +24$	V_1–$V_4 = 426$	t_1–$t_2 = +2$

It would be possible to specify the realization of a new system of world order in terms of these indicators, e.g., by positing a total for V_1–$V_4 = 2000$ and by requiring each of the WOMP values to have achieved an index number of 300 or more. Similarly, a decisive decline in world order quality could be identified at given thresholds, e.g., V_1–$V_4 = -500$ or at a point when any one of the four values has an index number of -600 or less.

EVALUATIVE ORIENTATION:
ACTOR VS. SYSTEM

In moving toward a preferred world, there is a shift from one set of dominant attitudes, practices, and structures to another. This shift will have a different ratio of costs and benefits for principal actors. In evolving a preference model, WOMP/USA has presupposed a distinctive relationship between its particular national perspective and the international system as a whole. It is certainly not correct to presume that

U.S. national interests as presently understood would be compatible with a preferred world shaped by the four WOMP values. The United States is in a privileged and powerful position—albeit a vulnerable one—within the existing world order system. We expect to encounter domestic reluctance, if not resistance, to any serious effort to identify national destiny with the wider global destiny which embraces very large numbers of people presently living in a condition of misery. President Lyndon Johnson expressed openly on one occasion what has been the implicit character of official American policy: "There are three billion people in the world and we have only 200 million of them. We are outnumbered fifteen to one. If might did make right, they would sweep over the United States and take what we have. We have what they want." [16] This kind of neo-Darwinian outlook is likely to be intensified by the emergent sense of resource scarcity and by the implications of the limits to growth debate. Up to this historical period of crisis, the liberal view of world poverty was that a dynamic growth process in the rich countries would trickle down to the poor ones and could be abetted by intergovernmental philanthropy (foreign aid). But given ecological constraints—with respect to planetary growth prospects—the only way for the rich to help the poor is by redistributive policies (i.e., altruism). Such a voluntary course of altruistic behavior is a very unusual response by the rich and powerful to a situation of community danger. The more common response is to freeze the status quo by coercive means, accepting as inevitable or unavoidable the persistence of poverty and the periodic occurrence of famine. The WOMP orientation is "countercultural" to the extent that it repudiates the domineering and dominant Hobbesian–Machiavellian tradition of guidance for a national actor, and opts instead for enlightened altruism for reasons of practical survival and positive human and national development.

A series of *national* calculations of gain and loss need to be made in relation to the four WOMP values, and there is also a *systemic* or *global* level of appraisal. We must take care to separate these levels of analysis and not presume naively a sentimental harmony, or even a convergence, of distinct national priorities and interests. The pursuit of additional values (see p. 31) within key national ruling groups will determine, to a large extent, the degree to which conscious, voluntary action can be taken in concert to achieve a new world order system. That is, unless intangible values associated with harmony, dignity, and solidarity gain far greater prominence than they presently possess, the tangible inequalities of power and wealth will produce sharp conflicts between the more and less privileged sectors of world society. Such conflicts might be muted by some new form of imperialism (that is, by denying the validity of equalizing claims) or by tradeoffs (that is, by compromising the differences in position so that all actors perceive gain, but not in the same way). The imperial solution is so at odds with WOMP values that it can be viewed as leading to a new type of world order system, a variety of *dysutopia* or negative preference model. It is possible that the United States and the Soviet Union might, for instance, encourage a world order bargain by compromising on V_2 and V_3 in exchange for progress in relation to V_1 and V_4.

Part of the purpose of WOMP/USA is to achieve a better understanding of disparities and convergencies with regard to the world order agenda of principal actors. Here, two issues are involved: the relationship among the perceptions, goals, and policies of different actors with respect to world order issues; and the relationship between actor orientation (including sub-systemic or regional patterns) and the overall character of the system.

We need, therefore, to calculate national differences as they bear on prospects for WOMP values, and also to specify as objectively as possible the gap between national approaches to value realization and the requirements of world order. In the first instance, we would end up with a rank-ordering of national governments vis-à-vis WOMP objectives and in the second instance, an assessment as to whether governmental actors are capable—because of role, tradition, or perceptions— of world order reform of the sort contemplated by WOMP values. In effect, the system of states as it has evolved induces patterns of behavior that are inconsistent with the realization of our preference model by the year 2000. The main implication of such an assessment is that governmental actors cannot be expected to become the main agents of transformation during a period of transition.

Thus, it becomes necessary either to build nongovernmental domestic and transnational sources of power to challenge the primacy of governmental authority in world affairs, or to redirect that authority in more helpful directions. This is a formidable task, as governments presently enjoy preponderant control over policy-making in the international system, although challenges are being made by global corporations and by certain functional international institutions.

OPERATIONAL VALUES AND WOMP VALUES: TWO FORMS OF DISCREPANCY

It is obvious that there is a major gap between values served in the existing world order system and the preference model projected for the

1990's. In large part, this gap can be conveyed by contrasting a state-centered zero-sum competitive approach to power, wealth, and prestige with a cooperative approach by governments to these same national objectives. Although the ideals implicit in the four WOMP values are consistent with the proclaimed aspirations of most statesmen, these proclaimed aspirations do not in any serious way correspond to the real aspirations of most statesmen.

There appears to be no evidence that richer, more powerful actors are disposed to jeopardize their relatively privileged (if, nevertheless, increasingly hopeless) position in the world system. Furthermore, there is only scant evidence that governments are prepared to realize these WOMP values within their own domestic societies, where their discretion is clearly greater. The operational code of many national elites is either to sustain or reform structures of stratification, in certain cases encouraging modest amelioration in living and social standards, in others seeking more drastic changes. "The ruler's imperative" is above all to rule on behalf of the interests of that sector of society responsible for his rulership. These interests usually presuppose the maintenance of a particular pattern of inequality and domination. To maintain such a pattern normally requires reliance on superior force, on threats and police methods in both internal and international affairs—although successful governments often are able to pacify their populations with various justifications of the existing socioeconomic order.

The existence of "enemies" of the established order within and without the society helps justify the role of coercion as a form of self-defense; a self-fulfilling kind of mystification tends to occur in any hierarchical political system in which ideals of harmony are constantly subordinated to the actualities of conflict. Such a situation helps explain the inability of world order reform to achieve its goals in the past, despite constant rhetorical support and even some apparent implementing steps (for instance, the deglorification of war and empire, the establishment of international organizations, and the formal renunciation of war as an instrument of national policy). Without a change in the motivations of elites with respect to international and national hierarchy and rivalry, the new rhetoric and institutions can be more accurately understood as facades that disguise the old order, than as agents of a new, more benign system. Therefore, we need a politics of world order reform that includes the activation of innovative elites who identify their interests with the pursuit of WOMP values on *all* levels of political reality. This process of activation of new nongovernmental elites depends, in the first instance, on mobilizing those who suffer most acutely from the inequities of the existing world order system, i.e.,

oppressed peoples and their genuine leaders. In some Third World
states such genuine leaders do control the apparatus of government
and could provide a basis for a substantial movement for world order
reform, although systemic factors make it very difficult for these governments to deviate very far from statist logic. Hence, the more progressive governments are mainly concerned with introducing greater
equity into the *existing* system of world order. At the same time there
is great variance among political leaders and social orders as to their
degree of responsiveness to WOMP values or to their receptivity to
world order reform.[17]

At present, many disadvantaged nations are ruled mainly by leaders
who identify their own well-being with the perpetuation of the present
world order system, including its great economic disparities. Thus,
these elites and their supportive groups may enjoy a high standard of
living amid a society that is generally impoverished. In such cases,
public policy will be designed to satisfy the concerns of the small
privileged class (perhaps 1–10% of the population) rather than to meet
the mass needs of the society.

There is, too, a tendency for short-run internal and regional conflict
to dominate governmental concerns, and for poorer governments to
compete for material help or to attract investment from the rich and
powerful countries within the operational code of the present system. It
is essential to understand that, until the real aspirations of peoples and
their leaders are linked to the realization of a world order system based
on WOMP values, the prospects for progress toward realization are very
poor. True, the rhetoric of world harmony may induce marginal progress, but the great proportion of energies and resources will continue
to serve the war system, to sustain patterns of domination and stratification, and to encourage a pursuit of wealth, power, and prestige in
which it is evident to all that there are "winners" and "losers," and that
it is essential to "play the game."

If significant progress is to be made toward our preferred world, it
will be necessary to subvert present value sets by introducing orientations toward world affairs that are more expressive of WOMP values.
As matters now stand, it is totally unrealistic to attribute to governing
elites any serious commitment to the creation of a new world order system.* In particular, there is little evidence of an orientation toward in-

---

* Such a generalization may pass too severe a judgment on the capacity of governments
to participate positively in a movement for world order reform. If a critical mass of governments comes to believe that transition to a new global order by voluntary planning is
the only alternative to traumatic transition or to the further disintegration of the present

ternational affairs that transcends the constraints of ideology, nation, race, class, or religion; the ideal of world community that is at the center of any approximation of WOMP values is not a significant element of the political consciousness that guides the participation of most large-scale organizations (governments, corporations, international institutions) in the present world order system.*

ACCELERATION OF VALUE CHANGE

The rapidly changing context of human activity is closely associated with the forward momentum of technological innovation.[18] Basic relationships of time, space, knowledge, and work are being altered in very fundamental ways. The impact of automation and computer technology will increase remarkably over the next thirty years. Such rapid change influences value perspectives regarding both the context of earlier values, and the growth of new value preferences.

We are aware of the need to reassess periodically the adequacy of value positions implicit in WOMP/USA proposals. There is a need for regular auditing procedures that enable a redirection of preference models of world order. Such audits should be especially concerned with interpreting and taking account of information flows, and relating feedback mechanisms to learning processes and educational activities.[19] At various points it may be desirable to reconsider the WOMP values in light of changes in world and national circumstances. Also, improved techniques for measuring value progress may evolve as new kinds of data become available, or if techniques relied upon seem to produce misleading interpretations.

---

system, an alliance, probably tacit, between a nongovernment transnational movement for world order reform and an intergovernmental coalition of reform-minded governments may be a plausible and significant development. Such a development can not be anticipated with any confidence before, at the earliest, the 1980's.

* The value base of nongovernmental actors is rather obscure. The globalism of the multinational corporation does not have a clear position on reform except to diminish the economic distortions of market and trade that result from the intrusions of policies designed to serve the distinctive interests of a particular nation. As the crisis in the present system deepens, the multinational corporate elite will have to choose between a status quo and a reformist orientation on world order issues. There will be pressure in both directions. A more detailed consideration will be found in Chapter VI.

THE PROBLEM OF MATERIAL CAPACITY

Hannah Arendt argues that in the past, revolutionary movements have been led in demonic directions by their inability to fulfill their promise to alleviate human misery. In her judgment, the material basis has not existed to permit a real solution to problems of equitable distribution and so the revolutionary regime is led to neutralize the expectations of its adherents by stressing "the enemies of the revolution." [20] The American Revolution did not go awry, according to Arendt, because it never claimed that national independence would also solve the problems of the poor, whereas the French and Russian Revolutions were doomed to failure by their messianic promises to deliver their citizenry from the clutches of misery.*

On a world level such an issue is rarely considered at all. A bland assumption is often made that the reorganization of world society around a community ideal would lead to the disappearance of the most serious human afflictions, especially poverty and war. But does enough material wealth exist to enable its just distribution, to provide everyone with the material requisites (food, shelter, schooling, health, security) of a decent life? The response is not obvious, and no serious effort has ever been made to deal with this problem, especially as it is linked to a prognosis of population growth. It is well-known that if, at the present time, the annual food production were divided equally among the human race, everyone would go hungry. Such a situation is different from the American failure to distribute available food to hungry people; within a national setting, there is every reason to suppose that the present American population could be given what it needs for a decent life.[21] The problem for America is to overcome *political* and *social* constraints on distribution. On a global level, however, given the size and growth of the population, limited supply of arable land and resources, and a variety of ecological constraints, it is not clear that a decent material existence could be provided for everyone, even postulating major reforms in economic, social, and political organizations. Certainly, at some point in the near future there would be a need for stabilization or reduc-

---

* This is the basic argument of *On Revolution*, by Hannah Arendt. There are two main currents of revolutionary energy: first, the liberation of the domestic order from foreign rule and domination; second, the drastic reconstitution of the domestic order on a more equitable or socialistic basis. The revolutionary movement in Vietnam embodied both objectives, which necessarily meant that it would split the domestic polity and cause confusion among those who favored the first objective but were opposed or ambivalent about the second.

tion of population growth; it would also be necessary to identify points of balance between world population and the carrying capacities of the earth. We require considerably more research before we can define such concerns in relation to specific policy proposals.[22]

Moreover, we need to relate the analysis to more creative conceptions of adequate life-style. The image derived from high-consumption societies of the West, with their heavy emphasis on luxuries, detached living units, and planned obsolescence, could not be generalized on a world scale without inducing ecological catastrophe. Therefore, a simpler life-style has to be accepted as the basis for securing material well-being of the human race, although diverse life-styles may be voluntarily adopted by different societies to embody their value priorities and to maximize their own potentialities.* It would be very helpful to define these life-styles with sufficient precision to allow a determination of material requirements.

It is difficult at this point in time to make a sensible judgment about material constraints. We do not know whether the neo-Malthusians or the technophiles are correct in their assessment of the future. It is difficult to determine whether current concern with the so-called "energy crisis" is a transitory phenomenon associated with the shift from fossil fuel energy sources to nuclear energy sources, or whether it is but the first of a series of crises arising from resource scarcity. It is also not yet evident whether technological potentiality is itself a function of political and social organization and, hence, whether what is technologically feasible is not relevant until "liberated" by appropriate organizational adjustments.

Some recent analysts—for instance, Buckminster Fuller and those influenced by him—have argued that technology is in a position to liberate all of mankind from poverty and burdensome abundance. Buckminster Fuller says that "Humanity has not yet learned that it could afford to employ science and technology to make all of humanity a success." [24] Edward Higbee, a Fuller disciple, says this technological potentiality presently confronts mankind with a choice between "an imaginative, deliberately created urbanization that fully employs the

---

* Tanzania's emphasis on intermediate technology and self-reliance is one positive example of a creative reconciliation of freedom and necessity in development planning. There need not be a master plan of life-style austerity, provided that the dynamics of adjustment can be initiated well before a breakdown of the world system occurs. Also, in all developed countries there are unregimented populist movements that involve a voluntary renunciation of high-consumption life-styles.[23]

wonder of modern technology for the ecological welfare of total world humanity, or universal genocide." The exercise of choice depends on the potency of the city as an organizing force in human affairs to facilitate the optimal application of technological possibilities. According to Higbee, the positive potentiality of the city requires an early abolition of the war system: "The capital now wasted on warfare is required to build new resource-making urban technologies." The abundance that could exist would stem from the application of Einsteinian ideas of relativity to the available energy supply at human disposal, more exactly the $E = MC^2$. Such an energy base implies virtually unlimited productive capacity, but it can happen only within a re-altered social, economic, and political structure. For Higbee, international business operations with their urban base and nonterritorial focus provide a foretaste of the future. He believes that ". . . the truest revolutionaries of our time are the managers of modern globalizing industries." [25] Such an assertion of belief places great emphasis upon the organizing patterns that dominate wealth-producing processes and motivations; it also exhibits a somewhat unwarranted confidence in their capacity to solve "the social question."

This kind of technological optimism remains highly speculative until the feasibility of using the energy supply, as measured in these Einsteinian terms, has been clearly demonstrated. Even then, beneficial consequences depend on transforming the political landscape, specifically by doing away with the war system. Neither in Fuller's writings, nor elsewhere, is a convincing scenario of transformation set forth; nor is it clearly shown that it is *necessary*, as distinguished from *desirable*, to eliminate war as a social institution in order to achieve the sort of material abundance that might be brought about by the evolution of new energy technologies. Therefore, it seems highly premature to conclude that the social question can be solved even if present levels of population were to remain stable, and if the only material goal were the complete elimination of poverty.

Indeed, there is reason to believe that the spread of urban life-styles and modes of economic management is likely to hasten an ecological catastrophe, and to incline political leaders of dominant states to maintain their control by relying on large-scale violence. Besides, the Fullerian view cuts against the most basic ecological imperative, namely, the need for limits, the reality of finitude, and the importance of organizing human affairs around a conservation ethic that pays particular attention to the management of resources over time. [26]

It is also not clear that such a series of techno-adjustments would adequately fulfill WOMP values, even if their realization could be envisioned within the relevant time frame. In this regard, the character of a preferred world must be considered in relation to a longer-term conception of human development than is implicit in the WOMP time frame and in its emphasis on rescuing the planet from an obsolescent and dangerous system of world order. A world of high-consumption living in which American patterns of affluence are globalized certainly might be an improvement upon the present circumstances of misery, but it might also carry mankind on an Orwellian dead-end road in which nature itself becomes subordinate to plastics of the new technetronic age. Fuller's image of cities under air-conditioned domes are suggestive of a utopia that might well be indistinguishable from a nightmare.

THE EXCLUSION OF NUCLEAR CATASTROPHE

Our inquiry into world order prospects presupposes that no nuclear catastrophe will occur between now and the 1990's. Such a presupposition is not intended to imply any confidence in or support for mutual deterrence as a catastrophe-preventing set of policies. Indeed, it is the appreciable risk of a nuclear catastrophe, and the negative effects of even threatening mutual annihilation of entire civilian populations, that have decisively deepened and exposed (though not created) the world order crisis of modern times.

World Wars I and II, as well as the post-nuclear conventional wars in Korea, Vietnam, the Middle East, and the Indian subcontinent, have caused widespread opposition to the war system as the basis for order and readjustment in international affairs. In fact, the League of Nations and the United Nations were the creations of a pre-nuclear political climate that purported to accept the necessity for a drastic reorganization of international affairs. Such efforts at reorganization, although not negligible as international experiments, have failed to secure the capabilities or political attachments needed to enforce peace against large-sized states. The atomic attacks on Hiroshima and Nagasaki in the closing days of World War II emphasized the necessity of carrying on the League experiment in the slightly altered form of the United Nations, but they did not induce any greater willingness by principal national governments to abandon the war system and centralize the pursuit of security. The United States enjoyed an atomic monopoly at the time, and did propose a far-reaching plan for nuclear disarmament in 1945 (the Baruch–Acheson–Lilienthal Plan), but it has never been clear whether the proposal actually sought its proclaimed end, or sought merely to demonstrate the peace-mindedness of the United States in order to keep the cork on the bottle with the nuclear genie more securely in American hands. Such ambiguity arises because the proposal coupled a serious disarmament mechanism [27] with procedures designed both to assure political control of the process by the Western alliance, and to maintain a one-sided American military advantage in the event that the disarmament system collapsed.*

After these early proposals, no serious effort has been made by either side to achieve drastic disarmament, though there have been periodic upsurges of support for arms control arrangements designed to stabilize deterrence or cut the costs of the arms race. The risk of nuclear war has been widely appreciated and has led to a series of arms control measures designed to stabilize the war system at the strategic level. Also, superpower diplomacy has evolved patterns of crisis-management, and since the 1962 Cuban Missile Crisis, crisis-avoidance. The USA/USSR détente has greatly increased the prospects for a continuous process of arms control. This process involves the negotiation of agreements under the bilateral auspices of SALT, and the creation of a climate of good relations through summit meetings and the exchange of visits by heads of state. In the Brezhnev–Nixon 1973 agreement on the Prevention of War, each side agreed to avoid "provocations" that could lead to crises or to outbreaks of nuclear war and to be guided by such considerations in their "formulation of . . . foreign policies and in their actions in the field of international relations." † Whether this improved superpower atmosphere will proceed beyond stabilization of the war system to a genuine disarmament process is far from clear. Arms spending and sales continue to increase on a global basis, and there is no evi-

---

* It is not clear that the United States would have ratified a drastic disarmament treaty, even if drafted along the lines of its own government's proposals. It should be recalled that the Senate refused to ratify the Covenant of the League of Nations after World War I even though that treaty was more a product of American influence than that of any other country. American leadership groups have been split between a hard-line "realism" based on preserving the full panoply of sovereign prerogatives, and a more idealistic "realism" based on the moderation of the state system and the development of a complementary structure of international institutions. Thus, there is no way, in all probability, to probe the true American intentions; it is only possible to offer a speculative assessment as to the relation of forces within American society in the event that the Soviet Union had accepted the basic bargain in the Baruch proposals. See more on this in Chapter VII.

† Article II.

dence that the war system has been rejected as the touchstone of foreign policy for the majority of powerful and rich governments.

Nevertheless, it seems evident that a risk of nuclear war continues to exist, that the risk is difficult to assess in probability terms, and that as matters now stand there is an adjustment to the unregulated possession of these weapons by at least five national governments.* Nuclear weapons—and the apocalyptic vision they appropriately induce—have not led to the abandónment of conventional warfare, nor have they provided the political motivation for a powerful new world order movement.

At the same time, there is a widespread sense that survivors of large-scale nuclear war would insist on a new world order structure that was less vulnerable to catastrophe.[28] Underlying this expectation is the idea that only a traumatic course of events provides the learning experience needed to bring about modifications in the organization and values underlying human existence. Educational efforts, appeals to history and reason, warnings about the eventual breakdown of the system and even crises at the brink are not able to overcome the rigidity of vested interests, habits of affiliation, and bureaucratic practice. Non-traumatic challenges directed at the existing order do not generate an organized demand for change and the willingness to struggle for its attainment. World order goals remain abstract for most people—not related tangibly to their life circumstances except possibly during the infrequent intervals of global crisis—and remain antithetical to the current practice of politics on the national level.

We do not deny the weight of such pessimistic perceptions. That is, we comprehend the formidable obstacles blocking a pre-holocaust approach to the transformation of the world order system. Yet we remain convinced of its necessity and feasibility. Indeed, our world order proposals assume (1) no intervening nuclear catastrophe and (2) the possibility of seeing a relatively non-traumatic process of drastic change develop from voluntary initiatives.

A final point: the danger of nuclear catastrophe remains a social fact that will persist for the indefinite future. This fact poses the issue of

---

* There is also the problem and prospect of *latent* possession of nuclear weapons by such countries as Israel or South Africa. It is these beleaguered governments that are most likely to feel obliged to rely on nuclear threats in the future to uphold vital state interests; in some instances, regional conflicts are so linked to global relations that pulling the nuclear trigger in one limited context could generate a wider escalatory response. The explosion of a nuclear device by India in May, 1974 gave rise to a new wave of anxiety about nuclear proliferation.

human destiny—quite literally, of human survival—in stark terms, and creates an absolute foundation in reason and will for the active work of drastic global reform. If this work is to have any prospect of success, it must combine education with action, and must acquire a political dimension (i.e., an ideology and a movement) at the earliest possible opportunity.

THE EXCLUSION OF ECOLOGICAL CASTASTROPHE

Reinforcing the sense of global danger, although quite separate from the risks of nuclear catastrophe, is the possibility of ecological collapse. Such a possibility is a consequence of the interplay between increases in population and rising economic growth, especially in the large industrial societies of Europe and North America. The United States and the Soviet Union, by virtue of their immense industrial development, are the most strategic actors with respect to the ecological as well as the nuclear agenda.

Specifically, it is plausible to anticipate irreversible contamination of the oceans or the atmosphere, induced changes in world climate, and desperate shortages of critical resources during the decades ahead that would make life on earth impossible, or virtually so. There is every likelihood of a series of local ecological and resource disasters—oil blowouts, tanker collisions, smog attacks, leakage into the air or water of ultra-toxic wastes, shortages of materials and energy supplies—in the years ahead. Serious dangers also arise from cumulative processes consisting of a multitude of imperceptible actions that may cause no sense of alarm until irreversible thresholds of ecological decay have been crossed. Many lakes, streams, and rivers have been polluted beyond rehabilitation by rates of decay that were imperceptible and hence unheeded, until almost the point of collapse.

The state system encourages irresponsible environmental policies on a world level. Each government seeks to maximize its economic product and to shift some of the costs of waste disposal to areas outside its boundaries of responsibility. Indeed, every industrial firm and individual has a similar incentive. Recent studies demonstrate that even socialist societies—wherein no profit motive operates—pursue economic policies that lead to ecological decay. The unifying pursuit of all national economies at the present time, whether grounded in the ideology of the market or of the state plan, is to keep the GNP growing as rapidly as possible, without sufficient concern for environmentally harmful forms of growth. Meeting the ecological challenge in terms consistent with our primary world order values requires a series of very fundamental adjustments in the costing of industry, the habits of consumption, and the patterns of human fertility.

There are several features of this deepening ecological crisis that encourage a world order learning experience:

1. Although the burdens of ecological collapse do not fall equally on weak and strong or poor and rich, all are adversely affected.

2. The process of ecological decay can be measured and is highlighted by sporadic disaster; hence, there are storm warnings.

3. The pressures generated to satisfy consumption demands (e.g., energy) are often in conflict with the pressures generated to maintain environmental quality.*

4. The pre-catastrophe impacts of ecological decay cause a steady erosion of the quality of life.

5. The hyper-modern technology that has accelerated the advent of the ecological crisis can also be used, in the correct organizational settings, to alleviate ecological damage.

6. The functional case for central guidance is not derived from any existing political perspective; therefore its neutral derivation and character can serve as the meeting ground for the convergent concerns of every major world ideology.

Hence, it seems important to build the case for world order change by emphasizing the emerging ecological agenda. Such an emphasis also

---

* The resource shortage and pollution control dimensions of the ecological crisis are often at odds. For instance, the national controversies over the location of refineries, power facilities, and pipelines are often contests between environmentalists and those groups concerned with the adequacy of energy supplies. Here again the degree to which this inconsistency is a technical and political problem (i.e., using the extra funds needed to assure that resource adequacy is not achieved at the expense of environmental quality) is not clear. Power companies contend, for instance, that underground transmission of electric power is more expensive by a factor of 20, but it would eliminate most of the environmental hazards and blights attributable to large-scale overland transmission.

follows from V4 (resource conservation and environmental quality). As a result, the ecological and nuclear challenges operate both to underlie central goals for the preferred world of the 1990's and to objectify the argument for drastic change during the transition process.

We do not know the extent to which political consciousness is shaped by the danger of man-induced catastrophes that could imperil human survival and the habitability of the planet.[29] Such a dimension of consciousness clearly exists and may provide part of the stimulus for a movement for world order reform or revolution. The annual commemoration in Japan of the Hiroshima attack arises from an intense belief that this localized catastrophe should be used as a world order learning experience that might help form a more general human disposition to avoid future catastrophes of a similar or worse character.

The cumulative impact of the nuclear and the ecological challenges also remains highly speculative. The constituency for ecological concern is somewhat broader, as this issue is more directly related to the quality of daily life. To the extent that the prospect of ecological collapse is associated with decay rather than disaster, its effects are pervasive and concretely experienced. The danger is not an abstract one, as the image of nuclear warfare tends to be. The dimension of catastrophe is creeping as a shadow cast across the life of the planet, providing recurrent proof of its actuality and demonstrating the planet's vulnerability to further deterioration unless there is a global reorganization of man's political and economic relations.

Therefore, although we exclude post-catastrophe planning from our inquiry into world order prospects, we are greatly influenced by the risk of catastrophe in carrying forward this effort. The seriousness of such risk gives an objective grounding to our pleas of urgency and gives shape to the sort of world order solutions that are responsive. Additionally, we should take note that certain parts of the world system experience disaster and catastrophe at the present time, either as a consequence of intense warfare or as a result of famine, disease, or extreme poverty. The heavy bombardment throughout Indochina; the widespread famines in Asia and Africa; the severe floods, storms, and earthquakes which periodically victimize communities around the world; the genocidal or semigenocidal massacres that have taken place in Bangladesh, Nigeria, Burundi, Brazil, and Paraguay, are all events that are experienced as "catastrophes" by the affected peoples. One early priority of a world order education program should be to interpret these tragedies in the wider context of international reality. Such constituencies of victims could easily provide some of the most persuasive and authentic spokesmen for world order reform.[30]

THE UNITED STATES' POSITION IN
THE WORLD ORDER SYSTEM

Our proposals for a preferred system of world order are consciously developed from an American perspective. That is, we adopt the WOMP values as governing the treatment of the subject matter, but inevitably approach their content with an American perspective and agenda of concerns, although not necessarily from a typical or mainstream American outlook.* Of course, this does not mean an endorsement of America's present role in world affairs. Quite the contrary. WOMP accepts as self-evident the need to reorient American public and elite opinion; hopefully, this country can be encouraged to play a less domineering global role, and to share its wealth and income with the world community on a far greater scale.†

Such objectives imply a strong link between domestic political developments and progress toward world order goals. In this sense, the domestic political arena of the United States is also a critical world order arena, perhaps even the single most critical one.‡ Without fundamental changes in the U.S. world role, no substantial progress toward world order goals can be realistically envisioned, except possibly in a post-catastrophe setting;§a redefinition of the U.S. world role by an increasing adherence to WOMP values would lead us to be relatively optimistic about the prospects for non-traumatic progress toward the preferred world, although response patterns in other critical domestic arenas, especially those in Soviet society, would be crucial.

---

* There are two intertwined, somewhat divergent, ideas present: first, the document has the provinciality of American authorship; second, this provinciality does not imply that it is a representative statement of American views on the future of world order. Such representative views are more accurately presented in the platform positions of the two main political parties, the statements and preferences of national leaders, and the content of the Nixon–Kissinger design for world order reform that has generally elicited bipartisan support.

† This kind of critique of existing American behavioral patterns is not the essence of WOMP/USA, which is fundamentally concerned with instigating the dynamics of a more positive world order system that will be beneficial to Americans as well as to others.

‡ This view of the critical role of domestic reorientation is elaborated in Chapters V and VI, and is also exhibited in most other WOMP group documents. Ebert argues interestingly that the most positive prospects for domestic reorientations favorable to drastic world order reform exist in the democratic and socialist states of Central Europe. See Ebert, *World Polity*, esp. pp. 11–15.

§ But the enactment of the United States role does not have to precede other changes in the world setting, including value reorientations in a series of domestic arenas that move in a WOMP direction.

There is a variety of other critical domestic arenas, and the parallel course of events within them will have important interactive effects.* That is, domestic arenas are themselves not insulated from external impact, no more than the patterns of international diplomacy are insulated from domestic impacts.[31] Although such an assertion seems on one level self-evident, it has not been usual to emphasize domestic politics in studies of world order problems.†

The WOMP/USA approach is informed by several closely related considerations: the development of an American perspective toward the pursuit of a preferred world by the 1990's; a stress on the domestic arena as critical to the prospects for world order reform; and the ways in which domestic developments might be constructively linked to specific models of world order change.

THE NEED FOR CENTRAL GUIDANCE

A preferred world can have many shapes and forms, provided only that it tends to promote the substantial realization of the four WOMP values. Such a constraint does not imply a unified interpretation of these WOMP values, nor does it entail any particular world order solution in structural terms. World government and anarchism are both theoretically compatible with a commitment to the realization of WOMP values. A wide range of differences among reasonable men may exist regarding the selection of a preference model from the array of alternative structural reform possibilities in the world system (see Chapter III for the array and Chapter IV for the rationale of the WOMP/USA selection), and the design of a transition process that maximizes the prospects of its his-

---

* Value shifts, especially in their early stages, would occur in an atmosphere of controversy and tentativeness; only part of the community would be convinced of their wisdom. Hence, such shifts could be retracted by bad learning experiences, especially by a confirmation of Hobbesian and Machiavellian warnings that altruistic tendencies are weaknesses in international life and will be exploited by the strong. Reciprocity in perception is a key feature in sustaining such dynamics.

† Note, though, that such emphasis is explicit in the thinking of Immanuel Kant (especially in his monograph *Perpetual Peace*) and implicit in the revolutionary visions of a new world order espoused by Lenin. Indeed Kant and Lenin share the view that world order problems can be solved by the emergence of progressive societies on a domestic level and that there is no need for any kind of supranational structure. Of course, these were pre-nuclear, pre-ecological approaches to world order reform.

Figure 1–2. The Real World Context of the World Order Models Project—The Principle of Continuous World Order Learning Cycles

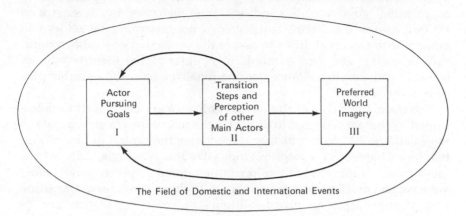

I. Present orientation—the tactics and strategy of national participation in the evolving world order system

II. Middle-range perception of reform potentialities, including reactions to behavior of other actors

III. Long-range perception of aspirational goals, including models for their realization

torical realization by nonviolent means. It is analytically consistent with this position to contemplate disarmament at the national level without any substantial buildup of police and military capabilities at the world level. At the same time, our assessment of the world order potentialities for the near future suggests the importance of working toward some greatly augmented capacity for central guidance in world affairs, including some increase in coercive authority. For this reason, we give priority to the design of a central guidance system in the WOMP/USA proposals.

Note that a central guidance system need not amount to "a world government" solution. Central guidance implies a unified capacity for policy-formation, -coordination and -implementation, especially with respect to issues closely related to WOMP values. Both the nuclear and the ecological crises seem to point toward a more centralized system of security and environmental management. State sovereignty impedes rational management of these issue-areas at present; national governments are too large to be susceptible to external pressures and too small to be able to protect national populations from adverse planetary developments. This rigidity and vulnerability of the sovereignty-based state system suggest a focus for transition efforts: to dilute the significance of national sovereignty, especially among developed countries. The state as an organizational center for political life need not disappear; so long as principal governments condition their behavior by deference to WOMP values, a substantial number of nongovernmental actors will emerge with the capabilities to assure the protection of world community priorities, and new symbols of popular global identity and allegiance will gain precedence over nationalistic ones for a sizable portion of mankind.

Therefore, the shape of the central guidance system is further determined by the posited need to diminish the role of the sovereign state in world affairs. We do not further characterize the central guidance system (see Chapter IV), except to emphasize that no single, fully articulated model of a preferred world can be offered as prescriptive before we have had much greater experience with the early stages of transition (see Figure 1–2). The broad contours of central guidance can be sketched in tentative terms, but such contours are subject to alteration during the transition process, which is above all else a world order learning experience for activists who engage themselves in the movement for a preferred world.*

---

* The stress in WOMP/Latin America on "prospective actors" who act now in a manner that anticipates the preferred future is a most important way to express the dynamic link between present behavior and future vision.

REFERENCES

1. For one important analysis along these lines, see John Herz, *International Politics in the Atomic Age*, New York, Columbia University Press, 1959.

2. Discussed further (in world order terms) in Richard A. Falk, *This Endangered Planet: Prospects and Proposals for Human Survival*, New York, Random House, 1971; among the numerous books that depict the ecological crisis see Paul Ehrlich and Anne H. Ehrlich, *Population, Resources, and Environment*, San Francisco, W. H. Freeman, 2nd rev. ed., 1972; René Dubos and Barbara Ward, *Only One Planet: The Care and Maintenance of A Small Planet*, New York, Norton, 1972.

3. A number of writers have done important work that facilitates quantitative tests of the extent of war system activity at various points in time. See e.g., Bruce M. Russett, ed., *Peace, War, and Numbers*, Beverly Hills, Calif., Sage, 1972; but also see the writings of Karl Deutsch, J. David Singer, Quincy Wright.

4. See e.g., Raymond Aron, *Peace and War: A Theory of International Relations*, 1st ed., Garden City, New York, Doubleday, 1966.

5. Herbert York, *Race to Oblivion: A Participant's View of the Arms Race*, New York, Simon and Schuster, 1970.

6. *Ibid.*, pp. 238–239; but also consider Gabriel Kolko, *The Roots of American Foreign Policy: An Analysis of Power and Purpose*, Boston, Beacon Press, 1969; Seymour Melman, *Pentagon Capitalism: The Political Economy of War*, New York, McGraw–Hill, 1970.

7. See Fred Charles Iklé, "Can Nuclear Deterrence Last Out the Century?" *Foreign Affairs*, 51: 272–285(1973).

8. This is well documented by Melman, *op. cit.*

9. Considered in Edward C. Higbee, *A Question of Priorities: New Strategies for our Urbanized World*, New York, Morrow, 1970. There are very basic issues of human nature and social goals at stake: Why national power? Why wealth beyond needs? Are these aspirations inevitable in any world order system?

10. See the chapters by Weisskopf, Hymer, and Sunkel in Jagdish N. Bhagwati, ed., *Economics and World Order: From the 1970's to the 1990's*, New York, Macmillan, 1972.

11. See Ted Gurr, *Why Men Rebel*, Princeton, Princeton University Press, 1970.

12. For a penetrating discussion of the unity of need and the diversity of aspiration, see Barrington Moore, Jr., *Reflections on the Causes of Human Misery and Upon Certain Proposals to Eliminate Them*, Boston, Beacon, 1972.

13. For a thoughtful discussion on this subject, see Moore, *op. cit.*, pp. 24–39.

14. Zbigniew Brzezinski, *Between Two Ages, America's Role in the Technetronic Era*, New York, Viking, 1970, p. 111.

15. These issues are considered in Gerald Feinberg, *The Prometheus Project: Mankind's Search for Long-Range Goals*, Garden City, New York, Doubleday, 1968.

16. Quoted by Richard J. Barnet, *Intervention and Revolution: The U.S. in the Third World*, New York, World, 1968, p. 25.

17. A very stimulating assessment of possibilities for world order reform along these general lines is Theodor Ebert's "World Polity: Futuristic Ideology or Concrete Utopia," *Contact*, 2: 3–18, 1973.

18. For a popularized account of this assertion see Alvin Toffler, *Future Shock*, New York, Random House, 1970.

19. Important interpretations that have a bearing on these issues can be found in Karl Deutsch, *The Nerves of Government*, New York, The Free Press, 1966; David Easton, *The Political System: An Inquiry into the State of Political Science*, New York, Knopf, 1953; Ervin Laszlo, *Introduction to Systems Philosophy*, New York, Gordon and Breach, 1972; Ervin Laszlo, *The Systems View of the World*, New York, Braziller, 1972; and especially, Ervin Laszlo, *A Strategy for the Future: The Systems Approach to World Order*, New York, Braziller, 1974. There is a major need at the present time to integrate systems thinking, cybernetics, and learning theory with respect to politically significant forms of value change. It will be important to relate value change to forecasting and futurist speculation.

20. Hannah Arendt, *On Revolution*, New York, Viking, 1963. For a helpful account of this revolutionary process as it has been embodied in South Vietnam, with its indigenous feudal pattern of landholding and its socially conservative religious and tribal groupings, see Frances FitzGerald, *Fire in the Lake*, Boston, Little, Brown, 1972.

21. But whether the United States could produce enough food from its own resources is not clear; present agricultural productivity relies heavily on imports of feeds from Third World (food-importing) countries. See Georg Borgstrom, *The Hungry Planet: The Modern World at the Edge of Famine*, New York, Macmillan, rev. ed., 1967; *Too Many: A Study of Earth's Biological Limitations*, New York, Macmillan, 1969.

22. Edward Goldsmith et al., *Blueprint for Survival*, New York, Houghton Mifflin, 1972.

23. One impressive formulation is in George Lakey, *Strategy for a Living Revolution*, New York, Grossman, 1973; see also Ebert, *World Polity*.

24. Introduction by B. Fuller to Edward Higbee, *A Question of Priorities*, p. XXLX.

25. Other quotations in paragraph are from Higbee, *op. cit.*, pp. 196, IV, and XIV, respectively.

26. My own appraisal of these issues is developed in *This Endangered Planet*, esp. Chaps. 1–4.

27. For analysis of governmental behavior in the disarmament negotiations see Richard J. Barnet, *Who Wants Disarmament?* Boston, Beacon Press, 1960.

28. The perspective of world order rigidity in a pre-World War III context and fluidity in a post-catastrophe setting seems to be at the center of Carl F. von Weizäcker's approach to world order reform; see "A Skeptical Contribution," in S. H. Mendlovitz, ed., *On Creating a Just World Order*, New York, Free Press, forthcoming.

29. Underlying questions of symbolization and consciousness are dealt with in path-breaking fashion by Robert J. Lifton in a series of books. See especially *Death in Life: Survivors of Hiroshima*, New York, Random House 1968 [© 1967].

30. For Lifton's discussion of the status of anti-war veterans as victims and then as positive forces for societal renewal, see *Home from the War: Transformations of Vietnam Veterans*, New York, Simon and Schuster, 1973.

31. One creative insight into the interactive features of the process is depicted by Charles E. Osgood, *An Alternative to War or Surrender*, Urbana, University of Illinois Press, 1962.

Chapter Two

TRENDS AND PATTERNS
IN WORLD SOCIETY

INTRODUCTORY NOTE

This chapter seeks to analyze the main features and apparent trends of the increasingly complex system of world order which we now know. Our appraisal leads us to conclude that the present system of world order is performing inadequately with regard to the four primary WOMP values set forth in Chapter I, and that it will probably deteriorate still further unless reforms can achieve fundamental changes. A contrasting system of world order which we favor—our preference model—is outlined in Chapter IV, and Chapter V sets forth possible strategies for accomplishing the desired transition as humanely, rapidly, and safely as possible.

Unfortunately, we have only a rudimentary understanding of the causal interconnections among different realms of human experience. For instance, we can sense intuitively that demographic developments will importantly influence the future shape of world order, but we are unequipped to say just what this influence will be. Population pressure and further urbanization might generate a disposition toward strife and warfare, but they might just as well lead to apathy and repression. Nor can we predict the future impact on world society of the growth and spread of knowledge; the emergence of a global communications network; the development of cheap, clean energy or energy scarcity; mining of the oceans, or the capacity to control the weather.

Despite the difficulties inherent in predicting the results of developments still to come, it is nonetheless possible to identify at least the general character of probable impact by analyzing current tendencies within the present world order system. The general direction of change with respect to the fundamental processes of population growth, technological innovation, environmental management, cultural transformation, and economic development is toward the interdependence and transnational linkage of sovereign states. These trends are likely to expose the inadequacy of the old system of world order based on a statist logic of competition, rivalry, and warfare. As the years pass, it will become increasingly clear that the state system that we have known is obsolete, unable to fashion responses required to coordinate activity on a planetary level.

The globalist imperatives for control will not necessarily be resolved by reorganizing the state system to allow coordination to take place; such reorganization to permit *voluntary coordination* of all planetary peoples is a central feature of the WOMP/USA preference model depicted in Chapter IV. It is also quite likely that the dominant centers of power and wealth will respond to these globalist imperatives by seeking to reorganize the planet along even more *hierarchical* lines than at present. A basic transitional concern is whether the state system (1648–1974) is being supplanted in a hierarchical (coercive) or in a coordinational (contractual) spirit. A second transitional concern is whether the world order reorganization will involve a reconstitution of the global authority system on the foundation of *existing* power centers (i.e., dominant governments) or whether the reconstitution of global authority will be accompanied by a corresponding reconstitution of power centers. The WOMP/USA proposals depend upon a substantial disintegration of state power centers as the basis for evolving a voluntary and equitable set of responses to globalist imperatives.

THE COMPONENTS OF THE
PRESENT WORLD SYSTEM

A world order system is a set of concepts and images that appear useful for generalizing our experience of the world. These concepts and images are themselves the product of dominant cultural traditions, reflecting the thought and beliefs of several centuries. Such traditions do not easily adapt to new circumstances, and adaptive potentialities must be related to the particularities of each tradition.[1] In our view, part of the difficulty of feeling, thought, and action regarding world order issues arises from bondage to a largely outmoded nomenclature and set of guiding concepts.*

In particular, the traditional nomenclature appears unable to cope with such new developments as the rise of transnationalism in economic, social, and cultural areas, and the rise of supranational functionalism which now characterizes international cooperation. The persisting tradition of speculation continues to limit the scope of world order inquiry to the external relations of national governments. We require a more inclusive conception that encourages new ways of feeling, thinking, and perceiving so as to enable us to take into account— descriptively as well as cognitively—the role of transnational, supranational, and subnational actors and developments.[2]

New nongovernmental actors—transnational corporations evolving from the organizational tendencies of international business operations, and supranational agencies formed to cope with some of the effects of technological change—are transforming the present system of world order by evolving new types of nonstatist diplomacy, during a period marked by the simultaneous erosion of traditional national boundaries which had formerly delimited subject matter. In particular, the basic boundary between internal and external (or domestic and international) politics seems much less sufficient for descriptive and explanatory purposes than it did in an earlier world of less complex and pervasive interactions and perceptions.[3] Indeed, the rise of these new actors is closely connected with the inability of governments to operate effectively themselves within many relevant fields of action. However, just when governmental action is demonstrably less efficacious than it used to be, governments all over the world are being confronted with a series of escalating domestic challenges from population growth, urbanization, and internal security, in addition to accelerating demands for great contributions to general well-being. The pressure to focus on these domestic agendas may make governments turn their attention away from important transnational problems, at the very time when

---

* *Feelings* underlie our assessment of evidence, give direction to our *thoughts,* and prepare the grounds for *action*. The triangular relationship between feelings, thoughts, and actions is an interactive one, connecting realms whose linkages should be studied. World order studies have tended to confine their inquiries to the province of thought, thereby ignoring the roots of feeling that make people receptive or antagonistic to certain ideas or ways of presenting ideas, as well as to overlook the critical process by which ideas are implemented in various fields of action. Zones of feeling, thought, and action relevant to world order reform should be depicted separately, in dynamic interrelation, and from a variety of cultural, ideological, and geographical perspectives.

these wider concerns are becoming more urgent and central to planetary life.[4]

On the basis of these introductory ideas, we turn now to an examination of the main features of the present world order system. This discussion will be oriented around the four central WOMP concerns: war, poverty, oppression, and ecological balance. Taking up first the main concepts traditionally used to describe the system, we shall focus on the role of governments and on the network of intergovernmental relations, because governments still remain the dominant actors in the world system and retain for themselves the authority to modify voluntarily the structure of the world order system. Governments are generally the most *powerful* actors because of their monopoly over military capabilities, except in those few national settings where counter-governmental or unofficial armies enjoy a favorable balance of power or exert quasi-governmental control over a portion of territory. As far as wealth is concerned, corporate actors are increasingly competing with governments; in Lester Brown's [5] ranking in terms of the size of annual product (GNPs for governments, gross sales for corporations) in 1970, there were 58 governments and 42 corporations on a combined list of 100 top entries.*

THE LOGIC OF WESTPHALIA

The basic coordinates of the present world order system are contained in the Peace of Westphalia which brought the Thirty Years War to an end in 1648.[6] According to Westphalia logic, the world order system is constituted *exclusively* by the governments of sovereign states. These governments have complete discretion to rule *national space* (or territory), and can also enter into voluntary arrangements (e.g., treaties) to regulate external relations and interconnections of various sorts. But these governments are *sovereign* and *equal* by juridical fiat, rather than by virtue of some higher authority within the world order system. No one government is entitled to greater formal status than another by reasons of wealth or power or size. In such circumstances, "law and order" rests upon the volition of governments and upon their perception of common interests.

---

* The size of corporate sales is not an altogether satisfactory indicator of political influence or status, but it does disclose comparative scales of various actors.

These perceived common interests provide a durable basis for agreement in those situations where interests are shared or reciprocal, and in which relative positions are unlikely to change as a result of alterations in power, technology or perception. The protection of foreign diplomats from national abuse—expressed formally in the concept of diplomatic immunity—or the governance of international postal service or telecommunications, exemplify obvious shared interests that are sustained through time by durable conditions of reciprocity. By contrast, the rules of warfare have broken down where technological innovations have shattered mutuality of advantage; the development of the submarine and the airplane as weapons of war, for example, superseded intentions to confine the impact of naval warfare to combatants. And now we are even observing the erosion of diplomatic immunity—not because this is no longer of mutual interest, but because governments can no longer dominate all *political space;* and counter-governments (or liberation groups) with no reciprocal interests in the security of diplomats have found that it is a useful tactic to kidnap foreign diplomats.* The use of air-hijacking by liberation groups as a bargaining and attention-drawing tactic is another example of the disruption of a common-interest intergovernmental arrangement—here, the security of international commercial aviation—by an actor who lacks any attachment to that kind of government interest.

Where interests are adverse or positions dissimilar (for example, in relation to competition for scarce power, wealth, and prestige among differently situated actors), there is a very small scope indeed for effective regimes of "law and order." Occasionally, areas of common interest can be identified within these larger spheres, such as the "hot-line" agreement linking the White House and the Kremlin by direct telecommunications contact during a period of intense Cold War rivalry, or the general (but by no means uniform) improvement of the treatment of

---

* Unlike traditional warfare between sovereign states, modern civil war often involves the most heterogeneous antagonists, each of which pursues its quest for victory by emphasizing its areas of comparative advantage. Thus, the government (incumbent antagonist) relies on military technology, torture of opponents, and general repression of dissent, whereas the insurgent antagonist emphasizes disruptive tactics relying on surprise and terror, and on generalized support available in an abused populace which resents, to varying degrees, the policies and practices of the government. The main point is that the law flourishes only where there exists a symmetry of relations and perceptions as to the character of self-interest, whereas modern civil war is dominated by asymmetries of the most fundamental sort. To the extent that civil war of various sorts becomes the characteristic form of modern warfare, the capacity of Westphalia to provide minimum boundaries is seriously undermined.

prisoners of war through negotiated treaty rules. But, by and large, these spheres of vital state action have been unregulated zones, facilitating and even legitimizing the domination of the weak by the strong.*

The main point to observe here is the *volitional* basis of intergovernmental action to protect world interests. The unreasonable or negligent government, especially if it is powerful and rich, cannot be regulated in any generally reliable way. If a government allows registry of unseaworthy oil tankers to obtain foreign exchange or disposes of nerve gas or radioactive wastes in defective containers, a portion or even the entire community of states shares the risk of these actions, although the responsible government cannot be held accountable in the event that something goes wrong.† In other words, there is considerable *decentralization of authority* in the present world order system that governments could voluntarily overcome for limited purposes. But governments tend to construe their interests, define their goals, and understand their positions in drastically dissimilar ways. The effort to secure a universal prohibition on nuclear testing in the atmosphere presents a vivid and important illustration. France and China have refused to accept the rules of prohibition agreed to by the United States and the Soviet Union in the Limited Test Ban of 1963. China, in particular, argues that total renunciation of nuclear weapons is the proper threshold for minimum

---

* Traditional international law, for instance, gave formal status to the entire colonial system, including capitulary regimes by which nationals from colonial countries were exempted from many aspects of territorial law.

† Obviously, preventive standards and implementation are needed to protect the world community against negligent or malicious risk-taking by a particular government, perhaps even if the burden of risk falls entirely within territorial limits, but certainly if its impact is extra-national. The point in this context is that even if an imprudent risk actually inflicts harm, then there is no assured way to compel adequate reimbursement by the responsible government. Indeed, given the extreme traditions of sovereignty, there is no orderly way to enjoin similar risk-taking in the future. A vivid illustration of this process was the French defiance of an order by the International Court of Justice to desist from further atmospheric testing of nuclear weapons until the prospects of actual harm and legal status could be fully and fairly assessed by the Court. France's refusal to accept the outcome and validity of this procedure initiated by Australia and New Zealand is indicative of the persisting vitality of Westphalia logic even in Western Europe, where it has been played out for the longest time and where two world wars have spread a wide swathe of death and destruction. In fact, despite the wide geographical orbit of risk and the highly charged symbolic content of nuclear weapons tests, there is no widespread international effort to bring pressure on France to respect the World Court determination. Governments are extremely sensitive about encroaching upon claims of sovereign prerogatives; here is one area of international life where statecraft seems to give expression to the "golden rule."

agreement, but the governments with nuclear superiority are unwilling to renounce or restrict their nuclear option.*

The current hard bargaining to develop an international regime for the regulation of the seabeds occurs in a different kind of setting, where the primary bargaining constituencies are those of the developed countries, the less developed countries, and the organized international community. President Nixon's proposals of May, 1969 tried to strike a bargain by offering incentives to each of these three constituencies. Other actors, by virtue of position and perception, regard a different sort of bargain as reasonable for purposes of allocating the mineral patrimony of the seabed. The reformist potentialities of a world order system organized along Westphalia lines depend considerably on the extent to which perceived interests can be made to coalesce around authoritative tradeoff bargains. That is, there is an increasing need to extend "law and order" into domains where *diverse* interests and positions exist, by establishing agreed-upon *tradeoff formulas*. Of course, such a process is rendered highly unstable if the negotiating elites do not represent the genuine interests of their populations, or if changes in circumstances and consciousness occur so rapidly that what appears to be reasonable in 1970 seems grossly inequitable to principal participants by 1975 or 1980.[7]

In matters of national security, the logic of Westphalia entails a primary reliance on self-defense, abetted by alliance relations. Governments are not precluded from recourse to war, and there is no higher authority than the warring governments to differentiate just from unjust causes of war.† Part of self-defense is the entry into alliance relationships that confront a prospective enemy with the prospect of aggregated force. In essence, within the present world order system, the

---

* This comment in the text is not meant to criticize China or France vis-à-vis other nuclear superpowers. It seems reasonable for secondary nuclear actors to claim testing prerogatives equivalent to those exercised by primary nuclear actors. Denuclearization of world politics is at least as worthy a goal as the termination of nuclear testing. In essence, both categories of nuclear actors are pressing certain statist demands and presenting them as issues of international morality. The United States criticizes further atmospheric testing; China criticizes the nuclear use and threat option, i.e., the legitimacy of nuclear weapons. Both states would gain in statist terms by the acceptance of their claims, and yet both claims also have genuine moral content and significance for world order reform.

† It is true that the United Nations Charter and modern international law seek to restrict governmental discretion and to draw a distinction between legal and illegal wars, but such a formal development has not had any major operative impact on the discretionary status of resort to force by governments pursuing what they conceive to be their vital interests.

prevention of war depends on deterrence or partnership. For instance, the security of Canada or Mexico vis-à-vis the United States rests on the cordiality of their relations, on their common heritage and outlook, and on their shared posture of opposition to other international power groupings. However, the discouragement of war between the United States and the Soviet Union (or between North and South Korea, or the Soviet Union and China) rests more heavily on a deterrence arrangement, in which a potential disturber of the status quo is confronted by an inhibiting prospect of retaliation.

Since 1928, the date of the Kellogg–Briand Pact, it seems that governments have in some respects renounced their discretion to make war. By virtue of this treaty, which has been confirmed by other treaties and by the statements of various national leaders, governments can use their war capabilities only for purposes of individual or collective self-defense. It might seem that such a modification of Westphalia logic would greatly alter the status of war in the world system by prohibiting other war-initiating pretexts and by classifying non-defensive uses of force as illegal. In fact, however, the absence of impartial higher actors and established procedures allows each government to describe its recourse to war as an occasion of self-defense, and to ignore contentions to the contrary. The League of Nations, set up in 1920 to prevent a recurrence of general warfare, lacked any enforcement capability; its voting procedures were based on the principle of sovereign equality (valid decisions required a unanimous vote, and therefore any negative vote was tantamount to a veto), there was no common definition of self-defense nor any institution entitled to adjudge opposing claims of self-defense, and several important states were either excluded or chose not to participate. Thus, the world order response to World War I involved a new *normative* orientation toward war—in a sense, a return to the medieval stress on the "just war" doctrine—but brought about no corresponding political or institutional shift capable of moderating the logic of Westphalia. There was some effort to accomplish more fundamental changes by means of disarmament, but it proved impossible to discover formulas of perceived self-interest for arms reductions that satisfied rival actors in diverse positions.*

The state system continued to maintain peace, if at all, as a result of

---

* This impossibility was not the fault of unimaginative negotiators, but reflected the continuing hold of the war system on the pursuit of value-conserving (defensive) and value-expanding (offensive) goals of the state. There can be no path to drastic disarmament that does not include an uprooting of the war system in the depths of human consciousness, as well as in the sinews of the bureaucratic structure of a modern state.[8]

national self-reliance, alliance relations, deterrence and domestic opposition to war-making. National governments, despite the normative
reorientation away from war, continued to reserve for themselves both
the effective discretion to wage war, and unrestricted control over the
instruments of warfare. Furthermore, the competitive dynamics of the
geopolitical struggle, especially after it was hardened into ideological
rivalry by the triumph of Communism in Russia, took precedence over
any attempt to assess which side in a conflict was the victim of attack.
The search for peace by Westphalia logic was based on the imagery of
"balance," "equilibrium," and "moderation" among the competing
units, and this continues to be true. Such a system is inconsistent with
ideological or normative commitments which ultimately entail a diplomacy based on *sympathies* rather than on *power*. An equilibrium system, relying on deterrent postures, ultimately rests on governmental
perceptions of relevant capability and on the credibility of the threat to
attack or resist. If discrepancies among perceptions emerge, then the
temptation to test the reality of the balance grows great, especially if
genuine revisionist grievances are felt, ideological tensions are acute,
and domestic political and economic pressures support the idea of external retribution.* Such factors were in the background of World
Wars I and II, although authoritative explanation of their origins remains controversial.

THE LOGIC OF WESTPHALIA APPRAISED

The basic "logical" difficulty with the statist approach to world order
arose from the recurrent tension between *equality in theory* and *inequality in fact*. As a world order system, the state system involved the formal
domination of the national societies of Asia (with the exception of
Thailand and Japan), Africa, and, indirectly, Latin America, by Europe
and the United States. Formal doctrines of nonintervention and territorial jurisdiction gave way to imperial and hegemonial incursions, reconciled in extreme cases by conferring legal status upon unequal relationships established by the colonial system.

---

* War-proneness also engenders irrational politics (high risk-taking) and facilitates as-
cent to power of desperate men (great oversimplifiers; Hitler's rise to power in Germany
is an extreme instance). Desperation in the future may not take such an explicitly pathological form, but may be adapted to the technological potentialities of the age and involve extreme depersonalization of attitude.

Furthermore, the notion of keeping the peace by offsetting alliances was constantly vulnerable to the irrationality or ingenuity of rival leaders, as well as to the real or supposed breakthroughs in the technology or strategy of warfare. The arms race is just a metaphor for the pervasive uncertainty associated with a peace system that depends on shifting calculations of advantages on the part of leaders in rival governments. Westphalia logic could never provide governments with more than a series of armed truces.

If in a particular historical period international society happens to be dominated by a series of moderate governments that subscribe to a more or less *common* ideology, conflict tends to involve *smaller stakes* and the incidence and magnitude of warfare is less. However, if any principal actor adheres to a more radical interpretation of the international situation and develops a set of revisionist demands, backed up by revisionist strategies, the danger of war exists. The danger is accentuated when ideology reinforces geopolitical claims, lending credence to the belief that it is necessary not only to pursue or resist particular claims, but also to eliminate rival actors (or at least drastically alter their domestic structure of authority). The Cold War has given some evidence of the extent to which this ideological dimension intensifies statist conflict and interferes with the overriding world order imperative of equilibrium in a general atmosphere of moderation; likewise, the ending of the Cold War demonstrates the degree to which formerly intractable issues of geopolitical rivalry now appear to be either negotiable or of marginal importance.

Nor can an equilibrium system cope very successfully with a large number of autonomous or semi-autonomous centers of decision. It has been argued by theorists of international relations that five actors provide the optimal conditions for managing the state system through reliance on balance of power mechanisms. It is notable that a revival of five-power thinking in the Nixon Era has accompanied the new moderation in superpower relations.[9] In the present world setting there are several interacting layers of power relationships, including bipolarity for matters of nuclear balance, and pluripolarity for matters of regional balance. When power relationships are conceived as encompassing economic relations, the structure of the international system is even more complicated and variegated.* International institutions, liberation

---

* Much of our thinking about international relations has been premised upon a military security paradigm, in which a few strong governments are the principal actors and a managerial objective is to secure balance and moderation in their relations with one another.

movements, business organizations, and transnational groupings of various kinds participate in conflict situations going on around the world. The proliferation of state actors and the emergence of these new kinds of international actors make it difficult to conceive of the multiple effects of any given action in terms of equilibrium, much less to premise behavior on the assumption that equilibrium can be achieved.

The Westphalia system fails to fulfill minimum requirements for progress toward realization of the WOMP value dealing with collective violence. Although the logic of Westphalia does provide a measure of confidence that large-scale nuclear war will not occur in the immediate future, it affords no longer-term assurance, especially given the prospects for proliferation of weaponry.[10] Furthermore, the consequences of failure are so serious that even a small risk seems intolerable, provided of course that lower-risk world order systems can be brought into being within the near future.* With respect to subnuclear levels of warfare, the complexity of the modern world, together with the immoderateness of political struggle, make the logic of Westphalia an unsatisfactory basis for attempting to minimize violence in world affairs.

Such a paradigm does not fit most international economic subject matter, where the identity of actors is likely to be different and where the managerial objectives tend to seek more unity and coherence. For instance, the international monetary system is dominated by market economies in the advanced industrial countries (especially the United States, Western Europe, and Japan). Advanced socialist countries and Third World countries, even the largest and most important, play virtually no role as compared with third-rate military states such as Switzerland or Belgium. Furthermore, nongovernmental actors, "the gnomes in Zurich"—whether speculators, multinational corporations, or governments with temporary foreign exchange surplus accounts (e.g., oil exporters in the Middle East, especially Saudi Arabia)—play a significant role in generating "crises" in money markets or in providing reassurance. Whether governments can reorganize the monetary system to assure their greater control over its fluctuating behavior remains uncertain at this time. Our main point here is that in terms of spatial scope, actor participation, and world order requirements, there are very important distinctions to be drawn regarding the state system's operation in relation to different subject matter areas.

* "Lower-risk" systems do not necessarily entail arms control, much less disarmament. The prevailing view among policy-makers is to approach existing risks as an *engineering* problem calling for better "command and control," more accurate and survivable weapons so that an irrational enemy will not be tempted, and safer techniques for storage, testing, and transportation of nuclear weaponry. The political, psychological, or moral dimensions of risk are not considered, or at least are not generally considered susceptible to reduction. We intend, of course, to encompass a much more drastic and less mechanical range of lower-risk systems within our inquiry. See Chapters IV and V for a consideration of lower-risk structural options and a rationale for the design of a preference model from the array.

When it comes to the realization of the other three WOMP values, the logic of Westphalia achieves even less satisfactory results. An extraordinary degree of poverty, hunger, and misery exists in the present world order system. The disparity of average per capita incomes between some sectors of world society exceeds 30:1. A great proportion of mankind exists at or below the poverty line, whereas a small proportion experiences the bounties of affluence. These matters will be explored in greater detail in Chapter VI, but suffice it to say that the discretionary basis of intergovernmental relations means that rich countries acknowledge no duty to transfer their resources to poor countries, or to expand their goals to include the improvement of economic conditions in these countries. An effort by Third World governments to impose a tax, or even to suggest voluntary contributions of one percent of GNP on rich countries to finance development efforts, has had almost no success, although a few countries (for instance, Canada) have been moving in the direction of accepting an informal obligation to provide development funds at about that level of magnitude. The present aid-giving policies of the rich countries continue to be carried out in the spirit of philanthropy as completely voluntary expressions of enlightened self-interest by the more fortunate, and as palliatives that will inhibit more desperate tactics by the poor countries. The amounts given by the rich countries over the years seem small in relation to either the capacity to give, the gap to be overcome, or the need for assistance.

The logic of Westphalia works against obligatory or substantial foreign aid by emphasizing the critical importance of sovereign consent in the emergence of new standards of international conduct. We cannot expect the existing system of sovereign and economically unequal units to rectify these disparities by voluntary action, at least not while present attitudes persist. One might have expected socialist governments to initiate a more altruistic set of relations, at least with one another or in dealing with problems of extreme poverty or disaster; to date, however, aid-giving by socialist states has exhibited the same combination of minimal help and influence-seeking, except in some instances where the geopolitical stakes are high (e.g., Cuba).[11] Also the expense of a security system based on national defense drains funds that might otherwise be devoted, at least in part, to improving economic well-being throughout the world.

With respect to the protection of human rights, Westphalia logic is similarly unsuited to the realization of minimum standards. The state system has been unable to combine its forces effectively to oppose abhorrent domestic policies, even when national governments have shared a high degree of consensus. The treatment of Jews in Nazi Germany and the treatment of blacks in South Africa suggest the impotence of the world order system.* Indeed, there is a normative contradiction, as the affirmation of internal sovereignty gives a government complete authority to decide how to treat its own *subjects*. Since governments have a mutual interest in upholding internal sovereignty, especially in a period of ideological strife, efforts to protect human rights rarely progress beyond the stage of censure—even when, as with respect to Rhodesia, the international community has agreed to impose economic sanctions. Statist interests take precedence over the pretensions of international solidarity and concern for human rights.

Similarly, with respect to the problems of environmental management that are beginning to be placed on the world order agenda, there is no tradition which encourages insistence upon a common framework for control and guidance. To the extent that the perceived common interests exist, it might be possible to develop collaborative institutions, but early evidence suggests that the diversity of economic and physical position among societies at different stages of industrial development will preclude any common approach beyond the endorsement of lofty aspirations and, possibly, the creation of machinery to gather information on general environmental trends and to respond quickly to certain kinds of international disasters (e.g., tanker collision, oil blowout, space accident).

On balance, the logic of Westphalia now seems unable to protect the most vital needs of most of humanity. It no longer provides sufficient security against attack, nor permits reasonable progress in attaining social and economic justice; it cannot protect the environment from deterioration, or satisfactorily allocate and conserve the scarce minerals and resources that will be taken from the oceans. Although a further proliferation of states, especially via secession from the larger advanced industrial states, might considerably improve the capacity of the West-

---

* The refusal of most Western liberal democracies to help Jewish refugees during the Hitler period is one of the most depressing confirmations of the general unwillingness of governments to pay any national price whatsoever to promote respect for fundamental human rights. See Eugene Davidson, *The Nuremberg Fallacy*, New York, Macmillan, 1973; Arthur D. Morse, *While Six Million Died*, New York, Random House, 1968. It appears that issues of human rights receive substantial governmental support only when it is geopolitically convenient to do so (e.g., when it was desirable to mobilize American public opinion behind the government's Cold War stance) or when a politically and financially potent domestic constituency can exert effective leverage on policy-makers (e.g., pressure on Soviet government to allow Jews to emigrate without paying an exit tax).

phalia system to promote WOMP values, such a development is not likely to occur in the foreseeable future.*

THE LOGIC OF THE CHARTER

Superimposed on the state system, to some extent as both its complement and supplement, is the ideology and reality of the United Nations Organization. The United Nations, as a network of institutions active on a global level, needs to be distinguished sharply from the lofty language and ambitious goals embodied in its organic law, the UN Charter.[12] The Charter looks toward the emergence of a peace-keeping force sufficient to implement decisions of the Security Council. However, the provisions of the Charter (contained in Chapter VII) have never been acted upon, and in this critical symbolic and perhaps actual sense, the monopoly of state control over military (and even police) power has remained undisturbed during the almost three decades of UN existence.

The Charter provided veto power for the five Permanent Members of the Security Council. But because of the veto, the decisional center of the UN system—itself a hierarchical innovation designed to reduce the gap between the Westphalia idea of sovereign equality and the real world actuality of great power status—has been virtually immobilized as an autonomous actor. The idea embodied in the Charter, and carried over into the organization of the Security Council, was that the UN could be more effective if it took formal and explicit account of the international power structure as it was understood to exist in 1945. In part, this step was designed to overcome a perceived weakness of the League of Nations, which had adhered more rigidly to the logic of Westphalia in all formal respects, including sensitivity to sovereign equality and voting rules requiring unanimous decisions.

---

* That is, we acknowledge the possibility that a certain structural modification—the breakup of advanced states into a series of smaller states—might produce very significant world order reforms *within* the state system. Such a possibility would be increased if the secessionist tendencies were themselves promoted by groups sharing allegiance to WOMP values or to a closely aligned value pattern. However, we do not consider this prospect sufficiently likely, nor are we optimistic enough about its impact on V_2 (well-being) and V_3 (human rights) to regard it as a preference model at this stage of our awareness of future world order prospects.

The Charter also embodied a further compromise by its reaffirmation in Article 51 of arrangements for collective self-defense, and its related deference to regional security operations. These arrangements, which amount to *actor-oriented* rather than *norm-oriented* notions of collective security, make it almost impossible to achieve a *community-based* consensus on the aggressor's identity. If countries continue to devote primary emphasis to alliances and rivalries, it then seems self-evident that in the event of armed conflict, a body with members from both sides will hold contradictory views as to which side is the aggressor and which is the victim of aggression. Norms of constraint cannot be relied upon to mobilize a unified community response under these conditions, although in certain circumstances where the facts of armed attack are reasonably clear, a norm-oriented consensus has been reached and implemented. The most prominent occasion of this sort was the UN response to the Suez campaign of 1956 initiated by France, Israel, and the United Kingdom.* The Charter approach often seems almost like a mirage. The discrepancy between the grandiose undertaking of its Preamble, and the meagerness of its implementation throughout UN history, has caused widespread disappointment and even embitterment among those who had expected the establishment of the United Nations both to reduce the frequency and intensity of warfare, and to increase the community aspects of international relations. These expectations of a major UN impact on the state system were, of course, unrealistic for several principal reasons:

The Charter logic incorporated Westphalia logic into its formal rhetoric.

There was no shift in power or loyalties, i.e., there was no political preparation for a shift from the state level to the UN level.

---

* Such a judgment is controversial, especially as it pertains to Israel. See Julius Stone, *Aggression and World Order*, Berkeley, University of California Press, 1958. The jurisprudential question is whether the norm of aggression should be so closely associated with priority of recourse to sustained military operations, as it was by the UN majority. The opposing view, which gathered some support in relation to the Middle East War of 1967 and the Indo-Pakistan War of 1971, argues that the norm of aggression should be associated with a wider context of considerations, including para-military and diplomatic provocations, threat behavior, and severe deprivations of human rights. The choice between clarity and reasonableness of normative standards is especially difficult with respect to a highly mobilized political arena such as the United Nations. Perhaps the reality of politicization would take precedence in any event, where the identification of an aggressor is determined primarily by the relative amount of political support each contender can mobilize. In actual practice an either/or approach is probably not helpful; norm-defining clarity plays a role for some actors most of the time and for almost every actor some of the time. Hence, the jurisprudential issue may not often be decisive, but it is nevertheless significant.

The alliance among the Permanent Members of the Security Council during World War II proved to have no durability after the defeat of the Axis powers.

The United Nations is hampered by a very small budget and enjoys virtually no financial independence, especially in relation to big powers.

Under such circumstances a Charter for the United Nations—even when given the solemn form of an international treaty—cannot hope to alter ingrained patterns of thought and action, especially within the social, economic, and political conditions of domination and inequality that exist throughout the world. Among Third World governments * there is a growing tendency to endorse violence by liberation groups in South Africa and to create an important legislative exception to the absolute prohibition on nondefensive force found in Article 2(4) of the Charter.

The United Nations does, however, provide a forum in which Third World countries can articulate their views and justice demands, and where all countries are encouraged to search for consensus in areas of controversy. This UN role will not often produce dramatic solutions for the leading problems of the day, but it may at least help activate the consciousness needed during a period of global reform and systemic transition. Thus, although the Charter's logic is burdened by the realities of Westphalia logic, it also embodies the vision, assuredly in primitive form, of a new system of world order based upon a concert of national governments and even capable, under appropriate circumstances, of moving from an intergovernmental to a supranational presence in world affairs. Given our conception of world order, the Charter seems excessively focused upon war prevention—precisely the sort of objective least appropriate for an intergovernmental body which lacks the attributes of supranationality. A new Charter, even if negotiated by governments, would probably be formulated and conceived around a *series* of values, including (we think likely) the four values emphasized in WOMP. The international community has been undergoing a generally encouraging learning process regarding the char-

---

* Of course, the category "Third World governments" is a gross one, including governments whose *political orientation* ranges from far left to far right and whose *governing style* ranges from passive to active in relation to domestic and foreign affairs. Also, there are important distinctions between resource-rich less-developed and resource-poor less-developed countries. The range extends from the main Arab oil-producing states with their enormous capital wealth, to the drought-afflicted countries of the African Sahel. The poor countries without the resource base needed for development are sometimes identified now as belonging to the Fourth World.

acter of world order. Of course, much of this learning is a direct consequence of the increased participation of Third World states on a basis of
sovereign equality in the United Nations setting, and it is not without
some counter-tendencies.*

THE LOGIC OF SUPRANATIONALISM:
INCREMENTAL FUNCTIONALISM

There has been an exponential growth in the activities of international
institutions concerned with technical cooperation among governments
in matters as diverse as postal service, health, communications, maritime safety, and commercial air transport. The expanding scope of technical capacity makes national boundaries less relevant in an increasing
number of critical areas.[13] There is considerable disagreement as to the
world order significance of these functional developments, and it remains too early to discern whether an increase in functional cooperation at a supranational level demonstrates the adaptive capacities of
the state system, or whether such cooperation is likely to gradually
displace the present nexus of nationally organized power and authority.[14]

Some of the international institutions that have been most successful
in impact and quality of performance, such as the International Bank
and the International Monetary Fund, have been dominated by leading
governments; in some of these institutions all of the participating governments are noncommunist. Under these conditions, supranational
forums can become adversary forums that embody international factionalism in much the same way as do alliance structures such as NATO
or the Warsaw Pact. That is, the proliferation and growth of supranationalism does not necessarily imply a movement toward the organization of a unified world community.

The degree to which a given subject is treated as one of *universal* concern (e.g., in conformity with WOMP values) varies with the issue, and
is influenced by matters of ideology, subject matter, tradition, and
knowledge. The world economy seems to be especially split, in its
supranational aspects, into partial groupings based on ideological af-

---

* Especially, a growing view in the advanced industrial countries that some form of
neo-Darwinian (competitive, hierarchical) solution to the neo-Malthusian problems of
scarcity is both possible and desirable. We find very little evidence of world order idealism of the sort embodied in WOMP present in the programs or statements of leading governments.

finities. The economic commissions of the United Nations which are continental in scope (e.g., Europe, Africa, Latin America, etc.) do represent an effort to establish more ideologically inclusive arrangements at the regional level, but their accomplishments to date are meager.[15]

The global potential of incremental functionalism is very unclear at the present time. The next decade will provide a very significant indication of the rate of supranational development and its impacts on the underlying character of the present world order system. In particular, it will be important to monitor two kinds of developments:

1. The capacity to accommodate pressures for functional cooperation by consensual processes of intergovernmental negotiation; the extent of progress here will depend on whether bargains can be struck among governments with very diverse positions and perceived interests in international life (e.g., regulation of oceans, environmental problems, and nuclear energy).

2. The capacity to implement effectively the schemes agreed upon. It remains to be seen whether governments that are unequal (in size, wealth, and level of development) and diverse (in matters of domestic political and economic organization) can develop cooperative approaches toward such major subjects as the allocation of ocean minerals and regulation of satellite communications.

In any event, as of 1974, there is no reason to suppose that incremental functionalism will substantially contribute to a fuller realization of the four WOMP values. Agreement on limited forms of supranational treatment in the areas of arms control, conservation and development of ocean resources, economic cooperation, environmental management, and human rights may decelerate certain trends toward deterioration and collapse of the present world order system in the years ahead. But these effects on international life would be system-maintaining, and would not be inconsistent with the persistence of warfare, economic and social injustice, racial discrimination, and pollution. In this respect, the growth of supranational cooperation will not challenge the dominance of Westphalia logic, nor will it overcome the principal defects of the state system as the organizational basis of international relations. On the other hand, if the development of supranationalism proceeds as favorably as might realistically be anticipated, then it could, in conjunction with other developments, weaken or transform the loyalty of citizens to national governments. In a climate of expanded supranationalism, both substantive and institutional progress toward a preferred world in the WOMP sense might become more feasible.

However, even such guarded optimism about the future of functional cooperation does not seem warranted, at least so far as the next decade is concerned.

The extent to which incremental functionalism alters the world order system seems heavily dependent on the orientation of domestic governments in principal societies. If most of these governments become more oriented toward supranational solutions, then world order prospects improve greatly (especially if early experience with functionalism seems to inspire confidence, or if the failure or refusal to achieve supranational solutions is widely perceived to cause negative results). A learning process based on supranationalist experiments will help determine the degree to which authority is voluntarily transferred beyond the nation–state. In any event, the dynamics of incremental functionalism will clearly not overcome the value insufficiencies of the present world order system by the end of the century; this kind of supranational development may be important in relation to the transition process, but seems incapable of providing the main substance of a preferred world, as specified by WOMP values.

THE LOGIC OF TRANSNATIONALISM

There are strong economic, technological, and political factors underlying the remarkable growth of transnational structure and sentiment during the last two decades. By "transnational" we mean the movement of goods, information, and ideas across national boundaries, without significant direct participation by governmental actors. This movement establishes transnational linkages, and is beginning to generate new types of organizational entities that are exerting an international influence not easily comprehended within Westphalia or Charter logic nor even within the notion of supranationalism.

The range of transnational activities is considerable. On the one hand, it includes efforts by militant minority groups in the United States to relate their aims directly to Third World liberation struggles. (The Black Panther Party has even sought to coordinate these transnational relationships by opening an Information Office in Algiers, Eldridge Cleaver's place of exile.) * But transnationalism is more typically

---

* For a variety of personality and organizational reasons the Black Panther efforts to establish a Third World presence in Algeria have not been successful. One of the reasons for

and pervasively illustrated by the multinational corporation's dramatic rise to prominence. This rise is a consequence of the spreading of corporate activities to all corners of the earth, a spread that is made feasible by a world economy that remains relatively open to capital flows.[16] Judd Polk of the U.S. Council of the International Chamber of Commerce has recently compared the rise of the multinational corporation with the earlier drive in the United States to open up a continental market in order to absorb the products of the industrial revolution. The "new industrial revolution" seeks to organize itself in relation to the world as a whole: "The state of industrial technology—very much including world electronic communications and computers—has created the situation in which, for the first time, men are in a position to treat the world itself as the basic economic unit." [17]

A central unresolved world order question is whether the large multinational corporations are pursuing "a foreign policy" that is compatible with that of leading national governments, whether such governments rule over market or state-controlled economies. The corporate search for profitability and unencumbered access to as large a marketing zone as possible may very well conflict with a national emphasis on full employment and maximum economic autonomy leading to protectionist policies in critical industries.[18] These issues are complicated and yield no easy, across-the-board generalizations. World order specialists should closely track the behavior of these corporate actors and observe whether the statist drive to regulate these corporations prevails over the corporative drive to elude national regulation by adopting an *a-national* identity, i.e., an identity beyond the reach of the state system.

A further world order focus should examine whether the transnational effects of the multinational corporation have a positive or negative effect on WOMP values within the existing world order system, and whether their net effect is positive, negative, or neutral with regard to transition prospects relative to the realization of our preference model (see Chapter V) by the end of the century.

Many other forms of transnational activity may be much more compatible with WOMP than the ambiguous consequences of increased multinational corporate activity. Especially in the area of human rights, transnational pressure groups clearly seem to have a positive impact in relation to V_3, and also with regard to weakening the absolutist links between the state and the individual that have been so characteristic of

---

disappointment was also a consequence of a conflict between the statist role of the Algerian government and the transnational radicalism of the Black Panther Party; this conflict became explicit when hijackers or "fugitives from justice" increasingly sought to use Algeria as a sanctuary because that country had accommodated Cleaver.

the state system. In addition, transnational efforts to promote human rights such as the emancipation of women may turn out to have spill-over effects on other value dimensions (for instance, encouraging the adoption of birth control, thereby alleviating population pressure, and improving the national and world capacity to raise living standards in accordance with V_2).

Some human rights issues that are attracting transnational support have to do directly with domestic dissent or international mobility. These issues are therefore symbolic for a future world order system based on human solidarity, free movement, and "continuous revolution" (or more restrainedly, continuous growth and development).

In the more general economic sphere, involving monetary stability and prosperity through world trade, there is a growing realization that state boundaries impede rather than facilitate national management. The transnational behavior patterns are becoming so pronounced and nongovernmental actors so significant, that traditional mechanisms of intergovernmental *ad hoc* consultation seem insufficient. The realities of transnational patterns are forcing an awareness of the state system's obsolescence upon even the most reactionary and entrenched forces, and are creating a certain receptivity to central guidance as at least "a necessary evil."

Thus, it seems evident that various transnational phenomena will become increasingly important over the next several decades. It will be critical to relate this transnationality to WOMP concerns, and to evaluate developments in light of our preference model. Transnational pressures can cause reforms to be made, but they do not seem likely to precipitate by themselves a voluntary process of transition to a new world order system organized around WOMP values. Indeed, at present the strongest transnational pressures are those in the economic sphere, largely motivated by value clusters that are either indifferent or antagonistic to WOMP values, although such pressures can still be used constructively to stimulate world order reform and augment transitional tendencies.

CONCLUSION

Westphalia logic, Charter logic, functional cooperation, and transnational formations are the main organizational energies manifest in the present world order system. Many nonorganizational developments—in the area of science and technology, politics, and social change—are exerting a formative influence on the evolution of the world order system. In the next chapter we will consider the world order impact of some of these nonorganizational factors.

It is important to bear in mind the distinction between two types of world order transformations: those that are brought about by the ongoing dynamics of international life, under conditions of accelerating change of all basic variables, and those which result from conscious reform. In our view the evidence vindicates the WOMP assumption that these ongoing processes of world order adaption and change, although substantial, are insufficient to meet the mounting challenges against the existing world order system, and consequently that the existing system must be supplanted as rapidly as possible by deliberate action oriented around the four WOMP values.*

INTERNATIONAL TRENDS, SOME CRITICAL VARIABLES, AND THE FUTURE OF WORLD ORDER

In this section, we will try to assess some general tendencies in international society. In the present global system we discern four inconsistent world order trends, of varying strength and desirability, which will constitute the main world order tendencies for the rest of the century:

1. The net deterioration of the existing world order system: a growing deficit balance will reflect the excess of decay over reform ("decay" and "reform," that is, in relation to the four WOMP values); as time proceeds, the system as a whole will grow increasingly vulnerable to catastrophic breakdown.

2. The net amelioration of the existing world order system, but without any drastic rearrangement of its basic components by the 1990's; here, unlike (1), a strong reformist movement succeeds in making

---

* By referring to WOMP values, we intend mainly to offer our shorthand designation for progress toward or the achievement of an *adequate* system of world order. We do not intend, however, to attribute any special significance to our value-set; we recognize that other conceptions of world order adequacy are ethically and pragmatically plausible. Our only claim is that the WOMP set underlies a coherent program of world order reform that concentrates especially on requirements for a supportive, but not overbearing, authority structure. Such a structure comprises our preference model for the 1990's and is depicted in Chapter V.

net gains in relation to the four WOMP values; violent struggle, economic misery, political injustice, environmental deterioration persist but are being dealt with in significant fashion.

3. The world order system is consciously altered to enable a better realization of the four WOMP values; this alteration would consist principally of an agreement to establish a major governmental presence
   on a world level and to eliminate (or drastically confine) the control
   of military capabilities by national governments.

4. An inward-turning emphasis on the part of principal world states,
   especially the two superpowers, likely to be quite easily reversed
   over the next several years.

We cannot yet be certain which of these four tendencies will prevail
by the end of the 1990's, but a straight-line projection of tendencies and
moods in 1974 would yield a clear expectation of (1). No existing countervailing forces seem formidable enough to offset the emerging encounter between the state system's economic and political style, and
growing threats to human survival. Neither is there any significant
trend toward more equitable distribution of national income or toward
a more progressive outlook on the part of national governments with respect to issues of world order reform. The emphasis on maximizing economic development, whether measured in national accounting terms of
GNP or in multinational corporate accounting terms of world sales and
profits, creates the dynamics underlying continuously intensifying
pressure on a world of finite space and resources. These dynamics are
reinforced by an ideology of "modernization" and "development"
which is ascendant throughout the world and is almost everywhere associated primarily with accelerating economic growth. Given the inequality of sovereign states, their competitive rivalries for resources
and markets, and their possession of weapons systems that are subject
to rapid and uncertain rates of obsolescence, there is little prospect for a
consensual shift toward a central guidance system for the world as a
whole. National elites appear increasingly disposed to turn inward in a
vain effort to satisfy, or frequently to neutralize, the demands generated
by their domestic political systems. These critical elite groups situated
at national centers of power, wealth, and authority give no evidence of
receptivity to major world order change.

The potentialities of tendencies (2) depend on a constructive response
to the negative consequences of (1), especially in the 1980's. Such a constructive response would seem to presuppose both a series of intense
warning signals on the ecological–equity front (pollution disasters,
famines, pandemics), a series of moderating developments in the ri-

valry among principal governments, and the ascendancy of national elites committed to programs beneficial for the *whole* of their national societies, but with priority given to progress for their fundamentally deprived sectors.* In such circumstances, the prospects for innovative forms of cooperation at the international level might increase dramatically. The growth of this kind of cooperation would tend to produce a more elaborate system of coordinating links to manage the world of intergovernmental and transnational activities. Many of the old elements of world order would persist, but Westphalia logic would grow less rigorous and its effects less menacing, enabling relations among states to proceed more generally in accordance with Charter logic.† There must be general understanding that environmental quality could not be achieved at the expense of the poorer portions of world society, and therefore, that the higher costs of ecologically sound modes of industrial development would be shifted by tax, aid, and trade mechanisms to more affluent societies and to the richest sectors of these societies. It is highly uncertain whether the reformist line of (2) would be able to meet the range of emerging survival challenges and still achieve a satisfactory rate of progress in relation to the other three WOMP values. However, the shift from (1) to (2) might under certain circumstances hasten the advent of (3) and help assure its peaceful emergence; under other circumstances, the deficiencies of (2) could lead to a reversion to some variant of (1) occasioned by militancy or extremist policies prevailing in a principal domestic arena (quite possibly, although not necessarily, for reasons almost entirely related to domestic political struggles).‡

The shift toward (3) depends on a positive learning experience in

---

* As earlier noted, we emphasize that a humanistic and non-repressive approach to governance on a domestic level is directly linked to the prospect of WOMP-oriented reforms on the global level. Such linkage is a necessary, but not sufficient, condition for reforms; it is also essential that a wider global consensus emerge on the direction of world order reform, and this process of consensus-building requires a genuine consideration of world order prospects by all actors participating prominently in global affairs.

† Such developments would also have a dramatic effect on the status, orientation, and role of the United Nations Organization as an actor in the world order system. In fact, the strengthening of this second tendency might support the judgment that the degree and quality of central guidance predicated by the WOMP/USA preference model (see Chap. IV) could be achieved by the evolution of existing institutional arrangements, including their adaptation to this more favorable international atmosphere.

‡ We have in mind here principally the international effects of some new form of "the Hitler problem," i.e., a dynamic, aggressive national leader or oligarchy that threatens the basic security (military, political, economic) of other states, including important states, by pursuing policies of military or para-military expansion.

relation to (1) and (2). This positive learning experience is likely to involve a combination of net negative feedback arising out of the persistence of the state system, and a growing consensus throughout the
world that new forms of world order would be both desirable and possible. This shift to (3) is very much contingent on the course of developments within the principal domestic arenas of the United States and the
Soviet Union; probably in China, Japan, and India; and quite possibly
in other less obvious states as well. It is also contingent on the gradual
acceptance by influential elites of a *world order interpretation* of the inadequacy of present modes of existence on earth. This latter contention
needs to be properly understood. Failures to maintain peace, achieve
social, political, and economic justice, and maintain environmental
quality can be attributed to inherent characteristics of human nature, or
to the peculiarly destructive tendencies of rival actors or ideologies. The
first view leads to immobilism, the second to a "holy war" mentality.
We are arguing here that the evidence for neither position is persuasive, although each may at a given historical moment shed light on
political behavior. Our basic contention is that in order to satisfy the
value requirements of the modern age, it is essential to focus upon the
incapacity of a world order system constituted primarily by sovereign
states of unequal size and wealth. These value requirements can be met
if, and only if, fundamental world order reform takes place in the form
of *rapid transition* to a type of world order system that embodies an adequate *central guidance* capability. Such transition would necessarily involve *substantial demilitarization* on a national level and a *substantial buildup of authority and of responsibility for planning, coordination, and
cooperation* on a global level.

   In grasping this orientation toward the future, it will be helpful to
consider several specific conditioning variables that are likely to shape
governmental behavior. The number of variables is large and their interplay is only very slightly understood. Causal statements can be made
with varying degrees of confidence. We are not trying to predict the future, but only to depict those dimensions of probable development that
will require constant monitoring in light of our basic assessment of the
vulnerability and inadequacy of the present world order system.

THE INTERNATIONAL POLITICAL SYSTEM

The dominant motif of international politics is competitive diplomacy,
structured very largely by the war system until the late 1960's; in the

most recent period, economic interactions have become an increasingly significant dimension of statecraft.* Since World War II, the principal focus has been upon the various dimensions of East–West conflict, dominated by the United States on one side and the Soviet Union on the other, and centering on the danger of a nuclear World War III. This central conflict has been premised on the West's ideological opposition to Communism, and has never strayed far from the possibility of war. The Soviet acquisition of nuclear weapons, and subsequent development of long-range delivery capabilities, generated in the early 1950's a strong impulse to shift the idea of security from *defense* to *deterrence*. [19]

The shared interest of the United States and the Soviet Union in avoiding nuclear war has not prevented other forms of large-scale warfare at the *margins* of great power concern. The Korean War and the Indochina War are the main arenas, to date, where the United States has actively used its military power to prevent the expansion of Communist control in world affairs. The Middle East and Central Europe have been the scenes of recurrent crises, and military interventions by the two superpowers have taken place in Eastern Europe and Central America. In addition, covert military intervention has been a prominent feature of bipolar diplomacy throughout the Third World, although it seems clear that the United States role has been much larger than that of the Soviet Union.

There are at least four trends now evident in bipolar relations. The first involves the dramatic muting of conflictive relations, and the affirmation of cooperative and friendly relations. The annual exchange of visits by Brezhnev and Nixon, with TV broadcasts to the host population, the rise of Soviet–American trade and other economic relations, the routinization of arms control negotiations, and the virtual elimination of hostile propaganda, have led observers to conclude that the cold war is over and that a new phase of superpower relations has begun. It is too early to assess the character of this new phase of relations. A great deal will depend on the future drift of the Sino–Soviet conflict, on the one side, and the economic relations among competing industrial states

---

* There are two elaborations on the generalization in the text: first, Marxist tradition has not acknowledged a distinction between the war system and the economic rivalries among principal capitalist states, regarding the latter as the premise of the former; secondly, the displacement of the national security paradigm as central to the functioning of the state system is only just beginning to take place. The whole Morgenthau approach is based on the overarching and pervasive character of the security system. Generalized metaphors about "balance," "stability," and "equilibrium" refer to relations among potential adversaries in a war, even though the claim of such international relations theorists is to deal with world politics as a whole.

on the other. If these intra-ideological conflicts deepen, then Soviet–
American friendship might further solidify to the point where desig-
nations of an emerging "condominium" would seem to be no more
than one latent potential line of development. If intra-ideological conflicts are resolved or muted, either a period of moderate international
relations organized around a "concert of powers" fulcrum, or a renewed period of ideologically fraught conflict (Cold War II), might
ensue.

The second tendency evident in bipolar relations is the uninter-
rupted arms competition between the two countries, despite the ending (or at least the waning) of the Cold War. In both countries, this
competition continues to sustain huge defense budgets and to induce
a continuous search for improved weapons systems. At the same time,
neither in Moscow nor Washington do leaders indicate any serious interest in disarmament or even in the denuclearization of international
politics. In view of the removal of a plausible external menace, the
persistence of the arms race under these altered world conditions must
be seen, in part, as a reflection of domestic pressure groups in both
societies. The continuation of the arms race may also be explained by
a tacit interest on the part of Soviet and American leaders in sustaining their joint military dominance in world affairs. Many past arms
control arrangements—including the Limited Test Ban Treaty and the
Non-Proliferation Treaty—can be understood in a vertical sense as
seeking to freeze the bipolar hegemony, and in a horizontal sense as
stabilizing bipolar interrelations. The bilateral nature of SALT talks is
also susceptible to this double interpretation and has been attacked by
resentful states, especially the People's Republic of China. The NATO
allies of the United States have also been restive about bilateral arms
control arrangements which may have an impact on their own security
positions but which are negotiated without their participation.

The third broad tendency, implicit in the first two, is a weakening
of alliance relations on both sides. The Cold War pattern is both less
necessary and less possible in this new era of great power amity. The
apparently successful Sino–American accommodation further disorga-
nizes the ideological patterning of statecraft that had been the prime
diplomatic reality in the two decades subsequent to World War II. The
failure of ideological cohesion on the Communist side is matched on
the western side by the collapse of postwar economic arrangements
based on United States dominance. The American disaster in Indochina and its complement, the Watergate scandals, have further
eroded American prestige and leadership. Similarly, the Soviet acquiescence in America's role in Indochina, its dependence on large food

imports from market economies, its pattern of domestic repression and its willingness to intervene to control deviant developments in its European "satellites," have all weakened the Soviet claim to lead a world Communist movement or even to be the spearhead of progressive tendencies in the world system.

The fourth and final tendency, perhaps the most transitory, is an inward-turning withdrawal by superpowers from a generally activist foreign policy.* Of course, such a development is, in part, a by-product of détente. It also represents a decline of concern about the evolution of most parts of the Third World, or at least a tacit delegation of that concern to other actors, principally the multinational corporation. Whether shortages in critical resources—for instance, the energy crisis—will lead to a revival of interventionist diplomacy is not certain. And, of course, a low-profile American counter-insurgency role in many countries persists. In the absence of ideological fervor, these links between Washington and military dictatorships around the world seem better understood in terms of maximizing United States power, or as an expression of the influence exerted by economic pressure groups to protect existing and possible future investments.

These governments are further compromised as international leaders by their failure to solve domestic problems. The Soviet government remains repressive and unresponsive toward the bulk of its own population, and despite its socialist claims has failed to provide its own poor or minorities with a discernibly more satisfying life than have the "capitalist exploiters" in the West. In addition, ideological and governmental considerations have produced an impression of unprecedented bureaucratic presence in the life of ordinary Soviet citizens, extending to gross invasions of human privacy and blatant denials of elementary civil liberties. As a result, new forms of alienation within Soviet society have made it unattractive as a model for the socialist societies which have subsequently emerged in international life.†

---

* The 1973 Middle East War suggests that any systemic generalizations can be misleading. The Soviet Union seems to have been actively engaged from the outset of the October War, especially in relation to the Syrian effort. The United States and the Soviet Union both became massive resuppliers of military equipment lost in the early days of the war. As with Korea, Indochina, and earlier wars in the Middle East, superpower weaponry and involvements fuel shooting warfare in Third World contexts.

† This loss of idealistic appeal by the Soviet system should not lead observers to neglect the contributions that the Soviet Union has made to progressive political causes in the world. As a consequence of objective interests and of opposition to the West, Soviet foreign policy has consistently supported progressive tendencies in the world system, al-

Similarly, the United States government has also been unable to produce a society that exhibits contentment or success,* despite its fantastic wealth, its democratic creed, and its relative insulation from debilitating warfare. Excessive consumerism and materialism undermine national self-confidence of the sort that existed earlier in the country's history. Racial discrimination persists, the principal cities are ugly, unhealthy, and unsafe, many among the young and the intelligentsia are disillusioned and cynical, if not deeply alienated; and the physical environment, once a source of pride, seems to be rapidly deteriorating. In addition, the status of women and of the aged seems completely unsatisfactory, given the ethical and political ideals of the society. And finally, conditions of work in what is increasingly described as a post-industrial society appear to be causing severe problems of disaffection and malaise, because job prospects rarely provide opportunities for creativity or individuality. This atmosphere engenders feelings that life is meaningless, and a sense of personal inadequacy grows widespread. The absence of a vital ideological myth, and the declining vigor of religious institutions, have further generalized this societal condition of malaise.

As of 1974, it remains unclear which set of tendencies will prevail in the U.S. and USSR and how their attitudes toward each other will develop, although it appears that neither side is prepared to exert an effective leadership role in any movement for world order reform of the sort that stresses WOMP objectives. The major conflicts of interest—the four divided countries and the Middle East—remain largely unresolved, and are not easily susceptible to compromise. However, the new moderation in Soviet–American relations makes these issues seem far less menacing than they did at the height of the Cold War.

By 1980 it seems likely that within the advanced industrial sector of

---

though not as ardently or materially as some would prefer. But the outlook and existence of the Soviet Union seems an important factor in the struggle against colonialism and reactionary government in the Third World, and in the effort to induce governments in leading capitalist countries to pursue more enlightened social and economic policies. The revolutionary option, as historically embodied, has been an important force for change in the world. With détente and the buildup of Soviet vested interests, it seems uncertain whether this progressive influence will persist; China seems to regard itself, with good reason, as the Soviet Union's successor as the principal governmental spokesman for progressive social, economic, and political policies in world arenas. It is China who has taken the lead in putting forward a progressive view in relation to such varied subject matters as disarmament, environmental cooperation, and the distribution of ocean resources.

* The situation in the United States is discussed in more detail in Chapter VII.

the world, the main line of ideological conflict will swing farther away from the issues of property ownership and state plans versus market allocations, and will focus on questions of international stratification and dependence. These issues are not purely political even in appearance, and involve above all else the use of existing power by rich countries to resist the revisionist claims and policies of poorer governments. The tactics of nominal accommodation by way of international assistance will probably not succeed in maintaining even a facade of harmony with respect to international priorities and goals. Confrontation will be more likely, as a result of increasing links and rising awareness among the elites representing the interests of poorer societies—despite the fact that these elites are themselves often in tacit alliance with rich foreign interests, and therefore represent vested interests which are at odds with the welfare of their own societies.[20] The globalizing influences of the multinational corporation will be very strong, and may coordinate a transnational business class whose widely shared concerns and goals will not require any explicitly political nexus of authority. In any event, present trends suggest major shifts in the next decade from East–West geopolitical conflict to North–South and intra-West patterns of geo-economic conflict.

Undoubtedly this shift will be difficult to detect because of a variety of inconsistent developments. Competition by great powers for influence in the Third World will continue into the 1980's and will partially obscure the relevance of geo-economic motivations.* Whether this competition will produce large-scale military struggles of the Vietnam type cannot now be predicted, although it seems inevitable that clashes among opposing factions throughout the Third World will provide occasions for intervention for the remainder of the century. Whether these clashes will be linked to wider patterns of conflict is less predictable. It is also unclear whether weapons and doctrinal developments will cause a decisive and consistent shift in the balance of influence to insurgent or to incumbent elites. A major reformist undertaking would involve strengthening the peacekeeping capabilities of the UN, perhaps including the creation of a standby police force; if the UN had such a capabil-

---

* For instance, if the advanced industrial sector evolves a cheap source of energy, such as fusion power, which does not require reliance on critical raw materials from Third World countries, the struggle for influence may indeed diminish, perhaps virtually disappear. On the other hand, if critical shortages emerge or if radical developments in the Third World threaten to close off large parts of the world economy to corporate actors, pressure for control mounted from within the rich and technologically superior countries is likely to grow intense.

ity, it might succeed in decoupling internal conflicts in Third World countries from geopolitical rivalries among principal states.

POPULATION AS A WORLD ORDER FACTOR

In a profound sense, population trends constitute the most basic factor in human affairs. Only in the last few decades have we begun to understand that there is "a population problem" of grave magnitude. More recently, widely read books by Paul Ehrlich, the Paddock brothers, and Georg Borgstrom have depicted world population trends in alarmist terms, comparing population growth to a global time bomb with a short fuse; these works have generated widespread concern and awareness.[21] Not only is there an increasing realization that current rates of population growth cannot persist much longer without resulting in catastrophe, but also that the present size of world population, combined with growth prospects, greatly complicates the task of eliminating poverty, improving the quality of life, conserving finite resources, and sustaining environmental quality.[22] Our intention here is to deepen these perceptions of population as a world order factor.

Facts

The explosive population growth throughout the world has been a direct consequence of successful efforts to achieve "death control," especially by improving mass hygiene in relation to the birth process, and by reducing susceptibility to disease. As matters now stand, the annual birth rate for the globe is approximately 34/1000, whereas the annual death rate is about 14/1000. The gap between birth and death rates results in a net annual increase in world population of 20/1000, or two percent. Given the present world population of more than 3.5 billion, a two-percent growth figure results in seventy million more people on earth each year. This rate of growth amounts to adding a population group equivalent to the present population of the United States or the Soviet Union—205 million—every three years. At this same rate of growth, the population of the earth will double in 35 years. This steep incline in world population has taken place during the last several decades.

The scale of population growth is so large, especially in Third World countries, that natural checks such as war, famine, and disease—even when they are of great magnitude—do little to inhibit growth rates.* Birth rates are very high in Africa (47/1000), Latin America (38/1000), and Asia (38/1000), as compared to Europe (18/1000) and North America (18/1000). As a result, growth rates are 2.6% in Africa, 2.3% in Asia, 2.9% in Latin America, while only 0.8% in Europe and 1.1% in North America. These figures obscure an even greater discrepancy in growth potentials because annual death rates remain at 20/1000 in Africa and 15/1000 in Asia, whereas they are only 10/1000 in Europe and 9/1000 in North America. These regional discrepancies are thrown into relief by calculations showing that whereas world population doubles every 35 years, African population doubles every 27 years, Latin American population every 24 years, Asian population every 31 years, North American population every 63 years, and European population every 88 years. In sum, population growth is unevenly distributed throughout the world and is heavily concentrated in the poorer sectors which are already the most congested. As a result, already overburdened governments are confronted with accelerating demands that must be met just to maintain the existing, woefully inadequate, quality of services. Furthermore, the age distribution of a population tends to reflect its rate of growth: the more rapid the growth, the higher the proportion of young people. Such a comparison can be made in relation to the age/sex pyramids of a rapidly growing population like India's (2.16% per year), and a reasonably stable population such as that of Sweden (0.8%). The importance of these age profiles is twofold: first, the proportion of the population under fifteen years constitutes dependent members of the community; second, the more pyramidal the structure, the harder it becomes to reduce population growth to parity in a short period of time. Thus, India's dependency ratio is far higher than Sweden's, and a higher proportion of Indians than Swedes will be of childbearing age within the next decade. Finally, the annual additions to the labor force

---

* That is, since the world population is growing at six million per month, even large-scale disasters in which hundreds of thousands of people die have no depressant effect whatsoever on aggregate population trends. In 1973, prior to monsoon rains, eighty million people in India were reportedly threatened with starvation; at the same time, 25 million or more inhabitants of six central African countries were threatened with mass famine. In such instances, the threatened loss of lives, by its sheer magnitude, may have an important "educational" impact, alerting people in many parts of the world to a crowding crisis in a way that books cannot do. To date, also, it has not been helpful that the alarmist books are written by Americans but apparently have their most direct applications to the attitudes and life-styles of Third World peoples.

are an outcome of the age pyramid; if massive unemployment exists to begin with, as it does throughout the Third World, the situation is aggravated by large additions to the work force—both absolute and per-centage-wise—each year.

The projections available for the remainder of the century suggest a continuation of the present pattern of explosive growth. Even assuming a somewhat diminished birth rate for the rest of the century, the popu-lation by the year 2000 will be almost double what it was in 1963 when the projections were originally made. But those who are most knowl-edgeable in this field seem to agree that from a resource and environ-mental perspective, the existing population is already too large. There-fore, the prospect of additional growth of this magnitude is a cause for despair, as it cannot help but complicate immeasurably, at every level of social organization, the tasks of reforming and transforming political order.

Our consideration of population as a factor in world order analysis encompasses three principal dimensions of concern: Malthusian, Marx-ist, and Ecological. These dimensions are often intermingled, with bad effects, in discussions of "the population problem." The diagnosis of the problem then becomes too vague, and the tactics and strategies too little related to specific manifestations of population pressure that are of paramount concern in a given place at a particular time.

The Malthusian Dimension

The popular understanding of population issues is connected with the adequacy of world food supplies. Thomas Malthus, writing at the end of the eighteenth century, made a set of gloomy predictions about the future of mankind. Asserting that food supply could only be increased at an arithmetic rate, while population would increase at a geometric rate, Malthus foresaw a growing gap between food supply and de-mand that could only be closed by the brutal impact of disease, fam-ine, and warfare. Man's productive ingenuity has exceeded Malthu-sian predictions, and food supply has increased at least as rapidly as population. It is estimated that there is today a similar proportion of hungry people as when Malthus wrote, and it is possible, although not likely, that this proportion will diminish during the next three de-cades despite prospects for rapid population growth during this period.

In one sense, however, a Malthusian problem already exists. The most accurate estimates now available suggest that ten to twenty mil-lion people die each year from malnutrition and starvation, and that anywhere from one-half to more than one-third of the world's population is undernourished and malnourished.[23] Georg Borgstrom, the food expert, points out that "equal distribution of all available food would only make hunger universal and shared by everyone."[24] Evidence also shows that malnutrition impairs child development. Insufficient food and inadequate diets, especially protein deficiencies, seriously deplete human potential in large portions of the world. It seems doubtful that existing governments will have the capacity to provide food for poor populations which will be, on the average, twice as large within the century, especially in view of the fact that these burdens fall in *inverse* relation to the ability to bear them. For instance, some of the governments least successful in meeting existing fundamental needs of all their people may have, by the year 2000, a population that has tripled or even quadrupled over what it was in 1970.

The organization of economic life on a national level, especially in relation to agricultural production, means that surplus food production cannot consistently be used to overcome food shortages. Despite world conditions, the U.S. Government has for years paid farmers several billion dollars a year through the Soil Conservation Bank to withhold as much as 22 million acres of land from production (although these market/price policies have now been virtually eliminated under the combined pressure of rising food prices and expanding market opportunities, especially large Soviet purchases).

The high productivity of the agricultural sector in modern societies is heavily dependent on feed imports from poorer countries. As Borgstrom points out, during the period of European empire there was a buildup of European food production at the expense of colonial peoples: "As late as 1939 shipload after shipload of peanuts left starving India to fatten cows of the distant empire rulers of the British Isles."[25] The character of international trade flows continues to deprive poorer countries of agricultural products they need to feed their own populations.

As Borgstrom puts it:

> Few seem to realize that European dairy production is dependent for its high productivity upon the influx of high-protein-concentrate feeds from the hungry world of tropical Africa and Latin America. The Nigerian sale of peanuts on the world market deprives this country of an amount of protein which is approximately half of what it needs to fill the present protein gap. . . .[26]

Such inequities are unlikely to be corrected by the existing state system and may be the source of desperate strategies by those who suffer their consequences in the decades immediately ahead. National and regional famine threats are becoming a recurrent feature of the international scene. The breakup of Pakistan in 1971 and the establishment of Bangladesh seemed triggered in part by population considerations. Although the impact of population pressure may be difficult to explicate in precise causal terms, its influence may be a conditioning factor that tends to push political controversy in extreme directions.

The Marxist Dimension

The issue posed can be summarized on one level by the question, "Will the green revolution turn red?" by which is meant, "Will the political discontent engendered by rapid agricultural development generate revolutionary politics in the Third World?" The question might also be phrased, "Will the green revolution turn black?" that is, in the direction of rightist repression, as governing groups perceive the dangerous political consequences of an adverse demographic matrix. Here the issues are generated not so much by the size of a population, or even by its rapid growth, as by its uneven distribution, especially the growing concentration of discontented people in cities. The cities of the Third World are already notable for their mass misery, sprawling slums, deficient hygiene, massive unemployment, and underemployment. The migration from the countryside is accentuated by pressures associated with increasing food production. The introduction of intensive farming depends on large-sized farms and a considerable substitution of machines for human labor. As a result, poor farmers are dispossessed of their land, opportunities for rural employment diminish, migration to the cities is encouraged and a counter-insurgency psychology infuses the governing process.

As Neil Chamberlain points out, because land is fixed in quantity, it tends to advance in price as population grows.[27] Such growth makes land increasingly scarce relative to demand, and limits its acquisition to those portions of the population—institutions of government or the upper classes—that can accumulate the capital needed for purchase. This structure of relations tends to intensify the already existing economic and social inequalities.

Most population growth in the remainder of the century will occur in the cities, the increases in the rural population being just about offset in most places by rural–urban migration. It seems clear that such rapid urbanization will lead to a labor force that is expanding much more quickly than job opportunities. For instance, George Tobias estimates that during the next decade in India alone there will be a net increase of

63 million workers in the labor force.[28] It is worth noting that the "manpower explosion" situation will not be affected in the near future by any impact family assistance programs may have on fertility patterns. India's labor force for the next fifteen years *is already in being.*

Of course, it is not certain what consequences this kind of manpower pressure will bring, but it is a virtually universal phenomenon that will clearly have an impact through the 1970's and 80's and probably into the 90's. Men rebel and governments repress when severe deprivation exists.[29] The conditions of manpower surplus in crowded and miserable cities would seem to stimulate a strong sense of deprivation.[30]

In many countries the *distributive* demographic profile is more significant than the aggregate totals.* A deterioration of the demographic matrix could be largely avoided in the United States through the 1990's, if expected additions to the population could be concentrated in sparsely settled regions of the country, spurred perhaps by a Model Cities Program sensitive to the possibility of demographic planning.

The Ecological Dimension

Additions to human population impose added burdens on the environment: many kinds of environmental decay increase in almost direct proportion to increases in human population, and efforts to increase food supply depend on the use of often-harmful insecticides and chemical fertilizers. On the other hand, from an ecological point of view, most of the pressure arises from industrialization, which has proceeded furthest in countries with relatively low rates of population increase. Thus, Australia, sparsely populated as a whole, is still confronted by the standard pollution problems of advanced industrialization in the vicinity of Sydney. In the United States, the concentration of people in and around cities living at high income levels and accustomed to high energy life-styles, rather than the total number of people living within national boundaries, provides the real basis for concern about population size and growth prospects.†

---

* Indeed, the traditional Marxist analysis of scarcity is based on the notion of capitalist exploitation; hence, in societies in which exploitation has been ended, no problems of scarcity would remain, including food, and there would be no reason to limit population growth. China's adoption of an ardent family planning program suggests a rejection of this ingredient of the Marxist dimension.

† Of course, this entire discussion is conditioned by a focus on "problems" rather than "policies" or "values." There is a tacit assumption in the population literature that concern with demographic patterns becomes well-founded only when it causes dramatic

Indeed the interplay of GNP per capita and marginal additions to population can be analyzed in such a way as to convert even a rather modest projection into an occasion for alarm. Thus, Paul Ehrlich writes:

> Assume for the moment that the demographic projections, so often mistakenly low in the past, are accurate, and that in the year 2000 the population of the United States is "only" 280 million people. What might that mean to us and to the world:

> Each American has roughly fifty times the negative impact on the Earth's life support systems as the average citizen of India. Therefore, in terms of ecosystem destruction, adding 75 million more Americans will be the equivalent of adding 3.7 billion Indians to the world population (predicated on the optimistic assumption that Americans do not pursue even more environmentally destructive activities in the interim). [31]

In partial response to this kind of presentation, Ansley Coale and others have pointed out that since the major part of ecosystem destruction comes about through life-style patterns, a stress on population growth projections is misleading in view of its trivial contribution to the total problem. For instance, if mass transit displaced the automobile, or if a clean engine replaced the internal combustion engine, or if Americans adopted a more austere pattern of living, then the pressure taken off the ecosystem would be many times greater than if fertility rates were reduced to replacement levels. GNP per capita is growing far faster than population, making it probable that life-style patterns will impinge even more on environmental quality in the future. In such circumstances, it is a mystifying distraction, some argue, to shift attention from these considerations by emphasizing population cut-backs as critical for environmental quality.*

However, on a global basis, it is also important to emphasize the extent to which agricultural developments needed to feed additional people will lead directly to ecological complications. Food planning expert Lester Brown, initially enthusiastic about the green revolution, has argued: "Whatever measures are taken, there is growing doubt that the

---

damage. A population *policy*, in contrast, would try to identify thresholds, distribution patterns, and growth dynamics that maximize other social and human values, a complex but essential process if human society is to take an active role in shaping its own destiny.

* For Americans, in other words, value changes and control over industrial pollution are needed, whereas a stabilized population is a matter of virtually no ecological significance (and may have negative side effects by making the population as a whole older, less dynamic, and more despondent).

agricultural ecosystem will be able to accommodate both the anticipated increase of the human population to seven billion by the end of the century and the universal desire of the world's hungry for a better diet. The central question is no longer 'Can we produce enough food?' but 'what are the environmental consequences of attempting to do so?' " [32]

In other words, although we do not know the exact extent to which improved technology can increase agricultural production, we do know that serious environmental consequences are associated with modernizing agricultural production.*

Prospects for International Control

It seems self-evident then, that there are powerful incentives to reduce population increase as rapidly as possible, and eventually to a level that is compatible with long-term ecological stability and environmental quality. The present world political structure means that population/agricultural policy is governed by national decisions and priorities, even though the cumulative impact of these policies may be felt throughout the global ecosystem. Such dissociation of authority and consequence is a further indication of the state system's obsolescence in relation to the world order agenda of our time.

Nationalist perspectives continue to dominate thought about population policy. Japan, despite its high population density and severe problems of crowding and pollution, is experiencing a labor shortage as a consequence of the incredibly rapid growth of its industrial sector. Instead of importing surplus labor from other Asian countries, or sacrificing optimal conditions for continuing economic growth, Japan has officially adopted a policy of encouraging population growth. Such a position illustrates the distortions of population policy that result from accepting nationally bounded labor markets, and from according such a high priority to maximizing economic growth. In a more rational and humane world system, not only would there be greater labor mobility; there would also be a calculus of cost/benefits such that side effects of population growth and environmental decay would be taken into account.

In a competitive world, there also remains a strong association between size and influence, and one of the components of size is numbers of people. This kind of rating schedule is exhibited in proposals for

---

* For further discussion of these issues, see pp. 125–129.

weighted voting in world institutions when such proposals are at least
partly correlated with relative population size. Thus, a country trying
to improve its relative and absolute rating in world power/prestige
hierarchies will tend to associate an improvement in position with population expansion and vice versa. Obviously, such an association will
not necessarily prevail over countervailing considerations bearing on
improving per capita living standards, but it clearly exerts a psychological influence supportive of pronatalist policies.

The main point is that governments regard population policy as a national matter unsuitable for international regulation. These governments are not likely to concur on the desirability of stabilizing or reducing the existing world population (whose global optimum may
conceivably be as low as 500 million), or on a common set of tactics to
achieve this objective.* The subject of population policy touches on
matters of human privacy, ethical and religious conviction, and varying
national priorities. As such, it is difficult, as American experience
shows, to evolve a population policy even on a national level in a society that is both democratic and pluralistic when it comes to race and
religion. Indeed, the most that can be done internally is to dramatize
the general consequences of unabated population growth and to provide the means (educational and technological) that will prevent the
birth of most unwanted children, in the hopes of approaching what
Charles Westoff has usefully labeled "the perfect contraceptive society." Where living standards and literacy rates are high, such a national

---

* The optimal global size involves matters of resource adequacy for future generations,
and concerns time horizons and judgments about the process of technological innovation.
The more future-oriented the assessment, the more likely it is to advocate a low global
population size; also, the more dubious about technological capacity, especially with respect to cheap energy supplies, the smaller the global population optimum. Part of the
issue is psychological—does one plan for the future of the planet by worst-case or almost-
worst-case analysis, does one project the past on a surprise-free basis, or does one introduce a continuous Prometheus factor into the future such that technology satisfies
human needs as they emerge? A wider part of the issue is aesthetic and ethical—does one
want an aristocratic culture in which the entire population experiences the highest available standards of enjoyment, including access to museums, zoos, parks, and wilderness
areas, or is one content with ultra-elitism that limits these finite resources to a tiny
proportion of the population? And does one restrict access by reference to total capacity—
as in a sports arena—or by consideration of conditions of optimal enjoyment, i.e., a far
smaller number? These factors are part of what must be considered in working out the
preliminary outlines of a population policy. It is a process common for more privileged
families who quite often consciously decide how large a family they would like to have—
given economic, vocational, personal goals—and then take steps to implement their
decision.

orientation is likely to cut population growth quite dramatically.[33] However, in societies where there is resistance to birth control or an inability to use it effectively, where women are unemancipated * or where parents want large families, then the goal of a perfect contraceptive society is both elusive and insufficient.[34]

On an international level there is practically no prospect in the 1970's of formulating, much less implementing, a global population policy, although there major data collecting and aid dispensing capabilities may emerge. Governments are likely to resist any international pressures on matters of domestic concern that touch directly upon individual lives. At most there may be a gradual and geographically uneven acceptance on a world level of an ethical consensus that individuals should confine reproduction to replacement levels.† It is even conceivable that a world movement will emerge to enshrine the standard of "zero population growth" in some kind of international declaration of population policy for the world community. Such an international declaration would be persuasive rather than coercive in character, and might be regarded as hypocritical if endorsed by governments that seemed committed to pronatalist conceptions of national interest.

The importance of curtailing population growth, and the means by which it can be done, remain matters of much international controversy. In particular, spokesmen from the advanced industrial countries favor doing whatever can be done to discourage population increase, whereas spokesmen from poorer countries regard such a call for family planning as premature, given the prior failure to eliminate misery. In this sense, stabilized population dynamics will be a product of rapid economic development, not the reverse. Of course, this kind of tactical perspective tends to overlook ecological constraints. The point is, however, that the prospects for mass family planning on a voluntary

---

* "All our preliminary findings point to the conclusion that the emancipation of women from traditional roles is indeed a prerequisite to the voluntary adoption of small family norms," writes Helvi L. Sipila, Assistant Secretary General for Social Developmental and Humanitarian Affairs at the United Nations, and involved in a major UN study on the links between status of women and family planning throughout the world. Letter to the *New York Times*, July 8, 1972, p. 12.

† It seems likely that such an ethos will emerge earliest in the richest societies and in the richer portions of all societies; it will accompany rising educational levels and standards of living. Hence, there will be great variations between and within countries as to whether the question of family size raises an ethical issue, and if so, of what character. Issues of religion and political ideology are also relevant to the ethical question, and to the capacity to encourage or coerce a value change.

basis do seem interrelated with substantial progress toward economic and social well-being (i.e., V_2 in WOMP framework).

Finally, on a world level, the issue of population pressure seems to have been conceived primarily (and overly much) in the context of disaster-avoidance. We have contended that just as enlightened families take an active part in deciding how large a family they would like to have, so enlightened societies should begin to take a similarly active part. An enlightened world community could then begin to engage in the same process of defining its goals in response to positive factors, as well as in order to avert disastrous consequences.* An interesting feature of most utopian visions is that quite a lot of attention is given to desirable population size, and that in most plans the ideal size is considerably smaller than what the utopian thinker was accustomed to in the world around him.

THE WAR SYSTEM: BASIC CONTOURS

Rewards and punishments in the present world order system largely reflect the dynamics of the war system. Governments protect or pursue their interests by the effective use of military power, including the indirect reliance on military power implicit in alliance relations. There is no immediate prospect for the elimination of frequent, large-scale violence within the realm of international statecraft, although there is some reasonable probability (at a level of assurance impossible to assess) that general nuclear war can be avoided until after the year 2000.[35] Reorientations of foreign policy and of defense posture by major actors, especially the United States and the Soviet Union, could substantially reduce the risk of nuclear war, could cut the costs of military competition, could produce international agreements that stabilize the arms environment to a considerable extent, and could set the stage for a reverse or negative arms race culminating in drastic disarmament and accompanying changes in the world order system by the end of the century.†

---

* Of course, the issue of means is much more troublesome on a *collective* level, than it is at the level of the single family.

† It may be misleadingly simplistic to project a chain of mutually reinforcing positive development flowing from more benevolent policies in Washington and Moscow. There are also less optimistic possibilities implicit in such shifts which might produce mixed or even negative world order results (as measured by WOMP criteria). For instance, secon-

Indeed, the image of a preferred world developed in Chapter IV and of the transition process in Chapter V presuppose at least the possibility of such a dramatic series of positive developments. But it must be stressed that such developments are not very likely, given the present world setting. The relation of domestic forces in all principal states continues to reinforce tendencies toward global disintegration; these tendencies arise from the combination of modern technology with competitive patterns of international behavior, which in turn are reinforced by threats and reliance upon military power.

The persistence of the war system in the nuclear age is a consequence of a large number of factors: bureaucratic inertia; vested interests; inequality of size and wealth per capita of states; competition for access to and control over scarce resources associated with wealth, space, influence and prestige; contradictory ideologies relating to international justice and to procedures for change; and a lingering glorification of war and the myth of the warrior hero.[37]

The persistence of war is not challenged by statesmen of major nations, and has been questioned only by leaders whose role is not dependent on a military or territorial base of power: the Secretary General of the United Nations and the Pope.

At present, no government has opted out of the war system in any decisive way, although several have limited their participation by a variety of devices. Sweden and Switzerland have long been committed to *neutrality* as a basic posture of national security, and as a result have refused to join in wars or in alliance arrangements. Both Sweden and Switzerland managed to preserve their neutrality under pressure from both sides during World War II. However, in both instances, the technique of maintaining neutrality entailed heavy expenditures on military capabilities, in order to raise the costs of attack to a potential aggressor. Sweden, according to 1967 statistics, ranked eighteenth among all states in total GNP but fourteenth in military expenditures, and fourth in per capita military expenditures; Switzerland was twenty-second in GNP, but thirty-first in military expenditure and sixteenth in

---

dary governments or alliances may be tempted to embark on their own programs of military expansion—the Hitler problem in some form—in an international atmosphere in which superpower complacency exists alongside persisting grievances. The revisionist option could then generate either a more feverish arms competition than ever before, preemptive modes of warfare, or even the outbreak of full-scale warfare between adversaries that we cannot now identify. Such an alternative future is particularly ominous because the rapid spread of nuclear technology will gradually globalize the capacity to produce nuclear weaponry.[36]

per capita military expenditure. Additional figures also demonstrate the extent to which Sweden and Switzerland are locked into the war system: In 1967, Swedish military expenditures of .9 billion dollars were more than double those of South Africa and were equal to those of Brazil, whereas the Swiss expenditures of .4 billion dollars were double those of Mexico and about equal to those of Yugoslavia.[38]

The Japanese Constitution limits military expenditures to so-called "defense forces," and Japan has renounced war as an instrument of national policy under all circumstances. In recent years, however, this Constitutional provision has come under increasing attack and its future in the 1970's is far from secure.* In any event, Japan has had the benefit of America's nuclear shield and has been able to achieve, or even exceed, traditional standards of national security by entering into a defensive alliance with the United States. This alliance has been made credible by American military personnel in Japan, bases nearby, and large naval capabilities in the Pacific area. Furthermore, Japan's defense expenditures have themselves been climbing to the point that by 1967 Japan was the thirteenth-ranked state in the world with $1.1 billion, a ranking ahead of Sweden and Poland and not far behind India. Therefore, Japan's apparent withdrawal from the war system is at best only partial and at worst only temporary. It is also significant that Japan has signed (3 Feb. 1970), but not deposited, its ratification of the Non-Proliferation Treaty, and since the decline of relations with the United States, has accelerated its program of remilitarization, thereby provoking an intense debate within the country.

There are other sectors of international society where reliance on military capabilities is associated only marginally with national security, as in the relations between Canada and the United States, among the countries of Western Europe since World War II, and the relations among states in most parts of Latin America. However, these "security communities" are rendered less impressive by close examination. Canada and the United States are so unequal in capability as to make even a deterrent posture very difficult for Canada to achieve or sustain; besides, informal penetration by American capital into the Canadian economy gives fairly high assurance that the Canadian government will not pursue a line of policy radically at variance with American interests;

---

* At the same time, working in the opposite direction, has been a decision by a Japanese court in 1973 which holds that existing defense forces violate the constitutional prohibition and are illegal under domestic law. The decision is under review at the present time within the Japanese judicial system.

and finally, the general world position and ideological orientation of the two countries is so similar with regard to either East/West or North/South issues as to provide an objective foundation for continuing intergovernmental compatibility.

The combined experiences of two highly destructive world wars, a common Soviet threat, and shared dependence on American protection seem to have overcome the long, bloody history of state relations in Western Europe. The functional imperatives of economic competition with the United States and Japan have also fostered the development of a multinational economy on the mainland of Europe, and have given rise to the institutions and traditions of the Common Market which, to a certain extent, supplant national consciousness with regional consciousness. In Western Europe, as in Canada, American economic penetration has been deep enough to shape a common outlook and also to create a common problem for the Europeans. Such developments, while significant as dampeners upon the recurrence of war within Western Europe, do not in any sense involve any withdrawal by European states from the war system. Indeed, "of the $200 billion estimated to have been spent [for weapons] in 1969, the NATO countries accounted for $108 billion, or 54 percent, the Warsaw Pact countries for $63 billion, or 32 percent." To the NATO total the United States contributed $82 billion, while the Soviet Union contributed $56 billion to the Warsaw Pact total.[39]

In Latin America, there have been periodic outbreaks of international violence since the last major conflict—The Chaco War—in the mid-1930's. The Latin American countries are absorbed by the dynamics of internal conflict and have rarely the energy or capability to pursue an independent foreign policy. Besides, once again American hemispheric dominance and Latin American dependence have tended to subordinate foreign policy initiatives of any sort, and have served also to establish the United States in the dual role of common benefactor/adversary. Recent purchases of arms by Latin American governments suggest, however, that the prospect of warfare in Latin America is by no means remote during the period of the next few decades. The degree of domestic political violence in Latin America, often of a prolonged and brutal variety, suggests that inter-group conflicts of a fundamental character in this region are often dealt with by violent means.

In short, it is necessary to conclude that warfare remains *endemic* in international relations. The form and locus of warfare are likely to reflect several sets of forces: shifting political alignments; changing foreign policy orientations of principal national governments; and technological and doctrinal developments in warfare.

Shifting Political Alignments

Recent international history suggests the possibility of rapid and unexpected changes in political alignment during the years remaining in this century. The pattern of rivalry that dominates international society will also have an important bearing on the character and likelihood of major warfare. The chasm between rich and poor, and the gap between capitalist and socialist ideologies, make it relatively unlikely that international conflict will diminish in intensity, although shifts in focus and modality are quite probable.

The structure of the world economy provides such a permanent basis for revisionist claims on the one side and for structures of domination on the other, that patterns of conflict may well remain centered in the mainstream of international politics for many years to come. Certain extrinsic factors, however, such as signs of ecological deterioration or the emergence of a pathological leader and/or movement in a principal state, may induce rapid development of international solidarity on an unprecedented scale.

At least through the 1970's, alliance politics will serve as the basis of collective security for secondary and tertiary national actors. The United States, the Soviet Union, and probably China will rely principally on their own nuclear deterrents to provide national security. A small international police force (10,000–50,000) may be created under UN auspices during the decade to provide a safer and cheaper alternative to competitive great power intervention, to decouple local and regional wars from wider international competition, or to provide an instrument of statecraft useful in certain conflict settings. It is unlikely, however, that any disarmament initiative of significance will occur until there has been a widespread, global dissemination of WOMP (or WOMP-like) values. We believe that the persistence of the war system is assured, however irrational from the perspective of national or species interest, so long as domestic repression, social injustice, and economic misery are widespread. Contrary to liberal humanist ideology, the elimination of war and violence as the main engines of social and political change in human affairs cannot be separated from other elements of world order reform. In this sense, the decline of interest by leading statesmen in disarmament, and their shifting of emphasis to arms control, represent a welcome abandonment of hypocrisy and embrace of realism. The message is clear. One needs to be either naive or a knave, both dangerous, to regard the war system as detachable from the present world order system with its distribution of values and capabilities, its traditions and expectations, and the entrenched role of violence as a mode of domestic governance.

Changing Foreign Policy Orientation

If more moderate national elites rise to power in principal countries, they may be able to de-emphasize international conflict and risks of war. Domestic pressures on principal governments to meet national or internal demands will create incentives to shift resources away from national defense. It seems likely that by the mid-1970's the United States and the Soviet Union will enjoy such moderate leadership, and that this fact might influence the whole climate of international relations. Moderate U.S. leadership might mean an end to both foreign military bases and to the willingness to help governments fight against largely internal enemies. Again, the longer-term results are difficult to anticipate; further retreat from an interventionary foreign policy would be possible, but if such a retreat produced adverse geopolitical consequences, a sharp counter-reaction would also be possible.

However, the main point here is that orientations of principal governments will influence one another greatly, as well as shape the type of warfare to be expected in future decades. There is likely to be a certain interactive tendency, with moves toward isolationism either opening up opportunities for expansion or inducing comparable moves of geopolitical retreat. At present it is not possible to tell whether the main thrust of this interactive influence will be imitative or dialectical.

Technological and Doctrinal
Developments in Warfare

Principal governments will remain preoccupied with avoiding nuclear war. At present, it is not anticipated that either the Soviet Union or the United States can achieve technological or doctrinal breakthroughs which would make plausible a nuclear war or frontal attack initiated by one side against the vital interests of the other. There may be more or less anxiety, depending basically on the success of the SALT talks and their interpretation by others.* Unless there are important shifts in the domestic bureaucracies of the USA and the USSR, it will be quite likely that pressures for weapons development will continue to take precedence over stabilizing pressures. The decision to deploy MIRVed warheads on the Minuteman and Polaris missile force, and the decision to

---

* The dramatic evolution of Soviet–American détente, especially when combined with the initiation of a new era of friendly relations between China and the United States, does create a new international situation, as of late 1973, that makes subsequent developments even more difficult to anticipate than previously.

develop the Safeguard ABM system as "a bargaining chip," represent the kind of 60–75 percent victory for hard-line defense advocates that has been characteristic of the nuclear age. It was a victory achieved despite a virtual consensus among nonaffiliated academic specialists on the desirability, feasibility, and benefits of reaching pre-deployment arms control agreements with the Soviet Union.[40] Similar pressures from the defense department appear to exist within the Soviet bureaucracy, although Herbert York seems correct when he blames the United States for initiating virtually every new phase in the arms race since the end of World War II.[41] As matters now stand, the relation of forces in Congress is closer than it has been at any time since the end of World War II, and the constituency favoring arms control has some prospect of scoring a major breakthrough in the decade, partly for reasons of ideology and partly for reasons of budgeting priorities.[42]

The relation of strategic competition among the superpowers to issues of weapons proliferation is difficult to predict and will reflect the influence of various other variables. The technological base enabling the effective development of weapons of mass destruction will be widely spread by the 1980's,* but whether or not it will remain a latent capability remains uncertain. The US–Soviet relationship will also determine the extent to which regional and local arms contests are linked to the arsenals of the superpowers. The rapid proliferation of conventional weaponry of the sort that took place in the Middle East in the 1960's will have a considerable impact on the future magnitude of regional and local warfare.[43]

The further development of exotic weaponry is likely to continue. The Vietnam War may be the last war in which a superpower relies substantially on its own men as instruments of sustained battle. Future warfare of the Vietnam type is likely to be electronic, in which the low technology society provides whatever manpower is needed, in exchange for the equipment and direction of its high-technology ally. The Nixon Doctrine enunciated in 1969 moves in this direction, although whether it survives Nixon's presidency remains to be seen.† In any case, clearly

---

* It should also be understood that a nuclear capability for a vulnerable country attains credibility much more easily than do the mutual, assured, deterrent systems of the United States and the Soviet Union, or even the nuisance capability of France or China. No elaborate or assured delivery capabilities are needed to achieve a desired degree of credibility for a beleaguered country like Israel or South Africa, especially when its probable targets are themselves much less adept at securing the inviolability of territorial space.

† The large-scale air war in Cambodia, carried out mainly by B-52 bombers, provides an image of a war which can be fought in the Third World without relying on the presence

the direction of counter-insurgency thinking is to minimize reliance upon the foot soldier, and to prepare for warfare in the cities as well as in the countryside. It is too early to know what adjustments national revolutionary movements will make to these shifts in counter-insurgency tactics and capabilities.

In conclusion, the war system is likely to remain intact so long as the state system persists as the main organizational nexus of international relations. Major powers will stress avoidance of nuclear war, for high levels of destruction would be its almost inevitable result. This emphasis may induce greater efforts to slow down or even reverse the arms race, thereby saving money and cutting risks, although so far these efforts have not been able to overcome pressures for continued self-reliance and a reliance upon security through strength. It seems likely that until the mid-1980's no major governments will press openly for the elimination of the war system, but that thereafter such pressures will mount until the end of the century, as the state system begins to manifest in more dramatic form its insufficiency to meet the needs of principal societies. These kinds of projections could be seriously altered by the rise of a strong challenging power or coalition from the Third World, or by a sense of ecological emergency arising from the consequences of mass famine or a large-scale pollution disaster. Such occurrences, or even their near-occurrence, might stimulate a much more rapid movement within and between states to change the world order system. Or contrariwise, technological breakthroughs with respect to fusion power or pollution control, or an era of great power moderation, may considerably defer the perception of the state system's imminent collapse, as well as obscure the constructive possibilities for promoting transition to a preferable world order system.

ECOLOGICAL PRESSURES

Before 1970, concern with the international environment was not a world order issue of any consequence. To be sure, there were a series of international issues with environmental content. Some were even serious—concern about contamination resulting from atmospheric testing of nuclear weapons, for instance. Others mobilized small constitu-

---

of U.S. ground forces. In the course of a 1971 news conference, President Nixon described the air war in Cambodia as "the Nixon doctrine in its purest form" (Nov. 12, 1971).

encies; for instance, several conservation groups felt deeply about achieving international regulation of the whaling industry in order to preserve several endangered species of the great whale. By and large, however, these issues were of a marginal character and could be dealt with by low-visibility conferences of specialists who would work out intergovernmental agreements in the common interest. No issues of sovereign prerogative seemed involved, and there was a generalized confidence in the capacity of the international system to deal adequately, even if not optimally, with environmental problems having an international dimension. Surely the literature of world order written before 1970 contains no suggestion whatsoever that a system of sovereign states is obsolescent in part because of its inability to prevent environmental decay or collapse.

Indeed, the literature of domestic society did not give emphasis to environmental concerns until the end of the 1960's. In their book *The Year 2000*, published in 1967, Herman Kahn and Anthony Wiener seem oblivious to the relevance of ecological pressures for the rates and consequences of the rapid economic growth that they project. And in *Agenda for the Nation*, a book prepared by the Brookings Institution in 1968 to assess public policy issues at the threshold separating the Johnson Presidency from the Nixon Presidency, only passing parenthetical reference is given to environmental issues.[44] In one of the most dramatic breakthroughs in political history, President Nixon not only admitted the environmental quality issue to the political agenda, but elevated it to the top place in his 1970 State of the Union Address:

> The great question of the seventies is, shall we surrender to our surroundings, or shall we make our peace with nature and begin to make reparations for the damage we have done to our air, our land, and our water? *

The process of depicting the environmental challenge on a world level has proceeded more slowly and with greater controversy. The UN Conference on the Human Environment in Stockholm in 1972 suggests both that the global problems associated with ecology are receiving atten-

---

* After 1970 President Nixon backed away from his strong support for environmental initiatives, and yet enough momentum was created by the initial burst of concern to give rise to a major set of governmental efforts in the environmental area, and to an extraordinarily increased sensitivity to adverse environmental impacts from a variety of undertakings previously regarded as automatically beneficial because they contributed to economic prosperity. For a general assessment see Walter A. Rosenbaum, *The Politics of Environmental Concern*, New York, Praeger, 1973.

tion, and that there are enormous difficulties in securing a basis for co-operative international action on a suitable scale.[45]

The world processes of population growth, urbanization, increasing energy consumption, and industrial development are building up pressures upon the global environment that increasingly present a risk of ecological collapse by causing basic ecosystems of land, air, and water to deteriorate.[46] We would contend, in other words, that environmental policy will maintain its status as a world order issue of prime consequence; that any adequate conception of a preferred world order system will have to make provisions for environmental quality; and that an important new constituency for world order change is present as a result of ecological pressures. These factors will be considered further in the following chapters. Here, our purpose is to indicate the basic facts and trends in order to suggest some limitations of response that can be attributed to the structural and dynamic characteristics of the state system.

The Basic Facts and Trends

Environmental pressure arises from the *quantum* and *quality* of human use of the natural environment. *Population is a factor.* The numbers of people on earth are a basic variable, and increasing demands for resources of all kinds at fixed levels of consumption are directly related to numbers of people. Population pressure in poor countries can only be dealt with by increasing productivity as rapidly and cheaply as possible, regardless of environmental consequences; in practice, this means relying upon agricultural and industrial processes that cause serious pollution. As noted earlier, the green revolution presupposes massive dependence on hard pesticides of the DDT variety and on chemical fertilizers, and reliance on these products increases geometrically with increasing productivity of the land.[47] Under conditions of extreme poverty, the pressure to increase industrial output tends to overwhelm countervailing arguments directed at longer-term consequences, such as national environmental quality or harmful impacts on the global environment.* As the problems of poverty diminish, the problems of

---

* Note that there are two dimensions of constraint: *time* (national planners tend not to be concerned about deferred effects on their own society; in general, the greater the immediate pressure, the nearer the time horizon of relevance); *altruism* (national planners tend not to be concerned about negative externalities, especially if the source of harm cannot be identified or the victim is in no position to retaliate; in general, the greater the im-

environmental quality tend to increase because industry is prevalent
and consumption patterns tend to be more harmful to the environment.
Jean Mayer, the Harvard nutritionist, has pointed out that whereas the
world environment could accommodate 700 million poor Chinese, it
would not survive the presence of 700 million rich Chinese. It seems
clear that the earth can support a few who are very rich or many who are
poor, but it is less obvious what size population can be supported at
moderate in-between levels of affluence and well-being.*

Technology as a Factor

The scale of technological development impinges more and more directly on the global environment. The process by which man becomes
capable of doing more potent things also involves an unavoidable interference with basic natural processes. The rate of technological innovation is itself accelerating, and the pressure of technology on the environment is likely to continue to grow in the years ahead, especially as
the more populous societies of the world attain new levels of industrialization.

There are various ways to illustrate this cumulative trend toward environmental pressure arising from technological development. For instance, in 1930, oil tankers were under 20,000 tons, whereas by the mid-
1970's there are prospects for tankers of 800,000 or more tons. Such a
factor of 40 indicates an increase in pressure many times more rapid
than that associated with population growth, itself proceeding at an explosive rate. The increase in energy consumption, per capita and in the
aggregate, is another useful indicator of overall pressure on the environment. Estimates project a continuing average rate of energy growth
on a world level at 5.2 percent (as compared with two percent for population growth) for the period between now and 1980.[48]

Of course, the environmental impacts of technology are not all negative. Indeed, there is a substantial prospect that if fusion power is de-

---

mediate pressure to engage in activity to promote self-interests, the smaller is the degree
of deference to community well-being).

* Such an uncertainty is further complicated by the ambiguities implicit in the notion of
support: do we mean support only in the minimum sense of making life possible, or do
we mean support to include conditions for self-realization? Do we intend the idea of support to take account of future generations and to assure these generations parity of support?

veloped on an economically viable basis, environmental pressures will diminish despite vast increases in aggregate and per capita energy use. It is also clear that in an appropriate political climate, technology can be made to serve the cause of environmental protection in impressive respects.[49] The point is not to build an attitude hostile to technology, but to make it clear that the mindless marriage of technology to economic growth priorities produces increasingly destructive results on a crowded planet. This mindlessness is strengthened by the various factors of greed and need which sustain economic growth priorities in *all* portions of the world.

Categories of Problems

1. *Environmental disasters.* The Torrey Canyon tanker breakup, the Santa Barbara oil blowout, the possibility of a "nuclear Torrey Canyon" (resulting from a collision of nuclear-powered submarines or other vessels), or the occurrence of a nuclear war suggests cases in which a discrete event causes dramatic damage to the environment for a specific period of time. These kinds of dramatic events have become regular features of international life, and are predictable consequences of the present level of technological development.

2. *Cumulative deterioration.* The more characteristic environmental problems arise from activity which takes place in a form that does not appear to be intrinsically harmful (or at least each perpetrator makes such a trivial contribution to the harm that costly forbearance does not seem justifiable). Also, the chain of causation may be remote and speculative, separated by time, distance, and intervening developments. For instance, the sustained use of DDT gradually increased in concentration as it passed up the food chain from plankton and algae to such animals as the peregrine falcon, whose calcium metabolism was eventually disrupted, causing faulty formation of eggs and hence their persistent breakage; the result was a virtual brake on reproduction. No particular farmer, nor even any nation's pattern of farming, could be held very clearly accountable for these consequences.

3. *Ultrahazardous activities.* Another interrelated set of dangers to the environment results from using or disposing of certain materials in a way that turns out to have extremely serious risks or consequences. There are the obvious problems of disposing of radioactive wastes, and storing and disposing of weapons stocks of nerve gases and biological toxins. The widespread use of herbicides by the United States in the In-

dochina War disclosed patterns of unintended side effects, either in the form of ruining fertile soil or by evidently inducing a high incidence of miscarriage and birth defects among the exposed population.

4. *Ecological catastrophe*. There is also some speculation about possible interference with the oxygen supply or with the earth's climate, as a result of cumulative pollution of the oceans and atmosphere. Ecological scenarios have portrayed coastal flooding by the end of the century as a result of the melting of polar ice caps, or alternatively, a new ice age due to increases in the density of particulate matter in the atmosphere which will lead to a cooling of earth temperatures. As matters now stand, we seem unlikely to be confronted by such extreme consequences of environmental pressure by the end of the century, although our present knowledge about global environmental processes is so rudimentary that evidence exists to lend some credibility to both doomsday prophecy and facile reassurances; as a consequence, we are surrounded by confusion and controversy. It is an atmosphere reminiscent of Babel. Monitoring and data collection capabilities will have to improve before we can discuss with confidence whether the oceans are dying or whether a new kind of climate is being brought into being by man's actions on the planet.* By the end of this decade, anxiety connected with some causes for alarm will create a widespread demand for better knowledge and for a global capability to take preventive action before thresholds of irreversible change are crossed.

Systemic Considerations

As we have already made clear, the existing world order system rests largely upon the ordering capacities of national governments. With respect to domestic events, an idea of community well-being influences policy-making and political discourse; the government, despite pressures from and favors for special interest groups, purports to rule on behalf of the entire society. With respect to external events, however, authority is exercised, if at all, mainly to protect a national society or

---

* It is an interesting observation on human nature that the conservatism of military planners does not extend to environmental risk-takers. One has the impression that most cautious analysts of Soviet intentions, who insist on worst-case planning, are generally optimistic about worst-case prospects in relation to the environment. In fairness, it is also true that worst-case thinking by environmental alarmists is accompanied by a bland confidence in deterrence capabilities regardless of their quality, and independent of any reasoned approach to the intentions of possible war rivals.

special interest groups from the harmful behavior of others. There is some nominal deference to the notion of a world community, of course, but its actuality is not generally evident in international society and is in any case inconsistent with the competitive dynamics of the state system. These broad observations have particular relevance to the establishment of a coordinated system of authority in relation to environmental concerns. The combination of exclusive national jurisdiction over territorial activity and of relative nonregulation of oceanic and other forms of transterritorial and nonterritorial activity constitutes a very difficult but altogether crucial domain within which to establish an effective and enlightened global environmental authority.*

Until recently, certain basic characteristics made the world order system operate reasonably well with respect to matters of environmental quality:

1. The limited external impacts of domestic agricultural, industrial, and human activity

2. Sufficiency of unused capacity in the oceans and the atmosphere with respect to the accommodation of waste disposal (the ratio of waste to the ecosystem was not high enough to cause major disruption)

3. The small-scale release of ultratoxic substances, and the infrequency and confined scope of ultrahazardous activities made the absence of regulatory authority of little consequence

4. The compatibility among various uses of the ocean, and between major land uses and oceanic quality

The emerging characteristics of the planet include:

1. Global interdependence of significant and diverse variety

2. The disappearance of unused capacity in the oceans and the atmosphere

3. An increasing variety of ultratoxic substances and ultrahazardous activities in the world environment

4. Growing areas of potential and actual incompatibility among various uses of oceans, and between land use and ocean quality

These characteristics are producing a situation of great environmental vulnerability. The fact that the interests of governments are so diverse

---

* *Enlightened* here is a shorthand reference to the normative orientation of the four WOMP values, considered in interaction with one another; *effective* refers to the capacity to implement an agreed program of action.

as a result of their varying size, distinct stages of economic development, and divergent cultural, historical, and ideological perspectives,
makes it difficult to secure and implement agreements to prevent
serious environmental harm. Given the structures and traditions of the
state system, existing processes for forming and implementing agreements in areas of diverse interest are very inadequate.

An underlying condition of a different sort arises from the universal
commitment by national governments to maximize their own economic
growth. Protecting the environment against deterioration, especially
under conditions of planetary crowding, is inconsistent with the priority accorded continuing growth of the gross national product. Of
course, some strategies of growth—particularly those related to patterns
of transportation and of energy consumption—are far worse environmentally than are others. As we have suggested, it is not necessary to
assume an anti-technological, anti-growth posture in order to maintain
that the dominant modes of economic development in all major societies have tended to pass onto the environment some of the real costs—
hidden from national accounts—of economic growth. Hence, as matters
now stand, it seems more than likely that future economic growth will
engender further deterioration of the environment.*

Hence, the prospect of a rapidly expanding GNP, especially for advanced countries, is not an ecologically comforting one. U Thant,
speaking as UN Secretary General in Austin, Texas, on May 14, 1970,
voiced his concern about the prospect of continuing increases in GNP
for the U.S. (1957: $453 billion; 1969: $728 billion, a sixty-percent increase; 1980: a further fifty-percent increase). Part of the new pattern is
exponential growth in relation to an already large base. Thus, as U
Thant points out, American economic growth between 1950 and 1970

---

* The position here is complicated. See text on p. 139 for a brief consideration of the
positive potential of technology and of the possible compatibility of technology and development goals. It must be stressed, however, that the technological momentum is so
closely tied to growth/profit considerations that it may be tactically essential to adopt an
anti-technological, anti-growth position in order to get a fair hearing. Only after the extreme position has been asserted is it possible to make reasonable reforms and to induce
conciliatory responses from those who control wealth and power processes. In this sense,
regardless of the intrinsic merits of their claims, doomsday analysts such as Paul Ehrlich
and Barry Commoner have created a situation in which more measured and specific
reforms can be made and a less absolute view of technological inevitability prevails. Environmental alarmists are definitely not crying wolf. There are real wolves; at most, they
may be overestimating the number of wolves, their ferocity, and their proximity. In this
sense, the successful Senate campaign in 1971 to withdraw Federal support from the SST
was a major symbolic victory.[50]

was as great as the entire extent of growth between 1620, when the Pilgrims arrived at Plymouth Rock, and 1950. As U Thant concludes: "An increasing gross national product was, until recently, regarded as an entirely desirable goal, but now we must also see this goal in terms of demands on resources, in terms of waste disposal and pollution problems and of other serious consequences, social and economic." As elsewhere, it will be difficult to induce governments to practice unilateral self-restraint, unless their leaders are convinced that national welfare requires it! *

In the developing world, heavy emphasis on economic and social development understandably tends to override all other priorities. Third World governments are reluctant to undertake any activities which interfere with their primary goals, particularly when such activities involve the expenditure of already scarce resources. Therefore, although Third World governments may offer rhetorical support for efforts to protect the global environment, they are unlikely to implement standards which may burden the modernization process.[51]

Although Third World attitudes in the area of environmental protection may be understandable, if held uncritically or dogmatically they are nevertheless short-sighted and counter-productive for several reasons:

1. There are serious environmental problems on a local level even at early stages of development.

2. The adoption of a planning perspective could permit the choice of development paths that substantially reconcile environmental quality with maximum economic growth; for instance, a preference for urban communities based on bicycles rather than automobiles.

3. The failure of Third World pressures on advanced countries to take steps to protect the environment risks an ecocatastrophe of planetary scope, and also may have major impact on access to and costs of resources that will be needed by poorer countries in the future.

---

* The 1973 energy crisis, global in scope and abetted by the selective oil embargo imposed by Arab producers, has encouraged a series of unilateral measures of self-restraint—reduced speed limits, bans on Sunday driving, appeals for voluntary compliance with standards calling for reduced energy consumption, and the likelihood of rationing. In the United States one early casualty of fuel shortages has been environmental quality standards. These standards have been suspended with respect to oil with high sulphur content. In general, the energy crisis is likely to weaken environmentalist pressures with respect to such critical issues as refinery and pipeline construction.

Given the planetary scope of environmental issues, all governments share an interest in assuring that satisfactory approaches emerge. The character and quality of a nation's immediate interest will vary, however, depending on the particular issue and on the country's place in the international system. But participating in the establishment of international cooperative environmental schemes offers a country some protection against eventual discovery that its options have been foreclosed. Countries which are still free of evident environmental dangers do have a stake, therefore, in the world community's adoption of enlightened and effective universal standards.

The Soviet Union, with its stress on carrying out state plans, fulfilling production quotas, and overtaking the capitalist West, has been afflicted with many of the same environmental problems as have the United States and Western Europe. The obstacles to reversing the trend in Russia are comparable to those in the West, including ideological and bureaucratic pressures associated with maximizing economic growth.[52] There is some still-inconclusive evidence that China may be more concerned than the Soviet Union with preserving environmental quality even if it burdens, to some extent, the process of economic development. However, it is too early to tell whether socialist economies in general will be more or less responsive to environmental challenges than market economies, in terms of both domestic and international policy.*

In conclusion, it seems likely that during the 1970's governments throughout the world will take increasing cognizance of ecological issues, although at an uneven rate and possibly in inconsistent ways. Official attitudes are likely to conflict actively with accustomed deference to economic/technological imperatives, on the one hand, and with mounting insistence on rehabilitating man's relationship with nature, on the other (even if economic growth or technological innovation must be sacrificed to some degree).

The 1980's will probably see more of these struggles, primarily on the

---

* Soviet bloc countries have been very reluctant to enter into any international agreements that infringe symbolically or substantially on territorial sovereignty. Environmental protection, to the extent that behavioral standards and their enforcement are involved, presupposes varying degrees of intrusion on sovereignty. As yet there is no indication whether the new international atmosphere of détente, called by some virtually irreversible in Soviet–American short-term relations, might lead to less anxiety about participation in international regulatory processes. After all, if Pepsi-Cola and Avis can operate in Moscow, why not the WHO, FAO, or the UN Commission on the Human Environment?

domestic level. Their outcome will be heavily influenced by the kind and frequency of environmental disasters, by technology's capacity to rectify its own mistakes, and by governmental success in dealing with other fundamental economic, social and political issues.*

SOME MISCELLANEOUS ISSUES OF TECHNOLOGICAL INNOVATION

Dramatic and fundamental technological innovations—which may impinge seriously upon basic modes by which man organizes his individual and collective existence—will probably be introduced into active use during what is left of the twentieth century.

However, the prospect of continuous technological change is no longer heralded as an unmixed blessing. The negative effects of technology are most obvious in the military arena: as military technology advances, warfare becomes ever more destructive. Unless significant steps are taken to control the situation, it will become easier for all countries to acquire modern weaponry—nuclear as well as conventional—and new technology will continue to be applied to military use.

Recent doubts about technological innovation stem not only from the realization of our increasing capacity for destructive behavior, but also from a growing appreciation of the need for environmental protection. The public has seen that many technological innovations have negative side effects—including the exacerbation of ecological problems—which are greater than their alleged advantages. Such suspicion runs counter to widely-held earlier assumptions that technological innovation was almost automatically beneficial and, in any case, virtually inevitable. The aroused concern about environmental quality—crystallizing in the United States around such issues as the SST—gives notice that the public will no longer necessarily support technological innovations as generously as before, unless they can survive an increasingly elaborate process of ecological scrutiny.†

---

* Resource constraints can, as we have suggested, contribute to environmental decay by forcing the suspension of quality standards. Thus the pressures associated with V_4 may lead, in some sense, to diminished performance, despite heightened awareness of the ecological dimension.

† The 1973 energy crisis is likely to have an impact on the whole process of innovation in the economy, placing a premium on low-energy or energy-conserving innovation and creating a bias against high-energy and energy-wasting innovations. One result of this

There are, however, contradictory pressures which also have an ecological origin. For example, fuel shortages of the early 1970's create
pressures for the development of domestic oil fields, especially on the
Alaska North Slope, which offset injury to the environment and overcome the objections of environmentalists.[53] The same dilemma also underlies disputes over the construction of new refineries along the coast
of northern New England. Thus the *resource* side of the ecological ledger
may, on occasion, outweigh the *environmental* side.

Of course, this process of scrutiny places a premium on technological
innovations that are compatible with ecological considerations, and
thereby, hopefully, provides incentive for the design of technologies
which will minimize environmental damage. One of the central human
dramas in the years ahead will be the "race" between technologies with
potentially hazardous side effects (e.g., nuclear reactors which produce
radioactive waste) and technologies which are more benign.*

Especially challenging, perhaps, are the unsettling prospects for high
order computer intelligence and genetic engineering, including cloning.[54] In the absence of social and political intervention, within several
decades computers will be able to make judgments about complex
choices which formerly called upon men to exercise their highest capacities. Thus, computer technology could lead to the depreciation of
human achievements and talents, both past and present.†

Will man, as inventor and programmer of such computers, be able to
maintain a sense of relevance and dignity under these circumstances?
Because the consequences of the new technology may not be appreciated until the early decades of the next century, we can only guess

---

perspective on energy consumption may be to reduce the volume of pollutants dumped
into the atmosphere. Compare this effect with the opposite effect arising from greater in-
dulgence of low-quality fuel.

* The shortage of energy supplies will undoubtedly accelerate reliance on nuclear
power (including dangerous breeder reactors that rely on fission processes), and overcome objections to stepping up coal mining in the most economical, but not the most en-
vironmentally-beneficial, fashion.

† Many philosophical questions are embedded in such a general statement bearing on
the nature of thought and creativity, the distinctive quality of human consciousness, and
the nature of computer achievement. It is not certain that the objective capacity of computers would displace comparable human efforts, or even that computers are inherently
capable of leaps of the imagination. Also, it may happen that human dignity is restruc-
tured into a hierarchical relationship of deference and devotion to the computer, making
computer experts a kind of new priesthood and giving computerology a kind of religious
role in the culture of the future that could even be regarded, in some sense, as a respiritualization of individual and collective life.

whether, from among myriad possible effects, a kind of collective depression or psychosis might ensue or, on the contrary, whether the depreciation of elite achievement might not finally lay the basis for a non-hierarchical social and political order and actually move men to a higher stage of human development beyond specialization and the division of labor. In this positive vein, the supercomputer of the future might provide humankind with a far superior basis for self-realization, measured more by intrinsic than extrinsic indicators of personal achievement and leadership.*

Genetic engineering will also pose issues which are difficult to fathom at this time. Cloning might alter the relevance of death to the human experience and hence alter the search for death-transcending symbolism and experience in human affairs, thereby eroding still further the role of war and military exploits.[55] The capacity to select sex, a rather likely development over the next few decades, might help stabilize population growth, especially in societies where there are strong economic pressures to have one or more sons.†

In essence, there is a strong temptation to see positive genetics as a tool for promoting planetary survival. One could even imagine serious advocacy of a world academy of genetic design, with a mandate to develop benign leaders who would act as positive forces for social fulfillment. Of course, less benevolent human types could also be created; there are those who might wish to develop a race of "supermen" to "take over." Although no such nightmare is likely to materialize within this century, its very existence as an active possibility is bound to influence somewhat the public mood. The potential of genetic engineering will also add a further dimension to the already troubled status of tech-

---

* That is, such a computerized superculture might create a real basis for democratic humanism as a civic religion, endowing life with quality and excitement (rather than the other way around). In the context of our discussion of transition in Chapter V, this spread of enlightened awareness might provide a normative climate in which the shift from our preference model of $S_{2(WOMP/ USA)}$ might further evolve in the direction of S_3. (The notational symbols introduced here are explained as follows: S-stands for a world order system. S_1 is the present world order system based on sovereign states; S_2 is a more globally integrated sequel to S_1; S_3 is a more individualistic sequel to S_2; $S_{2(WOMP/ USA)}$ is the version of S_2 preferred by the American group in WOMP and depicted in Chapter IV of this book.)

† Of course, implementing such capabilities involves making complicated ethical and political decisions, and effective implementation in such an area of traditional human autonomy raises the most profound conceivable questions about the limits of government and the proper allocation of authority in private and public realms of concern.

nological innovation, raising the basic issue of whether such developments represent a blessing or a curse.*

Despite these prospects of rapid and basic technological change, there will not necessarily be corresponding alterations in the *structure* of world society. In reviewing the international impact of recent technological change, one close student of the subject, Eugene Skolnikoff, observes that "the underlying assumptions governing international relations, in particular the dominance of the national state system as an organizing concept of the international system, have not been seriously modified." Professor Skolnikoff feels that "against this background, one may view with a skeptical eye the possible impact of future technological developments and applications, notwithstanding the great temptation to attach dramatic potential to some of them. In fact, I believe that over the decade the implications of advances in science and technology are unlikely to cause anything but marginal, though important, changes in international affairs, barring, and it is a major caveat of course, any catastrophic events in military and political areas." [56]

However, Skolnikoff's caveat is most significant. It undermines somewhat his confident forecast of technology's marginal impact, and highlights some basic and, at present, open-ended questions. How in fact will future technological innovations affect the present world order system, including its military and political dimensions? Will these innovations be likely to intensify or to bypass those tendencies in international life which might produce a dramatic change for the better in the decades ahead? Can we predict whether particular technological developments will facilitate or impede a transition from the present world order system in the direction of WOMP preference models?

In this, as in other areas of knowledge, we lack a solid foundation on which to base predictions. The experience of the past, at least when taken at face value, does not necessarily provide an appropriate basis for assessing the future. However, when attempting to identify undramatic processes which may eventually culminate in dramatic events, it is often useful to extrapolate from the past. Slow buildups of pressure over time gradually and often imperceptibly exceed the peakload capacity of the system, giving the lie to earlier assumptions that the system

---

* Our view is that such a debate is cast in such general terms as to be useless, at least once the influence exerted by mindless technophiles has been effectively challenged. Real inquiry should be more specific—what kinds of technology, for what sorts of problems, with what sorts of priorities? In essence, we need to develop a mood and structure for assessing technology that is as responsive as possible to WOMP values.

could adequately absorb increases in use. Power failures, crowded telephone circuits, and declining pasture land acreage all illustrate the failure to adapt thinking from a context of relative abundance (unused capacity) to one of relative scarcity (approaching peak load limits).*

At present, we have only a very limited understanding of the possible ramifications that technological innovation may have for the existing world order. We do not know, for example, whether the technological capacity to launch long range nuclear-tipped missiles tends to promote or to thwart *any* kind of world order change, much less whether it leads to the kind of change advocated by WOMP.

In general, therefore, it is exceedingly difficult to foretell the ways in which future technological innovation may affect the present international structure, whether the changes will be marginal or major, which features of the current structure will be strengthened by the changes, and what causal connections there may be between technological developments and global reform.

In more traditional writing, technological innovation is expected to have its major impact not on the *structure* of international relations, but upon the *relation of forces* or *modes of* conflict within it. Henry Kissinger, before becoming President Nixon's principal foreign policy advisor, expressed this important judgment:

> The traditional criteria for the balance of power were territorial. A state could gain overwhelming superiority only by conquest; hence, as long as territorial expansion was foreclosed, or severely limited, the equilibrium was likely to be preserved. In the contemporary period this is no longer true. Some conquests add little to effective military strength; major increases in power are possible entirely through developments within the territory of a sovereign state. China gained more in real military power through the acquisition of nuclear weapons than if it had conquered all of Southeast Asia. If the Soviet Union had occupied Western Europe but had remained without nuclear weapons, it would be less powerful than it is now with its existing nuclear arsenal within its present borders. In other words, the really fundamental changes in the balance of power have all occurred *within* the territorial limits of sovereign states.[57]

---

* Of course, technology redefines the parameters of resources, and creates a belief, often misfounded, that earlier concerns with scarcity were excessive. For example, confined grazing based on high protein feeds has replaced range or pasture grazing in the American meat industry, making large acreage apparently unnecessary. But should feed shortages emerge, as seems quite possible, then resort to older patterns of grazing may have to be revived.

In a subsequent essay, Victor Basiuk has extended Kissinger's point to encompass the entire spectrum of technological innovation. Basiuk writes that an important trend in the 1970's will be "the increasing importance of nonmilitary technology as an area of direct relevance to national security." Indeed, he argues that "the possibility of changing the distribution of world and regional power through nonmilitary technology is increasingly greater than the possibility of changing the distribution through military technology." [58] Basiuk gives the following evidence for this rather startling assertion:

> Computers provide a major impetus to the growth of other areas of technology and facilitate economic planning, investment, and the marketing strategy of corporations, providing a differential advantage for the countries and regions leading in this area of technology. Capability for the development of marine resources opens up new vistas in a virtually unexplored, unexploited, and unsettled three-quarters of the globe with concomitant geopolitical implications. Countries which succeed in reducing the costs of energy sooner than others will be able to enjoy major advantages in world markets and strengthen their industrial capability and leverage of influence in the less-developed world. Global television and weather control techniques can have the same implication. [59]

Such analyses of future international political, economic, and technological developments assume the basic stability of the global structure, and are rather insensitive to considerations of planetary peak loads. According to Basiuk, "the perils of the new technology" may include a loss of relative power for the United States and its allies, and threats to the domestic viability of the state. On the latter, he writes: "Not all societies will be equally successful in controlling the impact of technology, but the price for failure can be large. It may involve extensive social dislocation, widespread personal insecurity, and a serious weakening if not collapse of governmental authority and capability for defense." [60] Such internal developments can have a very decisive impact on world order if they occur within principal states, and could also engender a new political consciousness that rejects or greatly revises the idea of competitive relations within foreign policy. According to Basiuk's line of thought, the dominant form of international relations will become a technology race and as the competition in military technology declines, the arms race will slow down accordingly. In essence, adapting Clausewitz, technology would undertake to carry on politics by other means, and war—for various reasons including cost and indecisiveness— would become less central to thought and action. Hence, a fairly successful war prevention system, at least for the technological leaders, could emerge within the *present structure* of world order during the decades ahead, although the realization of other values would not necessarily be any closer at hand.

In fact, in a world characterized by continuing interstate competition and gross inequality, if greater equity is not achieved along with disarmament, extreme repression and stratification would result almost inevitably in all social, economic, and political relations. A crude neo-Darwinian ethos would encourage an Orwellian process of dehumanization.* Under such oppressive conditions, an increased resort to violence could be expected. Given access to the black-market plutonium which reportedly can already be purchased by the kilo, any sufficiently discontented portion of world society can potentially wield a threat of mass destruction.

Furthermore, it is not at all clear whether national governments will be able to maintain control over the spread of nonmilitary technology, and to orchestrate its application in accord with the dynamics of international political competition. The multinational corporation is increasingly moving to universalize its ideology, its base of operations and its image of a preferred world order system, and may gradually emerge as an *antagonist* rather than as an *agent* of any particular government. Courtney Brown, former Dean of Columbia's Graduate School of Business Administration, anticipates the incorporation of nonnational companies operating under an international charter: "Such a company would make no national distinctions among personnel from top to bottom, would remain rigidly nonpolitical, and would resist being the instrument of any national policy." [61] In the future, even principal governments may well be unable to impose their special interests upon the operations of large-scale business ventures. Government's future role will also be influenced by the framework within which ocean resources are developed: whether under international auspices, or as a consequence of competitive relationships regulated by national governments. These developments are difficult to assess at this time, but deserve continuing scrutiny.

Given the difficulty of assessing the interplay between technological innovation and the emergence of new social forces, we offer no firm conclusions regarding the impact of technology as a whole, but wish

---

* Oppressive domestic relationships can be sustained in most national societies by reliance on police and para-military capabilities, especially if no inhibitions on the application of terror exist. Such "police state" potentialities should also infuse our consideration of the role of force in our preference model. Eliminating the war system in a strict sense may still require a vigilant and imaginative approach to the *quis custodiet* area of concern.

only to draw attention to the risks arising from our limited knowledge. In the remainder of this section we shall briefly consider some specific areas of technological development that are bound to be consequential for all aspects of human well-being, and which are likely to shape future world order tendencies: energy, food, weather, and information.

Energy

The political implications of energy have not been generally appreciated by political scientists or by the main lines of world order analysis.[62] And yet it now seems clear that the *form* and *quantity* of energy which a social order relies upon have far-reaching consequences for the society's organization, the values of its leaders, and its external relations. Furthermore, the process of transition from one energy base to another seems to be a profoundly unsettling experience, on both domestic and international levels.* This is particularly relevant to our concerns, because the decades ahead will almost certainly require a rapid transition from liquid fossil fuels to less accessible coal reserves and nuclear energy produced by various techniques.[63]

Much of the debate about technology's relation to society centers on man's ability to develop cheap, safe, and abundant sources of energy for the future. Buckminster Fuller and his followers optimistically contend that the prospects for energy production are so favorable that all of mankind can live in permanent affluence and harmony, if human attention would only focus on this central task. Fuller embodied his optimism in a poem of sorts that he sent to Senator Edmund Muskie when Muskie was the leading Democratic Party candidate for the 1972 Presidential nomination:

---

* Other aspects of energy policy are considered in Chapter VI, pp. 363–366; the global oil shortage in 1973 is undoubtedly a turning point in consciousness and will provide many clues as to the relative strengths of neo-Darwinian and cooperative approaches to international relations. The Common Market countries are confronted by the present choice of whether to share some of their short supplies with the Netherlands, or whether to maximize their own position, as well as maintain as good a relationship as possible with Arab exporter governments. Because of the Arab–Israeli conflict, such oil diplomacy could shake up other geopolitical relations—if, for instance, the United States finds itself isolated with regard to its support for Israel and feels itself abandoned by its European allies.

> There is a dawning of world-around comprehension
> Of the existence of a significant plurality
> Of alternative energy source options
> Available for all Earthians' vital support.

Fuller goes on to assert that we now have the knowledge to harness extraterrestrial energy potential, but are held back by archaic patterns of thought, feeling, and organization:

> But originally permitted ignorance
>   No longer may be, self-excusingly, pleaded
> As justification for failure to employ
>   The now known to exist
> Omni-self-supporting technical capabilities
>   To produce unprecedentedly advanced
> Standards of living
>   And freedom of thought and actions
> For all humanity,
>   Without any individual
> Being advantaged
>   At the expense of another,
> All of which feasibilities
>   Are inanimately powerable
> Well within our daily energy income
>   From extraterrestrial sources
> And all accomplishable without pollution.

This technological vision rests on the adaptation of solar energy to human needs:

> Modern physics renders it incontrovertible
>   That celestial energy is nonexhaustible
> Only the fossil fuel account
>   And perishable human muscles . . .
> Humanity's economics are as yet ignorantly geared.

Fuller also regards the present period as one of great transitional magnitude:

> . . . That unwitting earthians
>   Gradually are being shifted
> Over an epochal threshold
>   Successful crossing of which,—

If not totally frustrated by reflexive inertias,—
  Will witness the successful gearing of all humanity
Into the eternally, inexhaustible, energy system
  Of omni-self-regenerative celestial mechanics.*

Thus, according to Fuller, "an energy revolution" could end the competitive struggle for dominance over shares of *scarce* energy. In his view, the elimination of *scarcity* would simultaneously undermine structures of *hierarchy* and *domination*, and provide mankind with a set of *objective conditions* favorable for *liberation*. Fuller's vision here goes even beyond the realization of the four WOMP values, by discovering that the basis for human fulfillment can be provided at all levels of social organization.

However, Fuller's argument raises serious questions of (1) technical feasibility (is it correct to anticipate plentiful energy at low cost in the event celestial sources could be mobilized?); (2) time horizon (how long will it take to create a world economy powered by such a new energy source?); and (3) ethical, political, and ecological ramifications (what assurance is there that existing structures of hierarchy would not endure?). Most analysts of energy potential do not anticipate such a radical transformation of the energy base by the end of the century. On the contrary, there is far more concern over the rapid depletion of existing energy supplies. Efforts to accelerate global industrial development will depend critically on the extent of energy available. In this respect the idea of *energy surplus* is a useful adjunct to the earlier stress upon capital surplus or labor surplus. Limits on societal development may be most clearly assessed by studying relative and aggregate expected energy surplus for various states and regions in the world. Energy surplus has been defined as "the energy available to man in excess of that expended to make energy available." [64] The distinction between rich and poor societies is magnified by relative rates of energy consumption. [65] In low-energy societies—those dependent on the physical output of men and animals—the surplus is insufficient to enable high living standards, leisure, or rapid technological change.

Faced with emerging energy shortages at the same time that demand for energy is steadily increasing, the high-energy societies are rapidly trying to develop new energy technologies. In recent years, this task has grown more complex and multifaceted, for the energy-developers now

---

* Buckminster Fuller to Senator Edmund Muskie. Used by permission. Published in the *New York Times,* March 27, 1971, p. 29.

have to contend with a new political constituency which advocates stringent environmental quality constraints on the processes of energy production. Thus, despite summertime "brown-outs," power failures and fuel shortages, effective citizen action has prevented the construction of additional power plants and refineries on the grounds that such facilities are principal sources of air and water pollution. Citizens concerned about the accidental release of radioactive waste are also taking defensive action to obstruct the development of nuclear energy. In fact some observers feel that much stronger attempts should be made to retard the development of nuclear energy, because the potential hazards from this source might be so immense.[66] Opponents of this view debate inconclusively the extent to which nuclear energy may be more dangerous than other energy sources.*

A related but much broader debate concerns the overall level of energy consumption per se, and its possible relation to the peakload crisis confronting mankind with planetary danger of ecocatastrophe. Many observers disagree with Buckminster Fuller, noting that past energy increases have been directly correlated with environmental decay, and that in recent years the energy curve has been rising at an incredible rate.[67]

In the United States, energy consumption has been doubling every decade; McHale reports that despite the slow rate of industrial growth in developing regions, "some already show a growth rate of electricity consumption of 15 to 22 percent between 1963 and 1964." [68] Demand for energy has induced recourse to sub-sea oil, and has encouraged larger tankers and a rapidly rising volume of oceanic oil transport. The rising demand for oil and gas in the United States, especially when combined with economic and geopolitical advantages of minimum reliance on im-

---

* There are two kinds of major issues: first, prospective nuclear energy facilities based on fission methods of production are dangerous and susceptible to dreadful accidents through negligence, wear and tear, or sabotage; thus, safety standards need to be made more rigorous; the second central issue is whether fission-based energy capabilities should be developed at all in view of these risks and costs (which also include diversion of weapons-grade fissionable material, and problems associated with the disposal of radioactive wastes); an alternative strategy would be to increase research and development in fusion technologies and plan for an energy transition from fossil fuels to fusion-based nuclear power. This latter course was probably available and clearly preferable, but it has been effectively foreclosed by now by the investment in the fission option and by the momentum associated with vested interests arising therefrom. In this setting, the main hope is the modest one of imposing safeguards on completed facilities, and in devising procedures for dealing with accidents and sabotage which might occur at nuclear power plants.

ports, creates pressure to build the trans-Alaska pipeline.* Clearly, the congruence of expanding energy needs with the depletion of nonrenewable energy sources poses some of the most serious environmental dangers of our time.

It is difficult to anticipate the political implications of a shift in the scope and character of the energy base. Karl Wittfogel has argued that the hydraulic character of Oriental civilizations led to despotic forms of government. The word "hydraulic" was used by Wittfogel to designate a farming economy "that involves large-scale and government-managed works of irrigation and flood control." [69] Only with the invention of agriculture did men begin to possess an energy surplus that made possible class structure, urban settlement, and political hierarchy. On the other hand, Buckminster Fuller believes that the utilization of inexhaustible and abundant solar energy would, by assuring permanent supplies of energy, eliminate man's impulse toward conflict and domination. But it is unlikely that the urge to dominate is solely or even predominantly a function of access to resources. Basic human drives, along with ethnic, class, and ideological factors, may also be responsible for the use of coercion to sustain structures of inequity.

A shift to nuclear energy could possibly induce a movement toward greater centralization in the world political system. The problem of establishing adequate safety standards seems to be of global scope, and to require a supportive global consciousness.† In addition, electric power grids could be more efficiently plotted if national boundaries were ig-

---

* As noted earlier, there is growing economic pressure to minimize dollar deficits by avoiding oil imports to the extent possible, especially as the oil-exporting countries are not trading partners and there are thus no offsetting export flows. Furthermore, dependence on oil imports involves certain noneconomic considerations. Since much of the oil import supply comes from the Middle East, especially Saudi Arabia, there is a kind of foreign policy impact arising from vulnerability to export stoppages. The United States may opt to pursue a more even-handed, or pro-Arab, policy in the Middle East conflict or, in contrast, it may initiate or support interventions in Saudi Arabia or elsewhere to prevent adverse political developments.

† In this connection it is worth pointing out that Canada and Sweden joined with such regional governments as Japan, Australia, and New Zealand in protesting French nuclear testing in the Pacific during July and August of 1973; this protest suggests the emergence of an intergovernmental global consciousness that has some world order significance. It is also encouraging to note that the governments of Australia and New Zealand supported individual acts of conscientious resistance to the tests (such as violations of the prohibited zone by test opponents), and that domestic labor groups instigated a boycott of French goods. Even more noteworthy, perhaps, was the decision by Peru to break diplomatic relations with France as a protest against the tests. Reported by the *New York Times*, July 25, 1973, p. 9.

nored, especially in less developed regions where annual energy needs per square mile are low and where the size of countries is relatively small. Although Cottrell argues that the impact of differential energy technology tends toward international stratification and dominant regional political systems (North America, Russia, Europe), rather than toward a universal system,[70] his analysis rests on the assumption that "coal is the basic fuel for high-energy society. Any political system based on high-energy technology must, then, either be possessed of coal or operate in a world which guarantees continuous access to coal-bearing regions." [71] We are not familiar with any world order analysis that argues that by the 1990's either nuclear energy or solar energy will provide the basis for new forms of social and political organization appropriate for high-energy technology. However, the current projections do seem to suggest a gradual displacement of coal by oil, nuclear power, and thermal power as the main energy sources.

Food

Technology has drastically improved the prospects for averting famine in some of the poorer countries of the world, at least during the early 1970's. The advances in agricultural technique that produced the green revolution have primarily involved the development of new seeds for grain cereals (especially wheat, rice, maize) in irrigated areas. These technological innovations are excellent examples of the transnational migration of knowledge: the research and developmental work was mainly done in Mexico, while its most spectacular applications to date have been on the Indian subcontinent. Norman E. Borlaug, Head of the International Wheat Research and Production Program of the International Maize and Wheat Improvement Center, described these exciting developments in his acceptance speech for the 1970 Nobel Peace Prize, awarded for his contributions to the green revolution:

> The green revolution in India and Pakistan, which is still largely the result of a breakthrough in wheat production, is neither a stroke of luck nor an accident of nature. Its success is based on sound research, the importance of which is not self-evident at first glance. For, behind the scenes, halfway around the world in Mexico, were two decades of aggressive research of wheat that not only enabled Mexico to become self-sufficient with respect to wheat production but also paved the way to rapid increase in its production in other countries. It was in Mexico that high-yielding, Mexican dwarf varieties were designed, bred and developed. There, also, was developed the new production technology which permits

these varieties, when properly cultivated, to express their high genetic grain-yield potential—in general double or triple that of the best yielding among older, tall-strawed varieties.[72]

The seeds are not inherently "miraculous," but depend on a variety of supporting efforts involving "heavy doses of fertilizers" and "a broad spectrum of disease resistance." The green revolution combines in one technological package "seeds, fertilizers, insecticides, weed killers and machinery—and the credit with which to buy them." [73] This initial success with wheat has since been repeated with a high-yielding dwarf variety of rice, IR8, developed at the International Rice Research Institute in the Philippines, and with maize and cereal grains.*

It seems clear, however, that the green revolution has not solved, but merely deferred and mitigated, the overall food crisis of mankind.† First

---

* The magnitude of the achievements can be appreciated by Lester R. Brown's summary of progress: "India's production of wheat, expanding much faster than that of other cereals, has increased by 80 percent over the last four years. Present estimates indicate that India, provided that basic political stability is maintained, may be economically self-sufficient in cereals by 1972—that is, India's farmers will be producing as much as the economy will absorb at prevailing prices. In one of the most spectacular advances in cereal production ever recorded, West Pakistan increased its wheat harvest nearly 60 percent between 1967 and 1969. This brought Pakistan—a nation of 130 million people and as recently as 1967 the second largest recipient of United States food aid—to the brink of self-sufficiency in cereal production. In Ceylon the rice crop has increased by 26 percent in the last three years. The Philippines, with four consecutive record rice harvests, has ended a half-century of dependence on rice imports and has become a rice exporter. Among the other countries that are beginning to benefit from the new seeds are Afghanistan, Burma, Indonesia, Iran, Laos, Malaysia, Morocco, Nepal, Tunisia, Turkey, and Vietnam." [74]

† Indeed, by 1973 a new wave of pessimism had emerged about the capacity of poor countries to feed their populations and avert famine. A drought in 1972 sharply reduced crops in several parts of the world, including Asia, Africa, and Central America, producing grave famine and threats of mass starvation. As George Brown writes, "The problem of food shortages does not arise primarily from the failure of the Green Revolution . . . the basic problem, as the Paddocks foresaw, is that population growth has kept pace with, if not exceeded, increases in food production in those areas of the world where the Malthusian food-population squeeze has always been most acute." From "Too Many to Feed," the *New York Times*, May 30, 1973, p. 39. Brown adds that the Paddocks' grim prophecy expressed by their title *Famine 1975* may become a reality as early as 1974. While Brown attributes much of the difficulty to an inability to reduce population expansion, others point to the ineffectiveness and injustice of most governments as more fundamental, and emphasize China's relative success, as compared to India and Bangladesh, in getting food to people who need it and in stemming population growth. Hari Sharma writes, for instance: ". . . critics are charging that, as always in India, the government's action is too little, too late. They ask why 'democratic' India has failed to build irrigation systems, when Communist China, once equally underdeveloped, has managed so well. China is being hit by the same drought, in her case, the worst since

of all, the technology of production does not overcome the obstacles of distribution to 50 percent of the world's population who are undernourished, or to the 65 percent who are malnourished (most of whom are undernourished as well). The purchasing power needed by poor people depends on the overall employment picture, and there are few encouraging signs on this scene. Indeed, as mentioned earlier, the green revolution aggravates the employment problem to the extent that its success depends on substituting machines for human labor, and increasing the unit size of farms to take full advantage of required capital outlays.

Second, it is not fully clear whether the gains associated with the green revolution can be permanently maintained. There is some concern about the vulnerability of the new cereal strains to plant diseases, and the need for more and more insecticide per acre. Third, there are significant ecological and social side-effects of the green revolution. The technology entails ever-greater reliance on chemicals for fertilizers and insecticides; economic pressures place a premium on minimizing unit costs. Hence, it will be difficult to persuade farmers and governments that environmental quality should be taken into account. Furthermore, we may anticipate that in market economies, the beneficiaries of increased production will be the privileged classes and not the enmired masses. The domestic gap between rich and poor will widen still further, intensifying perceived discontent, accentuating moods of frustration, and stimulating recourse to desperate strategies. It is perhaps accidental, perhaps not, that Pakistan, the prime success story of the green revolution, also gave us in 1971 a demonstration of the cycle that leads from discontent to insurrection and repressive violence.

In any case, there are serious doubts about the new agricultural technology's capacity to produce enough to keep pace with population growth in poor countries. Given projected population growth through 1985, it would take an annual rate of growth for food production of between 3.2 and 3.8 percent, just to maintain present abysmal nutritional levels. Ernest Borlaug has admirably described the provisional nature of the green revolution's relation to an expanding world population:

> The green revolution has won a temporary success in man's war against hunger and deprivation: it has given man a breathing spell. If fully implemented, the revolution can provide sufficient food for sustenance

---

1920, when twenty million died—yet suffers no famine and remains nearly self-sufficient in grain." From "Famine in India: The Politics of Starvation," *American Report*, July 16, 1973, p. 9.

during the next three decades. But the frightening power of human reproduction must also be curbed; otherwise, the success of the green revolution will be ephemeral only.[75]

In other words, according to optimistic calculations, it might be possible to avert mass famine and indeed, to alleviate hunger in many parts of the world over the next three decades. But such a "breathing spell" will not by itself overcome the underlying crises caused by trying to exceed the peak load limits of other planetary capacities.

The prospects for increasing food production are not confined, of course, to the green revolution. Various other ongoing efforts involve the synthetic production of food through the techniques of modern chemistry, and harvesting food resources from the oceans, including, quite possibly, the large-scale development of "aqua-culture." There is no consensus, at present, on how much success to expect from technological breakthroughs, or on the acceptability of such new foods to the human diet. At best, technological innovations in food production may be able to shift the issue of population policy away from a strictly Malthusian frame of reference.

A further set of issues concerns the relation of trade patterns to problems of hunger and food sufficiency. The poor countries have been exporting feed for animal husbandry to the rich countries, thereby depriving their own population of important nutrients. The pressure for this kind of trade generally derives from the poor countries' need to earn foreign exchange, in order to support upper classes' imports and to keep the industrial sector developing at a rapid pace. Borgstrom views this dimension of international stratification as leading to eventual catastrophe for the poor countries.[76] The perception of this kind of exploitative dependency could also produce a north–south confrontation, and might lead to the emergence of a new kind of world order coalition.

In summary, the brightest appraisal of technological prospects for food production over the period 1970–2000 does not promise any relief from the basic world order crises. Even if all, or even most, people could be given enough food to eat (an achievement of formidable social and political intricacy), it would still not relieve, and might even aggravate, ecological strains on the planet's life-support systems. Furthermore, the task of providing the citizenry with enough food to live on imposes immense organizational burdens on the limited problem-solving capacities of governments, and thus renders them less able to deal effectively with other human problems.*

---

* Such an observation seems to pertain to efforts directed at the reform of domestic political systems, but may not be applicable to drastic upheavals in the social and political

From a normative perspective, the provision of food is the most basic element of social justice. As Borlaug puts it: "Almost certainly . . . the first essential component of social justice is adequate food for all mankind. Food is the moral right of all who are born into this world . . . Without food man, at most, can live but a few weeks; without it, all other components of social justice are meaningless." [77] This assertion seems unexceptionable on one level, but from a world order perspective it would seem easier to realize WOMP values for a world of 2–4 billion, than for the world of 6–8 billion which is likely to exist by the early years of the next century. What seems to be an ethically mandatory precondition of individual human dignity at one level adds to the peril of the species and the planet and jeopardizes human fulfillment at another level.

Weather

Prospects for economic development are often closely tied to matters of climate. Water shortages exist in many parts of the world and can be overcome, if at all, only by large capital investment. Natural calamities—hurricanes, cloud-to-ground lightning, floods, hailstorms, tornadoes, droughts, fog—inflict heavy damage upon human society. To date, man's great technological prowess has been able to master the weather only in experimental settings, and even then, merely to a marginal extent. Furthermore, the global buildup of industrial activity and proliferation of a high-energy life style are causing changes in atmospheric conditions that might have an eventual impact on the weather, though as of 1974, experts continue to disagree on what the cumulative impacts on earth temperature or weather patterns will be.

The National Science Foundation Special Commission on Weather Modification has reported that major opportunities exist in the field of weather modification. As advanced experimental techniques and application of sophisticated concepts in statistical design promise to reduce uncertainty in interpreting field experiments, the scientific exploration of weather and climate modification is passing out of the speculative phase. Within reach are mathematical and laboratory modeling techniques that permit the simulation of atmospheric processes. By these

---

structure that permit governments to mobilize available resources and energies in a far more efficient fashion. On this kind of possibility rests the contention that the China–India comparison is of critical importance in assessing problem-solving capacities of governments.

means it should become possible to assess in advance the probable consequences of deliberate intervention.*

It seems clear that man's capacity to manipulate weather conditions will increase over the next decade and, depending on its allotment for research and development, could obtain dramatic results by the 1980's and 1990's. This new capability will cause several different kinds of international control problems:

1. The capacity to discern and assess *unintended* detrimental consequences of *intended* forms of weather modification, as when weather modification in state A does indirect harm to states B, C, D, to region X or Y, or to the globe.

2. The capacity to inflict intentional harm on foreign societies through the conscious manipulation of weather modification techniques, whether as a tool of hostile statecraft or an instrument of warfare.

3. The capacity to inflict unintentional and possibly undetected harm on overall global climate by weather modification.†

4. The alteration of global climate by activities unrelated to weather modification, such as the atmospheric disposal of toxic wastes and particulate matter.

---

* The Commission sets forth a series of conclusions that underlie its general appraisal of prospects:

1. Several cubic miles of super-cooled cloud droplets can be transformed into ice crystals by seeding with dry ice or silver iodide. Super-cooled fog on the ground can be dissipated. No practical approach to the dissipation of warm fog is at hand. 2. While the evidence is still somewhat ambiguous, there is support for the view that precipitation from some types of clouds can be increased by the order of ten percent by seeding. If the results are confirmed by further studies they would have great significance. The question of corresponding decreases of precipitation outside the target area is unresolved. 3. Results from attempts to suppress hail in the United States are as yet inconclusive but more promising results in other countries are leading to the establishment in this country of a program that should provide a more definitive answer. 4. Experts in lightning suppression are beginning to show some promise. 5. Modification of hurricanes has reached the stage of preliminary field experimentation but the results, so far, are inconclusive. 6. Changing the course or intensity of extratropical cyclones and altering climate over large areas remain as problems for the future. 7. Inadvertent changes in climate as a consequence of human activity (e.g. urbanization, air pollution, increase of atmospheric carbon dioxide by burning fossil fuels) are amenable to analysis and deserve early attention.[78]

† Here, as elsewhere, the definition of "harm" may be controversial, and the perception of good and bad in relation to weather modification may relate more directly to interest groups than to territorial units. For instance, what is good for tourism is generally not good for agriculture.

In each case there must be a way to establish the facts authoritatively, to create procedures and criteria for balancing benefits against costs and risks, to impose safety limitations on efforts at weather modification, and to assess damage and liability arising from weather modification damage. In the field of weather modification, as elsewhere, the cumulative impact of intentional and unintentional consequences on the world community would seem to require regional and global institutions of information gathering, data assessment, crisis management, and regulatory control. The present structure of fragmented authority cannot expect to achieve coordinated results, given the uneven rate of technological development and the diverse interests of states with different climatic patterns.*

Finally, if weather modification can produce economic and social benefits, to what extent and under what auspices should such information be shared, especially with low-technology societies not able to engage in their own research and development? † This problem—the terms and auspices of transfer, whether the transfer is a tradeoff, a gift, or a matter of community sharing—arises throughout our discussion of the prospective relevance of technology.‡ In the area of nuclear energy, the nuclear powers struck a bargain, at least temporarily, offering their assistance in the development of nuclear energy if the non-nuclear states would sign the Non-Proliferation Treaty. In the field of agriculture, the transfer, perhaps because it is related to food for subsistence, has largely been accomplished by a combination of philanthropy (promoted by large U.S. foundations) and self-reliance (the domestic priority of modernizing the agricultural sector).§ It is presently unclear how the technology of weather modification will be transferred from

---

* A weather modification capability to mitigate disasters associated with floods and droughts would clearly serve the sort of humanitarian values embodied in the WOMP mandate for world order reform, or in even more modest mandates.

† A somewhat comparable problem arises from the identification of mineral deposits and fisheries through the use of satellite technology, available only to the superpowers at present, to conduct a geological survey. The ability of satellites to identify foreign or oceanic deposits certainly involves world interests of a sort not dealt with in traditional doctrines of territorial sovereignty.

‡ For further discussion see p. 139.

§ Such transfer was also undoubtedly motivated by competitive diplomacy and imperial goals. When one country is providing another with its basis of subsistence, the former can "justifiably" maintain a presence and exert its influence. Just as the Peace Corps has been accused of having a link with imperial designs comparable to that of religious missionaries in an earlier era, so the foreign agronomist has a somewhat comparable role even if his own individual services are given out of a sense of pure dedication.

the main innovating societies to other parts of the world. Part of the answer will depend on whether the transfer moves via the state-based open market, or is assigned to some international managerial system responsible for sharing knowledge and regulating its application.

Information

One of the most critical areas of technological innovation is that of information processing and its dissemination. In the last two decades, no technological change has had a greater impact on advanced societies, and it will surely acquire an even more fundamental significance in the years ahead. Information means knowledge, and skillful application of knowledge increasingly means power. But information, like other instruments of power, can be used for positive or negative purposes (no matter how these normative terms are defined).

Inequality is measured in many respects by radically uneven access to information. Secrecy—the withholding of information—has become a central political issue in American political life; it highlights once more the tension between political ideals, and the political reality which sometimes induces the suspension of those ideals. Many of the Watergate disclosures, including the so-called "White House horrors," involved extravagant efforts by those in power to assure their capacity to keep secrets from Congress and the public.

On the other hand, the new information technology does enable a far better-informed citizenry, and *could* assure its immediate and effective participation on concrete issues of social choice. Informational technology may even hold the key to the reinvigoration of democratic political forms. Although the technology itself is morally neutral, its dual potential is evident: to serve or to thwart human well-being.

Information technology has obvious implications for a global system of guidance in which information and policy are considerably centralized, but authority and implementation procedures are widely dispersed. Our preference model in Chapter IV assumes the availability of information technology as a major element in its design of a non-hierarchical model of central guidance.

The technological capacity to collect, store, and disseminate information will increase dramatically in the near future, making information on a variety of subjects quickly and cheaply available. These capacities could lead to a cumulative trend toward decentralization or centralization; the new technology is Janus-faced, and can serve either end. In the short run, a great deal will depend on the attitudes national governments take toward various kinds of information dispersal. It is quite likely that access to technical information will be widely dispersed even in totalitarian and authoritarian societies, while access to "sensitive" information will be closely held. What different governments regard as "sensitive" may in the future become an important expression of fundamental political differences.

The changes in information technology are proceeding so rapidly that any discussion of their significance is unreliable. What seems a bold projection in 1974 is quite likely to appear naively conservative when looked back upon in the year 2000. Furthermore, very complicated political decisions will be required in order to choose among a series of options made available by the new technology, because information technology brings its dual potential to such sensitive areas of life as traditional values of privacy and autonomy, and the quality of political participation.

The new information technology may contribute to the formation of a global consciousness, by seriously preventing most national governments from controlling information flows to their respective citizenries. Conversely, the security of governance—especially in societies with important unresolved grievances—will come to depend increasingly on the ability to control major forms of news dissemination. Such control is already institutionalized in authoritarian societies, and pressures to obtain this power are increasingly visible even in countries with strong traditions of a free press and of civil liberties like the United States. Communications technology is capable of wielding enormous influence. As statesmen find themselves more and more forced to cope with demands for resources which have been growing progressively scarcer, they may be tempted to draw upon the media's power in order to neutralize public expectations or opposition movements. As a result, public policy toward information technology and the media is likely to constitute a principal arena of controversy over the next decade.

However, the economic advantages of computers and electronics are so enormous—including cheaper per-unit and per-mile collection, storage and dissemination of information—that in the long run the new technology may have a progressive impact on society. The scope of the industry's development is described by Ben Bagdikian:

> There is an enormous growth in the capacity for transferring information from point to point, and this growth will reach even greater capacities. In the past fifty years the number of continental electronic-communications channels has increased from six to 100,000. In the next thirty years the number could easily grow to one billion. Devices for entering information into such a system and for taking it out are proliferating. There is an ex-

pansion of forms for the display of information—voice, moving pictures, print—and in ways for the individual to find desired data from the expanding reservoir.

The several ingredients of this communications upheaval are still new. Semiconductors of germanium, silicon, and gallium arsenide duplicate the work of bulky glass vacuum tubes. Invention of the transistor in 1947 started the revolution that made electronic equipment cheaper, smaller, more portable, and demanding less power.[79]

Many related inventions, including vastly more efficient means of providing integrated circuitry,* have contributed to this process of miniaturizing electronic equipment, and the end is not yet in sight.

Substitutes for paper documents also began to proliferate until by now it is possible to use microphotography to record thirty-two hundred typewritten or printed pages on a single four-by-six transparent ultramicrofiche card. It is possible to carry the equivalent of a thousand books or of sixty hundred-page newspapers in the breast pocket of a man's suit, and read them on a projector, still expensive, but already as portable as a briefcase.[80]

The potential consequences are phenomenal: virtually all human knowledge can be within the reach of every section of every society—indeed, within the reach of every home. The new information capacities could be used for both general education and special purposes, didactically and interactively. In addition to economically-designed educational programs which would benefit everyone, many time-consuming and traffic-producing sales, marketing, and consumer transactions could be conducted by computer selection and response equipment. In this way, information technology might liberate people somewhat from daily chores, and would also help to reduce pollution and urban decay by inducing less mobile patterns of individual life. Indeed, the need to conduct business in urban centers might decline markedly, if many routine transactions could be accomplished instead by closed-circuit two-way television tied to computer transfers of information. For newly industrializing societies, it might make much more sense in economic

---

* Bagdikian notes, "In less than ten years, the cost of an integrated circuit dropped from $600 to $2.50." See note 80, Chapter VII. Such a cost drop, in an inflationary period, gives a sense of the scale of technological advance and its growing availability to various kinds of specialized information consumers.

and social terms to invest in computer capability than in a highway system.

Another major line of development is related to the improvement of cable transmission of TV broadcasts. Cable TV, or, as it is generally known, CATV (Community Antenna Television), now provides 42 channels, and may eventually provide eighty or more. These cable facilities can be used to transmit all kinds of information into the home, including stock-market quotations, weather reports, continuous news bulletins, and television programs imported from distant cities. In this respect, the capacities of cables are far greater than are the capacities of electronic transmission through the air. To quote Bagdikian once again,

> The long-range significance of cable is not its ability to duplicate existing television programs. It is the potential for two-way communications between the home and a vast array of information services; twenty-channel cable has forty thousand times more capacity than telephone wires. . . . Outgoing signals from the home by cable already are being used for automatic reading of household utility meters and burglar and fire-alarm systems, transmitted to a centralized location where the reading from each home can be identified.[81]

CATV can also provide a much greater variety of programming, thereby giving minority perspectives and deviant life-styles a better chance for representation in the media. Cable technology is, in many respects, very threatening to mainstream broadcasting, and to the monopoly on wired communications held for so long by telephone companies. Considerations of function and efficiency may help to resolve some technological management problems in a cosmopolitan fashion, but may not necessarily produce the kind of cosmopolitanism embodied in the four WOMP values.*

Conflicts may often involve bombarding target audiences with contradictory images of what is desirable. In many settings, hostile propaganda broadcast appeals might come to be widely accepted as a substitute for open warfare; domination might be achieved by thought

---

* Globalization is not necessarily beneficial, given a WOMP value outlook. We have tried to make this point clear with respect to the double potentialities of centralizing power and authority (the *quis custodiet* problem cluster) in a new world order system of multinational corporate formations (see Chapter III, pp. 225–228), and of homogenizing cultural and ideological variations. It is crucial, in conceiving of S2(WOMP/ USA) (see note, p. 236), to keep in mind the *value priorities* and *orientation* of principal actors, and the *procedures* and *substance* of diversity in the various dimensions of human existence.

control and brainwashing rather than by police techniques. While such a shift in governmental techniques might avoid bloodshed and eliminate the war system from human affairs, its costs could be very great in terms of human development. Men might be shaped from the time of their birth in the direction of docility and submission. Individuals might find that they are *inmates* rather than *citizens* in whatever political communities persist or emerge.*

In all events, because information technology clearly will play a central role in either advancing or impeding any movement for a better world order, vigilance and continued awareness of its double potential are most important. The development and application of information technology will both condition and reflect the character of political order at all levels during the decades ahead. One aspect of this impact, possibly with major significance, is the degree to which large-scale organizations need no longer be pyramidal in structure. Such an impact can be mentioned now only as a remote possibility, but it might be of great relevance to world order concerns. Without the need for a centralized bureaucratic structure, central guidance systems for planetary affairs could be designed without having to create the institutional nexus of a world government. Therefore, the information–communications revolution may help overcome "the Frankenstein problem," namely, the objection to central guidance based on the belief that any large bureaucracy, regardless of its original animus, would eventually deteriorate into some form of tyranny that might prove very resistant to reform.

Some General Considerations

The next thirty-year period is critical in determining whether the cumulative effect of technological innovation will be disintegrative or integrative. Major innovations are inevitable. The enlarged scale of technological capacity and economic efficiency makes the constraining boundaries of the state artificial, if not irrelevant. There are accumulating strains that will test the capacity of the planet to absorb pressures

---

* In essence, even world peace (V_1) secured in conjunction with economic well-being for virtually everyone (V_2) could still eventuate in an undesirable form of S_2 (see note, p. 321) unless V_3 and V_4 are simultaneously preserved and promoted. The WOMP perspective on world order reform stresses the *interrelations* among the four value dimensions, and is keenly aware that advances on one or another of these dimensions might be associated with setbacks on others.

upon basic ecosystems, as well as challenge the adaptability of the world order system to sustain minimum modes of societal coexistence. In the following sections, a few general considerations relating to the challenges and threats created by rapid technological innovation will be discussed.

S–Curve Phenomenon

In a stimulating essay, John Platt asserts:

> The essence of the matter is that the human race is on a steeply rising 'S-curve' of change. . . . In the last century, we have increased our speeds of communication by a factor of 10^7; our speeds of travel by 10^2; our speeds of data handling by 10^6; our energy resources by 10^3; our power of weapons by 10^6; our ability to control diseases by something like 10^2; and our rate of population growth to 10^3 times what it was a few thousand years ago.[82]

These awesome magnitudes of change place immense pressure on problem-solving patterns and structures which have altered little, if at all, over the last century; indeed, except for superficial changes in norms and institutions, the structure of international society is in 1971 what it was in 1871. The particular novelty of Platt's analysis rests, however, on the assertion that the era of exponential change will soon come to an end.:

> What many people do not realize is that many of these technological changes are approaching certain natural limits. The "S-curve" is beginning to level off. We may never have faster communications or more TV or larger weapons or a higher level of danger than we have now. This means that if we could learn how to manage these new powers and problems in the next few years without killing ourselves by our obsolete structures and behavior, we might be able to create new and more effective social structures that would last for many generations.[83]

That is, if we can regain control over technological trends, then "we might be able to move into that new world of abundance and diversity and well-being for all mankind which technology has now made possible." Such a diagnosis regards the present period as one of transitional crisis, in which either necessary adjustments will be made or else mankind will be disabled by a series of catastrophes involving war, famine, disease, ethnic hatreds, or political struggle. Underneath Platt's views are two problematic assumptions: (1) that prior to this period of exponential change the structures and behavior of human society were generally, or at least, sufficiently, adaptive to permit the development and evolution of the human species; and (2) that existing and emerging technological capability appropriately mobilized can deal successfully with the array of outstanding human problems.

Platt's analysis fails to give attention to "the peak load" perspective, which emphasizes the disappearance of excess capacity and the expanding scope of impact, making the distinction between local and global less firm. We have no evidence, in other words, that earlier patterns were any more adaptive, but only that their nonadaptive attributes did not eventuate in a catastrophe of planetary scope. But the S-curve analysis is helpful in suggesting that the buildup of certain kinds of pressure may be levelling off as a result of automatic corrective measures (after all, most people can't use, don't want, or can't afford more than two cars per family or specialized knowledge beyond certain levels), and that if these pressures can be contained through the 1980's, then nothing worse than what is already on the horizon is likely to emerge in the foreseeable future.

Platt argues principally that these problem clusters are formidable, but potentially manageable, if a suitable human response were mobilzed. Thus, transition to a new era of relative harmony and confidence depends upon a world order movement potent enough to meet the challenges being posed. Without such a movement, these challenges might eventuate in catastrophe for the species and the planet, regardless of the long-run reassurance implicit in the S-curve phenomenon.

Vulnerability and Complexity

The course of technological development will entail still greater complexity, more interconnecting parts, a vaster organic web of operations and activities. The techniques of disruption can therefore wreak correspondingly greater havoc, and the systems upon which organized life depends are vulnerable to very large-scale breakdowns. The incidence or frequency of breakdown may be less, but the consequences of particular breakdowns may be greater. When more primitive systems of organization are disrupted, only very local interests are at stake—when the wind blows out a candle it extinguishes only a faint single source of light. But the present stage of technological innovation tends to produce such complex interconnectedness that redundant systems, as well as rapid checking and repair capabilities, are absolutely essential.*

Stratification and Transfer of Technology

A persisting issue concerns the transfer of technological innovations from the advanced, dominant sectors of international society to the dependent sectors, as well as from one sector to another within a single nation. This concern involves a number of separate issues:

1. The extent to which technological advances are shared
2. The extent to which international institutions govern the transfer of technological innovations
3. The impact of the transfer on the national autonomy of the recipient society
4. The terms of transfer, the extent of subsidy, and the participation of the recipient society in designing applications

In essence, the world order issue here is whether technological development is handled primarily as a matter of global and humanistic concern or primarily as a matter of relevance to the functioning of a profit-oriented state system. Of course, the reality is likely to be mixed and to vary from innovation to innovation. Nevertheless, positive world order prospects will be greatly enhanced to the extent that the process of technological transfer is decoupled from the competitive logic of interacting states of unequal size, industrial development, and capital. The internationalization of technological transfer is a field for constructive international action that bears resemblance to the buildup of international peace-keeping capabilities as an alternative to great power competitive interventions. Educational opportunity for disadvantaged societies and

---

* Our image of technological development involves a series of increases in size, speed, and initial capital cost. Ocean tankers or commercial aircraft are typical specimens of such a technological progression. In the future, technology might concentrate on engineering detachability, working against the interconnectedness and economy of scale it has been generally creating up to this time. There is no necessary priority in technological momentum that dooms the human race to evolve an interconnected self-destruct habitat by the mindless pursuit of profit-oriented or GNP-oriented innovation. Soft technologies could be developed for efficiency at the neighborhood or community scale of operation.

disadvantaged individuals is crucial to building a climate for technology-sharing in an atmosphere of mutual respect.*

Functional Imperatives

The scale of technological operation and impact is constantly increasing, and extending beyond the jurisdictional confines of national and even regional markets. Business operations governed by profit criteria are pushing toward transnational networks of operation. The consequence of this pressure, given certain favorable conditions, may be a "green revolution of institutional innovations" on the world level, an unprecedented proliferation of supranational actors managing behavior at the forefront of human development.

Space/Time

Technological development is increasingly capable of integrating widely separated events, making central guidance a practical administrative potentiality, while rendering the relations of proximity and contiguity less significant. Even at great distances there are more possibilities for persistent interaction, as the flow of information and images increases in speed and decreases in unit costs. Also, functional drives to minimize costs generate much larger geographical areas of relevance—with respect to labor, materials, and creative endeavor.

CONCLUSION

This survey of trends and patterns has sought to raise the issues that will dominate the world order agenda in the decades to come. The

---

* The transfer of technology, without the existence of an autonomous capacity to make beneficial use of it, is not likely to be especially constructive. The Soviet transfer of arms to North Vietnam as compared to the Soviet transfer of arms to Egypt illustrates a relation of mutual respect in the former instance and ineffectual tutelage in the latter. The whole controversy in the area of foreign aid is relevant here, as is the counter-controversy in Third World countries dealing with the compatibility between foreign aid and a posture of national self-reliance.

cumulative effect of these issues, we believe, makes evident two factors: that the state system will experience increasing pressure from various sources and that it will, at best, be barely able to cope with this pressure. There is no serious likelihood that the problems which produce the pressure can be eliminated or even alleviated unless there is a serious and responsive reorganization of power and authority in international society. This is the principal reason that the remaining pages deal with the substance and strategy of global reform.

Not all directions of global reform respond to these pressures in ways which are beneficial from the perspective of the values set forth in Chapter I. In fact, we would anticipate almost as much danger from regressive varieties of global reform as from the persistence of the status quo. The basis of this concern will become clearer in Chapters III, VI, and VII. The type of global reforms that we support will be described in Chapters IV and V.

REFERENCES

1. See F.S.C. Northrop, *The Meeting of East and West,* New York, Macmillan, 1944; Adda Bozeman, *Politics and Culture in International History,* Princeton, New Jersey, Princeton University Press, 1960; see also Myres S. McDougal and Harold D. Lasswell, "The Identification and Appraisal of Diverse Systems of Public Order," in McDougal et al., *Studies in World Public Order,* New Haven, Yale University Press, 1960, pp. 3–41.

2. The anticipation of new political and legal forms—the embodiment of world order reorganization—by symbol-forming processes in the human imagination deserves serious study. The work of Robert Jay Lifton is very suggestive in these regards. See, in particular, final chapters in *Home from the War: Vietnam Veterans—Neither Victims nor Executioners,* New York, Simon and Schuster, 1973.

3. Transnational phenomena are carefully assessed in Robert O. Keohane and Joseph S. Nye, Jr., eds., *Transnational Relations and World Politics,* Cambridge, Harvard University Press, 1972; see also Samuel P. Huntington, "Transnational Organizations in World Politics," *World Politics,* XXV, No. 3, April 1973, pp. 333–368.

4. Well-considered as a general tendency in Harold Sprout and Margaret Sprout, *Toward A Politics of the Planet Earth,* New York, Van Nostrand, 1971, pp. 348–376.

5. Lester Brown, *World Without Boundaries,* New York, Random House, 1972, pp. 214–215; this issue is considered more fully in Chapter VI, pp. 382–387.

6. Such an account is developed in Falk, "The Interplay of Westphalia and Charter Conceptions of the International Legal Order," in Richard A. Falk and Cyril E. Black, eds., *The Future of the International Legal Order,* Princeton, New Jersey, Princeton University Press, Vol. I, 1969, pp. 32–70.

7. Bargaining for international agreements in authoritative treaty form is increasingly a matter of securing a *global* consensus among a highly *heterodox* group of participating actor governments. Heterodoxy exists on several dimensions: size, stage of economic development, skill in negotiations and knowledge of subject matter, orientation of governmental elite, tradeoff potentialities, aggregations of bargaining caucuses, and so on. In a *homogeneous* setting—greater similarity among actors—and where the system of negotiations involves only a small number of significant participants, the possibilities for negotiating without tradeoffs to neutralize heterodox elements are much greater. Some general theoretical background of these issues can be found in Raymond Aron, *Peace and War, A Theory of International Relations,* Garden City, New York, Doubleday, 1966.

8. Two important, very different approaches to this problem are Richard J. Barnet, *The Roots of War,* New York, Atheneum, 1972, and Robert Jay Lifton, *Home from the War,* especially pp. 329–378.

9. The initial formulation of a pentagonal design for world order reform was by Richard Nixon in a speech delivered to Midwestern newspaper executives in Kansas City, Missouri, on July 6, 1971. Text in *Vital Speeches*, August 1, 1971, pp. 611–615; for interpretation see also James Chace, *A World Elsewhere: The New American Foreign Policy*, New York, Scribner's, 1973.

10. This confidence may not be warranted; the system of deterrence, on the basis of its logic, is vulnerable to certain risks of irrational behavior by leaders (the Hitler problem), of unauthorized behavior by subordinates, and of accident. The extent of these risks is not possible to assess, but they are clearly greater than negligible and can never be eliminated by technical means, however ingenious. For a perceptive, if conservative, sound of a warning alarm see Fred Charles Iklé, "Can Nuclear Deterrence Last Out the Century?" in *California Arms Control and Foreign Policy Seminar*, January 1973, pp. 1–45.

11. The prominent dissident Soviet physicist, Andrei Sakharov, has proposed a twenty percent tax on the national income of all advanced industrial countries as a basis for solving the problem of world poverty; Sakharov's proposals were explicitly spurned by the Soviet bureaucracy and Sakharov has been treated as "an enemy of the state" despite his earlier role as "father" of the Soviet hydrogen bomb. See Andrei Sakharov, *Progress, Coexistence, and Intellectual Freedom*, 2nd rev. ed., New York, Norton, 1970.

12. The gap between the United Nations as actor and the Charter is examined in some detail in Falk, "The United Nations: Various Systems of Operation," in Leon Gordenker, ed., *The United Nations and World Politics*, Princeton, Princeton University Press, 1972, pp. 184–230. Of course, such a gap is not a *static* quantity, but must be constantly reassessed in relation to changes in the operation of the United Nations as *actor* and of the Charter as organic law. These assessments could also be usefully disaggregated in relation to each of the four WOMP values (see Chapter 1) and aggregated in relation to the overall, integrated role to provide the international system with central guidance.

13. See Robert C. Angell, *Peace on the March: Transnational Participation*, New York, Van Nostrand, 1969; see also Keohane and Nye, *Transnational Relations* and Huntington, "Transnational Organizations," cited note 3.

14. For a leading exposition of the functionalist approach to world order reform, see David Mitrany, *A Working Peace System*, Chicago, Quadrangle, rev. ed., 1966; for a challenging exposition from a neo-functionalist perspective that shares Mitrany's focus and goals, but disputes his reliance on apolitical strategies of transition, see Ernst B. Hass, *Beyond the Nation–State: Functionalism and International Organization*, Stanford, Stanford University Press, 1964.

15. For an assessment of this relatively unfamiliar organizational presence in international life see Robert W. Gregg, "The UN Regional Economic Com-

missions and Multinational Cooperation," in Robert S. Jordan, ed., *Multinational Cooperation: Economic, Social, and Scientific Development*, New York, Oxford, 1972, pp. 50–109.

16. The world order significance of the multinational corporation is considered somewhat more fully in Chapter VI.

17. *Business Week*, Dec. 19, 1970, p. 61.

18. Raymond Vernon, *Sovereignty at Bay: The Multinational Spread of U.S. Enterprises*, New York, Basic Books, 1971; see also Hugh Stephenson, *The Coming Clash: The Impact of Multinational Corporations on National States*, New York, Saturday Review Press, 1972.

19. This shift was decried by certain American strategists as unduly subordinating our comparative military advantage. Henry Kissinger's *Nuclear Weapons and Foreign Policy*, New York, published for the Council on Foreign Relations by Harper, 1957, is, perhaps, the most influential example of an effort to reassure American policy-makers that even nuclear wars could be threatened or fought without creating large risks of World War III. In essence, America's world role in the early Cold War depended on neutralizing Soviet advantages in manpower, conventional capabilities and geopolitical position by "a forward position" involving foreign bases and a credible willingness to meet Soviet non-nuclear provocations, especially in Europe, with a nuclear response.

20. Such a contention is elaborated and supported by considerable evidence in Thomas E. Weisskopf, "Capitalism, Underdevelopment, and the Future of the Poor Countries," in Jagdish N. Bhagwati, ed., *Economic and World Order*, New York, Macmillan, 1972, pp. 43–77.

21. See Paul R. Erhlich, *The Population Bomb*, New York, Ballantine Books, 1968; William and Paul Paddock, *Famine 1975! America's Decision: Who Will Survive?* Boston, Little, Brown, 1967; Georg Borgstrom, *Too Many: A Study of the Earth's Biological Limitations*, New York, Scribners, 1969. There is also a lively debate as to the relative significance of population in the context of ecological pressure. Among thinkers who regard the population factor as much less significant than technological developments and life-style, see Barry Commoner, *The Closing Circle*, New York, Knopf, 1971; Ansley Coale, "Man and His Environment," in Daniel Callahan, ed., *The American Population Debate*, New York, Anchor, 1971, pp. 168–181.

22. Among several books that relate these factors see Paul Ehrlich and Anne H. Ehrlich, *Population, Environment, and Resources*, San Francisco, W. H. Freeman, 2nd rev. ed., 1972; Edward Goldsmith et al., *Blueprint for Survival*, Boston, Houghton Mifflin, 1972; Richard A. Falk, *This Endangered Planet: Prospects and Proposals for Human Survival*, New York, Random House, 1971.

23. See Ehrlich and Ehrlich, *Population, Environment, and Resources,* p. 72; but see Ansley Coale, "Man and His Environment," who argues that these statistical assertions are not founded on appropriate evidence.

24. Borgstrom, *op. cit.,* p. 323.

25. *Ibid.* p. 321.

26. *Ibid.* pp. 328–329.

27. Neil Chamberlain, *Beyond Malthus; Population and Power,* New York, Basic Books, 1970.

28. *Population Bulletin,* November 1970, pp. 9–10.

29. See Ted Robert Gurr, *Why Men Rebel,* Princeton, Princeton University Press, 1970.

30. But see Barrington Moore on the poor prospects of revolution from an urban base, *Reflections On the Causes of Human Misery and Upon Certain Prospects to Eliminate Them,* Boston, Beacon Press, 1972.

31. The *New York Times,* Nov. 4, 1970, p. 47.

32. "Human Food Production as a Process in the Biosphere," *Scientific American,* Vol. 223, No. 3, Sept., 1970, p. 170.

33. See Larry Bumpass and Charles Westoff, "Unwanted Births and U.S. Population Growth," in Callahan, *The American Population Debate,* pp. 267–273; and Charles Westoff and Leslie Westoff, *From Here to Zero,* Boston, Little, Brown, 1971.

34. See Paddock and Paddock, *Famine 1975!*

35. Cf. Benjamin S. Lambeth, "Deterrence in the MIRV Era," *World Politics,* Vol. 24, pp. 221–242, 1972, with Fred Charles Iklé, "Can Nuclear Deterrence Last Out the Century?"

36. For a balanced discussion of this diffusion prospect see Mason Willrich, "Civil Nuclear Power: Conflict Potential and Management," in Black and Falk, eds., *The Future of the International Legal Order,* Princeton, Princeton University Press, Vol. III, 1971, pp. 252–270.

37. For a very important effort to study a group of American anti-war veterans of the Vietnam War from the perspective of the waning of the myth of the warrior hero, see Robert Jay Lifton, *Home from the War,* especially pp. 25–31, 331–378; for a very perceptive account of the persistence of the warrior myth in the setting of World War II, see J. Glenn Gray, *The Warriors— Reflections on Men in Battle,* New York, Harcourt, Brace, 1959.

38. For an even more negative interpretation of the parasitic relations of these states to the war system see Moore, *Reflections On the Causes of Human Misery,* pp. 20–22; the essence of Moore's skeptical view is contained in the

following assertion: "The peaceful situation of the weaker and peaceful states exists on the sufferance of the strong and more bellicose ones; the happiness of the former depends upon the simple fact that aggression against them is not worthwhile." (p. 21). I believe this judgment to be an exaggeration that overlooks the extent to which a peace-minded ideology helps organize a peace-minded foreign policy. It was no accident that Sweden was the most outspoken noncommunist governmental critic of America's war effort in Indochina, even though such criticism jeopardized Sweden's posture of non-participation in geopolitical rivalry.

39. *World Military Expenditures,* U.S. Arms Control and Disarmament Agency, 1969, pp. 1, 2.

40. E.g., McGeorge Bundy, "To Cap the Volcano," *Foreign Affairs,* 48: 1–20 (1969); Abram Chayes and Jerome B. Weisner, eds., *ABM: An Evaluation of the Decision to Deploy an Anti-Ballistic Missile,* New York, Harper, 1969; Herbert Scoville, Jr., "Toward a Strategic Arms Limitation Agreement," New York, Carnegie Endowment for International Peace, 1970; George W. Rathjens, "The Dynamics of the Arms Race," *Scientific American,* April 1969, pp. 15–25; George W. Rathjens, "The Future of the Strategic Arms Race: Options for the 1970's," New York, Carnegie Endowment for International Peace, 1969.

41. Herbert York, *Race to Oblivion: A Participant's View of the Arms Race,* New York, Simon and Schuster, 1970.

42. For a very persuasive analysis of the obstacles to arms control and disarmament since World War II and the prospects for their circumvention in the future, see Harold Feiveson, "Arms Control and Disarmament," in Black and Falk, Vol. III, *The Future of the International Legal Order,* pp. 336–369.

43. For a discussion of the problems associated with the global spread of conventional weaponry see William B. Bader, "The Proliferation of Conventional Weapons," in Black and Falk, Vol. III, *The Future of the International Legal Order,* pp. 210–222. Competitive economic relations among governments, especially given large trade deficits of arms suppliers, create formidable pressure to earn foreign exchange and contribute to a favorable balance of payments situation.

44. Herman Kahn and Anthony Wiener, *The Year 2000: A Framework for Speculation on the Next Thirty-Three Years,* New York, Macmillan, 1967; Kermit Gordon, ed., *Agenda for the Nation,* Washington, D.C., Brookings Institution, 1968.

45. See Maurice Strong, "One Year After Stockholm: An Ecological Approach," *Foreign Affairs,* 52: 690–707 (1973) for a relatively optimistic assessment of the UN effort at Stockholm.

46. Among the most prominent efforts to state an alarmist case are Edward Goldsmith et al., *Blueprint for Survival;* Donella Meadows and others, *The*

Limits to Growth, Washington, Potomac Associates, 1972; for a more reassuring view of global danger from environmental decay see *Man's Impact on the Global Environment*, Report of the Study of Critical Environmental Problems, Cambridge, Mass., MIT Press, 1970. We do not presently possess the data or the interpretative skill to assess the risk of ecological collapse.

47. See *Man's Impact*, pp. 280–282, especially Tables 6.5, 6.6.

48. *Man's Impact*, pp. 294–95, Tables 7.3, 7.4.

49. This general orientation animates Max Nicholson's fine book, *The Environmental Revolution*, New York, McGraw-Hill, 1970.

50. A. Shircliff, *S/S/T and Sonic Boom Handbook*, New York, Ballantine Books, 1970, well-depicted in brief by Paul A. Rosenbaum, *The Politics of Environmental Concern*, New York, Praeger, 1970, pp. 8–9.

51. For a helpful statement of Third World perspective see Founex Report and related papers in "Development and Environment," *International Conciliation*, No. 586, Carnegie Endowment of International Peace, Jan. 1972.

52. See Marshall I. Goldman, *The Spoils of Progress: Environmental Pollution in the Soviet Union*, Cambridge, Mass., M.I.T. Press, 1972.

53. See the illuminating article by Edward Cowan explaining the Senate victory of Alaska pipeline advocates in The *New York Times*, July 22, 1973, Section 4, p. 3. Mr. Cowan lists four factors to explain the political outcome, the first of which is that "the major oil companies, several of which would be the principal owners of the pipeline, spent a small fortune advertising their case. Aligned with them were the White House and many conservative members of Congress."

54. For a general assessment of fundamental impacts see Gerald Feinberg, *The Prometheus Project: Mankind's Search for Long-Range Goals*, Garden City, New York, Doubleday, 1968.

55. See the works of Robert Jay Lifton for a probing consideration of the role of death symbolism in contemporary life forms. Cf. especially, *Home from the War*, and *Death in Life: Survivors from Hiroshima*, New York, Random House, 1968; *Revolutionary Immortality: Mao Tse-Tung and the Chinese Revolution*, New York, Random House, 1968.

56. Both quotations from Eugene Skolnikoff, "Implications of Science and Technology on International Relations in the 70s," Conference on Trends Affecting International Relations, Council on Foreign Relations, Dec. 7–8, 1970, p. 2.

57. Henry Kissinger, "Changing Concepts in Foreign Policy," in *Agenda for the Nation*, p. 590.

58. Victor Basiuk, "Perils of the New Technology," *Foreign Policy*, Spring, 1971, p. 58.

59. *Ibid.*, p. 59.

60. *Ibid.*, p. 60.

61. *Business Week*, Dec. 19, 1970, p. 58.

62. Basic perspectives developed in Karl Wittfogel, *Oriental Despotism—A Comparative Study of Total Power*, New Haven, Yale Univ. Press, 1959; and William Frederick Cottrell, *Energy and Society, The Relations between Energy, Social Change, and Economic Development*, New York, McGraw-Hill, 1955. Among modern thinkers, Buckminster Fuller is one of the few who sees energy costs and supplies as fundamental to the shape of world order and the character of human destiny.

63. The shape of this transition, as presently appreciated, is discussed by John McHale in *The Future of the Future*, New York, Braziller, 1969.

64. Cottrell, *Energy and Society*, pp. 11–12.

65. McHale, *The Future of the Future*, pp. 110–111, for tables of energy consumption based on national comparison.

66. See Richard Curtis and Elizabeth Hogan, *Perils of the Peaceful Atom*, Garden City, New York, Doubleday, 1969; Sheldon Novick, *The Careless Atom*, Boston, Houghton Mifflin, 1969; also Mason Willrich, *Global Politics of Nuclear Energy*, New York, Praeger, 1971.

67. McHale, *The Future*, p. 51; see M. King Hibbert, "Energy Resources," in Preston, Cloud and others, eds., *Man and Resources*, San Francisco, W. H. Freeman and Co., 1969, pp. 157–239.

68. McHale, *The Future*, p. 118.

69. Wittfogel, *Oriental Despotism*, p. 3.

70. Cottrell, *Energy and Society*, pp. 284–86.

71. *Ibid.*, p. 295.

72. Borlaug, "The Green Revolution, Peace and Humanity," Population Research Bureau Selection No. 35, Jan. 1971, p. 3.

73. *Ibid.*, p. 3.

74. Brown, "The Social Impact of the Green Revolution," *International Conciliation*, No. 581, Jan. 1971, p. 7; Brown is somewhat less enthusiastic in his later book, *World Without Boundaries*, see e.g., pp. 3–12.

75. Borlaug, "The Green Revolution," p. 8.

76. Borgstrom, *Too Many*, pp. 312–340.

77. Borlaug, "The Green Revolution," p. 8.

78. As quoted in Howard J. Taubenfeld, *Controlling the Weather*, New York, Dunellen, 1970, p. XIII.

79. Ben Bagdikian, *The Information Machines: Their Impact on Men and The Media*, New York, Harper and Row, 1971, p. XV; see also John Kemeny, *Man and the Computer*, New York, Scribner's, 1972.

80. Bagdikian, *The Information Machines*, p. XVI.

81. *Ibid.*, pp. XXIV and XXV.

82. John Platt, "What We Must Do," *Science*, Vol. 166, Nov. 28, pp. 1115–1121.

83. This quotation and the one that follows it are both found in Platt, "What We Must Do," p. 1115.

Chapter Three

DESIGNING A NEW WORLD ORDER

A DESIGN PERSPECTIVE

We believe in the importance of rooting proposals for world order reform in the soil of current political, social, and economic reality. Therefore, our emphasis is upon the process of transformation from the world that is to the world that might be if certain conditions can be established. By emphasizing non-traumatic modes of transformation we are also seeking to avoid the costs of trauma and violence. In this chapter we will attempt to do two main things: (1) set forth a design perspective that should influence the presentation and understanding of our preference model for the 1990's (which will be depicted in Chapter IV); (2) highlight the main world order building blocks that exist within the present world order system, and consider their potential both with regard to further development and as structural settings suitable for the maximum realization of the four WOMP values.

In presenting this material, we are hoping to encourage a way of thinking about world order that is dynamic rather than static and that conceives of the future in terms of alternatives rather than as a single dogmatic possibility. It is important to realize that the literature of world order reform has heretofore been noncumulative, consisting of isolated visions or conceptions about how the world ought to be organized given the preferences and interests of the author. In accord with our view that global reform needs to be a continuous learning process, one that is never completed—because man as a biosocial species is characterized by the *need* to evolve in new directions—our conception of a preference model is intended only to orient the *next stage* of effort. It is a beginning, not the end, of the work of any would-be world order reformer. In this sense, the contrast with mainstream utopography should be obvious.

MAN AND NATURE AS A
WORLD ORDER ISSUE

A distinctive feature of our perspective is the extent to which man's relations with nature, as well as with other men, become part of the *ethical* and *political* foundation of the new world order. For centuries men have assumed that nature—except for the cataclysms of storms, quakes, volcanoes, and weather shifts—was domesticated, resilient, something that could be taken for granted because it was virtually immune from enduring abuse.[1] Now we are beginning to understand that the natural setting of human existence imposes limits on development in every sphere, and that the timely discovery and clarification of these limits is a task of great importance to mankind. There is an approaching need to agree upon limits that apply to such fundamental matters as human numbers and per capita life-style. How many people, at what levels of consumption, *can* the world support for the indefinite future? Would it be desirable to have population totals and life-style standards at levels below some theoretically-possible maximum? A serious posing of these questions constitutes an essential focus for inquiry, discussion, research, and consensus-formation in the years ahead. It is especially important to relate current planning for human development and survival to the life chances of furture generations. Such a futurist perspective, while difficult to assert until we find solutions to the tasks of dealing humanely with the present world population, nonetheless should no longer be deferred.* The failure to transcend the immediacies of the present, however urgent, endangers the future and in a most irresponsible way imposes on later generations crises that by then may be

---

* The balance between man and nature is, of course, a dynamic one. Man, as an important ingredient in the life processes of the planet, inevitably intervenes. The seeming ideal of noninterference with nature is as illusory in the ecology sphere as it is in the realm of foreign policy. The proper end is to avoid destructive forms of intervention, especially those forms that imperil basic life processes or set in motion large-scale degenerative modes of impact. It is also assumed, herein, that the diversity of natural forms is a positive attribute of human existence, especially with regard to higher orders of life, e.g., birds, mammals.[2]

past correction, or at least, will require corrective steps of a drastic and anguishing character.

These considerations bear on such diverse issues as: population policy, resource policy, environmental policy, technology assessment and control, arms control and disarmament, and management of the world economy. Our proposals presuppose the need for planning and coordination with regard to these spheres of activity; this need for integration on a global level is considered at various points in Chapters II, IV, and V.

THE FALLACY OF PREMATURE SPECIFICITY

There is some temptation to become enthralled with the intricacies of constitutional forms whenever proposals for new world order arrangements are made. This temptation should be resisted because it undermines the credibility of the basic recommendations and encourages a static mood toward the future. It is impossible to anticipate, from this vantage point in time, the details of institutional structure that would be agreed upon once the requisite political consciousness emerges that would engender a revolution in world order. Despite a measure of interplay, the mechanics of administrative management are an outgrowth of political consciousness rather than its source.

At the same time, a proposed world order model requires a certain amount of concreteness to elicit support and facilitate understanding of what is being recommended. It is desirable to work out the basic principles of organization without contending that these principles are rigid ingredients of the model as it might be realized in an actual historical process, or that the inherent reasonableness of such principles will by itself generate widespread support among power-wielders in the present world order system. Our concerns emphasize the need to overcome present forms of unreasonableness, but it would be naive to think that reasonableness of position is a potent political tool. What is needed is a new political energy, on the one hand animated by planetary goals and a coherent vision, and on the other propelled to action by self-interest and a sense of urgency. Our plans seek to contribute to this end, but not to shift the focus of action from the *transitional processes* to the contemplation of a *terminal model*. A terminal model helps orient action and reshape belief systems, thereby overcoming feelings of uncertainty and futility that will probably otherwise arise from the perception of increasingly serious danger. But the precise design of institutional forms, reconciling issues of effective operation with reasonable assurances against abuse, is a task that needs to be performed collaboratively in relation to the particular setting of deep transition. At this time, we can only indicate how general principles of constitutional structure can be used to overcome some of the obstacles to establishing central guidance mechanisms as the basis of a reformed world order. In this sense, the work of institutional specification can be conceived as a preliminary and highly provisional sketching exercise. Such work does not commit the fallacy of premature specification, provided there is ample discussion of transition processes and a flexible but comprehensive approach to power and change (i.e., the politics of transformation) embodied in the set of world order plans.*

TOWARD THE IMAGERY OF EQUILIBRIUM

The new world order system needs to be conceived in relation to the limited, finite circumstances of life on earth.[3] We can easily visualize how earth space is limited; now we must begin to plan for sustainable and beneficial existence within these limits. Such an outlook emphasizes that desirable limits may be much more constraining than feasible limits. Why foster a population policy, for instance, that crowds the planet? Why not begin to design policies that identify the optimal size and distribution of human population, given other goals of self-realization and community welfare?

The idea of limits and their immediate policy relevance is critical also to the more distant future. If we accept some sense of obligation to maintain, if not to improve, the life prospects of future generations, serious attention must now be given to the role of limits. Putting such stress on limits has profound implications for the control of family size, national population policy, GNP and GNP per capita, energy output

---

* These elements in our approach are configured in Chapter I and set forth in an approach to transition in Chapter V. There is some conflict between clarity of communication at any one point in the argument and fidelity to the overall orientation, which requires a continuous emphasis on the interplay between issues of fact, of tendency, and of goal. We hope to minimize this conflict by a good deal of cross-referencing and some degree of repetition of the central strands of the argument.

and consumption, the design of national, regional, and global transit systems, and reliance on detached dwelling units.

The basic alternative idea to current presuppositions about continuous expansion and growth is that of a steady-state society with a fixed population, age composition, economic output, and life-style.[4] Because national societies and world regions are now at such different stages of development, it would be necessary to diversify plans for reaching steady-state thresholds.

In effect, the idea of *equilibrium* for social and economic communities needs to be associated with notions of equality for individuals and groups. That is, the poorer sectors of rich societies must be allowed—indeed, helped—to grow economically and in terms of life quality until thresholds of dignity are attained. Therefore, the specific content of global equilibrium has to take account of the need for substantial increases in material and social well-being for most of the world. The complicated relationship between equilibrium and equality needs to be expressed in increasingly more operational terms.* Our present knowledge is so incomplete that it is impossible to select equilibrium points in any systematic way. A top research priority should be to identify meaningful thresholds of human activity in relation to the capacity of ecosystems of differing magnitudes.

THE DISPLACEMENT OF COLLECTIVE VIOLENCE

A central ingredient of the new world order system will be a full appreciation of the disutility associated with large-scale collective violence as a technique for conflict-settlement. Such an appreciation implies, above all else, that groups seeking change or the satisfaction of grievances be

---

* This relationship does not necessarily imply a *condition* of overall tension between satisfying values associated with ecological balance and those connected with the promotion of economic and social well-being. For one thing, technological innovations can help reconcile economic developments with the maintenance of ecological quality, or at least minimize detrimental impacts. Second, the pursuit of material and social well-being need not, and for value reasons, should not be conceived mainly in GNP terms. Third, redistributive reforms within state boundaries can contribute greatly to the realization of material and social well-being at existing levels of output. And fourth, further development of human potential in the richer sectors of the world could come to involve almost exclusively nonmaterial forms of improvement that make life more healthy and enjoyable, and that make work more satisfying.

presented with nonviolent options which not only encourage the presentation of demands for change, but which also favor the implementation of a mandate for change. In addition, the role of violence in sustaining the governing process within and among states will have to diminish. So long as power is maintained by violence, it will be challenged by violence.* In this sense, the displacement of collective violence in human affairs involves a comprehensive, although gradual and not necessarily total, substitution of modes of mediation, compromise, and persuasiion, as well as a growing appreciation of the greater utility of nonviolent techniques of control and transformation.†

Interim efforts to moderate the effects of "the war system" by way of arms control and partial disarmament may diminish the likelihood of apocalyptic warfare, but will not necessarily reduce the incidence of large-scale collective violence in domestic and international life.

The position taken in our proposals is that the reduction of large-scale violence depends on a number of fundamental and interdependent developments:

The loss of confidence in the value of violence as a means of social control and social change

---

* The control of deviance is an important issue. Police protection of the citizenry is needed for the foreseeable future, but the scope of protection should be confined as well as possible, so that dissenting views and life-styles are permitted to flourish. Such toleration for diversity will itself have to be worked out in accordance with the diversities of culture, national politics, and prevailing ethical norms, but the global ideal seems clear enough. Certain shared minima—the contents of a human rights code—seem appropriate and necessary ingredients of central guidance and comprise V_4 of the WOMP value set.

† During this period of displacement it must be understood that reasonable men may resort to violence for social and political ends and that reasonable men will pronounce such recourse as efficacious, moral, and even necessary to secure valued ends that correspond with WOMP priorities. In other words, although the bloody historical record and the awesome menace of modern war technology puts into question the whole tradition of "just war," it seems premature to resolve the question once and for all in relation to all persons in every situation. At the same time, two assertions can be made: first, the costs, risks, and record of violent approaches make it a strategy of last resort; second, the potentiality of nonviolent but coercive strategies warrants the most ardent and serious study, and may connect intimately with overall prospects for species development and even survival. Up to a point in human evolution violence may have been functional for the species, and beyond that point it may become increasingly more dysfunctional, although the image of a spiral is probably more apt than that of a straight-line decline. The unevenness of cultural evolution may place different portions of the human species in a distinctly different relationship to the functionality of violence.

The rise of confidence in the prospects for nonviolent means of social control and social change

The growth of convergent lines of consciousness in various parts of the world, including an increasing adoption and pursuit of the four WOMP values

The development of reliable institutions for the settlement of disputes, and the growth of respect for their procedures

The widely shared perception of tangible progress, at a tolerable rate, toward a life of social, political, and economic dignity for all people

Without fulfillment of these conditions, it is naive to suppose that reliance on violence will diminish in the decades ahead.* Furthermore, these achievements will have to be made in opposition to many entrenched centers of power and authority which at the present time continue to rely heavily upon violence to neutralize actual and potential opponents at home and abroad.

AN OPEN SYSTEM OF WORLD ORDER

The model of world order set forth by WOMP/USA is both provisional, with respect to institutional design, and temporary, in the sense that its own dynamics will lead to constantly evolving patterns of relationships.† The basic image of authority is "central guidance," relying on minimum coercion and bureaucracy to coordinate activities of smaller collective entities in the world system. Central guidance implies

---

* Indeed, there are voices in the Third World that regard accelerated armament as essential to the pursuit of all goals of reform. In effect, not until there is "parity" along the North/South military axis will there be parity in the geopolitical division of spoils. Such a perspective, the validity of which can be sustained by an analysis of world history or even of contemporary United States/Soviet relations, may introduce a dynamic new element of danger into international relations—namely, a universal, multi-actor arms race. Most of our understanding of arms races has been based on dyadic relations between dominant states or alliances, but the prospect of polyadic arms races may increase instabilities by several orders of magnitude, especially if new low-cost technologies (e.g., high-powered lasers) become ingredients of the arms proliferation process.

† The dynamics of process—entailing a continuous reshaping of means and ends—is illustrated to some extent in Chapter V. The horizon for world order reform must always be readjusted in relation to the specifics of time, place, and consciousness. Even the WOMP values are shared only as labels, and perhaps as limiting conditions, but their interpretation and derivative implications for action are conditioned by the observer's situation, including his participation in the observed phenomena. Physicists and psychoana-

a stress on process, on checks and balances, and on self-corrective procedures. The degree to which central guidance will entail "a governmental presence" on a global level depends largely on the character of transition, and on whether the growth of transnational economic, cultural, and social relations can weaken from below the hold which national governments now exert upon the loyalties and resources of their populations: *the weaker the governmental presence becomes on a national level, the smaller the governmental presence that will be needed on a global level.*

A COMPOSITE IDEA OF STRUCTURE

Our basic design for a new world order system is founded upon a synthesis of ordering structures that have been or are in being at the present time, as well as reliance upon institutional and procedural innovation. The existing world order system is itself a composite of several elements, including global and regional organizations, specialized agencies, great power concerts, spheres of influence, and alliance relations. This mixture of elements continues to be dominated by the sovereign state, especially with regard to matters of war and peace, resource use and conservation policy, economic development, human rights, and environmental protection. The state as the organizing fulcrum of international life is increasingly unsatisfactory for a variety of reasons that have been touched upon in earlier chapters: dangers of catastrophe; rise of egalitarian and welfare consciousness; global interdependence of economic affairs; and the expanding scale and increasing complexity of technological arrangements.

Our model is designed to alter this balance among the aggregation of global ordering elements in such a way as to make WOMP values more nearly realized, or at least realizable. The quantum of *power* and *authority* within world affairs is not a constant; in essence such power can be concentrated further (in imperial actors or in world institutions at the regional or global level) or it can be *dispersed* at or below the national level (by disarmament, by regionalization or federalization of the national governmental power-authority nexus, and by the decline of statist functions in the area of security and welfare). There is a spectrum of

---

lysts—the one concerned with atoms and particles, the other with the vagaries of the human psyche—have both emphasized this essential implication of the subjective vantage point in the objective account.

alternative strategies and probable outcomes with regard to the mixture of power, authority, and bureaucratic structure.

One major choice is that between *transfer* and *dispersal* models of the new world order system. Conventional thinking on world order reform sees central guidance as synonymous with a massive buildup of central institutions, which would follow the transfer of functions from the state to the global level. This prospect seems accurate and inevitable with respect to certain *functional* allocations of competence and capability that will require centralized guidance to achieve WOMP goals. However, because of the inhibitions and dangers associated with such centrist conceptions of world order, it seems desirable to take advantage of opportunities for dispersal both in presenting the scheme and in implementing transition strategies. In this regard, the drastic insights of anarchism and the less severe conceptions of confederalism are as relevant to world order reform as are the more governmental predelictions of world federalism. The decentralizing possibilities created by certain new technologies provide important instruments for reconciling centralizing and decentralizing needs.

In a sense, the elements of a new world order are latent in the present scheme of things. The essence of transition is to hasten and shape a redistribution of functions that is already underway, and to oppose certain regressive features of this structurally redistributive process.* The old system is crumbling, but it is not clear what it is giving way to or at what rate. A critical uncertainty involves the extent to which national governments will participate constructively in building a new world order system. National governments dominate the existing world power system and most of them will resist efforts to dilute their power-authority nexus or to give status and roles to nongovernmental actors.† Whether the reorientation of political consciousness on an individual or transnational basis can overcome this resistance is one of the great unresolved world order issues of the near future.

In the next section, diagrams and brief descriptions of main organizing patterns in various world order systems will be presented. By this

---

* Structural redistribution refers to shifts in actor functions, as distinct from resource or equity redistribution which refers to shifts in patterns of wealth and income.

† Enlightened governments, at least in the advanced industrial sector of world society, may be increasingly identified by the extent to which their sense of national purpose is identified with world order reform that includes a diminished status and role for state actors. The international behavior of the Scandinavian countries, especially Sweden, is suggestive of the possibility and significance of a redefinition of national purpose in the world system. In these national instances, relative prosperity and security, as well as peace-oriented internal developments, have undoubtedly contributed to the adoption of a

means it will be possible to gain insight into the complexity of a world order system and to assess *the organizing options* more clearly.

THE ELEMENTS OF STRUCTURE IN WORLD ORDER SYSTEMS: NOTES ON PAST, PRESENT, AND FUTURE

In depicting the structural outlines of several world order systems, we are concerned with the following objectives:

1. To make it clear that the pattern of present relations in world affairs constitutes *a system of world order* in the sense used in this project.

2. To emphasize that its inadequacy is largely a consequence of its incapacity to realize the four WOMP values, as construed by WOMP/USA.*

3. To clarify changes in the present world order system by briefly depicting structural developments that have taken place over the last several centuries.

4. To improve the understanding of the potential range of future structures by differentiating among the main organizational alternatives.

5. To contribute to a better appreciation of the transition process by disclosing the extent to which the design of a new world order involves the redistribution of functions among existing actors and organizational opportunities, in addition to the creation of new ones or the elimination of *old* ones.

---

relatively globalist perspective. A country such as Japan may be moving in a similar direction, although in response to very different influences, most especially the trauma of World War II (including Hiroshima and Nagasaki) and the economic success and ambiguities of its post-war recovery. Poor countries with low levels of integration at the national level may require a period of augmented government in order to overcome entrenched sectors of the domestic social, economic, and political order opposed to dealing equitably with the needs of the population as a whole. The degree of enlightenment exhibited by a particular government must be assessed in its particular context, even if WOMP values are used as the principal yardsticks to assess enlightenment.

* There are, of course, eight participating WOMP groups, and a reading of their final documents will confirm what might be obvious in any event: that their shared acceptance of WOMP values does not assure any commonality of judgment about the adequacy of the present world order system, the feasibility or desirability of particular alternatives to it, or the selection of transition tactics and strategies. At most, we can assert that the four WOMP values provide a common set of labels that convey the impression of a shared point of departure.

6. To underscore the extent to which the model of a preferred world order system for the 1990's is a *composite model.*

7. To stimulate the study of world order issues within a setting of *comparative systems of world order.**

The notes and diagrams in this section are tentative and experimental, and are presented in a heuristic spirit. It is hoped that this section may help a reader, however skeptical, to consider more intelligently the proposals for a new system of world order sketched in Chapter IV.

THE PRESENT SYSTEM OF WORLD ORDER: A STRUCTURAL OUTLINE

The present world order system is very complex, though its principal structural elements can be presented in relatively simple form. For the first time in human history, largely as a result of modern communications and transportation systems, there is a continuous pattern of interaction that embraces virtually the entirety of the land areas on the globe. These land areas are assimilated into an increasingly coherent world order system that continues to be dominated in its characteristic activity by the organizational presence of the sovereign state.†

The governments that represent these states on an international level control nearly all of the military power in the world and make, or at least appear to make, almost all decisions about the existence and functioning of non-state international actors. The most important of these non-state international actors are themselves intergovernmental in character, depending for political and financial support upon the direct

---

* Over the last several years I have been experimenting with a seminar that tries to evolve a disciplinary focus for the study of comparative systems of world order. It has two main features: (1) past, present, and plausible future systems are compared; (2) modes of comparison and judgments of plausibility draw upon imaginative literature (utopography, fiction, science fiction), as well as upon social science (systems theory, futurology, world order studies). A syllabus is available upon request.

† In economic affairs, multinational corporate actors increasingly challenge governmental actors in many policy-making contexts. Nevertheless, on the ritual stage of international diplomacy, state actors sustain their monopoly of the forms and symbols of interaction among the peoples of the world. As a consequence, the system appears to be almost exclusively a state system, and non-state actors are not allowed to have formal

participation of governments. Within state territories there are many instances of political struggle and confrontation, mainly waged to determine which domestic group or faction will control the internal governing process and represent the state in external affairs. As yet, these internal struggles for power are rarely concerned *directly* with world order issues, although issues of geopolitical orientation may be so clearly at stake that foreign governments intervene to influence the outcome. However, at present, these contending domestic elites are not inclined to alter the *patterning* of relationships in world society through drastic world order reform, whether the method be general and complete disarmament, or the buildup of capabilities by the United Nations or regional organizations. In fact, there is a virtually universal consensus among governmental actors to limit reformist goals to intra-systemic dimensions; indeed, intra-systemic reform pressures derive almost exclusively from *nonconstituted* elites, i.e., elites which function outside governmental and even opposition party circles. Such actors as the UN, specialized agencies, and regional organizations, are generally viewed as marginal instruments for the realization of *statist ends* on a global level, and not as precursors of a new supranationality.

The inequality of governments in all relevant dimensions leads to relationships of dominance and dependence in external affairs, and to a wide range of domestic governing strategies. This inequality also creates opportunities for intervention by the more powerful governments in the affairs of weak states, thereby eroding the realities of national independence and sovereign equality which are formally attained with statehood.

The politics and techniques of security policy also lead to *sectorial* alignments within the world, based on ideological defense or imperial considerations; *alliance* relations among national governments are far more significant in the security field than are the undertakings of international institutions.

In Figure 3–1 the existing world authority/power system is portrayed to underscore the following characteristics: The relative integration of the global system as a whole; the centrality of the state mechanism, as *the main* actor in world affairs; the existence of a global actor; the existence of several regional actors; the existence of a group of *specialized actors*

---

status in any highly visible international arena. In more specialized arenas, however, such as the International Labor Organization, entities such as labor unions and business organizations participate directly alongside governments. Such composite arrangements are virtually unknown to the public at large.

dealing with functional concerns of global scope; and the degree of inequality among state actors.

It should be noted that Figure 3–1 does not portray alliance relations or trade and investment flows; nor does it include functional organizations at the regional level. Figure 3–2 illustrates the significance of alliance relations by showing the formal commitment pattern underlying U.S. foreign relations.* No effort has been made to portray the structural role played by summit diplomacy, either in the form of superpower conferences or in the form of meetings among dominant state actors concerned with specific categories of issues.†

In Figure 3–3 we make a crude attempt to take account of variations in the internal political arrangements of state actors in the present system of world order. The smaller the diameter of the internal black circle, the more directly the prevailing governing perspective appears committed to the promotion of WOMP values, and vice versa. The size of the inner black circle expresses the degree of militarization (size of military budget, military budget as proportion of national budget and of GNP), the extent of social privation (proportion of population at subsistence level or below, provision of basic life necessities), the extent of political privation (number of political prisoners, protection of civil liberties, existence of an active opposition movement), and the extent of ecological privation (extent of pollution, responsiveness to ecological consequences of policy). We contend that the values around which existing governmental centers of power and authority are organized correlate directly with their capacity and willingness to participate in a peaceful process of transition to a more beneficial system of world order. Simplistic views with respect to the responsiveness of national actors to WOMP values are bound to be misleading. We recognize that a given government might have a good record on social welfare and a poor one on political liberty or peace-mindedness. We also recognize that a domestic disposition toward or away from WOMP values does

---

* Note that to obtain a fuller sense of formal structure it would be desirable to have an illustration of alliance patterns similar to Figure 3–2 for each state in the world.

† Summit communiqués, especially among great powers, impart considerable structure to relations among governments. Such diplomacy also makes certain kinds of expectations very explicit, and works to establish a mood of moderation with respect to the pursuit of antagonistic ends in world affairs. The Nixon–Brezhnev meetings, and the documents they produced, have played an important part in conveying the impression that the cold war is over and a new era of superpower relations has commenced. However, these documents, including the celebrated Declaration of Principles issued after the 1972 Moscow summit, have virtually no substantive content, and are mainly expressions of goodwill or elementary restatements of norms embodied in general international law and in the United Nations Charter.[5]

Figure 3–1. Existing World Order System

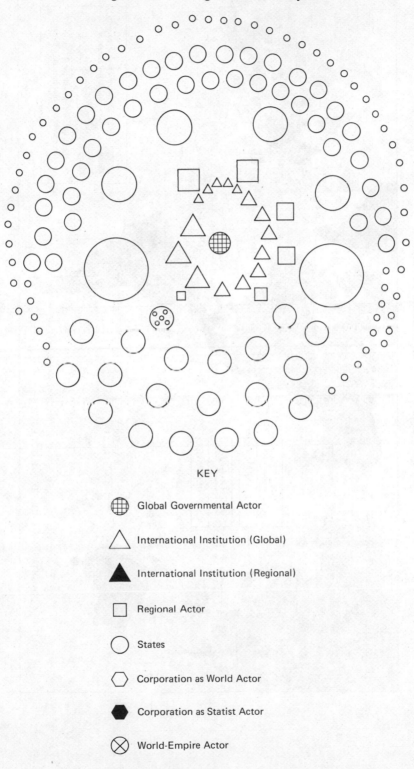

KEY

⊕ Global Governmental Actor

△ International Institution (Global)

▲ International Institution (Regional)

☐ Regional Actor

◯ States

⬠ Corporation as World Actor

⬢ Corporation as Statist Actor

⊗ World-Empire Actor

◉ Colonial Cluster

Figure 3–2. U.S. Alliance Patterns

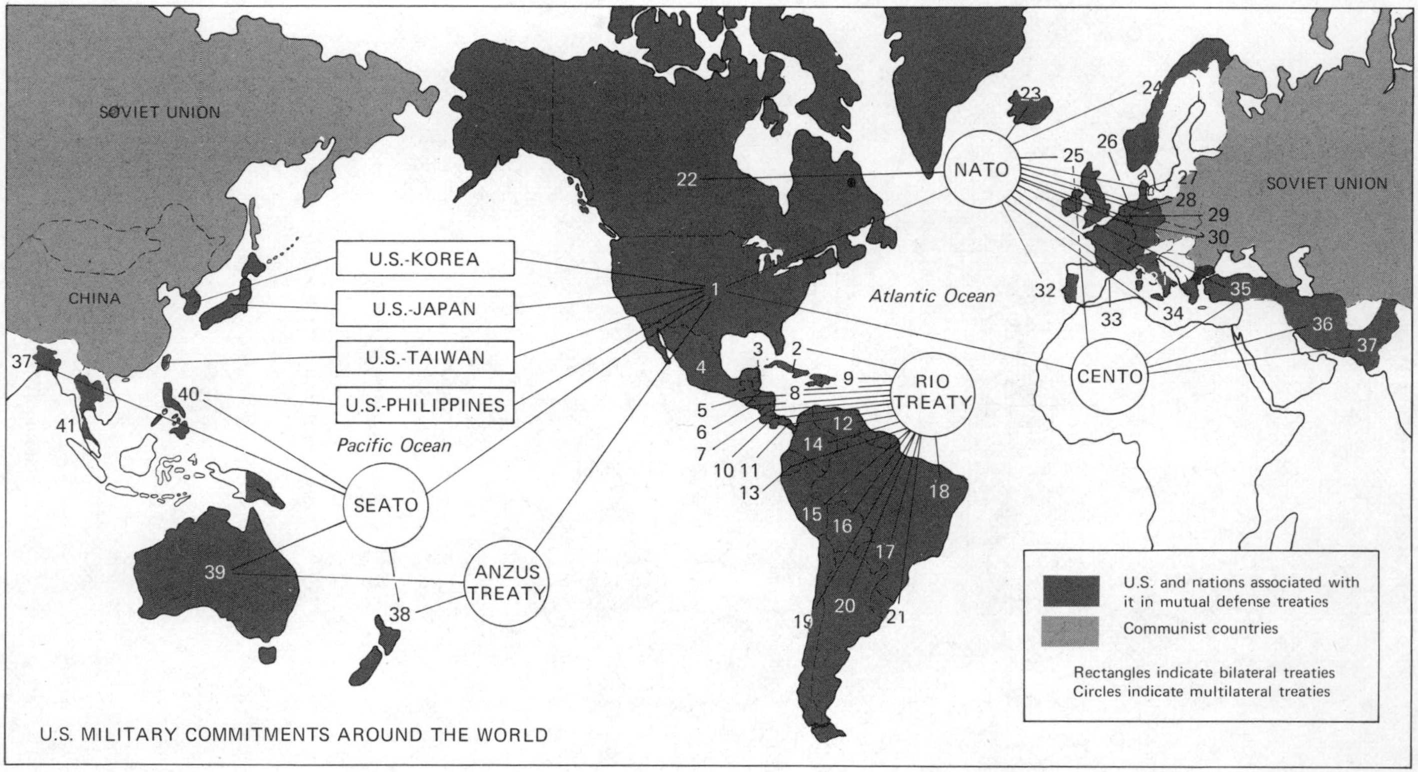
SOVIET UNION
CHINA
U.S.-KOREA
U.S.-JAPAN
U.S.-TAIWAN
U.S.-PHILIPPINES
Pacific Ocean
SEATO
ANZUS TREATY
NATO
Atlantic Ocean
RIO TREATY
CENTO
SOVIET UNION
1
2
3
4
5
6
7
8
9
10
11
12
13
14
15
16
17
18
19
20
21
22
23
24
25
26
27
28
29
30
32
33
34
35
36
37
38
39
40
41
U.S. and nations associated with it in mutual defense treaties
Communist countries
Rectangles indicate bilateral treaties
Circles indicate multilateral treaties
U.S. MILITARY COMMITMENTS AROUND THE WORLD

RIO TREATY

Nations pledge themselves, in the event of aggression, to provide assistance on request Members are:

1 UNITED STATES	8 HAITI	15 PERU	
2 CUBA *	9 DOM. REP.	16 BOLIVIA	
3 HONDURAS	10 COSTA RICA	17 PARAGUAY	
4 MEXICO	11 PANAMA	18 BRAZIL	
5 GUATEMALA	12 VENEZUELA	19 CHILE	
6 EL SALVADOR	13 ECUADOR	20 ARGENTINA	
7 NICARAGUA	14 COLOMBIA	21 URUGUAY	

*Still formally a signatory though not participating.

NATO

Members agree to regard an attack on one as an attack on all. Members are:

1 UNITED STATES	29 BELGIUM
22 CANADA	30 LUXEMBOURG
23 ICELAND	31 ITALY
24 NORWAY	32 PORTUGAL
25 UNITED KINGDOM	33 FRANCE
26 NETHERLANDS	34 GREECE
27 DENMARK	35 TURKEY
28 W. GERMANY	

ANZUS TREATY

Members acknowledge that an attack in the Pacific against any will involve all. Members are:

1 UNITED STATES
38 NEW ZEALAND
39 AUSTRALIA

SEATO

In case of aggression members are to "consult immediately in order to agree to measures which should be taken for common defense." Members are:

1 UNITED STATES	36 NEW ZEALAND
25 UNITED KINGDOM	39 AUSTRALIA
33 FRANCE	40 PHILIPPINES
37 PAKISTAN	41 THAILAND

CENTO

The U.S. is not directly a member of CENTO but has pledged to cooperate in mutual defense. Members are:

25 UNITED KINGDOM
35 TURKEY
36 IRAN
37 PAKISTAN

SOURCE: *The New York Times*, May 6, 1962, © by the New York Times Company. Reprinted by permission.

Figure 3–3. Existing World Order System: Internal Dimensions

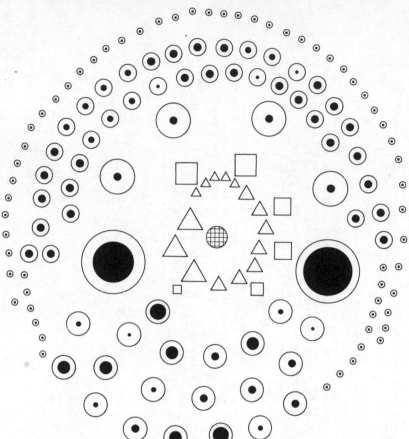

not *necessarily* correlate with attitudes toward the direction and preferred character of world order reform. But we do believe first, that the
value priorities of domestic governments are relevant to prospects for
world order change, and second, that there is a tendency for attitudes
toward world order reform to reflect domestic value priorities. Thus
Figure 3–3 augments Figure 3–1 by contending that states not only dominate the existing world order system, but that their distinctive influence significantly reflects their domestic orientation toward the four
WOMP values.*

---

* The relevance of domestic orientation to world order structure is one principal tradition in the literature of global reform, tracing back at least as far as Immanuel Kant's

Figure 3–4. Nixon–Kissinger Design

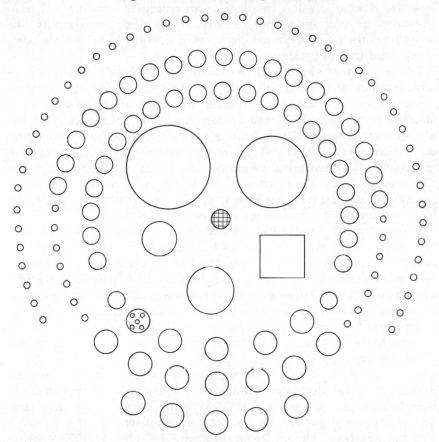

The five-power variant of the existing world order system in Figure 3–4 represents an effort to display the Nixon-Kissinger-Brezhnev(?) world order design based on the contained or moderated competition of five principal actors (the U.S.A., USSR, China, Japan, Western Europe). This model of world order is premised on maximizing certain oligopo-

---

monograph *Perpetual Peace*, first published in 1795. Leninist conceptions of global reform also emphasize revolution on the national level, and do not discern any need for altering the state system as the principal basis of global organization. The fissures within the Communist realm suggest that adherence to a common ideological tradition is no assurance that governmental forms will be either uniform or harmoniously interrelated. Indeed, the history of intense belief systems confirms the pervasiveness of sectarian tendencies and a complementary obsession with heresy.

listic tendencies in the existing system. It attempts to diminish the destructive risks of rivalry, to adapt to an emergent condition of multipolarity in economic and security affairs, and to simplify the procedures for mainstream cooperation in a world of increasing complexity and interdependence.

The five-power variant on the existing system is basically an intergovernmental managerial notion without any normative reforms contemplated. The main world order objectives are to eliminate destructive forms of political and military rivalry by encouraging moderate relations among existing centers of power and wealth. Ideological differences are respected and minimized; a condition of efficient global management is ideological tolerance. The status and role of supranationalism is diminished beneath current levels, although specialized functional tasks may be assigned to specialized institutions under the effective control of principal governmental actors.

The prevailing agenda of world order issues does not accord priority to values of social well-being or political dignity. A five-power scheme is fully compatible with the "toleration" of high levels of poverty and repression within the system as a whole. Even violence is acceptable if carried on outside the framework of great power relations, and no major emphasis is placed on peace-keeping or nonproliferation of weapons. Environmental quality is a fit object of interactor cooperation, but again it is presumed manageable through cooperative undertakings of the dominant international actors.

The five-power design is, in significant respects, an improvement over the cold war alignments, provided it does not encourage an era of complacency and does not itself degenerate into a two-power condominium arrangement. The emphasis on a bilateral setting for SALT and the Brezhnev–Nixon Declaration of Principles in 1972 provide grounds for fear that the nuclear superpowers are seeking duopoly control over the rest of the globe, and that the imagery of five participants was a tranquilizing disguise. Even on its own terms, the five-power design fails to affirm ideals of human solidarity or to seek ways of overcoming the immense inequities and miseries endured at present by such a high proportion of the human race. This five-power conception also tends to underestimate the ecological constraints and risks arising from continuing patterns of uncurtailed economic growth in a decentralized world order system. Finally, a concert of principal actors denies participation to many other important actors in the global arena and is eventually likely to produce a mode of bitterness and opposition from excluded sectors. Principal actors excluded from a managerial role, such as India, Brazil, Nigeria, and Indonesia, may be induced to seek access or to organize rival groupings, or at least be expected to object to any claims of pentagonal legitimacy of primacy.

SOME ILLUSTRATIONS OF PAST SYSTEMS OF WORLD ORDER: 1890, 1920, 1950

Though the evolution of world order systems has been continuous throughout international history,* the basic units of interaction have changed, the degree of global interrelatedness has increased, and the intensity of violent conflict has grown. These trends are not linear, but the thrust of long-term movements is unambiguous. We make no attempt to present schematically or otherwise the character of these long-term trends; [6] we aim merely to present the shifts in the organizational structure of international society that are visible in recent history. The purpose is to show elements of continuity and discontinuity over intervals of 20–30 years, the time span which corresponds to that projected for our futurist designs.

The basic continuity that is visible in recent international history is the preeminence of the sovereign state, which emerged definitively at the Peace of Westphalia in 1648 and has not been altered since in any fundamental respect. Until after World War II, references to world order systems were basically concerned with the organizational structure of a Eurocentric system. The rise of a universal system of world order (that is, of planetary scope) was originally a consequence of European colonizing movements; over the last several decades decolonizing movements in all major regions have produced state actors who participate directly in the dynamics of the world order system.

A focus on organizational structure is insufficient to the extent that it leaves out of account the level of technological achievement, including military technology, communications, and transport; trade and investment flows; human travel; and cultural, ideological, ethnic, and mythic patterns.

---

* "Continuous" in the sense that the number, size, and interactions of principal actors have been in flux through time. Each phase in geopolitics is distinguishable; cumulative tendencies with respect to a world order system can be referred to as its evolution. The issue of change *within* a world order system (reformist perspectives) as opposed to change from one system to another (revolutionary perspectives) is discussed in Chapter V. The boundary between system–reform and system–change may appear arbitrary in the same sense as does the boundary between Gothic and Renaissance art.

A Study of Future Worlds

If this were a mapping exercise, many maps would be needed to navigate along the different dimensions of international life. Such work is necessary to develop the historical dimension in the study of comparative world order system.

The 1890 World Order System

In 1890, as can be seen in Figure 3–5, the only international actors of consequence were sovereign states (a comprehensive designation which

Figure 3–5. 1890 World Order System

includes imperial clusters of dependent societies). The world order system was Eurocentric; the United States and the Soviet Union were not preeminent among states. The system was a simple structural grid that rested almost exclusively on traditional modes of diplomacy among a few powerful state actors. Alliance relations played a major role in this world order system, and no central guidance mechanism of even a nominal sort existed. It took World War I to shake the confidence that statesmen and world public opinion had had in the capacity of interacting governments to sustain a tolerable level of world order.

The 1920 World Order System

This world order system is displayed in Figure 3–6. Note the existence of a global political actor, the League of Nations, though several important state actors did not participate directly in its activities, and its competence and autonomy were severely compromised by its intergovernmental character. The League embodied the Eurocentric system of world order that survived World War I. The non-European world was "represented" through the participation of the main colonial powers. Important countries like the United States and the Soviet Union (until 1933) did not take part in League activities. America was relatively inactive in global politics because of domestic isolationist sentiment, whereas participation by the Soviet Union was restricted by the revolutionary nature of its regime and ideology, and the counterrevolutionary responses generated by the victory of Soviet socialism.

A few functional agencies had been established by 1920 to carry out minimal tasks of international cooperation in technical matters. No regional actors existed at all, although formal and informal alliance patterns continued to provide the foundation of international security. Serious disarmament negotiations were held in the 1920's, but their impact was diluted by geopolitics.

The 1950 World Order System

By 1950 (see Figure 3–7) the world order system had altered structurally in several significant respects. The United Nations had replaced the League and was in the process of becoming a more nearly universal actor.[7] Decolonizing trends culminated in the 1950's and were accompanied by the collapse of all colonial systems except that of the Portuguese, and by the rapid increase of Afro–Asian membership in the

Figure 3–6. 1920 World Order System

United Nations. In the 1920's (see Figure 3–6) several colonial systems, although diminished, were still in being. By 1950, the complexity of international life greatly augmented the role of global functional agencies. Increasingly, tasks of technical, economic, and social coordination needed some kind of specialized organizational focus, not necessarily removed from the political dynamics of international relations, but concentrating on a particular subject matter.[8]

In addition, the impetus toward some kind of generalized cooperation among states closely aligned by geographical position, traditional affiliation, ideological outlook or ethnic identity has generated regionalist tendencies in several parts of the world in the period since World

Figure 3–7. 1950 World Order System

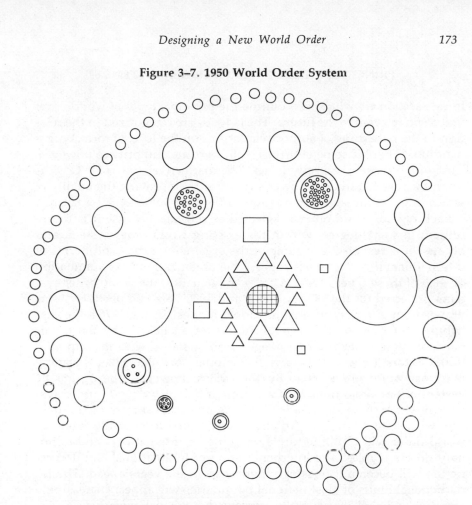

War II. There is a great deal of literature assessing the character of and prospects for regionalism, but it is evident in any case that the emergence of a variety of regional actors who to some extent engage in intergovernmental cooperation has produced a prime structural change on the world level. These developments may lead to some degree of national integration at the regional level, although at very uneven rates.* Such integrative tendencies on a regional level have been accompanied and strengthened by the rise of transnational relations of all kinds.

---

* The extent of unevenness is likely to be great, ranging from rather good prospects for supranationality in Western Europe, to highly disintegrative rivalry in East and South Asia.

PRINCIPAL TYPES OF WORLD ORDER SYSTEMS

In this section we will briefly outline the principal types of world order that seem relevant to the future. These types are categorized in the relation to the patterning of authority relations on the level of formal organization.* There is some effort, as well, to relate authority to power, at least in the sense of capacity to act. The distinctive stress of WOMP is upon the role of authority/power structures in improving the quality of world order as measured in relation to the four value axes.

Each type of world order is selected as relevant because it is represented, to some degree, within the existing world order system, and because it is responsive to some of the organizing needs and norms of international life. The charts suggest the organizational consummation of each of these types of world order. In actuality, the world order systems projected for the 1970's, 1980's and 1990's are composite systems drawn from a variety of organizational modes. In the 1970's the distribution of function and capability is skewed heavily by the dominance of state units and by linkages among states, with the supranational actors (whether universal, regional, or specialized) playing marginal world order roles. By the 1990's, however, the optimistic variant of our projections for transition anticipates a world order system in which these supranational actors play critical roles in conjunction with state actors, who in any realistic projection of the future of world order will continue to play significant international and dominant domestic roles. The interpenetration of international and domestic life will become increasingly pervasive in the years ahead. The jurisdictional limits of most national boundaries will appear increasingly artificial and will be generally perceived (for most purposes) as inconsequential.

To some extent, the conception of structure relied upon here is overly "statist" in its stress on formal organizational actors that are either

---

* The focus on authority structure represents an effort to convey an understanding of the outcome of a world order movement. This focus, however, needs to be connected with our emphasis on the formative character of the transition process. It is out of the ferment of transition that a new system of world order will emerge. The function of the preferential modeling considered in Chapters III and IV is to provide a point of departure for world order activists who are committed to the realization of WOMP values as soon and as nonviolently as possible. The feasibility of the preferential model is only slightly affected by its inherent attributes; feasibility will be determined by whether changes in consciousness and public understanding can be brought about and by whether a world order reform movement can be organized.

states or that require statehood for membership. For the sake of making the main assertions clear, transnational movements, international business entities, and nongovernmental international organizations are treated as structurally invisible elements of a world order system, although these kinds of actors are likely to play important world roles in the years ahead.

Most past proposals for world order reform have been almost exclusively concerned with achieving war-prevention goals. The more diverse WOMP goals are not quite as easily related to any given power/authority organizational structure.[9] The broadened purpose of world order reform sustains the general tradition of substituting some form of *effective central guidance* for the dispersed structure of power/authority in the state system.

New patterns of conflict—reflecting both the proliferation of instruments of manipulation and intervention and the shifting efficacy of military force—may have distinctive structural consequences. For instance, the role of technological innovation in concentrating control capacities in new elites, and the levers of manipulation relating to monetary and trade policy, may require special institutional responses that are not encompassed by traditional world order thinking on shifts in power/authority from national actors to supranational actors (whether universal, regional, or functional). *Informal* elites may now be concentrating and using power/authority in ways that will greatly impair the attainment of WOMP values—for instance, in the area of environmental quality or large-scale disruption of societal processes.

Despite these reservations, the focus on formal arrangements of power/authority continues to be most useful for world order analysis at the systemic level.[10]

Image No. 1: An Enhanced State System

The most easily attainable *positive* development that can be envisaged in the world order system would probably involve an overall ameliorative trend.* In essence, the structure of the world system would not be redesigned by conscious intervention (or rebuilt after a catastrophic breakdown), but the managerial capacities of the existing system would be improved and the cumulative trends relative to power, wealth, and

---

* To envisage is not to predict; it is to call attention to a course of development that is possible, given present trends.

dignity would be *modestly positive* as measured by WOMP primary values. By "modest" we mean average annual increments of about one percent.

In more specific terms, the following changes in structure could be anticipated:

The elimination of all colonial and racist regimes

The growth of the United Nations as a significant actor in relation to all four value sectors

The expanding size, role, and powers of specialized international agencies

The continuing development of regional cooperation through institutions

These developments would help stabilize international relations, especially if certain nonstructural changes could be postulated, such as:

Moderate governments in principal states

A rising and spreading appreciation of ecological issues, and a growing consensus on satisfactory responses

Decline in ideological conflict at the strategic level

Expansion of transnational business operations in a regulatory setting based on a WOMP orientation toward the world interest

Progress toward the establishment of a world currency

Control of the strategic arms race at reasonably stable levels and some international regulation of arms sales

Growth of transnational contact of all kinds, and of international cooperation in response to the independence of major aspects of modern life

This meliorist vision of the future is basically the liberal formula of combining moderate hopes with realistic limits on what is possible.* The program of incremental reform accepts the statist basis of world

---

* Such liberalism is associated with faith in reason and progress, and has its modern origins in the industrial revolution; this position is skeptical of any grandiose program of reform, either because it accepts the flawed or sinful condition of human nature, or because it believes that drastic strategies of change are virtually doomed to produce bloodshed, excess, and a new reign of oppression. See Hannah Arendt, *On Revolution,* and William Irwin Thompson, *The Imagination of an Insurrection* (Oxford Press, 1967). Advocates of gradual reform or, as it is sometimes called, meliorism, find it as detrimental to seek too much reform as it is to seek too little. The well-attuned reformer finds the middle way that takes advantage of the constructive potential of the present order without unleashing a new configuration of destructive tendencies.

order, but attempts to move toward central guidance by taking a series of small steps that add up to something in their net effect. Even if the basic outlook is correct, there are many gross uncertainties about specific scenarios of reform, and about the impacts they may have. That is, there are many ways of improving the capabilities of the present world order system, but we have no system of appraisal by which to anticipate or compare a large array of definite possibilities. The important integrating feature of this image is that world order reform does not depend explicitly on *drastic disarmament* at the national level, nor on a massive military buildup at some level of international organization. The state unit remains the central actor in war/peace issues on an external plane, and the main formal participant in the world authority system (i.e., in regional, functional, and universal international organizations).

This evolutionary image of the future is a popular and prevalent one, for it combines benevolence with realism, but it is not especially promising either in *predictive* or *normative* terms.[11] Regarding its predictive ability, this meliorist image underestimates both the pressures building on the existing structure, and the counterpressures that the state system will mount to maintain its control over the politics of the globe. We argue that the needs for central guidance within the relevant time frame are likely to be too great to accommodate within a reformist framework, especially with respect to war/peace, well-being, and ecology issues. Furthermore, the array of existing states in the world is too unequal in position, outlook, and size to enable an effective system of enduringly cooperative relationships to develop out of present circumstances.*

With respect to *normative* factors, the image of an *enhanced* state system accepts as virtually permanent the present *structure* of inequality, violence, oppression, misappropriation of resources, and poverty. The human costs, wastes, and risks associated with this ordering structure are so characteristic as to disqualify it as a preferential model of the future. Obviously, in contexts of immediate choice, it may be desirable and even important to support meliorist projects (for instance, arms control measures) to retard the disintegration of the world order system or to stem a worsening of the situation as measured by WOMP values, but such support is only *tactical* in nature.

---

* By enduringly cooperative, we mean based on perceived mutual benefit. Note that relations of domination and dependency may be cooperative even if objectively and subjectively exploitative, because the dependent participant is or acts as if it is helpless.

Therefore, although the most obvious path to world order reform lies in improving the existing structure, we conclude that such an emphasis is neither promising nor desirable, given our diagnosis of the present world crisis, unless it is one aspect of a wider vision. It offers little hope of achieving substantial progress toward WOMP values by the year 2000, and it tends to reinforce the prevailing psychology of "business as usual" with respect to matters on the world order agenda. In this respect, meliorism induces a pacified mind-set that is a great convenience for vested interests. Those who are dissatisfied with the existing order are reassured about the direction of change, and yet are discouraged from questioning matters of basic equity or from challenging the existing arrangements of power and wealth. Hence, this kind of piecemeal, *ad hoc* approach to reform, so characteristic of the Anglo–American world, is positively suspicious of any grand strategy for transformation. By contrast, WOMP/USA believes that a grand strategy of aspiration is needed at the present time, to relate the parts to the whole and to build an orientation toward action in the world. Meliorism, as we have indicated, should be appreciated as *a part* of the whole, but as no more than that.

Image No. 2: A System of World Government

The standard solution to the problems of a statist system of world order is to advocate the emergence on an international level of a governmental presence similar to that which exists on the national level of a well-organized state. This attitude partly reflects the historical progression in human affairs from smaller units of political control to larger ones. In particular, the disorganization of the feudal world order system seemed to be largely overcome by the appearance in the middle of the seventeenth century of national units that were precursors of the modern state. Now, several centuries later, given an increasingly global scale of human activity, it can be reasoned that the disorganization of the statist world can be most successfully overcome by a shift to a federated world.

Most of this thinking reflects a primary world order concern with war/peace issues. In this issue area it seems that the prospects for disarmament at the state level depend upon an effective governing presence on a global level. Again, the experience of disarming feudal principalities seems to bear out the belief that disarmament can proceed successfully only if accompanied by centralization of the power/authority structure that dominates the newly-disarmed units. Of course, a statist system is based upon a logic of multiple units competing for finite resources of power, wealth, space, and influence. A world government system would be a *totalist unit* of control that manages competition among its sub-units and deals with possible insurrectionary challenges, but would not be confronted with any need to prepare for external competition with one or more formally equal and militarily powerful actors.* As with most governments in the poorer sectors of international society and with almost all governments of smaller states, a world government would be, in this case, an "inward-looking" bureaucracy.

Many structural variations are consistent with a general image of world government. We offer some principal variations in Figures 3–8, 3–9, 3–10, and 3–11. The basic feature of this world government system is the central actor's dominance on issues of power and authority in relation to regional and state actors (functional actors can be understood as specialized adjuncts of the central actor, and hence as forming part of the global governmental presence).

In Figure 3–8 we illustrate a model of world government, designated Type A, in which state actors are dramatically reduced in power, the large ones divided up; central guidance roles are widely dispersed among regional, functional, and universal political actors; in effect, this version of an S_2 solution presupposes the disappearance of "the Great Powers" and of geopolitics as it has been known in the state system. Figure 3–9 makes less drastic assumptions. World Government Type B relies mainly on the *proportional* reduction of relative power by state actors, the massive buildup of the universal political organs, and the steady growth to significance of regional actors throughout the world; note that unlike Type A, it is not necessary to postulate the end of geopolitics in the setting created by the establishment of a world government within the contours set by Type B. Model C, depicted in Figure 3–10, is a compromise between Models A and B, allowing state actors to be relatively more or less strong, but allowing no one to be strong enough to challenge the authority of the central guidance system. And finally, Type D, displayed in Figure 3–11, extends the notion of dispersing central guidance functions among non-state actors beyond that suggested in Type B (Figure 3–9); the significance of state actors is diminished proportionally to a point where it would be difficult for even the

---

* Science fiction is replete with wars against aggressors from outer space. Such wars provide the motive for global integration—an external enemy. Some thinkers have emphasized that if the notion of an external enemy falls away, the motive for cooperation becomes so weak that disintegrative pressures mount. In any event, whether the dangers of world order collapse can function as a moral equivalent of an invasion from outer space, is a major open question as we confront the future of the species and the planet.

Figure 3–8. World Government (Type A)

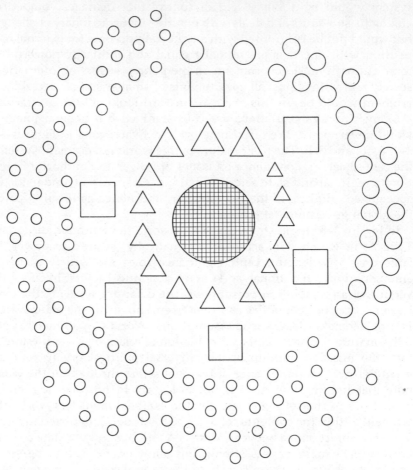

largest national government to challenge effectively the authority of
the central guidance system.

As a preferential model of the future, the world government system
would have to be principally devoted to the tasks of realizing the four
WOMP values. Such a normative nexus is not at all a matter of organizational necessity. There is nothing intrinsic about the idea of world government that precludes elitism, mass poverty, ecological decay, or even
large-scale violence. The orientation of the system depends on how it
comes into being, on public or community expectations, and on the objectives of the ruling groups. The range of possible governmental orien-

Figure 3–9. World Government (Type B)

tations at the national level can certainly be paralleled by a comparable range of alternatives on a global level. The most that can be affirmed is that a structure of central guidance makes it *possible* to realize WOMP values.

There are also important differences in organizational character. The extent to which the world government involves a dual sovereignty system, the extent to which non-state actors participate in world institutions, the extent of direct taxation, control over communications media, educational experience, and the degree to which the world government is based on notions of "social contract" and "the consent of the governed" are some of the important variables. A world government image relevant for the 1990's would probably represent an accretion to the ex-

Figure 3–10. World Government (Type C)

isting structure of world society. That is, a world government pow-
er/authority structure would be added to what exists, powers and capabilities would be redistributed, but the basic system of indirect
representation of peoples would persist. Most probably, national governments would decide voluntarily to form a world government in
order to facilitate realization of their interests. An intergovernmental
compact would provide the initial assurance that the new global arrangement possessed the consent of the people, that is, the citizenry of the
new global polity. Of course, it would be desirable if the new arrangement included provisions for enfranchising all people with respect to

Figure 3–11. World Government (Type D)

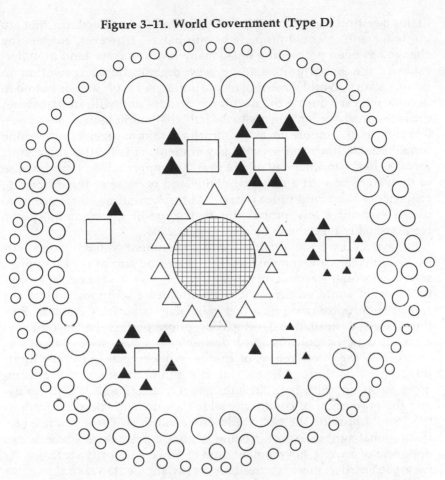

the operations of the world government; it would be desirable to fashion some compromise between the persistence of *statist* accountability and representation (i.e., accountability by the global mechanism to national governments), and the emergence of *populist* accountability and responsibility. In any event, given the short time interval for value changes and given the exclusion of traumatic and imperial transition scenarios, the prospect of world government, to the extent that it is reasonable at all, presupposes a *conservative variant*—minimal roles for the global bureaucracy, without any burgeoning forth of global political identity or widely shared sentiments of human solidarity.

Is this Image No. 2 perspective on world order reform so unrealistic within the time frame of the project as to be irrelevant? If the response to this question were to be based on "surprise-free projection," then, in our judgment, it would properly be affirmative. However, accelerating change has been proceeding on so many levels that we tend to underestimate the opportunities for a new organizational revolution in human affairs. World government as a horizon of aspiration is bound to become relevant during the next three decades and will, in that sense, provide a world order "enemy to the left" that might help create a political climate of support for major structural reform, even if not for the formal establishment of a world government. Finally, the apocalyptic mood is likely to intensify as the year 2000 approaches, both because of the nature of such a millenial divide and because of the deepening character of the world order crisis.[12] At the same time, there seems to be an exceeding low probability that a world government system would actually take shape before the year 2000.

But even if it were attainable, world government would not necessarily be *desirable*. Governmental presences can be and often are oppressive, ineffectual, wasteful, diversionary. It is essential to retain a skeptical view of world government as a world order solution, while at the same time proposing designs that maximize its positive features. Further analysis is needed to develop conceptions of the type of world government which would be most desirable, if at all, its conditions of emergence, the effectiveness of checks on its excesses, and the limits imposed on its duties.* In general, the minimum amount of government consistent with both the substantial realization of WOMP values and the promotion of conditions which accord with post-2000 priorities, would provide the best world order solution. There is a need for institutional agnosticism, for being neither a premature advocate nor opponent of a world government form of power/authority structure. As we argued earlier, there is a need for greatly augmented *central guidance* mechanisms in relation to the four WOMP values, but whether this entails a basic reliance on *governmental implementation* (i.e., by institutional policy-making and policy-applying) remains necessarily uncertain from our vantage point in time.

---

* See Chapter IV for an outline of a preference model of WOMP/USA. In this paragraph we are not arguing in favor of an S_2 solution based on world government, but only supporting the view that among world government models, certain design features are favored over others. It may also be the case that the label "world government" will be attached to any institutional arrangement that achieves a requisite degree of global coordination. Finally, centralized governmental notions may or may not, depending on other adjustments, especially at the national level, add to the net governmental presence in human affairs.

Image No. 3: A Regionalist Nexus
of Power/Authority

Great attention has been given to regional movements of economic and political integration, especially the European efforts, as the most promising approach to international cooperation among states situated close to one another and/or joined by cultural, ideological, or economic affinities.[13] Some specialists have speculated that the momentum gathered by economic integration "spills over" into areas of "high politics" involving security policy and issues of sovereign prerogatives. There is an unresolved debate in the economic integration literature as to whether present forms of regionalism are constrained by the limits of cooperation in a statist system or whether such limits are removed by building up the logic and structure of supranationalism.

A neglected perspective is *the sum* of regional initiatives at given historical moments—for example: $(R_{EEC} + R_{OAU} + R_{OAS} + R_{AL} . . . R_n)^{1971}$. This leads to the question of whether the *cumulative* impact of various regional plans can be assessed in world order terms (i.e., as a positive or negative force in relation to WOMP values).

It may also be helpful to consider whether a regionalist solution to the world order challenge is best conceived of as a realistic compromise between the status quo and world government. Regionalism can also be regarded as a preferable transitional power/authority structure that will "draw the fangs" of national sovereignty without moving too quickly into the Frankensteinian realms of super-government. The buildup of regional power expands the locus of human loyalties within the domain of a specific community that is only part of the whole human community; it thus preserves diversity and pluralism within the world system as a whole, and allows political identity to take shape around a "we" that is understood in contrast to the "they" who live beyond regional boundaries. The unevenness of present regional prospects (in the sense that regionalism is more feasible and desirable in some regions than others) is probably no greater than the unevenness among other types of actors in the world system. Little attention has been given, as yet, to creating regional peace-keeping forces as buffers between superpower diplomacy and internal disintegration or local war in some regions.

There seems to be ample reason, therefore, to take Image No. 3 seriously as a building block for the future of world order. By the 1990's it is possible to envision a rapid acceleration of integrationist projects, and many power/authority transfers from the national to the regional level. The orientation of regional actors depends on several variables that together define the political culture. There are clearly dangers in

Figure 3–12. Regional System (Type A)

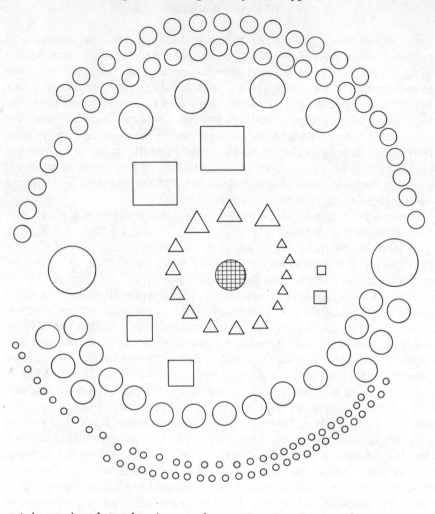

certain regional tendencies, such as attempts to use the mantle of regional action to vindicate the sort of coercive claims against a dissenting state that would not be permissible if undertaken by a single state. The efforts of the OAS to mobilize coercive pressures against Cuba under Castro, or by the pre-1967 moves by the Arab League against Israel, illustrate these dangers. But these dangers would exist in any movement toward centralization of the power/authority structure, although specifically regional biases might be neutralized or cancelled out in a world government system. Thus, action by the OAU against

Figure 3–13. Regional System (Type B)

South Africa enjoys virtually universal support, whereas OAS action against Cuba is, at most, a matter of only regional statist consensus.*

Our accompanying charts depict the basic world order structure envisioned, emphasizing what is probable and desirable by the 1990's.

---

* The OAS has been dominated by the United States, an actor with only dubious claims to regional membership. An OAS mandate, especially directed against Cuba during the height of the Cold War in the early 1960's, was largely an expression of United States

Figure 3–14. Regional System (Type C)

We project three principal forms of regional solution, to illustrate the range of organizational options that exists even within the regional category. Figure 3–12 presents Type A regionalism which emphasizes an expansion, although not an even one, of regional actors in all parts of the world system; regional actors become very significant, if not dominant, participants in many realms of international life, whereas state actors and global institutions remain more or less constant. Figure 3–13 illustrates Type B regionalism, in which the growth of regional actors is

---

foreign policy rather than any genuine expression of regionalist sentiments. The same problem of hegemonial regionalism exists in Eastern Europe, perhaps most dramatically in connection with the regionalist decision to intervene in Czechoslovakia in 1968 to unseat the Dubček regime.

complemented by the absolute and relative decline in the capabilities and competencies of the main state actors. And, finally, Figure 3–14 illustrates Type C regionalism, in which there is a growth and proliferation of regional actors, both political and functional, complemented by a drastic falling off of status and capability by state actors. Figures 3–13 and 3–14 indicate how an increase in central guidance within the world order system could be reconciled with a net reduction in the aggregate bureaucratic impact on human affairs.

At minimum, we favor taking the regional strategy of world order reform seriously within the time value horizons of WOMP, both as an indication of what can be done by the year 2000, as a transitional stage in world order between some kind of state system and some kind of world government system, and as an integrationist tendency that may produce a negative impact on the quality of world order under certain conditions. A further phase of world order reform would aim for new systems of central guidance by the year 2030 or so. To achieve coordination and to underscore the regionalist character of the world order system, one might consider adding a Council of Regional Representatives to the United Nations (or its successor organizations); depending on other developments, this Council could become in the 1990's the most important organ of UN affairs. The most doubtful aspect of these speculations stressing regional potentialities may involve their underestimation of "the global village" atmosphere that is likely to be created within the next two decades by the interplay between communications and transport developments, space travel, ocean use, and eco-management structures. Despite these globalizing tendencies we believe that world order analysts should give careful attention to the prospects and desirability of a shift from *statism* to *regionalism* as the basis of world order in the 1990's. Note, also, that an uneven endorsement of regionalism may also be made—i.e., good for Europe and Africa, bad for Asia, bad for Latin America unless the United States were excluded, and so on.

Image No. 4: A Functionalist Nexus of Power/Authority

As with other principal world order reform images, there is a wide range of functionalist approaches. More so, in fact, because each functional solution can be developed in relation to the technical and political features of a given problem area. The regulation of space with only two main actors is a different functional context than the regulation of ocean use, where every state, even those which are landlocked, deems itself a claimant to some extent. Figure 3–15 depicts a functionalist buildup on both the regional and global levels; in actuality, also, there are arrays of two- to n-party functionalist arrangements that would accompany a marked increase in intergovernmental cooperation. In Figure 3–16 the main evolution is with regard to global functionalism, suggesting the extent to which problem areas will require central guidance of planetary scope. In Figure 3–17 the emphasis is on functional expansion at the regional level, suggesting a model based on some degree of diversity and decentralization. Our design point is simply that functional arrangements can take a variety of forms, and that the principal patterns of these forms produce significantly different varieties of world order reform.

There has been a long tradition of thought in this century which argues that the creation of international institutions to deal with specialized functions represents the most fruitful approach to world order reform. David Mitrany evolved the view that specialized international institutions would engender a technocratic momentum within the scope of their concerns, and by excluding issues of a "political" charac-

Figure 3–15. Functionalist System (Type A)

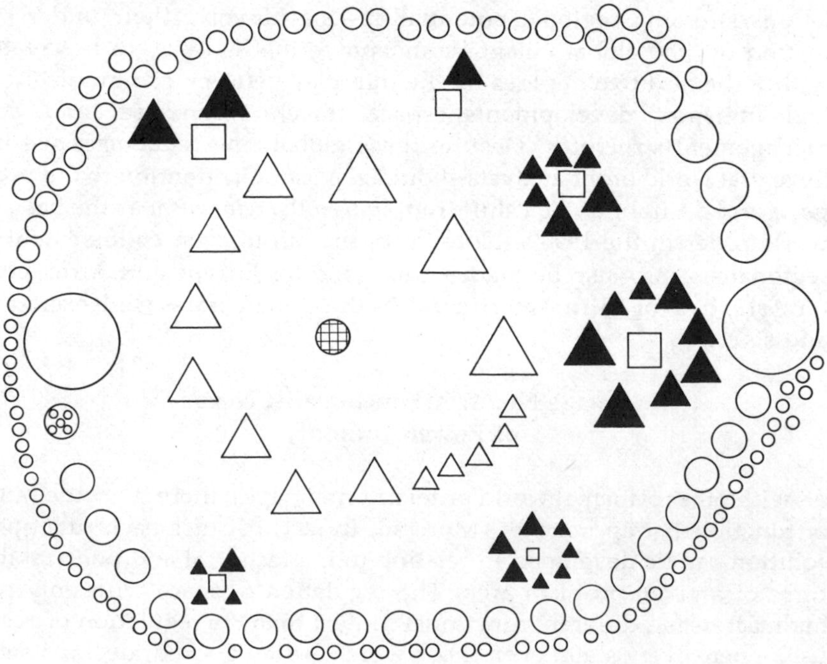

Figure 3–16. Functionalist System (Type B)

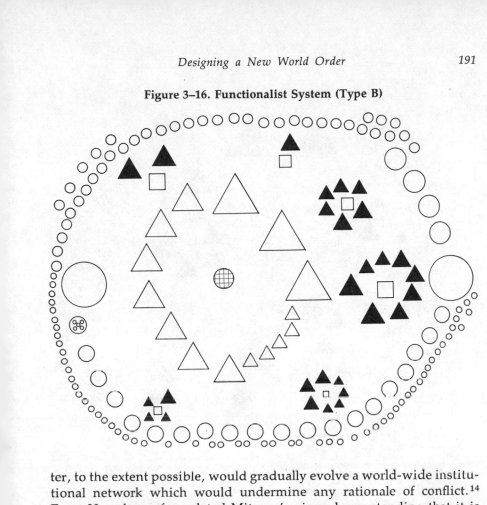

ter, to the extent possible, would gradually evolve a world-wide institutional network which would undermine any rationale of conflict.[14] Ernst Haas has reformulated Mitrany's views by contending that it is the *injection* (rather than the *exclusion*) of political issues that gives functionalist logic its sovereignty-cutting impact; Haas' views have been particularly shaped by a very detailed study of the ILO, where he finds many telling examples of "political" goals (e.g., East/West issue on rights of trade unions) later converted into precedents serving to implement technocratic standards of judgment (e.g., to condemn trade union restrictions in Portuguese colonies). Without the original political impetus, Haas suggests, the technocratic use of the standard would never have taken place.[15]

Regardless of the merits of the functionalist logic or of the debate among functionalists, what does seem clear is the remarkable rise in international institutions of a specialized kind over the last several decades. As Wallace and Singer have shown, the numbers of these institutions have increased from one in 1815 to 192 in 1960.[16] The increase in the number of functional actors at the regional level has been particu-

Figure 3–17. Functionalist System (Type C)

larly great. The expansion in the *number* of actors dealing with specialized functions is only one indicator of whether functionalism is an increasingly important element of the present world order system. Another indication would be the growth of the principal international institutions falling within the functionalist category, whether such growth is measured by *budget*, by an assessment of *role*, by the extent of *community participation*, or by the *stature* of the actor in the world system.

It would be helpful to distinguish between the use of specialized organs as *instruments* of cooperation within a statist system of world order and as autonomous actors within an altered system organized principally around the realization of the four WOMP values. This latter possibility is our focus. We regard a functionalist world order system as the culmination of very important technocratic trends in the most industrialized states. The newest arenas of mineral wealth and discovery—the oceans—may be a principal testing-ground of technocratic versus statist logic. The technocratic perspective, also present in such transnational actors as the multinational business corporation, may be reinforced by values of community and of social and economic justice at the world level. In essence, functionalist tendencies look toward the organization of various aspects of international life that are of concern to two or more states. The specialized organs that exist are dominated by national governments, by and large, despite some innovations in nongovernmental representation, and are dependent for their budget on national contributions; these specialized institutions operate as subordinate actors in the state system.* There is as yet no indication, even on the regional level, that specialized organs of international cooperation *transform* a statist system into a *community mechanism* of *central guidance*.

Indeed, even the most advanced regional experiments, those of Western Europe, seem to have made relatively few inroads on traditional matters of sovereign prerogative. At the same time, there is evidence to suggest that a high degree of functional integration by institutional means may achieve substantial progress with respect to WOMP values. Western Europe, because of its affluence, its adversary relations with Communism, and its painful experience of two world wars, is certainly not a typical regional sector of the world system. Nevertheless, the success of functionalist cooperation in reducing the prospect of large scale warfare among Western European states is an accomplishment with possibly wider implications.[17] Collective European efforts to prevent gross abuses of human rights, as in Greece since the 1967 coup, to redistribute income among the members of the community, or to work cooperatively on regional problems of environmental quality, have not been comparably impressive.† Even more negative is the view that European economic cooperation tied in with associate membership status for ex-colonies amounts to creating a new kind of imperialistic relationship.[18]

It is difficult to determine at this time whether "the security community" that has emerged in Western Europe is largely a response to a shared sense of external danger and unresolved grievances vis-à-vis the Soviet bloc, an outgrowth of the anguish ot two intra-European "world wars," or an expression of economic convenience and self-interest.

---

* Indications of relative dependence can be developed by reference to assessments, budgets, expenditures, voting patterns and rules and trends discerned over time for various international institutions.

† Nor have the efforts of large federal states been impressive with regard to the elimination of comparable deficiencies in their sub-units. Consider, for instance, the failure of the Federal government in the United States to secure equal treatment for black Americans at the state level, with respect to the most elementary issues.

Nevertheless, the European experiment in functionalist cooperation has been sufficiently successful, despite some periods of grave difficulty and some negative conjectures about past and future roles, to justify its study as a world order image for the future. On a global level, the efforts at international cooperation have been even more bland, and have rarely moved beyond such relatively noncontroversial activities as collecting information and discussing areas of possible intergovernmental agreement on common problems. Where there have been efforts to set world standards, their effectiveness has depended on the existence of strong incentives for compliance. Rules of maritime safety can be generated and are likely to be respected. But when specific monetary interests are at stake—when it comes to the discharge of oil at sea or the preservation of an endangered species of whale, for example—it then becomes difficult to establish appropriate standards, unrealistic to expect voluntary compliance, and impossible to achieve an effective regulatory arrangement. The obstacles to cooperation here, as elsewhere, become formidable when governments perceive adverse interests of a substantial kind arising from effective regulation in the community's interest.

Summarizing the present outlook for *specialized organs* of a *functional character*, the following conclusions seem reasonable:

1. These organs will increase in number, grow in size, and expand in function at the regional and global level during the remainder of the twentieth century.

2. There is considerable reason to believe that such organs, especially at the regional level, can make substantial contributions to the *quality* of world order (relation to WOMP values) in the decades ahead.

3. The encouragement of functional cooperation can and should be adapted to the particularities of each problem; there is no master functional model, but only a general conviction that functionalist solutions may help realize WOMP values under certain conditions, as well as help facilitate transition from S_1 to $S_{2(WOMP/USA)}$.

4. There is no present basis for believing that functional logic, as embodied in specialized institutions, can by itself transform the world order system by the year 2000; the growth of functionalism in accordance with propositions (1) and (2) is fully consistent with an expectation that the state system will persist through the period under study.

Given these judgments, does it still make sense to consider seriously an Image No. 4 solution of the world order crisis? We adopt a positive outlook, but without high expectations for dramatic successes in the near future. There are significant uncertainties about the role and degree of autonomy of functional actors in critical areas over the period of concern. For instance, pro-supranationalist resolutions of these uncertainties in the areas of ocean resources, satellite broadcasting, international aviation, and ocean waste disposal might create a powerful functionalist momentum that could virtually overwhelm the statist character of the present world order system. It will be very important to discern constitutional trends, if any, in the world of specialized agencies, especially on issues of representation, voting, and financing. Our general conclusion is that there is a possibility significantly greater than zero, but far less than .1, that a functionalist solution to the world order crisis will take shape by the end of the century.

In our view, the functionalist solution is probably not viable unless associated with other supranationalizing trends, such as expanded roles for regional and global political actors. In any event, the functionalist solution can take many value directions. By itself, it implies no particular commitment to WOMP values; such a commitment would presuppose reorientations of political consciousness, especially in the main national policy-forming arenas. We can envision a functionalist solution by the year 2000 that would go a long way toward substantial realization of the four WOMP values, but such a result would be virtually impossible without an immense prior effort to orient functionalist developments in a WOMP direction. Movement in this direction might be signalled by the early creation and expansion of a World Environmental Authority and an International Office of Human Rights; in functionalist settings, issues of social and economic well-being would have to be emphasized far more than in the past. Regional, as well as global developments, would have to be assessed in relation to their contribution to WOMP values, to determine whether emerging patterns of organization would indeed constitute *solutions*, rather than elaborate perpetuations, of *the problem*.

Image No. 5: A World Empire Nexus of Power/Authority

The idea of *unity* has often been the cardinal principle of proposals for world order reform *—to bring mankind under a single sovereign

---

* It is true that much utopian literature has been devoted to urban reform rather than global reform. The utopian tradition taking shape in the era of city–states was concerned with imagining the perfect city. The larger vision of organizing mankind around some benevolent principle has been characterized by a stress on unity and unification.

center and thereby establish the political basis of a wholly integrated human community. This quest for unity has many origins, some of which contradict others. Leaders of expanding states have built empires and indulged in the fantasy of world conquest. Religiously-inclined thinkers have sought a universal organization for bringing mankind together in harmonious unity. Early dreams of world peace—in East and West—involve breaking barriers and building a single world state that would govern all men everywhere. For both benign and demonic reasons, men have long conceived of an imperial solution to the world order crisis.

Not every large state is, or need be, an empire. It is useful to emphasize the distinction. Image No. 2—world government—embodies the power/authority structure associated with a state on a national level. An empire, in contrast, emphasizes the notion of a *core* dominating a subordinate *periphery;* the existence of an empire also involves a prior integration by *conquest* rather than by *contract.* Empire builders are conquerors who have imposed their will on subordinate areas, on behalf of the imperial center. In a world setting, "empire" would imply that a successful series of conquests by a state actor had eliminated or subdued all centers of autonomous, external authority and had extended the imperial prerogative to the entire world. Such an imperial model would do away with (or reduce to nominal roles) international institutions created by intergovernmental cooperation within a statist world order system. Because of its coercive roots and administration, the structure of an empire is probably not easy to reconcile with the full realization of WOMP values, except over a long time span. Its relevance to our analysis is mainly to suggest one main line of war prevention. Successful empires represent the most extensive experiments with large-scale coercive integration in human experience, and have often established high degrees of "peace" within imperial boundaries for relatively long periods. The collapse of imperial structures through the course of human history—their greater instability than state structures—suggests the difficulty of ruling over large areas where no natural bonds of affiliation exist.[19] Because the thirst for political independence seems so prevalent among many self-conscious political and ethnic groups, there is almost no prospect of securing a voluntary relationship between the governors and the governed in an imperial setting. By the logic of the system, the governed—those outside of the privileged core area—are or sense themselves to be exploited, and seek opportunities to overcome alien and disadvantageous control. The idealistic overtones of some imperial systems—bringing culture and technology to backward areas—can never overcome the basic relationship of dominance and exploitation, for the arrangement rests on violence and intimidation, rather than on consent and mutual interest.

With new modes of technology, the capacity to administer from a distance seems to be growing rapidly. It seems that the technological base for a totalitarian world empire will exist by the 1990's. That is, the capacity to sustain dominance, once established, might make an imperial system even on a world level relatively stable.

Figures 3–18 and 3–19 suggest two principal types of imperial world order reform. Figure 3–18 involves a total imperial consolidation of power/authority comparable to that associated with a well-administered totalitarian society, whereas Figure 3–19 involves a more hierarchical conception of world empire, with favored sections indicated by

Figure 3–18. World Empire (Type A)

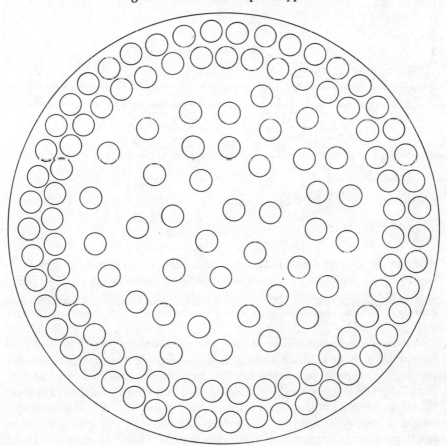

Figure 3–19. World Empire (Type B)

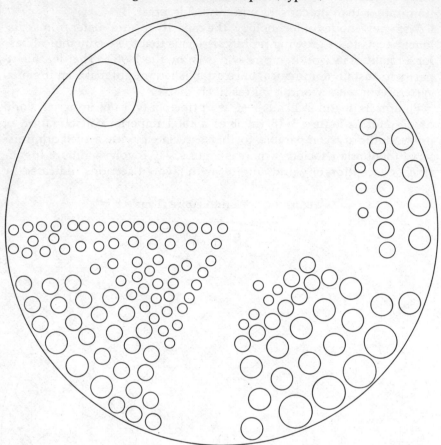

primary zones and darkened circles, and subordinate zones in descending order of secondary and tertiary realms of subordination. The point is that the empire can be based on a single polity of global scope and citizenry, or it can be organized around a more elite conception of core and periphery.

With the declining utility of war and war-making, shifts in political competition from explicit to informal patterns of control, and the dependence of poor countries on the rich ones, new patterns of imperial diplomacy seem to be emerging. For some nations, these international patterns involve maintaining the emblems of independence, while in reality assuming a subordinate status in an arrangement of relations that is imperial in critical respects. Thus, despite the rapid decline of "colonialism" and the more active and autonomous role of many new states, the currents of imperial expansion nevertheless run strong in modern diplomacy.

On a global level, the prospects for world empire over the next several decades seem virtually non-existent, although large portions of the world remain "colonized." [20] The nature of modern weapons demands that large-scale conquest be "deterred," for fear of provoking mutually-catastrophic results. The madness of a plan for world conquest is much more obvious today than in earlier periods of history. Resistance to any plan of imperial expansion would probably draw together the defensive energies of all but the imperial actor. The world community's eventual reaction of collective defense against Hitler's challenge is notable in this respect. At present, it certainly seems implausible that an imperial fanatic could successfully complete his plans, although it is true that the scale of technology now makes *global plans* feasible.* For instance, nonmilitary strategy of imperial conquest, possibly implemented in large part by nongovernmental actors, might be developed. One can imagine a plan to reorganize the world to serve the interests of the multinational corporation. Such a plan might even have a large idealistic element, promising prosperity, ecological management, and peace. Perhaps the imperial administrative center would be constituted by a superdirectorate of corporate managers, technocrats, and media chiefs rather than by a group of politicians or generals.† But these exotic extensions of the imperial idea do not yet seem plausible within the time span of the 1990's, although, as with Images 3–5, imperial tendencies in this direction may become more prominent during the relevant period.‡ Imperialism of the future is likely to impinge on the quality of

---

* It is always possible that a technological breakthrough in weaponry would enable a nuclear power to move from a position of parity to one of superiority. One can imagine a capability of a disarming first strike, coupled with a threat of a crippling second strike directed at industrial and population centers. The technological feasibility of such a breakthrough, depending on reliable antisubmarine weaponry, is in dispute. Beyond this, the costs of failure are so catastrophic as to inhibit the most ruthless leader, even if he were convinced that he had a foolproof first strike strategy. Nevertheless, political pathology is frequent in human history and one should not rule out the possibility of some mad scheme to establish a world empire once and for all.

† The administrative center could be a computer rather than a capital city, and the principal policy-makers need not even meet to reach critical decisions.

‡ Our concept of plausibility is extremely time-bound. From the perspective of 1935, world disarmament was totally implausible, but by 1945 it became briefly plausible, only to become more implausible than ever a few years later. The world order activist must be ready for the opportune moment when the constellation of forces suddenly seems favor-

world order according to the degree to which the manipulation of interdependence becomes concentrated in self-conscious elite groups acting
in concert. Whether the control of such levers of manipulation becomes
global or not within the century, will partly reflect the extent to which
central guidance of monetary, trade, resource and environmental policy
is established and leads toward an integrated world economy. Therefore, it seems important to include the imperial idea, and especially its
newer, nonterritorial, nonmilitary, nonstatist features, as one element
of an evolving post-statist world setting.

As far as desirability is concerned, it is difficult to assess the potentialities under Image No. 5. WOMP values can clearly be achieved by one
elite's conscious manipulation on behalf of the community. The sorts of
elites, however, that pursue imperial goals are rarely benevolently
inclined. The acquisition of control almost inevitably entails repression
of those elements who resist. Inequality and structural violence is built
into the very idea of empire. Nevertheless, on matters of "peace," welfare, environmental quality and even human dignity, a world imperial
elite could conceivably make considerable progress toward the realization of WOMP values. We can even imagine the possibility of a self-
constituted elite seizing power to help solve the world order crises in
the face of statist obstructions. We can also imagine counter-statist
elites with a technocratic, business, or anarchistic orientation working
toward the creation of a benevolent empire, perhaps even conditioned
on notions of a minimalist imperial structure, as the basis of a new system of world order.* The attraction of world empire is that it is likely to
come about, if at all, over the opposition of statist forces and would
therefore be the bearer of new values.† An imperial power/authority
nexus is not likely to be brought about by voluntary agreement among
national governments; rather, imperial control is quite likely to be extended, if at all, with no dependence on conventional governmental
presence. It is still accurate to characterize such a nongovernmental en-

---

able to drastic reform strategies. Therefore, it would be a mistake for advocates of WOMP-
type world reforms to become too literal about feasibility, merely in the interest of conveying a sense of world order realism.

* A neo-anarchist movement could easily form around the view that its foremost priority was to crush state power, and that the most efficacious and least destructive way to
achieve this outcome might involve toleration of an interim weak imperial transition.

† We are not seriously entertaining the prospect of a world empire of a conventional
territorial character with its authority nexus in the capital city of an existing sovereign
state. The neutralizing impacts of nuclear deterrence are sufficiently great, it seems, to
exclude this imperial eventuality from our thinking.

tity as imperial, however, because it constitutes an identifiable elite—fixed in time, space, and function—which would extend its control over the entire political order, and would decide upon the forms and roles of political, social, and economic organization at various levels of human activity.

Image No. 6: A Power/Authority Nexus Based on Concert of Principal Actors

Ever since the birth of the state system at the Peace of Westphalia, statesmen have felt some impulse to establish a managerial directorate. This directorate would serve the will of the dominant governments, establishing a consensus on the rules of the game which govern international diplomacy. The concert of Europe in the eighteenth century and the "conference diplomacy" of the nineteenth century are the principal historical examples of the concert model in operation.[21] Actually these examples are of regional scope, although the conferences in the late 1800's included agreements among European governments regarding the disposition of colonial claims, especially those in Africa. Recourse to mechanisms involving a concert of principal actors embodies several related issues: (1) dominance of the real world by a relatively small number of effective centers of power/authority; (2) the insufficiency of mechanisms of balance, dynamic equilibrium, and spontaneous stability to preserve the security and economic interests of the dominant centers of power/authority; (3) the perceived benefits of maintaining forums for communication and consensus-formation to link rival centers of power/authority; (4) the perceived benefit of excluding formally significant but relatively powerless authority centers from the process of "arranging" the course of international diplomacy.

The concert image is a more modest managerial alternative to the sort of unidirectional and highly concentrated nexus of power/authority embodied in the main conceptions of world government or world empire. As a move toward central guidance, the concert image represents a definite organizational advance over the highly dispersed nexus of power/authority that is world feudalism or world anarchy. The concert notion tries to provide the basis—with or without a formal structure of treaty obligations, fixed site, periodic meetings, institutional machinery—for contact between the principal actors in a given world order system. Because our experience has heretofore been connected primarily with a statist world order system, the idea of concert is identified with meetings among governmental representatives. The function of a concert is to work out the interests of these governments and there is no pretension, except in pious public rhetoric, that a world community interest is of foremost concern. The European invention and use of concert diplomacy made no effort to evolve any international voice of conscience of the sort associated with the role of the Secretariat and the Secretary General in United Nations affairs. Therefore, the background of the concert idea is deeply imbued with "the great power" side of international diplomacy. As we have already suggested, the post-Cold War era of international diplomacy is characterized by neo-concert designs for world order reform.

However, this background should not divert us from appreciating the relevance of Image No. 6 for world order reform. Again, it is important to keep in mind the distinction between a new world order *system* organized around the concert idea, and the concert idea as one *element* in an evolving world order system of mixed characteristics. The positive potential of the concert idea depends on whether it can be used to realize WOMP values within the time frame of the 1990's.

There are various implicit moves in the concert direction. The whole emphasis on "summit diplomacy," the excitement evoked by Nixon's journey to China, the SALT talks, and the various proposals to let the leading industrial states organize environmental defense arise from a concert approach to global reform.[22] All these illustrations maintain the statist bias of the present world order system and make use of the concert setting as an *instrument* of statist diplomacy. In thinking about the future of world order, it will be useful to conceive the possibility of heterodox concert mechanisms composed of national governments, regional actors, functional agencies, and transnational movements. These concert mechanisms can be related either to specific issue-areas (e.g., arms policy, environmental protection) or to general world order issues (e.g., an open agenda). Image No. 6 provides a flexible instrument of cooperation and control that can be shaped to carry out prevailing world order tendencies. Figures 3–20 to 3–22 illustrate this flexibility. Figure 3–20 is a statist variant of the concert notion as a world order construct. Figure 3–21 illustrates some heterogeneity in the form of regional political and functional actor participation in the overall central guidance scheme. Figure 3–22 is a variation on the mixed actor concert, stressing global functional participation.

Given the drift of the international system, is it realistic to suppose that the concert image might form the basis of a world order solution along WOMP lines by the 1990's? Given the present situation where no one solution is realistic in the sense of being probable, it would seem necessary to give a negative response. However, if concert tendencies were maximized in the 1970's, especially in relation to such functional

Figure 3–20. Statist Concert

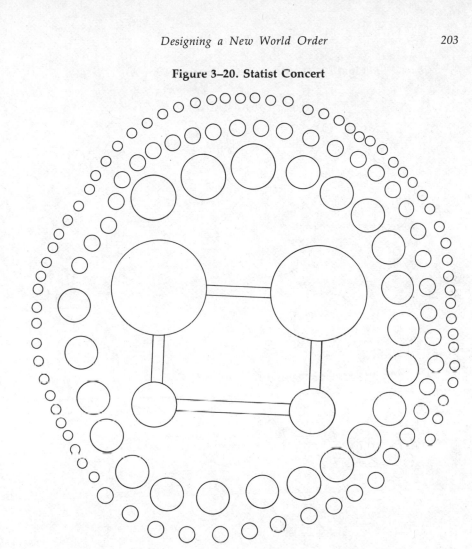

areas as arms control, environmental protection, and ocean resources, this approach to a world order solution might become promising by the late 1980's in a manner impossible to conceive of in the early 1970's. As matters now stand, image No. 6 activity is mainly *statist* in conception and execution and often contributes to the satisfaction of *hierarchical* interests rather than to WOMP values (that is, the dominant governments are likely to use concert mechanisms to impose their will on the world community as a whole). Recourse to concert mechanisms is likely to reflect distrust and disappointment with reliance upon more universal actors, such as the United Nations, that purport to be dedicated to a more idealistic view of the world. Therefore, it seems reasonable to

Figure 3–21. Mixed Actor Concert (Type A)

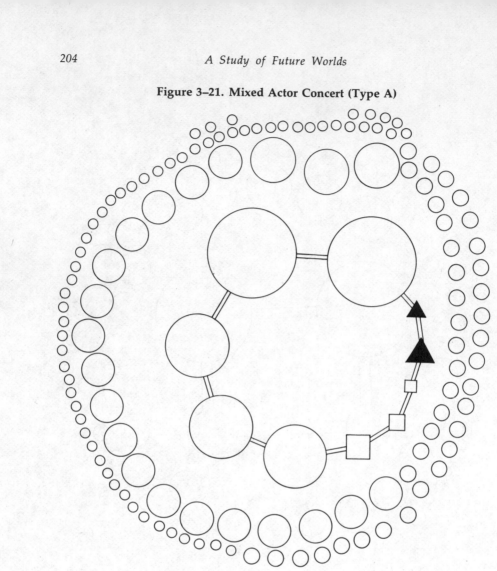

conclude that concert ideas might become very relevant as part of the world power/authority nexus during the remainder of the century, but will probably exert a fairly conservative overall world order influence,* and are not likely to provide "a solution" or its main inspirational foundation.

---

* The value impact of concert diplomacy may vary considerably from substantive context to context and from phase to phase. The goals of world leaders are likely to determine whether a given concert approach is progressive or regressive from the double outlook of WOMP—that is, by assessing impact on WOMP value criteria and by assessing impact on prospects for a shift to an $S_{2(WOMP/USA)}$ world system.

Figure 3–22. Mixed Actor Concert (Type B)

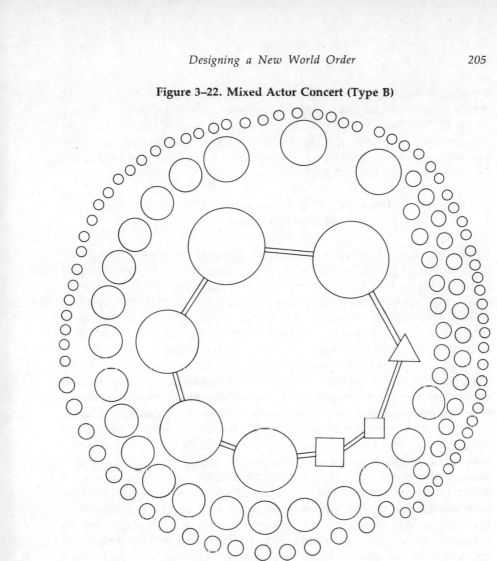

As far as desirability is concerned, a careful distinction has to be made between statist uses of the concert mechanism and *mixed-actor* contexts. If world order experiments with nonstate actors get started around the concert image, positive contributions are likely. Environmental quality and resource conservation issues may provide good testing grounds. In both settings there are persuasive reasons for organizing international responses on the basis of a mixed-actor mechanism: large governments, regions, functional agencies, and some transnational institutions (e.g., citizens' groups concerned with environmental quality). The concert mechanism might be able to shatter the stereotype that significant world order settings are constituted exclusively by governmental bodies. If so, this framework could help considerably to create a political consciousness predisposed to a world order solution along WOMP lines (i.e., post-statist reconstruction of the world order system). In any event, the concert mechanism warrants prominence, but not uncritical approval, in any plans for a new world order system by the end of the 1990's.*

Image No. 7: A Condominium Nexus of Power/Authority

By *condominium* we mean a cooperative arrangement among the dominant centers of governmental power to act together on key world order issues, in accord with pre-set procedures. Figure 3–23 illustrates a condominium approach to world order organized around principles of Soviet–American cooperation. At this historical moment the primary referent of condominium is a pattern of increasing U.S./Soviet cooperation in the security area: more or less formalized through agreements, through forums for continuous negotiation and communication, and by isolating bipolar diplomacy through summit meetings, hotlines, and other devices. There is also some possibility of *covert condominium*, whereby governments cooperate tacitly to attain joint goals, but fail to acknowledge the power/authority nexus thereby created. The idea of condominium is a logical consequence of bipolarity, in a period when expensive and mutually dangerous nuclear weapons are proliferating to secondary and tertiary actors. Statist imperatives tend to lead powerful actors toward status quo (equilibrium) or revisionist orientations (expansionist). The nuclear stalemate induces a status quo orientation in the main arenas of wealth and influence. However, it is expensive to maintain at a time of rising domestic demands, vulnerable to breakthroughs or alleged breakthroughs by the other side and hence subject to periods of intense anxiety, and also vulnerable to intolerable consequences if deterrence fails. The dynamic of a nuclear arms race creates national incentives to stabilize the rivalry on an improved basis, by diminishing the competitive feature of arms competition, stabilizing boundaries of influence, and establishing zones of mutual tolerance.

In large measure, these forces have already transformed the Cold War ideology of earlier decades. This new phase in geopolitics has been en-

---

* Unlike other world order reform imagery, the concert image is more attractive for its feasibility features than for its mainstream value impacts. That is, it is easy to imagine an emphasis on a world order concert by existing political leaders, but difficult to imagine directing the concert instrument toward WOMP ends.

Figure 3-23. World Order Condominium

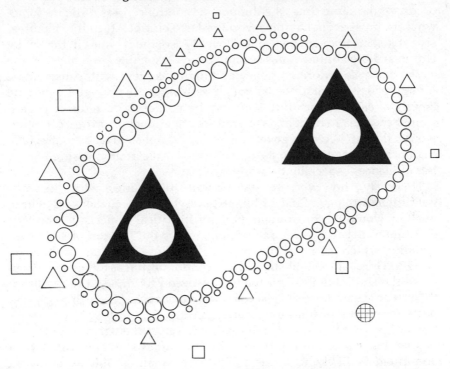

couraged on the Soviet side by the Sino-Soviet split and by the general appreciation that ideological affinity does not necessarily produce international harmony. On the American side, key factors have been its failure in the Indochina War and a growing sense that a foreign state's national identity may be more critical than its ideological creed. In this respect, both sides in the Cold War seem to have generally rediscovered the logic of statism, which implies the management of power relations to assure mutual advantage on an intergovernmental level. Part of this rediscovery has to do with the shared, although unacknowledgeable, U.S./Soviet interest in maintaining their relative dominance vis-à-vis secondary powers or "emerging superstates," to borrow Herman Kahn's label for Japan. The Non-Proliferation Treaty (unaccompanied by any renunciation of the nuclear option on the part of the nuclear powers) is an illustration of bipolar cooperation in the interests of maintaining hegemony.

The condominium approach is appealing because it fits in so well with the present power/authority nexus. No transfers of power or authority are required. No buildups of international institutions need occur. At the same time, the duopolistic control centers mitigate somewhat the prospect of having a world order "solution" turn into a repressive statist mechanism on a global level.* Also, the regimes in the Soviet Union and the United States seem to be in reasonable agreement on the *means* and *ends* of foreign policy and highly content with conservative foreign policy orientations, although both sides are prepared to pursue targets of easy opportunity and may be preparing to redirect expansionist energies in light of an altered set of national priorities.† In other words, the gap between governing groups is not so great as to preclude a cooperative relationship designed to evolve a certain measure of central guidance, especially on war/peace issues.

There are, however, several obvious difficulties with the condominium strategy. First of all, it tends to unify challengers whose position would be constrained, perhaps in critical respects, by the condominium. Second, a condominium shatters the illusion of sovereign equality, which is one of the main legitimizing principles of the state system. Third, the establishment of a condominium assumes the capacity of the United States and the Soviet Union to impose their wills on the rest of the system, at least for selective purposes. Fourth, the prospects for condominium are severely limited by the ideological traditions of both regimes, not only with respect to their rivalry with one another but also with respect to the sort of international setting a condominium is likely to achieve. Fifth, the main problems of world order—as defined by WOMP values—require the voluntary participation of many additional relevant governmental centers of power and authority.

As with several other images of future world order, the condominium seems more relevant as an *element* of a new order (or movement toward one) than it does as a *solution* for the present deepening crisis. Even as an element, however, the condominium image may be regressive or ambiguous over the next several decades. If U.S./Soviet cooperation seeks, above all, to perpetuate international inequality, it is likely to

---

* The economic notion of duopoly may be an important orienting concept. The maintenance of a duopoly may not involve explicit coordination or an outright conspiracy so much as tacit coordination and conscious parallelism. There would be many ideological reasons why a condominium, precisely if it did become a real organizing objective, would seek to operate as covertly and informally as possible.

† Control over the supply of such critical resources as oil may dominate great power foreign policy in the decade ahead, whereas considerations of market access for corporate operations, investment or political access, may diminish in importance.

hamper, rather than contribute toward, the elimination of poverty and oppression. In addition, the condominium idea seems like a way of extending the life of the state system at a time when this system itself comes under increasing pressure. Although principal governments will cooperate to sustain their prerogatives and to mitigate the dangers of imminent collapse, such cooperation does not seem likely to prepare the way for a new world order system, but rather to keep up false hopes about the serviceability of the old one. In the opposite vein, however, if condominium efforts can cut the costs and dangers of the strategic arms race, then they probably can gain time and reduce the risks of nuclear catastrophe. In this sense, limited acceptance of the condominium as an interim organizing strategy seems desirable during the period of transition. The identity of condominium principals does not necessarily have to remain fixed; it could evolve in the direction of a concert of principal actors, and expand its functional competence beyond issues of nuclear war prevention, arms limitation, and world security management.

Therefore, from a WOMP perspective, the condominium image has a limited role. Its relevance seems confined in substance to strategic armaments, and its desirability seems partially related to its adherence to these limits. That is, if the idea of condominium were to become part of a new world order ideology that gained the support of governing groups in the Soviet Union and the United States, its implementation would almost certainly diminish rather than strengthen WOMP values. Also, to the extent that the condominium scheme succeeded, it would engender serious countervailing international movements that would themselves endanger nuclear peace. As a matter of prediction, we regard the condominium image as *marginal* to both prospects and preference in the future, possibly evolving as a dangerous expression of statist resistance to more drastic and progressive modifications of the world order system, but conceivably important in arms and security matters.

Image No. 8: A Small-State Nexus of Power/Authority

If feasibility constraints do not prove too great, one of the most obvious directions for world order reform would involve the breakup of the largest sovereign states. The proliferation of states, especially if arising from secessionist movements in principal states, would tend to diminish greatly the dangers of large-scale warfare and erode the capability of governments to carry out extensive programs of external domination.[23]

Figure 3–24. Small State System (Type A)

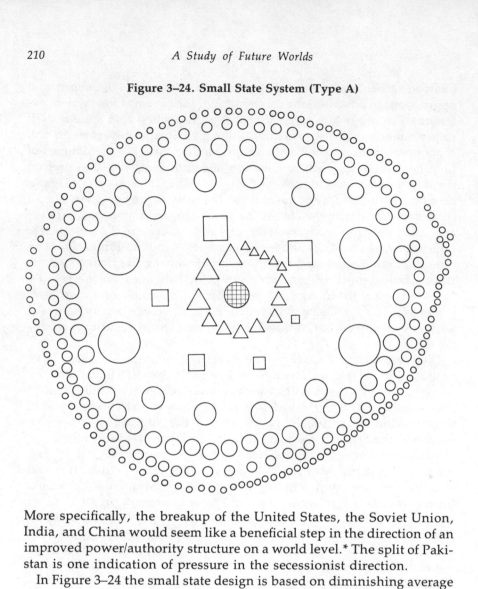

More specifically, the breakup of the United States, the Soviet Union, India, and China would seem like a beneficial step in the direction of an improved power/authority structure on a world level.* The split of Pakistan is one indication of pressure in the secessionist direction.

In Figure 3–24 the small state design is based on diminishing average state size without any buildup of the central guidance mechanism,

---

* Size of constituent units is an important world order variable often neglected in reformist literature. We would emphasize two points: first, size should not be associated exclusively with space, power, or wealth; second, the specific value impacts of unit-splitting or unit-merging vary with each context. Hence, a given secession may have a positive or negative value impact. Nevertheless, the net value impact of unit-splitting seems beneficial over the short-term, especially with respect to the main state units. One could take, overall, a dialectical view of unit size, levelling down at the top and levelling up at the bottom of the international status ladder.

whereas in Figure 3–25 modest increases in central guidance capabilities are also projected. In the latter, the small state system is combined with a modest variant of the global functionalist strategy. It would also be possible to include a small state system that involved a buildup of the smallest and weakest state units as well as size reductions for the biggest and strongest ones.

Among the attractions of a small-state solution to the world order crisis would be reduced pressure to provide central guidance by building up a statelike apparatus. The central political actors would need a far smaller capability vis-à-vis governmental actors to provide reasonable assurance on matters of peacekeeping and enforcing disarmament. Given the character of evolving information and communications technology, the diminished scale of actors in the advanced industrial sector of the world would strengthen greatly the network of interdependence,

Figure 3–25. Small State System (Type B)

and make mandatory a far more extensive system of functional coordination. A growth in the number and relative equality of governmental actors would reduce the likelihood that leading governments could dominate international machinery to serve their particular interests.

Furthermore, large states are frequently artificial political communities that tend to rely upon ideological manipulation and contrived symbols of coherence, if not outright coercion, to secure popular allegiance. That is, "the consent of the governed" is more difficult to acquire and maintain in a multi-ethnic society with varying regional traditions and interests, especially if the state mechanism exercises control over a vast geographic expanse. The rise of subnational militancy throughout the world, including those in the "old" states, suggests the renewal of the quest for political communities that correspond to genuine shared experience and real identification. The Soviet Union has a problem of latent internal colonialism involving the relations among its various nationalities, and between its core and periphery republics; the United States has similar problems arising from the subjugation of minority races. The Indian subcontinent is torn by religious, tribal, linguistic, and ethnic strife, as are many countries in Asia and Africa. In some areas of the world, the breakup of the state system might well be accompanied by the re-establishment of units of control comparable in scale to what existed in feudal Europe.

The new technology of war and the new interdependence of economic activity means that a national government, however strong and efficient, can no longer insulate its population from either the ravages of war or the vagaries of international economic fluctuations. The functional basis of large sovereign states has been considerably undermined by these developments, with a consequent decline in national allegiance. A rise in cosmopolitanism has accompanied the growth in transnational affiliation, the deglorification of war and conquest, and the beginnings of a world culture. This incipient world culture is symbolized by the imagery of a unified globe, resulting from space exploits, touring arts groups, and the instant communication links made possible by the Intellsat system. Conversely, these universalizing forces also help weaken the hold of state governments on their own populations, inducing the seeming paradox of smaller and wider patterns of identification simultaneously impinging upon the state's central position of symbolic eminence.*

_____

* Again we would suggest a dialectical reconciliation to the problems of optimal unit size from the perspective of personal identification. In some contexts, nation-building—

Of course, this small-state vision of the future is beset with practical difficulties. The large states possess increasingly effective capabilities for domestic pacification. The technology of surveillance and counter-insurgency gives a well-organized bureaucracy an enormous advantage over a hostile citizenry. The objective of a government confronted by sub-national challenges is to fragment its opposition. Totalitarian regimes have successfully atomized resistance and opposition efforts, making the initiative of individuals appear futile, and tending to rein-force rather than disrupt the control exerted by the repressive regime. In developing countries, the technological buildup of the central gov-ernment and the international bias on behalf of a statist outcome of civil strife (i.e., aid flows consistently discriminate in favor of the consti-tuted elite) have made it difficult for an independence movement to break away and form its own state.* In this sense, the wars in the Congo, Nigeria, and Pakistan are all bloody reminders that the relation of internal forces strongly favors the incumbent government, unless the balance is upset by external, cross-border factors. In the more advanced sectors of the world, government is in such a commanding position that the populace has almost no prospect of organizing against it. Even in the more moderate large states, radical separatist movements tend to be sporadic and are without the capacity to sustain a real secessionist challenge. The largely negative experience in wars of secession should be contrasted with the record of anti-colonial wars, where the enemy is "a foreign power" that rules from a distance measured in both miles and ethnic identity.†

Do these considerations make the small-state image irrelevant as a world order *solution* for the 1990's as conceived along WOMP lines? We think not. Again, this image offers no prospect of reorganizing the world by the 1990's, but it has a reasonable chance of exerting influence upon transitional developments between now and then. We view the breakup of large sovereign states as inevitable in the future unless the grip of totalitarian rule is imposed or maintained; i.e., the large state is an unstable political unit if its existence depends on the dynamics of

---

enlarging personal zones of identification—has very positive value effects enabling the growth of a more humane and successful national polity. In other contexts, nation-breaking—shrinking personal zones of identification—has very positive value effects enabling the emergence of a more consensual and communal type of national polity.

* International institutions constituted by governments have a strong anti-secessionist bias, almost regardless of the merits of a specific claim. It is difficult for the secessionist group to obtain a fair hearing for its position.

† The distinction between wars of secession and anti-colonial wars should not be drawn too sharply. On many occasions the secessionist issue is essentially colonial in character, as in the Indo–Pakistan War of 1971 which led to the emergence of Bangladesh.

voluntary or even semi-voluntary association. The continuing assertion of subnational claims for autonomy may generate compromises on the part of more moderate governments, including domestic experiments with more dispersed power. In France, the United States, and the Soviet Union, various experiments of this kind are likely to take shape in the 1970's. The small-state vision need *not* be tied to the *formal* breakdown of large states; it might be substantially accompanied by a major dispersal of the domestic power/authority nexus within orginal state boundaries. Therefore, it seems reasonable to regard the small-state image as at least a conditioning element in a positive world order solution for the 1990's. This does not mean that large states will disappear from the world political system by the year 2000, but only that their capacity to mobilize their internal resources might be greatly diminished by more autonomous sub-units, and by internal checks on action taken in the name of the entire state. If the state as such becomes less of a power/authority nexus—sharing power/authority with sub-national units of political control, with transnational actors such as the multinational corporation, and with supranational actors, especially of a functional kind—the small-state (or diminished) vision may play a very central role in world order reform. The immediate outcome would not necessarily entail superseding the state system so much as its beneficial reordering.

Image No. 9: An Anarchistic Power/Authority Nexus

An important tradition of radical political thought has maintained that reliance on governmental presence to order human affairs is the basic source of almost everything wrong in society. It is obvious that the consolidation of power/authority in a bureaucratic actor creates the capacity and incentive to manipulate for special advantage. The experience of our century with socialist revolutions gives great weight to that part of the anarchist argument which warns that the replacement of one bureaucracy by another will be accompanied by a betrayal of revolutionary ideals, however drastic the repudiation of the old order turns out to be. The experience with political revolution on the national level is not uniform, and is subject to many interpretations. It does seem clear, however, that because of the statist setting of world affairs and the ruler's imperative in domestic affairs, all principal existing governments are induced to adopt policies of pacification and militarization at home, and domination and interventionary diplomacy abroad. Such tendencies have been accentuated by technological achievement, and by the greatly expanded arena of intergovernmental rivalry which potentially embraces the surface of the entire earth and, in the not too distant future, much of the solar system as well.

There are many problems that the anarchist position either overlooks or handles inadequately. The most basic of these is probably the human impulse to survive and dominate. There are virtually irresistible pressures in our highly interdependent world toward counterrevolution from within and intervention from without. A major national revolution would probably be crushed by the statist order unless it armed to protect itself. But arming initiates the vicious logic of internal and national security which inevitably leads to an emulation of systemic behavior: a strong political order at home and an aggressive foreign policy. To achieve the capital surplus needed for a modern defense establishment and an active foreign policy, a huge amount of resources must be transferred away from the needs of one's own population. Such a transfer requires an ideological justification and transmutes government propaganda into some new form of mystification; the new rulers may need to be protected against their enemies by a secret police. When resources are transferred to these security functions, bureaucracies—especially those under real or imagined pressures—are inclined to proceed in a destructive fashion. This direction of governmental policy produces a negation of most WOMP values.

There is a wide array of ways to organize international life around a basic anarchist concept. We present some principal variations in Figures 3–26 to 3–29. Our main anarchistic emphasis is upon the breakdown of bureaucracy at the state level, although hostility to bureaucracies at all levels follows from the basic anarchist commitment. In Figure 3–26 the virtual disappearance of state bureaucracies is accompanied by the retention of an apparatus for central guidance consisting of global and regional actors. Figure 3–27 regards the central guidance role as best discharged by principal reliance on universal functional actors; note the virtual disappearance of regional and global general purpose organizations. In Figure 3–28 the anarchist success results in greatly diminished capabilities for state actors, but with their role still considerable by comparison with other institutional actors; in this variant, Type C, state actors would have to use cooperative procedures to satisfy the central guidance needs of the altered world order system. In contrast, Figure 3–29 conceives of a world order system in which state actors have disappeared altogether and all institutional roles are discharged by a network of international actors of all principal types.

Does the anarchist perspective have any world order relevance? In some ways an extreme variant of the small-state image, the anarchist

Figure 3–26. Anarchistic World Order System (Type A)

image has been very influential in "counter-culture" thinking, combining an anti-government view with an anti-technology position. In this sense the image is alive, especially among young people seeking to preserve individual autonomy and personality in a world whose dominant trends are dehumanizing.[24] If large states are world order arenas, the anarchist vision (especially if broadly defined to include all liberation programs which seek to dissolve the bureaucratic power/authority nexus to whatever extent possible at every level of institutionalization) clearly has some prospect of influencing the predominant orientation of major societies, including leadership groups. Charles Reich is "romantic" to the extent that he envisions the ascendance of Consciousness III without an intervening struggle against overwhelming odds, but he is correct to call our attention to the emergence of a novel human orientation as a principal datum for post-industrial societies experiencing social ferment in the years ahead.[25] The form of this ferment may change its shape rapidly and frequently over the years ahead, but its persistence seems clear.[26]

Consequently, within those states that allow the political market

Figure 3–27. Anarchistic World Order System (Type B)

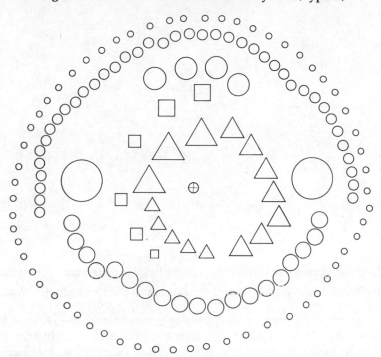

mechanism to operate, there will be a strong and very possibly a growing constituency (depending on population trends) that challenges the basic assumptions of statism as a world order system. At present this anarchist challenge is formulated largely in national terms. Its political goals include opposition to the military–industrial complex, to domestic exploitation of minority races and the poor, and to destruction of the environment on behalf of a profit-impelled cult of economic growth. The logic of coping with these national concerns is to cut the defense budget, reduce the interventionary side of foreign policy, encourage policies to promote well-being on a global level, and favor international cooperation in such areas as disarmament, environmental protection, and the promotion of human rights.* In other words, a certain amount

---

* The anarchist ethos does not necessarily assure concern with the problems of others. Many self-styled anarchists seem rather egoistic and self-centered. Therefore, the world order spill-over attributed to anarchistic approaches depends on stimulating an active involvement in the problems of the world as a whole. Such involvement, besides being a

Figure 3–28. Anarchistic World Order System (Type C)

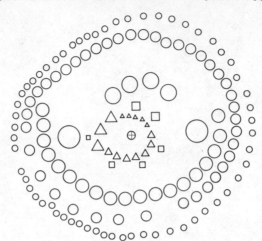

of anarchist success within states might help set the stage for a *positive* world order solution along WOMP lines. Furthermore, during this period anarchist groups are likely to develop a persuasive interpretation of the link between a world order solution and the realization of domestic aspirations. These developments could plausibly take place within the next two decades if the anarchist perspective takes greater hold in political consciousness.

In this sense, Image No. 9 is *relevant* and *positive* as an *element* of a solution, because of a very special kind of conditioning effect on the world order scene. There is no realistic prospect that governmental authority will be dissolved within the time period, but there is a considerable possibility that the more moderate governments will reach partial accommodations with anarchist challenges mounted from within and across their boundaries. Therefore, the WOMP/USA proposals treat anarchism seriously as a political movement with quite substantial world order implications. We do not expect any of the anarchist rearrangements of the world order system, as portrayed in Figures 3–26 to 3–29, to become feasible by the year 2000. As matters now stand, it is almost inconceivable that national bureaucracies can be drastically curtailed in more than a handful of countries, and even these are likely to

matter of moral expression, could also safeguard local anarchist gains in influence. The anarchist life style is naturally compatible with a peaceful life of harmony with nature, which animates WOMP/USA's whole approach to the quest for world order.

Figure 3–29. Anarchistic World Order System (Type D)

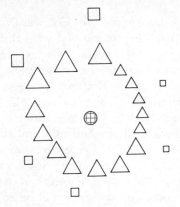

be small or medium-sized states. However, the anarchist value position will quite possibly influence the political climate in non-authoritarian post-industrial societies, presupposing the persistence of relatively open national political contexts. It is this prospect of influence, rather than the plausibility of anarchist solutions *per se*, that makes the anarchist position of interest to WOMP/USA. The anarchist outlook also provides an antidote to the pro-governmental bias so characteristic of world order reform literature.

CONCLUSION ON IMAGES

On the basis of the charts and accompanying discussion, we have tried to clarify the prospects for world order change in the decades ahead. As is evident, we do not believe that any world order solution is likely to emerge in this century by the abrupt substitution of one system for another. We observe, however, a series of positive tendencies toward world order development that might make an important difference if their cumulative impact is not offset, or reversed, by negative tendencies toward the deterioration of international life. There is a tension between the emergence of new organizational forms capable of handling intensifying challenges, and the disintegrative effects of these challenges upon an archaic and overburdened organizational structure (or, in the sense we have emphasized, in relation to the primary power/authority nexus of the existing world order system). This tension is dynamic, and can be conceived as a competition among contending forces.

Our preference model, set forth in Chapter IV, is derived from these organizational potentialities, combined with the assessment that there are no realistic prospects for a system change—as a deliberative undertaking at a given time—within the century. At the same time, as we made clear at the outset of this chapter, we reject a gradualist approach to reform as insufficient. As will become explicit in subsequent chapters, we are most optimistic about a sequence of changes that could bring about over time a dramatic and coherent set of results: first, value change via education; second, the growth of a world order reform movement via organizational activism; third, the institutional implementation of a new global consciousness via institutional innovation. Evaluation of this process at any time will be concerned with shifts in the capacities of the world system to realize WOMP values and broader changes in the global setting that favor or disfavor the attainment of $S_{2(WOMP/USA)}$, or some other S_2 option.

At present, these images are both weak counter-tendencies in the current world order system and building blocks for the future. Their relevance to the present is to help structure a feasible vision of a world order solution and to provide an intellectual basis for the preference model depicted in the next chapter.

If we are to avoid *ad hoc* problem-solving in the international arena, which is so often dominated by the interplay of vested interests, then public consciousness must become convinced of the need to plan deliberately for the evolution of a new world order system. It is our hope that this presentation of power/authority alternatives may improve the analysis of world order options, and encourage the promotion of innovative world order solutions by the more enlightened segments of world public opinion. Every level of human activity has a world order dimension that needs to be understood, in order to evolve more adaptive patterns of belief and behavior than have prevailed in the past.

REFERENCES

1. For a well-documented argument that natural disasters will be the principal energy of global reform see Alfred L. Webre and Phillip H. Liss, *The Age of Cataclysm*, mimeographed manuscript, 1973.

2. See, generally, David Ehrenfeld, *Conserving Life on Earth*, New York, Oxford, 1972.

3. *Ibid.*

4. See Chapter VI, p. 400 for a discussion of a steady-state world economy. For a generally excellent collection of papers on this subject see Herman E. Daly, ed., *Toward a Steady-State Economy*, San Francisco, Freeman, 1973.

5. For text of principles see *Survival*, July/August 1972, pp. 188–191.

6. Among thoughtful interpretations see Morton A. Kaplan, *System and Process in International Politics*, New York, John Wiley, 1958; Richard N. Rosecrance, *Action and Reaction in World Politics*, Boston, Little, Brown, 1963; Harold Sprout and Margaret Sprout, *Toward a Politics of Planet Earth*, New York, Van Nostrand, 1971; K. J. Holsti, *International Politics: A Framework for Analysis*, Englewood Cliffs, New Jersey, Prentice-Hall, 1972.

7. On actors in international politics see O. R. Young, "The Actors in World Politics," in James N. Rosenau, Vincent Davis, and Maurice A. East, eds., *The Analysis of International Politics*, New York, Free Press, 1972, pp. 125–144.

8. See Robert C. Angell, *Peace on the March: Transnational Participation*, New York, Van Nostrand, 1969; Robert S. Jordan, ed., *Multinational Cooperation*, New York, Oxford, 1972; see also J. David Singer, ed., *Quantitative International Politics: Insights and Evidence*, New York, Free Press, 1968; J. David Singer and Michael D. Wallace, "Intergovernmental Organization in the Global System, 1815–1964: A Quantitative Description," *International Organization*, 24: 239–287 (1970).

9. For a sophisticated depiction of the emergent international setting see Stanley Hoffmann, "International Organization and the International System," *International Organization*, 24: 389–413 (1970).

10. For other efforts directed at behavioral trends see John McHale, *The Future of the Future*, New York, Braziller, 1969; Jay Forrester, *World Dynamics*, Cambridge, Mass., Wright-Allen, 1971; Donella Meadows and others, *The Limits to Growth*, New York, Universe, 1972.

11. Perhaps the most effective presentations of this position are to be found in Louis Henkin, *How Nations Behave*, New York, Praeger, 1968; Wolfgang Friedman, *The Changing Structure of International Law*, New York, Columbia University Press, 1964; see also Myres S. McDougal and Florentino P.

Feliciano, *Law and Minimum World Public Order: The Legal Regulation of International Coercion*, New Haven, Yale, 1961, pp. 261–383.

12. Among important expressions of the apocalyptic mood see Doris Lessing, *Briefing for a Descent into Hell*, New York, Knopf, 1971; Walker Percy, *Love in the Ruins*, New York, Farrar, Straus, 1971; Mary McCarthy, *Birds of America*, New York, Harcourt Brace, 1971.

13. For a sophisticated assessment of regionalist trends see Joseph Nye, *Peace in Parts: Integration and Conflict in Regional Organization*, Boston, Little, Brown, 1971; see also Bruce Russett, *International Regions and the International System: A Study in Political Ecology*, Chicago, Rand McNally, 1967; on regionalism in relation to WOMP see Falk and Saul H. Mendlovitz, eds., *Regionalism and World Politics*, San Francisco, Freeman, 1973.

14. For Mitrany's fullest statement see David Mitrany, *A Working Peace System*, London, Royal Institute of International Affairs, 1943.

15. See Ernst B. Haas, *Beyond the Nation–State: Functionalism and International Organization*, Stanford, Stanford University Presss, 1964.

16. Wallace and Singer, *Intergovernmental Organization*, p. 272.

17. The argument that encouraging functional interdependence is the most effective strategy of world peace is well stated in Vincent Rock, *The Strategy of Interdependence*, New York, Scribner's, 1964.

18. This argument is the main theme of Johan Galtung, *The European Community: A Superpower in the Making*, London, Allen and Unwin, 1973.

19. This position is effectively supported in Amitai Etzioni, *The Active Society: A Theory of Societal and Political Processes*, New York, Free Press, 1968, pp. 580–583.

20. For a consideration of superpower patterns of hegemony see Richard A. Falk, "Zone II as a World Order Construct," in Rosenau, Davis, and East, *Analysis of International Politics*, pp. 187–206.

21. See Rosecrance, *Action and Reaction*, pp. 55–148.

22. One clear exposition to this effect is contained in George F. Kennan, "To Prevent a World Wasteland," *Foreign Affairs*, 48: 401–413 (1970).

23. See general development of theme in Leopold Kohr, *The Breakdown of Nations*, London, Routledge and Kegan Paul, 1957.

24. See Theodore Roszak, *The Making of a Counter Culture: Reflections on the Technocratic Society and its Youthful Opposition*, New York, Anchor, 1969; for a more fundamental critique of technological society see Jacques Ellul, *The Technological Society*, New York, Random House, 1964; cf. P. B. Medawar, *The Art of the Soluble*, London, Methuen, 1967.

25. Ideas developed in Charles Reich, *The Greening of America,* New York, Random House, 1970.

26. For a popularized account see Alvin Toffler, *Future Shock,* New York, Random House, 1970.

Chapter Four

DESIGNING A PREFERRED
WORLD POLITY

STATEMENT OF OBJECTIVE

Chapter III depicted world order building blocks and considered the basic orientations toward structural reform in the political realm. In this chapter, we set forth a specific preference model that is designed to maximize prospects of feasibility and realization of values. This preference model of WOMP/USA is only one of several possible models that could be set forth in compliance with the WOMP mandate. In our judgment, however, this particular model is the most viable one for a global movement committed to a program of drastic reform by the end of the century, without recourse to violence and without the sort of systemic shock that might be administered by global warfare, pandemic, widespread famine, or major ecological collapse.

Our objective here is to outline a preference model that can be appraised, altered, reconsidered. We initially seek to encourage its analysis and hope that assessment will ultimately enlist support and help focus a worldwide social and political movement of global reform. We are eager to strengthen the role of world order ideas and ideals in the world, and to help in making the realm of thought and imagination serve as a stepping stone between the realms of feeling and of action. Only by an organic process of triangulation among feeling, thought, and action can we hope to create a world order movement that is neither naive about its origins, sterile in its implications, nor reckless about its consequences.

PREFERENTIAL MODELING: THE IMAGERY
OF PREFERENCE AND OF PROCESS

The WOMP approach combines a stress on preference with an emphasis on the processes by which preferences are realized. The value dimensions of this approach have been set forth in Chapter I. In Chapter V, we will consider the process of reform—the transition process—by which the existing world order system might be transformed in the direction of our preference model. Because of the inevitable ambiguity of language and intentions, it is probably important to reiterate that we are not making world order *predictions* in the spirit of futurology. We hope, rather, to show what is *possible* and to clarify our convictions as to what is *desirable*. Explicating the possible in a persuasive fashion will hopefully create a magnet for potential world order activists, nothing more. Whether the magnet will be powerful enough to attract adherents is an open question. Another is whether other normative magnets pull enough adherents toward comparable fields of force in other parts of the world to engender a genuine movement for global reform. Charting a course is not at all the same thing as provisioning a vessel for voyage or setting forth from safe harbors of observation.

To orient the preference model's presentation we anticipate the next chapter's discussion of transition, especially by suggesting here, in a series of charts, the stages of structural reform. As we have already suggested, the process of structural reform will occur neither as a result of a single constitutional event nor as a consequence of steady institutional expansion at the global level. In essence, we expect dramatic modifications of the central guidance system to be deferred until the end of the transition process; these modifications might then result as expressions of an altered value consciousness and climate of aspiration. Indeed, if these normative preconditions cannot be satisfied, the structural reforms will remain a pipe dream, no more helpful (or harmful) than past flights of world order fancy.

In the decades ahead, various categories of actors will show different growth curves. The average growth that to us appears likely for each main category of actor is indicated by Figure 4–1. Note that a particular member of any one of these categories may have a pattern of growth or decline at considerable variance from that of the average member portrayed by the actor curves. Also, it should be clear that these curves do not portray steady rates of growth or decline; if a world order movement gains momentum, the rather stable world order structure projected for the next two decades will be significantly modified in the third decade or so, especially with respect to the construction of the

Figure 4–1. Projected Growth Curves for Actors in the World Order System

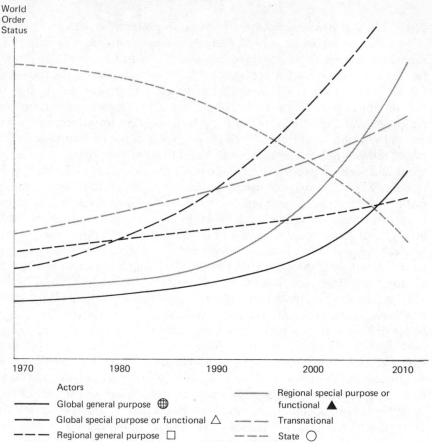

central guidance capability. As we will make clear in the chapter on transition, our concept of process is expressed through the image of stages whose duration is almost impossible to project but whose completion is essential for the initiation of the subsequent stage.

Our basic assumptions are that the preference model will result from a major buildup of functional agencies at the regional and world level, a steady growth in regional general-purpose actors, an accelerating rate of growth in the organs of the global general-purpose actor, and stagnancy followed by a shrinkage of state actors, especially the largest ones. Figure 4–1 charts these pathways to a preferred future in graphic form. On this basis we project a power/authority nexus for the year 2000 that has the following relationship to that which exists as of 1974:

1. A United Nations Organization or its equivalent, with a *doubled size* and *status*

2. A set of universal functional agencies that have *four times* their present size and status

3. A set of regional general-purpose actors with *doubled size* and *status*, with the European regional actor expanding at a more rapid rate to four times its present size and status

4. A set of regional functional agencies that have *four times* their present size and status

5. A network of state actors that have, on the average, half of their present capabilities: the largest states would diminish most rapidly, whereas most of the smaller and middle-sized states would increase their relative capability and influence *

6. A tripled number of transnational actors enjoying on the average a quadrupled increase in status and influence †

These six dimensions of the power/authority structure are intended only to convey an approximate sense of changes in magnitude that would be reflected in the preference model for the late 1990's. Our anal-

---

* The reduction in state capability would not necessarily be reflected by shrinkage in state size. The important expression of reduced ability would involve the elimination of military capabilities as an instrument of foreign policy and the decline of governmental function—as measured by budgetary allocations—over life within national polities. Thus, the demilitarization of foreign policy and dispersion of governmental roles in domestic policy areas would be the main measures of declining state capability. The size of the state actors on our charts is a measurement of *capability*, not physical *size*. It is possible, of course, that secession could produce a reduction of size that entailed a proportionate decline in capability as well, although such a direct correlation is neither necessary nor obvious. Indeed, one could imagine a successful secessionist movement that left both units as more potent actors than the one combined unit had been. France, after 1962 when Algerian independence was realized, has seemed stronger than in the decade before, when its boundaries included Algeria. State units can be weakened by strong centrifugal pressures that require the devotion of much energy in order to sustain territorial identity.

† We have not included transnational actors in the charts in Chapter III because they would so complicate the presentations as to inhibit understanding. We do regard transnational actors as important, if indeterminate, agents of change and control in the evolution of the world order system. Multinational corporations are especially important transnational actors, although it is not yet clear whether a positive (+) or negative (−) sign should be associated with their cumulative impact. It is uncertain whether the multinational corporate category of actor will function primarily as a regressive extension of statism, or as a generally progressive anticipation of and link toward a WOMP-oriented world order system. It is important to assess the prospects for such a positive role and the extent to which these prospects can be improved by conscious effort.

ysis of the specific *structural* attributes and the operating guidelines for institutional actors does presuppose the basic realism of this presentation. Figures 4–2 to 4–4 depict the main stages in the *process* by which the preference model can be brought into being. The duration of each stage cannot be accurately foretold, but we regard it as *possible* for the three-part process to be completed by the year 2000.

STRUCTURAL ATTRIBUTES OF THE PREFERENCE MODEL OF WORLD ORDER

This presentation of the preference model will be focused upon the general-purpose and functional actors at the global level; that is, the

Figure 4–2. Preference Model (Phase I)

Note: See page 163 for Key.

Figure 4–3. Preference Model (Phase II)

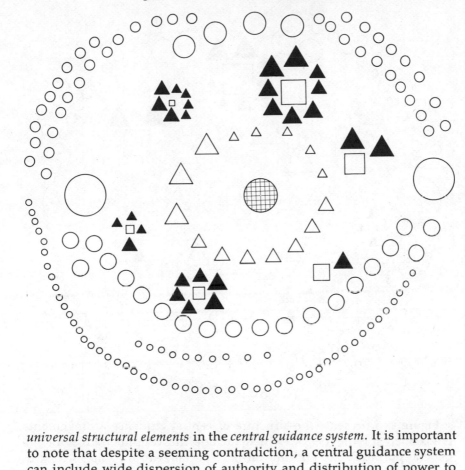

universal structural elements in the *central guidance system*. It is important to note that despite a seeming contradiction, a central guidance system can include wide dispersion of authority and distribution of power to other actors, and that our preference model is not based on "a world government solution" that would be accomplished mainly through shifts of authority and power from state actors to a general-purpose global actor. As noted earlier, the preference model illustrated in Figures 4–2 to 4–4 relies heavily on a buildup of role and capability for all categories of non-state actors, coupled with a shift in orientation, more than a reduction in power/authority, for state actors. Global functional actors—specialized agencies of universal scope—are closely related to the general-purpose global actor. Nevertheless, the most important structural changes will occur in relation to the central guidance capability.

Figure 4–4. Preference Model (Phase III)

Figure 4–6 presents the structure of central guidance arrangements envisioned for the 1990's, which include the combined roles of the general-purpose actor and the various specialized functional actors. In Table 4–1, we also present information on the costs of the UN system between the period of 1946 and 1969 to indicate the scale of the enterprise.[1] The designation "actor" may be misleading. We have in mind, of course, a label that covers the activities of a large-scale organization composed of many distinct bureaucratic entities and decision-makers, with linkages which are more or less close, and internal relationships of authority/power which are not necessarily hierarchical. Indeed, a fair amount of autonomy has been evident in the relations among different bureaucratic entities within the United Nations setting (see Figure 4–5). For instance, consider the relationship between the International Court of Justice and the General Assembly after the decision

Figure 4–5. The United Nations System

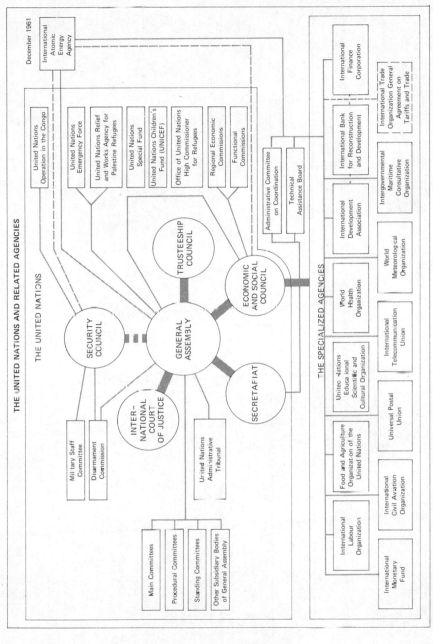

THE UNITED NATIONS AND RELATED AGENCIES

THE UNITED NATIONS

December 1961

International Atomic Energy Agency

United Nations Operation in the Congo

United Nations Emergency Force

United Nations Relief and Works Agency for Palestine Refugees

United Nations Special Fund

United Nations Children's Fund (UNICEF)

Office of United Nations High Commissioner for Refugees

Regional Economic Commissions

Functional Commissions

SECURITY COUNCIL

Military Staff Committee

Disarmament Commission

INTER-NATIONAL COURT OF JUSTICE

GENERAL ASSEMBLY

Main Committees

Procedural Committees

Standing Committees

Other Subsidiary Bodies of General Assembly

United Nations Administrative Tribunal

TRUSTEESHIP COUNCIL

SECRETARIAT

ECONOMIC AND SOCIAL COUNCIL

Administrative Committee on Coordination

Technical Assistance Board

THE SPECIALIZED AGENCIES

International Monetary Fund

International Labour Organization

International Civil Aviation Organization

Food and Agriculture Organization of the United Nations

Universal Postal Union

United Nations Educational, Scientific and Cultural Organization

International Telecommunication Union

World Health Organization

International Development Association

World Meteorological Organization

International Bank for Reconstruction and Development

Intergovernmental Maritime Consultative Organization

International Finance Corporation

International Trade Organization General Agreement on Tariffs and Trade

SOURCE: Inis L. Claude, Jr., *Swords into Plowshares: The Problems and Progress of International Organization.* New York, Random House, 1964, p. 446.

United Nations, Specialized Agencies, Special Programs and the International Atomic Energy Agency Total Program (Expenditures or Authorizations), Calendar Years 1946–1972 (In Thousands of Dollars)

	Cumulative Total 1946–1962	1963	1964	1965	1966	1967	1968	1969	1970	1971	Estimate 1972	Cumulative Total 1946–1972
United Nations, Specialized Agencies and International Atomic Energy Agency:												
United Nations	876,300	92,200	102,900	107,100	118,600	130,500	141,200	156,800	168,400	194,100	208,700	2,296,800
Food and Agriculture Organization	114,200	16,800	18,000	23,600	27,800	29,700	31,700	36,200	38,300	43,300	46,700	426,300
Intergovernmental Maritime Consultative Organization	1,200	400	500	900	800	800	800	1,200	1,200	1,600	2,000	11,400
International Atomic Energy Agency	26,000	6,900	7,300	8,800	10,000	9,300	10,000	11,200	12,200	14,000	16,600	132,300
International Civil Aviation Organization	57,900	5,800	6,100	6,400	7,500	7,000	7,600	7,700	8,400	9,700	11,000	135,100
Joint Financing Program	24,200	3,300	3,400	3,800	4,200	4,200	3,600	3,900	3,900	4,100	5,100	63,700
International Labor Organization	116,500	14,500	17,000	21,500	23,500	26,500	29,000	31,100	31,300	32,900	41,200	385,000
International Telecommunication Union	30,300	4,100	4,100	5,600	7,000	6,800	7,200	7,700	8,700	10,400	10,100	102,000
U.N. Educational, Scientific and Cultural Organization	166,500	19,700	21,300	27,200	28,600	32,900	37,300	41,800	43,700	49,500	54,400	522,900
Universal Postal Union	7,700	800	1,200	1,100	1,300	1,500	1,500	2,100	1,900	2,400	2,600	24,100
World Health Organization	168,400	29,800	33,900	42,100	48,200	56,300	61,100	68,800	75,000	85,500	96,200	765,300
World Meteorological Organization	5,000	900	1,100	1,500	2,000	2,400	2,600	3,100	3,500	4,500	4,800	31,400
United Nations, Specialized Agencies and International Atomic Energy Agency	1,594,200	195,200	216,800	249,600	279,500	307,900	333,600	371,600	396,500	452,000	499,400	4,896,300
United Nations Peacekeeping Forces:												
United Nations Emergency Force	128,700	18,900	23,500	18,900	15,000	11,400						216,400
United Nations Operation in the Congo	267,200	78,700	22,300									368,200
United Nations Force in Cyprus			15,300	23,900	19,400	19,000	18,300	14,300	12,700	12,700	15,000	150,600
United Nations Peacekeeping Forces	395,900	97,600	61,100	42,800	34,400	30,400	18,300	14,300	12,700	12,700	15,000	735,200

Special Programs:

												Total
International Atomic Energy Agency Operational Program	7,500	1,300	1,800	1,800	2,000	2,200	3,100	2,300	2,600	3,300	3,700	32,100
United Nations Children's Fund	355,500	38,300	39,800	31,200	35,400	39,200	45,900	50,700	50,600	56,900	61,400	805,500
Nigerian Relief						4,700	1,900					6,600
Humanitarian Assistance: India/Bangladesh										17,100	17,400	34,500
U.N. Technical & Operational Assistance to the Congo	93,500	37,300	13,000	14,200	9,100	4,000	3,000	2,500	1,400	1,300		179,800
United Nations Development Program	364,600	83,200	106,800	119,500	158,500	170,800	195,400	232,900	257,300	317,100	340,100	2,346,200
U.N./FAO World Food Program		8,500	15,700	19,500	38,300	40,900	58,100	84,400	149,200	134,600	174,000	723,300
United Nations Fund for Drug Abuse Control										100	3,600	3,700
United Nations Fund for Population Activities							100	1,200	6,700	8,600	27,000	43,600
United Nations High Commissioner for Refugees Program	31,600	6,600	2,800	3,400	4,200	4,700	4,800	5,900	6,500	5,900	7,300	83,900
Humanitarian Assistance: India/Bangladesh											184,300	184,300
Relief Program for Asians Expelled from Uganda											2,800	2,800
Southern Sudan Relief Operation											13,900	13,900
United Nations Relief and Works Agency	437,400	36,200	36,900	37,100	37,000	39,900	44,000	46,200	47,900	48,400	52,100	863,100
U.N. Relief Operation in East Pakistan/Bangladesh										36,000	177,000	213,000
United Nations Institute for Training and Research			100	500	600	900	1,100	1,200	1,500	1,200	1,300	8,100
U.N. Research Institute for Social Development				200	300	500	400	400	400			2,200
United Nations Volunteers Program											200	200
Special Contributions for Viet-Nam		1,100	1,900	200								3,200
WHO International Agency for Research on Cancer				400	700	700	600	1,700	1,900	2,200	2,400	11,600
WHO Special Programs [1]	19,500		1,200	1,900	1,100	800	100	200	400	2,400	5,000	34,800
WMO Voluntary Assistance Program							800	3,400	400	2,400	4,500	17,200
UNITAR Stevenson Memorial Fellowships							100					300
United Nations Programs for Southern Africans				200	100	500						1,000
UNESCO Special Programs [2]	8,400	13,000	12,000	6,000	6,000							45,400
International Refugee Organization	412,700											412,700
United Nations Hungarian Refugee Relief Program	12,000											12,000
United Nations Korean Reconstruction Agency	148,400											148,400
Special Programs	1,891,100	228,400	230,100	235,700	294,200	304,700	359,200	433,600	535,200	827,700	893,500	6,233,400
TOTAL	3,881,200	521,200	508,000	528,100	608,100	643,000	711,100	819,500	944,400	1,292,400	1,407,900	11,864,900

[1] WHO special programs are the Malaria Eradication Special Account, the Medical Research Program, the Community Water Supply Program, the Drug Monitoring Program and the Special Cholera Account.

[2] UNESCO special programs are Aid to African Education and the Nubian Monuments Program.

SOURCE: U.S., Congress, House, Committee on Foreign Affairs, *United States Contributions to International Organizations*, 93rd Cong., 1st sess., 1973, facing p. 86.

in the South West Africa Cases was handed down in 1966; * or, the relationship between the Secretary General and important members of the Security Council in relation to the Congo crisis in the early 1960's.[3] It will be important to clarify areas of semi-autonomous and of hierarchical linkage within the central guidance pattern of the 1990's, although it is virtually impossible to anticipate the impact of practice which will encompass a variety of unpredictable factors. This pattern of coordination projected for the 1990's can be thought of either as a drastic extension of the United Nations system or as a new approach to central guidance.

At this point it hardly matters whether our preference model of the general-purpose actor is called "the United Nations" or not.† Nevertheless, to make clear the discontinuity between the existing and the preferred world order systems, we will refer to the proposed central guidance capability as The World Polity Association. Such nomenclature does not intend to dispose of the issue of whether the new guidance capability can be evolved out of the United Nations Organization or whether a new constitutional conference would be required to give codified expression to the structural changes implicit in $S_{2(WOMP/USA)}$. However, it does seek to convey the organizational discontinuity between what is now known as the United Nations and what we are proposing on behalf of WOMP/USA.

The proposed changes in structure, role, and capabilities will be extensive, as will the changes *external* to the general purpose and specialized actors, particularly the orientation of the principal state actors and the overall setting of international life. Figure 4–6 presents our concept of the internal bureaucratic structure of the central guidance capability embodied in the preference model of WOMP/USA. At this point we offer no more than an institutional *profile*, although we will provide "an operating manual" later in the chapter and will describe the functions of each bureaucratic element in the central actor's domain. This skeletal

---

* The ICJ decision precluded inquiry into the propriety of South African administration, including its racial policies, of the mandated territory of South West Africa (now known as Namibia). Such a judicial outcome was so unpalatable to most governments that the General Assembly adopted Resolution 2145, which terminated South Africa's right to act as mandatory power.[2] The point here is that the United Nations as a composite actor spoke with several voices on the issue of the disputed mandate. Nor is each agency itself always a coherent actor.

† It is important to realize that by *central guidance capability* we refer to both the general-purpose and specialized agency sectors of institutional effort. The label "United Nations" has been used in this same comprehensive sense to cover both types of actors.

Figure 4–6. Central Guidance in the Preference Model

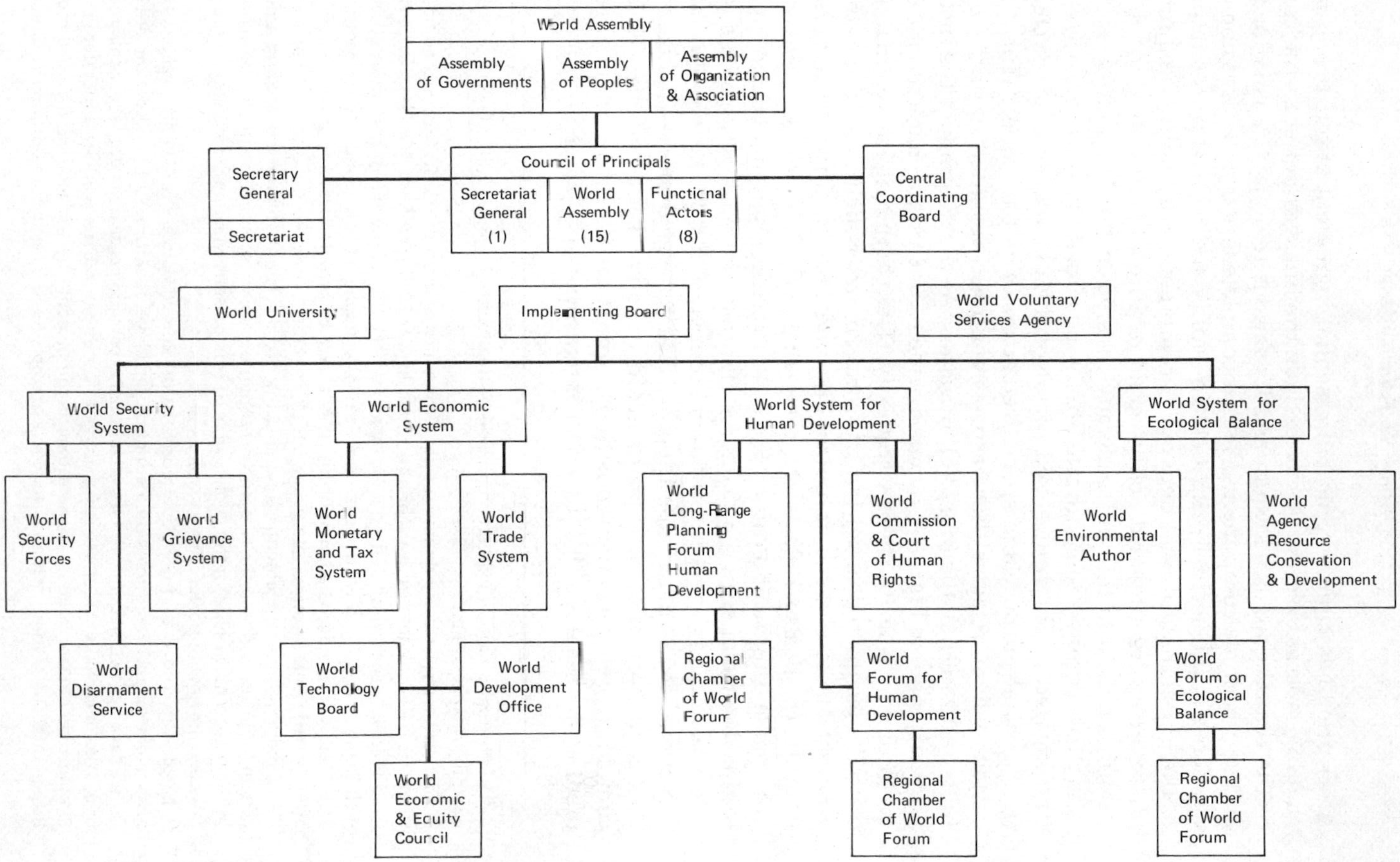

description is a cumbersome but essential ingredient of our proposal-shaping process. We purposely exclude the linkages between the core of the central guidance system and its various regional, transnational, and sub-national components. This incompleteness is an expression of our sense of intellectual priorities. To avoid a mechanical presentation of the global institutional network, a comprehensive institutional profile for an emergent world polity would require a lengthy, but not very useful, addition to the topics already covered in this chapter.

In this section we will indicate briefly the *substantive scope* of each entity engaged in the centralized sector of the overall guidance system (i.e., general-purpose and specialized actors of global scope).* The discussion will emphasize those aspects and roles designed to produce a fuller realization of the four WOMP values. As the diagram of the institutional profile in Figure 4–6 makes evident, one prime characteristic of the future will be its sheer complexity. The complexity arises mainly from the technological setting of world affairs, which makes nongovernmental actors much more mobile and less confined to national boundaries. It also reflects the view that economic competition will grow more intense and difficult to contain within national boundaries, in the absence of strong procedures and institutional arrangements for effective and equitable international cooperation.†

National economic competition has also generated increasingly complex regulatory mechanisms to avoid negative social effects. Thus, complexity generates demands for coordination, control, and management as the scale and frequency of interactions increase.‡ Such an ex-

---

* See textual note that explains omission of treatment of noncentralized sectors of the central guidance system, p. 227.

† Indeed, we regard the domain of geo-economics as the most critical conflict arena in the years ahead, renewing fears of a third world war in altered form. The ending of the Cold War has been stimulated, in part, by an appreciation of the extent to which national well-being is associated with geo-economic rivalry among advanced industrial countries. The great world order challenge of the 1970's may be whether emerging conflicts over money, trade and resource allocation can be contained, or even deflected into international cooperative arrangements. By displacing direct anxieties about warfare and arms-race instabilities between the two nuclear superpowers, these more recent conflicts could bring about a new phase in the evolution of S₁ (the present world order system), a phase replete with new opportunities as well as new risks.

‡ Unless preceded by normative reorientation in accordance with WOMP values, the growth of organizational roles on a supranational level is not likely to be very beneficial (as we have defined beneficial). Organizational expansion *per se* does not seem at all positive. We can envision an efficiently managed, highly centralized world order system that is more deficient in value attainment than is the present one. Actor *orientation* is a more important focus of inquiry than is actor *role* or *scope*. Such an assertion reinforces our gen-

pansion in the number, size, and influence of transnational actors is probable regardless of whether other desirable kinds of world order reform take place.

WORLD ASSEMBLY (WA)

The World Assembly will be the principal policy-making organ in the world system, with particular responsibility for the promotion of the four WOMP values. It will set world standards and render binding decisions by achieving a four-fifths majority vote within each of its three chambers having 200 votes apiece.* It can make recommendations, as distinguished from decisions, by securing a two-thirds vote of its three chambers. Decisions of the World Assembly (WA) can be appealed to the World Court for review by the initiative of any ten representatives in any of the three chambers of the WA.† If the WA decision requires immediate implementation, and so directs, executive organs of the World Polity Association will consider it valid pending judicial review. The World Court will, in this event, provide petitioners with an expedited review procedure that would seek to reach a preliminary conclusion within thirty days, and may propose preliminary measures to safeguard various threatened interests. If the Court, by a majority, concludes that there seems to be a substantial probability of invalidity, then it can enjoin further implementation of the WA decision pending its final judgment and decree.

The WA can then meet in plenary session and maintain the validity of its decision by reaffirming it in the form of an overall four-fifths vote, or by establishing a state of global emergency in relation to the specific decision by a four-fifths vote that authorizes suspension or revision of the judicial outcome.

The rationale of this system of "checks and balances" is to reconcile constitutional restraint with an interest in organizational effectiveness. For this reason, there needs to be some review procedure of all WA undertakings, enabling substantial constitutional issues to be authorita-

---

eral view that issues of constitutive order are secondary (although linked) to issues of *normative orientation*.

* The composition of the ⁴/₅ majority may reflect weighted voting schemes discussed below. Also, 200 votes do not necessarily imply 200 representatives.

† For a fuller explanation see discussion of World Grievance System, p. 248.

tively considered; in addition, a set of extraordinary procedures is needed to enable suspension of normal judicial review, either by moving beyond the World Court's view of constitutional restraint, or by dealing with a condition of perceived emergency that could, in the view of the relevant majority, deteriorate dangerously if action were delayed. Ultimate authority and responsibility are thus placed in the WA, with the idea of giving judicial review a central braking role, but not in an absolute or final form.

Each chamber of the WA will have 200 votes. The distribution of these votes will be a complicated task of institutional design. Criteria of membership will also be complicated, especially with respect to the Assembly of Peoples and the Assembly of Organizations and Associations. The Assembly of Governments will roughly resemble the General Assembly, although its role as a decision-making body will be increased and its internal pattern of operation may be influenced by the adoption of a weighted voting scheme.

There is no way to avoid the potential paralysis that might prevent a WA response in the event that the formal requirements for voting majorities could not be met. Some kind of emergency standby authority could be vested in a steering committee of the WA or in the Secretary General to keep a check on a deteriorating situation, if possible, until WA action is forthcoming; also, it should be possible to suspend the normal voting requirements by majority decision in each of the three chambers of the WA. But in the event that the Chambers reach incompatible or inconclusive results, then the WA may be unable to act at all. To forestall such a situation would require greater unification of power/authority than seems feasible or desirable. We are choosing, in effect, to subordinate considerations of *effectiveness* to those of *community consensus*.

COUNCIL OF PRINCIPALS

This new organ will be in continuous session and will be able (1) to propose action to implement valid WA decisions; (2) to take action in the event that the WA does not reach a decision; (3) to act in the event that one or more of the three chambers proclaims by majority vote that a state of "world emergency" exists; and (4) to act when power has been delegated by the WA.

The Council will be composed of the Secretary General and seven representatives from each of the three chambers; the commissioner of each specialized agency or his designated representative will participate in a non-voting capacity when the Council is dealing with subjects encompassed by his agency's activities. The Secretary General will vote only to break a tie.

The Council would be the main executive body with a normal responsibility for implementing directives of the World Assembly. The Council would have no power to question the validity of Assembly decisions, but it could delay implementation if the appropriate organ of the World Grievance System certifies in advance that a substantial question for review exists. The Council could also take emergency holding action until the Assembly is able to act with respect to rapidly deteriorating or dangerous situations in any of the four sectors of principal concern: peace and security, environmental quality, economic equity and relief, and human dignity.

The composition of the Council is designed both to reflect the mixed character of the emerging world order system—by including seven representatives from each of the chambers of the tripartite World Assembly, and to provide continuing coordination and oversight with respect to routine transactions and issues by providing for the participation of representatives from the main functional entities. The staff of the Secretariat will provide administrative back-up for the Council's work. Along with its recommendations, the Council can forward original proposals or suggestions for action by the Assembly; either the Council or the Assembly can seek studies or proposed courses of action from the Secretariat, which will assume, increasingly, the character of an international civil service. Members of the Secretariat will be given the opportunity (and perhaps at a later time will be required) to renounce, or perhaps better, to couple national citizenship with world citizenship.[4] This option will carry with it the right to travel with a World Passport.*

CENTRAL COORDINATING BOARD (CCB)

A Central Coordinating Board (CCB) will serve as a supervisory body to assure that directives of the WA and Council of Principals are carried out by other actors in the system. The CCB will be expected to make regular progress reports summarizing problems and achievements as-

---

* High mobility of people, ideas, and things would be an attribute of $S_{2(WOMP/USA)}$.

sociated with implementation. The CCB will also serve as a conduit for negative feedback that might even seek a modification of the initial mandate. For instance, if the WA has instructed World Security Forces to maintain checkpoints on the border between X and Y states, then it might receive feedback from the administering agency, or petitioners from X and Y, that the checkpoints are hampering trade without securing an embargo on arms shipment and should be accordingly revised in specific respects. Of course, the particularities of each context make it difficult to illustrate the real-world operations of the CCB, but its principal role would be to supervise and organize the information flow in both directions with respect to activities initiated by the central guidance capabilities, including the flow of information among various entities and individuals assigned a role in the overall concept of central guidance.*

The CCB might be initially staffed and departmentalized in relation to the four WOMP values. The Board itself would be constituted by fifteen men of international stature, five members to be elected by each of the three Chambers for three-year terms. One function of the Board would be to report back to the Assembly and Council on problems arising from incompatible directives, or to raise issues for further consideration whenever it appeared that directives were inconsistent with one or more of the four guiding values. For instance, if the Council prescribed a five-percent annual growth in GNP *as a condition* of eligibility for accelerated developmental assistance, it would seem to be strengthening pressures to maximize the output of goods and services at the expense of environmental protection. It would be important for the Board to discover and report such inconsistencies in normative impact to whichever body of the World Polity Association had initiated the directive. In general, the Board would not be a policy-making organ, but merely an institutional device to encourage effectiveness in the *process* of central guidance, and to maintain some kind of systematic concern about the relationship between the normative mandate (here associated mainly with realization of the WOMP values) † and the actual operation of the central formal actors in the world system.

---

* Despite our focus on the centralized or formalized sector of the central guidance capability, a continual effort will be made to disperse authority, function, and role as widely as possible. Facilitating such a sharing of participation will be an essential feature of stability and of the voluntary character of the World Polity Association.

† It would also be a part of the normative mandate to assure a continuing expansion of value horizons within the new world order. One feature of *dysutopia* is a sense of stagnancy. S_2, in our nomenclature, would be transitional to S_3. Maintaining a sense of

Another function of the Board would be to coordinate policy with any actor in the world system, when needed. In particular, on behalf of the central guidance system, the Board would process feedback from state or nongovernmental actors for distribution to participants in the relevant phase of work.

CENTRAL IMPLEMENTING STRUCTURE

There is a need to entrust distinct organizations with the separate tasks of implementing the directives of the political organs, maintaining contact with developments within the scope of special responsibility, and reporting back on progress and obstacles. We propose an organizational structure that reflects the normative mandate and whose activities are coordinated by a small administrative group called World Implementing Board (WIB). The WIB will be the basic link between the Council of Principals and the specific implementing organizations (vertical coordination) and among the separate implementing organizations (horizontal coordination).

The basic proposal here is to highlight the central actor's normative mandate by giving special institutional recognition to the four value goals. The more loosely linked functional actors also form part of the central sector of the central guidance system and contribute indirectly to the realization of the value goals. This kind of institutional differentiation is provided to convey an understanding of the organizational priorities that will exist in the 1990's (or whenever $S_{2(WOMP/USA)}$ might be realized); there is no intent to offer a blueprint of institutional design, an undertaking that would illustrate the fallacy of premature specificity. As is evident in Figure 4–6, the value goals entail certain organizational groupings. The scale and character of these organizations will be shaped in relation to the Organizing Principles, especially the Principle of Bureaucratic Effectiveness and the complementary and offsetting Principle of Bureaucratic Minimization. The buildup of an organizational presence at the center will be accompanied

---

dynamism, especially in terms of normative progress, would be an important dimension of activity in the World Polity Association. The human species needs always to feel it is developing toward an ideal point to avoid a serious sense of relapse and alienation. See note, pp. 400–01.

by an erosion of the authority/power nexus at the state level; therefore, the implementation of the normative mandate would not necessarily require enormous bureaucratic structures. At the same time, the existing structures will be operating on such a small scale—for example, their financial base—relative to the magnitude of world order tasks that some considerable expansion of budget, staff, and activities will be needed.*

WORLD SECURITY SYSTEM

The organizational entities clustered here will focus on minimizing large-scale violence. The Central Committee of the World Security System would be composed of the three Directors of the constituent implementing organizations: World Security Forces, World Disarmament Service, and World Grievance System. This Central Committee would try to coordinate activities directly related to war prevention. Obviously, the causes of international violence must be dealt with by activities situated elsewhere in the World Polity Association's overall power/authority nexus. The World Security System is needed only to buttress war prevention goals of S_2 and to act in the event of sporadic failures to maintain peace.†

World Security Forces

The task of the World Security Forces would be to maintain international peace under all possible circumstances. Its functions would include Peace Observation along troublesome frontiers or other trouble spots, and the coercive implementation of disarmament obligations

---

* However, a principle of maximum geographic dispersion will be part of the operating code of the World Polity Association. With a judicious use of computers and other technology it will be possible to combine administrative efficiency with decentralized organizational conceptions; with a judicious emphasis on mobility, this kind of decentralization can be combined with travel and with job rotation, to overcome a loss of personal identity and help achieve a widely shared feeling of global neighborhood.

† The main purpose of the World Security System would be one of *deterrence*, i.e., to deter military adventurism by irresponsible but not wholly irrational elements in the S_2 world.

should serious violations be verified by the World Disarmament Service. The World Security Forces could also undertake other missions if so authorized by votes in the World Assembly or the Council of Principals. Verified reports of abuses of human rights might well lead to humanitarian intervention under the revamped auspices of the central guidance mechanisms available.

The World Security Forces would try to operate as a police force rather than as an army.* A premium would be placed on effective action with minimum damage and loss of life. A great effort would be made to evolve weaponry that could temporarily and harmlessly neutralize—rather than kill, maim, or injure—hostile "targets." The success of such an effort would depend on the overall world climate, and especially on the extent to which disarmament would have prompted the abolition of national military establishments and turned grievance-oriented groups away from violent methods; it would also depend on the extent to which regional security forces would implement values relating to the minimization of violence. The character of the undertaking confronting the World Security Forces would also be influenced by the extent to which international disputes would be approached as occasions for nonviolent resolution.† This development would depend mainly on socializing governments into a new nonviolent grievance-resolution system; this process of socialization has been initiated with respect to the monopolization of violence by national governments in post-Medieval Europe, and by the gradual elimination of "the blood feud" from the settlement of private disputes.‡ Socialization in the use of a new settlement procedure is a slow process; relapses occur, its pace is uneven (varying according to the actors' relative world situations), and its progress depends on the extent to which the use of nonviolent grievance machinery appears to yield positive results. Does the griev-

---

* The distinction between army and police concepts is not always easy to draw in practice. We would emphasize, however, that World Security Forces would be expected to respect constitutional rights of individuals and groups and would be administered by civilian rather than military leaders.

† The rise of nonviolence as norm and as stratagem is extremely important as a conditioning factor during the transition period. There are two separate dimensions: first, the renunciation of violence; second, the development of a sophisticated approach to nonviolence—assuring its efficacity—and establishing a civic bargain by which neither advocates of change nor supporters of the status quo resort to threats of force or force itself.

‡ Of course, governments were motivated primarily by reasons of self-interest in their insistence on drastic, internal disarmament. The current controversies over gun control in the United States are concerned with how far this internal disarmament process shall be carried.

ance machinery sufficiently embody prevailing notions of equity to build confidence in the nonviolent paths to conflict resolution? Basic to this underlying movement away from violence as the energy of change, challenge, and control will be a perception that the world economic system is performing its distributive functions more justly (greater equality within and between states), and that it is successfully trying to eliminate extreme human privations. In this regard, the international elimination of violence is tied to the elimination of intranational violence; the value of minimizing violence is not made absolute in relation to other values. Furthermore, when in operation, all control mechanisms (including the World Security Forces) must place great emphasis on nonviolent strategies of policing, while regarding recourse to violence as a last resort. This will require the reorientation and redirection of the entire power/authority nexus toward the new prevalence of nonviolence.

The type of military equipment and the number of personnel involved are very difficult to project, partly because of technological uncertainties. It may be possible for many of the undertakings of the World Security Forces to rely on relatively non-intrusive electronic surveillance and incapacitation. For instance some, or conceivably all, borders might be monitored by a satellite observation system.

The most difficult issues for collective security in $S_{2(WOMP/USA)}$ would be posed by a well-armed adversary determined to engage in expansion by military means, and not amenable to nonviolent procedures nor even to rational deterrent pressures. What is to be done about "the Hitler problem" in the disarmed world of the 1990's, where the technological climate would enable even a relatively small-scale aggressor, possibly even a nongovernmental actor, to mobilize an immense destructive potential? The dilemma here is profound: either build up a relatively sophisticated nuclear-equipped capability at the global level, or subject the entire community to disruption, destruction, and conquest by a single actor.* With some major qualifications, we have decided to accept the latter risk as preferable to the creation of a highly efficient capacity for mass destruction located in the World Security Forces. We are confident that other steps can be taken to mitigate the Hitler problem in

---

* Another related issue is the degree of surveillance that will be needed to detect and control groups or individuals intent on disruption, nuclear blackmail, or even a military coup aimed at the central administration of the World Polity Association. Vulnerability will be considerable, but the political and human costs of guarding against it seem even greater. To embark upon effective surveillance would inevitably do away with the sense of individual liberty, which is dependent on a truly protected private realm.

S$_2$. Some kind of screening procedure might be agreed upon to identify dangerous psychological traits in aspiring leaders, reasonably discreet procedures possibly comparable to conflict-of-interest or loyalty checks now relied upon in the course of making appointments to high office in a large democratic society. Early warning procedures could also be established, and perhaps some challenge and removal arrangements could be agreed upon as a matter of global necessity. In any event, the avoidance of a Hitler problem is not something that can be categorically assured, while the creation of a huge fine-meshed security net could most likely provide only little protection but much interference with a desirable political atmosphere in S$_2$.

However, to provide a capability for dealing with pathological tendencies, it does seem desirable to maintain a minimal kind of nuclear deterrent under the control of several centers of power/authority at the regional and state levels. These residual nuclear forces—dispersed for reasons of effectiveness as well as to avoid providing the World Security Forces with any temptation to seek world domination—would act as a check against both encroachment by the central guidance system and the special danger of dealing with some principal variants of "the Hitler problem." This capability might consist of fifty missiles deployed far underground for survivability and reliability, and subject to activation only by the dual action of the repository authority and of the Director (or his deputy) of the World Security Forces.* Here, too, the pressure to deal with one set of risks generates another set. In this instance, the veto, in effect, given to the leadership of the World Security Forces, creates the possibility that a nuclear repository actor could be a member of a coalition seeking world domination. Such a possibility could either be countenanced, because of its unlikelihood, or the various repository actors could each be put in a dual control relationship with a distinct organizational official in the central guidance structure. It does not seem possible or necessary to carry the resolution of these issues any further at this early stage of speculation, beyond identifying some of these underlying complexities.

In military terms it would be desirable to pursue further such matters as nonviolent peace keeping missions, minimum-violence weaponry and tactics, and appropriate training for regular police units. The size of

---

* Note that one would want an indestructible deterrent that could not be fired too rapidly or too easily. As with any form of nuclear deterrence, the whole enterprise is beset by likely means/ends contradictions in the event that deterrence fails and the capability must either be used or withheld.

the permanent constabulary might be a police force of 200,000, or even less, supplemented by regional constabulary establishments of 50,000–75,000 and by much larger standby militia forces specially trained under national auspices for emergency international service. The whole orientation of the effort would be away from the notion of "fighting men" toward one of "peacemaking men." In fact, this constabulary might undertake most, if not all, of its functions without benefit of arms. These police forces would also regularly engage in emergency relief operations in disaster areas and help relieve hardships resulting from food shortages or disease. Rigorous training programs would be relied upon. Participation in these security activities would be a great honor and would be rewarded with high pay. Members would receive a sophisticated education and would be expected to be exemplary citizens of the World Polity.

World Disarmament Service (WDS)

We are assuming here that arrangements calling for drastic disarmament will have been agreed upon and at least partially, if not fully, implemented. The modalities of this disarmament process need not concern us here; the goal of disarmament will be to eliminate national military establishments. Residual and nominal nuclear arsenals of fixed specifications will be maintained in ten centers of power/authority, each subject to dual control activation and requiring the participation of a designated official, or his appointed deputy. The purpose of these arsenals will be to moderate fears that erratic behavior, by even a small actor, could disrupt the entire world order system in a totally disarmed environment. The basic mission of the World Disarmament Service would be to supervise the agreed process of disarmament, to report violations immediately to the World Security Forces and the Council of Principals, and to verify compliance with the terms of the disarmament arrangement so as to maintain confidence. The overall objective would be to provide reliable supervision with regard to disarmament, while minimizing the intrusion of inspectors on the life of the community. Sensor technology, surveillance at critical checkpoints associated especially with facilities that produce fissionable material, and a careful educational effort designed to delegitimize nuclear weaponry and military strategies should all provide effective, if imperfect, assurances in the preferred world. The role of cultural inhibitions on recourse to certain types of weaponry should not be understimated; delegitimized weaponry—for instance, poison gas and tools of biological warfare—has been rather effectively inhibited despite ease of access by both governmental and nongovernmental actors.

The WDS would be a branch of the professional international civil service. This civil service would be educated from an early age at several of the campuses of the World University, and would be trained at the specialized institute for professional disarmament trainees connected with a graduate program in International Administration.* The basic orientation of this personnel would involve the cosmopolitan values of the preferred world, but the program would not involve indoctrination or the imposition of rigid dogma. There would be general acceptance of the need for free inquiry, and above all, for the understanding that the preferred world is itself a transitional phase of the continuing search for improved world order. The main idea here is that the international civil service trained to deal with subject matter as sensitive as disarmament would be fully socialized into the overall belief system of the preferred world and would not, accordingly, tend to perpetuate coercive and hostile patterns of interaction in the course of discharging its official role.

This effort to keep the world disarmed presupposes some success with at least two other aspects of the preferred world's program: (1) substantial, perceived progress toward the realization of economic equality, and especially toward the alleviation of human misery and blatant exploitation; (2) widespread acceptance of the fairness and suitability of nonviolent approaches to conflict resolution and political management. These two central projects themselves depend on man's ability to achieve some kind of equilibrium with nature, especially regarding energy and resource consumption, and waste disposal procedures.† That is, disarmament's efficacy and acceptability is likely to depend largely on the acceptability of other aspects of the world order system.

---

* It would be important to develop a non-specialist training and education program for the entire civil service of the World Polity Association. The student and faculty would shift campuses to assure exposure to several world cultures during the course of education. Provision would have to be made to allow a sense of place and a feeling for family and locale to be part also of the long training and education process. In this way, job rotation would discourage the formation of entrenched elites or of a military caste within the WDS. Such a civil service concept could also serve as a model for a new approach to work in the world of S_2, and seems to far outweigh the case for specialization.

† The parameters of these ecological constraints are still uncertain for a variety of reasons associated especially with technological prowess and ethical consciousness. Will cheap, clean, abundant energy be made generally available? Will mankind evince concern for life prospects of future generations? Will reproduction rights be collectivized to some extent, i.e., determined as a matter of group policy toward population size?

Regional and nongovernmental actors could be given important roles in implementing the disarmament process, both to provide a "check" against unwarranted intrusion by the WDS and to augment central supervision with a regional capability that might be more familiar with particular causes of and cures for grievances.*

The WDS should alert the Implementing Board immediately if it detects (1) a verified violation of the basic terms of the disarmament undertaking, and (2) a political or social situation in which aggrieved parties seem to be contemplating using armed force, especially on a large scale. The initial communications should be confidential unless an emergency is deemed to exist by the investigators. An important consideration here is to employ pressures for nonviolent resolution before the parties commit themselves to armed force. Similarly, there should be an effort to avoid magnifying technical or nominal violations beyond their true character, and to create an atmosphere in which disputes involving the WDS can be resolved in a conciliatory way.

A government or individual that believes the WDS is exceeding its own competence could bring a complaint before the Central Commission of the World Grievance System. This Commission would hold a private hearing on the complaint, and in the event that parties could not agree and could present substantial evidence of abuse, would decide whether a more elaborate proceeding would be called for. All efforts at settlement would emphasize mediation. A more adversary posture would be taken only after clear indications that the preferred world's basic normative postulates were being repudiated. Until such repudiation became evident, the WDS would do its part to avoid coercive or self-righteous forms of international administration.

World Grievance System (WGS)

Our guiding presupposition is that conflict will persist in the preferred world of S2(WOMP/USA), but that its character will be increasingly expressed in nonviolent forms. We would emphasize that the socialization process of the transition interval would seek to discredit recourse to violence on both pragmatic and moral grounds, and to accord tech-

---

* Perhaps a private organization, comparable to the International Committee of the Red Cross, could play a large support role in relation to the World Security System, and, indeed, with regard to the entire gamut of activities of the World Polity Association. In this sense, a private, civic-minded association administered by individuals could be a model organizational form given greatly expanded roles and enhanced status in S2.

niques of nonviolence greater status with respect to both acceptability and effectiveness. Nonviolent tactics may be coercive, however, as in the case of a general strike, boycott, or mass demonstration. Such coercive strategies do seem consistent with the maintenance of a dynamic atmosphere of change in the preferred world.

Part of the reorientation toward dispute settlement requires more responsive institutional means of grievance resolution. We would downgrade the role of courts in this respect, because a judicial technique tends to be cumbersome and rigid in relation to the complex issues of controversy which are likely to bear on world order concerns. Courts depend on adversary presentations and tend to select the winning or "right" litigant; consequently, the judicial capacity to bring about compromises and mutually satisfying outcomes is exceedingly limited. Therefore, in dealing with disputes the WGS will be strongly disposed toward mediational procedures and flexible solutions. The principal role of courts within the World Polity Association will be to maintain constitutional restraints on the operation of its main organizational actors. Here, the adversary setting will help establish, maintain, and alter boundaries on the competence of these organizations to act. Such judicial scrutiny will be one of the integral "checks and balances" designed into the central guidance system, to protect the peoples of the world to the most practicable extent against unwarranted extensions of power/authority by world institutions.

In view of our preference for the most decentralized level of institutional involvement consistent with equity for the aggrieved parties, the WGS system will either rely upon regional chambers or work in conjunction with Regional Grievance Systems wherever appropriate. Also, specialized mediational units will be attached to particular functional actors concerned with technology, environment, resources, human rights, and international trade and investment. However, an appeal procedure will be available to enable any party dissatisfied with the outcome at the regional and specialized level to obtain review by the WGS.*

The activities of the WGS will be organized by a Central Commission of World Grievances. This Central Commission will review all grievances forwarded to it as best it can, both by maintaining an independent fact-finding service and by inviting the alleged wrongdoer or opponent to present a full statement on its position, including suggestions

---

* As with implementing procedures, provision for a grievance procedure organized by civic-minded citizens should be explicitly made. See parallel note, p. 250.

for further fact-finding. The Central Commission would seek only to certify the existence of a substantial grievance and to propose to the parties a recommended mode (or a choice of modes) of settlement. Any individual, nongovernmental organization, government, or intergovernmental institution could forward a grievance to the Central Commission. The Central Commission would certify the grievance as substantial if it found significant factual support for the aggrieved party's complaint and concluded that a world order issue was present. Any issue that dealt significantly with obstacles to the realization of the four WOMP values would be considered a world order issue.*

After the Central Commission certified the question for further action, a preliminary hearing would be held to consider procedural recommendations. The Commission's recommendations would be used to initiate discussions in the hearing. Each side would respond to these recommendations by accepting them, or modifying some aspects, or by proposing alternatives. The Commission's recommendations as to procedure would be binding only if the parties accepted them or could agree on no alternative. The Commission could also make use of an expedited procedure for resolution in the event that rapid action was essential.

If the facts were simple and more or less commonly perceived, the Commission might even recommend a compromise solution to the parties, although in this case there would be no compulsion to accept the recommendations.

The Commission could recommend any of several channels for settlement procedures:

Confidential Conciliation Council

World Conciliation Forum

Confidential Arbitration Council

World Arbitration Forum

In some cases, grievances can be more suitably resolved by confidential discussions, whereas other grievances arouse suspicion and resentment if kept secret. Therefore, if further action is needed, the Central Com-

---

* We realize that this is a broad mandate, perhaps overly so, but any narrowing down of competence at this point would seem arbitrary. The specific charters of competence entrusted to the various entities comprising the central guidance capability will have to be drafted in light of the specific concerns that predominate in the late stages of transition. See Chapter V.

mission should take a stand on this issue, which is subject to acceptance or rejection by the parties. A distinction should also be made between conciliation and arbitration, the former involving a passive third-party role and the latter a more active one.

In all important cases, implementation of an outcome of the grievance process will be left to the general machinery of the system. The Central Commission of the WGS will issue a report on implementation to the Implementing Board. Routine cases will be transferred by the Central Commission to the province of the World Security Forces to assure prompt realization of the outcome. As elsewhere, maximum emphasis will be placed on nonviolent, and indeed on non-coercive, procedures for implementation or a voluntaristic resolution of differences in the spirit of give-and-take that underlies WOMP values.

WORLD ECONOMIC SYSTEM (WES) *

The purpose of the WES would be to facilitate world economic development consistent with *considerations of well-being* (i.e., alleviating human misery), *equalizing* goals (i.e., promoting inter-group and intra-group equality of economic status), and *ecological balance* (i.e., assuring an equilibrium between human activity and ecological capacities regarding waste disposal and resource use; also, securing health and human satisfaction by exhibiting concern for environmental impacts).† These normative guidelines orient the mission of the WES. Given expected levels of international complexity and interrelatedness, it will also be essential to assure adequate central guidance with respect to the operation of the world economy. If the other goals are to be attained, the world economy must be kept as free as possible from the dangers of monetary crises, trade wars, protectionist policies, cartelizing tendencies, and drastic price fluctuations.

Pressures felt in the early 1970's for greater cooperation in the establishment and maintenance of an international economic system will reach dramatic proportions by the 1990's. Indeed, a major feature of the

---

* These sections on the WES should be read in conjunction with Chapter VI.

† The concern with ecological quality is dealt with directly in a series of sections beginning on p. 268. Here, we are merely concerned with making it evident that world economic policy could not be evolved in an ecological vacuum.

WOMP preferred world will be to shift control over economic policy away from governmental actors, especially with respect to economic relations among the more advanced industrial countries, and in the broad links between national societies at different levels of industrial and technological development. National governments will retain large measures of discretion over the domestic economic organization and priorities chosen to help move their respective societies toward acceptable levels of mass consumption.*

By the 1990's the entire world economy will be an integrated whole, although with different levels of development. The relative insulation of the socialist sector which now exists will virtually disappear as a feature of the world economy.

The transition period will cause many difficulties in economic policy. The logic of international rivalry is opposed to cooperative policy-making, and will therefore introduce pressures to thwart moves for an integrated, economically just and eco-supporting economy. Given, for instance, the unevenness of wage levels, it is difficult to obtain competitive parity in world trade without recourse to protectionist policies. To avoid persistent distortions in the healthy growth of the world economy, a successful world movement to secure equal pay for equal work will have to take place.† One goal of the preferred world is to maximize mobility of people and ideas, as well as goods and services. The emerging technology, including the further refinement of compu-

---

* Both the market and the plan, as organizing concepts, will be regarded as compatible with WOMP/USA. No necessary conclusions are drawn about whether and under what conditions social ownership of the means of production at the national level is a world order issue. The value impacts of real world state socialism and state capitalism are both problematic, although for different principal reasons, and we offer no assured image of the nature of economic reforms needed at the national level as part of the transition process to $S_{2(WOMP/USA)}$. In our view the variation in national circumstances is so great that no single reform pattern is very relevant. None of the current world ideologies have yet devised satisfactory solutions for the formidable problems of distribution of goods and services, the elimination of waste through manipulation of consumer taste, the conservation of scarce resources, the promotion of aesthetic forms of industrial development, and the need to make work more satisfying for the worker.

† If such a movement takes place too unevenly from country to country, it distorts trading options and gives the socially regressive economies a competitive advantage as a result of their lower wage scales. These distortions may produce prosperity for the regressive economies and high unemployment recessions for the more enlightened economies. If such results then stimulated a reaction, a negative learning experience (from the WOMP perspective) would be likely to encourage a repudiation of enlightened policies. Therefore, an early consensus on issues of social equity would be helpful in facilitating a smooth transition process in the WOMP direction.

ters, provides the basis for integrating the world economy into a functioning whole that serves rather than undermines the values of the new world order system. A committee composed of directors of the separate organs will coordinate the activities of the WES. This committee will refer problems of wider scope to the Central Coordinating Board, which will then recommend further action if a voluntary resolution of the difficulties cannot be achieved.

The main components of the WES respond to familiar divisions in world economic policy: trade, development, and money. In addition, special bureaus would be established to deal with global aspects of technological development (especially its economic effects; environmental effects will be dealt with by the World System for Ecological Balance, p. 268), and with issues of economic planning and equity (how to develop and maintain a steady-state world economy, and how to implement goals of human welfare and equality).

World Monetary and Tax
Policy Council (WMTPC)

We assume that in S_2 there will be a single paper currency that can be used anywhere in the world for international transactions. As a consequence there will be no problems associated with exchange rates and balance of payments. However, some schedule will be needed to regulate the amount of money in circulation and to establish the original distributive ratio of relative values and quantities. Also, rules governing the movement of money may need to be established to protect societies against short-term liquidity crises and longer-term structural challenges involving chronic money shortages or gluts. We shall assume, however, that these problems have been more or less solved, and that the principal task of the WMTPC will be to regulate the quantity of money in circulation. Obviously a government can go bankrupt in such a system by being unable to pay for all of its purchases, or by pursuing a precarious set of economic policies. National governments will not be allowed to increase the money in circulation except by a grant of authorization from the WMTPC, but there would have to be "special drawing rights" arrangements to provide buffers against contingencies.*

---

* If these "contingencies" were structural or chronic, strains and resentments would grow. It is not clear whether such a prospect would require some rights on the global level to exercise an extraordinary power of economic supervision with respect to national policies.

The WOMP values will guide the activities of the WMTPC in accord with the basic commitment to move toward a steady state world economy.* Since this commitment needs to be reconciled with raising and equalizing living standards throughout the world, transfers of money or other forms of wealth from the rich to the poor sectors of the world economy must occur.† Close coordination between a world taxing authority and the policy on the circulation of money will be needed as well. We have combined these two functions in a single institutional setting.

The tax division will obtain revenue from:

1. Internationally administered activities, including licenses granted to withdraw minerals from the sea bed or the ocean floor

2. A graduated progressive tax payable by all governmental and non-governmental organizational entities eligible to participate in the Assembly of Organizations and Associations.

3. A direct personal tax levied on incomes above a certain level, possibly to be collected by national governments on behalf of the world institutions ‡

The revenue obtained by the WMTPC will be used to pay for the activities of the World Polity Association and to promote such world order goals as the elimination of poverty, the equalization of individual and group living standards, and the preservation of the environment. The budget of the World Polity Association will be prepared by its Secretariat and then submitted to the separate chambers of the World As-

---

* The image of a steady-state is derived largely from the need to reconcile economic development with ecological quality. Satisfying this need may not be tantamount to "no growth," but only to "no dangerous growth," "no depleting growth," or "no wasteful growth." It would still be possible to develop the service side of national output at a rapid rate in all parts of the world.

† High degrees of factor mobility might accomplish the same result in a more efficient and less coercive manner. If labor, capital, and managerial skill were allowed to flow freely in the world system, equalizing tendencies would be automatically enhanced. But such a flow, aside from reversing the protectionist ethos which is as old and as fundamental as the state system itself, would presuppose equality of education and of other forms of human development. In conceptualizing our image of the economic order in our preferential model, it is best at this stage to rely on a combination of approaches; thus, both transfers of wealth and income and increases in factor mobility will be necessary and desirable transition features that will persist in S_2.

‡ Perhaps, here too, a nongovernmental association of citizen benefactors would be the most appropriate agency of tax collection, i.e., building upon and extending the concept of the International Committee of the Red Cross.

sembly for approval; disagreements among the chambers will be worked out in a conference committee, if possible, and by vote of the World Assembly as a whole, if necessary.

The WMTPC can recommend increases or decreases in either money supply or in tax rates to the Council of Principals. If the Council approves these recommendations, they will be submitted to the World Assembly for debate and concurrence. Changes will not go into effect without World Assembly concurrence.

The details of tax and monetary policy cannot be worked out very well in advance. For one thing, the transition will be very important in shaping attitudes about the role and scale of central guidance in relation to the world money supply, and to the use of tax policy for redistributing wealth and income within the world system. For another, it is difficult to anticipate the appropriate fiscal policies for a steady-state economy. To avoid freezing inequities into the preferred world, it will be essential to blend notions of "steady-state" with those of distributive equity. One strategy of mediation between these two positive goals would be to plan geographical shifts in certain ecologically burdensome growth-oriented activities to induce negative economic growth in the rich sectors of international society, while sustaining economic development in the poor sectors of international society. Obviously, such a redirection of economic growth in the post-industrial world is of fundamental importance and appears to challenge the whole image of human progress based on the increase of material goods and services.* The net effects on individual living standards below the level of super-affluence would be deferred as long as possible, and very hopefully avoided altogether.† Thus, even for rich countries, continuing progress

---

* Certain forms of growth would have to be eliminated in moving toward some variant of a steady-state world economy, but development could continue to proceed in all sectors of the world economy, including those which are currently existing at the highest consumption standards. Such development would involve redirected economic effort and might not be fully disclosed by current GNP accounting. New indicators, more closely related to revised views of economic development for advanced and affluent industrial societies, will have to be devised to measure more qualitative forms of progress. Also, we need to evolve an array of steady-state images of the global economy analogous to what we have depicted in Chapter III with regard to authority patterns. Such an endeavor deserves high priority in future studies. Let me reiterate that steady-state in our usage does not entail "no growth" or economic stagnancy. The idea of steady-state is conceived in deference to the notion of maintaining or even enhancing ecological quality. See Chapter VI, pp. 397–405.

† Such an assertion depends on readjusted measuring criteria. For instance, the substitution of bicycles for cars in certain urban situations might involve an increase in living standards even if it were accompanied by a decline in disposable income. If one can live *better* with less income, then living standards have increased despite falling income.

in improving the quality of life and raising living standards could accompany annual declines in the gross national product and even in
average disposable income.

The realization of these policy objectives requires considerable planning at all levels of social organization in the world. The learning process that will have preceded the acceptance of a steady-state world
economy as the basis of planetary well-being would include some conscious effort to redirect economic priorities in socially useful directions.* There is no reason to suppose that careful adjustments in priorities cannot combine a steady-state Gross Planetary Product (GPP) with
dramatic national progress for all societies. Of course, such economic
stability would be accompanied by a commitment to a demographic
steady-state system, and by other adjustments in life-style such as restrictions on the types and numbers of vehicles available for private
transportation. In all of these areas of concern it would be desirable to
implement the global policies of the WMTPC by regional, national, and
private efforts, and to rely upon tax and monetary policy as a tool of
dual economic reform. Achieving growth or decline would depend on
national position; growth, as such, would be regarded as less important
than improvement of the qualitative and distributive aspects of GNP
and GRP (Gross Regional Product). The reliance on planning should not
disaffirm the values of diversity, including especially individual freedom; tax and monetary policies should not seek rigid policy outcomes,
but should encourage broad shifts of priorities. The basis of these
priorities should be open to continuous reexamination. The preceding
period of transition will have shaped the political consciousness of society in such a way as to discredit the gospel of economic growth per se,
and to convey the sense that at this historical stage of human development, human progress requires continuous emphasis on *qualitative* and
distributive issues, rather than on *quantitative* and *material* indicators
alone.† Criteria of waste, corruption, and superfluity consequently
become central social issues for the politics of the near future. The cen-

---

* The character of the learning process, especially the extent to which it includes
responses to ecological and economic trauma, will condition the effort to reorder priorities at every stage. There are various modes of learning that can be roughly categorized as
educational and experiential.

† While we reject an uncritical endorsement of GNP criteria of development for any national economy, we are especially concerned with new measures of development for
richer sectors of the world economy. Where privation persists material requirements need
to be satisfied as a matter of urgent priority, but uncritical GNP thinking is still inappro-
priate as it overlooks the entire distinction between socially useful and socially wasteful
outputs.

tral role of the WMTPC is to provide leadership for this kind of reorientation by its policies in the ultra-symptomatic areas of monetary and tax policy.

World Economic Planning and
Equity Council (WEPEC)

The WEPEC will study the underlying economic position of the preferred world order system in $S_{2(WOMP/USA2)}$. It will be constituted by fifteen officials, five of whom will be elected by each chamber of the World Assembly for staggered six-year terms. The main job of the WEPEC will be to report back to the political organs on the degree of progress achieved toward realizing a desirable variant of a steady-state economy and on the particular obstacles to the eradication of inequities. In this capacity, the WEPEC needs to have a reasonably large staff of civil servants who will maintain a liaison with significant governmental and nongovernmental centers of activity throughout the world. They will also engage in investigative reporting to ascertain how the reorientation of economic activity is taking hold. Implementing the new economics will require excellent feedback mechanisms to permit early identification of problems, prompt responses, and curative remedies.

In the early years of the twenty-first century, the poor sectors of international society will probably still have "growth economies" as measured by current GNP yardsticks, but subject to qualitative standards of control.* Part of the task of the WEPEC will be to minimize adverse impacts of world economic policy on goals of well-being such as full employment and meaningful work anywhere in the world system. Perhaps these adverse impacts can be minimized partly by relying on the international mobility of labor, although the human costs of such mobility may be too high; these questions will have to be confronted in the context of world consciousness at that time.† Attitudes that now

---

* We intend no implication that poorer societies are less sensitive, even at present, to qualitative dimensions of growth than are the richer ones. In fact, China and Tanzania, although exceedingly poor in per capita GNP terms, have demonstrated a remarkable capacity to evolve economic policies that emphasize the qualitative side of development. It is those societies with little concern for the welfare of their populations *as a whole* that seem most committed to measuring national development by GNP rates of increase.

† These costs are mainly associated with rootlessness. It may be possible, if travel is cheap enough, to combine job mobility with a sense of place, enabling the positive side of cosmopolitanism to be integrated with a specific feeling for homeland, neighborhood, and family. It is also possible that the increasing mobility of capital will bring opportunity to where workers and resources are available.

exist will be altered or will be in a condition of flux by the time S_2 comes into being so that currently unacceptable policies may seem more acceptable. If national boundaries diminish in significance, movement across them for purposes of work and habitation may seem less objectionable, particularly if by then the cultural basis of "a global village" is widely shared. Ultimately, the acceptability of mobility depends on making credible progress in equalizing living standards. We project a world setting by the year 2000 in which abject poverty has been substantially reduced everywhere, and in which there is persuasive evidence that equalizing and humanizing trends are being implemented throughout the world system.

On the basis of extensive data collection, the WEPEC will prepare statistical projections setting forth national, regional, and world-wide targets for the future. These statistical surveys will emphasize *distributive* indicators of national income, and not just *aggregate* national accounts. The aspirational goals for the preferred world will seek to limit income inequalities among nations to a 10:1 ratio, with the base income set at a level designed to assure an adequate living standard.* The base income may vary from country to country, depending on the degree to which government services are freely provided and upon the kind of life-style associated with adequate living standards. Notions of national and regional equity will be formulated initially on a local level to assure the preservation of diverse living forms and to provide as much human participation as possible in the creation of world standards. Discrepancies in the formulation of national criteria of adequacy will be dealt with first at a regional level by a committee composed of national representatives. The WEPEC can also question the proposed national and regional standards. If negotiated agreements cannot deal with such issues of equity, either side can call for public hearings to consider arguments that relate to levels of adequate living standards and to proposed plans for attaining economic goals.

The WEPEC will also have a Commission competent to arbitrate disputes about planning activities and equity standards. This Commission will attempt to assess grievances and make recommendations to the WEPEC regarding revision of its practices and policies. The Commission's findings can be appealed to a specialized judicial organ

---

* Domestic ratios of individual incomes will be a matter of national policy, provided only that internal distribution patterns satisfy the globally protected human rights of individuals to receive the fundamental resources of money, materials, and opportunity needed for a decent existence. The establishment of such a threshold will be an imperative, if controversial, task.

within the World Grievance System or by petitioning any of the three assemblies of the World Assembly.

World Trade System (WTS)

The WTS will seek to assure that trade flows promote WOMP values to the greatest extent possible. In particular, the terms of trade will be shaped to some degree by redistributive and equalizing objectives. Trade regulations will also impose world duties on the transfer of goods that seem not to promote better living standards, but merely to embellish life with ornaments of super-affluence.* Thus, considerations of ecology, as well as of justice, will determine world trade policy. At the same time, the positive merit of diverse social orders will be protected by the WTS as fully as possible.

The WTS will have a basic commitment to free trade.† However, national, regional, or transnational actors will be able to seek special import tariffs or export subsidies if sound arguments along the four value dimensions can be advanced. The WTS will also try to avoid social injuries arising from shifts in trade patterns. A capital fund might be made available to reduce impacts on employment or national earnings arising from abrupt shifts in buying and selling patterns which stem from such diverse causes as the development of synthetic products, or the prohibition of imported items falling below environmental purity standards (e.g., fish containing lead or DDT).

The WTS might also have a research and analysis division that would identify opportunities for constructive trade expansions and help to capitalize related investments, either through its own lending resources or by recommendations to the banking division of the World Development Office. Such investment activities should be shaped by normative standards relating to the attainment of WOMP goals and, more generally, to the establishment of the overall conditions for an optimal man/nature equilibrium.

---

* At the same time, the objective is not some form of global austerity. Given value priorities, diversity in life-style preferences should be indulged to whatever extent possible. However, we do take a position of generalized opposition to "fashion" and "advertising" which encourage waste of resources and shallow horizons of personal aspiration.

† The whole image of "trade" may alter greatly over the next several decades, depending on the extent that business operations are multinationalized to embrace the entire world economy.

The WTS will also have a Commission that can hold public hearings on any aspect of trade policy which generates controversy. A conciliation mechanism that parallels in all respects the procedures already described on pp. 257–259 for the WEPEC will be established to expedite accommodations without assessing responsibility.

In general, the character of the world trade framework will be vastly altered by the underlying climate of the 1990's and by the diminished status of national governments as policy-making actors for economic affairs.

World Technology Board (WTB)

The WTB will provide general policy supervision in relation to technological development. Its basic role will be to stimulate beneficial applications of technology and to discourage or prevent detrimental applications throughout the world system. It will coordinate its activities with the World System for Ecological Balance. The WTB will formulate recommendations and submit reports to the Implementing Board in the event that specific action is required. The WTB will be made up of fifteen specialists selected by vote, five each from the three chambers of the World Assembly elected from a list of fifty submitted by a designated roster of world scientific, engineering, and humanistic centers of activities.

The WTB will be expected to assess information about potential harm and benefits from present and proposed technological applications, and to draw policy conclusions therefrom. The WTB will be empowered to hold public hearings, to create task forces of experts, and to seek cooperation from other international actors. The WTB can also recommend that the World Forum and Regional Forums consider a particular problem arising out of discovered social costs of specific applications of technology. Underlying the work of the WTB will be its mandate to promote the realization of WOMP values and to encourage the establishment of a multi-dimensional condition of *dynamic equilibrium* between man and the world environment (involving people, resources, wastes). A more specific mandate will involve a continuous scrutiny of human activity that could have ultra-hazardous consequences. If the WTB concludes that ultra-hazardous consequences might ensue, then the issue would be brought before the Council of Principals and the questionable undertaking could be suspended for an interim period of thirty, sixty, or ninety days. In other words, there should be community participation in any action that might endanger life or health on earth. This kind of risk should be accepted, if at all, only on the basis of careful assessment and shared responsibility.

Of course, the WTB might have to restrict the rate and character of technological development in ways that might occasionally prove costly in terms of material output. On other occasions, the WTB might pioneer technological advances that could be more rapidly developed and applied as a result of its research and development role.* However, the basic operating premise for the WTB is that improving the quality and distribution of output are far more important in the world of the future than mere quantitative increases. Indeed, an equilibrium goal for gross planetary product (GPP) presupposes such a shift in concerns, as well as the development of new indicators of progress. The fundamental reorientation of community attitudes toward technological development requires a considerable effort at clarification in the preferred world of the 1990's. The blind pro-technology bias of several centuries needs to be reshaped for the sake of ecological balance and for the promotion of humanistic values—but without impairing equalizing tendencies within and between countries, and without hampering the effort to alleviate human misery.[5] Such a shift in technological priorities requires an enormous readjustment in attitudes and behavior in the most advanced countries, but it does not require any wholesale rejection of technology.† The WTB can contribute to this reorientation by sponsoring studies, conferences, and publications dealing with these concerns. Also, the WTB could propose subsidies or loans to provide economic incentives for shifting the energies of technological innovation and application in the direction of the new value framework associated with $S_{2(WOMP/USA)}$.

---

* The WTB would seek to develop an even-handed view of technology as potentially, but not necessarily, harmful or destructive of human development. The WTB could play an increasing R and D role, either through its own laboratories or by selective grants to research and development units throughout the world. The ICRC model previously described could again play an important role in this context.

† Confusion arises because the ecology movement has generated a certain amount of free-floating hostility against technology *per se*. Such hostility has contributed to creative experiments with simplified life-styles outside of or on the edge of the mainstream money economy in principal market societies. Such experiments contribute to diversity and opportunities for human choice, but they do not provide societal standards for governing the status and role of technology. Our approach is governed by an instrumental view of technology; that is, that the net social effects of technology are determined by the wisdom and values of those who provide oversight. Judgments as to benefits and burdens have to be made in each controversial instance, both as to innovation and the range of applications, e.g., a new kind of dam may be needed for the Nile, but would produce disaster in other river systems.

World Development Office (WDO)

The WDO would be constituted in the same manner as the WTB. In addition, nominations would be secured from institutions with particular interests in economic development. The WDO would try to discern and encourage beneficial development patterns in these separate respects:

Growth for poor countries

Equalizing tendencies in all countries and between each major sector

Alleviation of mass misery

Qualitative improvement in the character of GNP

The WDS would be divided into three main divisions:

1. Capital assistance and labor mobility programs
2. Policy guidance studies and recommendations
3. Studies of work and working conditions

The annual activities of each division would be planned in advance and acted upon by the WDO as a whole. The capital assistance and labor mobility priorities and plans would be based on broad mandates formulated by the World Assembly and given more precision by the Council of Principals and the Implementing Board. Interpretations by the WDO would be guided also by the normative goals of the 1990's. The idea of beneficial development would be dominated by the concepts of work for human development rather than for industrial output, and production for *needs* rather than for wants; the concept of need would be flexibly developed with due regard for the positive effects of diversity of life-style upon the social milieu. Major research and analysis efforts would be made to improve the conditions of work along a series of different dimensions, including safety, satisfaction, and personality development. The effort to safeguard future generations from ecological deterioration would receive high priority. The WDO would administer a world-wide program of seminars and discussions to elicit widespread participation in formulating development priorities and boundaries.

WORLD SYSTEM FOR HUMAN DEVELOPMENT

At the very center of concern in the WOMP/USA vision of a preferred world lies a commitment to the process of improving the quality of human life. Part of this commitment will involve exploring the nature of "improvement" under contemporary conditions. The great English historian, Macaulay, exhibited a characteristic early enthusiasm for the value of technology when he observed that mankind would be benefitted morally and intellectually by each improvement of the means of locomotion. We no longer possess such confidence. We now know that technological advance does not necessarily enhance the quality of life, and that material or quantitative indicators of growth may, at certain stages of economic development, be inversely correlated with qualitative indicators.

The need to define goals for mankind will be a continuing feature of human existence in S_2. "The great unfinished business" of the preferred world will be to complete the transition from growth dynamics to equilibrium dynamics. Such a transition needs to be accomplished so as to maximize the prospects of development for social groups and for individuals. These prospects will be partly realized by the growth of a new political consciousness around WOMP values. Such a shift will help offset the depressant effects of negative growth GNP quotas. It will be necessary to cope with problems of man's identity under conditions of rapid change, especially those associated with scientific progress and technological innovation. A major challenge in the technological milieu of the future will be to design work which helps fulfill human potential and provides workers with a sense of satisfaction.

The development of man would become a special focus of concern in the preferred world; implementation of this concern depends initially on the availability of adequate models and procedures for discussion. Our goal would be to shape policies of importance for human development around innovations compatible with the progressive realization of human potential while reshaping, restricting, or even prohibiting those that were not. The programs of several existing international institutions such as the International Labor Office and the World Health Organization are relevant to this endeavor and need to be closely tied into the undertaking of the World System for Human Development.

World Forum of Long-Range Planning
for Human Development

This Forum will attempt to provide wide-ranging opportunities for exchanging ideas about the emergent future, by sponsoring activities such as conferences on specialized subjects, book translations, a journal in the major languages of the world, and films and programs on satellite television. Its objective would be to build international understanding by analyzing different perspectives on world order issues, goals, and procedures throughout the world. Therefore, this undertaking would seek both to enlighten mankind and to provide people of diverse cultures with intellectual tools for participation in the process of shaping the future of world order.

The World Forum would have a small professional staff that would orient its activities in response to the directives of a Council of Notables, perhaps drawn partly from recipients of Nobel Peace Prizes and partly, perhaps, by a lottery of all world citizens interested in belonging to the Council.* Individuals, associations, or governments could submit reports to the World Forum and petition the Forum to place a particular issue on the agenda of semi-annual meetings of the Council of Notables. The same right of membership would be given to all actors in the World Polity Association. This Council would set general priorities for the staff in terms of budget and educational activities, and it would organize the preparation of reports bearing on the long-range development of mankind. The Council would not try to impose its own judgments, but would seek rather to identify issues and problems and report on popular attitudes, patterns of response, and innovative approaches.

The Forum's main purpose is to achieve an explicit and systematic awareness of the future as a time span which will be affected by planning freedom and unforeseen developments. The normative focus is overt, but not static in content; the process of trying to chart more desirable directions of human development is never-ending. The preferred world would start off with the view that human fulfillment has to do with the adequacy of material and social opportunities for maximizing personal and group realization, and with the spiritual, cultural, and political opportunities for maximizing moral growth and individual creativity. Animating all of the World Forum's inquiries will be the question, "What makes life worth living?" In one sense the primary criterion of achievement in the preferred world will be the extent to which prevailing answers to this question are actualized in the life experiences of most people. "How many people find life worth living?" is a more utilitarian way of measuring minimal success and progress within the system. Higher goals of satisfaction and fulfillment should also be kept in mind.

One of the central value conflicts in the future, posed by new potentialities of electronic techniques, will be between *efficiency* and *privacy*.

---

* The recruitment criteria here would combine issues of efficiency with those of widely shared success. A major challenge in S_2 will be whether it will be possible to avoid elitism in the discharge of principal tasks.

It might become possible to have virtually perfect surveillance of individual behavior, but only by depriving individuals of sanctuaries wherein living experiments, including deviant ones, may be carried on with relative security.* Stifling such initiative may impose an oppressive burden of conformism, mechanism, and anxiety on the world of the future. Encouraging diversity and indulging some measure of disorder may be a low price to pay for keeping alive the creative and personal sides of life-patterns. In any event, this is the kind of issue that the World Forum should open up for full consideration.

Regional Chambers of the World Forum would be established along similar lines, to encourage regional perspectives on human development, interaction at the regional level, and continuing interchange with the World Forum. These Regional Chambers could also consider issues and proposals that had been brought before the World Forum.

The overall objective of this long-range planning undertaking would be to initiate multi-media town meetings on a global scale to deal with all facets of human development. The seriousness of the enterprise would depend on whether there was a general appreciation of the need and desirability of actively conceiving and planning responses to emerging problems of man and society.

World Forum for Human Development

This second World Forum will take up world order issues currently before other institutions in the Central Guidance System. Unlike the Central Coordinating Board, whose function it would be to keep track of various formal initiatives in the different organs of the World Polity Association, the World Forum for Human Development would appraise and influence current undertakings in terms of their impact on human development. The policy-making process would thus receive an input that is explicitly responsive to considerations of alternate lines of policy and decision on human development. Again, as with the long-range planning Forum, the image of human development will combine material and nonmaterial considerations. Particular emphasis will be placed

---

* The incentives and popular pressures for such surveillance may grow strong if disruptive terror by private groups becomes even more widespread than it is at present. Whether it will be possible to provide a grievance machinery that works well enough to discourage adoption of desperate strategies of terror is unclear. This uncertainty casts a pall over the prospects of creating a satisfactory balance between civil liberties and community security in $S_{2(WOMP/USA)}$.

on the impact that environment at work and home can have for health
and personality growth. Some effort will be made to plan all forms of
physical construction so as to facilitate the development of personality
and character along WOMP lines, while realizing that minimum provision of the necessities of life is a pre-condition for efforts to improve the
nonmaterial dimensions of life experience. Architects would become
critical actors in the World Polity Association.

The members of the Council of the World Forum will be nominated
by a Panel of Notables constituted perhaps by the Council of Notables
of the World Forum on Long-Range Planning. This Panel will nominate
at least fifty candidates who will then be voted upon by the entire membership of the three chambers of the World Assembly. The thirty nominees receiving the highest votes will be elected; each delegate can
vote for ten members.* Those elected will serve ten-year terms. The
Council will be assisted by a technical staff.

The World Forum will issue reports to other organs of the World
Polity Association, especially the Central Coordinating Board, either in
response to requests or on its own initiative. It will also receive petitions of concern and schedule hearings as appropriate from any entity
or individual in the world.

The Regional Chambers will seek to elicit regional views on the consequences for human development of existing or proposed policies of
the Central Guidance System. They will report to the World Forum,
which can then request an assessment of regional attitudes bearing on
given issues of human development. The main activity of the World
Forum on Human Development will consist of assessing current proposals, policies, and decisions throughout the World Polity Association
and of conveying to other organs concerns about human development.
Its reports will be published and made as widely and cheaply available
as possible.

World Commission and Court of Human Rights

The World Commission of Human Rights will receive all complaints
regarding abuses of human rights. Those complaints that have sub-

---

* The avoidance of elitist recruitment patterns is also a consideration here. Perhaps
some proportion of the Forum members should be selected from tax lists or electoral voting rolls, although such a process may not produce useful results unless accompanied by
other qualifications such as education, interest, and moral consciousness.

stance, in relation to world standards, will be investigated to assess the factual accuracy of specific allegations. The Commission will have the right to take depositions, hold hearings, and interview individuals. Non-cooperation or perjury will be regarded as an international delinquency which will be apprehended in the first instance by national courts. If the volume of complaints exceeds the Commission's capacity to deal responsibly with them, scheduling choices will have to be made by the Commission staff. These choices should be acknowledged and justified in the annual report of the Commission (which will be forwarded to the Implementing Board of the World Polity Association for review).

The Commission will prepare decisions that combine findings and recommendations. Any party alleged to be infringing upon internationally protected rights will be given an opportunity to explain his position. The domestic grievance structure, including informal privately administered procedures, will be urged to investigate situations where action seems appropriate, and each issue will be kept under scrutiny by the Commission until satisfaction is obtained. Each annual report will include an account of the disposition and progress of complaints and petitions that resulted in recommendations for rectifying action.

Failure by national institutions to implement the Commission's decision within a stated period would generate a right of recourse to the World Court of Human Rights. This Court would be structured to encourage flexible modes of conflict resolution, and to move away from rigid adjudication which explicitly seeks to determine "winners" and "losers." Rather, the Court would attempt to secure from both sides a "consent decree" that would appear to uphold the human rights claim, and to assure maximum publicity and visibility for any continuing abuse or delay in rectification. The process of accommodation should involve participation by all concerned groups, and possibly even a right of intervention on behalf of other claimants alleging analogous abuses. In addition to a specific complaint about noncompliance, the Court could be empowered to issue supplemental decrees that suggest applications of its judgment to other situations of human rights abuse falling within the same category of prohibition. Objections to such a decree would be considered at hearings convened shortly after the decision. These hearings would give an objecting party a day in court and yet minimize the prospects of repetitious litigation. Judicial craftsmanship, perhaps reinforced by fact-finding masters and advisers, would help create confidence in the reliability of this innovation in the scope of adjudication.

We are assuming that the period of transition to S2 (WOMP/USA) will see a great strengthening of the explicit commitment to minimum protection of the human person and to the pursuit of racial, sexual, religious, and economic quality. In this altered atmosphere, the threat and actuality of disclosure should help significantly to discourage blatant abuse. If such values have not become sufficiently pervasive to support these standards, then prospects for eliminating large-scale violence and misery from international life would also be doomed. Institutional intervention cannot realistically be expected to do more than reinforce existing attitudinal and behavioral trends, and introduce marginal pressure for compliance with basic norms. Such a modest role for institutional intervention is particularly likely in relation to the protection of human rights.

Of course, adherence may be uneven throughout the world, even if the basic shift in values takes place by the 1990's. The work of the Commission and Court is to diminish this unevenness as rapidly as possible and to generate responses by the more political organs of the Central Guidance System.

The ten-man Commission will be appointed by the Secretary General of the World Polity Association, subject to confirmation by the World Assembly. Confirmation will require a two-thirds vote; hearings will be normally held before a Joint Committee on Human Rights of the Assembly. The five-man Court will be elected by the World Assembly for nine-year terms, from a list of ten nominees submitted by the Panel of recipients of the Nobel Peace Prize, or some comparably oriented group, hopefully with less elitist connotations.

WORLD SYSTEM FOR ECOLOGICAL BALANCE

The basic challenge confronting WOMP/USA's model of the preferred world will be to achieve an orderly and humane transition from a growth orientation to an equilibrium orientation. As we have already indicated, this transition process will need to go on—perhaps at an accelerated pace—after the preferred world order system has already been established. The transition to equilibrium is motivated, above all else, by the need to avert eco-catastrophe and to safeguard the life-prospects of subsequent generations by sustaining ecological balance. It would also be motivated by goals such as environmental protection (including the maintenance of bio-diversity) and enhancement of the quality of life for groups and individuals. The optimum level of equilibrium may involve long-term maintenance of "excess capacity" beyond what is needed to sustain life at present levels.

These ideals involve complex economic, political, and ethical issues. It is essential to understand the alternative patterns of costs which would arise from various possible ways of stabilizing the world economy within the next fifty or sixty years. Furthermore, it is desirable to mobilize a consensus on both means and goals as early as possible. Finally, the prospects for equalizing world living standards must be examined in the course of the transition process. The radical redistribution that this implies will have to be initiated during the transition in ways which elicit the participation of the richest and most powerful actors. Therefore, the redistribution process will probably have to assume that self-interest will continue to motivate action, and consequently must be buttressed by arguments showing that qualitative increases in GNQ (Gross National Quality) will more than offset quantitative declines in GNP. Achieving adequate indicators of GNQ and related accounting measurements thus become essential aspects of this venture, both for building confidence and minimizing opposition.

Therefore, the work of the World System for Ecological Balance is much more fundamental than maintaining environmental quality and conserving resources. Its work will require close coordination with other parts of the Central Guidance System and some directives as to priorities from the principal political organs of the World Polity Association. Implementation will be a crucial issue. State sovereignty may wage its final rearguard struggle around the policies recommended for achieving ecological equilibrium.

World Environment Authority (WEA)

The WEA will be a specialized agency concerned with the maintenance of environmental quality. It will deal specifically with issues of pollution, waste disposal, climate change, disaster control, endangered species, and such concerns as oxygen depletion and polar melting. Environmental protection involves complex tradeoffs that have to be determined in settings more political than the WEA; in fact, the relation between benefits and burdens may be difficult to calculate. With respect to the use of DDT, for example, it is necessary to balance immediate health and food requirements against deferred burdens on environmental quality and possibly even on human health. One of the functions of the WEA will be to formulate policies to take account of these tradeoffs; when it cannot negotiate a satisfactory tradeoff, the WEA will have to determine its own view of the relative merits of competing claims.

The WEA will almost certainly have to fulfill several functions of such enormous complexity that we can consider them only in brief:

1. To build upon and improve the information base, resolving as much as possible reasonable doubts about environmental effects attributable to ongoing patterns of human and natural behavior; * the WEA should become an authority on environmental subject matter; also, the WEA ought to keep abreast of developments in the earth sciences and of all current regional, national, and subnational environmental issues; the WEA should disseminate this information globally through its publications.

2. To monitor principal changes in the environment by assessing the mineral content of the oceans and the atmosphere, measuring waste disposal of different kinds, and determining whether world weather conditions are undergoing detrimental changes due to either human or natural causes. Such monitoring activities would have to be combined with judgments as to critical thresholds of irreparable harm or irreversible decay; if monitoring efforts discloses danger points, various kinds of emergency standby action should be authorized, including special sessions for the Council of Principals.

3. The WEA would also make proposals about appropriate standards of behavior required for environmental protection; these standards would reflect certain priorities regarding the extent of environmental protection that is desired, given other claims on resources and outputs; such standards would also embody a judgment on whether environmental protection should seek merely to avoid deterioration and collapse, or to work toward a longer-term man–nature equilibrium. Both technical and political inputs will be needed to establish precise standards, which might appropriately be worked out by a Joint Committee on Environmental Policy drawing its membership from the Chambers of the World Assembly and from the WEA. The WEA might also prepare draft conventions for discussion and ratification at a standing World Environment Conference that would hold

---

* The WEA will also devote its attention to *natural* dangers to the planetary habitat arising from destructive storms, quakes, and volcanic activity. Improved capacity to predict and protect against such calamities can help greatly to diminish destructive effects.

annual negotiating sessions of the sort we now associate with activities in the areas of arms control and disarmament.

4. The WEA would be expected to report on compliance with existing environmental standards, and bring instances of significant or continuing noncompliance to the attention of the Implementing Board or Council of Principals (depending on the seriousness and character of the alleged violation); before reporting such noncompliance, the WEA should give the alleged violator an opportunity to either justify or rectify his conduct. Insignificant instances of noncompliance should be handled by negotiations between the WEA and the relevant actor. The WEA should be able to deal with regional actors on problems of regional scope, with a corporation or municipality on problems of transnational scope, and with privately constituted service institutions when appropriate.

5. The WEA would also have responsibility for responding to environmental disasters, whether man-induced or natural. As this responsibility would encompass both emergency relief operations and attempts to mitigate the effects of environmental breakdowns, it presupposes the availability of equipment, personnel, mobility, access, authority, and knowledge. To handle environmental disasters the WEA would need teams of trained personnel, the ability to put these teams into effective operation anywhere in the world, right of access to the disaster site (or to the place where the activities causing the disaster were taking place), authority to establish and implement emergency regulations, and expertise in dealing with various classes of environmental disasters.

Decentralized action would be favored whenever practicable. The WEA would cooperate with other actors responding to environmental problems of urgent magnitude by supplying requested advice, information, personnel and/or equipment.

The definition of a "disaster situation" calling for emergency action is, in part, a political choice that may have major economic and social repercussions. Suppose the WEA determines that the rising content of DDT in the water is endangering the existence of a given species of fish, declares the situation a "disaster," and suspends the use of DDT until further notice. Such a decision may very quickly have adverse affects on crop production and malaria control. Therefore, in emergencies, the WEA should schedule hearings before the Implementing Board, at which time it would seek authorization and affected actors could respond. The Implementing Board would then forward recommendations to the Council of Principals, which would give the issue immediate priority on the agenda. If the disaster allows no time for this procedure, the WEA has authority to act but it must report immediately to the Implementing Board and seek the same procedure to review its initiatives.* In the event of arbitrary action, affected actors would be entitled to treble damages collected through some dispute settlement process, possibly under the auspices of the World Grievance System. A punitive approach to dispute-settlement would have no place in the preferred world, *except in deterring arbitrary or excessive claims by the family of actors comprising the Central Guidance System.*

Finally, the WEA could invoke the authorization procedure immediately upon identifying a situation that would lead to environmental disaster within a specified time interval. The objective would be to prevent environmental disasters, but such a program could involve considerable and intrusive regulatory activity that might impede or defer industrial expansion, a cost that would have vastly different human consequences in different parts of the world.

6. The WEA would also have some kind of specialized dispute-settlement machinery to cope with the complexities of environmental subject matter. Any actor could seek relief, whether injunctive or monetary, but the Arbitral Panel of the WEA would have flexible authority to fashion equitable solutions. If the WEA were a party to the dispute, then it would be handled by reference to the World Grievance System. However, in any environmental dispute the Director-General of the WEA could submit a brief setting forth the global interest. It might also be desirable to allow the World Polity Association's Secretariat to initiate proceedings (or to intervene in others) for the purpose of upholding global interests. Regulatory agencies tend to reflect the interests of those they regulate; hence, "checks" need to be designed to maximize the potency of community perspectives.

The WEA will be operating in an altered climate of awareness and concern. The environmental dimension of world order has barely made its way onto the international agenda at this time. In the future, the further crowding of the planet under conditions of global industrial

---

* This sort of controversy should also be referred to the World Forum for Human Development and to the appropriate Regional Chamber for Human Development, as well as to the World Forum on Ecological Balance. Complex tradeoffs will benefit from discussion and reflection of this type.

growth is likely to give these issues increasing prominence. A major, unresolved, area of conflict for S₂ will involve issues of cost-sharing and priorities where environmental damage seems evident.

World Forum on Ecological Balance

As with the Forums convened for the World System of Human Development, the World Forum on Ecological Balance will seek to elaborate an ideology for ecological policy that takes account of diverse perspectives. The Forum will be receptive to all approaches and considerations, but will consider specifically the interaction of goals of well-being and equality with policy positions involving environmental defense or preserving life prospects. There are apparent conflicts between simultaneously maximizing equity and development *in space* and *through time* that will have to be continuously considered throughout the world.

Tradeoffs between qualitative and quantitative measures of life will probably give rise to many specialized problems connected with ecological risk-taking in the face of uncertainty of knowledge, and involving apprehension about the conformity that could result from a global approach to ecological protection. These problems will, in our view, be at the very center of human concern by the end of the century. Even if substantial progress is made toward other goals, serious problems of ecological danger are likely to remain within the preferred world, and to arouse acute anxiety and intense controversy. Ironically, in the probable event that the fundamental dynamics of demographic and economic growth persist, the apocalyptic prophecies associated with the present system of world order could actually gain a wider following in the preferred world.

The World Forum would facilitate greater understanding of the facts, risks, and choices facing the control centers of the preferred world. Given the strong bias toward voluntary behavior, the World Forum would concentrate on identifying areas of consensus and on strategies to mitigate dissent.

Specialized commissions of experts from different parts of the world could prepare reports for discussion by the Forum. The Forum would be constituted in the same manner as the Forum on Human Development; indeed, it might consider joint sessions and projects, and intentionally seek some degree of overlapping membership. The Forum could itself issue Advisory Reports that would be acted upon by the WEA and then would be referred to the Implementing Board for presentation to the Council of Principals and World Assembly.

The World Forum should also administer a program of publications and general education, but with care to avoid taking set positions on issues still in controversy. Reactions and discussion should be sought in all parts of the world. To this end a system of Regional Chambers of the World Forum will be established to carry forward the *central ethos of governance* by *participatory dialogue*.

World Agency of Resource, Conservation, and Development Policy

Along with WEA, this agency is conceived as a specialized operation staffed by international civil servants, with its leadership selected on a representative basis from around the world. Its main function will be to link resource policy, conservation programs, and developmental opportunities. The character of these linkages will depend upon the extent to which world public opinion and the leadership of the World Polity Association are committed to promoting ecological equilibrium, and the degree to which this objective can be harmonized with ending poverty and diminishing inequality. The World Agency will derive its mandate from the Implementing Board, as program interpreters for the Council of Principals and World Assembly.

At minimum, the Agency should serve as a clearinghouse for principal information on such issues as resource supply and demand, population trends for endangered species of wildlife, and conservation standards and policies in different regions and nations. The Agency might also work out a series of threshold indicators by which to direct the attention of the World Forum and central organs to emerging resource shortages. In more advanced stages of central guidance, this Agency might draw up plans for allocating resource quotas among claimants, thus combining efforts to ration in the face of scarcity, with allocation on the basis of need, equity, and developmental aspirations.

The World Agency could also ascertain future prospects for profitable use of low-grade ores, mining of deep-sea deposits, and new energy sources, and could report on these prospects as objectively as possible.

It would also be desirable to present information on global resource distribution relative to population distribution. To arrive at some kind of equitable distribution relative to existing standards and emerging expectations requires information on both existing and anticipated shares of resource stocks. Obviously, also, there must be some assessment of the degree to which poorer sectors of the world economy can effectively use more resources than are now available. Underlying such concerns are quasi-philosophical and highly political issues bearing on the character of "effective use" and on the extent to which market mechanisms should be subordinated to considerations of conservation and fairness.

The World Agency might also be given the job of assessing compliance with international standards of resource use. It would be desirable to achieve an agreed framework of restraint based on voluntary patterns of behavior, but confidence in such voluntarism must await more information about actual behavior. Success with such arrangements may decrease the need for surveillance, whereas failure will give the Agency a police and supervisory role.

CONCLUSION

This chapter has set forth the main elements of structural reorganization that seem desirable to realize the four WOMP values. Other structural patterns are, of course, possible, and may either be more likely to come about or may be more apt to realize the mix of objectives embodied in our vision of a preferred world. We have tried to develop the most plausible arrangement of structural elements, given our knowledge and awareness at this time. There would undoubtedly be differences if we set about the same design exercise in 1980 or 1990.

Furthermore, by stressing the structural elements of a preferred world order system, we do not mean to imply that structure is the most significant aspect of global reform. Changes in attitude and behavioral tendencies are likely to be more important features of a transformed world than its bureaucratic profile. Nevertheless, this structural emphasis seems justified, for several reasons. First, it provides a clear expression of present preferences, and includes both the evolution of central guidance mechanisms and various checks on their operation to guard against their misuse. Second, it seems possible to depict the structural elements with less arbitrariness than new psychological states or behavioral patterns. Third, a world order emphasis seems most appropriately constructed around the patterning and repatterning of power and authority structures, although we agree that additional or alternate emphases might also be helpful.

REFERENCES

1. On the role of the United Nations, see Inis L. Claude, Jr., *Swords into Plowshares: The Problems and Progress of International Organization*, New York, Random House, 4th rev. ed., 1971; Leon Gordenker, ed., *The United Nations in International Politics*, Princeton, Princeton University Press, 1971; James Barros, ed., *The United Nations: Past, Present, and Future*, New York, Free Press, 1972.

2. On the dispute over Namibia (South West Africa) see John Dugard, ed., *The South West Africa/Namibia Dispute*, Berkeley, Calif., University of California Press, 1973; see also Solomon Slonim, *South West Africa and the United Nations: An International Mandate in Dispute*, Baltimore, Johns Hopkins University Press, 1973.

3. See Donald W. McNemar, "The Post-Independence War in the Congo," in Richard A. Falk, ed., *The International Law of Civil War*, Baltimore, Johns Hopkins University Press, 1971, pp. 244–302.

4. On the reconciliation of national and global loyalties, see the perceptive essay by John H. Schaar, "The Case for Patriotism," *American Review* 17, New York, Bantam, 1973, pp. 59–99.

5. For perceptive accounts see Ezra J. Mishan, *The Costs of Economic Growth*, New York, Praeger, 1967; Jacques Ellul, *The Technological Society*, New York, Knopf, 1964.

Chapter Five

THE TRANSITION PROCESS

AN ORIENTATION TOWARD THE
TRANSITION PROBLEM

In world order studies it is traditional to propose a better system of world order and then argue for its adoption.* Such an approach tends to be "utopian" or "romantic" in the sense that it overlooks the transition from "here" to "there." It is also utopian to the extent that it premises prospects for change upon the reasonableness of the arguments or the general ethical attractiveness of the world order vision. Those who benefit from existing arrangements of power and interest are unlikely to be swayed, except in marginal or cosmetic respects, by appeals based on argument or values. Power can be transformed only by counter-vailing power, although not necessarily or exclusively by violence and its threat. No world order solution which presupposes the substantial modification of the state system can be achieved unless the advocates of the new system are aligned with important social and political forces within the existing world structure. Education and related strategies of persuasion can help to mobilize or even "create" social forces commit-ted to world order change.

---

* The character of improvement that makes a proposed system "better" has usually been taken for granted. The claim is made that the new system would assure peace and justice in a manner that contrasts with the chaos and injustice of what presently exists. Often, however, the claimed improvements are self-serving, helping to extend the sway of values existing in one part of the world and to make them serve as the foundation for a unified, global system. Dante, for instance, in his essay *De Monarchia*, proposed an exten-sion of the Roman Empire to global proportions as the only tenable solution to the world order failures of the fourteenth century. It is necessary, then, to pierce the veil of reformist rhetoric and sentiments to discern whether proposals for global reform are self-serving, whether wittingly or not.

Concern with transition, then, calls for an analysis of political prospects over the relevant time period. This analysis has a number of distinct features:

Identifying actors and social forces receptive to world order change

Mobilizing receptive actors and social forces to support transition to a preferred world organized around WOMP values

Creating a public climate of support for global reform

Identifying potential areas of transnational cooperation on a regional and intergovernmental scale which will strengthen the prospects for the endurance of the present system of world order, while building experience with more cooperative approaches to international problems.

Action bearing on transition issues can occur in any political arena, but the most critical arenas in the next decade or so will be the domestic societies of principal states. Therefore, the highest priority for transition efforts will involve orienting national elites or portions thereof to regard drastic global reform of a carefully specified character as necessary, desirable, and feasible.* A second critical arena will involve the activities of various transnational elites, especially corporations, professional associations, church organizations, labor unions and liberation groups. A third set of critical arenas involves activities of specialized international institutions and those areas subject to multilateral uses of the treaty process.†

This chapter attempts to describe the transition problem, provide some thoughts on method, and give some ideas on transition tactics and strategy.

DEFINITIONS OF THE TRANSITION PROBLEM

There is a great deal of unplanned change taking place on all levels of human activity, including the international one. Over a period of years,

---

* Political parties, labor unions, church groups might become identified with specific proposals for or approaches to global reform; that is, the domestic politics of democratic societies would come to include global reforms on its primary agenda. Such a development would have profound significance. In the past, only in post-war contexts have issues of global reform been emphasized as such.

† Ocean use, environmental quality, control of aircraft hijacking, arms control, and regulation of satellite broadcasts are the sort of subject matter likely to be dealt with significantly by international institutions and by treaty-making multilateral diplomacy.

a variety of technological, ecological, and political changes have modified the world order system which evolved from the Westphalia system of sovereign states. At what point the cumulative impact of these changes results in a system change is for an interpreter of the international scene to judge. We are using the concept of transition in a more precise way, as confined to planned and value-directed change that deliberately facilitates the shift from one system of world order to another. And more particularly, our views of "the transition problem" involve the specific effort to describe the process by which the preferred world outlined in Chapter IV might most reasonably and beneficially be brought into being by the end of the 1990's, or more realistically, by a sequence of changes stretched out over a time span that cannot be associated with definite chronological intervals.*

Our use of the word "transition" is quite different from its more popular association with a new era of international relations ushered in by the moderation of "the Cold War." W. W. Rostow, in a lecture at Leeds University in 1967, organized his thinking around the idea of "a great transition" that was concerned with "our common central task—the building of a viable world order." [1] Rostow oriented his conception of the future around a sentence in President Johnson's 1967 State of the Union Address: "We are in the midst of a great transition—a transition from narrow nationalism to international partnership; from the harsh spirit of the cold war to the hopeful spirit of common humanity on a troubled and a threatened planet." [2] For Rostow this more "hopeful spirit" entailed four elements that bear some resemblance to WOMP goals:

Deterring aggression

Economic and social progress in the world as a whole, but especially in the developing countries

The buildup of international organization on the regional and global level

The search for reconciliation so as to create a basis for cooperation among adversaries and the realization of the objectives of the United Nations Charter as outlined in Article 1.

Carrying Woodrow Wilson's idealism into the contemporary context, Rostow based his liberal program of reform and progress on the possibility that the existing state system would give birth to a reformed

---

* We can conceive of stages of development for a global polity, but it is difficult to correlate those stages with ten- or fifteen-year intervals or to suppose that the intervals will be of equivalent duration.

type of world order that was, in a fundamental sense, beyond power politics. No preconditions were indicated. The modalities of transition were not specified, nor did Rostow give any persuasive rationales for the withering away of the war system in the aftermath of the Vietnam War. In this central respect, the liberal vision is utopian—it heralds the possibility of transition to a better world order system without entailing any change in the present structure of international society and without providing any political basis for taking on the shape that one favors.* Only a few years later, the persistence of conflict, violence, poverty, economic plunder, and statism seems assured, despite the fact that the United States is no longer militarily involved in Indochina and the Cold War has been virtually brought to a halt. It seems much more likely that the Cold War Era will be followed by Richard Nixon's concept of a "five-power world" oriented toward an economic rivalry condominium, rather than by a just and peaceful world order system remotely resembling the preference model depicted in Chapter IV.†

The idea of transition held by statesmen involves "intra-systemic" and marginal adjustments in the world order system; i.e., the distribution of power and values remains about the same, and major structural modifications are neither needed nor likely to occur. This conventional wisdom of statesmen underestimates the extent to which the war system, with its periods of violence and tension, is inextricably bound up with the internal and external dynamics of sovereign states. Implicit in WOMP's idea of transition is the need for "intersystemic" transformation, making the transition process eventuate in a new system (S2) of world order; transition tactics and strategy involve accelerating the process and devising ways to assure its completion in accordance with our specified value preferences. In this sense, it adopts an *activist* or *engineering* posture, in contrast to the *passive* perspective of statesmen such as Johnson or Nixon, who report that a historical transition is underway and that our main task is to relate to its actuality in a positive and self-interested way. We agree that convulsive changes of historic proportion

---

* There are two senses in which utopia is used. The first sense is negative: utopian thinking is wishful thinking that gives false hope and distracts attention from real problems and the search for genuine solutions. The second sense is positive—the use of imaginative powers to embody aspirations in a concrete vision of desirable social and political arrangements. As such it directs human effort toward a vision of the future, thereby sustaining hope and justifying effort. Rostow's utopianism illustrates the negative sense.

† We will consider dominant images of the future of world order held by governing groups in the United States in Chapter VI.

are taking place, but we regard the basic tendencies of adjustment as ill-conceived and insufficient to avoid world catastrophe, as well as heedless of positive opportunities for improving value realization. In other words, the intensification of conflict, the deepening awareness of deprivation, the proliferating technology of modern warfare, the crowding of the planet, the prospects of resource scarcity, and the alarming increase in global pollution present a cumulative profile of *systemic decay*. This international profile is reproduced in domestic settings as well; it is reflected in the rise of repressive politics and in the virtual collapse—even in societies with strong democratic traditions—of procedures for the accountability of rulers to the ruled.[3]

Thus, we hold a view that is more closely associated with the British document "Blueprint for Survival." Endorsed by prominent scientists, it contends that the principal bases of industrial society are "not sustainable," and that the only choice is whether fundamental change will take place "against our will" in catastrophic form or "because we want it to" in a series of "thoughtful, humane and measured changes." [4] WOMP, the Club of Rome, Lindisfarne, and a variety of proposals now under consideration express the judgment that S_2 is almost certain to be a disastrous sequel to S_1, unless we reorient world order values in a decisive and specific fashion through the intervention of activist education and progressive politics. In contrast, prevailing official views suggest that adequate world order reforms can be carried out within the confines of S_1.

Furthermore, we believe that the prospects for a humane and non-traumatic transition to a preferred form of S_2 would be greatly enhanced if an accurate diagnosis of the need for world order change were to take hold of public and elite imagination in the next several years (or, in our more schematic terms, as near in time to t_0 * as possible). Additionally, the early initiation of a transition process oriented around the pursuit of WOMP values will also increase the likelihood that S_2 will be an improvement in value terms over S_1 for most individuals and groups in the 1990's, rather than a steep regression as is likely to be the case given the drift of present dominant tendencies. The projected future is likely to be a regression from the present, unless intervening forces can reshape developments in the direction of an alternate preferred future. Our selection of $S_{2(WOMP/USA)}$ represents our judgment as to the most promising preference model. Other reasonable judgments can, of

---

* t_0 designates the time at which speculation about world order developments originates. It is the present, and could be also designated by year, e.g., t_{1974}.

course, be made regarding the shape of the preferred world and the most appropriate means of achieving it.

A PROSPECTUS FOR TRANSITION

In this section we will set forth some ideas about a systematic orientation toward the transition process. Our initial emphasis will be upon the relation between time (designated either as t_1, t_2, t_3, t_4 . . . t_n, or as t_{1974}, t_{1984}, t_{1994}, etc.) * and arena (A^n = national arenas; A^r = regional arenas; A^g = global arenas; A^{tn} = transnational arenas). The dual system of notation for the transition period takes into account both analytic stages of temporal progression (t_1 . . . t_n) and historical time points (1970's, 1980's, 1990's). For the sake of carrying out the mandate of WOMP we can correlate these notations by equating T_1 with the 1970's, and so forth, but it should be clear that there is no empirical basis for assuming that the duration of a "t" will be a decade, or that the three intervals will total thirty years or that they will be each of uniform length. A more satisfactory concept of the transition period would separate the two notions of world order development, thereby acknowledging our rather feeble command over mapping the future in historical time. It is one thing to envision and work to achieve a sequence of developments, and quite another to correlate the sequence with a specific historical time period. Given our current degree of insight into world order change, the relative prophetic humility of the analytic notational system is far more in keeping with our state of knowledge.†

With respect to shifts in consciousness (public attitudes) and behavioral patterns over the period of planned transition, we postulate the priorities set forth in Table 5–1.

The transition process is to be completed by 2004, at which time S_2 exists; a new transitional process would be projected in relation to S_3. The broad pattern of development over the time interval t_1–t_3 will be

---

* The t_1, t_2, t_3 sequence refers to a logical sequence, whereas the t_{1974}, t_{1984}, t_{1994} sequence refers to specified time durations set in the history of the future.

† Our objective is not to predict or forecast. It is rather a planning perspective: If we seek to attain $S_{2(WOMP/USA)}$ by the year 2000 we should seek to do thus and so in the 1970's or during the first planning period (t_1), and so on. There is also a broader intellectual purpose. If we seek to understand how $S_{2(WOMP/USA)}$ might come about, our transition scenario with its three analytic stages (t_1, t_2, t_3) provides a framework for thought and action.

Table 5-1. The Transition Sequence

					Arena
A^n $\quad$ A^{tn} $\quad$ A^r		A^g			Arena
$t_{-1} \longrightarrow t_1 \underset{t_0}{\longmapsto} t_2 \longrightarrow t_3 \longrightarrow t_4$					Temporal Progression
	1974 $\quad$ 1984	1994	2004		Historical Time
$S_{-1} \longrightarrow S_1 \longrightarrow\!\!\!\!\longrightarrow S_2$					Systemic Progression

considered in relation to both *political action* and *political arena*. In terms of political action we anticipate t_1, the 1970's, to be the decade in which value changes occur mainly on the level of *political consciousness*, i.e., orientations toward action.* In t_2, the 1980's the main value changes will involve *mobilization for action* to achieve the new value priorities, while in t_3, the 1990's the focus will be on *action to achieve transformation of institutions and organizations*, both to alter value and goal priorities and to adapt organizational forms to the emerging value consensus. However, like a musical round, the processes initiated in each time interval persist and continue to operate in successive stages until arrested by new challenges.

With respect to considerations of *political arena*, in the initial decade (t_1) efforts to reorient national outlooks need to be emphasized; in the second decade (t_2) the growth of transnational developments would be emphasized; and in the third decade (t_3) global developments of a structural sort would be emphasized.

We can summarize these comments about political action and political arena in very schematic terms of chronological time intervals as follows:

In the 1970's: *Political Consciousness and the Domestic Imperative*

In the 1980's: *Political Mobilization and the Transnational Imperative*

In the 1990's: *Political Transformation and the Global Imperative*

---

* Our use of t_1 and the 1970's as equivalent is to illustrate parallel modes of planning: first, how can we conceive of $S_{2(WOMP/USA)}$ by the year 2000? Second, how can we conceive $S_{2(WOMP/USA)}$ coming about at *some* time in the future? In this portion of the text we have treated the two modes as identical, i.e., by treating t_1 as equalling the 1970's. However, in general, the two modes should be kept apart, so as to enable global reform to be planned both in relation to *a certain time* and in relation to *some time* in the future.

We believe that it will be helpful to organize our inquiry into the transition problem in a manner responsive to these categories. In addition, we believe that *value* dimensions need to be taken into account during the transition period. To inquire systematically into value dimensions we propose to organize material around a matrix, as shown in Table 5–2.

Table 5–2. Value Emphases During the Transition Process

	War Prevention V_1	Economic and Social Well-Being V_2	Human Dignity V_3	Ecological Quality V_4
t_1				
t_2				
t_3				
t_4				

We suggest lines for comprehensive inquiry. As noted in Chapter 1, we seek to put world order issues in a form that enables operational tests of progress or regress so as to encourage more objective and precise assessment of trends and prospects. These quantitative measures will require data not now available and the use of sophisticated techniques of presentation and evaluation.* The prospects for plausible projection diminish as the future time interval increases. As a result, it is appropriate to anticipate a line of rather specific proposals for reform and reorientation that arise from the present social and political context. The continuation of positive trends in t_2 depends on so many variables that it becomes less appropriate to depict transition steps other than in an illustrative form (i.e., the sort of undertaking that would seem instrumental in relation to WOMP values and in relation to the organizational model of a preferred world as outlined in Chapter III). Finally, the effort to write now about t_3 is bound to be highly speculative, given the

---

* It is an urgent task of global reform to collect data and develop appropriate indicators. Peace research groups around the world might usefully cooperate in this endeavor, which has important elements of preference and cannot be safely entrusted to the "objective" methods of any single person or group.

decisive conditioning of intervening developments that can be fore-seen, if at all, in only the most general way. In one respect our objective is to provide a coherent account of how a transition process from t_1 through t_3 might eventuate, so as to establish a realistic link in the imagination of readers between the present world order system and the emergence of a preferred world by the late 1990's.*

We have already indicated a general scenario for the transition process in Chapter IV, pp. 225–228. This general scenario focuses on the altered pattern of authority in the late 1990's, the alterations being envisioned from the outlook of smooth growth curves (see Figure 4–1 on p. 226) that reflect the ascending and descending organizational roles of various categories of actors in the world order system.† Such a scenario takes some account of trends over the last two decades and of anticipated functional pressures on statist modes of problem-solving in the near future. For instance, the technological setting of the late 1970's and 1980's will encourage unprecedented efforts to achieve international cooperation in relation to exploitation of ocean resources, weather control, international communications, world trade and monetary relations, and environmental quality. These efforts may fail, in whole or in part, but it does seem reasonable to anticipate an increased role for functional institutions of regional and global scope. We also envisage a continuing reluctance by most national governments to shift their traditional prerogatives directly to central political institutions of global scope (that is, to strengthen a UN-type system).

Our prospectus for transition embodies several assumptions that shape its content:

1. The importance of providing a coherent account of the entire transition process

2. The virtual impossibility of comprehending transition prospects in relation to traumatic or disruptive eventualities that would make the organizations' growth curves much more jagged

---

* And hence, to structure *present* action. A real question for reformers is what to do *now* in light of where we would like to be by a given date in the future. In a sense, the description of a transition process should be thought of as *a work schedule* for a movement of world order reform.

† These smooth growth curves are not of various organizational actors on the world scene; rather, they should be associated with the basic transition sequence of t_1 (consciousness), t_2 (mobilization), and t_3 (transformation) that constitutes our view of the best hope to achieve $S_{2(WOMP/USA)}$ by or about the year 2000 without recourse to violent or inhumane means.

3. The dual intellectual task of presenting an organizational model of a preferred world and of assessing progress in terms of WOMP values

4. The absence of any prior relevant method for transition studies that combines trend analysis (futurism) with prescriptive analysis (social planning and engineering) in a world order context

In this chapter, we aim to provide a basis for linking Chapters II and III in terms of the growth of political consciousness, value change, and structural modification. We purport to do no more than provide a framework of inquiry relevant for the study of transition phenomena, given our value preferences and our basic judgment that in any event S_1 will come to an end some time during the next few decades. We are well aware of the need for more systematic studies that devote careful attention to the range of potential arenas within which it is possible for relevant value developments to take place.

FOCUS ON POLITICAL ACTION

WOMP/USA emphasizes those aspects of the transition process concerned with a shift in the locus of power/authority vis-à- vis the critical value-realizing process.* Unlike many earlier studies of global reform which have limited their effort to the exposition of a coherent set of world order preferences, our inquiry concentrates upon the process by which our preferences can be realized within a set historical framework. This emphasis reflects a criticism of the apolitical quality of much global reform literature, and also expresses our own political commitment to work for global reform in an effective and humane way; in other words, we want to know how to reach our goals, as well as how to formulate them. Moreover, by focusing more concretely on action-in-transition, we will be in a better position to test the wisdom of contending proposals. If there is no plausible way to reach the promised land, its presentation as a solution becomes merely an opiate to be overlooked altogether, or else a vision whose unattainability enhances the staying-power of adherents to the present world order setting. The

---

* We do not claim that this change in power/authority structure is the fundamental feature of a successful transition process, but only that it represents a proper focus for social science at this stage of human understanding.

Christian stress on other-worldly salvation involved just such distraction from real-world possibilities for reform and transition.* In a quite literal sense, world order visions can, like religion, act as opiates. Emphasis on transition considerations helps anchor preferential modeling. It is necessary to practice, as well as preach, global reform, and to embody world order values in present public policy choices.†

THE ERA OF CONSCIOUSNESS

In t_1, the 1970's, the main field of "action" will be the terrain of political consciousness. On an international level, it will be desirable for governmental leaders to attain a high degree of consensus on world order problems and goals. In our judgment, it would be helpful if global understanding crystallized around an awareness of the need to achieve ecological equilibrium while simultaneously giving high priority to the equity imperative (that is, overcoming poverty and reducing inequality).

The ecological challenge is beginning to be perceived by ruling elites as a global problem. However, the early indications are that the dominant response is based on control by the powerful rather than participa-

---

* It seems to us that the cult of progress which has accompanied the Industrial Revolution, the dominance of science and technology, and the stress on rationality have performed a comparable social and political function. As these opiates fail, there is recourse to real opiates. Drug culture and a revival of occultism have followed the hyperrationality of the earlier period, as part of the continuous search for opiates in a civilization that cannot satisfy elementary human needs. That drug culture should, in turn, inspire repressive forms of crime control is a further turn of the rack. Demystification is an essential component of any viable strategy for drastic global reform, including the renunciation of popular opiates that mislead mind or body by inducing spurious feelings of contentment. What is spurious must be approached with a sensitive appreciation of complexity, and with due deference to human rights considerations implicit in V_3.

† We believe that existing conflicts provide an opportunity to embody world order values in the life of a national polity. In this sense, joining the anti-apartheid campaign, or opposing on world order grounds the confirmation of Henry Kissinger as Secretary of State, constitute consciousness-raising arenas. It is not essential for these efforts to succeed. Indeed, it is in their nature to fail because they do represent a normative orientation that is counter-systemic. Put differently, if an $S_{2(WOMP/USA)}$ perspective were politically viable now, we would be much further along on the transition path than is in fact the case. Our political arenas, especially in principal states, are dominated by an S_1 normative orientation.

tion by the weak. There are two lines of response to the issue of scarcity in a situation of inequality: accentuated inequality via reliance on mystification and power, or shifts toward equality by levelling down of the high consumers and levelling up of the deprived consumers. S_1 logic drives its practitioners toward the first line of solution; various S_2 alternative logics do not even receive a real hearing at the present time.

It is more likely that the ecological and equity challenges will be sharply dissociated, the response to the former negating the claims of the latter. Related issues associated with the war system are important; increasingly, the technology and material needed for the production of nuclear weapons will be available to all governments and, quite possibly, to nongovernmental actors as well. In the 1970's, then, the United Nations might help shape a world order consensus in which a diagnosis of deepening danger is widely shared by governments of differing persuasions and positions. However, the intergovernmental character of the UN would probably mean increasing controversy over the implications of the diagnosis, and sharp disagreement over the selection of an appropriate therapy. This disagreement might become so fundamental that it could induce a dissolution of the United Nations, or at least hamper the further development of parallel constitutions representing different governments.

The international process of heightened, but quite possibly fragmented, consciousness needs to be complemented by comparable realizations within the main national societies of the world. Because there are a variety of national political systems, the form of this awareness may differ from society to society. In essence, our goal would be to raise public consciousness to the point where "conventional wisdom" about the future approaches the kind of interpretation embodied in the "Blueprint for Survival" or the Club of Rome "Limits to Growth" study.* Such a development in public consciousness is being resisted at the present time. The strongest institutions in the major societies of the world are committed to the capacity of technology to evolve solutions that can moderate the strains of growth without disrupting the growth ethos itself. There are numerous examples of this regressive counter-attack by advocates of values associated with nationalism and growth. For instance, on most vital issues of public policy, President Nixon has coupled rhetoric of ecological concern with a pro-growth,

---

* We have criticisms of these studies, especially of *The Limits to Growth*, but we share the essential position that the dynamics of S_1 are not sustainable and that a shift to some type of S_2 is necessary. See Chapter VI, pp. 397–405.

pro-technology stance. Mobil Oil advertises widely that "stagnation" (i.e., equilibrium) is a principal form of "pollution." The debate is highly ideological in the sense that ideas are presented so as to serve the cause of vested interests.[5]

In this setting of controversy, the role of independent educational efforts could be very significant. It is essential that the public be given access to diverse assessments of the world situation and to an array of possible responses that are not influenced by the special goals of the assessor. Many of these efforts will be carried on through the initiative of private individuals and groups acting outside conventional educational settings. Universities have tended to resist efforts to deal comprehensively or systematically with the crisis of understanding posed by the cumulative effects of the ecological challenge in a setting of nuclear weapons, continuing economic growth, and rising population. Symptomatic of this educational lag is the large number of proposals now being developed for the creation of institutes, academies, and independent learning centers that will be institutionally and financially autonomous. Part of the task in t_1 is to gain greater access to conventional educational resources by penetrating school structures at all levels with materials and courses that are more realistically related to the world order situation and more enlightened about lines of response. The Institute for World Order has been pioneering along these lines, but its efforts have been largely confined to achieving *mechanical penetration* of existing curricula rather than aiming at the *organic reorientation* of the educational program, which is what would enable students to develop an understanding of what is needed, what is desirable, and what can be done. By *organic reorientation* we mean more than new materials for old courses, or even curriculum revision; we mean, in essence, changing the implicit symbol and belief systems that underlie the whole way citizenship, national goals, and even personal fulfillment are approached in the educational system.*

In universities the organic reorientation would entail shaping new institutional identities that are not as vocationally rooted as present departmental boundaries. Such a task would be difficult to accomplish, as educational policy is controlled by groups largely integrated into the value/belief patterns of system maintenance vis-à-vis S_1, such as boards of trustees and parent–teacher associations.

---

* We also mean a richer concept of knowledge than now prevails. Within the realm of knowledge we would include the domains of feeling and action, in addition to the domain of thought where the sciences and humanities seek to test and study ideas.

There is one major caveat that relates to this educational emphasis. Especially in the context of WOMP, it may appear that such concern with education is tantamount to advocating student indoctrination. It is important to be clear about a number of issues; first, covert indoctrination now takes place in the form of an acceptance of the permanence of the state system and the viability of a nationalist ideology built around flag and country;* second, the reassessment of the wider reality is not indoctrination, but exposure to critical arenas of human concern; third, the objective is to initiate a relevant response, not to preach about the proper solution; WOMP is a methodological exercise that posits one *possible* solution, but it invites alternative solutions and urges others to embark upon world order reformist efforts that posit different values and pursue different transition strategies. All that is being urged is a need to think prescriptively about the future of world order, given a diagnosis which is pessimistic about accomplishments to date, and even more so about prospects for the future.

Relevant education during this period is likely to be largely accomplished outside formal institutions of learning. The course of events will disclose the limited capacity of earlier value/belief systems to cope with basic human problems. The menacingly obsolescent character of the outmoded power/authority structures will impinge negatively on human consciousness, widening the receptivity of all kinds of groups to appeals and proposals for world change. One of the tasks of a world order movement is to provide people everywhere with better tools to understand both the costs and dangers of the present world order system, and the realistic prospects for its decisive improvement.[7] This understanding would help explicate current issues of policy and choice in all major arenas of action as they bear upon the agenda of world order concerns.

The main objective of the 1970's is to crystallize a world order consensus, beginning with issues of diagnosis, proceeding toward the affirmation of WOMP values, and implementing some early transitional steps. In t_1 the main priority relates to political consciousness in national arenas, hopefully creating orientations toward new forms of action. Obviously, during t_1, direct efforts to mobilize and transform various components of the overall world power/authority structure will occur, but in our view these efforts will not be very consequential

---

* We intend no diatribe against patriotism. On the contrary, we believe in the revival of patriotism around a set of ideas that links the particularities of place and the specifics of national history with the general requirements of the species and the planet.[6]

without a prior reorientation in political consciousness for broad sectors of public opinion in several vital states. Until the groundwork is laid by widely diffusing an S_2 ideology that is grasped and affirmed by large numbers of people, challenges directed at S_1 spokesmen will be viewed all too often as naive, or worse, as utopian in the bad sense of being irrelevant.

Reform efforts to raise consciousness will persist in t_2 and t_3; and indeed, the "openness" of the preferred world emergent at the end of t_3 would create new horizons of opportunity for value realization and a world support structure. The basic need is to supplant the outmoded value/belief system associated with the state system in a pre-ecological age. The emergence and diffusion of a new value/belief consensus is a vital precondition for the kind of active politics that would accomplish the transformation of the structures of power and authority in subsequent periods of time. In t_2, the evolving political consciousness would help assure that mobilization efforts were responsive to WOMP values, and would provide a continuous reconsideration of the means and ends of global reform in light of new developments. In t_3 a comparable effort would be needed, to assure that emerging structures were realizing WOMP values to the greatest possible extent, and that an S_3 horizon of aspiration was beginning to take shape. At each stage, the level of consciousness determines what is possible on the level of action, in addition to providing a critique of projects for change. In moving toward a world order solution, it will be very important to avoid bureaucratic centralism or ideological dogmatism, once a consensus in principal countries is mobilized in support of drastic modifications of the existing world order system. However, it is anticipated that adjustments in consciousness will be of diminishing relative significance as we proceed from t_1 to t_3, and beyond. However, this sense of future context may underestimate the demands for continuous shifts in political consciousness, not just a single, coherent reorientation sympathetic to organizing the transition $S_1 \rightarrow S_2$ as humanely and as quickly as possible.

We do believe that the basic shifts in orientation must come before their embodiment in effective action, and that the critical changes involve two steps, both of which must be substantially taken in t_1: first, a realization that S_2 is possible and necessary, and that human efforts can have a positive effect; secondly, a determination that $S_{2(WOMP)}$ is the preferred objective of global reform as compared to other orientations toward S_2. Note that we do not believe that $S_{2(WOMP/USA)}$ must also be chosen from among $S_{2(WOMP)}$ proposals. And we mean $S_{2(WOMP)}$ in a non-dogmatic way, implying a concern for the construction by humane means of a world order system devoted to peace, economic well-being of the planet, ecological quality, and human dignity.

THE ERA OF MOBILIZATION

By the end of t_1, we postulate the emergence of a new consensus on the character of world order problems and on the broad contours of a solution (see Chapter IV). The priority task in t_2 will be to translate that consensus into a politically effective movement. This movement will take distinct forms and shapes in different arenas. On a national level, the mobilization of change-oriented social forces in the United States may proceed along a path quite independent from that arising in the Soviet Union or Japan.

It should be understood that we postulate a rather widespread, but diffused, receptivity to WOMP values by the end of t_1 throughout the world. This receptivity may be uneven and not entirely coherent. Thus, in country X, there may be a widespread acceptance of V_1, V_2, V_3, but not V_4; in country Y there may be an insistence on V_5 and V_6, and in Z a rejection of V_4 (environmental quality) as an element of an S_2 solution. Yet, there will be a general repudiation of S_1 as a viable world order basis for the future, coupled with a conception of global reform that is drastic in terms of change and possesses affinities to the WOMP scale of value priorities.

It is also likely that positions of power and authority will continue to be dominated by those who accept a pre-ecological variant of the Westphalian view of the world. In our judgment, the progressive forces in most principal societies will be denied significant access to power in the 1970's, although there may be some instances of success in middle-size countries and in middle levels of the bureaucracies of large-size countries.*

The focus for mobilization will depend on tactical opportunities that

---

* Such a situation can produce many changes in domestic political organization. At best, it will stimulate genuine debate and political competition between advocates of S_1 and of $S_{2(WOMP)}$. Incidentally, this competition can take different forms in different political systems and need not necessarily involve party politics. Also, depending on the global setting, as the debate deepens it may shift from S_1 versus $S_{2(WOMP)}$ to $S_{2(n)}$ versus $S_{2(WOMP)}$, with n representing a range of normative orientations incompatible with WOMP objectives.

seem to exist at the beginning of t2. It may be, for instance, that a world order input into movements for minority rights, women's liberation, or dignity for the aged, would be the best way to gain access to power centers. It may be, in other national contexts, that mainstream party politics provides major opportunities to serve as a bearer of new demands for social and political change. And, in still other national settings, the debate and change may have to come about within the narrow confines of ruling oligarchies and governing elites. Possibilities are also available for using transnational, regional, and global arenas to relate WOMP consciousness to the activities of effective pressure groups. It may even be, as Ralph Nader has demonstrated with respect to consumer affairs, that dedicated individuals can mobilize enormous resources to mount campaigns for change. The example of Gandhi also illustrates the capacity of one individual to mobilize a receptive citizenry toward a preferred future. The success of Zionism in establishing Israel, despite the "utopian" character of the initial project, is also highly suggestive; it is true that the Nazi persecution of the Jews and the twilight of British colonialism after World War II lent viability to the Zionist vision, but it is also likely that without its "unrealistic" phase and nucleus of fanatical leaders there would have been no capacity to "seize the day."

Although t2 is described as the "Era of Mobilization," the efforts to mobilize will begin in t1. Indeed, a variety of pressure groups are already organized on behalf of world order values, although their strength is not now great and their objectives are generally vague and unrealistic, lacking a coherent view of world order and of the transition process. The point of our approach is that mobilization efforts are a logical sequel to a receptive consciousness, and that this receptivity cannot exist until after a massive educational effort has influenced the value/belief systems which now prevail.* Therefore, the concept of t2 is based on the need for a decent interval separating the impact of a new consciousness on behavioral patterns and the consequent steps of structuring a new world order system.†

---

* This educational effort will not proceed in a vacuum. Many developments in the world will confirm the obsolescence of a laissez-faire world order ideology and of the fragmented structures of power and authority implicit in the state system.

† This decent interval is associated closely with the insistence that global reforms be brought about by peaceful and humane means. The duration of the interval will depend on many factors, including the extent of pressure to evolve $S_{2(WOMP)}$ structures, the degree of resistance from S_1 social forces, and the extent of competition from negative conceptions of S_2.

At the end of t₂ mobilization efforts do not cease. There will be a continuing occasion in t₃ to mobilize new groups, to create new forms of mobilization, and to consolidate earlier mobilization gains.

We presume that by the end of t₂, significant elites in power/authority structures in various world arenas will be receptive to proposals that would help realize WOMP values.* We can identify the beginning of t₃ by noting the building phase—the institutionalization of WOMP values will become an express objective of many governing groups, and such efforts will enjoy strong public support.

THE ERA OF TRANSFORMATION

In t₃, political consciousness presumably will have crystallized in support of WOMP values and important efforts to mobilize for action will have been completed. The overriding emphasis during t₃ will be upon the institutional structure needed to cope with an S₂ world. Of course, some institutional changes would have been initiated in t₁ and t₂, and so the developments in t₃ will be more a culmination than a completely fresh beginning. Nevertheless, we do not anticipate that the full institutional impact of the changes in world order values will be evident until the end of t₃, or perhaps even beyond.†

As with other efforts to promote peaceful and humane transition, the prospects for constructive use of institutions in *all* arenas depend on building a political base for effective action. We also expect the forms of institutional modification to incorporate varying national, cultural, ideological, and regional perspectives, a feature of S₂ which will allow and encourage maximum flexibility for institutional experimentation. The whole imagery of "central guidance" underscores our commitment to minimizing the degree of bureaucratic and coercive centralism in the

---

* Given V₄, such receptivity presupposes the humanization of relations between governments and their own populations in many countries. From our current perspective, perhaps this presupposition is the least hopeful element in our program for transition.

† The attainment of S₂ may precede its realization. We may create a new world order system without being fully aware of the process until sometime after its completion. (It is worth noting that "the state system" did not exist as a *mental construct* until long after 1648, when it can be said to have begun its existence as *a social fact*.) The extent of awareness will probably depend on whether the final steps in t₃ are formal and dramatic (e.g., a world constitutional conference) or involve the intensification of existing tendencies (e.g., expanding budgets of global actors, contracting defense budgets, etc.) carried on over a number of years and eventuating in enormous cumulative changes.

preferred world that we postulate for the end of t_3. This attitude toward the benefits of diversity should be linked with the attitude toward the benefits of human mobility, giving individuals the right to travel as freely as possible, to obtain political asylum, and to exercise as much choice as feasible with respect to their country of residence.*

It also seems evident that although periods associated with consciousness-raising and WOMP mobilization will establish an unprecedented consensus on the character of world order goals, there will still remain important differences in priorities and political styles. We anticipate neither the disappearance of group conflict nor a total renunciation of the instruments of violence during t_3. However, we do believe that t_1 and t_2, if satisfactorily consummated, will be powerful learning experiences for most peoples and leaders of the world, and will create strong dispositions in favor of nonviolence, equity, and ecological equilibrium. At the same time, S_1 resistance movements are likely to grow; desperate strategies may be sought by those who identify their interests with either the persistence of S_1 or with the creation of a counter-WOMP variant of S_2. There is no reason to expect a harmonious transition to $S_{2(WOMP)}$, particularly in its latter stages, when impacts on resource allocation and access to power become more evident. Indeed, given probable lines of technological innovation and its geographic diffusion—especially in relation to nuclear power production—the capability for large-scale systemic disruption will be increasingly accessible to governmental and nongovernmental actors with small power/wealth authority bases. The possibilities for "hijacking" spaceship earth will inevitably grow into a more serious problem. Thus we not only envision t_3 as a period in which the dominant consciousness and many of the main organizational forms are oriented toward achieving world order changes and adjustments, but also as a period when minority efforts and deviant reactions could be desperate and dangerous, thereby generating a cycle of threat, disruption, fear, repression, and rigidity.†

---

* All rights and goals must be balanced against competing claims. There can be no absolute claims in $S_{2(WOMP)}$ without encroaching on claims based on other protected values. The value setting is constituted by complementary and dialectical relations, and value reconciliation will be a major task challenging the humanism and wisdom of policymakers called upon to choose how far to extend a given right (say, mobility) into the domain of another right (say, ethnic autonomy).

† Progressive forces mobilized in various arenas to achieve S_2 may become deeply divided themselves on the question of dealing with S_1 challenges or with counter-WOMP S_2 movements. Stalinism was not a *necessary* sequel to the Russian Revolution, but it was a *plausible* one. The 1973 overthrow of the Allende government in Chile discloses the vulnerability of drastic reformers who choose largely peaceful and humane tactics, but who neither convert nor eliminate their opposition.

A further observation has to do with relying on cumulative tendencies rather than on abrupt constitution-building. It is quite possible for t_3 to proceed without a dramatic confrontation between opposing groups on the issue of world order organization. We do not foresee any kind of occasion comparable to a formal constitutional conference of national governments and other principal world actors, nor, on the other hand, do we rule it out altogether. We foresee a period of confrontation beginning in late t_1, and continuing on through t_2, between the adherents of statist values (or their S_2 equivalent) and the world order values associated with WOMP. However for world order developmental purposes, we define t_2 as continuing as long as necessary to assure that the new values are dominant in political consciousness in the main centers of power/authority throughout the world. In t_3 there may be various kinds of regressions, despite the overall drift toward $S_{2(WOMP)}$. Tension in the atmosphere accompanying dramatic reforms and the consolidation of structural adjustments should be anticipated. The degree of manifest tension may be inversely related to the extent to which these structural changes are mere continuations of tendencies already initiated in t_1 and t_2, tendencies which have increased their support through time as a result of problem-solving and value-realizing achievements that are generally associated with the emergence of a central guidance system of the $S_{2(WOMP)}$ variety.

A NOTE ON S_2 AND ITS RELATION
TO THE TRANSITION PROCESS

The rate and character of institutional and constitutional development during t_1 and t_2 will provide positive, negative, or mixed learning experiences for power-wielders and other groups concerned with order and justice in human affairs. The prospects for smooth transition, by which we mean a process that is largely nonviolent and cumulative, will depend on the extent to which a positive learning experience is widely shared throughout the world in relation to early efforts to pursue the new agenda of world order values.* In the rich developed countries

---

* "Widely shared" does not imply identical; the important ingredient of "learning" in this sense is the commitment to a continuous process of global reform, more or less in accordance with the WOMP priority schedule, but allowing for important variations in emphasis.

with liberal democratic traditions, such a positive response seems closely associated with developments that promote the structures of world peace and ecological quality without jeopardizing political autonomy or economic sufficiency.* In the less rich but developed socialist countries, a positive response is likely to be associated with successful world trade and internal economic development, with progress toward a more secure peace in a world setting that discourages confrontation and is more genuinely committed to the values of political and ideological diversity. Whether the poor countries have a positive learning experience in t_1 and t_2 depends very heavily on the degree to which alleviation of mass misery and a reduction in civil violence and intervention are associated with the promotion of WOMP values.† For some poorer countries, world order priorities involve a movement toward greater *autonomy* in *internal* affairs and greater *participation* in *external* affairs of significance. Latin American spokesmen seem particularly sensitive to these considerations.

World order perceptions will also be influenced by demographic tendencies, especially by the success which poor and crowded countries have in stabilizing their populations early in t_2. We need a set of indicators to identify positive and negative learning experiences for various actors who have diverse, and sometimes inconsistent, value priorities. (See Figures 5–1 to 5–3.)

The other important point is that the degree of violence and disruption is likely to depend on the evenness of the change curves, both with respect to perceived learning experience and with regard to the construction of the central guidance system or global polity. This assertion can be demonstrated by a series of distribution charts that are offered

---

* The learning process will not be shared by all groups. One important issue is whether currently dominant groups pursuing their own self-interest can become bearers of global reform in the WOMP direction, or whether responsibility for such reform must be assigned to under-class change-oriented groups. This issue (discussed further in Chapter VII) must be considered in relation to every important subsystem in the overall global structure. The range of WOMP proposals might also be studied in relation to the location within social and political systems of the main energies for global reform (although early assessments along these lines will necessarily be tentative).

† This assertion may be misleading. There are many poor countries whose governments are not at all seriously concerned with the alleviation of misery. These reactionary governments are generally interested in achieving a maximum rate of economic growth and in equalizing the relation of rich and poor countries as measured in aggregate terms. The world posture of Brazil is indicative of a strategy of participation taken by a reactionary Third World country eager to raise its status *as a state* in the global system. For discussion see Chapter VI, pp. 378–380.

Figure 5–1. World Order Learning Experience: Some Illustrative Distribution Patterns for Ten-Actor World for t_1 and t_2

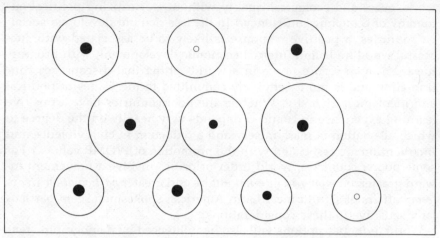

This is a largely positive learning experience suggesting prospects for accelerating a smooth transition process.

Code: Size of circles is roughly proportional to status of actor in the system.

Positive learning experience:

● 80% or more   ○ 30% or less   ● 55-80%   ○ 30-55%

largely for illustrative purposes. These charts are intended to report the situation as it exists late in t_2, assuming that developments up to then fulfill the transition prospects depicted in Figure 4–1 on p. 226. Figures 5–1 to 5–3 serve only to highlight the importance of positive learning experiences for smooth transition. At best, these distribution patterns are metaphors for the complexity that will be associated with engineering global reforms of appreciable magnitude over extended time periods.

For comparable purposes we suggest three institutional growth patterns characterized respectively by steady exponential growth, a rising slope of jagged growth, and a spiral downward until dramatically uplifted. (See Figures 5–4 to 5–6.) These patterns of structural development suggest some of the paths by which an adequate central guidance system might emerge. Again, their role is to underscore the complexity and the lines of plausible variability that might lead to eventual entry into t_3 and its culmination in S_2. These charts should be viewed as a more sophisticated, yet still very simplistic, consideration of the emergence of central guidance capabilities set forth on p. 235 and supporting text.

Figure 5–2. Mixed World Order Learning Experience

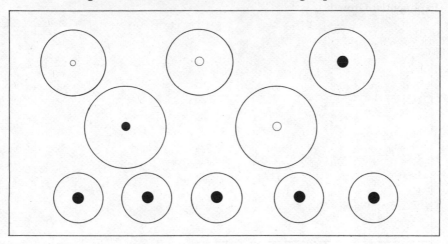

Mixed learning experience suggesting that prospects for t_3 are not bright and that smooth transition is not very likely; regressions possible, even likely.

Figure 5–3. Negative World Order Learning Experience

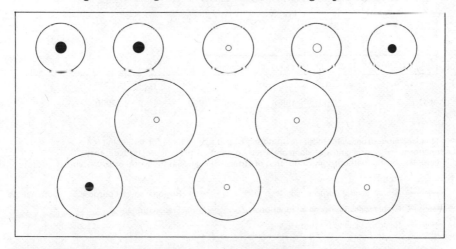

Largely negative learning experience suggesting likely disavowal of transition goals and regressive prospects for the future.

Figures 5–4 to 5–6 could be elaborated in greater detail, but their main purpose is served by showing that different patterns of actor growth and decline in t_1 and t_2 could create a variety of world order contexts within which t_3 might come into being. It is helpful to recall that t_3, by

Figure 5–4. Pattern of Institutional Development Characterized by Steady Exponential Growth

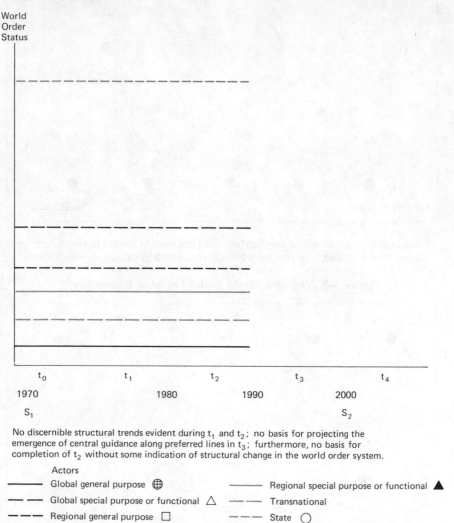

World
Order
Status

No discernible structural trends evident during t_1 and t_2; no basis for projecting the emergence of central guidance along preferred lines in t_3; furthermore, no basis for completion of t_2 without some indication of structural change in the world order system.

Actors
———— Global general purpose ⊕ 　　　　 ———— Regional special purpose or functional ▲
— — Global special purpose or functional △ 　 — — — Transnational
— — — Regional general purpose □ 　　　　 — — — State ○

stipulation, commences only after dominant political consciousness has been reoriented around a new set of world order values and after a worldwide movement for global reform has taken shape. However, t_2 could end with or without corresponding structural adjustments in actor roles. In general, if the end of t_2 is accompanied by appropriate

Figure 5–5. Pattern of Institutional Development Characterized by Uneven Growth

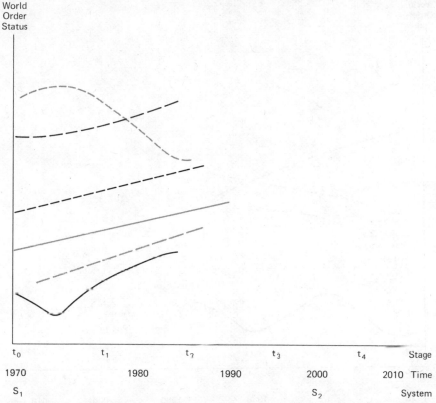

Withering away of state system amid a variety of structural trends vis-à-vis other categories of actors; cumulative trends are supportive of smooth transition through t_3 and the emergence therein of S_2.

structural change, t_3 is likely to witness a continuation of the adjust-ment process with, perhaps, a formal act of constitutional consolidation at the end of t_3 or early in t_4; if t_2 ends with no real institutional changes, t_3 is likely to be a period during which efforts to achieve dra-matic or abrupt institutional change are made, perhaps by a very bold strategy culminating in a single event of a magnitude comparable to that of the Peace of Westphalia. By our analysis, the initiation of t_3 implies a receptivity to the structural modifications needed to bring about S_2, and therefore it is a matter of finding the most efficient and humane formula. Our analysis also suggests, without insisting, that t_3 could commence approximately in 1990 and that S_2 could be realized in

Figure 5–6. Pattern of Institutional Development Characterized by Initial Downward Growth

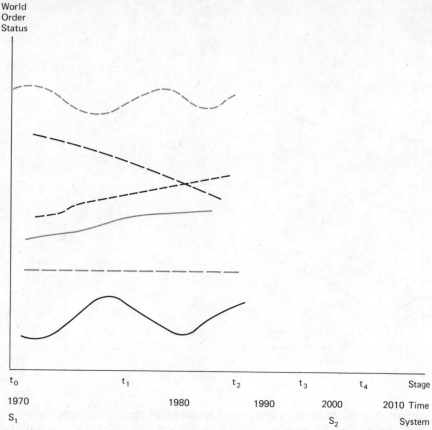

World
Order
Status

t_0	t_1		t_2	t_3	t_4	Stage
1970		1980	1990	2000	2010 Time
S_1				S_2	System

Dynamic structural tendencies are visible during t_1 and t_2, but it is unclear whether transition to t_3 will occur at all, or if it does, whether it will be smooth; trend lines are ambiguous.

the vicinity of the year 2000. Two final observations are relevant: first, as we have noted earlier, it may take several decades or more of experience in S_2 to comprehend the fact that the transition process from S_1 has been completed or should be so treated; there may not be a clear threshold occurrence, but rather a series of developments whose combined effects support a retrospective judgment that a new system of world order exists. History is often not as clear as historians. Second, the proposals we are concerned with are normative, as well as drastic. Hence, we seek a transition strategy that will result in a particular S_2 based on the value priorities embodied in the WOMP enterprise.* It is easy to contemplate an S_2 that is based on different values, for instance, one that accords primacy to war prevention and control of deviance. Such a world order system would be a nightmare for many individuals and sectors of the planet. There is an array of plausible S_2 outcomes for the transition process, and we designate desirable proposals for world order change by the notation $S_{2(WOMP)}$, thereby enabling comparison with $S_{2(World\ Empire)}$, $S_{2(World\ Police\ State)}$, $S_{2(Communitarian\ Anarchist\ Arrangement)}$, and so on.† Finally, we do not claim that $S_{2(WOMP)}$ or even $S_{2(WOMP/USA)}$ is the best of all possible S_2 outcomes, but only that it represents the array of outcomes that appears to best combine features of feasibility and desirability within the time frame of the relatively near future.

If the t sequence is rapid, and t_3 corresponds to the 1990's or earlier, the likelihood of a difficult $S_1 \rightarrow S_2$ seems quite great because such a rapid completion of t_1 and t_2 would occur only as a consequence of necessity (i.e., trauma and crisis), and because the WOMP value orientation would not have been very deeply assimilated by then even if dissemination efforts in t_1 are very successful.‡ If the t sequence is slower, it is possible that the transition $S_1 \rightarrow S_2$ will be a very positive period in which the notion of human progress and optimism about the future is reborn on the planet. In any event, from the vantage point of the present we can not do better than depict these alternate contours of t_3 that culminate in $S_1 \rightarrow S_2$. It may happen that t_1 and t_2 are only a decade long, but that t_3 is drawn out over a much longer period. There may then be a final spasm of adherence to S_1 structures and an outpouring of anxieties about impending changes on the global level.

We offer Table 5–3 to illustrate the alternative transition paths from $t_0 \rightarrow t_3$. The chapter has been written on the assumption that either each t interval equals about ten years, allowing the beginning of S_2 to coincide roughly with the year 2000, or that the length of the t interval is indeterminate and hence the sequence $t_1 \rightarrow t_3$ may theoretically take

---

* Even within WOMP each group has evolved its own preference model. There is no present analysis as to whether the various $S_{2(WOMP)}$ models converge with one another in critical respects.

† Of course, our special preference model is denoted $S_{2(WOMP)}$, which is one of eight models forming the $S_{2(WOMP)}$ subset of S_2.

‡ Only in the 1970's, after more than twenty-five years of post-war experiment, is a European consciousness emerging to complement specific national consciousnesses in the countries of Western Europe. This shift has finally taken place in the context of two destructive intra-European wars, pressure of a political kind from the Soviet Union, and pressure of an economic kind from the United States. Old patterns of identification do not give way easily, nor do power/authority structures dissolve quickly or voluntarily.

Table 5–3. Alternative Transition Paths

Interval of years	1	10	50	100
Specific t zone	t_1	t_2	t_3	
Patterns of t Sequences	$10t_1$	$10t_2$	$10t_3$	Path 1
	$10t_1$	$10t_2$	$50t_3$	Path 2
	$10t_1$	$1t_2$	$10t_3$	Path 3
	$100t_1$	$10t_2$	$5t_3$	Path 4

Note: The number before t indicates length of t interval in years; "Path" designates the pattern of $S_1 \rightarrow S_2$ transition in terms of sequence of world order developments as a function of intervals of time.

place over any period of time. As part of our methodology, however, it may eventually make sense to study distinct transition paths having different and uneven time sequences and durations, as depicted in Table 5–3.

FOCUS ON POLITICAL ARENAS

A second emphasis during the period of transition is on critical arenas of change and action. By arenas we refer to the milieu within which international actors derive their power and authority. Thus national governments, although capable of global action, are conceived as domestic arenas. The scope of formal competence as measured in jurisdictional terms—the legitimized capacity to govern events—further clarifies our use of the term arena. Actors whose formal mandate is somewhat nebulous may operate within certain ambiguous boundaries. The multinational corporation may be the most important example of an international actor whose arena of action is somewhat vaguely defined. In one sense, such a multinational corporation is controlled by a series of national charters of incorporation, but in another—and in our view more significant—sense, the multinational corporation is transnational rather than "multinational." * This transnational identity arises from the unity of corporate direction and control, the autonomy of its position relative

---

* On some occasions its identity is claimed to be a-national rather than transnational or multinational. Its a-national character would exempt it from any bonds of affiliation to a particular nation. Anti-American attitudes in the Third World create an additional incentive for avoiding an identity based on either the locus of a home office or of the capital ownership.

to many national governments, and the difficulty of imposing effective regulatory policies emanating from any particular national source. The multinational corporation is an elusive, yet formidable, new actor on the world scene with its own self-interested ideas about the proper course of global reform.

As with the evolution of an authority structure appropriate for S_2, our emphasis on critical arenas will be arranged in a sequence that corresponds to the three developmental stages (t_1, t_2, t_3) postulated as necessary for the completion of the transition process. These stages can, in turn, be roughly correlated with the three decades remaining in the century. To avoid undue complexity and because we are more confident about the validity of the developmental stages than their time frames, we will relate the role of distinct arenas to different t periods.

The focus on critical arenas is not meant to delineate mutually exclusive categories. Again, as with the sequence of consciousness, mobilization, and transformation, the sequence of critical arenas is meant to give some coherence to a process of plausible development. Obviously, throughout the transition process significant action will or can occur in all arenas, and in a very real sense the degree of interplay among arenas should be regarded as a significant variable during the successive stages of transition. This interplay will probably intensify through time, providing one index of the increasing degree of interdependence in human affairs, and we expect that it will be considerably greater in S_2 than in the later stages of S_1.

We project the following sequence of critical arenas:

Domestic Arena t_1	Transnational and Regional Arenas t_2	Global Arena t_3

Our rationale for projecting this sequence is as follows: The initial task, and the precondition for other steps toward $S_{2(WOMP/USA)}$, require a reorientation of governing consciousness in the principal sovereign states of the world. This process of reorientation, whether it occurs mainly by persuasion (including party politics) or by struggle (including violent revolution), will largely take place in a domestic context, although significant positive and negative learning experiences will be projected across national boundaries.* The outcomes in principal states

---

* For instance, the September 1973 overthrow of Allende's government in Chile will stimulate very different perceptions of how to accomplish drastic change. From a conser-

will influence both the pace and form of adjustment. The present situation seems to discourage any prospect that these domestic outcomes will be compatible with movement toward t_2. Nevertheless, in thinking about the future of world order it seems essential to stipulate that normative reorientations must occur within domestic arenas by the end of t_1, i.e., before the beginning of t_2. In theory, this may extend t_1 in chronological time well beyond 1980, perhaps for an indefinite period, but this possibility only indicates the uncertainty that attends the future. However, we do argue explicitly that $S_{2(WOMP/USA)}$ will only come about through a particular sequence of transition stages. We acknowledge that other sequences are also possible, indeed, that other sequences might attain $S_{2(WOMP/USA)}$ more rapidly, securely, and humanely than our image of transition, but we limit ourselves here to this principal transition path. It would be desirable for others who accept our proposals to set forth alternative transition paths that lead to $S_{2(WOMP)}$ or even $S_{2(WOMP/USA)}$, accompanying their recommendations with reasons for regarding them as preferable or more likely to occur.*

If and when t_1 does come to an end, in t_2 the critical arenas will be those within which transnational and regional actors operate. In t_2 we expect to find a large proliferation of transnational actors, and a particular set of economic crises involving the role and orientation of economic organizations operating within transnational realms.† We anticipate a central struggle to bring those progressive values now dominant in domestic arenas (this is the meaning of the completion of t_1) to bear on transnational operations, including especially activities associated with the multinational corporation in its various formats. As t_2 proceeds, we would also expect regional actors to gain increasing prominence as new world order system "experiments." Leaders of national governments in

---

vative outlook, the Allende experiment suggests that any drastic reform proposal destroys the framework of constitutional government and generates recourse to counter-governmental violence. From a radical viewpoint, the downfall of Allende confirms the Leninist contention that it is impossible to make a social revolution by parliamentary means, or, put differently, that a program of drastic reform will be crushed unless the reformers first destroy the apparatus of "the bourgeois state."

* It is important to keep in mind that other WOMP documents are based on different images of the transition process and different concepts of $S_{2(WOMP)}$. Our version of $S_{2(WOMP)}$ is identified as $S_{2(WOMP/USA)}$ and is attained by Transition Path 1 (Table 5–3).

† We acknowledge the possibility that we may have reversed the sequence of transitional developments. That is, crises in the world economy may occur in t_1 prior to reorientations of governing consciousness in domestic arenas. These crises may induce transnational resolutions which, in turn, generate value changes in domestic arenas that correspond roughly to the WOMP mandate.

t_2, although largely oriented toward S_2, will still have to maintain a degree of coherence in their domestic politics, and may be confronted by varying forms of regressive opposition that seek to maintain the behavioral and belief patterns appropriate for S_1. Hence, it may be especially disruptive to press forward prematurely toward central guidance in t_2; our preferred strategy of "drastic gradualism" would be to strengthen the progressive tendencies within national arenas by building more modestly in t_2 at the regional level. We stipulate that t_2 does not end until transnational and regional activities have expanded considerably over their magnitude in t_0 and until the values associated with $S_{2(WOMP)}$ have gained ascendancy at the transnational and regional levels.* As with t_1, there is real uncertainty regarding both the duration of t_2 and whether it can be brought to a successful conclusion. It is unclear, for instance, whether or not major multinational corporations can be influenced in such a way as to make them a positive feature in the movement for global reform along WOMP lines. Even strong national governments have had great difficulties in dealing with internal organizations (General Motors, Mafia, Ku Klux Klan) whose particular set of goals may, in general or on important occasions, come into sharp conflict with dominant national policies. We believe that t_3 should not be thought of as beginning until t_2 tasks have been substantially completed.

In t_3 the main reform undertaking will occur within the global arena, involving world order bargaining to create and sustain the sort of central guidance mechanism implied by the $S_{2(WOMP/USA)}$ preference model set forth in Chapter IV. Here, too, the incompleteness of the successes in t_1 and t_2 would indicate continuing reliance on the posture of drastic gradualism. There is a need to proceed on the basis of maximum consensus so as to weaken the appeals and prospects of those social forces throughout the world which continue to identify their interests with restoring some form of S_1. As the trend lines and political groupings become unmistakable, it is realistic to anticipate a very concerted effort in t_3 to organize counterrevolutionary world order movements and, possibly, to concentrate upon maintaining pockets of affiliation to an S_1 concept. Perhaps the toleration of diversity in S_2 could extend protection even to such "backward" or "primitive" experiments in political organization. The important point, and the principal challenge during

---

* We cannot be more precise about the degree of expansion in transnational and regional activities. The prospects for creating a global polity of an $S_{2(WOMP)}$ character will, at that stage, be influenced by the extent to which the value changes in t_1 have really reshaped outlooks and behavior patterns.

t_3, involves the construction of a central guidance system that is oriented around the four WOMP values, and yet is sensitive to the dangers of excessive concentrations of power and authority. Again, duration and outcome are contingent dimensions, but the completion of t_3 tasks is a precondition to the existence of $S_{2(WOMP/USA)}$. It is quite plausible, given our support for value reformulation throughout the process of transition, that a beneficial S_2 will be organized around values that are more encompassing or quite different from those we now emphasize. It seems likely that "the technological crunch" in the years ahead may give greater prominence and universality to the human crises now commencing in the most advanced countries on issues relating to the nature of work, human identity, and alienation. We do not prescribe the normative orientation of S_2 beyond suggesting that it involves a humane and peaceful embodiment and extension of the four WOMP values.*

We realize that this outline of developments is vaguer than desirable, but it proceeds without the benefit of established conceptual categories and still presents, hopefully, a program that is definite enough to be challenged by contending viewpoints. Our main purpose here is the modest one of providing a tentative framework for thought and action that might guide the formation of a global reform movement or, at least, provoke a better series of concepts on how to think and how to act in relation to global reform.†

THE DOMESTIC IMPERATIVE OF T_1

The dynamics of global political reform are closely associated with the power/authority nexus that exists in the latter stages of S_1. This nexus

---

* These four values seem to be minimum conditions for a humane and peaceful process of transition to a beneficial form of S_2. Additional values of the sort we have associated with S_3, or involving considerations about which we are insensitive, may very well become ingredients of the global reform movement during t_2 and t_3. The pace of value shift is very rapid, and it is extremely hazardous to project value priorities far into the future.

† Perhaps we have not stressed enough the dialectical character of a global reform movement. The work of embodying S_2 would proceed in the most personal and local spheres of human existence. The evolution of the central guidance system would be more a *symptom* of WOMP consciousness than its *essence*. We have, perhaps, perpetuated the errors of past reform literature by devoting too much attention to structures of governance, and not enough to the changes in the quality of life and patterns of experience that would become increasingly meaningful as the process of transition gathers momentum.

continues to be organized around statist symbols and concerns. Such statism is premised on a readiness for armed conflict, especially by the richest and most powerful. Cooperative endeavors between governments are based on their perceived and discretionary sense of self-interest. The basic postulates of state action involve competition for limited valuable goods and maximization of relative shares of wealth, power, and status within the world system.[8] There are several deficiencies in this form of world order, given the realities of the 1970's, but we will refer to two issues that are peculiarly relevant to this inquiry:

The diminishing capacity of governments to articulate and serve human interests

The growing incompatibility between a laissez-faire mode of world organization and the promotion of human interests on a global scale.

We need measures to assess the relative capacity and willingness of various governments to pursue a schedule of goals that corresponds to some sort of schedule of national well-being. In essence, governments in many parts of the world are not responsive to the needs of their own societies, but rather to the interests of a privileged ruling elite.* The following letter to the *New York Times* written from the town of Euluss, Texas expresses well this fundamental opposition between governmental and human interests. The letter was stimulated by a public controversy over whether the United Nations should insist that governments turn over captured hijackers to their country of origin:

The direction the U.N. takes is important, but I am doubtful of any solution which requires the return of the political refugee. The greatest service the U.N. can render is to gain acceptance by all nations of a Bill of Rights for mankind. . . . Man is important, not nations. We should be allowed to leave our valley, to climb our mountain, to cross the sea; to be free as the wind. That is our natural right.

How naive. How vulnerable to diplomatic argument. But how basic to man. We need the recognition of man—not nations.

Our diplomats have failed us. Look at Cuba. Our people did not fail the Cuban people. The Cuban people did not fail our people. The leadership of the countries failed us and continues to do so.

---

* We identify "needs" in humanistic and WOMP terms. We do not accept the Roman formula of "bread and circuses" or the Grand Inquisitor's prescription in Dostoyevski's legend of "bread, mystery, and miracle."

We should have normal air service and trade relations with Cuba today. Why not? They chop their sugar cane like we do. They fish the same ocean we fish. The put on their pants one leg at a time, etc., etc. If the people could break through the barriers maintained by leadership, we could have peace.[9]

This letter in many respects illustrates an orientation of domestic consciousness that needs to become much more prevalent during t_1. Even allowing for overstatement, the author basically realizes that governments should exist *to serve men*, not the other way around, but that international diplomacy in fact often acts to promote governmental interests at great human cost. This skepticism about the capacity of government to fulfill its proclaimed ends challenges the statist myth that national well-being in world affairs can be automatically associated with governmental policy.

Governmental actors, even if sincerely oriented toward the promotion of national well-being, are not well-suited by structure or tradition to solve the outstanding problems of mankind. In this respect, domestic education in world order studies would have to combine a critique of the failures and dangers of S_1 with the positive alternatives that exist in the form of $S_{2(WOMP)}$ and other S_2 models of preferred worlds. The domestic imperative cannot be satisfied in t_1 until the public and a significant proportion of leadership groups come to share this general assessment (i.e., that the organizational weakness of S_1 cannot meet the existing challenges of interdependence, insufficiency, and inequality). Public opinion must also understand that liberation is possible through massive social engineering designed to bring into being the most beneficial world order system, given the array of S_2 options. "Education" is used broadly to include learning experiences associated with domestic and world behavior that clarify the choices among various S_1 and S_2 orientations.*

At present, leaders in the large states cannot gain or maintain power unless they adhere, at least overtly, to some S_1 pattern of belief and practice. Acceptable orientations range from extremes of autarchy or self-reliance to extremes of expansion and conquest, although the pursuit of these extremes is generally tempered by considerations of prudence and limited capabilities. The point is that as t_1 proceeds, the

---

* Note that not every S_2 solution is an improvement over S_1, given WOMP criteria. For instance, imperial, tyrannical, or possibly even multinational corporate consolidations of power and authority in a unified structure seem likely to be more dangerous and costly than the state system in its post-mature stages.

perspectives of S_2 will have to become less alien to public opinion and to policy-making groups around the world. Among the decisive obstacles now preventing or retarding this attitudinal adjustment is the hold that S_1 power-wielders have on communications and education; the strange contrast in the United States between public and commercial television illustrates the tension between S_1 and S_2 realms of value, with governing groups tending, ironically, to align themselves mainly with commercial TV.*

Nevertheless, reality has a way of penetrating. Carefully documented accounts of what is wrong with S_1, and why S_2 can be both designed and attained through human endeavor, need to be disseminated as widely as possible. Limited critiques of S_1 patterns, such as are made by deprived groups—minorities, the poor, women, the young, the aged—need to be broadened to global dimensions. Those who already adhere to $S_{2(WOMP)}$ need to associate their advocacy, now so isolated from mainstream politics, with real social forces struggling for liberation. The only hope of satisfying the domestic imperative involves the formation of coalitions among change-oriented groups seeking constructive ends. In this regard an inwardly-directed progressive movement that gains power will almost surely contain a spill-over of attitudes favoring drastic global reform, a spill-over that will be inconsequential unless it is reinforced by specific positive results elsewhere. A progressive outward orientation by a government cannot endure hostile responses from other governments and sectors of the world system without hardening its own behavior. Positive reinforcement would probably be needed to sustain a major government in its determination to make serious efforts in t_1 to encourage really drastic forms of global reform along WOMP lines. In truth, however, if such a government—its leadership backed by public sentiment—were enlightened about the needs of and possibilities for global reform, it could not be so easily swayed from its course of advocating structural change in the world order system, no matter what the reaction of other governments. At most, its reliance on conventional techniques of persuasion and diplomacy might be shaken, and it might align itself increasingly with a nongovernmental global reform movement. Therefore, t_1 de-

---

* The irony is rather deep. Commercial TV, by and large, avoids raising fundamental questions. It helps tranquilize the citizenry and to induce compliant attitudes of respect and obedience. Public TV, because it tends to deal with more intellectual subject matter, probes discontent and often confronts official policy with severe criticism. The relative freedom of American society needs to be contrasted with the oppressive removal of options in a society that controls all forms of public communication.

pends on reinforcing developments throughout the world, but not necessarily of the same kind. Third world countries might still obtain great benefit from a modified S_1 orientation in their struggles to satisfy their minimum material needs and to provide their peoples with a sense of growth, cohesion, and autonomy. The highly industrial societies—where growth, cohesion, and autonomy are becoming costly social goals, often destructive of the general quality of life—need to move rapidly toward the double realization that S_1 is doomed, and that a credible vision of S_2 can rekindle human hope in the future for their countries and for the world.*

In more specific terms, it is unlikely that organized centers of power, communication, or education can take the lead in spreading the message of transition, at least not early in t_1. The early initiatives will have to be pioneered by progressive individuals and groups acting within "the open spaces" tolerated by beleaguered S_1 elites. These spaces may be closed off in various ways, or they may be widened somewhat. This central uncertainty will be resolved by a series of factors bearing on how domestic elites choose to respond to deteriorating public confidence, •or more aptly, to a spreading mood of subversion among enlightened segments of their own citizenry. It is evident that even societies which enjoy democratic traditions are moving in the direction of internal colonization because of their tacit acknowledgement that the social contract between governed and governors has been decisively broken.[11]

Without a better understanding of causal linkages, we cannot predict with confidence just how principal governments will react to the advocacy of global reform by their respective citizenries. More moderate external behavior by dominant governments may encourage a broader S_1/S_2 dialogue, or S_1 elites may reach external accommodations which enable them to concentrate even greater energy on isolating, destroying, or reshaping S_2 tendencies within their own societies.†

---

* The richest countries, of course, should also continue to be attentive to the needs of deprived segments of their own populations. Redistributive policies are imperative to eliminate poverty and mitigate the consequences of unequal opportunity for group and self-realization. In this sense, the warning of social reformers to resist the appeals of the ecology movement until the needs of the poor have been satisfied deserve a fair hearing.[10]

† National governments are not necessarily opposed to all S_2 options. Indeed, governments in principal states seem to be moving toward an acceptance of S_2 reform scenarios modeled along *condominium* or *concert* lines. See Chapter III, pp. 201–209. Other influential domestic groups associated with policy-making for some multinational corporations also endorse a kind of S_2 scenario that seeks a single world market. Neither of these S_2 options is in any way aligned with the WOMP schedule of value priorities.

It does seem likely that the reduction of warfare as a regular feature of international relations will encourage more movement toward benign concepts of S_2 on the part of relatively secure and prosperous state actors. This trend is already prominent in the Scandinavian countries. Perhaps the exemplary role of stable middle powers—advanced enough industrially both to have solved minimum material problems and now to be confronting post-industrial challenges—can serve as a basis of pressure throughout the world, especially by providing inspiration to counter-elites in the states whose governments are most determined to retain S_1 values and behavior patterns. During the Indochina War, appeals by American anti-war activists to the Swedish government demonstrated that during the period of transition, the act of soliciting support from a foreign government can be the very opposite of treason.* This sort of transnational link—between individuals of one country and the government of another—constitutes one of the potential sources of strength that will be needed to hasten the spread of $S_{2(WOMP)}$ thinking during t_1.

Webs of interdependence stimulate cooperative enterprises even for elites oriented toward S_1 values. These cooperative ventures tend to undermine purist notions of national autonomy, even when they are justified in S_1 rhetoric. S_1 patterns of justification are especially pronounced in the war/peace area, where the traditional Westphalia notion of the government as guardian of the people is most centrally at issue. Justification in American domestic arenas of SALT (Strategic Arms Limitation Talks) [12] agreements on grounds that they facilitate U.S. weapons development while retarding comparable Soviet advances, illustrates an extreme form of reliance on S_1 logic; it is particularly extreme when we take account of the fact that the arms environment is already replete with ultra-destructive weaponry.† That the debate should be between S_1 apologists and S_1 ardent loyalists suggests the extent to which we must understand our failure to move deeply into t_1. It re-

---

* The reference to treason may be obscure. We are arguing that those who oppose an aggressive war waged by their own government are in fact world order activists trying to serve the larger national interests of their society. In this sense, the appeal for help to foreign governments is anti-treasonous in intent and effect, designed only to promote the well-being of the country.

† Part of this internal debate has to do with the difficulty of negotiating a consensus among critical domestic interest groups. Some critics of Soviet–American arms control negotiations argue that on balance, they accelerate the arms race. The domestic military–industrial complex in each society is reassured that the really menacing weapons systems will not be regulated, so that the agreements reached make research and development (R and D) elsewhere in the military system more necessary than ever.

mains virtually impossible for a statesman in a leading country, however progressive he may be on other matters, to speak or act out of deference to $S_{2(WOMP)}$ aspirations, except in the vaguest terms of ritual rhetoric.* Despite this discouraging fact, the steady pressure to negotiate international arrangements tends to associate national welfare with cooperation rather than conflict and to require a greater understanding of world interests; † cooperation by agreement necessarily encourages the creation of procedures and institutions to implement, adapt, and sustain the arrangement.

Conversely, the perils and costs of unilateralism become ever more evident, whether the goal is protecting great whale species against the predations of the two main whaling countries or seeking to plan economic transactions in a reliable fashion.‡ Obviously, disasters associated with S_1 patterns of behavior can help to generate a reformist mood, especially if construed by progressive adherents of S_2 reform. Auschwitz, Hiroshima, Vietnam, Torrey Canyon, the peregrine falcon, terrorism at the 1972 Olympic Games, letterbombs in London—each is a metaphor of the "sealed fate" associated with the persistence of S_1.

Our fundamental point is that although the domestic imperative of T_1 will be difficult to satisfy, its satisfaction is essential in bringing about a new political consciousness which can then be mobilized in t_2 for action in t_3. The relation of forces within the most powerful states continues to be dominated by either S_1 attitudes and structures or by undesirable S_2 options. The gradual crystallization of one S_2 position is taking place among ruling groups in powerful states, but it is not the positive sort of development envisioned by $S_{2(WOMP)}$. We need a more politically sophisticated approach to the dissemination of positive forms of S_2 thinking in various national settings, so that a positive concept begins to be understood as part of the solution for a whole series of problems which are

---

* As Nixon and Kissinger prove, however, the movement toward some kind of S_2 option is increasingly acceptable to public opinion. Their conception of S_2 is managerial and hierarchical, and seems oblivious to considerations of equity or ecological quality.

† However, intergovernmental conferences may be unable to articulate human or planetary interests. The search for consensus among antagonistic and unequally placed governments leads to embodying contradictory goals in overarching declarations of allegedly shared sentiment. The consequence is irrelevance and incoherence. The Stockholm Declaration on the Human Environment of 1972 could be seen in this light. [13]

‡ Here, too, there are exceptions. It seems that increased unilateral claims vis-à-vis offshore resources are being made. Indeed, they are likely to be beneficial responses by poor countries to their situation of technological inferiority. China has recently elevated its claim of a 200-mile limit to the highest level of demand for S_1 reform.

now viewed as unrelated and susceptible to either an S_1 solution or to a regressive variant of S_2.*

THE TRANSNATIONAL AND REGIONAL
IMPERATIVES OF t_2

The altered national consciousness that exists by the end of t_1 is likely to cause a shift in critical arenas beyond the nation–state during t_2. For one thing, the new consciousness is, by definition, oriented toward WOMP values and acutely sensitive to the need for steps in the direction of S_2; at the same time, leaders of a movement for global reform will be seriously concerned in early t_2 about consolidating the gains of late t_1 and resisting backsliding tendencies that seek to re-establish S_1 patterns of thought and action in principal governments. Therefore, national governments are likely to be cautious about following through in t_2, although mindful of the need and desirability of doing so.† This assessment of the dominant political mood in early t_2 depends on a large number of uncertain conditions, especially on the extent to which the problem areas in S_1 are perceived as approaching or even crossing thresholds of disaster (whether in the form of war, famine, pandemic, economic collapse, ecological decay, resource shortages or pervasive *ad hoc* terror, as well as their interrelations).‡

In general, the greater the *perceived pressure* of problems upon the main nexuses of power/authority, the more rapid the transitional progress through t_2 is likely to be; on the other hand, the more rapid the pace of transition in t_2, the greater the chance of significant reversals of orientation in principal domestic arenas, as the move toward S_2 will be

---

* When we characterize S_2 options as regressive or negative we do so by reference to WOMP value criteria. The reasoning beneath these shorthand judgments is given elsewhere, especially in Chapter VII, pp. 442–448.

† It is reasonable to expect a wide range of national positions on the pace and depth of feasible steps of global reform early in t_2.

‡ In our discussion of transition sequence, we have not postulated a worsening of the international situation with respect to perceived problems. However, for reasons specified in Chapters II and III, we anticipate such deterioration. In this event, the completion of t_1 would have created the sort of political consciousness that might greatly accelerate reform prospects in t_2. The most formidable obstacles to global reform probably exist at the outset of the transition process. In this sense, positing symmetrical t periods may be misleading, and Transition Path 4 (Table 5–3) may be the most realistic conception; or, if transition is set within the WOMP time frame, then the following sequence: $20t_1$, $5t_2$, $5t_3$.

perceived as threatening entrenched groups.* Thus we would argue that early t_2 is likely to commence in a gradualist spirit that will be sustained only if problem-solving does not attain crisis proportions. If crises do occur, t_2 will probably exhibit more dramatic progress toward S_2 but, at the same time, be more vulnerable to relapse and "a turning back of the clock" to t_1 or even beyond.

Against this background, we think it likely that the critical arenas in early t_2 (t_{2a} in our notational system) will involve transnational relations, and in late t_2 (i.e., t_{2b}) will involve regional relations. Transnational arenas would provide somewhat ambiguous settings within which to carry forward a reoriented world order consciousness. These arenas would not involve any real break with S_1 structure or behavioral patterns, and yet would provide a basis for mobilizing the forces needed to accomplish the transformations which will be required during t_3. Technological complexity, the rising significance of ocean resources, space exploration, protection of the human environment, protection of communication and transportation from disruption, reliance on nuclear energy, the growth and dispersion of multinational capitalism and socialist state trade, the diffusion of culture and education, and trade control including narcotics, are among the transnationalizing forces that will be at work regardless of other world order tendencies. Assuming a successful completion of t_1, however, this rise of transnationalism also creates very important mobilization opportunities in t_2. Reoriented elites in national governments would seem highly motivated to experiment in transnational arenas with inchoate S_2 structures of control and participation, including—but not necessarily limited to—structures embodying incipient WOMP value priorities. We would also expect an explicit effort on the part of functional reference groups (students, blacks, workers, pilots, professionals, and others) to organize transnationally and to identify their political affiliations and goals in more cosmopolitan terms. S_2 movements, including one or more incipient world political parties, are likely to be founded, possibly dividing along presently unfamiliar ideological lines and differing with

---

* So long as global reform prospects are moderate there is a likelihood of acquiescence in the shift of political mood. But if the reform movement gains momentum and threatens the well-being of entrenched groups in fundamental ways, desperate strategies become more likely to thwart subsequent moves. It is at such a point that conservative forces in states might seize power and treat leaders of a global reform movement, including elected officials, as dangerous revolutionaries. The Chilean counterrevolutionary coup of 1973 may provide an ominous warning to global reformers that vigilance may be most needed *after* their hour of success.

one another on the degree of centralism appropriate for different political and economic functions.

We envision strong regulatory impulses to bring transnational arenas of action into conformity with the new world order consciousness. For instance, multinational corporations will, in all likelihood, become even more formidable centers of power and authority, oriented primarily around an S_2 outlook that is at odds with $S_{2(WOMP)}$.* Indeed, we may postulate a struggle between national leaders espousing transition toward $S_{2(WOMP)}$ and business leaders espousing transition toward $S_{2(MNC)}$ as the central conflict of early t_2. $S_{2(MNC)}$ is our symbolic notation for an S_2 option organized around criteria of market efficiency. The multinational corporation (MNC) would be the dominant actor and its concerns with sales, growth, and profits would be fully appreciated and protected. There is a wide range of judgments about social and political issues relative to our value priorities ($V_1 \rightarrow V_4$) that might accompany the realization of $S_{2(MNC)}$. It is possible to envision either an appreciable improvement in realization as compared to S_1, especially for V_1, V_3, and V_4, or a virtual repudiation of these goals except possibly V_1. It is hard to visualize the persistence in $S_{2(MNC)}$ of war as we have known it, although there may be severe struggles among competing corporate actors.

This overarching S_2 consensus is likely to prevail over reactionary efforts to rehabilitate S_1 in t_2, because the dominant elites in the most critical arenas of action are likely by then to share a system-changing orientation toward the future of the world. But in order to complete t_{2a}, it will be necessary to quell or reshape the tendencies toward $S_{2(MNC)}$, especially as these are now embodied in transnational business and functional elites. It is quite likely that specialized international institutions will be assigned regulatory functions in relation to transnational economic activities, particularly on the oceans and in space, and that these so-called international auspices will be socialized into the dominant $S_{2(MNC)}$ orientation.[14] The outcome of the struggle between adherents of $S_{2(WOMP)}$ and $S_{2(MNC)}$ will largely determine the ending of t_{2a} and the shift to a regional emphasis in t_{2b}.

In t_{2b} the focus will be on regional arenas. As with transnational arenas, regional arenas will become increasingly important throughout t_1 and t_2 as an almost automatic by-product of growing international complexity. This steady increase of regional activity will not be linear or

---

* On the other hand, some multinational corporations may adopt a WOMP outlook and join in promoting such a process of global reform.

evenly evident throughout the world, but trendlines in all regions are likely to exhibit cumulative growth over this period of time.* Again, the task in t_{2b} will be to convert regional actors into mobilization centers that facilitate transition to S_2. In this respect, it will be important to reorient the activities of these regional actors around WOMP value priorities. Such reorientations would be generally supported by national governments, given their t_2 perspective, and yet would not overly expose t_2 national elites to reversionary movements within their territorial bases of power and prestige. The reorientation of regional elites encourages experimentation with intermediate forms of central guidance that fall between the basic statist structure of S_1 and the more globalist structure of S_2. Also, the diversity of regional situations allows a series of distinct visions of $S_{2(WOMP)}$ to be tested to some extent, without altogether rupturing the more particularistic and conflictual images of world order that have evolved out of the Westphalia tradition and kindred political traditions in the East.† Regional prospects depend considerably on the genuineness of the cooperative, multinational nexus, which may in turn presuppose both the elimination of "superpower" participation from regional membership and the creation of stronger traditions of constitutionalism and autonomous operation within regional arenas. For t_{2b} to end, a substantial evolution of structural reform will be required in regional arenas, including a consensus among regional policy-makers that regional problems require drastic global reforms of the sort associated with a shift to $S_{2(WOMP)}$.‡

The combined accomplishments of t_{2a} and t_{2b} will reinforce disorganized social forces mobilizing around WOMP values within or across national boundaries. In this respect, t_2 carries forward the altered consciousness of t_1 to a point where drastic proposals for global institutional reform become realistic projects for t_3. While these steps are proceeding toward S_2, it will nevertheless be important to bear in mind the likelihood that problems of pollution, poverty, privation, and strife may grow worse in t_1 and t_2 than they were in t_0, and that pessimistic

---

* Regional prospects are very much conditioned by a series of specific characteristics that pertain to *each* regional subsystem. It is very difficult to generalize about the systemic phenomenon of regionalism.[15]

† It is well to appreciate the fact that the world order system associated with S_1 was not truly a global system except for a very short period of time during the peak of colonialism (say, 1880–1920). Throughout most of the time the Eurocentric system associated with Westphalia was the richest and most powerful subsystem, but it coexisted with other important subsystems that had quite distinct normative and political traditions.[16]

‡ If regional tendencies do evolve rapidly in t_{2b}, they may influence very significantly the structural modifications undertaken in t_3. Indeed, regional roles could become much larger than those posited in our preference model of $S_{2(WOMP/USA)}$.

images of S_2 prospects are likely to evoke attention and fear.* Such a negative balance-sheet of response contributes dynamic energy that always underlies progressive reform, but that also makes the passage to the future replete with risks and costs. Developments in t_1 and t_2 largely involve *organizing* to meet the challenges of world order problems, but do not appear likely to achieve their solution or even amelioration, given the underlying pressures consequent upon economic and demographic growth. There are likely to be conflicting interpretations in t_{2b} as to whether the $S_{2(WOMP)}$ program is a utopian mirage or a viable political undertaking.† A positive interpretation of S_2 prospects is likely to prevail, however, if the progress through t_2 manifests real reorientations in the outlook and behavior of principal actors in transnational and regional arenas. In turn, this kind of positive interpretation will create both a receptivity to and an impatience for the transformation of global structure that we associate with the final transition from $S \rightarrow S_2$. Indeed, alongside the reactionary views of S_2, a "progressive" redefinition will emerge in critical arenas by the end of t_2 that challenges advocacy of $S_{2(WOMP)}$ by positing a more perfect world order concept (S_3) as desirable and attainable, or by reformulating $S_{2(WOMP)}$ in such basic terms as to make earlier embodiments seem virtually irrelevant.

THE GLOBAL IMPERATIVE OF t_3

For t_3 to begin, by definition the mobilization phase must be substantially completed. The boundary line between t_2 and t_3 is obviously

---

* S_2 may not seem like the promised land, but more like an emergency reorganization of planetary existence undertaken during an hour of dire necessity.

† If scarcities become acute, neo-Darwinian S_2 options may engender strong minority followings even if more humanistic versions of S_2 achieve majority support. There is no assurance that the majority will prevail against determined neo-Darwinian efforts to accent hierarchy and privilege in the process of adjusting to the new challenges of scarcity. In that event, highly repressive and manipulative approaches to S_2 will become prominent in t_2. How to deal with these approaches is a formidable ethical and tactical issue. There is no easy resolution. To deal repressively with neo-Darwinian movements for global reform is to commence the vicious circle of repression begetting violence, begetting further repression, and so on. To tolerate such neo-Darwinian movements is to expose the transition process to elements that would thwart its most fundamental goals and send its most faithful adherents to jail or possibly, to their death. We can only recommend sensitivity to the dilemma; we see no assured way to overcome the twin set of dangers or, even, to choose between them in the abstract.

somewhat arbitrary and indistinct, and needs to be more objectively identified by reference to specific indicators. At present, in considering the shift from t_2 to t_3 we are concerned only with the reorientation of outlook within critical arenas. By the end of t_2 the shifts in national consciousness will have become more definite and less vulnerable to reversionary tendencies. Also, by the end of t_2 transnational and regional arenas will have become generally oriented toward $S_{2(WOMP)}$. There will probably still be important ambiguities relating to the choice of S_2 option, and whether $S_{1(WOMP)}$ is posited as an alternative to $S_{2(WOMP)}$.* That is, the value consensus at the end of t_2 may appear to obviate the need for structural changes related to $S_1 \rightarrow S_2$.

Put differently, given the value atmosphere existing at the end of t_2, there may be a sense of an emergent capacity to solve world order problems without any further centralization of functions. Thus, the reform energy mobilized behind the pursuit of S_2 may appear dissipated early in t_3. We think this kind of world order "complacency" unlikely to persist, if it does indeed develop, for two main reasons: first, world order problems are likely by then to have worsened, especially those relating to social and economic misery and ecological jeopardy; second, the evolving technology of production and consumption, including the source of energy, will be increasingly global in its scope of operations and impacts.† As a result, there is no reason to suppose that the appearance of a WOMP orientation is likely to engender widespread confidence in the capacity of S_1 to cope with existing world order problems—quite the contrary. Furthermore, the heightened interdependence, complexity, and scarcity characteristic of global affairs in late t_2 would seem to encourage receptivity to central guidance approaches to problem-solving.

Hence, in our view t_3 will produce dramatic action in the global arena as a stage-setting prelude to S_2. The precise character of this action is difficult to anticipate, but it would certainly involve, at the very least,

---

* $S_{1(WOMP)}$ implies a concept of global reform that combines realization of WOMP values with the structure and interstate dynamics associated with S_1.

In early t_3 there is also likely to be considerable factionalism among various adherents of $S_{2(WOMP)}$. Issues of priorities, leadership, ideology, and so on, may create very important divisions, especially if S_1 adherence weakens and there is no serious challenge posed by reactionary forces mobilized behind $S_{2(MNC)}$ or $S_{2(Condominium)}$.

† By t_3 there is also likely to be a strong sense of global identity in terms of affinities, symbolic identification, and belief system. As a consequence, the development of a central guidance presence may satisfy strong sentiments for tangible expressions of unity and solidarity in planetary affairs.

some administrative machinery to supervise drastic disarmament, a world program of economic assistance and disaster relief, and apparatus for the use, conservation, and allocation of shared resources (e.g., ocean resources and the renewable resources of earth, air, water). As we have indicated earlier, the WOMP/USA vision of a preferred world is nongovernmental and nonstatist in character.* We anticipate that new political forms will emerge in t_3 to deal with specific functional issues (see the institutional profile set forth in Chapter III) that seek efficiency by means of coordination and planning (rather than hierarchy), and that are strongly committed to "checks and balances," divided structures of authority and power, and the minimization of bureaucracy.

The process of transformation may itself be cumulative and gradual, with t_3 perceived only retrospectively (after some decades) as the interval during which $S_1 \rightarrow S_2$ took place. It is also possible, although less likely, that a ritual and formal transition $S_1 \rightarrow S_2$ will be consciously organized around a series of occurrences late in t_3, especially if this period should coincide with the year 2000. The main problems in the global arena may involve conflicts among defenders of competing images of S_2, possibly the survival or revival of $S_{2(MNC)}$ or a movement to achieve $S_{2(EMP)}$, $S_{2(CON)}$, or $S_{2(GOV)}$. $S_{2(EMP)}$ is an S_2 option organized around an imperial concept, with one or more centers of state power exerting direct control over subordinate areas or regions of the world. $S_{2(CON)}$ refers to a condominium or duopoly imposed by superpowers with more or less empathy for other actors and regions, either those less powerful or those less rich. $S_{2(GOV)}$ involves governmental centralization as the basis for order in world affairs, and allows for a wide array of types of governing ideology and bureaucratic structure.

There are likely to be conflicting images of $S_{2(WOMP)}$, depending on the differing priorities, perceptions, and world order experiences of different sectors of the world. A major task of central political organs

---

* Are all variants of $S_{2(WOMP)}$ nonstatist and nongovernmental in character? This is an empirical and an analytic question. Have other WOMP groups proposed world statist or world governmental mechanisms for their preferred world? Would it be plausible—from an analytic perspective—to design such mechanisms, given WOMP values? The issue here seems to hinge on whether such a degree of bureaucratic centralism is compatible over time with the commitment to V_3 (human rights). V_1, V_2, and V_4 could all be plausibly realized within the framework of a world state or world government. Indeed, the higher degree of centralization suggests greater efficiency than is likely to result in $S_{2(WOMP/USA)}$ and yet we are willing to sacrifice some prospect of efficiency because of the importance we attach to V_3. Realization of V_3 is also linked with preventing S_2 from becoming a closed system of a totalitarian type that forecloses (or tries to) the evolutionary move toward S_3.[17]

in the global arena would be to work for implementing a consensus regarding the specific structure of $S_{2(WOMP)}$ and the final transitional phase culminating in $S_1 \rightarrow S_2$. The learning dynamics of $t_1 \rightarrow t_3$ would include a feedback process involving continuous examination and re-formulation of the goal values of world order reform embodied in $S_{2(WOMP)}$. However, given our present level of understanding, we can-not now say whether the participants in this momentous dialogue will have convergent learning experiences, or whether like experiences will be similarly interpreted for purposes of action in the global arena dur-ing t_3.

It is evident, however, that the gains of t_1 in the national arenas, and of t_2 in transnational and regional arenas, will be carried forward to global arenas during t_3. Of course, action in all main arenas will take place simultaneously throughout the transition process, although we have indicated earlier why we believe that there will be a sequential relationship among critical arenas. During t_3 individuals throughout the world will increasingly replace their national identities with wider global symbols of identification.* In this context, the transition to S_2 will seem natural and inevitable (almost as the shift from a colonial to a statist structure began to seem natural and inevitable in the 1950's). Of course, if the transition is accomplished under severe ecological pres-sures, it may be a traumatic period, prone to risk and fraught with con-fusion and despair; in such a setting even S_2 may be perceived as too little and too late.

For our purposes here, it is necessary only to assert that the global arena will become the world order focus during t_3. Continuing develop-ments in the direction of $S_{2(WOMP)}$ will also occur in all other critical arenas. One important undertaking in the global arena will be to coor-dinate and link more limited arenas of international action so as to produce a more coherent overall world order system by the end of t_3.

CONCLUDING NOTE ON CRITICAL ARENAS

The correlation of critical arenas with transition stages represents our best judgment regarding the most likely sequence of developments on

---

* This widening of identity pattern is likely to be accompanied by an intensification of narrower identities associated with self, family, neighborhood, affinity group, and so on. The national identity bonds will loosen in response to this double set of pressures from above and below.

different levels of organized action in human affairs, during the progression from where we are now, to $S_{2(WOMP)}$. It is, of course, highly unlikely that any such sequence would manifest itself so clearly in actual historical developments. Furthermore, it is important to note that this sequence would become much less plausible either if S_1 persisted for a very long period (i.e., if t_1 did not end before, say, the year 1995), or if the transition path to S_2 were dominated by social, economic, and political forces oriented toward a different set of values and hence advocating a different set of behavioral and institutional outcomes to fulfill their S_2 vision. We readily admit that both of these possibilities are more likely than our prescriptive vision of the transition process. We are engaged in a preferential modeling exercise in which we are trying to identify the most plausible and desirable path to the most beneficial world order solution that seems realizable by the end of the century. Many favorable developments would have to occur before we could become confident that what *could* happen *will* happen. As matters now stand (t_0), the relation of forces is strongly arrayed in favor of S_1, or at most in moving toward an acceptance of certain negative variants of S_2.

A CONSIDERATION OF WORLD ORDER VALUES DURING THE TRANSITION PERIOD

To supplement our presentation of sequenced transition during the final phases of S_1, we will consider the relative prospects for value change in each of the t intervals. Such a consideration will be illustrative in the same sense as has been our discussion of phases of action on p. 283 and of successive critical arenas on p. 304. As with other discussions of sequence, we do not imply mutually exclusive categories of development, but only a sequence of evolving emphasis that corresponds with conditions of *perceived plausibility*. Specific world order reform steps are contingent upon developments that cannot be anticipated, such as those associated with the pressure of events (e.g., decay of the oceans or large inland lakes) or the political orientation of national leadership in the United States or the Soviet Union. It is necessary, of course, to ignore these contingencies while hypothesizing a plausible sequence of world order developments from a perspective of preferred values.

While our value perspective is shaped primarily by the four WOMP values, we would like also to take brief account of value developments relating to individual and group identity—developments that reveal the world order importance of personal alienation, the quest for participation, and inhumane government. Finally, on p. 333 we will consider briefly the value tradeoffs arising from inconsistencies among strategies for promoting a given value (e.g., helping protect the environment may interfere or seem to interfere with development plans to diminish poverty).*

MINIMIZING COLLECTIVE VIOLENCE (V_1) DURING t_1

It is our judgment that notable progress toward minimizing collective violence (V_1) will take place in t_1. This progress will both deepen and reflect the altered political consciousness in principal domestic arenas during this initial stage of the transition process. Progress toward the realization of V_1 may be assessed in terms of incidence of international warfare, numbers of battle deaths, and percentage of total government budget and GNP allocated for defense.† There is likely to be uneven progress in terms of time and region during t_1, and relatively little institutionalization of disarmament. Specific international conflicts, such as those in the Middle East, the Indian subcontinent, elsewhere in Asia, and southern Africa may produce fairly large-scale wars and high, sustained military spending. It is also quite likely that some governments, particularly in Third World countries, will try to attain great power status by acquiring nuclear capabilities, especially if the rich–poor gap continues to widen and to confront countries with an indefinite prospect of mass misery. India's explosion of a nuclear device in 1974 gives a morbid credibility to these concerns.‡ One can also imagine Japan, Iran, "Europe," Brazil, or even Saudi Arabia, under the pressure of eco-

---

* The role of tradeoffs has already been discussed somewhat in Chapter I. The further consideration here relates to tradeoff issues associated with the transition process.

† V_1 may also be realized through widening adherence to the ethics and tactics of nonviolence by both change-oriented and order-oriented groups. A declining confidence in the efficacy of violence might be the most important conditioning development of all to occur in t_1.[18]

‡ The current role of nuclear weaponry in improving a government's international status and bargaining power is bound to provoke reconsiderations of present determinations to forego the nuclear option. Only a serious effort by existing nuclear powers to denuclearize world politics can, over the next decade or so, effectively deter further proliferation of nuclear weaponry. Such proliferation is also encouraged by the growing ease of access, which may mean that governments will seek a nuclear deterrent so as to reduce their vulnerability to nuclear blackmail by their domestic adversaries.

nomic rivalries that are likely to grow more severe during t_1, deciding to accelerate arms spending and, possibly, embarking upon geo-political expansion. Finally, there is every expectation that the incidence and severity of civil strife will persist throughout t_1, and may not abate until fairly deep in t_2.

Despite these negative prospects, certain secular trends are operating to make t_1 a period in which the war system will begin to be dismantled as well as stabilized.* Such trends are closely linked to an assumption of the continuing moderation—and eventual elimination—of Soviet–American tensions, and the building of a domestic consensus in each country on the need for major resource transfers from the military to the nonmilitary sector. These developments will be reinforced by rising domestic demands for social services, national welfare programs, and environmental protection, as well as by a military technology that becomes increasingly expensive as its weapons systems grow more elaborate. Under such circumstances, there will be rising public pressure to translate an international climate of moderation into a national security posture based on some less grandiose conception of deterrence than that now prevailing. A reduction in nuclear capabilities is facilitated by increasingly effective command and control constraints, and by greater willingness on the part of the superpowers not only to accept mutual arms surveillance, but possibly even to establish shared surveillance capabilities for monitoring governmental and nongovernmental arms acquisition and deployment.† In late t_1, principal governments may begin to feel more threatened by counter-governmental adversaries than by intergovernmental war risks.‡

In more specific terms, early t_1 is likely to witness rather dramatic

---

* The inconsistency is only apparent. To eliminate war through negotiated disarmament it is first necessary to diminish the short-term prospects for its outbreak by stabilizing mainstream geopolitics. Of course, longer-term stability is not envisaged or needed, and is indeed structurally inconsistent with the dynamics of S_1.

† Such mutual surveillance can be carried on largely through satellite observation. Its role has evolved tacitly through the last decade and has contributed to the belief that the Soviet–American military balance is rather stable. Given a growing acceptance that nuclear stability cannot be realistically upset by technological breakthroughs, there is an increasing Soviet and American awareness that large budget cuts on both sides would allow each government to use its revenue more effectively. Andrei Gromyko's proposal to the General Assembly in 1973 to cut defense budgets in the United States and the Soviet Union by ten percent and use the money saved to help poor countries may be suggestive of a new attitude toward defense spending.[19]

‡ Many Third World governments presently regard their defense establishment as useful mainly for purposes of deterring and fighting against domestic adversaries.

declarations that will moderate the operations of the war system. The Brezhnev–Nixon Declaration of Principles on May 29, 1972, and subsequent bilateral arrangements on security issues, illustrate the kind of progress characteristic of early t_1.* These principles require no specific changes in behavior by either party, although they proceed on the assumption of a permanent condition of "peaceful coexistence" and of the mutual benefits deriving from "the renunciation of the use or threat of force." The moderate tone of these principles may be of more enduring significance than the specific substantive arrangements negotiated at SALT I to limit ABM and strategic missile deployment. (As noted earlier, the agreements themselves may, in the short run, be used to accelerate the next round in the arms race by creating a strong incentive to develop qualitative improvements in unregulated sectors of defense, thereby encouraging the development of ultra-modern weapons systems.) Of course, so long as the logic of S_1 dominates governmental elites, it is reasonable to expect apparent "limitations" on war-making capabilities to serve as inducements to circumvent the negotiated constraints by shifting efforts to unregulated sectors. As t_1 proceeds, however, a genuine conflict in domestic societies should emerge between those who are concerned with competing for control according to S_1 rules and modalities, and those who seek to overcome the risks and costs of S_1 by a belief in the feasibility and desirability of a reformed S_2.† Already the first signs of such a struggle in the domestic arena

---

* The Soviet–American Agreement on the Prevention of Nuclear War (June 22, 1973) is a more specific kind of declaratory instrument that includes an obligation to consult:

> If at any time relations between the parties or between either party and other countries appear to involve the risk of a nuclear conflict, or if relations between countries not parties to this agreement appear to involve the risk of nuclear war between the USA and the USSR or between either party and other countries, the United States and the Soviet Union, acting in accordance with the provisions of this agreement, shall immediately enter into urgent consultations with each other and make every effort to avert this risk (Article IV).

Note that the consulting machinery is not activated if the risk of nuclear conflict does not affect the U.S. or the USSR. Such a careful limitation on the scope of concern is presumably designed to avoid furthering the impression of a bipolar condominium or duopoly, but it is hard to imagine any conflict with a nuclear dimension that was not perceived as involving one or the other superpower directly or indirectly. Our main point here is that a communications process is established to implement purely declaratory undertakings.

† $S_{2(MNC)}$ and $S_{2(CON)}$ are compatible with the permanent militarization of world society, and may be dependent on such militarization. In S_2 the role of military power may be largely repressive, to deter and defeat insurgencies arising out of political orientations of an $S_{2(WOMP)}$ character. These negative outcomes of transition from S_1 to S_2 would probably produce new forms of coalitions between those who controlled the main wealth-

reveal fissures in the statist model of world order, and those fissures can be expected to widen in the principal centers of industrial power.

As t_1 proceeds, there will probably be some efforts to denuclearize world politics, and to end or at least erode the stratification of international society along nuclear/non-nuclear lines. Here again it is likely that the first move toward denuclearization will take the form of declarations, involving renunciations by nuclear powers of their right to initiate the use of nuclear weapons in situations of armed conflict. To satisfy domestic security constituencies, such declaratory steps will have to be accompanied by credible postures of non-nuclear defense, i.e., by making it evident that security interests can be upheld by non-nuclear weapons.[20] We regard denuclearization of world politics to be the most important development bearing on V_1 during t_1, and the most significant value accomplishment during t_1. Without denuclearization, the structure of international society would remain nonreciprocal with respect to the war system. Such an imbalance would make progress on other world values very difficult to attain by consensual means, just as it would make drastic disarmament virtually impossible to negotiate during t_2 and t_3. The shift to S_2, if it is largely consensual, presupposes a high degree of reciprocity and mutuality with respect to conditions of value-realization. Of course, some highly hegemonial variants of S_2 might actually accentuate the existing nonreciprocal aspects of statist participation in the war system. Note, however, that our proposals are based on the view that $S_1 \rightarrow S_2$ will only be beneficial if it proceeds in accordance with WOMP values.

In t_1 we do not expect any dramatic transfers of police and peace-making capabilities to the United Nations, regional organizations or some new international institution. As discussed on pp. 308–315, we expect the main kind of progress in t_1 to involve the character of political consciousness in domestic arenas. Other arenas may also be active in relation to V_1, and it is possible that superpower moderation, including limited zones of consensus, might be sufficiently secure by the end of t_1 to permit regional and global peace-keeping capabilities to be constituted for certain limited purposes, provided they were subject to stringent requirements of intergovernmental control and consensus. Nevertheless, the most notable development during t_1 is likely to be the degree to which war becomes more remote as a diplomatic option in cases of serious conflict among principal governments. It is now dif-

producing processes and those who managed the main instruments of legitimated violence (police power).

ficult to envision war between the United States and Canada or among the main states in Western Europe, but by the end of t_1 we would suppose that it will become just as difficult to envision war between any of the powerful governments in the world.* Regional wars may occur even late in t_2, but their scope is likely to be quite restricted and their superpower allies are likely to reach tacit decoupling arrangements to avoid escalating interventions.† By the end of t_1 there may be dangerous arms developments in all parts of the world, including the presence of significant nuclear capabilities. It is quite likely that the most serious threats of nuclear war will shift away from the epicenter of the state system to certain peripheral zones of conflict, especially in situations where a technologically sophisticated government (e.g., Israel, South Africa) finds itself threatened by a hostile regional environment.‡

The emphasis on V_1 is also predicated on the expectations that economic rivalry will displace military confrontations and that military and economic factors will be considerably independent of one another (i.e., no direct military backing or economic claims). This projection could be upset if a single state were to feel its basic viability threatened by the main currents of world economic rivalry, as Japan felt threatened in the period after World War I, or if the North–South rivalry should grow embittered by a perceived lack of progress toward greater equalization of world economic conditions. If resource scarcity and ecological pressures mount very rapidly in t_1 and if no bargain is reached on the sharing of the ocean's wealth, the overall tendencies toward moderation may be arrested or even reversed. The energy crisis in the early 1970's suggests the geopolitical implications of supplier leverage over a critical resource such as oil, which most advanced industrial countries must import in large quantities and on a continuing basis.§ However, given our antici-

---

* Such a general shift in attitude toward the role of war in S_1 is not inconsistent with the persistence of one or more intractable conflicts which sustain a manifest war potential. As of 1974 one thinks of the Sino–Soviet and Israeli–Arab conflicts over disputed territory, but there could be others that endure through time or arise in the years ahead.

† Or, more menacingly from an $S_{2(WOMP)}$ perspective, superpowers may allocate interventionary prerogatives in such a way as to manage conflicts in dependent areas of the world system. Such arrangements would foreshadow transition to $S_{2(CON)}$ and $S_{2(MNC)}$. It is also possible that governmental and corporate actors might reach a world order bargain that would eventuate in $S_{2(CON/MNC)}$.

‡ The unpredictability and danger of widely distributed nuclear capabilities, combined with increasing vulnerability to "resource blackmail" (i.e., where supplier countries manipulate production and delivery schedules to enhance economic and political bargaining positions) might reinforce the reasonableness of various hegemonial options: $S_{2(CON)}$, $S_{2(MNC)}$, $S_{2(CON/MNC)}$.

§ See discussion of energy crisis in Chapter II, p. 120, p. 125, and Chapter VI, p. 363.

pation that national governments will be increasingly disposed toward an $S_{2(WOMP)}$ solution of world order problems, it seems reasonable to expect important steps toward the minimization of collective violence in world affairs during t_1.

Both the incidence and magnitude of large-scale civil strife—of the sort that took place in Nigeria, Sudan, and Pakistan at the outset of t_1—may well diminish by the time t_2 begins. By t_2, nation-building dynamics are likely to have proceeded far enough in the main Third World countries to assure generally effective governmental control, or else to have produced successful secessionist outcomes (i.e., Bangladesh) or satisfactory internal compromises in the form of cultural, economic, and political zones of autonomy enabling more equitable participation in control functions.

In essence, t_1 will not change the objective status of the war system in S_1, but it may create a new kind of dominant mood that will facilitate further progress on V_1 during t_2 and t_3, and make possible subsequent progress with respect to V_2, V_3, and V_4.

In t_1, V_{2-4} are likely to undergo less dramatic development. V_2 will be influenced by whether some share of ocean resources, part of the common heritage of mankind, can be brought under world community control. The present outlook is not encouraging, except for certain nominal gestures of community-sharing; the basic prospect is that ocean resources will be allocated by market forces operating in the setting of statist competitive logic, and supplemented by the transnational logic of private multinational corporate growth. Indeed, in t_1 it is quite likely that no net progress will be made with respect to V_2, but rather that the quantum of misery and poverty will increase and will be even more concentrated in Third World countries, while the disparity between rich and poor continues to grow.

With respect to V_3, human dignity, it is likely that statist considerations will bar notable progress during t_1. Failures relating to V_2 may generate pressures which, in turn, may cause even more general and severe deprivations of human rights than is presently the case. A recent series of genocidal occurrences in the Third World suggests vulnerability of the present world order system to V_3 regressions of the most extreme character. Rhetorical commitments to V_3 will not be significantly implemented until the end of t_1, when the orientation toward $S_{2(WOMP)}$ begins to alter the relationships between the rulers and the ruled in large states.

Finally, V_4 is unlikely to make net progress during t_1. The dynamics of industrial development and growth-planning will probably contribute to a continuing deterioration of the world environment, although important efforts at environmental protection will be undertaken in some states and, possibly, in relation to certain regional issues. Some technological developments may lead to net reductions in pollution (for instance, as a result of new engine designs for ships, planes, and cars, or a breakthrough in the development of nuclear fusion technology); in our judgment these beneficial developments will be more than offset by the interaction between GNP and population increases during t_1. This dismal prospect is especially true with respect to environmental decay in locations outside the jurisdictional competence of state actors, e.g., oceans, upper atmosphere. S_1 does not possess regulatory traditions or capabilities to uphold global interests even where these interests are identified and appreciated by leading governments. Perhaps implementing processes will improve greatly during t_1, but from the vantage point of t_0 the case appears quite the opposite.

These brief comments on V_{2-4} are intended merely to suggest some general tendencies. The discussion seeks to convey an image of t_1 that helps organize thinking about the early stages of transition to $S_{2(WOMP)}$ and does not purport to make specific forecasts.*

MAXIMIZATION OF HUMAN WELL-BEING (V_2) AND MAXIMIZATION OF HUMAN DIGNITY (V_3) DURING t_2

In t_{2a}, i.e., the first phase of t_2, the maximization of human welfare (V_2) is the value that will be stressed. With reduced danger of war among the rich and industrial states, this would seem an opportune time to emphasize the range of world social problems associated with poverty and development.† In poor countries, these problems may well be even worse than at present, as a result of continued population growth and undiminished migration from the countryside to already overcrowded cities. Urban problems of crime, unemployment, and despair are likely to impair prospects for orderly and humane domestic politics, and to

---

* We want to organize a line of thinking that could undergird a global reform movement. We do not expect this thinking to prevail in the future, but we are convinced that unless it challenges regressive world order orientations, the prospects for positive adaptation to world order challenges are virtually nil.

† It may be that progress toward V_1 and V_2 will be more closely coupled than we have suggested in the text. Great powers may see these issues as linked in a way that relates directly to their perceived interests. Note the linkage suggested in the Gromyko proposal referred to on p. 325. See also the appeal to the self-interest of the rich in well-known statements by Robert McNamara and Andrei Sakharov.[21]

provide dramatic evidence of the need to handle these problems associated with poverty in the course of any realistic and enlightened program of world order reform. Hopefully, the changes in domestic consciousness postulated for t_1 would, in t_2, greatly improve receptivity to pleas for greater sharing of world resources.*

Consistent with earlier discussions, it is our view that transnational actors might provide the most important contexts within which to promote V_2. In particular, it is even possible that the multinational corporation might become reoriented in such a way as to make it at least a partial bearer of progressive values.† Indeed, we have postulated on p. 227 the multinational corporation's reorientation from the pursuit of $S_{2(MNC)} \rightarrow S_{2(WOMP)}$. In this milieu we can expect much greater levels of coordination between investment activity and human well-being, although this coordination presupposes that during t_1 changes in the domestic leadership of many Third World countries will have brought the objectives of the rulers into closer alignment with the aspirations associated with V_2.[22] Such a presupposition may be realistic because the renunciation of interventionary diplomacy during t_1 by principal governments is likely to facilitate the triumph of progressive groups in domestic struggles.‡ This outcome of the dynamics of self-determination, and respect for these dynamics by major governments, is a very critical conditioning feature of t_2. It could make t_1 such a bloody period of ferment that more coercive forms of S_2 may gain ascendancy despite the rise of WOMP consciousness. Nevertheless, we feel that it is reasonable to consider that t_2 begins with progressive national elites entrenched in many Third World countries, and hence, willing and able to cooperate in the pursuit of V_2.

By the end of t_{2a}, the leadership of poor countries should understand that the realization of V_2 aspirations depends heavily on the rapid transition from $S_1 \rightarrow S_{2(WOMP)}$, and that the progress in t_{2a} has only set the

---

* That is, we have presupposed the widespread acceptance of V_2 and V_3 prior to the completion of t_1; thus, the politics of empathy is assured a certain prominence by the stipulated character of t_2.

† This possibility seems absurd from a pre-t_1 perspective. It is only after a general shift in political consciousness has been achieved that we can imagine the corporate form adapted to serve general, as distinct from particular, interests. The role of private ownership in such a new atmosphere would be a delicate and critical issue requiring resolution in t_2.

‡ Such an outcome cannot be assured. A ruthless counterrevolutionary minority may be able to intimidate and pacify a society for a very long time without receiving any major support through intervention. Latin America exhibits several varieties of durable counterrevolutionary success.

stage for acquiring dominance over some agents of control and exploitation that have been operating under the auspices of S_1 (or are sponsoring shifts to various undesirable forms of S_2).

Similarly, in t_{2b} some initial progress will be made toward the maximization of human dignity (V_3). Most of this progress will come as an automatic consequence of more progressive leadership in national capitals. We postulate, in particular, strong regional initiatives to uphold human rights on a model that emulates and goes beyond what has taken place in Western Europe since World War II. Even African governments may become less sensitive to threats of internal dissolution, abandoning their characteristic post-colonial response of noninterference with systematic abuses of human rights, for one regionally sponsored collective intervention organized around a humanitarian rationale. This prospect in t_{2b} will depend considerably on whether Southern African issues are dealt with in a fashion that seems to represent a net human gain, i.e., whether the dynamics of humanitarian intervention result in an outcome that is generally less objectionable than continuing toleration of human abuse by deference to notions of "domestic jurisdiction" and "nonintervention." We do believe that t_2 cannot be considered completed without considerable moderation of domestic politics throughout the world. Totalitarian regimes seem incapable of sharing control over their territorial space, population, and resources, and hence by definition oppose deference to any extra-national political order such as is implicit in all S_2 models that are not based on formal or informal concepts of hierarchy and hegemony.* In particular, $S_{2(WOMP)}$ depends on consensual relations between people and institutional agencies of control, whether national, transnational, regional, or global. Therefore, some movement toward V_3 seems very critical in t_{2b} if the work of transformation in t_3 is to take place within global arenas and if $S_{2(WOMP)}$ is in some form to succeed S_1 as a world order system.

In t_2, developments relating to V_1 are also likely to go forward. However, we expect the basic achievements to be intensifications of what took place in t_1, rather than any disposition to dismantle the war system by agreement or unilateral action.† Governments will continue to domi-

---

*There are two main prospects for hegemonial patterns of global integration, the first organized on behalf of principal governments, the second on behalf of principal multinational corporations. In fact, a likely possibility is a hybrid hierarchical system based on coalitions between leading governmental and corporate actors.

† Unilateral cuts in defense budgets of leading states may become the most significant form of arms control in t_2. If such cuts occur on a reciprocal basis, a negative arms race could possibly be stimulated.

nate legitimate control over war-making capabilities, and will generally continue to devote between two to ten percent of their GNP to national security, but the disposition to use these military capabilities to solve national problems will become more and more remote, given our presuppositions about the new political consciousness.* These capabilities will be generally perceived, even by most leaders, as resources for pacifying internal social forces which remain aligned with S_1, rather than as critical instruments of national security foreign policy. It is possible that system-changing dynamics in t_2, combined with deepening social and political problems, will create an unstable situation vulnerable to the emergence of pathological leadership. Such an occurrence could imperil transition progress and might impede indefinitely the movement toward the realization of $S_{2(WOMP)}$. In such a context the frustrated pressures to move $S_1 \rightarrow S_2$ could provoke a global war. However, we regard the further erosion of the war system as an even more likely possibility in t_2. It is also quite likely that nongovernmental international and regional actors will play significant peacekeeping roles.

We believe that maximization of environmental quality (V_4) will be a significant dimension of global concern in t_2. However, the main action with respect to V_4 is likely to represent reformist, piecemeal responses to pressing particular problems. Realization of V_4 requires globalist appraisals and achieves a durable, if dynamic, equilibrium between man and nature. Central guidance for V_4 will have to be fully embodied in $S_{2(WOMP)}$, but it is impossible to achieve within the traditions and structures of S_1. However, by late t_2, the ecological imagery of interdependence and unitary policy will help encourage the shift from t_2 to t_3.

MAXIMIZATION OF THE HUMAN ENVIRONMENT (V_4) DURING t_3

The incompatibility between S_1 logic and structures and progress toward realization of V_4 is dramatic. V_1, V_2, and V_3 could, in theory, be substantially realized in a fragmented world order system composed of

---

* Such an optimistic anticipation depends on containing neo-Darwinian pressures to solve problems of scarcity by reliance on superior force. The transition process $S_1 \rightarrow S_2$ may witness a strongly financed movement to achieve assured control over critical resources; this might involve competitive struggles resulting in warfare between opposed coalitions of corporate and state actors. Even the shift in dominant consciousness implicit in reaching t_2 does not preclude policy take-overs by minority elites associated with either S_1 or anti-WOMP S_2 outlooks.

moderate governments and liberal social and economic sentiments. However, real confidence about dealing with issues of environmental quality and resource depletion seems to require central guidance of considerable reliability.* It therefore seems likely that not until t_3 will V_4 gain real prominence as the cause and agent of structural reform on a global basis. V_4 will help convey the case of $S_{2(WOMP)}$ as the necessary and desirable sequel to S_1. We believe that in t_3 the expectation of S_2 will become so normal that its actualization may not represent such a significant change. To the extent that $S_{2(WOMP)}$ is understood to be under construction at all, it will be regarded as a natural extension of earlier reforms rather than as a first approximation of utopia. Indeed, new compromises and vested interests will have been built up around the anticipation of S_2, so that the idealists in t_3 will increasingly define values and goals with reference to more distant goals associated with S_3.

The sense of planetary wholeness and organic interrelatedness associated with the active pursuit of V_4 can be expected to energize the movement for achieving central guidance of human affairs in t_3.† The basic normative imperative embodied in V_1 is to minimize violence as a mechanism of control and conflict, and this presupposes establishing a more *consensual* system among and within states (i.e., V_2 and V_3), but there is no complementary functional imperative suggesting the need for $S_{2(WOMP)}$ without relying on V_4.‡ Thus the political energy needed to complete $S_1 \rightarrow S_2$ will be based on the combined strength of the normative pressures mounted in t_1, and the functional pressures brought to bear in t_3. From these dual sources of pressure will arise a better appreciation of the objective requirements of planetary organization. By reasoning in this way we may be exaggerating the influence of analysis

---

* Therefore, if V_4 were not in the picture, it might be quite possible that the reformist mood would wither away in t_2 and there would be no real pressure to manage a humane transition to a desirable variant of S_2. Indeed, such a benign form of S_1 might be very popular, combining the strengths of cooperation with the checks of national autonomy.

† As a result, V_4 efforts will have generally positive side effects with respect to V_1, V_2, and V_3.

The preventive side of V_4 arising from the need to conserve and share resources and to protect the environment from abuse also calls attention to the need for central guidance to achieve efficiency.

‡ Mainstream world order thinking in the past has been built around V_1. The idea of peace—the "peace movement"—continues to be what most people have in mind under the rubric of global reform of a drastic charactor. We are arguing here that such reformist outlooks now are dependent upon incorporating V_4 if they are to make a persuasive case for central guidance along WOMP lines. The dream of world peace associated with V_1 continues to enjoy a dominant normative status, but it is not clear that peace can *only*, or can be *best served*, by moving to S_2.

upon behavior; by the time t_3 begins it is assumed that relevant leadership groups and arenas are already preferentially oriented toward $S_{2(WOMP)}$.

In early t_3 it seems likely that strong programs will be established to assure continuing progress for V_1, V_2, and V_4. In particular, dismantling the war system and sharing the world's wealth more equitably will be generally understood as preconditions for establishing procedures of central guidance for ecological purposes. The alternative to consensual shifts in t_3 will be a resurgent temptation in the richer and more powerful sectors of the world to organize a movement, perhaps on a transnational or counter-governmental basis, favorable to world order solutions of a more coercive and hierarchical variety.* In our view, the political and normative climate in t_3 will support institution-building relevant to the concerns of V_4, including planning and allocation of economic development on a planetary scale. All sectors will be allowed to develop, but the criteria will shift in such a way that "development" may entail negative economic growth for certain sectors of rich countries ("rich," that is, as defined by GNP criteria). Such prospects are deeply contingent on the chronological length of t_1 and t_2, the extent to which world poverty has been mitigated or accentuated by the time t_3 commences, and on whether the prevailing interpretation of V_2 is concerned primarily with *equality* of life prospects or merely with a shared *minima* that may be compatible with persisting inequalities of large magnitude.

As far as V_4 is concerned, it will be essential to alter the present structure of world authority in two very fundamental respects:

1. Events taking place on national territory but having significant effects on the world environment will have to be made subject to regulation via central guidance.

2. Use of the oceans will have to be beneficially managed to serve global community interests, including equitable distribution and preservation of the life chances of future generations.

---

* It is difficult to take proper account of our stipulated conditions that identify the ending of periods t_1 and t_2. Without these conditions the discussion of the transition process could not proceed in an orderly way. But the rigor of the stipulations is so great that it is highly unlikely that t_1 can be completed within the next five or ten decades, except by the interposition of factors that we have excluded (also by stipulation) such as a catastrophe or two. In effect, we must consider whether such value changes can be brought about in the near future, and if so, whether they can hope to contain the opposition which will arise at the same time.

A further concern derives from these two: namely, that the interplay between ocean and land activities must also be regulated in terms of an overall planetary perspective.

These objectives will require a considerable institutional presence in global arenas to guarantee adequate impartial information, and to insure the respect of participants in the world order system for governing outcomes reached by global procedures deemed generally fair to the divergent interests at stake. By contrast, the realization of V_1 and V_3 can occur mainly by means of "self-help" at the national and regional levels (drastic unilateral arms control and disarmament could become strong tendencies in international life during t_2 and t_3). In such settings global structures would be needed mainly for purposes of reassurance, and to undermine the contentions and strategies of those who oppose the realization of $S_{2(WOMP)}$. Even V_2 could be largely realized within an S_1 framework of institutional and behavioral patterns. Therefore, it is only V_4 which depends substantially upon central guidance mechanisms of an explicit sort. The creation of these mechanisms will be the central world order preoccupation in t_3. It is for this reason that we link t_3 with structural modification in the global arena and that we posit V_4 as the value to be stressed in this final transition interval that ends the birth pangs of $S_{2(WOMP)}$. This emphasis may cause some consternation at the present time, because it appears to overlook Third World development priorities in a global situation of widening economic gaps and massive misery. We believe, however, that we have specified a transition path to $S_{2(WOMP)}$ that will eventually encourage very great convergence with respect to the needs for global equity and ecoequilibrium. Therefore, we do not expect the present divergence on world order priorities to persist in t_3. By then it will be clearer that adequate equity procedures for the world can only be reliably evolved if tied to adequate provision for the various facets of ecological quality addressed by V_4.

A NOTE ON THE MAXIMIZATION
OF PERSONAL IDENTITY

All action on any level is a consequence of individual behavior. The relationship of individuals to various collectivities of peoples, symbols, and structures is of critical importance for the kind of politics that is possible at a given historical state. In particular, weakening the bonds of identification and subordination between individuals and state actors will be important throughout the transition process. It is important that $S_{2(WOMP)}$ appear to provide individuals, wherever situated, with the prospects of a more satisfying life experience. Such a perception will determine to a large extent whether populist support can be mobilized for the sort of global reform movement that we advocate. We do not, at the same time, want to introduce a personal identity dimension into the schema of $S_{2(WOMP)}$ by regarding it as a fifth value dimension (V_5).

Therefore, we would recommend that those who are concerned with global reform study problems of alienation and identity in their particular regional manifestations. A specific program for transition to $S_{2(WOMP/USA)}$ should address itself to these problems in such a way that reduced alienation is perceived as a by-product of the establishment of $S_{2(WOMP/USA)}$. In the United States this means that concerns arising out of worker alienation, exclusion of minorities from participation in authority structures, and various forms of de-spiritualization of everyday existence receive sympathetic attention. In part, the very process of designing and realizing a more peaceful and humane context for our national existence may itself kindle hope and restore meaning to the lives of ordinary citizens. Beyond this, however, the commitment to V_3 can be translated into a variety of other settings that involve eliminating demeaning forms and conditions of work. Sensitivity to these issues of personal identity also suggests the desirability of numerous channels, ranging from discussion to direct action, enabling individuals to participate in the process of drastic global reform.

Awareness of the personal identity dimension would also contribute to the realization that greater autonomy would result from global reforms of the right kind, despite the greater degree of central or planetary guidance in human affairs. This concern with autonomy, especially on the part of global reform groups, might reassure those who fear that global reforms would end up placing individuals in some Orwellian mold of existence.

In addition, there is a series of philosophical questions which involve the political ethics of $S_{2(WOMP)}$; these relate, especially, to the individual's coexisting bundles of duties and rights. Is there a duty to work or to contribute to global well-being? Is there a right to maintain group identities associated with race, culture, language, religion, or shared history? Are there any limits on personal or political deviance? How would advocates of a resurrected S_1 be treated, especially if these advocates threatened or used violence?

Concerning the transition from t_1 to t_3, issues of personal identification seem likely to contribute in t_1 to the reorientation of consciousness within principal domestic arenas. We believe that the discontent arising from the more prevalent forms of alienation has created a latent receptivity to change, especially change that promises to overcome meaninglessness and to end enchantment with death and destruction. A major challenge to advocates of drastic global reform is to formulate their proposals so as to reach this massive change-ordered constituency. In the past, world order advocacy has been unsuccessful in motivating support partly because of its inability to demonstrate the benefits it would hold for personal existence. It may also be fair to criticize WOMP/USA for being conceived in overly abstract, structural, and collective terms that are not directly enough related to individual fears, hopes, and latent drives.

In t_2 the objective tendencies of continuing economic development and urbanization around the world are likely to produce an intense focus on the domain of personal existence and create part of the political foundation for progress toward S_2, which we believe will take public shape in the form of an emphasis on V_4 during t_3. The sense of crowding, the dual process of weakening some and strengthening other traditional affiliations, ecological pressures, conditions of work in relation to the sense of potential human worth, a flourishing revival of spiritual and religious modes of thought—all are likely to stir an unprecedented effort to interpret the future primarily by reference to personal prospects. In particular, we might expect that by t_2, the advocates of world order would have set forth a concept of planetary destiny that can function as part ideology, part ethics, and part religion, vectoring behavior and aspiration toward a preferred future and stirring the imagination by visions of what can happen to individuals in a new world order setting.

In t_3 the reorientations of identity implicit in S_2 will be experienced by large numbers of individuals. But it will be in $S_{2(WOMP)}$ that the agenda associated with personal identity will become the new focus for world order change. $S_1 \rightarrow S_2$ will be primarily concerned with avoiding catastrophe, widespread misery and repression—a rescue operation in a situation of treacherous waters and near shipwreck. $S_2 \rightarrow S_3$ will be conceived in more positive terms, as a sea voyage to lands of enchantment, distant but attainable, on a ship that is not immune to danger but is also not nearly as vulnerable to disaster as our present vessel.

Thus, issues of personal identity impinge on the transition process, even if their resolution is not treated as a formal part of $S_{2(WOMP)}$. These issues will also be relevant to the extent that Consciousness III thinking inverts priorities for change by insisting that withdrawal from collective arenas is an authentic way to reshape society in terms of restoring meaning to the work, play, and dreams of concrete individuals.[23] We reject such a political ethic of withdrawal because it offers no challenge to entrenched elites; on the contrary, at best it can hope to survive (in chosen sanctuaries) only at the sufferance of these elites, i.e., only as long as this ethic does not appear to endanger larger edifices of power, wealth, and authority.* We believe that struggle and participation is an essential part of any program for political reform, whether in one's neighborhood or one's world.†

THE INTERPLAY OF VALUES
DURING $S_1 \rightarrow S_2$

As we have acknowledged throughout, the four primary WOMP values are neither mutually exclusive nor mutually consistent under all circumstances. We discussed this problem in Chapter I and referred to it in Chapter III, but not in agonizing contexts of concrete choice. Dostoyevski, disillusioned with the gap between revolutionary promises and performance, embraced a purist ethic toward the end of his life which he dramatized by asserting that if the perfect society could be brought into being with the loss of only one child's life, then it was still not worth it. Albert Camus, similarly disillusioned with political activism, remained silent during the Algerian War of Independence because he discerned evil on both sides.

In contrast, revolutionary ethics seem reconciled to human suffering. Lenin's phrase, "You can't make an omelette without breaking eggs," acknowledges the distinctive prelude to revolutionary reconstruction. Others are even less reluctant, viewing the violent upsurge of the oppressed as a therapeutic process of healing, valued for its own sake, regardless of the revolutionary sequel. More restrained positions, such as that held by Jean Paul Sartre, appear to argue that an individual should accept and support progressive tendencies that are alive in a

---

* Such sanctuaries or enclaves are also dependent on the basic competence of the governing elites to provide for their security and well-being. If nuclear war or ecological collapse ensue, those who have withdrawn will be destroyed along with others.

† At the same time, experiments in detachment are positive during a time of confusion and decay. Such experiments are, in effect, a judgment of repudiation. They help preserve learning and resuscitate spiritual energies during dark periods. William Irwin Thompson's own decision to leave the university and create the Lindisfarne Association is the sort of positive experiment I have in mind, which can serve as a source of inspiration and appraisal for those who are more actively engaged "in the world."

given historical period, despite an inevitable human toll and despite the ethical ambiguity of some of the means by which progressive change might come. From this standpoint, the progressive impact of decolonization objectively takes precedence over the ethical shortcomings of an independence movement that may rely on random terror and inflict gratuitous pain upon some of its victims.

These issues have stimulated fundamental debate for centuries. They remain relevant and unresolved. It is still necessary to choose and act in the face of agonizing value conflicts aggravated by factual uncertainty. We do not know whether the costs of the space program have been borne by the poor; we cannot calculate how many lives would be lost by recourse to a violent revolutionary strategy at a particular time or how much progress could be achieved by reliance on nonviolent tactics or what the relative prospects of success are for different strategies at different times. Put in world order terms, we cannot measure either the quantum of tradeoff between V_1 and V_3 or the quality of the exchange of lives for liberties. The absoluteness of Dostoyevski's scale of comparison seems far too rigid, confining mankind to a permanent and assured condition of repressive misery; the permissiveness of Fanon's scale of comparison seems to authorize violence without sufficient sensitivity to its negative consequences, and with no sense of proportionality between means and ends.* Many radical reformers take a middle position invariably mired in cant and mystification; that is, we claim a sense of proportionality between means and ends, without any tools for justifying the lines we draw. We merely assert a proportional relationship—if

---

* Frantz Fanon was born on the French colonial island of Martinique in 1925, studied medicine and psychiatry in France, and emerged as a leading intellectual advocate of the anti-colonial struggle. He worked in an Algerian hospital and his reluctance to leave the scene of struggle during the Algerian War of Independence seems partly responsible for his death from cancer at the age of thirty-six in 1961. Fanon remains one of the most profound and potent voices from below, whether in the context of domestic or international oppression, and he has been hailed throughout the Third World as a prophet. An unfortunate feature of his thought is its stress on the positive side of violence, and its failure to identify the dangers and costs of embracing violence even in pursuit of the highest social and political goals. Consider the following typical utterance: "Violence alone, violence committed by the people, violence organized and educated by its leaders, makes it possible for the masses to understand social truths and gives the key to them. Without that struggle, without that knowledge of the practice of action, there's nothing but a fancy-dress parade and the blare of trumpets." [24] I would not want to leave the impression that if Fanon is read in his full context his endorsement of violence is not without sorrow and qualifications. Nevertheless, the message of violence is the one that seems to have been delivered most effectively, and for which Fanon is best known and most influential.

we consider the problem at all—and feel excused from liability for whatever consequences ensue. Our leaders determine when it is worthwhile to inflict nuclear destruction upon a foreign society (or at least claim the prerogative to do so) by a virtually untested tradeoff calculation. Potential leaders of a liberation group have no real way at the outset to assess either their prospects or the human costs of their enterprise, and yet they embark on deadly violence (as do, incidentally, those who fight against revolution or those rulers who close off nonviolent avenues for human and social fulfillment). *

Several issues are linked in the preceding discussion:

1. WOMP values are not mutually consistent in many circumstances of choice and decision; priorities and tradeoffs must be made, whether consciously or not.

2. Degrees of uncertainty are so great regarding the consequences of various courses of action (and non-action must also be viewed as a form of action) that we cannot calculate even the most critical choices in any very rigorous way.

3. We possess no agreed formula for assessing relative value consequences; we cannot agree on how much violence is tolerable to diminish how much poverty or rectify how much abuse of human dignity or overcome how much degradation of the environment.

4. We cannot assess the short-term/long-term tradeoffs that arise from alternative responses to threats; when is a given quantum of violence worthwhile to avert a probably or possibly larger quantum in the future?

Part of our problem is a lack of useful information, but a greater part resides in the limited capacity of human beings to reach agreement on risk-taking, cost-bearing, and burden sharing. These limitations are further restricted by unequal life circumstances and dissimilar life outlooks. These difficulties are compounded by the radical indeterminism of our past experience—even if we can form a moderate consensus around an interpretation of what was done in the past (e.g., Munich as "appeasement"), we know this inference is simplistic and unidimensional; more important than this, we have no record or way of assessing what might have happened if different choices had been made, nor can we compile such a record by mere speculation, no matter how clever our computers become at tracking alternatives.

The tradeoff issue can thus never be satisfactorily resolved. We can set forth a preference for maximum explicitness, given our knowledge of the past and our best anticipations of the future. We can also make our choices with sufficient humility, so that every undertaking is tentative in the sense that it is subject to revision in light of reassessment. We can also adopt an ethical posture based on a preference for non-violent tactics, for persuasion rather than coercion, for wide sharing of what is deemed valuable, for endurance, for life-sustaining attitudes and plans, for integrity and openness. None of these prescriptive guidelines is very satisfactory as a basis for political action when the public so often expects a policy advocate to promise a particular outcome; without certainty people are rarely willing to take risks and accept the costs of change. But in working for desirable forms of drastic global reform, it will be necessary to base action on the best knowledge available.* Integrity in relation to the advocacy of change would itself represent an ethical advance, compared with the tendency of traditional politicians to understate or even deny uncertainty so as to command the respect of their citizenry.† The political discourse between rulers and ruled in $t_1 \rightarrow t_3$ would improve in quality to the extent that it was based on increasing degrees of integrity. This kind of integrity could underlie the revival or redrafting of the basic social contract between a truly democratic government and its citizenry.

Raising the problem of knowledge in this form might seem to undermine the basic reformist claim that $S_{2(WOMP)}$ would be better than S_1 and, hence, that it is worth making major sacrifices of position and privilege to achieve it by peaceful and humane means. We think not. Briefly put, the comparative merit of $S_{2(WOMP)}$ is not based on a static comparison of two world order systems, but on a continuous effort to improve the cumulative condition of mankind by reference to certain widely shared value predispositions that have been shaped in response to universally experienced problems identified with death, destruction, exploitation, and waste. By subjecting our action on the transition path to periodic audit, we can hopefully make general assessments about what constitutes desirable behavior. Of course, such judgments cannot hope to win universal approval; there will be purists who want no eggs broken,

---

* Education based on knowledge is itself a major reform tactic. As we have suggested, our view of relevant education is based on an organic sense of the links between feeling, thought, and action.

† Reliance by governments upon classification procedures and secrecy is often designed to exclude uncertainty from the public presentation of controversial or costly policies.

there will be apologists who want no new omelette, there will be idealists who reject any new taste that is not a perfect taste, there will be shallow sympathizers who will abandon the kitchen as soon as one egg cracks, and others who, in contrast, will grow impatient with the chef's degree of care. But, hopefully, a mainstream global reform movement can gradually define its character as the transition process proceeds.

As with other aspects of these proposals, we acknowledge the limits of our present knowledge and understand that there are some inherent limits associated with the human situation. We believe some of these limits can be removed by further work. We claim only that these WOMP proposals provide several beginnings for the work of world order activism, and that this work deserves our urgent attention at this time.*

In the next section we wish to set forth as briefly as possible some ideas about improving our concept of the transition process. We seek a systematic basis for including the transition intervals in our overall educational effort to encourage the serious study of comparative world order systems.

A MATRIX FOR THE TRANSITION
PATHS $S_1 \rightarrow S_{2(WOMP)}$

The matrix in Table 5-1 briefly summarizes the basic $S_{2(WOMP/USA)}$ concept of a transition path to a preferred world. We acknowledge, of course, that there are a variety of transition paths that could produce a comparable world order outcome and that there are a variety of preference models other than those constituted by WOMP values; furthermore, even WOMP values could be maximized in a variety of ways, especially if the year 2000 constraint is accepted as a boundary on the time available to complete the transition to S_2. Nevertheless, at this stage of inquiry a matrix might help to clarify the single transition path depicted in this chapter. A more ambitious use of a transition matrix would specify characteristic or expected developments in each box.

---

* In this sense, the array of approaches and preferential models present in this first phase of WOMP is itself a recognition that there is not yet a consensus on either the means or ends of global reform, even within the sort of humanistic framework suggested by the four WOMP values.

Table 5-4. Matrix for the Transition Path $S_1 \rightarrow S_{2(WOMP)}$

Value Dimension (V) / Critical Action Phase / Critical Arena	Consciousness Phase I / Domestic Arena	Mobilization / Transnational and Regional Arenas	Transformation / Global Arena	Consciousness Phase II / Personal Social Arenas
V_1	pp. 287–292; 308–315			
V_2		pp. 292–294; 315–319		
V_3		pp. 292; 317–318		
V_4			p. 292	pp. 294–296; 319–322
$V_{5...n}$				
Analytic Time Interval t_0	t_1	t_2	t_3	t_4
Chronological Time Interval	1970's	1980's	1990's	2000's
World Order System Interval	S_1	$S_{2\,(WOMP)}$ $S_{2\,(WOMP/USA)}$		S_3 $S_{3\,(WOMP)}$ $S_{3\,(WOMP/USA)}$

Explanation of Matrix

V	= Value
V_1	= Minimization of Collective Violence
V_2	= Maximization of Economic and Social Welfare
V_3	= Maximization of Human Dignity
V_4	= Maximization of Environmental Quality
V_5	= Maximization of Personal Identity
V_n	= Additional value dimensions that will become relevant during $S_1 \rightarrow S_{2(WOMP)}$ or during $S_2 \rightarrow S_{3(WOMP)}$
S	= World Order System
S_1	= Statist world order system prevailing since Peace of Westphalia
S_2	= An alternative, successor world order system to S_1, with characteristics unspecified
$S_{2(WOMP)}$	= An S_2 world order system constituted to give substantial realization to WOMP ($V_1 \rightarrow V_4$) values
$S_{2(WOMP/USA)}$	= The particular preference model set forth by the United States Group to maximize WOMP values; comparable preference models could be designated $S_{2(WOMP/JAPAN)}$, $S_{2(WOMP/AFRICA)}$, etc.
$S_1 \rightarrow S_2$	= The transition path between S_1 and S_2
S_3	= An alternative, successor world order system to S_2, with characteristics unspecified
$S_{3(WOMP)}$	= An S_3 preferred world embodying a new value consensus comparable to $S_{2(WOMP)}$
$S_2 \rightarrow S_3$	= The transition path between S_2 and S_3
t_1	= The first interval in the transition path that is completed only when certain specified conditions have been satisfied
t_2	= The second such interval in the transition path
t_3	= The third such interval the conclusion of which is stipulated to coincide with the end of S_1 and the start of S_2
t_4	= The first interval in the transition path to $S_{3(WOMP)}$ that is completed only when certain specified conditions have been satisfied

Consciousness

(Phase I)   = The shift in value priorities to WOMP $V_1 \rightarrow V_4$

(Phase II)   = The further shift in value priorities in $S_{2(WOMP)}$ to a new set of values associated with $V_s \rightarrow V_n$ and related to the quest for $S_{3(WOMP)}$.

WORLD ORDER INDICATORS

A major requirement for intellectual progress is a better data base for assessing relevant world order trends. This requires, in the first instance, a world order framework that would identify the sorts of data needed. It seems likely that our matrix $S_1 \rightarrow S_{2(WOMP)}$ provides some guidelines. It would be particularly important to obtain information that bears on value changes (positive and negative) and that assesses changing roles of world order actors and arenas. An immediate priority would be a world order data handbook that organized existing data to facilitate analysis by specialists in world order change. In WOMP discussions it has been proposed that an annual or biennial handbook of world order indicators be compiled and published, perhaps using as a model the SIPRI yearbooks on defense spending and on arms control negotiations.

Computer simulations of multi-dimensional change and computer modeling to study systemic behavior may also contribute to our understanding of world order behavior. Work is now proceeding that seeks to describe and quantify the world system as a whole. The Club of Rome study of the limits on growth generated one computer approach to a world model based on the systems approach of Jay Forrester. Although this model has been widely criticized, it has aroused unprecedented interest in world order issues, even if not always so phrased, and properly challenges its critics to do better.*

AGENTS AND AGENCIES OF
RECEPTIVITY TO $S_{2(WOMP)}$

Our concept of the transition path to $S_{2(WOMP)}$ has been influenced by judgments about social and political bases of a desirable global reform

---

* The limits to growth approach will be discussed in Chapter VI, pp. 397–405.

movement. We have stressed domestic agents and agencies of change as essential, especially during t_1, and have identified all change-oriented progressive movements, regardless of objective, as latent constituencies supportive of $S_{2(WOMP)}$. We need a more systematic global mapping of these constituencies and their principal arenas of action, in order to assess their relative capabilities and to develop tactics that would enable them to add strength to the world order movement during the long trek along the transition path, while at the same time adding to their prospects for achieving narrower and more partisan goals.

In addition, we require a more comprehensive concept of the politics of world order change.[25] In this connection it needs to be remembered that the tradition of world order speculation has been notoriously inattentive to these political dimensions underlying proposals for world order reform.[26] Most of the speculation has either been self-interested in a narrow sense of helping to extend the scope of a particular power/authority nexus (for instance, Dante's *De Monarchia*), or excessively confident in the capacity of reasoned advocacy to induce transformation (for instance, Clark and Sohn's *World Peace through World Law*). World order studies are beginning to take due account of the centrality of political factors in achieving reform. Given the seriousness of the problems, we believe that the development of an adequate concept of global reform poses an important challenge to the social sciences.

CONCLUSION

Chapter V has attempted to depict a transition path to $S_{2(WOMP)}$ that is responsive to Robert Heilbroner's incisive chastisement: "Like all utopias, it is a joy to contemplate. Alas, like all Utopias it contains not a word as to how we are to go from where we are to where we are supposed to be." [27] It provides our response to questions of feasibility and desirability associated with the structural proposals outlined in Chapter IV. This discussion of transition also anticipates our effort to relate the $S_{2(WOMP)}$ to the particular circumstances of the world economic setting that will be discussed in the next Chapter, and to the role of the United States, which will form the basis of Chapter VII.

REFERENCES

1. W. W. Rostow, "The Great Transition: Tasks of the First and Second Post-war Generations, *"State Department Bulletin*, 51:491–504 (1967).

2. *Ibid.*, p. 491.

3. For an important assessment see Noam Chomsky, "Watergate: A Skeptical View," *New York Review of Books*, Sept. 20, 1973, pp. 3–8.

4. Edward Goldsmith and others, *Blueprint for Survival*, Boston, Houghton Mifflin, 1972, p. 3.

5. See Edward S. Herman and Richard B. Du Boff, "Trickle Down, With Radical Chic," *Commonweal*, June 29, 1973, pp. 360–382.

6. For a very perceptive argument to this effect see John H. Schaar, "The Case for Patriotism," *American Review 17*, New York, Bantam, 1973, pp. 59–99.

7. One of the most successful and significant efforts in this regard is by Harold Sprout and Margaret Sprout, *The Politics of Planet Earth*, New York, Van Nostrand, 1971.

8. Richard A. Falk, "The Logic of State Sovereignty versus the Requirements of World Order, *The Year Book of World Affairs 1973*, London, Stevens & Sons, pp. 7–23.

9. Letter signed by Peter Landsman, the *New York Times*, July 4, 1972, p. 16.

10. For an eloquent and carefully reasoned argument to this effect see Richard Neuhaus, *In Defense of People: Ecology and the Seduction of Radicalism*, New York, Macmillan, 1971.

11. The most important and creative statement of this position is contained in Marcus G. Raskin, *Being and Doing: An Inquiry into the Colonization and Decolonization and Deconstruction of American Society and its State*, New York, Random House, 1971.

12. John Newhouse, *Cold Dawn: The Story of SALT*, New York, Holt, Rinehart, 1973, for narrative account; see also Elizabeth Young, *A Farewell to Arms Control?* Baltimore, Maryland, Penquin, 1972, for a skeptical view of the contribution of arms control to world peace.

13. For a positive assessment see Maurice Strong, "A Year After Stockholm," *Foreign Affairs*, 51:690–707 (1973).

14. For a perceptive analysis along these lines, see Beryl L. Crowe, "The Tragedy of the Commons Revisited," in Leslie H Roos, Jr., ed., *The Politics of Ecosuicide*, New York, Holt, Rinehart, 1971.

15. This is the main theme of Falk and Mendlovitz, eds., *Regional Politics and World Order*, San Francisco, W. H. Freeman & Co., 1973.

16. For a useful discussion of non-Western systems see especially A. B. Bozeman, *Politics and Culture in International History*, Princeton, New Jersey, Princeton University Press, 1969; F. S. C. Northrop, *The Meeting of East and West*, New York, Macmillan, 1944.

17. For an important, if overstated, indictment of closed system thinking see Karl Popper, *The Open Society and Its Enemies*, Princeton, New Jersey, Princeton University Press, 1950.

18. See excellent essay by Beverly Woodward, "Reason, Non-Violence, and Global Legal Change," in Virginia Held, Sidney Morgenbesser, and Thomas Nagle, eds., *Philosophy, Morality, and International Affairs*, New York, Oxford University Press, 1974.

19. For report of Gromyko's proposal see the *New York Times*, September 26, 1973, p. 3.

20. This argument developed in Falk, "Renunciation of Nuclear Weapons Use" in Bennett Boskey and Mason Willrich, eds., *Nuclear Proliferation: Prospects for Control*, Cambridge, Mass., Dunellen, 1970, pp. 133–145.

21. Robert S. McNamara, *The Essence of Security*, New York, Harper & Row, 1968, pp. 141–158.

22. For a helpful analysis of the extent to which Third World leaders fail to reflect the interests of their population as a whole see Thomas E. Weisskopf, "Capitalism, Underdevelopment, and the Future of the Poor Countries," in Jagdish N. Bhagwati, ed., *Economics and World Order*, New York, Macmillan, 1972 pp. 43–77.

23. William Irwin Thompson, *At Edge of History*, New York, Harper & Row, 1971.

24. Frantz Fanon, *The Wretched of the Earth*, New York, Grove, 1963, p. 117.

25. Three important very different recent efforts are Amitai Etzioni, *The Active Society: A Theory of Societal and Political Processes*, New York, Free Press, 1968; George Lakey, *A Strategy for a Living Revolution*, New York, Grossman, 1973; W. Warren Wagar, *Building the City of Man: Outlines of a World Civilization*, New York, Grossman, 1971.

26. For a critique of these legalist and moralist traditions see F. H. Hinsley, *Power and the Pursuit of Peace*, Cambridge, England, Cambridge University Press, 1963; Walter Schiffer, *The Legal Community of Mankind*, New York, Columbia University Press, 1954.

27. Said of the proposals offered by the authors of *Blueprint for Survival, op. cit.* in Robert L. Heilbroner, "Growth and Survival," *Foreign Affairs*, 51: 139–153, at 151, fn. 4 (1972).

Chapter Six

THE WORLD ECONOMY AS A WORLD ORDER DIMENSION: SELECTED ASPECTS

SCOPE OF INQUIRY

As a dynamic component of the existing world order system (S_1), the character of the world economy bears significantly on the prospects for a new system of world order (S_2), and on the selection of transition tactics which encourage the emergence of a new system that substantially realizes WOMP values ($S_{2(WOMP/USA)}$).* In this chapter our objective is to take note of some salient features of the world economy that are relevant for a movement of global reform. Although a more detailed treatment of these complex issues will be needed before economic considerations can be systematically incorporated into world order studies, we feel that previous world order studies, especially those conducted from a non-Marxist perspective, have unduly neglected this subject matter.[1]

The agenda for diplomacy has recently shifted discernibly toward economic subject matter, especially among principal governments in the advanced countries. As we have already noted, the apparent settlement of the Cold War,† the rapprochement between the United States

---

* There are other S^2 solutions that might realize WOMP values as well, or more successfully, than $S_{2(WOMP/USA)}$. Indeed, a careful consideration of other WOMP manuscripts from this perspective might be illuminating, both as to the range of $S_{2(WOMP)}$ thinking and as to relative persuasiveness on matters of attainability and desirability. There are non-WOMP S_2 perspectives that also should be considered. Here, however, to confine our analytic task we are identifying $S_{2(WOMP/USA)}$ with the optimal realization of WOMP values in S_2.

† The settlement of the Cold War in ideological terms seems clearer than its settlement in geopolitical terms. The 1973 Arab–Israeli War, the importance of oil diplomacy, implications by Americans that the Soviet Union might have introduced nuclear weapons, and "the world alert" of U.S. forces ordered by President Nixon to counter alleged Soviet moves in the Middle East, suggest that the Soviet–American rivalry may yet flare up in unsettling and dangerous forms.

and China, recurrent monetary and trade crises, and the growing realization that food and energy shortages may persist for years, if not decades, have all contributed to the recent prominence of international
economic issues. We are also witnessing renewed expressions of concern about the destructive and dangerous consequences of economic
nationalism. Managing the world economy is likely to dominate statecraft in the 1970's and may even induce major shifts in geopolitical
alignments by the end of the decade.

Unpredictable tremors might be caused by this renewal of economic
nationalism, in which rival states seek larger relative shares of world
markets or resources, and/or seek to secure their perceived needs
against the more effective assertion of claims by Third World states. It
seems evident, however, that the rate and character of the passing of S_1,
as well as the nature of transition from $S_1 \rightarrow S_2$, will be conditioned by
whether or not WOMP values generally come to predominate in critical
domestic arenas by the end of t_1. Of course, the educational effort to
promote WOMP values may also be influenced by the extent to which
policy-makers throughout the world perceive the economic consequences of such a reorientation as beneficial.

Advanced industrial countries like the United States must deal with
the realities of global interdependence on a daily basis. Can a series of
world order bargains be struck within the economic domain that will
perpetuate S_1? * The prospects for world order bargains relating to
money, trade, and resources depend mainly on agreement by relevant
governments as to what constitutes *a fair exchange;* this agreement
depends in turn on coordinating broad concepts of *equity* in intergovernmental relationships which are presently characterized by
great *inequalities* of position and capability.† The prevailing view in the
capitals of the rich countries is that these definitions of *fair exchange*
should be made on the basis of *subsystemic* considerations of equity,
rather than by applying global or systemic criteria.‡

---

* It is logically possible for S_1 to be perpetuated in a wide variety of forms that are more
or less positive from the perspective of WOMP value criteria. In our view, the pressures
that exist (see Chapter II) make it unlikely that S_1 future options will compare favorably
from a WOMP perspective with the actual S_1 conditions during the period 1970–1975.

† The position of a government may also be substantially shaped by special interest
nongovernmental groups and actors, including actors whose main locus of concern is
foreign. For instance, multinational corporations may have a considerable influence on
government positions in intergovernmental bargaining arenas.

‡ Thus, the United States as a subsystem seeks mainly its fair share, rather than seeking
as a member of the global system to distribute shares more equally among all people and
governments. The inequalities are so great and the unmet minimal needs of the poor so
large that we can discuss various nominal forms of deference to a systemic orientation.

Thus, the United States Government has emphasized the inequities in the present world economic order which have resulted in a decline of its relative position vis-à-vis West Germany, France, Japan, United Kingdom, and Italy since 1960.[2] The other advanced industrial countries, on their part, emphasize the continued gaps that exist on an absolute basis and identify equity not with trends, but with parity; note the similarity to discussions of force levels among rival states in arms control bargaining. Whether compromises can be negotiated will determine the extent to which principal economic actors on the world scene can work out a cooperative and stable system that satisfies their respective interests. It is significant that this center-stage world economic arena devotes virtually no attention to issues of fair exchange and equity with respect to the Third World, where two-thirds of humanity exist in the most extreme misery.

Since our primary concern is with $S_1 \rightarrow S_2$, it is not at all obvious which resolution we should wish for the present impasse in economic relations among advanced industrial actors. An era of economic harmony among the rich and powerful would tend to confirm for dominant actors the capacity of S_1 to meet *their* needs, without relinquishing their privileges or status; it might, therefore, delay transition to S_2, as well as defer the emergence of the kind of genuine global orientation needed to promote WOMP goals. Such stabilization might also deepen the conflict between the rich and poor in S_1, and encourage actors in the Third World to consider coercive and disruptive tactics and strategies. Such tactics, especially if reinforced by anxieties concerning resource supplies, might stimulate a new era of outright imperialist quest and control. The revival of intense economic nationalism might have important security spill-overs, perhaps encouraging nuclear weapons proliferation and possibly generating entirely new and dangerous configurations of great power rivalries. President Nixon's Fourth State of the Globe Message to Congress, transmitted on May 3, 1973, acknowledged that "the peace and stability we seek could be jeopardized by economic conflicts." The Message adds: "Such conflicts breed political tensions, weaken security ties, undermine confidence in currencies, disrupt trade, and otherwise rend the fabric of cooperation on which world order depends." [3] An atmosphere of economic nationalism would greatly inhibit transnational pressures to build a world community and might give governments a renewed capacity to mobilize their popula-

---

However, these forms of deference have no intention or prospect of making real inroads on structural inequality or poverty.

tions for purely nationalist ends. Such a prospect seems especially likely if economic nationalism generates domestic hardships through inflation, unemployment, shortages of food and energy, and a general climate of economic stagnation and recession. The temptation is practically overwhelming for hard-pressed domestic leaders to blame national economic misfortunes on the machinations of foreign states. Such hostility leads to self-fulfilling protectionist policies that can give rise to an escalatory spiral of the sort which has ended in outright warfare in the past. In this kind of world context, the false agenda of economic nationalism would displace the true agenda of global reform, greatly increasing the danger of catastrophic transition from $S_1 \rightarrow S_2$.

Two broad kinds of concern dominate our inquiry. First, will the handling of present economic concerns reinforce or undermine the viability of the state system? It is quite possible that international cooperative regimes might be established which would, in effect, supplant the state system while appearing to sustain it. If this tendency materializes, positive effects should be interpreted in relation to the wider $S_1 \rightarrow S_2$ transition context. Nongovernmental economic pressures, especially those associated with the multinational corporation, could also operate to supplant the state system by organizing economic life around the principles and ideology of a global market.

Second, will the persistence or aggravation of present economic concerns exert a discernible influence on the transition from $S_1 \rightarrow S_2$? Given the view that we are quite likely living in the final stages of S_1, the principal contingencies involve how and when the transition to S_2 will occur, and the manner in which S_2 will be organized. From this perspective it is obvious that the very salience of the world economic agenda may inhibit the energies of voluntary and humane transition.* Our understanding of causal effects is rudimentary. We do not know, for instance, whether an intergovernmental focus on apocalyptic concerns—World War III or ecological collapse—is or is not helpful from a consciousness-raising perspective. We have no reliable way of knowing whether the renewed significance of the economic agenda will operate as a new source of distraction and discourage an appreciation of the

---

* It is necessary to understand that *managerial* interests of dominant economic actors largely explain the new prominence of the world economy. These are the same sort of interests that focused attention on issues of strategic balance and arms competition during the more intense phases of the Cold War. The international agenda of the poor countries has been dominated by economic issues for decades, but it has been neglected by the geopolitical managers as irrelevant to their principal concerns, i.e., the security and prosperity of dominant actors.

more fundamental case for global reform. In recent years, mainstream elite and scholarly concerns have shifted from the war/peace-security agenda to the economic agenda; this shift is likely to continue during the next few years. The new primacy of economic issues has also tended to draw attention away from ecological issues.* Indeed, in the short-run, there is in many settings an increasingly well-understood antagonism between keeping the world economy functioning smoothly, and responding to the ecological challenge.† The former tends to entail GNP-maximization and unplanned expansion of the world industrial base, while the latter seems to involve forgoing some growth or even curtailing existing capacities in those sectors of industrial life where the negative externalities of production and/or consumption are high, jeopardizing the ecological balance of the region or planet.

ISSUES UNDERLYING AN ECONOMIC
APPROACH TO GLOBAL REFORM

On the basis of the orientation given on p. 353, it seems possible to indicate briefly the main issues that bear upon the management of the world economy in S_1, upon the encouragement of tendencies which increase prospects of establishing $S_{2(WOMP/USA)}$ by the year 2000, and upon the inhibition of either catastrophic transitional paths from $S_1 \rightarrow S_2$ or transition tendencies that generate an S_2 with net unfavorable value implications. Our discussion seeks to depict the main issues in a responsible way, so as to make readers aware of their relevance to the WOMP enterprise.‡

---

* Indeed, maintaining existing resource supplies at reasonable prices and protecting environmental quality are increasingly seen as competing goals; however, governing groups are more easily pressured by interests associated with resource considerations. The immediate impact of the energy crisis has been to weaken the political potency of environmentalist objections to various efforts to expand energy supplies, for instance, safety hazards from nuclear fuel plants, health hazards from fuel oil with high sulphur content, wilderness hazards from the trans-Alaska pipeline.

† In some settings economic and ecological factors seem congruent even in the short-run, e.g., managing ocean fisheries to sustain maximum yields over time. Over longer time intervals economic and ecological pressures will be reconciled, whether at low levels through depletion and pollution or at higher levels through planning, recycling, and conservation.

‡ A detailed analysis of the world economy is essential for the work of global political reform. We need a model of the world economy in S_1, a comprehensive guide to transition

RICH/POOR GAP

In many parts of this book we have emphasized economic inequalities that exist between

> individuals, age groups, sexes, classes, and groups *within* particular sovereign states;
>
> interstate and transnational regions, cultures, and races;
>
> state units.

We have also emphasized that the existence of these gaps is fundamentally inconsistent with the preference model $S_{2(WOMP/USA)}$, and is a principal barrier to its attainment via the preferred transition path. It is important to appreciate the extent, trend lines and projections of various economic gaps (as between different units of reference, e.g., state, social class, gender, race). World order discussions emanating from the mainstream of industrial governments tend to neglect the basic issue of whether such gaps—and an awareness of their injustice—are increasing or decreasing.*

The views of global reform prevailing in advanced countries still contemplate the persistence of wide gaps, making it difficult for them to be reconciled with more than a half-hearted commitment to the elimination of the war system. The gap structure presupposes that dominant units will maintain war capabilities to threaten, intimidate, or resist revisionist claims by economically deprived potential challengers. This link between a stable gap structure and the war system applies to all forms of political organization, including interstate and intrastate patterns of governance.

The extent to which a world order movement needs to implement gap-diminishing tactics and strategies is a complicated but basic issue, at least in relation to intermediate stages of transition (t_2). It is necessary to consider which economic gaps play a critical role and in what

---

tactics and strategies, and some preferential images of how the world economy might function in $S_{2(WOMP)}$.

* The question is whether human brotherhood can be accepted or demonstrated as an operative ethical ideal. The history of ethical thought does manifest great deference to the idealistic view that all persons are united in one great human family. However, our personal experience of friendship and enmity suggests that even within a close community one rarely, if ever, experiences brotherhood. On the other hand, the kind of global community essential at this stage of species development cannot function unless some degree of brotherhood is postulated. The international movement against slavery, and the more recent efforts to abolish torture and eliminate racism, represent a practical embodiment of brotherhood ideals, if only in minimal form.

sequence their reduction or elimination must occur. Levels of consciousness and levels of achievement are both significant. Thus, for instance, equalization of the sexes seems more critical in the United States of the 1970's than for most other parts of the world, where *class* and *ethnic* gaps predominate.*

Data are needed to enable a full graphing of *gap tendencies* with respect to the world distribution of goods and services among relevant units of reference. Table 6–1 attempts to portray the extent and pervasiveness of this gap by highlighting its salient features.† Figures 6–1

Table 6–1. The Development Gap

Indicator	Developing Country	Developed Country	United States
Per Capita GNP	230	$3,085	$4,756
Population (millions, mid-1971)	1,850	664	207
Population Growth Rate	2.6%	1.1%	1.1%
Literacy	40 %	97%	98%
Protein Consumption	54 g/day	97 g/day	—
Calorie Consumption	2,180/day	3,030/day	3,300/day
Life Expectancy	52 yrs.	71 yrs.	70 yrs.
Infant Mortality (death per thousand live births)	110	21	—
People per Physician	3,400	700	620
Per Capita Power Consumption (annual KWH output per person)	220	5,140	8,000

SOURCE: Robert E. Hunter (Project Director), *The United States and the Developing World: Agenda for Action*, (Washington, D.C.: Overseas Development Council, 1973), p. 123. Copyright © 1973 Overseas Development Council. Reprinted with permission.

* A rising class or group with high political consciousness tends to be a bearer of other values, sometimes progressive, and sometimes not. There is a natural bond between oppressed groups, but there is also a hostility toward those below by those who have escaped from the socioeconomic bottom, especially if their escape is recent, partial, or conditional.

† Fred Bergsten has a useful summary of the situation in poorer countries with respect to poverty: "Despite the impressive growth rates of the aggregate Third World in the 1960's, unemployment exceeds 20 percent in many countries. The per capita income of the poorest LDC's, which now contain half of the world population, has been growing by only 1.5 percent annually. The gap between the income of the richest 10 to 20 percent and the poorest 20 to 40 percent has been getting wider. There are 100 million more illiterates in

Figure 6–1. Gross National Product for Developed and Developing Countries, 1960–2000

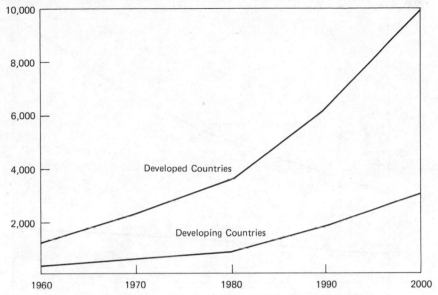

($ billions 1971 U.S. dollars)

Note: Data for 1960 through 1980 based on Bureau of Intelligence and Research, Department of State, "The World's Product at the Turn of the Decade: Recessional," September 12, 1972. Projections for 1990 and 2000 were arrived at by computing annual growth at 5 percent for developed countries and 6 percent for developing countries.

SOURCE: Robert E. Hunter (Project Director), *The United States and the Developing World*: *Agenda for Action* (Washington, D.C.: Overseas Development Council, 1973), p. 124. Copyright © 1973 Overseas Development Council. Reprinted with permission.

and 6–2 project major relationships until the end of the century, showing the extent to which population growth in poorer countries is likely to erode "the growth dividend" (even aside from the structural barriers which in most poor countries prevent a significant "trickle down" effect).

Figure 6–3 depicts a situation of uniformly increasing gaps among the three instances of some common unit of reference. Actual comparisons

---

the Third World now than twenty years ago, and two-thirds of all children there suffer from malnutrition." [4] Note that Bergsten's statement is extremely restrained, but imagine the consternation of a developed country if two-thirds of its children were deprived of some fundamental basis of human existence as the malnutrition statistic implies. Also, it should be appreciated that most, if not all or even more than all, of the 1.5 percent per-capita growth in income benefits the top 20 percent, or less, of the population.

Figure 6–2. Population Growth for Developed and Developing Countries, 1960–2000

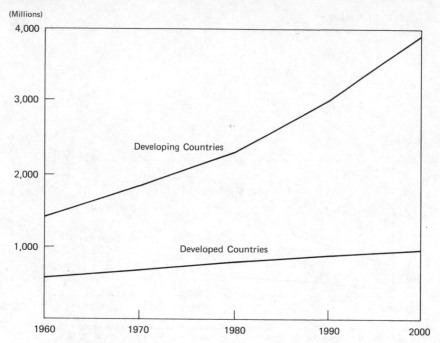

Note: Based on Office of Statistics and Reports, U.S. Agency for International Development. The projected annual growth rate used by AID for developing countries is 2.6 percent, and for developed countires, 1.1 percent.

SOURCE: Robert E. Hunter (Project Director), *The United States and the Developing World*: *Agenda for Action* (Washington, D.C.: Overseas Development Council, 1973), p. 124. Copyright © 1973 Overseas Development Council. Reprinted with permission.

through time for all world actors would assume great arithmetic complexity and would best be handled by computer programs. However, the approach in Figure 6–3 has quite general applicability. Time A, B, C, . . . n can be associated with calendar time (1974, 1980, etc.) or with analytic time (t, t₂, etc.); the units of reference could have any focus of interest for which personal income or other quantitative data exist (e.g., male/female; black/white/brown/red; old/young; Europe/North America/Africa; top 10%/bottom 10% of national population).

To gain an accurate picture, economic gap comparisons have to be adjusted for various nonmonetary factors—public welfare benefits, climate, nonmonetary forms of income, life-styles. Nevertheless, even crude gap comparisons are revealing for an analysis of world economic structure, and they unfortunately tend to be obscured by prevailing

Figure 6–3. Widening Development Gaps

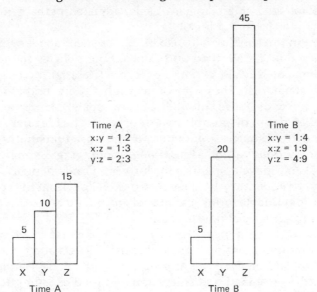

techniques that measure aggregate figures such as GNP rate of growth or per capita income levels.*

INCOME THRESHOLDS: MINIMA AND MAXIMA

It would also be important to fix minimum and maximum need thresholds for various groups within the world economic structure. These needs would include food, housing, clothing, medical treatment, edu-

---

* The per capita income figure is derived by dividing the size of population into the national income. There is no claim made that distributive shares are equally available to all sectors of the society. Thus, the poor may get poorer while the rich get richer, whether GNP rises or falls. Distributive flows are what determine whether a given GNP increase is benefiting all portions of the society or, equally, whether a static or negative GNP is hurting all portions. It is possible to imagine a society where for a period of time redistributive reforms are helping the poor during a period of stagnant or falling GNP. Studies of income distribution in different Third World countries are badly needed to assess the consequences of various development strategies.

cational and cultural opportunity. A minimum need threshold could then be established on a planetary basis, adjusted perhaps for climate and possibly for preferred life-style.

A maximum threshold would also be established, above which negative values would be attached and appropriate policies implemented. Such maxima could relate to both aggregate (state, group, region) and individual standards. These maxima might apply only to material goods (e.g., size of house, number of cars, boats, planes; level of income; level of wealth disposable by gift or will). The idea here is to conserve the earth's resources and to discourage wasteful patterns of living or governing without at the same time discouraging diversity, experimentation, and developmental incentives. Fundamentally, the establishment of upper threshold levels would follow from the conclusion that *certain* identifiable forms of material *growth* are destructive of individual, group, or special development.

To assess world economic structure from this perspective of thresholds would require identification of threshold levels and a massive effort to collect and analyze the appropriate data. A beginning can be made by utilizing statistics of starvation and food consumption, death in childbearing, longevity figures, hospital beds and schools per 1,000, and so on. It is important to establish as well as we can which portions of the human population are not now having their basic needs satisfied, and to map their relative densities so that distributional policies can be plotted within and between societies, regions, and ideological blocs. Obviously, it will be important to determine whether percentages of the population living below the minimal thresholds are increasing or decreasing for various categories of deprived people (i.e., class, race, gender, religion).

At this stage the concept of maximal thresholds for certain kinds of material consumption has primarily an *ideological* and *ethical* content. Maxima are ideological in the sense of transposing onto the level of economic distribution the consequences of *limits*—on space, resources, waste disposal facilities. Maxima are ethical in the sense of shifting growth and development goals—whether for the person, family, community, nation, or planet—from a material to a more spiritual axis. Thus, at levels below or just above minimum thresholds material considerations should certainly predominate, whereas at or beyond maximum thresholds nonmaterial ones should predominate.

We need extensive experimentation with social and political forms to identify thresholds in distinct settings. The current minimum needs thresholds for China or Tanzania seem much lower than the minimum thresholds for the United States or West Germany.* The shared need of all societies to respond to the ecological challenge accords some preference on a global basis to the Chinese model of minimum and maximum thresholds (i.e., elimination of poverty, but with relative austerity sustained for the entire population, including its leadership), at least from the perspective of bio-ethics.

As a matter of world policy, the most crucial issue at the present time is how to satisfy various cultural and physical concepts of minimum thresholds for anywhere from 60–98% of each national population. Enormous emphasis should be given to demonstrating existing failures of the world order system to satisfy fundamental needs, especially in the Third World, and to developing suitable explanations, remedial tactics and proposals. It is also necessary to connect the gap profile with the threshold problem, with respect to both the dynamics of S_1 and the prospects of $S_{2(WOMP/USA)}$.

Market-oriented economists tend to hold the view that the adoption of drastic remedies directed at overcoming international gaps would severely aggravate threshold problems. Indeed, the basic international growth model of the liberal ideological persuasion anticipates that the solution or improvement of the threshold problem must depend on ignoring tendencies toward widening gaps (it is argued that in order to help the poor sectors move from $50 to $300 per capita, it may be necessary to encourage the rich sectors to move from $3,000 to $20,000 per capita). On the other hand, planning-oriented economists who are equity-minded tend to argue that it is both possible and necessary to redistribute (i.e., diminish the gaps) on a planned basis in order to deal adequately with the urgent threshold requirements of the very poor. Planning perspectives tend to be very skeptical about the redistributive effects of growth-oriented policies, especially if implemented in a deformed social structure (where acute gaps exist and more than 25% of the population is at or below the poverty level) and executed mainly by profit-oriented multinational corporations (see pp. 392–396). UNC-TAD (United Nations Conference on Trade and Development) reflects this skeptical planning perspective with respect to world economic de-

---

* In this regard, it may turn out that poor societies are much more adaptable than rich ones during a period of resource shortages due to ecological pressure. North Vietnam's survival in the face of the American air onslaught from 1965–1973 was undoubtedly facilitated by the poverty and simplicity of the society, enabling degrees of autonomy at local levels and extreme decentralization of vital services that would be unimaginable in highly complex, interdependent portions of the world.

velopment, whereas GATT (General Agreement on Trade and Tariffs) or world monetary arrangements embody a market perspective on world economic development.

The link between economic thresholds and demographic growth is very important. Perhaps no upper threshold is more important to encourage than a reproductive one governing family size, but ironically, such encouragement appears to depend on prior success in reducing the prospects of misery for the population. There is what has been called "a demographic feedback" from successful programs of economic development that exerts a far more effective depressant on fertility rates than does the dissemination of birth control techniques and facilities. As Lester Brown has noted, "the historical record indicates that birth rates do not usually decline unless certain basic social needs are satisfied—an assumed food supply, a reduced infant mortality rate, and the availability of appropriate health and educational services." [5] Provision for the aged might also be added to Brown's list of factors. Ideally, such upper limits will be achieved by voluntary behavior induced by education and by governmental policies that assure social security for the aged. It is obviously desirable to minimize bureaucratic control over population growth, but easy family planning devices and backup abortion facilities would at least cut down on unwanted children. In a crowded world beset by scarcity, it is obviously helpful to eliminate, to the extent possible, the problems arising from an increasing global population. The global population currently rises by about two per cent a year, or just under eighty million; every three years this adds a consumer cohort whose size exceeds the United States or the Soviet Union, and every decade the 700–800 million growth total equals the population of gigantic countries such as China or India.

The causal links between population growth and other societal dimensions are generally controversial. Does one attribute famine to overcrowding or drought? Does one attribute communal violence and strife to overcrowding or bad government?

The ecological consequences of further population growth are manifest—more demand for all resources (other considerations being constant). The problem of establishing thresholds of need are intimately connected with issues of overcrowding the earth's facilities. Any kind of satisfactory program for global reform will have to include an effort to agree upon an *optimum* size population for the world and how to attain it. Such agreement cannot be reached in isolation, but will reflect attitudes toward sharing, the elimination of poverty and imperialism, mobility of people, and ethnic tolerance and security.

As an interim approach, an appeal for ZPG (zero population growth) by voluntary action should be included in any program for global reform.* Such a goal merely reflects the consensus that the planet's population is presently too large, that its further increase would be detrimental, and that such a situation calls for appropriate policies at all levels of social action. Paul Erlich and other pessimistic commentators on the world scene argue that ZPG is likely to be achieved by the 1980's not as a result of falling birth rates, but as a consequence of rising death rates. He anticipates famine, disease, warfare, and environmental decay to be contributing factors.

A GEO–ECONOMIC PERSPECTIVE

The "energy crisis" of the early 1970's is symptomatic of raw materials shortages likely to emerge in early t_1, and is itself likely to alter alignments in many respects. The process of decolonization, even if incomplete, has cut the advanced industrial countries off from direct control over raw materials critical for their continued functioning. The supplier countries may begin to organize for purposes of bargaining and leverage, as the Organization of Petroleum Exporting Countries (OPEC) has already done within the oil industry.[7] The Soviet Union, by virtue of its size and mineral wealth, is less dependent than other major world actors on external sources of raw materials supply.[8]

Middle East oil-exporting countries are building up huge foreign exchange surplus accounts.† These surpluses can be used to finance military ventures, to underwrite "a strike" against the industrial world, or

---

* However, the issue of population pressure should not be separated from the issue of environmental overload. Thus, from a global perspective it may be more important to achieve population control in countries with relatively low birth rates, but with highly detrimental consumption patterns. Estimates vary greatly as to whether each additional American is fifty or five hundred times the ecological burden of each additional Indian, but there is no serious disagreement that the difference in burden is significant and closely correlated with degrees of industrialization and personal affluence as calculated in material or energy consumption terms.[6]

† In October 1973 an unnamed "high U.S. official" warned that "In three years Saudi Arabia may have greater financial reserves than the United States, Western Europe, and Japan combined." In 1974 Saudi Arabia was expected to earn $15 billion in oil revenue, of which only $3 billion would be spent for internal development. At this rate it seems likely that by the end of the decade Saudi Arabia "may have accumulated $100 billion in reserves," thereby becoming "bankers of the world."[9]

to play havoc with existing money markets through speculative currency transfers.* Saudi Arabia is in a particularly strong position, with the world's largest quantity of proven oil reserves and 26.7% of the world total (the Middle East has about 62% of the world total, as compared with 6% each for the United States and the Soviet Union).

In his 1973 International Economic Report, President Nixon made the following statement:

> The oil-producing and oil-consuming countries are linked inextricably. In the most basic terms, neither side can do without the other. But this interdependence is no guarantee that the international oil trade will go smoothly. For oil is not just another commodity. It is of vital importance to consumer economies, and political and emotional overtones are far greater than for most other commodities.[10]

The United States has increasingly depended on oil imports to meet its energy requirements, and will continue to do so through the 1970's. In 1970 Western Europe imported about 80% of the 13 million bpd that is used, and is expected to increase this figure to 20 million bpd by 1980. In 1980 Japan is expected to rely on oil for at least 75% of its energy needs, and virtually all of this must be imported.†

The leading oil exporters from the Middle East, Africa, Latin America, and Asia, through OPEC, have gained a formidable bargaining asset vis-à-vis the oil companies and the importing countries. A sharp controversy presently exists as to whether an actual oil shortage is likely to emerge and if so, whether the importing countries can effectively resist economic and political pressures from OPEC. The bargaining process concerns not only the sale price per barrel for different grades of oil, but also the production schedule, policy on reserves, managerial control, and foreign policy problems. Through the Organization of Arab Petroleum Exporting Countries (OAPEC), the Arab members of

---

* These funds could also be used to promote Third World development and cohesion, although the major oil exporter governments seem highly nationalistic and exhibit minimal empathy for the plight of their own populations.

† The oil embargoes and cutbacks triggered by the 1973 Arab-Israeli War may alter these prospects considerably and in ways that are not now predictable. The United States, Western Europe, and Japan will both seek a better understanding with Arab oil producers, and take steps to encourage the accelerated development of other energy sources (e.g., coal, nuclear power, shale). Liquified coal, if economically feasible, might relieve the energy pressure for a considerable length of time. The shortage of oil, the rise in the price of oil per barrel, the prospects of governmental subsidies, and a huge market make it much more attractive to proceed more rapidly with new energy sources.

OPEC have instituted a production slowdown, as well as an embargo, hoping thereby to reshape the approach of the United States and other oil consumers to the Middle East conflict, and to induce a shift from a pro-Israeli posture to one that is either anti-Israeli or neutral. By favorably altering the price structure for oil, it is obvious that the oil producers can cut production *and* sustain revenues, thereby extending the time period over which oil reserves would be expected to last.

The OAPEC/OPEC model is important. It demonstrates the added potency that arises from aggregated bargaining. It suggests the political dimension of resource issues. It discloses the previously underestimated vulnerability of the advanced industrial economies to Third World pressures, at least with regard to energy supplies. As financial analyst Roy Vickers put it in November, 1973: "Now that it is here, the Arab oil boycott seems to be an extremely effective weapon, indeed, one which could soon squeeze economies of the whole Free World. No longer is the argument heard that boycotts couldn't happen, and wouldn't work very well if they did." [11] Various response strategies are being considered: more attention to alternative energy sources, reprisals in the form of withholding food exports to Arab countries, shifts in diplomatic alignment, vague threats of countermeasures, pressures for more cohesive relations among oil consuming allies, and accelerated efforts to negotiate a peace settlement in the Middle East. [12] In the background would seem to be the ultimate threat of military intervention, a threat somewhat neutralized (or deterred) by the Soviet military presence, by Arab commitments and by a change in norms with regard to such uses of military power. If the pressure increases we would expect more overall attention to be given to various uses of the military instrument, which is, after all, the main comparative advantage at the disposal of the United States. The Saudi Arabian official in charge of oil policy, Ahmed Zaki al-Yamani, has responded to these threats with his own warning that any military intervention would compel Saudi Arabia to blow up sensitive areas in her own oil fields, thereby depriving oil importers of Saudi Arabian oil for many years. [13]

We do not now possess enough information to determine several lines of future development:

Can the OPEC and OAPEC models be extended to other spheres of economic interaction (for example, other resources, or trade relations in general) between the Third World and the advanced industrial countries? Will they be? UNCTAD has not, so far, enjoyed notable success in this regard.

Will the squeeze in energy supplies prompt importing countries to adopt new counter-strategies such as aggregating their buying power (they might form an "Organization of Petroleum Importing Countries") or, more dramatically, undertaking to assure oil supplies by political and/or military intervention (either by maintaining a sympathetic government in power or by occupying the country in direct imperial fashion)?

In the face of new energy technologies (e.g., coal, solar, nuclear) will oil continue to have a critical geopolitical status through the 1980's and 1990's?

How creatively will the oil exporting nations use their economic leverage to promote global reform which helps the world's poorer sectors?[14]

Will the energy crisis generate a new wave of domestic repression and foreign imperialism to cope with growing challenges posed by scarcity?

Will these challenges be met by fission technologies that subject the populations of the world to numerous hazards arising from possible accidents, radiation exposure, and higher risks of nuclear blackmail (via diversion of weapons-grade fissionable material)?

These concerns suggest some of the uncertainties and intricacies that bear upon the geo-economic dimension of the future. Two anticipated countervailing tendencies are already becoming evident:

1. An unprecedented drive to manage the world economy for the mutual benefit of the rich and powerful in areas of money, trade, and investment

2. A new surge of unilateralism, arising from the diverse interests and pressures of principal actors, that may result in surprising geopolitical realignments

To some extent, these two tendencies are being played out in the Middle East. Back in 1956 it was the United States that was accused of betraying its closest allies by refusing to back the English–French–Israeli Suez Campaign, whereas in 1973 the United States accused Western Europe of not supporting its pro-Israeli diplomacy. In the background of 1956 lay European dependence on the Suez "life line," whereas in the background of 1973 lay greater European dependence on Arab oil in a context where military approaches seemed unavailable.* The point here is that geo-economic pressures are intense and that

---

* Western Europe, with the exception of Greece and Portugal, refused to support American efforts to resupply Israel during the October 1973 War, despite a massive Soviet

geopolitical strategies are diverse. In 1973, the United States and the Soviet Union could *cooperate* in establishing a framework for an Arab–Israeli settlement, as well as possibly securing for themselves a hegemonic role in the region. Beneath this banner of peacemaking lurks a new threat of hegemony and imperialism, which China alone among governments seems willing to condemn.

The competition for ocean resources is another dimension of geoeconomic conflict arising out of the wider crisis of world order.* Existing "rules of the game" waver between the right of the shore state to claim as much ocean as it deems appropriate, and an international limitation on the extension of territorial boundaries. According to one statist element of S_1 logic, the low-technology, large coastline states have a maximum incentive to support a territorial-based solution, whereas high-technology states, especially if their coastlines are limited, have a maximum incentive to support a high seas-based solution according to a complementary element of S_1 logic ("freedom of the seas"). Small, poor states and landlocked or shelf-locked countries (see Table 6–2) have a maximum incentive to favor a community solution based on the idea that ocean resources are "the common heritage of mankind." Nat-

---

resupply operation for Syria and Egypt. Arab countries threatened production cutbacks and embargoes in the event of any help to Israel, direct or indirect. This threat seemed effective, and left the United States in a diplomatically isolated role as Israel's sole major supporter. Even the United States did not want to deepen its identification with Israel, and resisted Soviet diplomatic efforts to have American and Soviet truce observance forces associated with respective allies. President Nixon made clear that the United States truce observers would be unharmed and would be on the scene only in response to a request (prearranged) by the Secretary General of the United Nations. Such an uncharacteristic American posture of deference to the United Nations seems clearly designed to avoid acting on behalf of Israel and further aggravating Arab governments, thereby possibly provoking even more serious oil reprisals.

* There are a variety of significant ocean resources: marine life, fossil fuel, minerals. Fishing disputes have grown more intense in response to scarcities, mobility of modern fleets, and concern about overfishing; "the cod war" between Iceland and the United Kingdom in 1973 concerning the relative legitimacy of coastal sovereignty versus high seas "freedom" suggests the need for new guidelines. Where states are close together as in Northern Europe, offshore oil drilling raises similar issues, in addition to provoking severe environmental problems from blowout and leakage risks. Deep sea mining of hard metals also is beginning to assume serious proportions. There are now reported to be over 100 subsea underground mines, off the coasts of more than a dozen countries. These mines have yielded minerals such as coal, iron ore, nickel-copper ores, tin, gold, mercury, barite, and limestone. Highly concentrated metallic deposits in manganese nodules on the floor of the seabed also contain large quantities of copper, nickel, and cobalt. While it is not presently feasible to mine them, active research and development programs throughout the world are working to improve such prospects.[15]

Table 6–2. Land-locked and Shelf-locked Countries

Land-locked (30)

Asian	Mali	*Others*
Afghanistan	Niger	Andorra
Bhutan	Rhodesia	Austria
Nepal	Rwanda	Czechoslovakia
Laos	Swaziland	Hungary
African	Uganda	Liechtenstein
Botswana	Upper Volta	Luxembourg
Burundi	Zambia	Mongolia
Central African Rep.	*Latin American*	San Marino
Chad	Bolivia	Switzerland
Lesotho	Paraguay	Vatican City
Malawi		

Shelf-locked (20)

Asian	United Arab Emirates	Finland
Bahrain	Vietnam (North)	Germany (East)
Cambodia	*African*	Germany (West)
Iraq	Togo	Monaco
Jordan	Zaire	Netherlands
Kuwait	*Others*	Poland
Qatar	Belgium	Sweden
Singapore	Denmark	

Note: A shelf-locked country is one with offshore areas that do not exceed 200 meters in depth.

SOURCE: Data for this table taken from "Indices of National Interest in the Oceans," by Lewis M. Alexander in *Ocean Development and International Law Journal*, 1:37. Used with permission.

urally, the third perspective is at the same time the weakest (because it challenges S₁ traditions of conflict resolution), and the most desirable from the viewpoint of global reform (because it brings an $S_{2(WOMP)}$ perspective to bear).

Can a world order bargain be struck among states so differently oriented? Governments themselves find it difficult to shape a coherent policy, being caught in the cross-fire of competing interest groups (for example, naval authorities want as small an ambit for coastal sovereignty as possible, whereas investors want the security and profitability associated with extensive national regimes). The one factor that does strongly encourage the search for a negotiated global solution is the perceived need for a common approach to control, exploitation, conservation, and environmental protection with respect to ocean activity. Whether this perceived desirability can be translated into a world order bargain remains to be seen, and will depend on whether governments can form a consensus around reasonable lines of compromise. An initial testing ground has been the Third Law of the Sea Conference convened in Caracas, Venezuela in the summer of 1974 and operating under a broad United Nations mandate to modify a fundamental component of S_1. As Dr. Sreenivasa Rao has put it: "What began as a modest enterprise to modify the law of the sea soon led to extensive questioning of the public order of the oceans. The third LOS conference now has a mandate not only to modify the existing law of the sea but to change it radically, if that can be accomplished within the contemporary political framework." [16]

What consequences do these geo-economic pressures have for a movement of global reform? In one sense, the pressures are themselves symptomatic of the breakdown of S_1, while in another, they induce preoccupations which distract attention from either the reform of S_1 or its displacement by a beneficial variant of S_2. The educational challenge presented at this time includes an interpretation of geo-economic settings as world order issues of prime importance; these settings raise transition possibilities which must be fully explored. Because of their relevance to daily routine, these issues touch the lives of ordinary citizens in ways that more grandiose problems of war and peace rarely do; hence, high priority should be given to consciousness-raising in t around WOMP solutions for geo-economic crises. One exceedingly interesting suggestion along these lines is Norman Borlaug's urgent call for the establishment of international granaries to avert food crises leading to mass famine:

> The time has arrived when international granaries of food reserves, financed by all nations, should be established for use in case of emergencies. These granaries should be strategically located in different geographic areas of the world in order to simplify logistics and also minimize the danger of disruptive railroad, port and shipping strikes in times of emergency. These grain reserves must be made available to all countries that need them—and before famine strikes, not afterwards. [17]

It is doubtful whether the structures of planetary culture are sufficient to overcome statist approaches to food supply, but as with energy and ocean resources, these issues provide testing grounds for the durability and ethos of late S_1 problem-solving. Contrast Borlaug's WOMP-oriented concept with Henry Kissinger's proposed response to the same

issue in his 1973 address to the General Assembly of the United Nations
shortly after his confirmation as Secretary of State:

> The growing threat to the world's food supply deserves the urgent atten-
> tion of this Assembly. Since 1969, global consumption of cereals has risen
> more rapidly than production; stocks are at the lowest levels in years. We
> now face the prospect that—even with bumper crops—the world may not
> rebuild its seriously depleted reserves in this decade.
> No one country can cope with this problem. The United States therefore
> proposes:
> —that a World Food Conference be organized under United Nations
> auspices in 1974 to discuss ways to maintain adequate food supplies,
> and to harness the efforts of all nations to meet the hunger and malnutri-
> tion resulting from national disasters.
> —that nations in a position to do so offer technical assistance in the con-
> servation of food. The United States is ready to join with others in provid-
> ing such assistance.[18]

This response exemplifies the statist philanthropic approach; while acknowledging the grave community threat, Mr. Kissinger is willing nevertheless to rely upon the wisdom and generosity of individual governments to deal with the situation. The contrast between Borlaug's and
Kissinger's approach to the world food crisis vividly illustrates "the
great debate" on a whole series of geo-economic issues that can be expected to ensue in the 1970's and 1980's. It is important for advocates of
global reform to participate actively in these debates which focus on
particular subject matters, as well as to link the specific problem at hand
to the structural constraints imposed by an S_1 framework, to show the
range of S_2 options that might lessen or remove such constraints, and to
evolve a response reflecting an $S_{2(WOMP)}$ outlook.

PROFITABILITY VERSUS MINIMUM STANDARDS OF HUMAN DIGNITY

Global consciousness, economic interdependence, and widespread
abuses of human rights have created a new, controversial set of world
order issues:

Should international institutions or national governments impose trade barriers as instruments of protest against abuses of human rights?

Should foreign investors be encouraged or coerced to promote human rights in their business dealings abroad?

Should economic favors (loans, credits, grants, subsidies) be made conditional upon the willingness of foreign governments to satisfy certain standards of human rights?

These very complex issues are relevant to all world order arenas, ranging from individual and private activity to the actions of governments and international institutions. Much of the debate has centered upon American and British business involvement in southern Africa, where official racism imposes such severe handicaps on the black majority population. For example, many churches and universities are now being asked by human rights-conscious associates to dispose of their holdings in companies that do business in southern Africa. Recently, another area of active debate has been whether the United States Congress should withhold most-favored-nation treatment from the Soviet Union until emigration restrictions on Russian Jews are lifted (the so-called Jackson Amendment). Questions have been raised in a less-defined way as to whether the United States and other governments should suspend economic and military assistance to governments whose policies contravene minimum standards of human rights.

These problems cannot be discussed in any detail here. Intricate questions of *principle* and *tactics* are at stake. It is important, first of all, to disentangle political and ideological values from genuine issues of human rights. American investors have been reasonably successful in securing legislation requiring the President to suspend foreign aid to a government that expropriates American-owned property without paying full compensation. Such a national posture cannot help but seem regressive when it transmutes a vested economic interest in foreign property into an international human right that allegedly warrants national protection. Similarly, the Jackson Amendment controversy mingles cold war sentiments of anti-Communism, pro-Zionist pressures for the free-flow of Jews, a general interest in upholding the rights of individual mobility, and concern that Soviet–American relations not be encumbered with special pleading on issues of human rights because of the overriding interest in achieving world nuclear peace.

There are also *tactical* questions. There is widespread disagreement as to whether overt, official American pressure beyond a certain point on the issue of Jewish emigration helps or hurts its supposed beneficiaries. It is argued, for instance, that in this context quiet diplomacy is much more effective than legislative insistence, and, indeed, current Soviet emigration policy has relaxed to the point where 35,000 Jews have received exit visas in the last few years, about as many as Soviet administrative machinery available for the purpose can process. In the South African context, it is analogously argued that foreign investors should be viewed as "Trojan horses" capable of contributing to the betterment of black workers and to higher employment standards in general. For instance, Louis Turner asserts that "withdrawal of investments would currently be a regressive step. . . . The correct strategy for anti-apartheid forces is thus to pressure multinationals into significantly improving the conditions of their black workers and into confrontations with the government." [19]

The more drastic tactical view asserts that foreign investors can be pressured into making some cosmetic changes in working conditions that do benefit a tiny proportion of African labor (see the Polaroid Experiment),[20] but that by disarming opponents who demand real structural changes, these reforms may blunt the incentive of investor governments (in this instance, mainly the United Kingdom and the United States) from taking any position harmful to these racist and colonial regimes. United Nations efforts to impose mandatory sanctions on the Smith regime in Rhodesia have evoked quite emotional responses. There is disagreement over the effectiveness of these sanctions, and one view maintains that such sanctions actually help the target nation's economy by forcing it to diversify and to evolve a more disciplined approach to national development.[21] Controversy in the United States has centered around Congress's repudiation of the United Nations boycott on Rhodesian exports (which the U.S. Government supported in the Security Council) by authorizing the import of chrome from Rhodesia (the so-called Byrd Amendment).[22]

In the present context the main point is to assess the links between economic interactions and the realization of V_3, especially during t_1. Consciousness-raising would generally seem to be promoted by asserting transnational demands, provided the human right in question had the backing of virtually the entire world community. For this reason, the anti-apartheid campaign is attractive. However, if the human right in question involves a self-interested assertion of claims by one group against another, with no agreement on the human right standard in question or where the abuse was less severe than others which are tolerated, then it is undesirable to use economic leverage to promote this right. The concreteness of many human rights issues and their capacity to engender individual concern make this area an important one in which to foster a transnational consciousness, as well as to expose, in operational terms, the deficiencies of S_1 as a system for protecting and promoting human rights.

NATIONAL DEVELOPMENT

In S_1, human goals are set primarily at the national level. A major governmental responsibility is the adoption of policies designed to promote proclaimed national goals. Virtually all national governments share the goals of achieving secure boundaries against foreign enemies, maintaining the formal aspects of political independence, and maximizing the income and wealth of the state. In this section we focus on national economic development as a world order issue.

NATIONAL ECONOMIC DEVELOPMENT
AND WORLD ORDER

Traditional approaches to global reform emphasize altered external relations among state actors. The focus of WOMP/USA is upon improved human relations leading to a more peaceful and just world; it relies upon a concept of world order which is comprehensive in the sense of encompassing both international and intranational dimensions of government. These principal dimensions have an influence upon the degree to which V_1, V_2, V_3, and V_4 are realized at any given point in time.*

Given the degree of poverty that exists in the world, it is obvious that the selection of national development options has a strong bearing on progress toward improved realization of V_2. Other WOMP values are also centrally at issue. The pursuit of incompatible development strategies—for example, capitalist versus radical socialist—tends to arouse political enmities across state lines, enmities which generate various types of political violence relative to V_1. The combination of gross economic inequality with interdependent economic activity leads the rich and powerful to be heavily involved in the political life of the poor and weak; it is not accidental that since 1945, warfare has been concentrated in the Third World. The pressure to develop economically—that is, the priority accorded to national enrichment—provides governments of both left and right with a rationale (or it is usually a rationalization?) for repressive policies which detract from the realization of V_3. And, finally, for similar reasons the primacy of development policies leads to the neglect or subordination of the various categories of ecological con-

---

* For depiction of subcategories encompassed by V_4 see p. 27; fuller descriptions of V_1, V_2, V_3, are also contained in Chapter I.

cern encompassed by V_4. Note that all societies, regardless of current GNP or standard of living, continue to pursue accelerated development strategies. Note also that there are underdeveloped portions of large developed societies. Whether "development" beyond a certain threshold of affluence becomes "overdevelopment" is a central political and ethical question for advanced countries.[23] Because such a high proportion of resource consumption and waste disposal is concentrated in rich countries, their debate on development options has the greatest immediate bearing on both sets of ecological concerns (resources, pollution) embodied in V_4.[24]

There are, then, several main points:

First, national development options are centrally linked to those WOMP criteria which guide appraisals of world order performance at a given time.

Second, interdependence of economic and political activity means that certain patterns of national development are more compatible with one another than others; these patterns are both *horizontal* (on given layers of economic activity, e.g., among advanced industrial, among relatively industrial, and among pre-industrial national societies as separate categories of relations) and *vertical* (across layers of differing economic development, e.g., advanced industrial in relation to industrial and pre-industrial national societies).

Third, some national development options and certain patternings of economic relations are more conducive than others to desirable types of drastic global reform.

Fourth, the continuing quest by rich countries for GNP-conceived development has an ecologically depressant impact.

Fifth, continuing population growth has an ecologically and economically depressant impact that makes it difficult for poor countries to translate aggregate growth into better living conditions.

This subject matter is complex and controversial. Our objective is to raise the appropriate questions for readers concerned with the dynamics of global reform. A further refinement would involve rating development options in terms of value impacts, societal effects, and systemic prospects for global reform. (See Table 6–3.)

NATIONAL ECONOMIC DEVELOPMENT OPTIONS

Every country in the world is presently pursuing a national development strategy centered upon positive economic growth—all share the

Table 6–3. World Order Effects of Development Options

World Order Effects / Development Option	(1) Value Effects	(2) Patterning Effects	(3) Systemic Effects— Global Reform Prospects
Country A	V_1	horizontal	S_1 reform
	V_2	vertical	S_2 reform
	V_3		$S_{2(WOMP)}$ reform
	V_4		$S_{2(WOMP/USA)}$ reform
Country B	V_1	horizontal	S_1 reform
	V_2	vertical	S_2 reform
	V_3		$S_{2(WOMP)}$ reform
	V_4		$S_{2(WOMP/USA)}$ reform
Country C	V_1	horizontal	S_1 reform
	V_2	vertical	S_2 reform
	V_3		$S_{2(WOMP)}$ reform
	V_4		$S_{2(WOMP/USA)}$ reform

Note: This table suggests a way of organizing data that is responsive to the concerns of global reform; it proposes a framework of inquiry for a detailed consideration of national economic development as a world order variable; the horizontal (relations among states of approximate equality) and vertical (relations among states of significant inequality) patterning in Column 2 need to be considered in relation to each value; the four types of systemic effects in Column 3 are categories of effects (i.e., there is a range of S_1 reform possibilities, not just one, etc.).

goal of increasing both the size of GNP and its rate of growth. No-growth positions are discussed only in rich countries, and then only marginally, in nongovernmental settings. Governments do vary in relation to the kind of growth they seek, and even in the extent to which they will make concessions in other areas in order to achieve maximum growth.* Governments also differ sharply over security policy, espe-

---

* The place of economic growth in a national priority schedule depends on a large number of contextual variables: defense of territory and political independence against perceived enemies of the ruling group takes precedence over all competing goals of government, especially if warfare is present or seems imminent; control of domestic discontent may also take precedence, if the ruling group feels that its position is endangered. In other contexts, ideological considerations may be preeminent, especially if the ruling group has seized power to set the country straight; for instance, China gave clear priority to ideological concerns during "the cultural revolution." The Chilean junta after taking power in 1973 emphasized its mission to save "the fatherland" from Marxist contamination, suggesting that ideological fervor exists on the right as well as the left, and might even be used to justify certain economic sacrifices.

cially over the degree to which national security should be based upon national effort and resources, and the extent to which internal and external threats are perceived. Security requirements generally take precedence over development priorities in government thinking, although the two policies are compatible to the degree that military preparedness involves economic activity that is reflected in GNP accounts.

Based on his study of comparative development options selected by African governments after their independence, David Apter has usefully distinguished governments by classifying them as being either mobilization systems, reconciliation systems, or modernizing autocracies.[25]

According to Apter, a mobilization system has five characteristics: "(1) hierarchical authority; (2) total allegiance; (3) tactical flexibility; (4) unitarism; and (5) ideological specialization." It relies on assured guidance from the state or single party, and implements a single national plan, by coercion if necessary. In this sort of approach to development, epitomized in different ways by the two Communist giants, China and the Soviet Union, there is in Apter's words an explicit effort "to mobilize . . . political energies and resources for a grand assault on poverty, ignorance, and backwardness." [26] Centralization, militancy, intolerance of deviation, and austerity generally characterize mobilization systems.*

A reconciliation system is more amorphous, there are greater variations from instance to instance, and the basic mode is vulnerable to crisis and challenge. For Apter a reconciliation system also has five parts: "(1) pyramidal authority; (2) multiple loyalties; (3) necessity for compromise; (4) pluralism; and (5) ideological diffuseness." [27] Most constitutional democracies and market economies are or purport to be reconciliation systems of some form, although there may be some limits on pluralism (e.g., Communists or fascists may be excluded) and on the extent of political participation that is sought (e.g., the poor or minorities may be excluded). In essence, however, there is competition for leadership, elections are held, and private centers of capital and policy-making place constraints on governmental functioning with respect to development. India represents one type of reconciliation system (al-

---

* In China, it is true, certain forms of carefully conceived decentralization have been encouraged and virtues of self-reliance praised. Nevertheless, the prevailing organizational and political atmosphere emphasizes a single path to national fulfillment that must be taken by all Chinese. Adaptation to variations in circumstances is indulged, but deviation from prevailing lines of interpreting Maoist thinking is not. The one hundred flowers that bloomed briefly have wilted, at least for the present.

though it has some characteristics of a mobilization system) and the United States represents another. Federal political systems are structurally committed to compromise and apportionment of power.*

The third type of system depicted by Apter is a modernizing autocracy. Here traditionalism plays a commanding role, and development goals are pursued within an inherited political framework which did not originally possess such goals. The characteristics of a modernizing autocracy are as follows: "(1) hierarchical authority; (2) exclusivism; (3) strategic flexibility; (4) unitarism; and (5) neo-traditionalism." [28] Apter gives as illustrations Morocco, Ethiopia, and especially Japan in the period of rapid modernization after the Meiji Restoration (1868–1912). There is a continuity with the past, pride in national heritage, and respect for a ritually endowed (and possibly sanctified) national ruler.

Of course, most actual societies are mixtures of these ideal types; in fact, some military coups have sought to combine elements of all three systems. Often, development priorities are also deeply influenced by the relative impacts of different national ethnic and interest groups. A major set of differences concerns whether the *needs* of the population as a whole are given immediate priority, or are viewed as deferrable at least until after a period of self-sustaining growth and supposed "take-off." Receptivity to and the extent and roles of foreign investment, technical assistance and foreign aid may all be significant factors.† Another significant variable is the capacity of ruling groups to create a development consensus that need not systematically rely on coercion. Obviously some countries are much more richly endowed with resources

---

* Note that federalism must be substantive, as well as formal, if this generalization is to hold; the Soviet Union has a nominally federal structure, but is appropriately classified as a mobilization system.

† Generally, so-called capital importing countries in the poor sectors of the world are in reality providing a net outflow of capital to rich countries. This assessment was made by a non-radical former Foreign Minister of Chile, Gabriel Valdés, in a statement delivered to President Richard Nixon at the White House on June 12, 1969:

It is generally believed that our continent receives real financial aid. The data show the opposite. We can affirm that Latin America is making a contribution to financing the development of the United States and of other industrialized countries. Private investment has meant and does mean for Latin America that the sums taken out of our continent are several times higher than those that are invested. Our potential capital declines. The benefits of invested capital grow and multiply themselves enormously, though not in our countries but abroad. The so-called aid, with all its well-known conditions, means markets and greater development for the developed countries, but has not in fact managed to compensate for the money that leaves Latin America in payment of the external debt and as a result of the profits generated by private direct investment. In one word, we know that Latin America gives more than it receives. [29]

than others; Middle East oil countries such as Kuwait and Saudi Arabia provide spectacular examples of national wealth, whereas the sub-Saharan tier of African countries are just as extreme in their impoverishment.

Can we choose a preferential model for the poor countries? For every national society? Or, does the configuration of national circumstances determine the relative merits of alternative options? Issues of magnitude and scale are significant; a large society faced by mass poverty, entrenched interest groups, and quite limited resources probably cannot make an impressive impact on social ills without proceeding along the mobilization path, although it may create an illusion of progress by achieving a respectable rate of GNP growth within the framework of a reconciliation system.

The crux of development is satisfaction of human needs. We are discovering a very important reality—that there is no *necessary* correlation between economic growth and a needs-oriented development concept. Indeed, there may be an inverse correlation. As Celso Furtado has put it: "The Brazilian economy constitutes a very interesting example of how far a country can go in the process of industrialization without abandoning its main features of underdevelopment: great disparity in productivity between urban and rural areas, a large majority of the population living at a physiological subsistence level, increasing masses of underemployed people in the urban zones, etc." [30] Thus, things can get worse despite a dramatic upward sweep in economic growth curves. This contradiction of the mainstream wisdom of economists [31] is a consequence of the fact that *structural* changes must be made in domestic society to assure that economic expansion will mean substantially improved lives for the people, not only aggrandizement for the elite classes: "Real *development* involves a structural transformation of the economy, society, polity and culture of the satellite that permits the self-generating and self-perpetuating use and development of the people's potential." [32] Despite satisfactory rates of GNP growth for Latin America over the past decade, the employment picture has deteriorated everywhere except in Cuba: "In both absolute and relative terms, unemployment, underemployment, and unproductive employment in petty services are steadily increasing in Latin America, as is underdevelopment of the system as a whole. Cuba alone has managed to eliminate unemployment and now has a labor shortage instead." [33]

In Asia, the China/India comparison is suggestive. China has appeared to put its domestic house in order—whether we consider order from the angles of poverty, demographic balance, security, or international stature—even though its record of GNP growth is worse than that of India. Brazil, too, scores high on GNP increase, but it has failed to distribute its growth dividend, to provide minimum social services or jobs for its poor, to allow human rights to flourish, or to compensate for the ecological side effects of rapid development, especially in the Amazon Valley.* Allende's Chile started out with a mobilization strategy, but without an adequate consensus among or control over influential groups. In that situation, the effort to establish the structural preconditions for genuine development invited counterrevolution. Allende's toleration of dissent, his reluctance to interfere with the military establishment and his desire to fulfill his commitments to the poor produced disaster for his followers. The lesson is clear: either tolerate the structure of dependence with its disparities, or proceed in a more revolutionary way as Cuba has done; reformist revolution is almost a contradiction in terms. At the same time, the Allende impulse to preserve civil liberties, to avoid convulsion and class war, represented an admirable reluctance to proceed down a coercive, probably bloody path which might also have produced a military coup—perhaps earlier, perhaps even bloodier.

The development option which would be most compatible with WOMP values can only be determined within a specific *context*. Internal conditions and external links are both important. The character of political consciousness is significant. In poor countries, the links between the national bourgeoisie and the military are important, as is the political consciousness of the military leadership itself. Structural changes are usually needed for genuine development in the overdeveloped sector as much as in the underdeveloped one. But structural changes are not easy to make unless the change-oriented group possesses a clear mandate, and such a mandate is difficult to attain through electoral politics. It comes about, if at all, by revolutionary politics. But a revolutionary animus is usually dependent upon large-scale violence—violence which the revolution must direct at its internal enemies in

---

* As William Moyer observes, "Even in Brazil, with one of the world's highest economic growth rates for five years, the Economic Minister estimates that only five million people are better off and 45 million people had their living standard eroded." Moyer correctly draws the conclusion that GNP per capita is not very illuminating as a basis of national comparisons with respect to the well-being of the population as a whole. For instance, the latest statistics suggest $133 GNP per capita for China compared to $342 for Brazil. As Moyer notes, "The Chinese success at ending poverty with only half of the Brazilian per capita gross national product reveals the absurdity of using economic growth as the major guideline to measure or guide poor nations' efforts to end poverty." [34]

order to attain and sustain power. The revolutionary threat also tempts counterrevolutionary interventions of various sorts, which in turn induce the revolutionary leaders to use more violent and coercive means in order to safeguard and justify their position. We have before us a series of instructive historical examples: Cuba, Brazil, Chile (before, during, and after Allende), China, India. These examples suggest the character of development tradeoffs. The dilemma remains: either avoid structural change and forego genuine, mass-oriented development, or attempt structural change and accept the uncertainties and risks associated with revolutionary goals.

THE RISE OF THE MULTINATIONAL CORPORATION

There is no longer any serious doubt about the need to take multinational corporations seriously in a study of world order. These corporate actors operating across many boundaries—increasingly welcome even in socialist countries—are the bearers of a significant ideology of global reform that poses a potential challenge to both the statism of S_1, and to the equity and ecologically oriented humanism of $S_{2(WOMP/USA)}$.* On a number of critical issues the multinational corporate outlook is diverse and still ill-defined: links to host country and to capital source country, amenability to unified global regulation, compatibility with the statist arrangement of power.

---

* A quite diverse group of actors are often embraced within the terms "multinational corporation" or "multinational business." Companies that do business in more than one country, companies with multinational management and ownership, and international entities that engage in certain quasi-public business operations are among the main categories of actors encompassed. George Modelski writes that the broad category of multinational business "denotes enterprises, and in particular corporations, whose business activities are located in a number of nations." He then adds, "Within this broad category, the most attention has so far been paid to the *giant corporations;* these need to be distinguished from enterprises of clearly global purposes, which will be referred to as *global businesses.*" Modelski gives General Motors as "a standard example" of a multinational giant, where great size and multinational operations are characteristic. But global business is a more functional concept: "Typically, such business would specialize in functions requiring world-wide knowledge, a capacity for cross-cultural contacts—hence, also a global identification." [35] As examples, Modelski gives INTELSAT (International Telecommunications Satellite Corporation), international banking, airlines, shipping, construction firms, management consultants.

We seek to consider a number of questions about the rise of the multinational corporation at this stage of international history.* Our special concern is to assess the short-term (t₁) and longer-term (t₂, t₃) impacts of the multinational corporation upon the WOMP/USA conception of transition.

Some sense of the scale of multinational corporate operation is suggested by John Diebold in the following passage:

> Business generated by multinational enterprises outside their home countries already amounts to about $350 billion worth of goods and services a year (three-fifths of it by U.S. companies). This is one-eighth of the gross product of the non-Communist world. The proportion is increasing rapidly, because the production of MNC's seems to be expanding at about ten percent a year. On a crude extrapolation of recent trends one could expect MNC's to be responsible for one-fourth of the production of the non-Communist world by the early 1980s. If the host countries continue to receive multinationals, there is a strong possibility that this last figure will prove to be an underestimate. Trends suggest that the growth of multinational corporate activity is likely to be even faster in the near future than in the immediate past. . . .[37]

The surge of foreign investment since World War II can be comprehended by reviewing Table 6–4.

The overall relationship is indicated by direct foreign investment totals accumulated by major countries as of 1967 and 1971, as seen in Table 6–5. The spectacular dominance of the United States is disclosed, as is the relative strength of other market economies. Table 6–6 elaborates these relationships in terms of the numbers of MNC's and their national identities. Table 6–7 demonstrates, with regard to the international economic role of the countries with most MNCs, the extent to which multinational corporate activity has dwarfed export trade. Table 6–8 breaks down the national distribution of MNCs in terms of scale of sales operations.

---

* There are international relations specialists who argue that the focus on direct foreign investment by the MNC has been exaggerated. George Modelski, for instance, points out that

> In 1914, the grand total of direct foreign investment (say $10 billion in 1914 book values) may have reached eight or ten percent of the world gross product. By 1965, foreign investment (say 100 billion in 1965 values, nearly two-thirds of it American) may have been less than five percent of world product. Overall, moreover, the salience of foreign investment in U.S. economic activity in 1965 (7.2% of GNP) may have been about the same as in 1897 (8.2%) or 1914 (6.7%).
> . . . Alarmist views to the contrary, however, multinational business as a whole today is a less dominant, and possibly also a more benign, form of interdependence than it was at the beginning of this century.[36]

Table 6–4.   Foreign Direct Investment by U.S. Corporations in
Manufacturing Subsidiaries (Book Value in Millions of Dollars) *

Year	World	Canada	Latin America	Europe and U.K.	All Other Areas
1929	$ 1,813	$ 819	$ 231	$ 629	$ 133
1936	1,710	799	192	611	108
1940	1,926	943	210	639	133
1950	3,831	1,897	781	932	222
1957	8,009	3,924	1,280	2,195	610
1964	16,861	6,191	2,507	6,547	1,616
1969	29,450	9,389	4,347	12,225	3,489

SOURCE: Raymond Vernon, *Sovereignty at Bay: The Multinational Spread of U.S. Enterprises*, New York, Basic Books, 1971, p. 65, Table 3–4. Copyright © 1971 by Basic Books Publishers, New York. Reprinted by permission.

The rise in income attributable to foreign direct investment (mainly MNC) has become "the foremost generator of income for the United States." [39]

Figure 6–4 also demonstrates that income from foreign investment activities has been increasing at a more rapid rate than capital outflows, thereby contributing a large surplus that helps create a favorable balance of payments situation for the United States. The trends are summarized in Table 6–9.

There is no doubt that multinational corporate structures are big and are engaged in disparate activities in a large number of separate states. As Lester Brown writes, "the emergence of the MNC and its rapid growth put the larger ones on a par economically with all but a small number of the largest nation–states." Charles Levinson observes that "investments by multinational companies are increasing two or three times as fast as the growth rates of most countries, and at least double the annual rise in exports. . . . Their financial vice-presidents, a fast-rising factotum in the corporate power structure are often more powerful than the Minister of Finance in many a small or medium-sized country." [40]

By ranking the first hundred state and corporate entities in terms of their GNP or gross annual sales, Brown found that "Of the top 50 entries in the merged list, 42 are nation–states and 8 are MNC's. Of the second 50 entries, 14 are nation–states and 36 are MNC's" [41] George Modelski gives a sense of size by using 1967 figures enumerating such vital statistics as number of affiliates, employees, sales, percent of sales

Table 6–5.   Market Economies: Stock of Foreign Direct Investment, 1967, 1971 [38]

Country [a]	1967		1971 [b]	
	Millions of dollars	Percentage share	Millions of dollars	Percentage share
United States	59,486	55.0	86,001	52.0
United Kingdom	17,521	16.2	24,019	14.5
France	6,000	5.5	9,540	5.8
Federal Republic of Germany	3,015	2.8	7,276	4.4
Switzerland	4,250 [c]	3.9	6,760	4.1
Canada	3,728	3.4	5,930	3.6
Japan	1,458	1.3	4,480 [d]	2.7
Netherlands	2,250	2.1	3,580	2.2
Sweden [e]	1,514	1.4	3,450	2.1
Italy	2,110 [f]	1.9	3,350	2.0
Belgium	2,040 [f]	0.4	3,250	2.0
Australia	380 [f]	1.9	610	0.4
Portugal	200 [f]	0.2	320	0.2
Denmark	190 [f]	0.2	310	0.2
Norway	60 [f]	0.0	90	0.0
Austria	30 [f]	0.0	40	0.0
Other [g]	4,000 [g]	3.7	6,000	3.6
TOTAL	108,200	100.0	165,000	100.0

[a] Countries are arranged in descending order of book value of direct investment in 1971.

[b] Estimated (except for the United States, United Kingdom, Federal Republic of Germany, Japan, and Sweden) by applying the average growth rate of the United States, United Kingdom, and the Federal Republic of Germany between 1966 and 1971.

[c] Data from Max Iklé, *Die Schweiz als internationaler Bank und Finanzplatz* (Zurich, 1970) for 1965 ($4,052 million) and 1969 ($6,043 million) seem to indicate that the 1967 and 1971 figures are probably relatively accurate.

[d] From the *Financial Times,* June 4, 1973.

[e] The figures for Sweden are for 1965 and 1970 instead of 1967 and 1971; they are in current prices for total assets of majority-owned manufacturing subsidiaries.

[f] Data on book value of foreign direct investment are available only for developing countries. Since the distribution of the minimum number of affiliates between the developing countries and developed market economies correlates highly with the distribution of book value, the total book value has been estimated on the basis of the distribution of their minimum number of affiliates. For Australia, the average distribution of the total minimum number of affiliates has been applied.

[g] Estimated, including developing countries.

Table 6-6. Multinational Corporations of Selected Developed Market Economies: Parent Corporations and Affiliate Networks, by Home Country, 1968–1969

Home country[a]	Total parent		Parent corporations with affiliates in				Affiliates	
	Number	%	1 country	2–9 countries	10–19 countries	Over 20 countries	Minimum number[b]	%
United States	2,468	33.9	1,228	949	216	75	9,691	35.5
United Kingdom	1,692	23.3	725	809	108	50	7,116	26.1
Federal Republic of Germany	954	13.1	448	452	43	11	2,916	10.7
France	538	7.4	211	275	42	10	2,023	7.4
Switzerland	447	6.1	213	202	26	6	1,456	5.3
Netherlands	268	3.7	92	149	20	7	1,118	4.1
Sweden	255	3.5	93	129	24	9	1,159	4.2
Belgium	235	3.2	137	88	8	2	594	2.2
Denmark	128	1.8	54	69	4	1	354	1.3
Italy	120	1.7	57	54	3	6	459	1.7
Norway	94	1.3	54	36	4	—	220	0.8
Austria	39	0.5	21	16	2	—	105	0.4
Luxembourg	18	0.2	10	7	1	—	55	0.2
Spain	15	0.2	11	4	—	—	26	0.1
Portugal	5	0.1	3	2	—	—	8	—
TOTAL	7,276	100.0	3,357	3,241	501	177	27,300	100.0

[a] Countries are arranged in descending order of number of parent corporations.

[b] Minimum number of affiliates refers to the number of links between parent corporations and host countries. Two or more affiliates of a particular corporation in a given country are counted as one link.

SOURCE: Centre for Development Planning, Projections and Policies of the Department of Economic and Social Affairs of the United Nations Secretariat, based on Yearbook of International Organizations, 13th ed., 1970–1971.

Table 6–7. Market Economies: International Production and Exports, 1971 (Millions of Dollars)

Country [a]	Stock of foreign direct investment (book value)	Estimated international production [b]	Exports	International production as percentage of exports
United States	86,000	172,000	43,492	395.5
United Kingdom	24,020	48,000	22,367	214.6
France	9,540	19,100	20,420	93.5
Federal Republic of Germany	7,270	14,600	39,040	37.4
Switzerland	6,760	13,500	5,728	235.7
Canada	5,930	11,900	17,582	67.7
Japan	4,480	9,000	24,019	37.5
Netherlands	3,580	7,200	13,927	51.7
Sweden	3,450	6,900	7,465	92.4
Italy	3,350	6,700	15,111	44.3
Belgium	3,250	6,500	12,392 [c]	52.4
Australia	610	1,200	5,070	23.7
Portugal	320	600	1,052	57.0
Denmark	310	600	3,685	16.3
Norway	90	200	2,563	7.8
Austria	40	100	3,169	3.2
TOTAL, above	159,000	318,000	237,002	133.7
Other	6,000	12,000	74,818	16.0
TOTAL, market economies	165,000	330,000	311,900	105.8

[a] Countries are listed in descending order of book value of foreign direct investment.
[b] Estimated international production equals the book value of foreign direct investment multiplied by the factor 2.0. The estimate of this factor was derived as follows: the ratio of foreign sales to book value of foreign direct investment has been estimated from 1970 United States data on gross sales of majority-owned foreign affiliates and book value of United States foreign direct investment. "Gross sales of majority-owned foreign affiliates" (approximately $157 billion) include transactions between foreign affiliates and parent corporations (approximately $20.3 billion) and inter-foreign affiliate sales (approximately $28.1 billion), which together account for about 30 percent of gross foreign affiliate sales. The book value of United States foreign direct investment in 1970 amounted to $78.1 billion. The resulting ratio of gross sales to book value is 2:1. This ratio has been used to estimate the international production of non-United States foreign affiliates.
[c] Includes Luxembourg.
SOURCE: Centre for Development Planning, Projections and Policies of the Department of Economic and Social Affairs of the United Nations Secretariat, based on table 5 and *Monthly Bulletin of Statistics* (United Nations publication), Vol. XXVII, April 1973.

Table 6–8. The 650 Largest Industrial Corporations [a]
of the Market Economies, by Country and by Size
(Sales in Millions of Dollars), 1971

Country [b]	Number of corporations with sales [c] of					
	Over 10,000	5,000– 10,000	1,000– 4,999	500– 999	300– 499	Total
United States	3	9	115	115	116	358
Japan	—	—	16	31	27	74
United Kingdom	—	1	14	22	24	61
Federal Republic of Germany	—	—	18	10	17	45
France	—	—	13	9	10	32
Canada	—	—	2	7	8	17
Sweden	—	—	2	6	5	13
Switzerland	—	—	4	2	2	8
Italy	—	—	4	2	—	6
Netherlands	—	1	1	2	2	6
Belgium	—	—	1	2	2	5
Australia	—	—	1	1	2	4
South Africa	—	—	—	1	2	3
Spain	—	—	—	—	3	3
Argentina	—	—	—	1	1	2
Austria	—	—	—	—	2	2
India	—	—	—	1	1	2
Brazil	—	—	1	—	—	1
Luxembourg	—	—	1	—	—	1
Mexico	—	—	1	—	—	1
Netherlands Antilles	—	—	—	1	—	1
Zaire	—	—	—	—	1	1
Zambia	—	—	—	—	1	1
Netherlands- United Kingdom	1	1	—	—	—	2
United Kingdom-Italy	—	—	1	—	—	1
TOTAL, number of corporations	4	12	195	213	226	650
TOTAL, sales (millions of dollars)	76,131	77,807	382,297	147,703	86,069	773,007

[a] Almost all the corporations included are multinational, according to the definition adopted in the text.

[b] Countries are arranged in descending order of total number of corporations listed.

[c] Sales are based on figures adjusted by *Fortune* and are not necessarily identical with those reported by corporations

SOURCE: Centre for Development Planning, Projections and Policies of the Department of Economic and Social Affairs of the United Nations Secretariat, based on the listing in *Fortune*, July and August 1972, of the 500 largest industrial corporations in the United States and the 300 largest industrial corporations outside the United States.

Figure 6–4. Direct Investment Income Related to Foreign Direct Investments

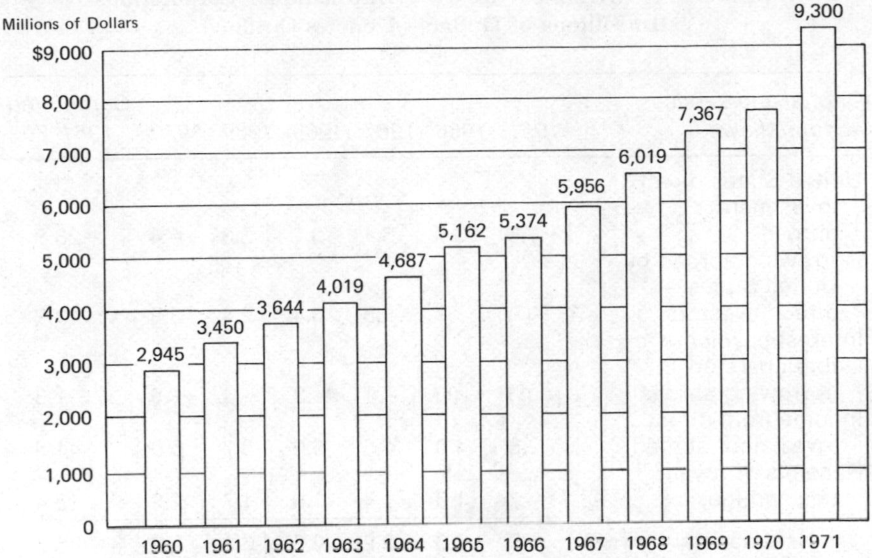

Millions of Dollars

outside headquarters country, and net income.[42] IBM, with its headquarters in New York, has 80 foreign affiliates, 222,000 employees, $5,345,000 annual sales, does 30% of its business in foreign countries, and had a net income of $652,000,000; Standard Oil of New Jersey, also with New York City headquarters, has 44 affiliates, 150,000 employees, $13,266,000,000 in annual sales, 68% of its business in foreign countries, and had a net income of $1,232,000,000; General Motors, based in Detroit, has 22 affiliates, 728,000 employees, $20,026,000,000 in annual sales, does 14% of its business abroad, and had a net income of $1,627,000,000. General Motors' sales were larger than the GNP of such substantial countries as East Germany, Belgium, Switzerland or Argentina for the same year.

It is difficult, however, to calculate the possible world order implications of multinational corporate actors. It is not clear, for instance, that sales are a particularly good indicator of power, or even of bargaining influence. After all, these corporate actors do not directly possess the capabilities to secure their economic goals if confronted by a hostile political atmosphere.[43] Various claims and charges have been made, ranging from heralding these corporate actors as the bearers of the most pro-

Table 6–9. Net Effect of Capital and Service Account Flows Associated with Direct Investment of U.S. Multinational Corporations (In Billions of Dollars—Denotes Outflow)

Capital and services account flows	1961	1966	1967	1968	1969	1970	Cumulated 1961–70
United States direct investment abroad	−1.6	−3.7	−3.1	−3.2	−3.3	−4.4	−28.8
Borrowing abroad by United States direct investors	(¹)	.7	.5	3.4	2.4	3.9	11.2
Interest payments to foreigners on borrowing abroad	(²)	(²)	−.1	−.2	−.4	−.6	−1.3
Income from direct investment abroad	2.8	4.0	4.5	5.0	5.7	6.0	41.8
Receipts of royalties and fees	.7	1.3	1.4	1.5	1.7	1.9	12.4
Net financial flows ³	1.9	2.3	3.2	6.5	6.1	6.8	35.3

¹ Not available.
² Less than $50,000,000.
³ Estimated.
Source: Robert Gilpin, "The Multinational Corporation and the National Interest," U.S. Senate Committee on Labor and Public Welfare, *Report*, October 1973, p. 23. Reprinted with permission from the July–August 1972 issue of the COLUMBIA JOURNAL OF WORLD BUSINESS, Vol. VII:4. Copyright © 1972 by the Trustees of Columbia University in the City of New York.

gressive values associated with peace and prosperity for all, to allegations that the multinational corporation is merely imperialism in a new guise, more sinister because more camouflaged.[44]

The positive case can be briefly stated. First, corporations provide an efficient mechanism for transferring technology and knowledge from advanced industrial to developing sectors of the world economy. Second, the corporate pursuit of profits is the most efficient and effective engine of economic development that is available. Third, the links of interdependence set up by world-wide corporate activity act as a brake upon interstate rivalry and, indeed, encourage a kind of "businessman's peace" in which globalist operations dependent on political stability displace the outward patterns of nationalist rivalries. Fourth, by making entry conditional and by revising the terms of business operations, host governments can now exert control over multinational corporate activity in a manner that was not possible when foreign investors confronting adverse local developments could be generally assured of military intervention by the home country. These political realities have led corporate leaders to seek a national status, both to free themselves from home country regulation, and to tone down their foreign identity in national arenas eager to control their own business assets. It is argued, in effect, that the business logic of the multinational corporation cuts against the grain of statism and imperialism; the integrative effects on the world economy which ensue from its normal operations will then bring peace and prosperity.* Furthermore, the spread of business operations reduces international wage and knowledge disparities, tending to equalize conditions in various parts of the world in a reasonably natural and non-disruptive fashion. John Diebold enumerates the arguments for and against the MNC in Table 6–10.

As one cautious analyst, Vernon, puts it, "The multinational enterprise as an economic institution seems capable of adding to the world's aggregate productivity and economic growth, as compared with the visible alternatives." [47] That is, if growth is the primary economic objective of governments, then the MNC is the best available mechanism for its achievement.

Vernon's argument is a curious challenge, suggesting that a positive appraisal of the MNC arises because of the absence of alternatives. By contrast, Richard Barnet notes "The most crucial intellectual and political task of the 1970's is the development of an alternative vision of a world economy based on the values of just distribution of economic and political power and the priority of human growth over economic growth." [48]

---

* Lester Brown makes this assessment:

> If the multinational corporations continue to expand their activities as projected, they will contribute importantly to continuing economic integration and indirectly to a reduced prospect of conflict between the more thoroughly integrated countries. Like nation–states, they have a strong vested interest in a smoothly functioning international system. To the extent that economic integration continues to make war a less practical instrument of foreign policy, the prospects will improve for creating a socially and politically unified global community and for restructuring the global economy to eliminate poverty. [45]

Brown's assertion about nation–states and world stability is obviously subject to a series of significant qualifications related to any government that adopts a revisionist posture toward the international system. Modelski also concludes that there is not much support for the allegation that MNC's contribute to international tensions by prompting military interventions to protect their investment equity: "A list of 65 substantial armed conflicts for the period 1945–1970 has been consulted, and a rapid survey does not disclose significant instances of participation of multinational business in their causation." [46]

Table 6–10. The Debate Over the Multinational Corporation (MNC)

Its Proponents Say	*Its Critics Say*
1. By focusing on *economic rationality,* the MNC represents the interests of all against the parochial interests of separate nations. It is the most effective available counter to rampant nationalism. Its only political weapon is that it can remove its benefits from developing countries that are politically unreliable or confiscatorily anti-business: and this is an incentive towards responsibility that is in the poor countries' own interests.	1. The MNC removes a significant part of the national economy from responsible political control without escaping improper political influence, including influence from the governments of the MNC's home countries. The MNC is an invasion of sovereignty and frustrates national economic policies. It fragments industries, causing proliferation without hope of consolidation.
2. The MNC is the best available mechanism for training people in countries for modern managerial skills.	2. *It does not train people in entrepreneurial skills* which is what a developing country most needs.
3. No more effective instrument has been found for the diffusion of technology.	3. The transfer of technology is often minimized because (a) R and D is generally carried out by the parent company; (b) the training of nationals of the host country for R and D posts is often neglected; (c) the technology itself is often closely held.
4. The MNC is the most promising instrument for the transfer of capital to the developing world and its role will be crucial in overcoming the income gap.	4. The cost of the capital brought by the MNC is far higher than the host government would be charged as a direct borrower in capital markets. The MNC invests relatively little of its own capital, and buys up foreign enterprises with local capital. The profits of the MNC are exorbitantly high, and too low a proportion of them are reinvested.

Table 6–10. (continued)

Its Proponents Say	*Its Critics Say*
5. The MNC's integrated and rationalized operations in many lands make it *incomparably efficient*. It has proven to be the only really effective instrument for economic development.	5. The rationalization of production is sometimes a *tax dodge*. The MNC distorts development programs by channeling its reported profits to countries where taxation is lowest, by manipulating charges for services and transactions to disguise real earnings.
6. The MNC enhances competition and breaks local monopolies. To the consumer, it provides a better product at a lower cost. To the host country it can provide a *new export industry for tomorrow*.	6. Its sheer size and scope represents unfair competition to local enterprises. It tends to preempt the fast-growing, advanced technology industries where profits are highest, ignoring older, more competitive fields.
7. Management of the MNC is becoming increasingly flexible, sensitive to local customs, and genuinely international in fact and in spirit.	7. The interest of the parent company must remain dominant and the MNC cannot ever become genuinely international. Often, the MNC has resisted genuine internationalization by declining (a) to put foreigners into management and (b) to make shares of its affiliates available to nationals of the host country.
8. The MNC is an agent of change which is altering value systems, social attitudes, and behavior patterns in ways which will ultimately reduce barriers to communications between peoples and establish the basis for a stable world order.	8. Far from breaking down barriers between peoples, the MNC aggravates tensions and stimulates nationalism. Moreover, there is every indication that these tendencies will intensify in years ahead.

SOURCE: John Diebold, "Multinational Corporations: Why Be Scared of Them?" Reprinted from FOREIGN POLICY 12, pp. 84–85. Copyright 1973 by National Affairs, Inc. Used by permission.

Fouad Ajami has usefully emphasized the oligopolistic consequences of the economic concentrations of wealth resulting from the MNC. In particular, he regards the MNC as a bearer of a materialistic, Western culture that is ill-adapted to the values and traditions of the non-Western world. Ajami contends that

> . . .oligopoly is quite detrimental for global pluralism and diversity. The value of pluralism obviously depends on the premium one places on it, and so far the oligopolists seem to show little tolerance for diversity and tend to behave as all large-scale organizations do when confronted with a complex environment: they attempt to increase certainty by reducing complexity and by wielding power and dominance. While the costs of such a strategy will be shared and felt by most, the burden is heaviest on non-Western cultures, where societies are open to currents, products, and styles over which they have little or no control.[49]

In effect, the MNC exports tastes and product preferences that have originated in its capital country, i.e., most often the United States.[50] In a sense, this kind of cultural imperialism is more insidious, even, than outright economic domination, as it shapes national sensibility from without. Concern about the expansion of the MNC has also been prominently expressed in Europe and Canada where it was looked upon, especially a few years ago, as an engine of American expansionism.[51]

The world order case against the MNC is essentially related to the contention that its impacts are imperialistic.[52] As Richard Barnet alleges:

> The essence of imperialism, regardless of the economic system from which it proceeds, is the unjust bargain. Human beings are used to serve ends that are not their own and in the process they pay more than they receive. The effort by two hundred multi-national corporations (or twenty or two thousand) to rationalize the world economy is part of an imperialist pattern in a new dimension . . . If the attempt of a few hundred corporate managers in multinational private and state enterprises to determine how and where the resources of the whole earth shall be developed is successful, these members of the new international managerial class will for practical purposes be the first world conquerors in history.[53]

Here, MNC's are seen as spreading across the earth's surface a system of exploitative control that is not at all responsive to human needs, especially those related to reducing poverty and expanding liberty. As Barnet continues, ". . . most of the earth's poor will be outside that economy [of the MNC], just as they are outside the money economy today." [54] Businessmen naturally desire predictability, and in the context of massive unsatisfied human needs, this imperative quickly leads to support for a counterinsurgency model. That is, if needs cannot be satisfied or assuaged, by definition a revolutionary potential exists which must be checked by control mechanisms if possible, by counterinsurgency mechanisms if necessary.

The Latin American trend toward military regimes sympathetic to foreign investment is quite instructive.[55] These military regimes reflect the "new professionalism" of Latin American armed forces which are no longer indoctrinated in warfare of the conventional sort, but rather in the military's domestic role and relevance during the fragile stages of nation-building. Thus, coups in Brazil, Chile, and Peru were not mere changes in elites, as in so many earlier Latin American military takeovers, but systematic efforts to safeguard the economic and social structure from radical elements. The multinational corporation can enter such an atmosphere with relative security because the regime's tenure is likely to be quite long, and its policies will favor rapid aggregate economic growth with rather little concern for distributing its growth dividend to the poor. As the Peruvian coup of 1968 suggests, the military regime may seek popular legitimacy at first by expropriating a foreign company, but will then move to attract foreign investment back to the country once its structures of control are firmly established. A background element here is that U.S. influence has been profound through its impact on officer training in Latin America, especially in relation to the military elite's shift away from a professional national security orientation, and toward a professional concentration on those who are increasingly defined as internal enemies by their Marxist or radical tendencies. The Chilean coup of 1973 against Allende exemplifies our fears about the impact of global corporatism: a radical social and economic program, including expropriation of MNC's, provokes a violent military coup and widespread repression; the U.S. almost immediately recognizes the military regime, which in turn invites foreign enterprise back into the country on a large scale.*

Can we properly blame the multinational corporation for such a pattern of development? As Paul Baran and Paul Sweezy state,

---

* The American world role cannot be so easily rationalized in non-economic terms, now that the cold war has subsided and removed the central pillar of anti-communism from American foreign policy. It should also be noted, perhaps without too elaborate comment, that the areas of maximum American effort in its counterrevolutionary mission roughly coincide with areas of heaviest foreign investment in the Third World. (There presently is no revolutionary threat to counter in the advanced industrial sector of world society.)

The multinational companies often have conflicting interests when it comes to tariffs, export subsidies, foreign investment, etc. But they are absolutely united on two things: First, they want the world of nations in which they operate to be as large as possible. And second, they want its laws and institutions to be favorable to the unfiltered development of private capitalist enterprise.[56]

In theory, a number of different kinds of national regimes, including rather progressive ones, could establish favorable operating conditions for the MNC. Some observers argue that the enlightened interest of MNC's lies in linking their activities with the goals of change-oriented domestic groups, even at times when such groups are on the "outs" because they oppose the current rulers.* As an appeal to business logic, this position rests on the assumption that sooner or later change will occur in these countries, and that when it does the MNC will be repudiated unless it is seen by the architects of change as an agent of positive social, economic, and political development.

This view of domestic politics can certainly be kept in mind, but the evidence is against it, either as a prediction or as an MNC perception. The basic MNC consensus is now probably quite pluralistic. It leads to adaptation to diverse national contexts by business managers who stress profit potential and a low profile for foreignness or national problem-solving, and who have close links to and a definite preference for stable conservative regimes.

In this general situation, most MNC's are likely to be oriented toward the well-established repressive regime that is organized in such a way as to achieve rapid economic growth while keeping the lid tightly on social unrest and political radicalism—that is, the Brazilian model.

Despite these effects of the MNC it is probably useful to emphasize its globalizing ideology. MNC board rooms often have on their walls a boundaryless map of the world or a spaceship photograph of the earth—images appropriate to their search for ways of assuring a global market freed from the boundary encumbrances which originate with

---

* George C. Lodge has developed an argument to this effect. His position is epitomized by this statement: "The operations of an MNC or indeed any other infusion from outside is bound to have an interventionary effect. It will sustain the status quo or it will sustain forces seeking to change the status quo. The choice is between conscious and conscientious intervention on the one hand or careless and shortsighted intervention on the other." [57] The question arises as to whether it is possible for the MNC to exercise the sort of change-oriented choice that Lodge proposes, within the structure of underdevelopment and dependency that characterizes much of the Third World. See pp. 38, 39n.

statist parochialisms. By contrast, counterinsurgent regimes are beginning to experience tension between the goals of stability on the one hand and of the free movement of ideas and goods on the other; repressive regimes are very boundary-conscious, fearing that "Trojan horses" of one sort or another can be brought across, or that plots can be hatched from beyond their boundaries.

We are not arguing that it is either the *foreignness* or *the private ownership* of the MNC that makes its world order role so problematic. As Shane Hunt has suggested, if the Chilean copper companies had been predominantly owned by the national bourgeoisie (rather than foreign companies), then the anti-Allende coup would have probably happened earlier;[58] that is, economic/military links within a society tend to be stronger if the ownership of critical assets is largely in national hands. Furthermore, the device of state ownership may involve a shift in the identity of "capitalists" rather than an ideological turn toward socialism:

> It would be wrong to think that the management of Standard Oil opposes government enterprise in the subordinate countries because of a naive belief that state action is identical with socialism. The explanation is much more rational: government enterprise and state action in these countries generally represent attempts on the part of the native bourgeoisies to appropriate for themselves a larger share of locally produced surplus at the expense of the multinational companies. It is only natural that such attempts should be resolutely opposed by the multinational corporations.[59]

The essence of the MNC effort, then, is to *concentrate power* beyond national control and to assure itself a stable set of market situations within which to operate. Its short-run effects are to—

transfer technology and knowledge to poor sectors;

standardize global consumptive patterns and preferences;

provide some employment and training opportunities in the Third World;

encourage counterinsurgency postures and counterrevolutionary outlooks throughout the Third World;

create a post-statist kind of global ideology.*

---

* Robert Gilpin has made a strong argument to the contrary, namely, that the growth of the MNC leads to a rise in statist activity, partly to safeguard national autonomy against outside pressures. As Gilpin writes,

These effects have a complex relationship to WOMP values; we can expect the MNC to bring in its wake a certain inhibition of war (V_1) especially to the extent that MNC and socialist trading actors increase their transactions with one another; a contribution to human social and economic well-being (V_2) to the extent that growth in poorer countries "trickles down" or is used to finance increases in social services for the impoverished masses; an undoubted discouragement of radicalizing movements for direct assaults on poverty, but a toleration over time of liberal party politics carried on within rather narrowly specified limits (V_3); a generalized insensitivity to ecological variables relevant either to conservation of resources or protection of environmental quality (V_4).*

There are some other issues of consequence for WOMP thinking:

The impact of the MNC on various categories of governmental actors

The impact of the MNC on the dynamics of interstate relations in S_1, along both north/south and east/west axes

The relative significance of the MNC as a stabilizing force in S_1, as an agent of transition to S_2, as an opponent of $S_{2(WOMP/USA)}$.

Contrary to the argument that the multinational corporation will somehow supplant the nation-state, I think it is closer to the truth to argue that the role of the nation-state in economic as well as in political life is increasing and that the multinational corporation is actually a stimulant to the further extension of state power in the economic realm. One should not forget that the multinational corporation is largely an American phenomenon and that in response to this American challenge other governments are increasingly intervening in their domestic economies in order to counterbalance the power of American corporations and to create domestic rivals of equal size and competence.[60]

If this American challenge has been increasingly met, as seems the case, in the advanced industrial world, then the nature of the MNC impact on the state as world actor will have to be reassessed. Note that Gilpin's comments do not apply to Third World contexts where there is no capacity by governments to intervene to create national MNC's of their own and, rarely, the disposition even to offset domestic economic impacts of the MNC.

* It is no accident that official spokesmen for a government like that of Brazil should invoke the specter of poverty to resist claims related to V_4 for restraint in the development process.[61] The Brazilian opposition to V_4 efforts is in actuality related to the desire for rapid economic growth as measured by GNP. As we have already discussed, this growth benefits a small fraction of the population and the government has no intention of implementing policies to distribute the growth dividend to the poor; but on an international stage the purported concern for national poverty provides an acceptable excuse for an anti-ecological position. This position should be sharply distinguished from that taken by Third World militants who genuinely feel that the alleviation of mass misery takes priority over environmental quality in the immediate future, at least for poor countries.

THE LIMITS TO GROWTH DEBATE AND
THE FUTURE OF THE WORLD ECONOMY

For several decades the planet's basic organization has supported the idea that profit maximization by economic operating units was a desirable mode of wealth production. On a national level this belief system generated confidence in the future. As technology enabled man to produce more goods with less effort, the economic surplus would grow, allowing all in society to share in the blessings of affluence. This has happened to some extent in North America and Western Europe, but the affluence achieved seems increasingly provisional, and significant segments of the domestic population have never been tied into the reward system. As a consequence, large pockets of poverty have remained even in the United States, the richest of capitalist countries.

Global liberalism envisaged the same pattern of achievement for the poorer countries. "Development" would supply the magic needed to turn rags into riches. The poor countries were regarded merely as latecomers to the development process; the sooner they started on that process, the sooner the removal of their terrible curse of poverty. The rich countries could speed up the process somewhat by a combination of charity (foreign aid, international assistance) and self-interest (foreign investment). As we discussed in pp. 35 and 67 this development utopia, even on its own terms, has always lacked substance: the GNP increases are siphoned off to benefit the higher strata of poor societies; the underdevelopment of Third World countries plays a functional role within the world economic structure; the charity of the rich, when carefully considered, represents a further extension of hegemony and exploitation rather than a contribution to self-reliance and genuine development.[62]

Traditional economic thinking continues to assume that because of the interdependence of the world economy, the rich must get richer if the poor are to get less poor. In a typical statement Carl Kaysen observes that "it is difficult or even impossible to conceive of continued substantial economic growth in the poor countries in general taking place in a context of economic stagnation in the industrialized world."[63] Indeed, it is often argued that the poor countries would suffer much more than the rich ones from any kind of decoupling process in the world economy—without rich customers for their exports, poor countries would have no way to finance their economic growth, and would stagnate as a result. The Chinese example stands out as a refutation of this claim, but only a partial one, as China is so large, and, after a period of isolation, has itself sought economic relations with the rich sector of the world economy. Growth dynamics are presented as the only reliable cure for poverty.

Within this context, the first ecological mini-bomb exploded in the late 1960's, raising deep questions as to whether the industrialization of the planet could proceed much further without imperiling the survival prospects of the human species and the habitability of the planet.* A rather furious debate has ensued over whether present growth dynamics are poisoning the planet at an unacceptably dangerous rate or are depleting scarce resources in an exceedingly shortsighted fashion. [64] The pessimists (in our view, the realists) argue that it is essential to begin now to plan a world economy based on an acceptance of ecological limits, whereas the optimists (in our view, the romantics) argue only that issues of global pollution and resource shortage make it desirable to proceed, as ever, but with *caution*, as concluded by Ross and Passell: "The most important lesson of ecology is caution: each step toward more sophisticated technology risks transgression against nature." [65]

Carl Kaysen has carefully formulated this optimistic canon:

> There are no credible reasons for believing that the world as a whole cannot maintain a fairly high rate of economic growth (though not necessarily the present one) over a long period of time into the future. Further, if it becomes necessary, for whatever reason, to slow down the growth rate, a relatively smooth transition from higher to lower rates will be perfectly possible, and not achievable only through catastrophe. [66]

There are two parts to the pro-growth, or more accurately, the anti-anti-growth position: (1) the ecological challenge has been exaggerated; (2) the existing system has a variety of market mechanisms, such as the pricing process, that will provide ample warning if serious curtailments of growth should become necessary. [67]

Pro-growth observers tend to discount present ecological strains, such as the energy crisis, as provisional, short-term problems which will disappear in a decade or so when new energy sources are developed. This position is fundamentally anti-Malthusian, believing that technology can innovate so reliably that man need not concern himself, at least for the indefinite future, with ecological limits. Whether concern is directed at the waste disposal or resource shortage side of the ecological challenge, the acceptance of the status quo with respect to behavior,

---

* See Chapter II, pp. 103–120.

values, and institutions reflects technophilia—cleaning up our air and water, finding new resources and new ways to ferret out the riches of the earth.

Anti-Malthusians often suggest that elitist and privileged groups have fabricated the ecological crisis because they are more concerned with preserving remote wilderness areas than with alleviating human misery.[68] The militant Oi Committee International issued a statement at the 1972 Stockholm U.N. Conference on the Human Environment expressly denouncing the most prominent presentations of the ecological challenge, such as the Club of Rome project carried out at the Massachusetts Institute of Technology by the Meadows' group and published as a report entitled *Limits to Growth*, and the study done for the English magazine *The Ecologist* entitled *Blueprint for Survival* and signed by well-known scientists.[69] The statement declares:

> We strongly reject models of stagnation, proposed by certain alarmist Western ecologists, economists, industrialists, and computer-fans and assert that holding economic growth per se responsible for environmental ills amounts to a diversion of attention from the real causes of the problems which lie in the profit-motivation of the systems of production in the capitalist world.

The Oi Committee Declaration regards as "at best diversionary" any approach to global reform that fails "to put the primary emphasis on the destruction of the profit-oriented system of production." [70] Here, the Oi analysis parallels other drastic views of the development process which argue that any "non-diversionary" approach must bring about a structural change in the circumstances of national underdevelopment. Hence, oddly, both the Oi Committee and Kaysen dismiss the limits to growth position as an instance of crying wolf, although the Oi group proposes the destruction of capitalism, while Kaysen advocates an even more efficient capitalist-dominated world economy.[71]

The ecological pessimists are alarmed by the interplay between growth dynamics, and the finite space and usable resources available to mankind. These pessimists foresee a steady deterioration of the quality of life as a consequence of further crowding and depletion. This deterioration could diminish the life prospects of future generations and may even precipitate an ecological collapse of catastrophic proportions.* Ex-

---

* Very difficult questions of choice and policy are posed. Roland McKean suggests that while most people "will make enormous sacrifices for their children and grandchildren," their willingness to help more distant generations is much less clear. As he puts the issue

amining the relationship between food supply and demand, the anti-growth school anticipates genuine Malthusian checks on population growth, and points to the drought famines of Asia and Africa as proof that acute problems of food shortage are already with us, but are only a foretaste of what is to come. In general, the pessimists are dubious about technology's claims to relieve the situation in more than marginal respects. In agriculture the technological potentialities, even if fully exploited, don't seem capable of meeting future needs for more than a few decades at the most.* In industrial sectors, optimistic assessments of recovery prospects for minerals only move the point of critical short-age a few decades ahead. Giving technological claims the benefit of every reasonable doubt does not constitute a response to the ecological challenge, but only allows a somewhat longer time period within which to shape the attitudes, behavioral adjustments, and institutional changes that will be needed. As we have earlier argued, the case for a central guidance solution to the overall problem of global reform rests heavily on the credibility of the ecological challenge (see Chapters II–IV). Therefore, WOMP/USA rejects the pro-growth view, although our proposals emphasizing structural transformations of domestic po-litical systems in t_1 are certainly compatible with arguments for going beyond a narrow focus on growth dynamics.

Richard Barnet was quoted earlier in the chapter on the need to evolve images of the world economy which facilitate national develop-ment on premises other than the ascendancy of the MNC. A related un-dertaking is to evolve a steady-state model of the world economy that enables meeting the ecological challenge without foregoing success in the areas of war, poverty, and oppression.† Some work is beginning to

---

in stark form, "I don't honestly know whether I would voluntarily give up one quarter of my disposable income even if this would, with 100 percent certainty, prevent extinction of the human race 1000 years hence." McKean speculates that "For most people the preferred compromise may be to profess, but not really demonstrate, concern about the distant future. Such a pretense lets us eat our cake and yet also satisfy our need, for the sake of sanity or a greater sense of purpose, to believe that mankind has a future." [72]

* Lester Brown has enumerated the following constraints on the expansion of world food supply: the withdrawal of acreage for crop use in densely populated countries; severe soil erosion; shortage of water for agricultural purposes; shortage of pasture land for animal grazing; limited reproductive capacity of cows; inability to increase per-acre yield of soybeans; marine protein capacity cannot be further enlarged. Brown does suggest, in balancing these comments, that underutilized crop acreage in the United States could be used to build a world food reserve and that agricultural development, especially on small farms, could increase yields and crop acreage in Asia and Africa. [73]

† As we have earlier stressed, it is also important to distinguish steady-state thinking from advocating stagnancy. The existence of new and open frontiers may be very crucial

be done on steady-state concepts which do take into account the necessary considerations of equity; such work must also be sensitive to a number of qualifications on the anti-growth position:[74]

A steady state can be achieved by increasing growth in poor regions and by decreasing GNP in rich regions, as well as by stressing consumer necessities, by phasing out consumer and public sector luxuries and waste, and by limiting the output of semi-luxuries.

A steady state that is responsive to the ecological challenge need not eliminate growth in service sectors of even the richest countries.

A steady state that is responsive to the ecological challenge can be achieved through recycling and anti-pollution technologies as well as through ceilings and reductions in output.

A steady state world economy need not be inconsistent with improving average life circumstances for an indefinite period in the future.

Thus we are arguing that the ecological challenge has grave implications for a world order system organized around a principle of virtually unrestricted and uncontrolled growth. Wasteful consumption patterns and environmentally destructive behavior should be reduced as quickly as possible; conservation policies must be adopted and implemented even-handedly. Such tasks cannot be performed by 140 or so governments each pursuing their separate interests, nor by business organizations working to achieve higher and higher profits. The logic of decentralization works against the requirements of ecological balance. A central guidance solution will become necessary in the next several decades. Whether this solution is brought about by conscious planning (see Chapter V) is an open question; another is whether central guidance is imposed to benefit the privileged few or is based on a voluntary, equitable role for everyone. As Robert Heilbroner puts this issue: "We might well ask whether the approach toward the ecological disaster point will encourage the equitable distribution of the means of life or will only serve to fortify the resolve of favored nations to preserve their own good fortune against the rest?" [75] Another formulation might be, "does the realization of the neo-Malthusian threat produce neo-humanism or neo-Darwinism?" In most respects the social and ethical

---

in a steady-state economy to avoid a collective mood of depression, even psychosis; bio-politics as an area of inquiry may help us appreciate the importance of keeping developmental frontiers open in a large political system so as to avoid stifling the species, i.e., conditions of ecological balance depend on satisfying diverse needs including, perhaps, a human need for a sense of "growth." Such a hypothesis would require the discovery of economic patterns that satisfy this need without overburdening the biosphere.

barriers to adaptation by voluntary action seem even more formidable than the material ones.

To date, state socialism exhibits no greater sensitivity than state capitalism to the dangers posed by the ecological challange.[76] The socialist mode of economic organization is anchored in an overall plan for the society centering on the notion of the public good however it may be defined; as such, it provides a basis for generalizing planning to encompass the globe. However, the public good as conceived by Soviet planners involves maximization of output,* and the character of the output has consistently reflected statist imperatives specified by the rulers rather than humanist imperatives specified by the citizenry.† More fundamental, perhaps, is the relative degree of closedness of principal state socialist societies; the logic of total state control seems to entail a reluctance to participate very seriously in global structures of cooperation, and an outright antipathy to any dilution of territorial sovereignty through transfers of sovereign functions to regional or global institutions.‡ As a consequence, the socialist sector has been the least willing to regard national economic policy as subject to criteria of globalist well-being.

The state capitalist societies have somewhat different but equally fundamental problems. Capitalist production schedules are manipulated by market forces, including advertising, and by state subsidies responsive to pressure groups and vested interests. As a result, planned obsolescence is built into the basic operation of the economy. The automotive industry is a prime example, but so is the entire industrial buildup around the arms race and military preparedness. The individualist ethos of capitalism is also antagonistic to state planning or to ex-

---

* Marxist analysis also attributed *scarcity* to capitalist exploitation of labor. With the socialist mode of production established, abundance was expected to result and the entire population was promised a permanent era of prosperity. The ecological boundaries encroach upon the utopian element in communist ideology, and suggest the need for a quite altered reformulation of socialist expectations.

† As always, there are a variety of reasons to explain this posture, including the need to protect the socialist experiment from its numerous foreign enemies. The Western Hemisphere's reception of socialist experiments such as those in Cuba and Chile suggest that this vigilance remains plausible even if its likely consequence is to betray the basic revolutionary promise of delivering the society into a more fulfilling and liberated mode of existence.

‡ Again, this Soviet insistence upon untrammelled state sovereignty seems reasonable on other grounds, namely, the extent to which global institutions are dominated by nonsocialist governments and civil servants. Globalist approaches are perceived as "Trojan horses," enemies disguised as beneficiaries.

tensive government efforts at redistributing income. Capitalist societies nurture a deep conviction that private property and personal wealth— even if inherited or earned in flimsy ways—are somehow deserved, and that the best way to promote the public good is to provide individuals with every incentive for attaining their own private or selfish ends.* At the same time, capitalist pursuits have evolved increasingly global ways of organizing and behaving. The MNC represents a globalizing evolution that threatens to cut the links between state and corporation. However, the MNC is geared for profits, not service to the public well-being or deference to ecological constraints. Government regulation is needed to prevent direct human abuse by corporate operations, whether the issues involve strip mining, marketing unsafe products, or dumping contaminating pollutants into the civic water supply. Hendrik Ibsen's nineteenth century play *Enemy of the People* was alert to capitalist priorities and to the contradictions between public well-being and private greed; † rather than the invisible hand of Adam Smith, it is necessary to have a very visible stick to assure that profit motives don't lead to the most elemental abuses of people and nature.‡

What sort of world economy will meet the requirements of the ecological challenge? We have to specify those requirements in some detail, including a position on our obligation to future generations. The

---

* William Ophuls correctly associates the capitalist ethos of American society with the thought of John Locke and Adam Smith.[77] Locke contributed ideas about the sanctity of private property, while Smith provided the reconciliation of public and private interests in a laissez-faire economy through his semi-mystical notion of "the invisible hand."

† A vivid recent instance concerns the depiction of "the medical–industrial complex" as it operates in the asbestos industry, to the horrifying detriment of workers.[78]

‡ The issue of selfishness pertains to all sectors of society; it is one thing to worry about the ecological challenge, but it is quite another to adapt one's life style in a responsive manner. Robert Heilbroner makes the following observation: "I have wondered . . . how many of the 100-odd signers of the 'Blueprint' and the 'Limits' have sold their automobiles or never take a taxi? I wonder how many have dispensed with all unnecessary gadgets in their homes, use both sides of the page when they type a manuscript, flush their toilets but once a day, and generally conduct themselves with the Spartan restraint integral to a program of economic limitations such as they urge?" [79] There is something cleverly unfair about Heilbroner's questions. It is one thing to favor systemic or structural change; it is another to accept the recommended restraints on an individual basis: My Spartan restraint is only socially valuable if it is also the effective norm for the polity as a whole. Volunteerism, as Garrett Hardin calls the voluntary action of enlightened individuals, may even be detrimental to the extent that it minimizes the need for systemic solutions. On the other hand, it is also possible to suppose that value changes have to begin with exemplary individuals; those who exhibit Spartan restraint possess credentials to lead a reform movement, having demonstrated their own sincerity through real sacrifices in comfort and convenience.

design of a feasible world economic model would be an important advance for the anti-growth position, as would a more careful statement of what would have to give way in a steady-state world economy. Perhaps more difficult than designing models is designing strategies to overcome resistance to change. Mobilization priorities are deferred to t_2, but it is necessary in t_1 as part of consciousness-raising to begin the effort to mobilize social forces.

At the present time, receptivity to a wide range of experimental probes will be helpful. E.F. Schumacher writes intriguingly about Buddhist economics as a source of adaptation to the ecological challenge:

> From the point of view of Buddhist economics, therefore, production from local resources for local needs is the most rational way of economic life, while dependence on imports from afar and the consequent need to produce for export to unknown and distant peoples is highly uneconomic and justifiable only in exceptional cases and on a small scale.[80]

Austerity, simplicity, self-reliance, communality are being reemphasized in a number of contexts ranging from Maoist China to the serious study of man/nature belief systems embodied in the traditions of American Indian tribes.* Also of relevance is the effort to respiritualize our political and economic sensibilities through such disparate activities as meditation and study of Eastern religions, and the related creation of spiritual sanctuaries where work is shared and material comforts renounced.† We require a new consciousness as a precondition for a new

---

* Some critiques of mainstream economic development strategies from non-ecological perspectives also assist in the process of ecological adjustment. For instance, Rasheed Talib's critique of development policies in India is based on the tendency to gear up production of consumer items for India's top ten percent without doing anything to alleviate the main societal problems of mass poverty and unemployment. Talib urges, instead, a development posture that is much more closely shaped by the country's prime needs, and which takes its main inspiration from national conditions, including such potential assets as a huge labor surplus and large undeveloped rural areas. In such a context, the Gandhian tradition of austerity becomes very useful for India and, in Talib's words, "has nothing to do with the sentimentalism of the Gandhians" but fits into "the rigorous framework of modern economics" as applied to India's problems. Such application includes emphasis on Schumacher's ideas about "intermediate" technology.[81] It is very encouraging to appreciate the extent to which such a development strategy for India combines economic reform with ecological restraint.

† One important initiative in this direction is the Lindisfarne Association started in 1973 at Southampton, Long Island, under the general direction of William Irwin Thompson. Within this "sanctuary" diverse traditons of rational and nonrational thought are studied,

approach to the organization of the world economy. Ingrained habits of expectation stemming from the industrial revolution need to be supplanted by earlier and more fundamental views of man's dependence on the earth as habitat. We do not believe that the political ideologies now on the scene can begin to deal with the problems embodied in the limits to growth position.

A CONCLUDING NOTE

We promised no more than an agenda in this chapter. The economic dimension touches on the four WOMP values in a very central way. It is sometimes argued that the development of legal and moral prohibitions on the use of force has at least eliminated the prospect of blatantly imperialist diplomacy, thereby shifting the terrain of conflict from the battlefield to a variety of economic arenas. As the ecological/equity crisis worsens, the direct reliance on military strategies may reemerge. For instance, it is not inconceivable to contemplate Western occupation of Middle Eastern oil fields before the end of the 1970's, either by direct action or through the medium of some form of indirect or proxy rule. Similarly, it is not inconceivable in the same period to suppose geo-economic terrorism spawned in the Third World, but challenging the neo-Darwinian pretensions of the rich countries.

In conceiving of economic relations it is crucial to distinguish between *peoples* and *governments*. No reification is more loaded these days than the assumption that the policies of a foreign government are tantamount to the preferences or interests of its population. Sometimes, the whole issue is hopelessly elided, as in Robert Hunter's statement that "In general, the methods open to the rich nations to secure the in-

---

dreams and culture are broadly investigated, and the survival of the group is conceived in simple, shared terms. The objective, perhaps not fully explicit, is to explore the dimensions of a new planetary consciousness that is inevitably emerging from increasing interconnectedness and the erosion of boundaries. Thompson's approach is anti-ideological in the sense that the new consciousness cannot be expected to produce a political program or even a line of response to the problems of the day. It seems correct, however, to expect such a respiritualization of consciousness (and downplay of materialism) to contribute positively to global orientations, to human solidarity, and to a more relevant view of time present, past, and future than generally exists, as well as to conceive man's relations with nature and the universe in more reciprocal terms.

terest they have in poor-country cooperation must be largely *positive* ones; that is, the developing nations must also gain some benefits from meeting the needs and the interests of the rich nations." [82] Hunter uses the terminology of "nations," but he mainly means "governments." However, if he means governments, then his statement is incoherent because many, if not most, poor-country governments are oriented toward the well-being and consumptive priorities of a privileged tiny minority, alongside repression of the population as a whole.[83] Striking such an intergovernmental bargain may have little, if anything, to do with satisfying the needs of a poor nation as a whole, although it may help the rich countries sustain their geo-economic hegemony for several more decades. The elites of the world share a strong common interest in confusing governmental preferences with genuine national aspirations. Indeed, the whole American effort to orient Latin American military leaders toward counterinsurgency seems designed to prevent governmental representations from expressing the dynamics of national self-determination. One can, incidentally, make the same kind of analysis with regard to zones of Soviet influence, such as Eastern Europe. Foreign governments in dependent sectors of the world order system often become agents of external economic and political interests rather than embodiments of national self-determination.

REFERENCES

1. One important exception is Jagdish Bhagwati, ed., *Economics and World Order: From the 1970's to the 1990's*, New York, Macmillan, 1972.

2. *International Economic Report of the President*, Washington, D.C., Government Printing Office, pp. 4–7, Figures 3–7.

3. *U.S. Foreign Policy for the 1970's: A Report to the Congress by the President*, Vol. IV, Washington, D.C., Government Printing Office, p. 162 (1973).

4. C. Fred Bergsten, "The Threat from the Third World," *Foreign Policy* 11, pp. 102–124, at 103 (1973).

5. Lester R. Brown, "The Changing Face of Food Scarcity," Washington, D.C., Overseas Development Council, Communiqué No. 21, August 1973.

6. This point is well-developed by Wayne H. Davis, "Overpopulated America," in Daniel Callahan, ed., *The American Population Debate*, New York, Anchor, 1971, pp. 161–167.

7. See M.A. Adelman, "Is the Oil Shortage Real? Oil Companies as OPEC Tax-Collectors," *Foreign Policy* 9: 69–107 (1972–73); for a quite different assessment of the oil pressure see James E. Akins, "The Oil Crisis: This Time the Wolf Is Here," *Foreign Affairs* 51: 462–490 (1973).

8. William W. Behrens III and Dennis L. Meadows, "Determinants of Long-Term Resource Availability," in Dennis L. Meadows and Donella H. Meadows, eds., *Toward Global Equilibrium: Collected Papers*, Cambridge, Mass., Wright Allen Press, 1973, pp. 291–306.

9. *International Economic Report*, p. 69.

10. Article by Harry B. Ellis in *Christian Science Monitor*, Oct. 10, 1973, pp. 1, 9.

11. "An Arab Oil Squeeze that Works," *Wall Street Journal*, Nov. 6, 1973, p. 22.

12. See Leonard Silk, "The Oil Weapon," *New York Times*, Nov. 6, 1973; also editorial in *Wall Street Journal* "To What End?" Nov. 6, 1973, p. 22.

13. The *New York Times*, Nov. 23, 1973, pp. 1, 56.

14. See Fouad Ajami, "The Global Populists: Third-World Nations and World Order Crises," Research Monograph #41, Center of International Studies, Princeton University, May, 1974.

15. John P. Albers, "Seabed Mineral Resources: A Survey," *Bulletin of the Atomic Scientists*, 29: 33–38 (1973).

16. P. Sreenivasa Rao, "Development and the Sea," *Oceanus*, 16: 6–13, 6–7 (1973).

17. Norman E. Borlaug, "Civilization's Future: A Call for International Granaries," *Bulletin of the Atomic Scientists*, 29: 7–15 (1973); see also Lester Brown, "The Changing Face of Food Scarcity."

18. Henry Kissinger, "A Just Consensus, A Stable Order, A Durable Peace," U.S. Department of State Bulletin, 69: 469–473, 472 (1973).

19. Louis Turner, *Multinationals and the Third World*, New York, Hill & Wang, 1973, pp. 247–248.

20. For a positive assessment see Michael Reisman, "Polaroid Power: Taxing Business for Human Rights," *Foreign Policy*, 5: 101–110 (1971).

21. Johan Galtung, "On the Effects of International Economic Sanctions: With Examples from the Case of Rhodesia," *World Politics* 19: 378–416 (1967).

22. See, in general, Leonard T. Kapungu, *The United Nations and Economic Sanctions against Rhodesia*, Lexington, Mass., D.C. Heath, 1973; Diane Polan, *Irony in Chrome: the Byrd Amendment Two Years Later*, Washington, D.C., Carnegie Endowment, 1973; Stephen Park, *Business as Usual: Transactions Violating Rhodesian Sanctions*, Washington, D.C., Carnegie Endowment, 1973.

23. On overdevelopment see Paul R. Ehrlich and Ann H. Ehrlich, *Population, Resources and Environment: Issues in Human Ecology*, San Francisco, W.H. Freeman and Co., 2nd rev. ed., pp. 419–421.

24. Robert Theobold and Stephanie Mills, eds., *The Failure of Success: Ecological Values vs. Economic Myths*, Indianapolis, Ind., Bobbs-Merrill, 1973, explore many of these issues in their American context.

25. David E. Apter, *Some Conceptual Approaches to the Study of Modernization*, Englewood Cliffs, New Jersey, Prentice-Hall, 1968.

26. *Ibid.*, pp. 277–278.

27. *Ibid.*, p. 278.

28. *Ibid.*, p. 278.

29. Quoted in André Gunder Frank, "The Underdevelopment Policy of the United Nations in Latin America," *NACLA Newsletter*, December 1969, p. 1.

30. Celso Furtado, "The Brazilian Model," *Social and Economic Problems*, 22: 122–131 (1973).

31. E.g., P.N. Rosenstein-Rodan, "The Haves and the Have-Nots around the Year 2000," in J. Bhagwati, ed., *Economics and World Order*, New York, Macmillan, 1972, pp. 29–42.

32. James D. Cockcroft, André Gunder Frank, and Dale L. Johnson, *Dependence and Underdevelopment: Latin America's Political Economy*, New York, Anchor, 1972, p. xvi.

33. *Ibid.*, p. xv.

34. William Moyer, "De-developing the United States through Nonviolence," *IDOC-North America* 52: 61–67, at 61 (1973).

35. George Modelski, "Multinational Business: A Global Perspective," *International Studies Quarterly*, 16: 407–432, at 415–16 (1972).

36. *Ibid.*, p. 415.

37. John Diebold, "Multinational Corporations: Why Be Scared of Them?" *Foreign Policy*, 12, pp. 79–95, 80–81 (1973).

38. Centre for Development Planning, Projections and Policies of the Department of Economic and Social Affairs of the United Nations Secretariat, based on table 11; Organisation for Economic Co-operation and Development, *Stock of Private Direct Investments by DAC Countries in Developing Countries, End 1967* (Paris 1972); United States Department of Commerce, *Survey of Current Business*, various issues; Bundesministerium für Wirtschaft, *Runderlass Aussenwirtschaft*, various issues; Handelskammer Hamburg, *Deutsche Direktinvestitionen in Ausland* (1969); Bank of England, *Quarterly Bulletin*, various issues; Hanc-Eckart Scharrer, ed., *Förderung privater Direktinvestitionen* (Hamburg 1972); Toyo Keizai, *Statistics Monthly*, vol. 32, June 1972; Canadian Department of Industry, Trade and Commerce, "Direct Investment abroad by Canada, 1964–1967" (mimeograph, Ottawa, 1971); Skandinaviska Enskilda Banken, *Quarterly Review*, No. 2, 1972; United Nations Department of Economic and Social Affairs, *Multinational Corporations in World Development*, New York, 1973, p. 139.

    According to the Organisation for Economic Co-operation and Development, *op. cit.*, p. 4, ". . . by the stock of foreign investment . . . is understood the net book value to the direct investor of affiliates (subsidiaries, branches and associates) in LDC's . . . Governments of DAC member countries decline all responsibility for the accuracy of the es timates of the Secretariat which in some cases are known to differ from confidential information available to the national authorities. . . . Any analysis of detailed data in the paper should therefore be done with the utmost caution. . . ."

39. Robert Gilpin, "The Multinational Corporation and the National Interest," U.S. Senate Committee on Labor and Public Welfare, *Report*, Oct. 1973, p. 23.

40. Charles Levinson, "Labour in the New Global Economy," *Yearbook of World Affairs 1973*, 27: 277–300, at 279.

41. Lester R. Brown, *World Without Boundaries*, New York, Random House, 1972, p. 213; for a full list of states and corporations ranked according to scale, see pp. 213–14.

42. George Modelski, *Principles of World Politics*, New York, Free Press, 1972, p. 323. Richard Barnet in *The Roots of War*, New York, Atheneum, 1972, p. 230, depicts the scale of MNC as follows: "In 1966 the U.S. exported $43 billion of goods and services produced by U.S.-owned facilities abroad came to $100 billion, or two and a half times as much. Kenneth Simmonds estimates that 71 of the top U.S. industrial corporations employ on an average about

one-third of their total payroll overseas. Sixty of the top American firms have factories in at least six countries."

43. For pertinent assessment of MNC influence see Louis Turner, *Multinational Companies and the Third World*, New York, Hill & Wang, 1973, pp. 41–43.

44. A helpful appraisal is found in Modelski, *Principles of World Politics*, pp. 416–430.

45. Brown, *World Without Boundaries*, pp. 254–255.

46. Modelski, *op.cit.*, p. 417; but see pp. 418–422 for discussion of indirect influence on coups and interventions. Modelski's main conclusion is only that "no case can be made for dominant causative influence."

47. Vernon, *Sovereignty at Bay*, p. 248.

48. Barnet, *The Roots of War*, p. 238n.

49. Fouad Ajami, "Corporate Giants: Some Global Social Costs," *International Studies Quarterly* 16: 511–529, at 517–518 (1972). Ajami views with some horror the image of the world, that others endorse with enthusiasm, as "a global shopping center."

50. The modes of cultural penetration—especially via the rise of global public relations (PR) activities of large advertising agencies—is vividly depicted in an innovative paper. See Herbert I. Schiller, "The Multinational Corporation as International Communicator," American Political Science Association, Annual Meeting, Sept. 8–12, 1970 (mimeographed).

51. The most celebrated European counterattack was that of J.J. Servan-Schreiber, *The American Challenge*, New York, Avon, 1969.

52. For a highly sophisticated and closely reasoned statement of the national interest case against the MNC (from an American perspective) see Gilpin, "The Multinational Corporation," esp. pp. 67–74; Gilpin's ideas will be considered in Chap. VII, pp. 468–472.

53. Barnet, *The Roots of War*, p. 237.

54. *Ibid.*, p. 238.

55. The following line of analysis is indebted to a public lecture by Professor Alfred Stepan at Princeton University, November 2, 1973.

56. Paul A. Baran and Paul M. Sweezy, "Notes on a Theory of Imperialism," in Kenneth E. Boulding and Tapan Mukerjee, eds., *Economic Imperialism: A Book of Readings*, Ann Arbor, University of Michigan Press, 1972, pp. 156–170, at 169.

57. George C. Lodge, "Multinational Corporations: Make Progress the Product," *Foreign Policy* 11, pp. 96–106; see John Diebold's reply, pp. 107–111 and Lodge's reconsiderations, pp. 111–112; the quoted language appears on p. 111.

58. Informal faculty–student discussion group, Woodrow Wilson School, Princeton University, October 30, 1973.

59. Baran and Sweezy, "Notes on a Theory of Imperialism," p. 170.

60. Robert Gilpin, "The Politics of Transnational Economic Relations," in Robert O. Keohane and Joseph S. Nye, Jr., eds., *Transnational Relations and World Politics*, Cambridge, Mass., Harvard University Press, 1972, pp. 48–69, at 69.

61. For a typical Brazilian statement see Miguel A. Ozorio de Almeida's commentary on the Founex Report on Development and Environment: "The Confrontation between Development and Environment," *International Conciliation*, No. 586, Jan. 1972, pp. 37–56.

62. See Teresa Hayter, *Aid as Imperialism*, London, Penguin Books, 1971.

63. Carl Kaysen, "The Computer that Printed W*O*L*F*," *Foreign Affairs* 50: 660–669, at p. 667; see also Peter Passell and Leonard Ross, *The Retreat from Riches: Affluence and Its Enemies*, New York, Viking, 1973.

64. Much of the evidence is carefully and convincingly considered by William Ophuls in *Prologue to a Political Theory of Steady State*, Ph.D. dissertation, Yale University, 1973; see also literature cited in Chapter II in connection with discussion of V4.

65. Passell and Ross, *The Retreat from Riches*, p. 35.

66. Kaysen, "The Computer that Printed W*O*L*F*," p. 666; for a more general affirmation of the capacity of the existing system to handle human problems for the indefinite future see John Maddox, *The Doomsday Syndrome*, New York, McGraw-Hill, 1972.

67. For a balanced assessment of principal issues, although perceived largely on a national rather than a global setting, see Mancur Olson, ed., "The No-Growth Society," *Daedalus* 102: 1–241 (1973).

68. One sensitive argument to this effect is to be found in Richard Neuhaus, *In Defense of People: Ecology and the Seduction of Radicalism*, New York, Macmillan, 1971.

69. For technical criticism of the limits to growth position see Sussex study, *Prophets of Doom*, 1973.

70. "Declaration of the Third World and the Human Environment," Oi Committee International, Stockholm, June 1972, pp. 1–4, at p. 1; see also Johan Galtung, "The Limits to Growth and Class Politics," *Journal of Peace Research*, 1–2: 101–114 (1973).

71. For a statement by the Club of Rome on the main issues in the limits to growth debate see Aurelio Peccei and Manfred Siebker, "Point and Counterpoint: A Summary of the Debate over 'The Limits to Growth,' " *IDOC–North America*, No. 52, April 1973, pp. 75–82.

72. See Roland N. McKean, "Growth vs. No Growth: An Evaluation," in Olson, "The No-Growth Society," pp. 207–227, at pp. 210–211.

73. See Brown, *World Without Boundaries*.

74. See especially Herman E. Daly, ed., *Toward a Steady-State Economy*, San Francisco, W.H. Freeman and Co., 1973; also Ophuls, *Prologue*.

75. Robert L. Heilbroner, "Growth and Survival," *Foreign Affairs*, 51: 139–153, at p. 152.

76. See argument set forth by Marshall I. Goldman, "The Convergence of Environmental Disruption," *Science* 170: 37–42 at 42 (1970).

77. William Ophuls, "Locke's Paradigm Lost: The Environmental Crisis and the Collapse of Laissez-Faire Politics," paper presented at 1973 Annual Meeting, American Political Science Association.

78. For an excellent exposé see Paul Brodeur, "Annals of Industry (Industrial Casualties-III)," *The New Yorker*, pp. 131–177, Nov. 12, 1973.

79. Heilbroner, *Growth and Survival*, at 150.

80. E.F. Schumacher, "Buddhist Economics," in Daly, *Toward a Steady-State Economy*, pp. 231–239.

81. Rasheed Talib, *A New Strategy for Growth*, New Delhi, Rachna Prakashan, 1972, p. 16.

82. *The United States and the Developing World:* Agenda for Action, Overseas Development Council, Washington, D.C. 1973, p. 25.

83. This analysis is well-put in Thomas E. Weisskopf, "Capitalism, Underdevelopment and the Future," in Bhagwati, *Economics and World Order*, pp. 43–77.

Chapter Seven

AMERICA'S STAKE IN GLOBAL REFORM

A QUEST FOR NATIONAL IDENTITY

The United States' relationship to global reform is complicated and confusing. This country has a tradition, deriving from its own revolutionary origins in an anti-colonial war, of favoring progressive reforms. At the same time, strong countercurrents have existed since the earliest years of the Republic. The brutal dispossession of Indian tribes from the land, imperial venturings in the Western Hemisphere and the Pacific, the institution of slavery and its various aftermaths, and the more recent militarization of foreign policy associated with world primacy have shaped America's role in world history up to the present time. Probably no other country currently important in world affairs has had such a curiously mixed balance sheet. The ultimate expression of this mixture is the persisting sense of a dual America that is benefactor and exploiter, at one and the same time the last best hope of mankind and the gravest menace to the pursuit of justice and tranquillity on earth.

This tension between polar tendencies shapes the American role in world affairs. It exists most obviously, of course, with regard to war-waging dispositions and capabilities. But it also exists with respect to values associated with social and economic well-being, human dignity, and environmental quality. The United States is an exceptionally mobile society in terms of providing its citizenry with opportunities for economic and social betterment, but paradoxically it is also one of the most hopeless for those who do not make it, either because they fail along the way or start life in a severely handicapped position.* The

---

* The anguish of failure is accentuated by the stress on success and by the myth that merit and work will be rewarded with wealth, influence, and prestige. The need to be a

United States is at once the birthplace of the world ecology movement and the scene of the world's most anti-ecological life-style and consumption patterns. America is a crucible of positive and negative potentialities for global destiny.

These poles of opposition are also reflected in the oscillations of national mood, shifts from foreign involvement to isolationist withdrawal, shifts from hope to despair, shifts from national assertions of pride to guilt, shifts from unbounded confidence in the capacities of technological innovation to profound anxiety about the dehumanization and environmental destruction following compulsive subservience to technological momentum.* At one pole of American experience are the words of Edward Everett at Harvard in 1824, in the course of a celebrated Phi Beta Kappa address: "When the old world afforded no longer any hope, it pleased Heaven to open this last refuge of humanity." Indeed Everett went so far as to call America "the last solemn experiment of humanity," and warned its inhabitants to heed "the eloquent ruins of nations" that "conjure us not to quench the light which is rising in the world." [2] This sense of America as the chosen land with a special historic destiny continues to inspire those who hold an optimistic view of the nation's future, and is shared by some foreign observers who believe that America may be the only national setting within which positive, progressive changes might occur and radiate their influence throughout the globe. [3]

The negative pole of the American experience, crystallized for many even before the agony of Vietnam, involved various forms of awareness that violent and destructive forces were strongly at work in the social and political order; these forces were made more menacing by the claims of benign intent and glorious achievement. There are many ways to make this point: to catalogue lynchings and riots, to set forth homicide and crime rates, to note the rise of drug culture, to examine "the economy of death" that creates a ghastly interface between the war system and the governing process, to depict the imagery and patterns of imperial reality within and without. [4] In many ways, Allen Ginsberg's

---

winner in America seems to distort the perceptions and behavior of even our highest leaders. Lyndon Johnson and Richard Nixon both seem almost incapable of acknowledging loss or defeat. It is almost as if espousal of unflagging devotion to the winners' creed were a tacit condition of advancement within the political process.

* Arthur Schlesinger, Jr., in his study of the American presidency, notes that "corruption appears to visit the White House in fifty-year cycles." He thus proposes that "Around the year 2023 the American people would be well advised to go on the alert and start nailing down everything in sight." [1]

long poem "Howl," turning Whitman's celebration and inventory of national virtues on its head, is the best national mood piece of the times. In its opening lines the poem anticipated an entire direction of contemporary response that did not become fully manifest until a decade after its 1956 publication: [5]

> I saw the best minds of my generation destroyed by madness, starving
>   hysterical naked,
> dragging themselves through the Negro streets at dawn looking for an-
>   other fix,
> angelheaded hipsters burning for the ancient heavenly connection to the
>   starry dynamo in the machinery of night . . . .*

Another poetic voice, Paul Goodman, writing in 1961, captured this loss of self-confidence in self, nation, and future:

> My poisoned one, my world! we stubborn few
> physicians work with worried brows and speak
> in low voices; dying in the epidemic,
> our quiet will is only what to do.
> The time is Indian summer and the blue
> heaven is cloudless, but the rains will reek
> with poison and the coming spring will be sick
> if fire has not blasted us in snow.

These lines, evidently provoked by atmospheric tests of nuclear weapons at the time and the all-pervading danger of nuclear war, also anticipate ecological concerns born almost a decade later. Goodman closes his sonnet significantly:

> we do not have the leisure to despair
> we cannot cope without new inspiration.†

This theme of engrained despair persists as the dominant national mood, strongly reinforced by the whole array of debasements stem-

---

* Allen Ginsberg, "Howl," from *Howl & Other Poems*, San Francisco, City Lights Books, 1956, p. 9. Copyright © 1956, 1959 by Allen Ginsberg. Reprinted by permission of CITY LIGHTS BOOKS.

† Paul Goodman, "The Russians Resume Bomb-Testing, October 1961," in Todd Gitlin, ed., *Campfires of Resistance: Poetry from the Movement*, Indianapolis, Bobbs-Merrill, 1971, p. 4. Copyright © 1972, 1973 by the Estate of Paul Goodman. Used by permission of Random House, Inc.

ming from the Watergate disclosures. At the same time there is an emerging realization that to accept despair is to convert the probability of disaster into a certainty; there is a healthy national effort to revive the spirit of hope despite all the evidence of accumulating doom. A credible vision of global reform could help direct this quest for hope into areas of constructive action. Without such a vision it is likely that the drift of national consciousness will persist in an aimless way until arrested by existing emergency or impending disaster.

The Vietnam War provided a focus for some of these anxieties. Daniel Ellsberg writes that "For over seven years, like many other Americans I have been preoccupied with our involvement in Vietnam. In that time I have seen it first as a problem, then as a stalemate; then as a crime." [6] Whether to view the war as "an honorable mistake," "a tragic mistake," or a grisly episode in a criminal enterprise (i.e., an imperial foreign policy) continues to divide Americans. The success of Nixon's foreign policy has been his capacity to rebuild a domestic consensus without altering the basic posture of American participation in the world, although it is uncertain whether this consensus can persist despite the loss of confidence associated with presidential leadership, especially as compounded by the energy crisis and by a hardening of Soviet foreign and domestic policies in the direction of re-stalinization. [7] As matters now stand, mainstream discussions of foreign policy do not call for a fundamental reappraisal of America's role in the world. They merely confine themselves to asking which margins of policy should be trimmed.* There is not yet any public demand for a new foreign policy, much less a new system of world order. The prospects for $S_{2(WOMP)}$ depend vitally upon generating such a public demand relatively early in t_1 in the United States.

It is also necessary to acknowledge that "world order rhetoric" has been considerably discredited among progressive social forces in the United States during recent years. For one thing, the architects of the Vietnam War during the Johnson and Nixon presidencies have themselves frequently invoked world order rhetoric and imagery to describe their vision of national goals. Hence, the affirmation of world order concerns and the pursuit of a militaristic foreign policy are linked in the

---

* Public acquiescence is surprising because the principal rationale for overseas deployment has been eliminated as a result of Soviet–American détente and Sino–American normalization. Whether this acquiescence will last very long is uncertain and depends on an array of domestic and global developments, especially relating to the economic and political factors.

political imagination.* For another thing, the notion of "law and order" in domestic society has been relied upon by those groups and forces that feel most threatened by liberalizing patterns of social change. Because an international variant of the "law and order" goal has often been adopted by conservative professional lawyers' associations, a focus on world order seems like one more effort to preserve a status quo favorable to the United States; the slogan "world peace through world law" is generally regarded as a conservative state-oriented appeal rather than as a call for drastic global reform.† Finally, there is justifiable disillusionment with the United Nations, partly as a consequence of its inability to contribute solutions to the great human problems of the day, and partly because these global institutions are perceived mainly as creatures of great power politics which apply one set of standards to Soviet–American behavior and quite another to small state behavior.‡

This chapter will consider the conditions under which public demand for drastic global reform might be made in the United States. We will also examine the standard approach of liberal realists who propose a strategy of global reform compatible with the logic of S_1 thinking.§

THE UNITED STATES AND THE PRESENT
WORLD ORDER SYSTEM ($S_{1\text{-}1974}$)

Three sets of concern will be briefly considered: matters of advantage, matters of equity, and matters of survival. In relation to each set of con-

---

* Of course, the deepest negative association arises from Hitler's frequent emphasis on his mission to create "a new world order." It is not surprising that global reformers are viewed either with suspicion—because they might deliver, or with scorn—because they have no prospect of fulfilling their quest.

† Beneath such a slogan many positions can flourish. The Clark–Sohn plan bears the title *World Peace Through World Law* and it is certainly a proposal for drastic global reform. The point is that change-oriented groups are not responsive at this time to law-based appeals.

‡ One way to put it is to suggest that there is nothing wrong with the United Nations except its members. But when we have said that, we are really saying that the Charter concept cannot be realized within a political framework based on the state system. In this sense it is hardly surprising to find a widening gap between the United Nations as *actor* and the Charter as *concept*.[8]

§ Liberal realists are identified here as those who presuppose the durability *and* correctability of S_1, and yet adhere generally to the same goals embodied by WOMP.

cern we emphasize two dimensions for purposes of world order appraisal:

Is there a rational basis for leaders representing the U.S. public interest to support the maintenance of $S_{1(1974)}$?

Is there sufficient evidence to justify supporting an American effort to facilitate transition to $S_{2(WOMP)}$, or, even more precisely, to $S_{2(WOMP/USA)}$ along Transition Path 1? *

The first of these questions raises a very serious preliminary difficulty. Disagreement exists about the extent to which our government is in a position to represent the best interests of the national citizenry, and the degree to which a government more responsive to these interests can reasonably be expected to gain effective power in the next several years. Such questions, while fundamental, will not be analyzed here. We will consider world order interests *on the assumption* that it is possible to have a government in this country dedicated to promoting the best interests of American society.[9] We are aware that the consequences of such an assumption may be seriously biased by the tendency to emphasize governmental action in relation to global reform.† It is quite reasonable to suppose that a movement to achieve $S_{2(WOMP)}$ can only occur, if at all, as a counter-governmental phenomenon. However, we believe that if $S_{2(WOMP)}$ is to be achieved sometime around the year 2000, it will be essential for the main governmental actors to become proponents of $S_{2(WOMP)}$ by the end of t_1. Indeed, as Chapter IV details, progress on Transition Path 1 is predicated on this assumption.‡

The second question concerns whether enough information presently exists to vindicate the adoption of $S_{2(WOMP)}$ or $S_{2(WOMP/USA)}$ as a focus for reformist action by individuals exercising power and influence within our society. It seems clear that as of t_0, the early 1970's, it would be virtually impossible for American leaders to take, or even advocate, action

---

* The distinctions between S_2, $S_{2(WOMP)}$, and $S_{2(WOMP/USA)}$ are important here. There is no doubt that a variety of S_2 options are being considered by American policy-makers. Our effort is to encourage a comparable consideration of $S_{2(WOMP)}$ options and to mobilize, in time, a consensus around the relatively specific $S_{2(WOMP/USA)}$ variant as outlined in Chapters IV and V.

† We believe that it will become possible for an American government to work for global reform along $S_{2(WOMP)}$ lines. But this possibility cannot come into being without a period of public preparation and general education.

‡ Such an assumption is not a forecast, but a consequence of political analysis. We are arguing that if $S_{2(WOMP)}$ is to come about within the relevant time frame, it will depend on the prior conversion of principal governments. We do not regard this prospect as probable, but it does seem possible, given a variety of pressures and the growing need to choose among S_2 options.

based on promoting transition to $S_{2(WOMP)}$. At present, to borrow Harold Lasswell's phrase, national leaders belong to "entrapped elites"; they are entrapped by the para-official and public acceptance of the mythology and ideology of an S_1 value structure. As a consequence, the open advocacy of an $S_{2(WOMP)}$ position of any kind by an American leader would be viewed, in a domestic context, as world order adventurism of the most dangerous kind.* At present, unacknowledged support for $S_{2(WOMP)}$, rhetorical endorsement of its ideals, and encouragement for reorienting educational undertakings are the most that can be realistically expected. Relatively early in t_1 symbolic world leaders such as the Secretary General of the United Nations or the Pope might espouse $S_{2(WOMP)}$ as a program for the future,† and national leaders in prosperous, homogeneous, and stable countries of intermediate size such as Sweden or Canada may also be led to lend open support. These kinds of external developments, together with much more vital citizen efforts within the United States, would initiate a world order dialectic within American politics that would begin to break down decades of adherence to S_1 and its infrastructure of values, perceptions, and institutions. No longer would the national leadership be entrapped in an S_1 framework, although it is likely that remnants of this elite would continue their adherence to S_1 or to an anti-WOMP variant of S_2, and would be opposed by other portions of the elite or by counter-elites adhering to $S_{2(WOMP)}$. The pressure and dominant perception of the international setting (especially linked to war, resource availability, environmental decay, world famine and disease) would help shape the position taken by national leaders and would tend to reflect the relation of forces in American society. In this regard, and perhaps in an overly paradigmatic spirit, we project a minority position for adherents of $S_{2(WOMP)}$ by the

---

* S_2 options of a self-serving kind are not yet openly avowed by entrenched political elites. Corporate elites have been willing to espouse a world without boundaries, a new globalism, which can be represented as $S_{2(MNC)}$. But no "responsible" leader has advocated the adoption of $S_{2(WOMP)}$ as national policy. The irony is that in the context of global reform American political leaders, however enlightened, are confined to the pursuit of "irresponsible" options. It is for this reason that a movement for drastic global reform based on WOMP values must win popular support before it can hope to receive official endorsement. A "Pope John" presidency is possible in which a leader acts "unpolitically," i.e., transcends conventional wisdom as to the limits of practical politics.

† Indeed, reaching such symbolic leaders should be a priority objective of the movement for drastic global reform. Their endorsement need not be a mechanical advocacy of $S_{2(WOMP)}$, but rather a show of serious support for drastic global reform of a coherent character that embodies an ethos of equality among peoples, and is sensitive to the solidarity of the species and the unity of the planet.

middle of t_1, gradually strengthening its following until it becomes dominant by the end of t_1. As we indicated in Chapter IV, throughout the transition period there will be situations of dangerous conflict containing regressive potential. There is no doubt that substantial energies will be devoted to thwarting a popular shift toward an $S_{2(WOMP)}$ orientation, including reliance on counterrevolutionary tactics by outmaneuvered elites and reversionary moods and movements among the general public.* Given the fundamental collision of value prospects, the strain on democratic procedures in the United States is likely to grow greater as we proceed through t_1, especially as this value collision may be replicated in intense fashion in relation to a variety of domestic issues. It should, perhaps, be recalled that we expect the main bearers of world order values associated with $S_{2(WOMP)}$ in t_1 within the United States to be those pressing for radical shifts on social issues—repressed minorities, youth, women.

Richard Nixon, speaking at a news conference on July 28, 1972, called the impending Nixon/McGovern election campaign one that offered American voters "the clearest choice in this century" and reflected "honest" differences of opinion on foreign, domestic, and defense policy.† This choice was not expressed in any manner that suggested an S_1/S_2 difference between the candidates, and indeed there may have been none, at least not on a conscious level. But the McGovern candidacy carried with it some of the seeds of S_2 adherence, and was so perceived by many supporters of an S_1 position.‡ (One might argue that the danger of a premature S_2 political success in the United States might be to authorize such an outlook before creating the public support

---

* The attractiveness of a neo-Darwinian global reform option should not be underestimated as the pressure for adaption grows. Americans may be misled to perceive their choice as one of sacrifice or domination, when the real choice is between a developmental and anti-developmental view of human nature and experience. It is a question more of spiritual growth than material allocation.[10] On another level, the issue is one of biological and ecological adaptation for the species rather than the ascendancy of any portion of humankind.

† The Watergate disclosures of efforts by Nixon campaign strategists to assure McGovern's candidacy provide a relevant irony. It was not the Democratic Party that wanted "the clearest choice" but the Nixonian re-election machine.

‡ Senator McGovern disguised his deviations from S_1 attitudes and goals during his national campaign. As such, his failed candidacy was worse than nothing. It vindicated the view that a presidential candidate must appear to espouse mainstream positions on foreign and domestic policies. It failed to make use of the national platform created by the candidacy to present a coherent challenge to S_1 ideology or an alternative to the sort of S_2 options attractive to Henry Kissinger or ITT.

needed for effective action.* As a consequence, the length of t_1 might be greatly extended because S_2 could be repudiated and temporarily discredited early in t_1, thereby reconstituting an S_1 position with even greater control over behavior and policy than it now possesses.)

Jean-François Revel also viewed the 1972 American elections as posing a basic choice, although not one of "honest" policy differences: ". . . the only question is: Will the American political system, the American constitution, manage to mint a new society or will they be blown up by the endless American crisis? If Mr. McGovern is elected, the basic changes will have a chance of occurring legally. If Mr. Nixon is re-elected, complete disintegration has even more of a chance of occurring, also legally." [11] Revel correctly (we feel) expresses the connection between the domestic and global arenas when he writes that "the real ability for a country to help in solving world problems depends on its ability to solve its own problems first." What is less persuasive in Revel's formulation is his conviction that the American domestic conflict has deepened to the point where a genuine revolutionary situation exists or is, at least, emergent. It seem more correct to suppose that the traditional forces of control in American society have been confronted by only a gesture of revolutionary challenge, a challenge that lacks a sufficient base in popular discontent and possesses neither the means nor prospect of acquiring power. Indeed, the challenge is now so feeble that it is useful to the ruling groups, by providing a popular pretext for tightening the grip of government on the processes of wealth and opinion formation among the general public.[12] In the post-Watergate setting, Revel's fears of government repression seem both naive (it was already happening) and alarmist (countertendencies have now been released that protect dissent, at least for some time).

The underlying premises of our approach are that S_1 is being undermined all the time by the main tendencies of objective circumstances, that transition to S_2 is inevitable, and that the main uncertainties concern the modality and timing of transition and the choice of S_2 option. Another relevant conditioning variable will be the degree to which the world order dialectic is able to function in the domestic arenas of other principal world actors, especially those now perceived as rivals.† As

---

* Political success could result from a situation in which the incumbent candidate is discredited, and a challenger wins an election—but before his program is either fully understood or revealed. Once its radical dimensions become plain, however, the position is precarious if the public has not yet been oriented toward the pursuit of drastic reform.

† The plight of Soviet dissenters as of 1974 indicates both the existence of such a dialectic, and an effort by Soviet rulers to choke it off.[13]

with arms races and international tensions, world order developments in a given direction within one national arena tend to encourage developments *in the same direction*—whether regressive or progressive—in other national arenas. Therefore, in considering prospects within the United States we must remain mindful of parallel developments within such critical national arenas as the Soviet Union, China, Europe, and Japan, each of which is part rival, part partner in security, economic, and functional arrangements underway to perpetuate S_1. National leaders in any of these arenas can alter the world order debate taking place in the United States, and vice versa.

In the next section we shall depict some features of America's participation in these final phases of S_1. The central question is whether anti-WOMP S_2 forces will prevail over WOMP S_2 forces during the next few decades; the future shape of global reform will be heavily influenced by this competition in the United States among aspiring designers of the future.

MATTERS OF ADVANTAGE, EQUITY, AND SURVIVAL IN S_1

It is difficult to grasp the interdependence of the war system and economic inequality, but it seems fundamental both in relation to the dynamics of S_1 and the conflict over the selection of an S_2 option. This interdependence is purposefully obscured by the rhetoric of equality embodied in the forms and rituals of the state system. It is also obscured by the degree to which control over Third World governments has been achieved by elites whose affinities and interests tie them to the dominant state actors rather than to their own dependent, impoverished populations. From a WOMP perspective there are grave distortions in S_1, even aside from the structural questions of guidance dealt with in earlier chapters. These distortions arise from the large extent to which world order is based on intergovernmental relations and the small degree to which governments respond to actual human needs.

The American contribution to this deformed world order system is very considerable. As the richest, most powerful and most august state actor, this country has the largest stake in S_1 and in assuring that its evolution does not disturb the hierarchical order of relations and benefits that now exists. In this regard, America's role in promoting reactionary counterinsurgency operations throughout the world needs to be more completely understood than it has been in the past. Vietnam was not an accident or exception. Wherever American power can be exerted at reasonable cost, it will be brought to bear in support of reactionary contenders for national control. These reactionary contenders eagerly seek American aid and investment; the bargain reached is to enrich a small segment of the native population in exchange for ceding a portion of national wealth and autonomy to the United States; it is a geopolitical variant of "the protection racket." The circumstances that led to the 1973 downfall of the Allende experiment in Chile, the quick recognition accorded the military junta, the junta's immediate invitation to American and other foreign investors, its program of returning previously expropriated companies, and the cruel repression of the political left in Chile, together exemplify the general pattern of America's role in the world. The Chilean case is especially instructive, because it was not necessary to use crude forms of intervention to bring about the desired result, and this is clearly the preferred way to obtain the ascendancy of counterinsurgent elites throughout the Third World.*

There is no doubt about the extent of American wealth and power as compared to that of the rest of the world; such a comparison is a matter of familiar statistics. There is also no doubt that other national governments would like to increase both their own supply of wealth and power and their proportion of the world's wealth and power.† Given the inequality of present global arrangements, there is little reason to doubt that disadvantaged actors would under certain circumstances resort to violence if it could facilitate the achievement of these goals.‡ Hence, there is also little doubt that the American effort to repress forces of change throughout the Third World reflects its support for the

---

* Although September 1974 official disclosures documented earlier allegations that the CIA had played a substantial role in "destabilizing" the Allende government.

† As we have suggested, most Third World governments are representing the interests of a tiny privileged upper class in their country, rather than the population as a whole. Hence, these governments are concerned with larger aggregate revenues so that their privileged classes can grow even more affluent. There is little or no concern with the development of policies that will spread the wealth or that will assure an equitable spread of the growth dividend to the impoverished masses. There are liberal governments in the Third World that are committed on paper to improving the condition of their whole population, but they are rarely willing or able to implement their goals. India might be the prime example in the world today.

‡ That is, wealth and power have in large part been acquired and maintained by reliance on force of arms. Therefore, there are no ethical inhibitions which might discourage disadvantaged groups from using violence to improve their situation. The only inhibitions would be pragmatic, the feeling that violence would not work. It is mainly up to the privileged and powerful to lead the way in dismantling the war system by embracing a more nonviolent view of social, economic, and political organization at all levels of human activity, from the family to the world.

Table 7–1. Per Capita Consumption of Energy

United States	11.1
Canada	9.1
Sweden	6.3
Czechoslovakia	6.3
Belgium	5.9
East Germany	5.9
Britain	5.4
West Germany	5.1
Netherlands	5.1
Soviet Union	4.4
Argentina	1.6
Mexico	1.2
Brazil	0.47
Egypt	0.26
India	0.19
Ghana	0.16
World Average	1.9

SOURCE: Reproduced from the *New York Times*, July 10, 1972, p. 8; © 1972 by The New York Times Company. Reprinted by permission.

socioeconomic status quo and is linked to the rich/poor gap, as well as to the struggle with communism for supremacy in this vast area of global ferment.*

These gaps in life circumstances can be portrayed in a variety of ways, and the United States is not at the top of the world pyramid in all relevant respects. Energy use per capita is considered the best overall indicator of material living standards at the present time. Table 7–1 shows how the United States dominates the world economic scene in this respect. For example, the ratio of America's use of energy per capita

---

* As the Cold War waned and as Great Power relations improved, the ideological rationale for American involvement in counterinsurgency activity throughout the world has been destroyed. And yet, the mission remains. The United States continues to prefer repressive regimes to progressive ones. Why? It is not an endorsement of repression or a residue of the Cold War, but it is a sense that these reactionary regimes want and need what we have to give and will not take away what we have previously established; i.e., the terms for a favorable bargain can be struck. In contrast, a progressive regime wants to get rid of foreign control of its economy, of foreign military bases, and is wary of new dealings. As happens, however, the progressive regime may be forced to choose between soliciting a new foreign presence (Soviet Union) as was the case with Cuba, or succumbing to counterrevolutionary forces (Chile).

to that of India is about 55 to 1 in America's favor. But this ratio is also relevant to assessing responsibility for contributing to global pollution and, thereby, disturbing the ecological balance of the planet. It also bears upon issues of resource depletion. It has been estimated that the United States, with somewhat less than 6% of the world's population, uses annually between 30 and 45% of the world's replaceable resources (depending on which statistical measures and minerals are considered).[14] This resource use by the United States does provide earnings to poor countries which would be even poorer without the American demand, but it also reflects a structure of pervasive inequality in which the poor depend for their existence on the maintenance of the rich.* The economic gaps tend to be reflected also in the more ultimate measures of life expectancy and infant mortality (see Tables 7–2 and 7–3). It seems clear that the advantage enjoyed by the United

Table 7–2. Life Expectancy

Sweden	female	76
	male	72
United States	female	74
	male	66.6
Japan	female	74.3
	male	69
U.S.S.R.	female	70
	male	70
Gabon	female	45
	male	25
Nigeria	female	36.7
	male	37.2
Guinea	female	28
	male	26

Source: Reproduced from the *New York Times*, July 10, 1972, p. 8, © 1972 by The New York Times Company. Reprinted by permission.

---

* Robert Osgood's explanation of why Third World efforts, through UNCTAD and elsewhere, have been generally so unsuccessful: "In bare power terms the fact of the matter is that the Third-World countries need economic relations with the developed countries more than the developed countries need economic relations with them." [15] The oil crisis and the organization among oil producers (OPEC) is an apparent exception. Resource scarcity combines with an increasing ability of producers to take a common position to give OPEC real leverage and, for the first time, to require rich countries to devise counterstrategies.

Table 7–3.　Infant Mortality

Sweden	11.7
Japan	13.1
United States	19.8
U.S.S.R.	24.4
Gabon	22.9

SOURCE: Reproduced from the *New York Times*, July 10, 1972, p. 8; © 1972 by The New York Times Company. Reprinted by permission.

States in energy use, passenger cars per capita, and GNP is not fully reflected in such social measures of well-being as life expectancy and infant mortality. Domestic structures of inequality in the United States as compared, say, to Sweden help explain why this country fails to translate our greater national wealth into longer lives and safer childbirth.

On the level of world order thinking, the driving assumption of American ideology has been to offer other societies an image of sustained economic growth as the best way in which to raise national living standards. In this regard foreign aid, investment, and trade are all conceived as ways to stimulate the development process in other parts of the world. This ideology has been increasingly challenged on both economic and ecological grounds. On economic grounds, some contend that the poor countries are victims of systemic underdevelopment, that their leadership is generally joined in a tacit transnational alliance with the richer sectors of world society, and that basic patterns of foreign aid, trade, and investment reinforce relations of dependence that are incompatible with genuine economic development.* On ecological grounds, it has been suggested in recent years that resource scarcity or pollution saturation will place fixed limits on the gross planetary product that can be accommodated, that late-comers to development will be "taxed" by the emergence of pollution control standards, and that further development by rich societies will soon directly limit the prospect for further growth on the part of poor societies.†

---

* In societies with impressive GNP figures there is often no "trickle down" effect of significance. Thus, a nation can be growing more prosperous, while the misery of its people is actually worsening, if measured in terms of numbers and proportion. In such a setting it is sheer mystification to rely on growth to "do the job" or to point with pride to a steady rate of GNP increase over a period of years.

† The growth issues are discussed in Chapter VI. The main point here is that the outcome of the struggle between neo-Darwinism and humanist perspectives on global

Underlying these issues is the question of whether present American advantages can and should be maintained over time, in view of the world's shrinking resource base and increasing ecological and demographic pressure. Does the advantageous relationship now enjoyed by the United States *depend* on keeping others poor and dependent, or is there an expanding pie of world wealth that can produce abundance for all? Eventually, although the time interval remains controversial, growth dynamics seem likely to induce collective catastrophe, although some optimistic voices still argue that we are or might be close to the start of an era of unprecedented energy and resource abundance.

Regardless of the intellectual debate on "limits of growth," the character of world order in S_1 seems clearly based on predominant adherence by national leaders to a "zero-sum" orientation in their relations between rich and poor, strong and weak.* As Richard Nixon expressed it in his 1972 State of the Union Address: "Strong military defenses are not the enemy of peace. They are the guardians of peace."

Such a basic outlook connects the Nixon promise of "a generation of peace" with an alleged American need to maintain an edge in the arms race. In his Annual Report as Secretary of Defense for Fiscal Year (FY) 1973, Melvin Laird argues that "second place" in the "technological race" governing weapons development and deployment "is simply not good enough." Given the secrecy and long lead time needed to deploy weapons systems (as much as two decades between proposal and development), there is a constant scramble to achieve "superiority," in order to be secure in the belief that a position of "inferiority" has been avoided.† Arms control arrangements are "sold" to the American

---

reform will determine whether ecological *costs* will be borne primarily by the rich, or whether they will be distributed more generally or even, in effect, concentrated in poor countries. By "costs" is meant the overall curtailment of economic activity that results from ecological constraints. The cunning of reason is such that the "costs" of ecological constraints may turn out to be "benefits," i.e., the poor countries may rely on low-technology development and avoid the materialism and dispiritualization that has resulted in the highly industrialized parts of the world.

* Here again the complexities are very basic. The zero-sum attributes refer to true interests humanistically specified; such a competitive situation does not pertain to the extent that the "poor" are identified with "the governments of the poor countries." As we have argued, these governments often act as agents for the interests of the dominant state actors. Similarly, the lateral relations among the rich can be developed in mutually beneficial ways by trade and interaction, although their military prowess is maintained at enormous cost, so that a zero-sum approach to relations among the rich and powerful does not seem too attractive. Deterrence is designed to convince potential military rivals that major geopolitical success is impossible without enduring catastrophic losses.

† That is, to be secure in the belief that defense capabilities are second to none, it is virtually necessary to sustain a position of primacy. The dynamics of weapons innovations,

Congress and public on the grounds that they inhibit arms development favored by adversaries, while enabling accelerated arms spending and development in areas not covered by the arrangement. Again Mr. Laird's formulation is useful: "So I repeat what I have said so many times: The American people may perhaps be willing to accept parity in regard to the deployment of strategic nuclear weapons; but, in my view, they will never accept a position of inferiority." [16]

One recent study has argued, with considerable power, that the American national tendency to depreciate militarism has led the country to underestimate the military contributions that have been made at each stage of American history. Its author, Raymond O'Connor, believes it to be a dangerous illusion for Americans "to think of themselves as peace-loving people in contrast to the warlike populations of other countries." Mr. O'Connor believes that "knowing how military power determined the course of events at crucial periods in the past might eliminate much of the confusion." O'Connor points out that not only was independence wrested by force of arms, but America's territorial expanse was secured by "the winning of the West," that is, by "wresting the land from the natives . . . through the use of force." [17] The main point is that the war system, including armed strength in periods of formal peace, has been an integral feature of America's rise to world preeminence.

Thus, it seems important to understand the links between the war system, a generally hostile American attitude toward revisionist aspirations of foreign societies, and international gaps in wealth and human well-being. It seems inconceivable that any real changes in this pattern of attitudes and relationships can occur within the confines of S_1. In this respect, we are locked within the statist frame of reference, including its tendency to regard other states as potential enemies and its inability to give real content to the affirmation of human community or planetary consciousness. The American position is accentuated by its advantages, as measured by criteria of success in S_1, and generates leaders who prize these advantages and regard themselves as "secure" only so long as the country can defeat any rival state by force.*

---

the long lead times, the secrecy surrounding Soviet defense planning, and the wide range of military contingencies are among the factors that account for this striving to be in first place, so as to be sure not to be in second place among world powers. Note that such relative capabilities have little to do with traditional roles of military power: to provide for national security in the sense of the defense of homeland or, even, an extended view of defense that includes helping with the defense of close allies.

* As we noted earlier, American leaders are exploring S_1 reforms as well as S_2 options that would sustain the relative hierarchy of the world system under the pressure of

Can these characteristics of dominance really be advantageous for the American people? If our national position is joined in a death embrace with a doomed dynamic of economic growth, then we as a people have much to gain by early transfers of allegiance to positive S_2 images of the future, where we could base the "security" of our material conditions on the welfare of others and create a world order system that is designed to express ideals of planetary coherence and human community.*

It thus seems clear that matters of advantage are intertwined with concerns of equity and of survival. The basic disclosure of social reality appears to underscore the desirability of an early shift away from the goal of maximizing a beneficial *position* in S_1, and toward joining in the work of creating a beneficial S_2. As we observed earlier, the transition to S_2 is inevitable, although we do not know whether S_2 can be generated in a humane fashion and with a beneficial cumulative effect. We believe that Americans need to redefine their goals by consciously adopting an $S_{2(WOMP)}$ program of transition. A first step in this process of redefinition is to comprehend the extent to which present efforts toward world order reform both express and support S_1 logic or, at most, facilitate S_2 options that are incompatible with the realization of WOMP values.

MAINSTREAM REFORM OF S_1

There are clear indications that world order reform is an explicit goal of leaders within American society. The character of this reform is subject to fairly intense controversy in relation to any specific undertaking, al-

---

change and heightened interdependence. S_1 leaders are exploring three main options: a moderated S_1, $S_{2(CON)}$, $S_{2(MNC)}$, as well as combinations of the three.

* Beyond the issue of ecological well-being lies the issue of civic well-being. The Watergate disclosures have finally conveyed to liberal members of the American Establishment what was long the first principal of the anti-war movement—namely, that there is a necessary interrelationship between lawlessness in foreign policy and in domestic governance. Nicholas Katzenbach, former Attorney General and Under Secretary of State during the Johnson Presidency and now Vice President of IBM, writes: "I am prepared to take some losses in our foreign affairs if by doing so we can restore the fundamentals of representative democracy to our foreign policy. As Watergate demonstrates, democracy is too fragile to be divided into foreign and domestic affairs. We cannot give the President a free hand in the one without eroding the whole of the governmental system that all policy seeks to preserve." [18]

though quite often the contours of reform are asserted as virtually self-evident efforts to reduce the risk of large-scale war, cut the costs of overseas military involvement, and assign a larger share of productive resources to domestic pursuits. In recent years, a national consensus of sorts has emerged around the goal of shifting "national priorities" from the defense to the civilian sector of the economy.* Even the Secretary of Defense concluded his Annual Report for FY 1973 with the claim that "a massive shift in priorities has already occurred, and that an adequate defense effort imposes a smaller economic burden upon the nation than at any time for more than 20 years." In essence, this claim reflects the declining percentage of GNP and of the federal budget on the part of the defense sector (Table 7–4).

The other part of the claim of shifting priorities is based on comparing *real* expenditures in which inflation-generated increases are eliminated. For example, if current dollars are used to assess defense spending, there is an increase from $50.8 billion in FY 1964 to a projected $76.5 billion for FY 1973, whereas if constant prices as of 1973 are considered, defense outlays have declined from $83.1 billion in FY 1964 to $76.5 billion projected for FY 1973. It is highly questionable whether shifts of this magnitude can appropriately be said to indicate "massive" changes in national priorities, even with regard to defense outlays. Nevertheless, it is clear that the guiding concept and proposed changes take for granted the persistence for the indefinite future of the present world order system (S_1). The debate on world order reform is almost totally devoid of any discussion emanating from an S_2 perspective. Most discussion of global reform is devoted to changes internal to the international system, and to the desirability of incurring a series of marginal adjustments as a consequence.

---

* In actuality, however, President Nixon had been leading an effort to reduce federal spending for domestic programs, an effort resisted by Congress but with insufficient political potency to override Presidential vetoes or to liberate impounded funds. In the Foreword to the Brookings study of the 1974 budget the authors note: "In any one year, presidents seldom propose major changes in the scope and role of the federal government. Such changes do occur, but usually in small steps whose implications are realized only after several years have passed. The federal budget for the fiscal year 1974, however, is a striking exception. Faced with the prospect of a substantial excess of spending over revenues in a period when large budget deficits would clearly be inflationary, the President decided not only to reduce the level of federal spending but to change national priorities. While leaving the structure of federal taxes and the current defense posture unchanged, he recommended a sweeping series of reductions in the domestic expenditures of the federal government, including elimination or sharp curtailment of many programs." [19]

Table 7-4. Defense Spending

	GNP (%)	Federal Budget (%)
FY 1950 (Pre-Korea)	4.5	27.7
FY 1953 (Korea peak)	13.3	62.1
FY 1964 (Last peace-time year)	8.3	41.8
FY 1968 (SEA peak)	9.4	42.5
FY 1970	8.2	38.4
FY 1971	7.5	34.5
FY 1972	7.0	31.0
FY 1973	6.4	30.0

Source: Annual Defense Department Report, FY 1973, p. 201.

Suggestive of these tight ideological blinders is the modest range of alternative spending patterns envisioned by the highly respected Brookings Institution annual review of the federal budget. For instance, in considering defense spending, the analysts compare the Administration's program for the period 1973–1979 with alternative budgets that reflect somewhat differing assumptions about the security requirements in each major mission area (strategic forces, ground combat forces, navy general-purpose forces, tactical air forces). The authors of the Brookings study insist that they have made "a deliberate effort to outline a relatively wide range of options." [20] But the lowest cost option considered for ground combat forces furing the 1973–1979 period would involve a reduction in average annual cost of only $2.3 billion from the Administration's program calling for an average annual cost of $22.2 billion.[21]

There is no effort to consider, even for illustrative purposes, the various possible revenue impacts over a five-year period of drastic disarmament, a cutback of the global security role to defense of homeland, or a national or bilateral shift to a strategic position of minimum deterrence. It is characteristic of reformist discussion to confine a consideration of options to those that can be accommodated without changing basic S_1 characteristics or the dominant United States role as primary global actor in S_1. The Brookings inquiry is regarded as "reasonable" and "responsible" partly because it does tacitly accept these constraints as boundaries on the range of its inquiry; such an acceptance helps fortify the governing consensus that any rejection of the basic assumptions of foreign policy would be "unreasonable" and "irresponsible." [22] This is the price that must be paid to gain access to the prevailing political dialogue. [23] Consequently, reformist perspectives are united in their effort to restrict public consideration of options to those that are system-maintaining. Indeed, the pressure is so great that the more clear-headed reformers tend to be labeled "way out," despite their advocacy of rather mild programs for change; they can become credible political figures only by providing constant reassurance of their allegiance to the system. For this reason also, a project such as WOMP, with its explicit system-changing focus, will be generally characterized as "way out," "naive," "idealistic," "impractical." As we have earlier suggested, the boundaries of "realism" will have to be significantly expanded during t_1.

A further reformist inhibition commonly seen in the United States is to accord prevailing orthodoxies complete "good faith" toward divergent points of view and to reject structural analysis of the self-serving motives which frequently infuse dominant groups or classes. In this regard, a comparison of budgetary options for defense spending is carried on as if the outcome of the debate depended on assessing the real defense needs of the country—the evidence for or against a particular arms posture is considered as if it were only a matter of assessing military missions and future contingencies. No plausible word is breathed in mainstream debates about the military–industrial complex, arms race momentum, the war system, and so on. [24] The Brookings study does consider the employment consequences of various levels of defense expenditures, but portrays the connection as just one additional factor to be considered in their overall effort at budget appraisal. These constraints on respectable analysis seem to function as elements of an ideology relied upon by a ruling group to maintain in existence the basic system of power/authority, including the world order system. Thus, especially in the United States, but elsewhere as well, it is difficult to penetrate S_1 frames of reference *even* for the sake of discussion. If an S_2 project should somehow be put before the government and the public, as was the case with general and complete disarmament (GCD) [25] in the early 1960's, it will be depreciated.*

---

* The temporary concern with GCD was a quite accidental mirror-image response to the espousal of drastic disarmament proposals by the Soviet government. The discussion of GCD became a charade, as neither side seemed genuinely interested. The Americans

These taboos on thought must be shattered. They function as mystifications at the present time, and quite literally frustrate the realization of the original American concept that government exists to promote the life, liberty, and happiness of its people. One way of thinking about world order education is as a way of renewing these domestic promises under vastly altered global circumstances. Our most fundamental claim is that the future of life, liberty, and happiness for Americans (and others) depends on the completion of $S_1 \rightarrow S_{2(WOMP)}$ within the next few decades, which would require taking the initial steps down Transition Path 1 as soon as possible.

Henry Kissinger, writing in 1968 before he became the top advisor to President Nixon, discerned that changes in relative power had become more a function of technological proficiency than territorial conquest, and that hence the acquisition of territory was of declining relative significance. However, he foresaw nothing more fundamental emerging from this development than an altered framework of conflict among sovereign states.[26]

It may be helpful to consider in greater detail the main proposals for global reform put forward by mainstream American statesmen in recent years. These proposals are basically concerned with *moderating* risks, costs, and inequities *within* the existing structure of a statist world order system. Nevertheless, there are important policy and normative variations that express different attitudes toward the agenda of existing world order problems. As with WOMP, it is common for mainstream statesmen to develop their reform proposals as specific responses to perceived problems.

Rostow–McNamara Proposals for World Order Reform

Walt Rostow and Robert McNamara, as principal advisors to Presidents Kennedy and Johnson, developed proposals aimed at world order reform. Their basic concern, of course, was to maintain sufficient strategic forces to deter the Soviet Union from provocative action, as well as from

---

were countering Soviet propaganda, and the Soviet Union lost their enthusiasm for disarmament when its propaganda value was lost. Both sides tacitly agreed to drop any serious effort to make disarmament proposals that its rival ought to take seriously and concentrated instead on making the status quo more safely manageable and the arms rivalry less financially debilitating.

direct attack. In their view, international "balance" and "stability" were associated with maintaining a credible deterrent. Convinced, also, that the Communist revolution was a threat to American interests, these policy-makers associated the prospects for Communist advance with instability and poverty in the Third World and reacted with acute sensitivity to Sino–Soviet advocacy of and professed support for "wars of national liberation." The Rostow–McNamara response was two-fold: they advocated a gigantic buildup of counterinsurgency capabilities to enable the defeat of liberation movements, and proposed major development assistance enabling conservative and reactionary governments to modernize rapidly enough to undercut the popular appeal of radical politics.

The Vietnam War was the crucial laboratory for this new "world order" concept. The hope of American policy-makers was to *defeat* a Communist-led insurgency—the prototypic war of national liberation—and thereby *deter* other potential revolutionary actors throughout the world; the American leaders hoped also to deter Moscow and Peking from providing support and encouragement. The task of counterinsurgency was understood to be only partly a matter of military prowess. Hence, the stress on "hearts and minds," "the other war," the so-called pacification effort to provide the government of South Vietnam with a social program that could command support, or more realistically, secure the acquiescence of the civilian population.[27] The basic objective was to maintain the international status quo as securely in relation to revolutionary violence as in relation to large-scale strategic force. As Walt Rostow argued back in 1967, lecturing at Leeds University in England, "if we have the common will to hold together and get on with the job, the struggle in Viet-Nam might be the last great confrontation of the postwar era."[28]

There were some notable variations. Robert McNamara, in a widely noticed 1966 speech delivered to a meeting of newspaper editors in Montreal, emphasized poverty more than Communism as a source of world tensions. He called upon the rich countries to assume a much larger burden in relation to the task of mitigating and overcoming world poverty. Indeed, Mr. McNamara seemed to be advancing the radical notion that national security had as much to do with feeding hungry people as with building missile silos. While speaking as Secretary of Defense in the midst of the Vietnam War, Mr. McNamara described "the central concept of security" as "a world of decency and development where every man can feel that his personal horizon is rimmed with hope."[29] If realistically implemented, such a vision would lead to positions that could move the country out beyond S_1, but such a radical proposal is not likely to proceed beyond the stage of rhetorical boldness.*

Walt Rostow, too, had elements of a transition strategy embroidering his "America first" vision of world order. He advocated sympathetic support for regionalist tendencies in the world as a preferred basis for structuring international political and economic relations. The development of regional arenas, he argued, would tend to erode statist logic and weaken national bonds of identification. Such a pattern of behavior would contribute momentum and centralizing direction to the $S_1 \rightarrow S_2$ transition; in fact, we project a similar course as a feature of Transition Path 1. As with McNamara's emphasis on poverty as a security issue, so Rostow's emphasis on regionalism as a security goal involved rhetoric with no prospect of translation into political reality. We find no specific ideas about how to overcome the statist logic that dominates political and economic behavior in every corner of world society (except Western Europe, where special circumstances were unusually conducive to the successful initiation of an ambitious experiment in regionalism).[31]

The Nixon–Kissinger Proposals for World Order Reform

A new emphasis in American foreign policy can be dated from 1968, when Richard Nixon became President. The basic objective of the Nixon Administration was to enable the United States to maintain its effective influence in foreign settings, but with considerably less expenditure of effort and resources—in order, hopefully, to diminish divisive strains in the domestic polity.

An essential feature of this approach was contained in Nixon's response to the Vietnam debate. This response was packaged as "the Nixon Doctrine" at the time of its original formulation at Guam in July, 1969, perhaps to invoke sympathetic associations with such generally celebrated presidential initiatives of the past as "the Monroe Doctrine" or "the Truman Doctrine." In Mr. Nixon's words, the Nixon Doctrine had three main elements:

---

* In McNamara's case there was a noticeable failure of follow-through or endorsement by President Johnson. At most, it was an unsuccessful trial balloon, released as an act of individual conscience by a strong-minded civil servant. Such bold suggestions for altered perceptions of national interest are more likely to come from counter-governmental voices such as Andrei Sakharov in the Soviet Union, whose proposals also proceed from the view that national security has to do with solving world social problems more than with weapons innovations.[30]

First, the United States will keep all of its treaty commitments.

Second, we shall provide a shield if a nuclear power threatens the freedom of a nation allied with us, or of a nation whose survival we consider vital to our security.

Third, in cases involving other types of aggression we shall furnish military and economic assistance when requested and as appropriate. But we shall look to the nation directly threatened to assume the primary responsibility for providing the manpower for its defense.[32]

The Nixon Doctrine is based on the central role of alliance politics in maintaining the United States' international position of preeminence throughout the Third World.* In Point 1, Nixon's reference to treaty commitments refers only to alliance treaties, not to a broad array of options in any emergent future situation. Point 2 is particularly disturbing in this respect. Who decides when a nuclear power "threatens the freedom" of a nation or what constitutes its "survival" or which nations are "vital to our security"? A reading of the *Pentagon Papers* shows, for instance, a highly exaggerated sense in Washington of North Vietnam's reliance on China's guidance vis-à-vis the struggle for control in South Vietnam, as well as an inflated view of the geopolitical significance of South Vietnam itself.

The Nixon Doctrine as applied to the final stages of the Indochina War meant several things:

A drastically increased willingness to use massive airpower and a decreased insistence on selective bombardment

An increased reliance on electronic warfare to inflict devastation without incurring battlefield casualties

An increased willingness to modernize national armies of allied governments

---

* Although the formulation is in general terms, its concerns were assumed to be focused on the American role in the Third World after Indochina. By affirming these alliance relations, Mr. Nixon was implicitly endorsing a continuation by other means of the counterrevolutionary role that led the United States to become involved in Vietnam. This endorsement was made clear by Nixon's subsequent claim of "peace with honor," by his unrelenting opposition to amnesty for draft resisters and evaders, by his diplomacy of support for counterrevolutionary regimes however brutal, and by appointment of such principal figures in the Indochina counterinsurgency program as William Sullivan, Mac-Murty Godley (confirmation refused by Senate Foreign Relations Committee), and William Colby to high positions associated with future counterinsurgency undertakings.

An increased effort to enter into burden-sharing partnership arrangements on security matters, especially with Japan in relation to Pacific affairs

In essence, a two-tiered system is employed: first order attempts—Vietnamization, Laotianization, Cambodianization; second order attempts—massive, virtually unrestricted American air and naval bombardment, reliance on the electronic battlefield, and the employment of mercenary forces as necessary (for example, use of Thai troops in Laos, and somewhat in Cambodia).

The objectives disclosed by the Nixon Doctrine are to uphold allied regimes by force, regardless of their capacity to govern and independent of the relation of forces within a given national arena of struggle. The new constraints involve carrying out this counterrevolutionary role without losing many American lives or generating a major outflow of U.S. dollars.

Mr. Nixon had been concerned with other changes in the world setting that should help reshape American foreign policy. Indeed, he decried "the tendency to almost totally obscure our vision of the world because of Viet-Nam." [33] The main changes since World War II that he perceived were:

A decline in military and economic power of the United States in relation to Japan and Western Europe

A narrowing, perhaps even a disappearance, of military advantage with respect to the Soviet Union and the absence of any prospect of securing such advantage in the future

The emergence of a strong and stable China that was isolated from the world and alienated from the Soviet Union

In these circumstances Nixon foresaw some shifts in emphasis at the strategic level:

The competitive horizons within the economic sphere were broadened to include political allies and the cooperative horizons could also be broadened to include political rivals

The basic framework of order in the world would be established by patterns of interaction among *five* centers of economic and military strength: the United States, Soviet Union, China, Western Europe, and Japan

Such principal power centers could probably be induced to negotiate differences rather than rely upon costly and risky confrontations. To attain these ends Nixon had encouraged China's participation in the world system, has negotiated arms agreements with the Soviet Union, has cultivated superpower détente, has inaugurated a new economic policy to improve the monetary and trade position of the United States relative to its European and Japanese allies, and has promised moderation in the pursuit of foreign policy goals

The Nixon–Kissinger approach is coherent, and reflects a determination to establish a new balance in world affairs based on their perception of the existing objective situation. It devotes almost no attention to the idealistic objectives generally associated with global reform or embodied in the United Nations Charter. The Nixon approach is based on stabilizing relations among the strong and rich, according little attention and less compassion to those sectors of the world confronted by widespread misery and oppression.* The Nixon Administration has made tangible demonstrations of support for such oppressive regimes as those in Greece, Haiti, the Philippines, and Brazil. At the same time it has not joined the international campaign to combat acute racism in southern Africa. Is this a realistic world order position? Does it maximize American interests in peace, power, prosperity, and prestige? † Is it desirable and possible for the United States Government to ignore poverty, oppression, dissatisfaction in the Third World?

The Nixon policies raise questions of judgment (i.e., which policies and practices will succeed, given traditional American foreign policy goals?) and ethics (i.e., what kind of priorities do we citizens want our leaders to have as a basis for dealing with the rest of the world?). The Nixon–Kissinger conception of global reform is based on "stability," "balance of power," "moderation"—that is, on an essentially nineteenth-century "concert" of actors.‡ As such, this Nixon–Kissinger

---

* Such a posture becomes more viable as a consequence of the muting of Cold War tensions, including a diminished sense of competition for influence in the Third World. There is a new willingness by the United States to rely on subtler forms of counterrevolutionary intervention than existed in the 1950's and 1960's, and to be less threatened by adverse political developments in a particular country. However, there is even less idealism than earlier, and hardly a pretense of objection to anti-democratic or cruel regimes.

† A very significant ambiguity surrounds the phrase "American interests." Do we rely upon our government to identify these interests? If we disagree with official policies which allegedly support these interests, to what higher standards of judgment do we appeal? Popular sentiment? Reasoned analysis of "true interests"? Moral or legal norms? A decent respect for the opinions of mankind? This book reflects the view that governing groups are locked into an obsolete system of values and beliefs and are, therefore, not capable of defining the interests of their populations.

‡ The nineteenth-century inspiration should not be taken literally. Kissinger is well aware of special factors in the present situation—the influence of nuclear deterrence, the

image of world order is fundamentally statist; * it lacks the Rostow–Mc-Namara humanitarian dimension of concern about world poverty and the internationalist commitment to the evolutionary buildup of regional and global institutions. Indeed, the Nixon Administration has used its influence to attack the United Nations in a number of ways: it has reduced American financial contributions, it has not energetically supported economic sanctions voted by the Security Council against Rhodesia, it has attacked the Secretary General for his "naive" expression of concern over reports in 1972 that U.S. bombs were falling on dikes and dams in North Vietnam, and it has not appointed leading national figures to represent the United States in the Organization. The Nixon–Kissinger orientation toward world order values does not advocate the promotion of WOMP values, even within the structure of S_1. The Rostow–McNamara program of reform (as distinct from its implementation) is generally consistent with WOMP values, although it failed to express any commitment to the $S_1 \rightarrow S_2$ scale of reform and it refrained from recommending major adjustments in America's world role.†

In our judgment, the prevailing world order debate is pretty much confined to these parameters of discussion. "Transition" is used to mean the passing of the bipolar era, the muting or ending of the Cold War, the fracturing of alliances, but not a shift in aspiration beyond the statist structures or normative priorities of S_1. Most influential formulations remain largely pre-ecological in character, either because they were developed before environmental concerns became salient or because these concerns are viewed as peripheral. Our view is that if the

---

heterogeneity of principal actors, the universality of scope. Nevertheless, the basic mechanisms and the overarching morality are reminiscent of this earlier age of Eurocentric diplomacy.[34] The concert image of global reform is discussed in Chapter III, pp. 201–206.

* The image is statist in an extremely hierarchical sense. It respects the autonomy and interests of the five or so dominant state (or statal, i.e., Western Europe) actors, not the autonomy and interests of the 140 or so states that constitute the state system. To the extent that the pentagonal concert achieves a degree of managerial control over global affairs it may be conceived as an S_2 option, and in a very basic sense is post-statal in character. We have also mentioned a possible coalition with globalizing efforts by leading corporate actors giving rise to an $S_{2(MNC)}$ option. As of t_0 or t_{1974} it seems most reasonable to regard the Nixon–Kissinger design as a saving strategy for S_1 rather than as a plea for a hierarchical variant of S_2.

† These absences of implementing strategy create some doubt as to whether these idealistic assertions were meant to be taken seriously. Can we endow the rhetoric of transformation with our approval if it is not directed toward actualization in history? The Nixon–Kissinger design is impressive partly because the reformist rhetoric was accompanied by appropriate implementing initiatives, the most spectacular of which was the Nixon visit to Peking in 1972.

Rostow–McNamara liberal strain of world order reform were reformulated today, it would give some emphasis to environmental quality issues, but that the Nixon–Kissinger conservative strain of world order reform is unwilling to accord these issues major status as real concerns of the present era.* The anxieties over assured overseas oil supplies represent an ecological issue of sorts, but the issue seems likely to revive a kind of neo-Darwinian quest for dominance, rather than a humanist assertion of the need to share scarce resources on some equitable basis. The ecological challenge will be posed with increasing frequency, and will compel governmental responses that are oriented either around neo-Darwinian or globalist principles of allocation.

MAINSTREAM WORLD DEBATE:
A NOTE IN CONCLUSION

For reasons expressed earlier, we find that support for S_1 has, if anything, been somewhat strengthened by recent developments.† The nonoccurrence of nuclear war since 1945 has engendered confidence in world stability and has discredited to some extent those who have argued that the emergence of weapons of mass destruction was tantamount to a death warrant for the human race. This confidence has been furthered, also, by the Soviet–American détente. Political credibility these days rests on relating proposals to programs of action that

---

* The Nixon Administration has made some gestures of support for a global approach to environmental problems, especially early in Mr. Nixon's first term. The United States urged NATO to expand its concerns to include environmental protection and it was the leading government supporting the 1972 Stockholm U.N. Conference on the Human Environment. However, on the level of action the record is disappointing—support for the SST subsidy, support for exempting the trans-Alaska pipeline from the Environmental Protection Act's requirement of an impact statement, reliance on environmental warfare in Indochina, and refusal to appropriate enough funds to the U.N. effort to make it a significant response.

† This S_1 strength may be deceptive. Globalizing tendencies arising from technological and economic developments are occurring at a rapid rate. The Great Power consensus could easily evolve into a managerial duopoly or oligopoly that amounts to an S_2 design. We may not be sufficiently sensitive to the extent to which the Kissinger–Nixon initiatives or the pleas of multinational corporations for "a-nationality" are part of an S_2 transition strategy. As with the $S_{2(WOMP)}$ options, we may not be in a position to identify their prospects until we can look back on them several decades hence.

seem attainable within a few years; that is, to marginal reforms that are compatible with existing political consciousness. Wider proposals for change are not being seriously considered in mainstream political discussion in the United States, although the beginnings of global populism and corporate globalism can be discerned in political discussion.

At the same time, unofficial world order speculation is spreading in scope and depth, and is shifting from the advocacy of $S_1 \rightarrow S_2$ to a serious effort to study how transition might be accomplished within a relatively short period of time. The critical emphasis of WOMP/USA on Transition Path 1, on the process of world order design, and on activating and orienting agents of change is suggestive of a new intellectual climate. It is important for those individuals who reject S_1 frameworks of reform or certain S_2 options to manifest their opposition in visible and constructive forms.* By itself the affirmation of an $S_{2(WOMP)}$ ethos is of little value. In fact, it may even be counterproductive, strengthening support for S_1 or repressive S_2 options by suggesting that adherents of the WOMP ideology are sentimental idealists unwilling to assume the risks of challenging current power-wielders with more than easy rhetorical flourishes.† Examples of such world order impotency are the various manifestos signed by famous men who profess their belief in a peaceful, human world community, without offering any challenge to the nexus of power/authority which sustains the present antithetical world order system.

---

* The sorts of action which seem "constructive" vary with time, place, and judgment. Symbolic actions may be the most effective kinds of initiative in t_1. The award of the Nobel Peace Prize to Henry Kissinger in 1973 represents one kind of challenge to the sort of value perspectives embodied in the WOMP approach to global reform; intelligent and dramatic forms of opposing such an award would be an example of visible and constructive individual action. For instance, suppose—by analogy with anti-war veterans who threw away their medals in a demonstration—that it would be possible to persuade Nobel laureates to renounce their prize.

† There is a serious issue of sincerity in relation to the advocacy of drastic global reform of a progressive kind. Proponents, virtually by definition, lack access to official power and rarely command large resources. If their words are not related to some conception of transformation, their commitment has a questionable status. If their actions are not an embodiment of their commitment, issues of sincerity are posed. However, we are not proposing absolute tests of commitment. We would not expect adherents of WOMP values to embody within their personal existence all of the implications of such a systemic adjustment, e.g., contribute their individual wealth to the alleviation of poverty. Perhaps leaders of a global reform movement, in order to be credible, would have to embody fully the values they propose in their present modes of existence.

THE CASE AGAINST S2(WOMP) AS THE PROPER
BASIS FOR U.S. FOREIGN POLICY

Our argument reflects the view that S_1 possibilities do not offer much prospect of solving salient human problems, that S_1 embodies serious risks of breakdown, and that the maintenance of security in S_1 is exceedingly expensive in financial and moral terms. These concerns existed in a pre-ecological setting. With the added set of concerns about the human environment, the fragmented and laissez-faire structures and attitudes associated with S_1 seem sharply incompatible with human welfare and survival over a time period as short as the next few decades. We do not know the exact magnitude of the risk and are not able to anticipate the date of ecological collapse, but we do observe a series of negative trends and we note storm warnings in various sectors of human experience.[35]

It could be argued that the United States should seek to maintain its privileged status in a world of scarcity and vulnerability. The United States enjoys sufficient material advantages for the entire population to have a decent life prospect, without seriously altering the American domestic economic and political system. Furthermore, American nuclear capabilities preclude an attack by a rival society. Constant improvements in "command and control," the moderation of Cold War antagonisms, and the frank avowal of a posture of mutual deterrence have reduced the risks of large-scale warfare to a practical minimum. American leaders contend that the costs of this security system, while high, are easily bearable and comprise a declining share of both the Federal Budget and GNP; defense was 8.3% of GNP in FY 1964; it is 6.4% in FY 1973; it represented 41.8% of the Federal Budget in FY 1964, 30% in FY 1973. These defense costs are far less, in relative terms, than are being borne by much poorer countries confronted by active dangers of war such as Israel, Egypt, India, China, and Pakistan.

With respect to world order itself, the case for S_1 includes the statist orientations of countries less advantaged than the United States. Both socialist and Third World governments are sovereignty-oriented, regarding globalist solutions as dangerous threats to their national autonomy. There is, in other words, very little evidence that other sectors of world society are currently receptive to the adoption of any S_2 projects. There is some concern, in fact, that the only plausible S_2 projects would perpetrate patterns of dominance rather than establish the more egalitarian kind of world order implicit in $S_{2(WOMP)}$. American advocacy of an S_2 approach to global reform is appropriately received with deep-seated suspicion and fear at the present time, regardless of how idealistic its rhetoric might be. From this point of view it would seem that any viable movement for system-change on a world level must originate elsewhere than the United States, and it especially must not be regarded as a goal of the government or the business elite.

A further line of resistance has to do with the fear of uncertainty. Systemic transitions have tended to be bloody and traumatic. S_1 itself came into being after a long grim period of bloodshed and barbarism, culminating in the religious wars of the seventeenth century known as the Thirty Years War. Challenges to S_1 have been associated with World Wars I and II. It is widely believed that a feasible S_2 proposal is contingent upon World War III as a *necessary* (although not necessarily a *sufficient* condition), making such an eventuality an occasion of horror rather than enhancement. There are compelling reasons why sane and moral men refrain from thinking too hard about the unthinkable.*

A final line of resistance to global reform arises from our inability to weigh comparative dangers in a convincing fashion. This inability makes many people prefer the known to the unknown. In a privileged society such as the United States which derives huge benefits from S_1, there are many reasons to remain conservative about reformist risk-taking. Americans have a lot to lose. For others, S_2 represents an inevitable concentration of planetary power somewhere else. This new power nexus, it is feared, would only generate new dangers of global tyranny of a particularly repressive character, possibly in such a consolidated form as to be irreversible. It is not worth sacrificing present levels of prosperity, security, autonomy, and diversity, given the propensity of power-wielders in every setting to impose their will by coercive means and given the technological possibilities that are beginning to make global administration a manageable undertaking. Furthermore, some believe that the scale of poverty exceeds the stock of resources in such a way that a sharing ethos would reduce everyone to a life of impoverished misery, rather than raise the poor to a life of dignity in exchange for skimming excess affluence.

It is probable that most Americans are habitual S_1 partisans and do not base their commitment on an explicit rationale. This habit of belief is fortified by power-wielders in the United States who affirm tradi-

---

* The phrase "thinking about the unthinkable" was aptly invented by Herman Kahn, whose work well illustrates what happens when amoral cerebral energy is turned loose on the ultimate jeopardies of the human race. Whether his subject matter involves "winning" in Vietnam, recovery from nuclear war, or the shape of the future, the same "liberated imagination" is demonstrated—liberated not from the false constraints of conventionality (as he would have us believe) but from the real concerns of the human species.[36]

tional patriotism as an intrinsic good, and refuse to present the public with a choice between S_1 and some beneficial variant of S_2. These power-wielders are generally sincere when they identify national welfare almost exclusively with the retention of existing domestic and global structures of wealth and power. The domestic commitment to private property rights in the United States, including virtually unrestricted rights to accumulate and transmit capital, reinforces a neo-Darwinian acceptance of the legality and justice of retaining fruits acquired through conquest and competition. Given this belief system, a "prudent" American politician is as yet unable to advocate an $S_{2(WOMP)}$ program of global reform. Even "radical" political programs involve no more than a critique of the U.S. role in the world system, and tend to refrain from "structural" proposals to achieve drastic global reform.*

THE CASE FOR $S_{2(WOMP)}$ AS THE PROPER BASIS FOR U.S. FOREIGN POLICY

We will not repeat earlier arguments bearing on the desirability and feasibility of $S_{2(WOMP)}$, except to relate them to the particular circumstances of the American situation. We also acknowledge that the position taken here reflects an underlying set of judgments and preferences. There can be no "demonstration" of several key contentions—that S_1 will collapse or be superseded, that some version of S_2 will be enacted in any event, and that it is desirable for Americans to support a particular version of S_2 associated with WOMP values. Our advocacy of $S_{2(WOMP/USA)}$ rests on six essential elements:

1. S_1 is disintegrating rapidly and dangerously.

2. Some alternative world order system (S_2) will take shape in the next several decades.

3. The best world order solution would involve some variant of an $S_{2(WOMP)}$ program of global reform.

---

* Domestic reformism often stops at the water's edge. European socialists have often demonstrated the primacy of their nationalist sentiments, even to the extent of supporting colonialist projects. For example, the French socialists supported the military efforts by France after World War II to keep Indochina within the French Empire. As yet, the cause of global humanism has not been espoused very consistently by politically potent groups, even if their domestic orientation is humanist in character. For this reason our initial stress in t_1 is upon educating the public on issues of global reform.

4. It is possible to influence the outcome of this transition process and to make the process itself less violent and dangerous.

5. The best strategy for Americans involves commitment to the rapid realization of $S_{2(WOMP/USA)}$ by means of Transition Path 1.

6. The best tactics available for Americans to initiate Transition Path 1 involve a combination of world order education and an active commitment to nonviolent change-oriented politics (associated with equity, dignity, and ecological balance) within the domestic arena.

S_1 seems destined to be superseded; the American position of relative advantage cannot endure in its present form.* There are too many perceived deprivations, scarcities, and capabilities for disruption in different parts of the world. The proliferation of disruptive capabilities is taking place at an accelerating rate; it is symbolized, but not exhausted, by the latent capacity to produce weapons of mass destruction in any part of the globe. The vulnerability of S_1 to disintegration also reflects the deepening ecological decay stemming from global processes of industrialization, urbanization, population increase, and GNP growth. The most affluent members of S_1 are increasingly anxious about their vulnerability to shortages of energy supplies or other resources. S_1 is a viable system only so long as conditions of *distance* and *abundance* characterize the basic world setting. But with the advent of modern weapons and communications technology, no part of the world is remote from any other; increases in world population and industrial wastes are exceeding the accommodating capacities of the planet. Under these conditions, a system of fragmented power and authority is increasingly unable to satisfy minimum needs for order, justice, and durability. The relative dominance of the United States and other advanced industrial sectors makes it harder to arrange for a peaceful and humane transition to a more coordinated world system, but it also creates an unusual opportunity for enlightened world leadership that combines self-interest with the genuine well-being of the planet.†

---

* As we have pointed out, there are two sets of options: an array of S_2 organizational patterns and a broad ethical choice between hierarchical domination and global sharing. The United States might be able to retain its advantaged position by means of implementing a hierarchical form of S_2. The most "romantic" outlook is to believe that collapse and chaos can be avoided by some mechanism of central guidance, without replacing the state system.

† The more likely adjustment by the rich and powerful is to entrust the managerial role to the governmental or corporate centers of dominance in S_1, i.e., central guidance, but in such a way as to subordinate equity claims. The rationale for such subordination will un-

Aside from considerations of interest and prudence, there are powerful intrinsic reasons to prefer $S_{2(WOMP)}$ options over S_1 or Darwinian versions of S_2. In S_1 we are violating the basic creed of human community by premising national security upon a persisting threat to kill millions of innocent victims in a foreign country and to wreak havoc on the planet. Such a threat can be morally indulged only if it is repressed, thereby alienating ourselves from reality in a basic way. The same results follow from paying farmers in America not to plant crops in a world suffering from mass malnutrition and widespread hunger, or to restrict food exports so as to keep domestic prices low.* Such profound inequality, whether at home or abroad, fragments humanity into privileged and victimized sectors, and creates an inevitable condition of exploitation and servitude with all the apparatus of mystification and repression that such a structure entails.

The affluence of our society is beginning to turn in upon itself so as to produce a range of negative effects including pollution, crowding, ugliness, despiritualization, and cynicism.† A laissez-faire social order proceeds at increasing costs even in domestic society, and its ravages on a world level are reflected in the fate of endangered animal species, and the general decline in the quality of the oceans and other large international seas. Further increases in *quantity* are no longer necessary for improvements in *quality*.‡ Enhancing the life experience of the affluent classes will depend on valuational and distributive processes,

---

doubtedly involve some version of "trickle down" thinking in which the poor are expected to share in the overall process of enrichment, but to no special degree. See Chapter VI, p. 378 for a critique of this line of thinking.

* American consumers are bearing the burden of food exports through higher prices in domestic markets, but it is not satisfactory to increase food supplies at home or fight domestic inflation by curtailing the right of foreign societies to purchase our food surpluses they need to feed their populations. Tax reforms and other social policies need to be adopted to avoid a regressive impact on the purchasing power of our least advantaged citizens.

† The American vision of the future as of t_{1974} is a "Clockwork Orange" vision—pervasive amorality and dulled feeling in a material environment constituted by plastic objects and neon colors. The traits produced incline society toward sado-masochism of an extreme character, illustrated by grotesque private and public criminality and by a growing loss of identification with victims of cruelty and violence. In this sense, ghetto crime and Indochina War tactics express the same psychic deterioration.

‡ For those many Americans without decent housing, health and recreation facilities, schooling, food, clothing, such an assertion is not accurate—increases in quantity do constitute increases in quality. But for two-thirds or more of the society, provided with the means to realize its needs, the additional resources at its disposal do not result in a better life. Part of the difficulty here arises from the society's failure to beneficially allocate public goods. For instance, the failure of the city and mass transit are, in part at least, a reflection of economic pressures brought to bear by the construction and auto industries.

building a social order based on liberty, dignity, and happiness. This building process depends on creating an $S_{2(WOMP)}$ consciousness that moves beyond an S_1 frame of mind, without embracing a coercive variant of S_2.

S_1 structures impinge on foreign policy-making in the United States, creating persistent contradictions between the political creed of this country and its pattern of overseas commitments. The leadership of the American government consistently supports rightist or militarist foreign governments that repress, and even torture, their own citizenry. Why? The Cold War seems more and more like a rationalization, rather than an explanation.* Such support preceded the Cold War, especially in Latin America and Asia, and will undoubtedly survive its moderation. The United States government has intervened overtly or covertly against progressive movements throughout the Third World (but especially in Latin America and Asia) to safeguard investments and influence, and to assure a climate conducive to the operations of international capitalism in the era of the multinational corporation. It should be noted that America's dominant position in S_1 creates a counterrevolutionary disposition to intervene in this regressive fashion; † comparable counterrevolutionary patterns exist in the socialist world, and are associated with Stalinist and neo-Stalinist support for regressive counterinsurgency in Eastern Europe. These patterns of rule and foreign policy are strengthened by anxieties common among power-wielders who tend to perceive threats in an exaggerated manner.

What we suggest, therefore, is that individual self-realization is increasingly difficult for Americans living in a world based on S_1 logic. This difficulty undermines also the conditions for democracy and human rights at home because of the government's need to cope with real or imagined militant challenges mounted by its own citizens against its domestic and foreign policies.‡ Counterinsurgency becomes

---

* In moving toward détente the Nixon Administration has been singularly undisturbed by growing evidence of Soviet repression of domestic political dissent. Why should the U.S. government be disturbed by Soviet behavior that is less severe than the sort of repressive tactics we endorse in Indonesia, Greece, South Vietnam, Haiti, Brazil, and elsewhere?

† It is not only intervention, but endorsement. The United States quickly recognized the military junta in Chile that overthrew Allende despite its repudiation of democratic principles and summary execution of political opponents on a massive scale (what has been called "the Jakarta solution," a reference to the bloodbath that followed the anti-Sukarno military camp in Indonesia in 1965).

‡ The Watergate testimony of James McCord, John Dean, John Ehrlichman, and H. R. Haldeman reveal how far this domestic "security complex" had gripped the Nixon leadership.

the characteristic stance of the government toward its own population and toward elected officials. Security policy and surveillance expand their role as the leaders increasingly rely on secrecy and deception; "checks and balances" and "the separation of powers" wither away, while an apparatus of informers, provocateurs, and inquisitors builds up. We contend that the adoption by the United States government of a counterinsurgency posture in domestic politics represents an almost unavoidable response by a powerful actor pursuing its interests in an S_1 world setting, and cannot be accounted for by the corruption or perversion of a particular elite.* The S_1 crisis exerts strains which produce a series of domestic crises, which in turn lead every major progressive social and political movement down the path of betrayal.† It is naive and foolish to suppose that we can reverse this situation without a drastic reordering of the world order system along the lines of $S_{2(WOMP)}$. The longer we defer this realization, the harder it will be for this nation to make the adjustments in behavior and outlook necessary to reach some variant of $S_{2(WOMP)}$.

LITMUS ISSUES DURING EARLY t_1

In this section, we will consider the possibilities of expanding world order and foreign policy debates within the United States to include S_2 goals as realistic alternatives to S_1 reform.‡ The initial step along Transition Path 1 involves reorienting domestic political consciousness, espe-

---

* The blatant abuse by Nixon of the constitutional order and the accidental aperture created by the Watergate fiasco have probably given the society "a breathing spell." However, the tendencies toward domestic counterinsurgency were pre-Nixon in origin and the pressures on the government to control citizen opposition will undoubtedly persist for a long time even though Nixon has departed from the scene.

† Such national movements become repressive to avoid vulnerability to their real or suspected enemies (i.e., a blood path) or expose their own followers to counterrevolutionary terror (i.e., a blood bath). The dilemma is pronounced and tragic, and suggests that we must try to change *the whole* (the path of global reform), as well as *the part* (the path of national reform).

‡ A first step in this direction would be to regard the range of S_2 options, including the negative ones, as relevant issues of foreign policy choice for the United States. As matters now stand, these globalizing tendencies are not perceived as system-changing challenges.[37]

cially in the United States. Certain "litmus issues" are particularly apt for testing the relative strength of various system-changing perspectives, and for identifying value positions consistent with the WOMP outlook.

In our view, potential ways of resolving these issues are at the present time almost always constrained by an S_1 horizon of aspiration. Even enlightened and progressive individuals who act within the power-authority nexus tend still to be so conditioned by S_1 reasoning and imagery that they take it for granted. Such individuals must be persuaded that feasible and desirable S_2 potentialities do exist, whose policy relevance and implications deserve at least to be examined. Or, to put the issue differently, these individuals must be educated to understand that since we are inclining toward an $S_1 \rightarrow S_2$ transformation in any event, the more important creative challenge is to find ways of working on behalf of a positive S_2 outcome.[38]

In an American context, principal prospects for drastic global reform can be distinguished as follows:

$S_1 \rightarrow$ Transition Path 1 $\rightarrow S_{2(WOMP/USA)}$ or any $S_{2(WOMP)}$

$S_1 \rightarrow$ Transition Path 2 $\rightarrow S_{2(IMP)}$ or $S_{2(CON)}$ or $S_{2(MNC)}$

$S_1 \rightarrow$ Transition Path 3 $\, > S_{2(Violent\ Anarchy)}$

As suggested in Chapter III, Transition Path 1, although turbulent, could probably be kept relatively nonviolent and non-traumatic in the course of moving progressively to realize S_2. In Transition Path 2, the process and the outcome would both be regressive, leading probably to American domination but conceivably to America's victimization.* In Transition Path 3, we would expect a global war fought with weapons of mass destruction or a major ecological catastrophe, leading to chaos and disorder such as that of the late feudal period, before power and authority were consolidated in state structures. These three transition paths to S_2 are intended only to suggest a broader range of world order possibilities, and to make clear the point that not all S_2 outcomes are beneficial.

---

* It is possible that geopolitical karate could shift the locus of dominance away from the United States and that instead of remaining dominant the country would become subordinate and victimized. It is also possible that Transition Path 2 would lead to a new world order system in which nongovernmental actors (probably business organizations) emerged as dominant.

STRATEGIC POSTURE IN RELATION
TO NATIONAL SECURITY

Throughout the Nuclear Age, one prime litmus issue has been the role of nuclear weapons in U.S. security policy. The American development and use of these weapons during World War II has given their role a special significance. After World War II, American proposals to internationalize the control over atomic energy were rejected by the Soviet Union. It is unclear whether this rejection was based on genuine Soviet concern over her own vulnerability to an American-dominated international control scheme, or whether it reflected primarily a preference for a competitive world system in the Nuclear Age.[39] In any event, an S_1 approach to nuclear weapons prevailed after World War II, generating a nuclear weapons race between the Soviet Union and the United States, and a proliferation problem of as yet uncertain proportions. It is symbolic, if coincidental, that the five nuclear powers in the world are also the five permanent members of the Security Council.*

Throughout the Nuclear Age, a continuous debate of sorts has focused on national strategy regarding two key issues: first, the proper role of nuclear weapons in security planning; second, the level of capabilities needed to assure the fulfillment of this role.

The debate still goes on. Do we expect nuclear weapons to deter a nuclear attack only upon the United States? Or do we also expect nuclear weapons to deter "provocative" initiatives anywhere in the world, whether launched by the Soviet Union, by other nuclear adversaries of the United States, or by a non-nuclear adversary?

Issues of "sufficiency" and "reliability" are often raised in connection with each of these roles. To deter a Soviet surprise attack, must we be able to destroy 100 percent of Soviet industrial capacity, 80 percent, 20 percent, or 5 percent? To deter such an attack, must we have 10, 100, 1,000, or 10,000 deliverable weapons that each have a 50 percent, 70 percent, 99 percent chance of surviving a surprise Soviet attack? Do we need to maintain land, sea, and air delivery systems? When do these systems become obsolete or obsolescent? [40]

To date, the Pentagon's view of these matters has generally carried

---

* Nuclear status, permanent membership on the Security Council, and participation in world monetary discussions are among the indications of hierarchy in the present phase of S_1. Such hierarchical arrangements may be less onerous for poor sectors of the world than for their colonial antecedents, but the world system is in no sense operating according to notions of sovereign equality embedded in the classical expositions of S_1 organizational logic.

the day: we need to plan for "the worst possible case" vis-à-vis our potential enemy's intentions and capabilities. Given secrecy and long lead times, this planning outlook encourages the acquisition of weapons far in excess of national defense needs.

There is also considerable debate as to whether excessive military capabilities primarily provide "bargaining chips" in arms control negotiations, or serve merely to strengthen the military orientations of adversary elites, each of whom makes a convincing presentation of its security needs on the basis of its own "worst possible case" analysis. The interactive features of the arms race are evident, especially given the fear or pursuit of a decisive technological breakthrough.

Only recently has the position of Pentagon planners been seriously challenged by Congress. The expense and waste of this security system is beginning, but only just beginning, to trouble Congress and the general public as well. Such questioning is deepened by the apparent muting of Cold War antagonisms and by the military oversell associated with maintaining a decade of support for an unsuccessful Indochina War. However, the basic momentum and logic of arms competition persists, and indeed a series of governmental requests for new weapons systems designed to increase both the flexibility and effectiveness of response in crisis situations was authorized as recently as 1972–1973. President Nixon favors creating enough response options so that decisions to retaliate with nuclear weapons can be made with high degrees of flexibility.[41] The insistence on intermediate retaliatory options may mean targeting "hard" targets and avoiding enemy population centers, thereby imposing greater accuracy and penetration requirements on weapons systems. But more accurate weapons by definition imperil strike-back capabilities; they therefore create a strong incentive for the adversary to strike first, should it perceive an attack to be imminent. A debate is also underway over the relative merits of threatening cities or weapons systems, for although it is allegedly inhumane to attack the former, to attack the latter might make nuclear warfare more routine and possibly more likely. This debate also extends to the deployment of defensive weapons systems [42] to protect cities or retaliatory capabilities.*

By and large, the American strategic posture has aimed at maintaining an enormous massive retaliatory capability based on redundant air, sea, and land systems. The missions and targets assigned are kept am-

---

* Defensive deployments have been sharply curtailed as a result of the 1972 ABM Treaty between the United States and the Soviet Union.

biguous, to discourage potential adversaries from taking various marginal risks. Naturally, our government would like the Soviet government to believe that a large number of moves on its part might trigger mutually-destructive nuclear war. But to make Soviet planners believe in this possibility, it is necessary to make the threat credible— that is, to demonstrate a credible willingness to act when challenged. Is this margin of ambiguity desirable, or useful?

We believe that the war system, the basic foundation of S_1, is increasingly, though still slightly, being challenged within the United States.[43] This early challenge will probably take the form of a *debate* carried on outside official circles, and become policy-relevant only after several years. Briefly, the three elements of the system-changing challenge are as follows:

1. A movement away from a flexible, deterrent posture based on maintaining R & D superiority, and toward a minimum deterrent posture in which nuclear weapons would be designed only to deter a direct nuclear attack on the United States; such a reformulation of national security might be accompanied by various efforts to secure "openness" or even a negotiated "freeze" on weapons development in rival societies.

2. The consideration and adoption of a "no first use" doctrine, either by declaration or agreement, as part of an effort to de-nuclearize international politics by outlawing these weapons except in retaliation for their prior use; in actuality a "no first use" position is embodied in the minimum deterrence posture.

3. The serious consideration of "general and complete disarmament" as a goal of national policy and as a subject for international negotiations; such seriousness would include developing proposals that ought to be accepted or at least taken seriously by other governments.* Earlier "general and complete disarmament" proposals have usually been propagandistic, in the sense that they were intended as palliatives for public aspirations for peace, rather than as either serious proposals to foreign governments or real options in domestic policy-making arenas.†

---

* "Ought to" in the sense of being formulated in an even-handed, reasonable, and precise manner, so that their rejection seems arbitrary to an impartial observer.

† There are a number of factors that make the reconsideration of GCD appropriate at this time: Soviet–American détente; Sino–American normalization; disillusionment with military options to secure foreign policy objectives; strategic stalemate; huge outlay of resources and energies to sustain the stalemate; a long list of domestic claims on

In t₁ we would expect each of these initiatives to be increasingly considered and advocated within the United States, if social forces favoring Transition Path 1 are achieving political alertness and gaining in their relative popular strength. During the past decade, disillusionment with military approaches to foreign policy as a result of the Indochina War, and rising pressures to divert more of the government budget to non-military uses, have combined to make S_1 logic less dominant in public consciousness. Hopefully, challenges from other perspectives can be mounted at this time. There is greater receptivity to innovative ideas, less tacit deference to Pentagon planners, more public skepticism about governmental preferences than in earlier years. On the other hand, a regressive S_1 variant remains dominant, and indeed is represented by a civilian ruling group that is particularly responsive to the outlook of the military–industrial establishment. This group has evolved a geopolitical design to sustain S_1 or supersede it by an S_2 variant that preserves its moral defects. It seems likely, however, that the distintegration of S_1 will be preceded by a period of polarization, in which the progressive portion of the national elite challenges the power-wielders from a position that moves toward an $S_{2(WOMP/USA)}$ outlook—tacitly at first, explicitly later on. Figure 7–1 presents one interpretation of the way in which national political parties will handle the challenge of transition with respect to defense spending.

ALLIANCE POLITICS VERSUS CONCERT POLITICS VERSUS CHARTER POLITICS

During S_1, the overriding issue in classical international relations involves devising a national strategy enabling successful participation in "the war system." [44] Indicative of the systemic or general character of this problem is the fact that every governmental actor accepts the premises of the war system as the foundation of its security. "Security" is an exceedingly ambiguous word that may include the use of force for purposes of economic, ideological, or territorial expansion. The perceived security needs of government X may be threatened by a political struggle in state Y, or by the invasion of Y by Z.*

---

resources devoted to military purposes; and prospect of a militarized world society in which danger of irrational war increases.

* National security for weak states means the maintenance of territorial integrity and formal independence. For somewhat stronger states it means territorial integrity and real independence in most essential respects. For the stronger states it means these attain-

Figure 7–1. Platform Advocacy of Defense Posture (as Measured in Dollars) by Principal Parties as Indicator of Consensus and Prevailing World Order Mood

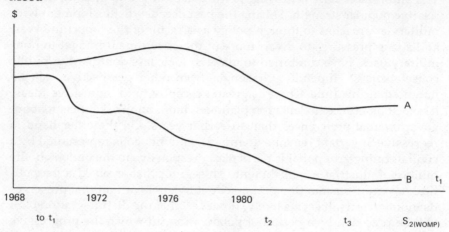

Party A consistently takes more conservative positions on defense spending, whereas Party B takes more progressive positions; we would assume that A is dominant until the middle of t_1, although more and more directly confronted; by the end of t_1, B would become the dominant position, reshaping a new political consensus that would persist in t_2 and t_3, and gradually build the basis for official American efforts to achieve $S_{2(WOMP/USA)}$; the graph is illustrative. Actually, A and B might reverse platform positions in response to struggles for ascendancy within their own party ranks, but we are assuming that the A position associated with S_1 thinking lasts until a substantial reorientation of political consciousness occurs within the United States.

International law has attempted to circumscribe the orbit of ambiguity by confining the *legitimate* threat or use of force to situations of self-defense (including collective self-defense), and designating all other national uses of force as "aggression." * In the wake of World Wars I and II

---

ments plus the maintenance of certain favorable geopolitical and geo-economic conditions. The Monroe Doctrine, for instance, staked an American claim as of 1823 to resist the extension of European influence to Latin America; no other Western Hemisphere government could have credibly staked such a claim. In 1968 the Soviet Union led an intervention into Czechoslovakia to depose Dubček, thereby positing a claim of geopolitical hegemony in Eastern Europe. The inequality of states and the diversity of foreign policy goals of governments (e.g., compare Weimar and Hitler Germany's foreign policies) make the idea of security in international affairs exceedingly imprecise.

* International law (a perspective based on equality, mutuality, and reciprocity) is in constant tension with geopolitics (a perspective based on inequality, hegemony, hierarchy), although both perspectives play significant roles in the logic and operation of S_1.

and the advent of nuclear weapons, every government has formally accepted these restraints on its discretion; however, the significance of this acceptance is far from clear. There are no adequate procedures for identifying illegal or wrongful uses of force, nor for prohibiting aggressive uses of force. Every government is, in effect, a self-judge, and international assessments are more likely to reflect political preferences than to implement legal norms. As a result, there is a great deal of cynicism about claims that international law can limit state violence. There is no general agreement as to what constitutes aggression or self-defense. There has even been a revival of national claims to use force for humanitarian ends, such as when communal strife turned genocidal in East Pakistan (1971) and Burundi (1972).[45] The insistence on national competence to use force in situations other than self-defense can be partially explained by the United Nations' inability to protect victim states from destructive violence.

Most governments rely primarily on a combination of self-help capabilities (i.e., their national defense establishment) and bilateral or multilateral alliances to sustain their security. Note, also, that the security needs of many governments may be far broader than those of states, as particular governments are often confronted by domestic opposition movements which threaten to use warlike strategies.* In S_1, decisions to intervene in foreign civil strife are generally treated as matters of national discretion, whether the interventionary claim rests on support for the just cause, or upon the legitimacy of constituted authority.

The United States, despite its awesome power, defines its security in diffuse and ambiguous terms which encompass a far wider range of concerns than simply defending national territory against armed attack or maintaining political independence. The United States has more than forty commitments in treaty form and a host of "vital interests" which, if infringed upon, would induce recourse to force.† Hundreds of American military installations dot the non-Communist world; naval fleets roam the western Pacific, the eastern Mediterranean Sea, and the

---

* Thus, a state may be under no threat of external attack, but still seek a close alliance with a powerful government willing to supply it with arms, training, and possibly "a presence" in order to deal with a militant insurgency. Indeed, the beleaguered incumbent subordinates the security of the state by inviting its foreign ally to enter the territory and maintain the security of the government.

† Note that these alliances are not mutual (with the possible exception of NATO), but constitute American commitments to help foreign governments; given the military characteristics of the Nuclear Age, it would be absurd for a country or even Europe to offer help to the United States (or the Soviet Union). These alliances are largely treaties of protection given to foreign rulers sympathetic to the United States.

Indian Ocean. For more than a decade, the United States has fought a major war to protect a non-Communist government in South Vietnam. Our space satellites are engaged in surveillance operations that encompass the globe. The United States is at once the strongest state in the world and also the one most willing to engage its military capabilities in distant regions of the world.

Since World War II this country has identified its own national security with the maintenance of "the Free World," i.e., the non-Communist sector of world society.* This security rationale has involved direct American military operations against Communist probes, most spectacularly during the Cuban Missile Crisis (1962) and in the Korean War (1950–1952). More characteristic have been the efforts to assist anti-Communist regimes faced with domestic challenges, especially if the insurgents seemed to be receiving aid or encouragement from major Communist centers of power. The American concept of security has meant deterrence, together with maintaining a far-flung alliance network.

In the Nixon period there has been an emphasis on "Concert Politics," bilateral summit meetings with rival leaders in China and the Soviet Union. These meetings were initially held in 1972 without prior consultation with such major allies as Japan and the NATO countries, and in obvious opposition to the wishes of the American "ally" on Taiwan. The Brezhnev–Nixon Declaration of Principles was evidently formulated on a bilateral basis without wider negotiation, provoking dismay in friendly foreign capitals.[47] These developments disclose an American effort to establish a framework for superpower coordination within which to conduct essential international relations.† This new diplomacy also reflects a growing sense among American leaders that economic relationships with former allies may provoke the most intense and dangerous international competition in the years ahead. Hence, geopolitics will soon see both the United States and the Soviet Union embroiled in deepening rivalries with their respective former allies, while the ideological identity of individual governments becomes less and less relevant as a basis for political affinity. The Soviet

---

* Whether the avowed anti-Communist crusade is a cover story for imperial adventure or is actually the real explanation is a matter of current controversy.[46] Both lines of explanation have probably played a part in influencing various policy-makers in various global situations.

† Such an American initiative may also be conceived as a possible move toward an $S_{2(CON)}$ option, either to offset renewed geo-economic rivalry, or to neutralize the growing anti-statism of the multinational corporate elite.

Union's counterrevolutionary relationship to political developments within its own society and in Eastern Europe, as well as the Chinese response to the Indo–Pakistan War and to Bangladesh's claim of self-determination, also suggest a drift toward statism within the Communist world, in the context of an accommodation with the West. Under such circumstances, détente is reinforced on both sides by trade prospects and other incentives which present tangible advantages for interest groups who might otherwise obstruct the movement toward an East–West political reconciliation. The 1972 U.S.–Soviet wheat deal is an excellent illustration of the economic spill-over of détente.*

These diplomatic moves represent primarily an attempt to rehabilitate the American role in S_1, given the collapse of the post-war world economic structure and the major loss of prestige in Indochina. This rearrangement is not being challenged in any serious way within mainstream American politics. There is widespread American support for moving toward more moderate participation in $S_{1(1970's)}$, and for giving greater attention to reforming the main international economic arrangements governing trade, money, and investment. At present, there is only sporadic concern within the United States about official America's disenchantment with the United Nations. It should be understood that the United Nations has never been accorded more than a modest relevance for foreign policy, but it often proved a useful arena for national policy-makers at the height of the Cold War, when American-oriented majorities could give a cover of global legitimacy to anti-Communist alliance-based security claims. There is no well-organized constituency that favors reorienting U.S. foreign policy around Charter principles.†
In fact, the main critique of the Nixon approach comes from those who, like George Ball, view Nixon summitry as adventurist, weakening the chief bulwarks of post-war security—our alliances with Western Europe and Japan. The participants in the debate are not interested in the U.S. relationship to the United Nations; they certainly do not view the United Nations as an embryonic central guidance system of the sort presupposed by $S_{2(WOMP)}$.‡

---

* The inflationary domestic effects of the wheat deal, and the evident failure to get a fair *quid pro quo* from the Soviet Union, may make American policy-makers more wary in the future about certain types of East–West trade.

† The anti-Israeli sentiment in the United Nations, especially since 1967, has also contributed to the dissipation of U.S. support for the Organization. Many of the most ardent proponents of a strong United Nations have also happened to be pro-Israeli.

‡ Note that other principal S_2 options depend on central guidance capabilities derived from statist or corporate sources and do not envisage an expansion of international institutional roles.

It is also appropriate to note that we see no evidence of a trend among non-U.S. governmental actors toward abandoning the war system or even making serious efforts to examine world order alternatives. One of the few encouraging signs comes from Sweden, where for a generation peace-oriented education has reportedly influenced the whole public attitude toward war and world order policy issues.* Even Japan, with its constitutional inhibition against a military establishment, has built up significant war-making capabilities over the last decade, to supplement an American "security" shield. The bilateral Okinawa Communiqué of 1970 suggests that Japan is even willing to extend its security role in the Pacific, in cooperation with the United States. A series of middle powers have pursued a generally constructive neutralist role in world politics, but they have not abandoned their reliance on national defense efforts or prerogatives, nor have they officially supported measures of drastic disarmament. India, with its tradition of Gandhian non-violence, has not seen fit to refrain from national uses of force, nor to propose a post-statist reorganization to achieve peace and justice. In other words, the world order system is fairly homogeneous with respect to governmental acceptance of the war system as the enduring basis of national security. We find S_2 advocacy of a positive kind only in nongovernmental circles—such as statements by Pope John XXIII or U Thant, manifestos of private groups, and individual writings.

During t_1 it will be very important to stimulate the reemergence of Charter politics in the United States, both as a serious moderating influence on national behavior in S_1 and as a transition step toward $S_{2(WOMP)}$. The revival of such a Charter-oriented interest in global reform could be initially signaled in the form of Congressional hearings and political debates in Presidential election years. In addition, it will be worth noticing whether public officials become more conscious of system-change as a foreign policy goal, and whether $S_{2(WOMP)}$, and $S_{2(WOMP/USA)}$ constituencies take effective shape in a variety of national settings. Above all, the gradual elimination of the overt and covert overseas American military presence would be a positive sign of new prospects for global reform along WOMP lines. Dismantling the alliance network would also provide important evidence of a shifting American political consciousness about the future of national security. Such action might generate either a period of national withdrawal (or isola-

---

* The Swedish experience has not been widely disseminated, but it is indicative of the impact that peace-oriented general education can have on public opinion over a relatively short period of time.

tionism) from the world scene, or a period in which a new vision of American participation in transition to S2(WOMP/USA) takes hold.

THE POLITICS OF COMPASSION

The American response to misery and oppression in foreign societies embodies many of the ambiguities that pervade our overall foreign policy, and reveals a curious Yankee blend of humanitarian concern and pragmatic self-interest. Attempts to dismiss either element are misleading. It is precisely because both are genuine that they produce confusion in thought and distortions in policy. As Cold War pressures have accompanied a rise in political consciousness throughout the Third World, these confusions and distortions have grown to gigantic proportions in recent years, culminating in the American crusade in Vietnam.[48] Political speeches by American government officials during the 1960's seem to contain genuine expressions of compassion for Third World societies, especially for their vulnerability to "aggression" and their severe forms of social and economic privation. These pronouncements also proclaimed an American willingness to act as benevolent catalyst of progress, and as disinterested guardian of peace for the weak.

Only recently have influential Americans conceded that empire-building and economic self-interest were behind the expansion of America's world role after World War II.* In the early 1970's, two major positions on foreign policy reform are evident:

Category A: Drop missionary claims to do good for others and concentrate upon those foreign relationships critical for American power, wealth, and prestige (i.e., Japan, Europe, Latin America).

Category B: Withdraw from military and economic involvement in foreign societies, and concentrate energies and resources on building a better America.

Both positions tend to downgrade the politics of compassion, the first by abandoning humanitarian pretensions, the second by reverting to

---

* This expansion was also facilitated by a number of factors: the collapse of the main European empires; the consequent emergence of weak states that were targets of opportunity; the perception of Communism as monolithic, expansionist, interventionary and evil; the "lesson" of Munich on the futility of appeasement; and the surplus capabilities and energies of post-war America.

isolationism. Furthermore, although A and B type positions (there are several variations of each) have distinct implications for global reform, both are delimited by S_1 horizons. Category A leads to a revived balance of power orientation; Category B leads to a classical Westphalian statism, in which independent sovereign units pursue their own interests as autonomously as possible.

We would argue, of course, that the politics of compassion has an important role to play in the transition period $S_1 \rightarrow S_{2(WOMP/USA)}$, and is related to strengthening all national commitments to V_2 and V_3. We believe that V_2 and V_3 will not be emphasized on Transition Path 1 until early t_2, although some actors may give them priority reasonably early in t_1.

As far as the United States is concerned, the most important shift in orientation would involve the serious development of a third position on foreign policy reform, a Category C alternative.

Category C: Large-scale American participation in a cooperative struggle to overcome world poverty and inhumane governance, relying heavily on supranational procedures and institutions—the politics of compassion would be revived on a national level, but implemented in a more cosmopolitan manner than in the past. National self-interest would be also served by defusing violent strategies, and by generating confidence in the capacity of the international system to make reforms and adjustments.* It is unlikely that a Category C position could be implemented in the United States until late in t_1, although governments in other countries might move earlier toward this enlightened position.

Basic national achievement relative to the politics of compassion might be gauged by specific criteria:

Quantum and mode of international disaster relief (e.g. flood, famine, disease, quakes in poor countries; compare with quantum and mode of disaster relief made available in domestic society)

Character and extent of support for humanitarian intervention to safeguard or liberate ethnic groups (e.g., response to problems of southern Africa) and balancing of humanitarian claims against counterclaims—for instance, the interests of American foreign investors

---

* Perhaps the greatest gain for America would be to bring a measure of coherence to its behavior in foreign and domestic arenas, making it plain that we would not engage abroad in tactics that we deplored at home, nor enter into friendly relationships with foreign governing groups that relied on repressive policies.

Quantum, mode, and national rationale for "foreign aid" to the developing world; procedures for capital transfer and trends relative to budgetary patterns.*

It seems likely that shifts in the United States toward a Category C position would presuppose the prior success of the politics of compassion within domestic society. Therefore, domestic treatment of issues of social, economic, and political justice will undoubtedly have international ramifications, although not necessarily in a mechanical way.†

WORLD ORDER BARGAINS AND BARGAINING

Formal international cooperation is increasingly required to efficiently handle a vast array of functional issues with global dimensions. An erstwhile laissez-faire confidence in "the invisible hand," harmonizing world community interests with the separate interests of national policy-makers, seems to be vanishing in all portions of the world.‡ Even the most powerful state actors require reliable international norms, procedures and regimes, in order to achieve desired levels of predictability and stability.§ The United States has a particularly high stake in

---

* It is significant to note that American development assistance is declining, relative to the size of the U.S. budget and GNP; as of 1972, development assistance was $3.5 billion, or less than 2% of the U.S. budget and less than .4% of GNP. These trends and totals compare unfavorably with most other developed countries. It should also be realized that, aside from India, the top aid recipients are all political clients of the United States—South Vietnam, Indonesia, South Korea, Brazil, Pakistan, Cambodia, and Turkey are all in the top ten.[49]

† For instance, one form of neo-Darwinian response to a global scarcity crisis would be to evolve principles of domestic equity, while sustaining a world structure based on dominance and extreme inequality.

‡ More important than the interplay of national and global well-being is the link between national behavior and species adaptability. The ecological challenge of the present era, unlike earlier challenges which altered man's behavioral patterns and relation to his environment, is man-caused and of global scope.[50] The appropriate line of response, then, needs to be of comparable scope in order to remove the threats now mounting against the species. It is our special contention that unlike earlier ecological challenges, the present one calls for a response centered around a movement for rapid global reform.

§ A more dependable international legal order does not signify a more equitable one. Legal arrangements reflect political arrangements, and the former will be as coercive and

promoting dependable forms of international cooperation, because its essential activities are spread out far beyond its own "jurisdiction" (i.e., its territorial domain), and its domestic equilibrium depends in intricate ways upon the dynamics of global interdependence.

In many areas of international life, including important economic relations, strong governments are at least temporarily less able and less eager than formerly to use direct action as a prime means of imposing their wills on the weak, even with respect to legal claims based on property rights.* When France and Great Britain attempted to enforce their economic claims on Egypt after Nasser expropriated the Suez Canal Company in 1956, the U.S. opposition to this military effort indicated a real shift in tactics. At the same time, the hostile U.S. reaction to radical regimes in Latin America and concomitant efforts to thwart their success suggest that we should not over-estimate the significance of this shift. The present world structure of economic dependency provides the United States with potent nonmilitary levers of influence, which bear on credit terms, foreign aid, tax schedules for exports and imports, and freezing foreign-held accounts and other assets.[51]

In some contexts, however, this leverage is limited by a paramount interest in maintaining cooperative links with foreign governments in matters of security and basic ideological orientation.

For instance, the United States government is reluctant to push its claims that Ecuador is illegally seizing and fining U.S. fishing vessels off its shores, because of its overriding interest in maintaining solidarity with respect to hemispheric security and geopolitical affiliation.†

---

exploitative as the latter dictates. Therefore, an expanded role for international law is not necessarily consistent with global reform as we have specified it. Its consistency will depend on whether a neo-Darwinian or humanistic ethos prevails in the relations of states and peoples, or whether some kind of "mix" emerges. In the likely event of a "mix" it becomes more essential than ever for international lawyers to become more alert to the value implications of given proposals for legal development. It might be helpful to assess systematically the annual output of the International Court of Justice, the International Law Commission, and other bodies of the United Nations from the perspective of probable impacts on WOMP goals.

* It is exceedingly doubtful that this renunciation of force by the strong would withstand real pressures on their interests, e.g., if the United States economy were as pressed in the 1970's by Arab manipulation of the market conditions for oil, as Japan was pressed in the 1930's by Euro–American manipulation of world trade conditions. Japan's military quest for control over resources essential to its national economy suggests the degree to which even a country with a relatively isolationist tradition can be induced to adopt an imperial strategy.

† What is suggestive here is the bargaining potential of weak governments when the military sanctions of strong governments are rendered inoperative either by self-restraint

Thus, the United States government has so far preferred to have its own taxpayers reimburse American owners of captured fishing vessels, rather than attempt even indirectly to coerce these governments into accepting the American position on territorial jurisdiction over ocean activity.

Similarly, government officials in the United States charged with halting the international flow of heroin, and aware that Thai officials are not taking steps to prevent heroin production on their territory, have opposed legislative efforts to penalize Thailand by cutting off $100 million in foreign aid.[52] In a setting like this, the diverse interests of governments may conflict, even in the face of shared nominal and rhetorical commitments to halting heroin use. As evidence has shown, foreign government officials may themselves benefit from the heroin trade, or may regard export sales as an essential source of scarce foreign exchange; it may even be (as has been convincingly alleged) that the CIA or other segments of the U.S. government do not really favor implementing the official national policy.[53]

Air piracy, or hijacking, is another problem which illustrates how interdependence, statist constraints, and diverse perceived interests can interact to offset one another. Nongovernmental actors with no positive interest in intergovernmental stability can all too easily block efforts to reach an effective world order bargain. Hijacking is also a metaphor for the growing vulnerability of the emerging world public order system to disruption by any group with deep grievances that are not susceptible to peaceful, orderly satisfaction. This vulnerability provides the ruling groups with a rationale and rationalization for repressive tactics, ranging from police prerogatives to intrusions on privacy. The complexity of the United States, the surfacing discontent of change-oriented groups, and the traditions of personal liberty and social contract, make our society a likely arena for the enactment of this drama in a form that has wider than national significance.

The domestic response to hijacking, and the related questions of kidnapping high diplomatic and business officials, are separate from the effort of the United States to strike a world order bargain. With regard to hijacking, the United States has strong incentives to strike a bargain: its interests are so spread around the globe that secure air travel and

---

(i.e., renunciation of force for non-defensive purposes) or by offsetting considerations (i.e., fear of provoking domestic radicalization or geopolitical defection). In this regard, even the puppet ends up pulling some of the strings, as the United States discovered in its anguished relations with the Saigon regime under both Diem and Thieu and in its relations with the Chiang regime on Taiwan.

unimpeded diplomatic and business intercourse are crucial, intrinsically as well as symbolically. Can such a bargain be struck? Are there genuine common interests that enable the negotiation of an effective world procedure? The more militant Arab governments have actually joined in celebrating successful hijackings and other acts of terror organized by extremist wings of Palestinian liberation groups; indeed, these disruptive undertakings are popularly viewed in the Middle East as spectacular exploits of courage and their perpetrators are treated as heroes. While much of the world was shocked by terror against Israeli athletes participating in the 1972 Olympic Games in Munich, the Black Septembrists who died there were brought to Libya to be buried amid exultant crowds. Obviously, such governments would be reluctant to commit themselves to an effective international anti-hijacking code. As long as there are deep-seated human conflicts in the world arena, those governments and groups who identify with the goals of the hijackers would not be inclined to adopt, much less support, a program designed to discourage hijackings. Israel might not be ready to cooperate with a procedure that compelled the return of hijackers to the country of origin; what if the hijackers happened to be Soviet Jews seeking to emigrate to Israel?

In certain contexts a procedure has been tacitly accepted whereby planes and ransom money are returned but the hijacker is granted asylum. Cuba and Algeria have apparently adopted this intermediate position, but these governments have mixed interests. In the Beirut Raid of December, 1968, Israel demonstrated that she was prepared to retaliate against Arab commercial air capabilities, as a way of punishing and deterring the support Arab governments had allegedly given to anti-Israel hijacking activities. Clearly, there are some objective conditions of vulnerability to various types of hijacking, a vulnerability increased by the diverse governmental attitudes toward the particular political *motives* involved. In any event, by definition, an intergovernmental bargain would not altogether prevent hijacking or kidnapping. The United States has been able only to reduce but not to eliminate domestic hijacking, despite a unified national policy of surveillance, regulation, and punishment. Indeed, a fully satisfactory world order bargain may not be possible in such an area. The competitive logic of S_1 (and the nature of the act itself) may virtually preclude an international solution.

The United States government would like to negotiate world order "bargains" that create reciprocal obligations by foreign governments in exchange for undertakings by the United States. Naturally, these bargains must be based on "tradeoffs" between governments that have diverse perceived interests. The Treaty on Non-Proliferation of Nuclear Weapons (1968) is an excellent example of an effort to strike such a world order bargain; the non-nuclear powers renounce their option to develop nuclear weaponry, and in exchange receive technical assistance to enable their development of peaceful nuclear technology and energy facilities.[54] Whether this tradeoff continues to be mutually beneficial over time depends on a number of uncertain factors, such as the overall character of world order, decisions made by non-signatory governments regarding their own nuclear status, the willingness of nuclear powers to denuclearize world politics, and satisfaction with the way the nuclear powers fulfill their pledge to render nonmilitary assistance. An existing treaty obligation indicates only that a bargain has been struck at one point in time, not that an accord will be maintained indefinitely. The Non-Proliferation Treaty explicitly recognized the conditional effectiveness of treaty arrangements by providing governments with a three-month right of withdrawal for unilaterally determined reasons of supreme national interest.*

We think the United States government should seek a series of world order bargains in this world of independent states and interdependent interests, because conditions of reciprocity need to be perceived by governments, and then established and sustained. Where reciprocity cannot be negotiated, the United States is faced with a series of options; the options range from deference to foreign claims, to the coercive use of military power. Obviously, nonviolent, collective means of persuasion are preferred strategies, in contexts where world order bargains are prevented either because interests diverge too sharply, or because the relevant governmental actors cannot negotiate mutually reasonable tradeoffs.

It is possible to complement world order bargains with unilateral nonmilitary sanctions which might be both effective and beneficial for community welfare. For instance, it seems desirable to encourage cooperative arrangements for protecting endangered species such as great whales and polar bears, by prohibiting the sale of product imports in American markets. Similarly, national legislation to prohibit foreign SST's from landing on American air fields seems like a desirable way to

---

* Such conditional effectiveness of treaty obligations on the continuation of perceived advantage to participating governments is a natural consequence of S_1 logic and dynamics. A particular government may, for egocentric reasons, conclude that its general interests in stability are better sustained by respecting a disadvantageous obligation of international law. However, this general sentiment is weak in world affairs, especially as dominant actors do not seem often to accord such general respect.

discourage further development of ecologically destructive and dangerous technology. Such "unilateralism" would exert American power on
behalf of widely shared community values.

Efforts like the Hickenlooper Amendment represent another brand of
unilateralism—the desire to impose special American policy on foreign
governments in an area of legitimate diversity. (In this case, national
law specifies the terms of compensation that a foreign government must
give an expropriated American investor; if proper compensation is not
made, the President is authorized to cut off foreign aid.) * The Hickenlooper enactment was a response to corporate pressure, and thus the
North American *legislative* definition of international legal requirements bears little resemblance to the requirements of either world justice or of existing rules of international law.[55]

The area of foreign investment illustrates a much more general problem with unilateral approaches to world order bargaining. The United
States government's capacity to represent the enlightened self-interest
of the nation as a whole is seriously affected by the differential access
which some special interest groups have to influential policy-makers.
International positions are skewed toward the outlooks of well-
organized and well-financed lobbies both inside and outside of government. For example, in connection with the attempt to establish a global
code for governing the exploitation of offshore oil resources, the oil industry has influenced the U.S. government to put forward an apparently non-negotiable offer which, if accepted, will virtually assure a
statist competitive scramble. As a result, an excellent opportunity to experiment with supranational arrangements for control and development of ocean activity has been jeopardized, and perhaps lost altogether.

A series of questions are raised about the capacity of governments,
including our own, to reach and sustain satisfactory world order
bargains that must simultaneously embody the reciprocal interests of
many governments. Experience with this bargaining capacity will one
way or another influence the American policy-making elites' general
perception of the feasibility of world order reforms and adjustments

---

* Unilateral efforts to coerce compliance by others with dubious international norms
(especially norms repudiated as expressions of nonvoluntary creations, as in the foreign
investment area) encourage retaliatory acts and embitter international relationships. Reliable law in S_1 is based on voluntary contracts among participating governments; imposed
contracts, such as peace treaties, have not fared well when the imposing power is removed; they characteristically inspire disrespect that is popularly supported.

within the confines of S₁. In any area where "national security" is at stake, such as assured access to oil, the "national solutions" argument is likely to prevail. Thus, despite expected environmental harm, the United States has decided to go ahead with the development of the North Pine Slope oil fields and the trans-Alaska pipeline, in order to reduce its increasing dependence on oil imports.* It is always difficult to distinguish special pleading (e.g., a "national security" cover for concern over company profits) from honest expression of the self-reliance ethic which girds the belief system of most power-wielders in S₁.

Can S₁ forms of order prevent destructive competition in nonmilitary realms, when its underlying structure so heavily depends on the war system and a wasteful, perilous arms race? When confronting critical functional problems, can an American government hope to crystallize bargaining positions that genuinely reflect its own national interests in world order stability, much less provide reasonable incentives to diversely oriented foreign governments? † Will foreign governments, especially those that are most sovereignty-oriented—either because of totalitarian tendencies toward exclusive control, or national self-assertion during a period of domestic nation-building—be capable of realistic world order bargaining? That is, even if the United States develops its side of the bargain in a reasonable manner, will enough other principal actors perceive the offer as "reasonable," or make a counter-offer that the United States government perceives (or should perceive) as reasonable?

We fear that the United States is not likely to develop reasonable proposals where critical world order bargains need to be struck and that, in any case, shared perceptions of reasonableness will not be forthcoming to sustain important forms of international cooperation. In this event, the problem-solving capacities of S^1 will appear obsolete even without

---

* Indeed, President Nixon's principal response to the American energy crisis, aggravated by an Arab oil embargo, had been to move deeper into S₁ patterns by proclaiming Project Independence for realization in 1980, i.e., making the United States independent of external supplies. In the European context, Henry Kissinger has taken a second line of approach, proposing in a preliminary way the shared management of energy supplies among developed non-Communist societies.

† In effect, this question asks whether special interest perspectives can be sufficiently neutralized so that the national position reflects the overall well-being of the United States. The evidence is not encouraging in critical areas where significant business opportunities exist.

consideration of the war system, and receptivity to S_2 type thinking is likely to increase.* Testing grounds for reform potential are likely to arise early in t_1, most probably with regard to negotiations on world monetary and trade relations, a global regime for the exploitation of ocean resources, the protection of ocean quality, and satellite broadcasting. These negotiations will probably fail unless dominant political consciousness in this and other critical national arenas proceeds at least to a mid-t_1 position of receptivity to $S_{2(WOMP)}$.† "Failure" in this context can occur because no bargain can be reached, or because only a nominal bargain with minimal behavioral consequences is negotiated. In other words, failure constitutes an inability to strike a world order bargain that achieves a generally satisfactory functional solution of global scope.

To date, the international economic system has been fragmented along ideological lines. What is generally described as "world trade relations" or the "world monetary system" has in reality been limited to relations among non-Communist actors. It remains unclear whether economic relations will be universalized by revived "balance of power thinking," the rise of inter-bloc trade, the presence of China in the United Nations, the decline of ideological politics in the main world capitals, the Sino–Soviet split, a shared rich-country consensus about the boundaries of their respective spheres of influence, and a statist ordering of world relations.

A major uncertainty surrounds the multinational corporation as world actor—whether it opts or is co-opted into a position of support for concert politics of principal governments, or whether it opposes neo-statist trends and seeks, on a relatively autonomous basis, to organize economic markets around its own interests.‡ The United States has

---

* There is already some elite receptivity to an S_2 approach to global reform, but its character is *hegemonial* rather than *egalitarian*, *elitist* rather than *equitable*. The sort of humanistic approaches to S_2 embodied in WOMP are not present in government or corporate visions of the future.

† It is a curious paradox that given present levels of governmental consciousness, reformist potentialities in S_1 depend greatly on an increasing acceptance of WOMP goals. This dependence reflects the fact that reformism requires the voluntary accommodation of unequally placed governments increasingly aware of their real situation. Even reactionary governments such as Brazil adopt a Third World outlook in world order bargaining situations to maximize the interests of their national elites.

‡ See Chapter VI, p. 381 for a discussion of the multinational corporation as actor in S_1. The ability of the corporate interests to deny anti-MNC individuals and groups access to national power will be a major influence on whether an independent $S_{2(MNC)}$ becomes a serious possibility. There is no doubt that the resources at the disposal of world business interests are so great that the MNC's preferences will either be realized or its autonomy

a particular relationship to the global role of the MNC. As Robert Gilpin notes in an important study of the link between the MNC and American national interests, "In large measure, the term 'multinational corporation' or MNC is a euphemism for the outward expression of America's giant national corporations." [56] Contrary to some popular impressions, the bulk of this investment has been in the industrial sector of the world economy, mainly Western Europe and Canada, although increasingly in Japan as well. Between 1946 and 1970, American direct foreign investment increased at a remarkable pace: from $7 billion to $80 billion. Europe and Canada have become very agitated about "the American challenge," and have felt that their national independence was being eroded, if not threatened, by the growing influence of American export capital in their societies.

Gilpin raises important complementary questions about the extent to which American state interests have been served by the outflow of capital, and the related tendency to substitute foreign investment for exports. His basic conclusion is that our national tax law provides American business with an extra incentive to make foreign investments. In the course of a sophisticated discussion of economic consequences, Gilpin persuasively contends that this basic pattern of exporting productivity (via investment) rather than goods is producing a *rentier* position for the United States. This position implies both a kind of parasitism vis-à-vis foreign productivity, and extreme vulnerability to changes in foreign investment circumstances. The extent of this vulnerability has been vividly demonstrated in the area of oil production. Gilpin also suggests that the national economy is being hurt by the insufficient rate of domestic investment, a diminished emphasis on increasing profits via technological innovation in domestic industry, and the tendency to deprive labor of its normal share of the economic fruits of increasing productivity. Therefore, the harm done to this country by the MNC arises mainly from its failure to allow the nation as a whole to enjoy the benefits of economic growth, and from the instability that may result from having such a large stake in maintaining a favorable investment climate abroad. It should be emphasized that Gilpin is not arguing the case against the MNC from a radical perspective. On the contrary, he is

---

destroyed by government regulation. Either governments will become captives of multinational business, or the other way around. At the present time, the split between corporate and sovereign perspectives has a healthy effect of dissolving the identity of interests that has united business and political elites in this country for several decades, producing a kind of state capitalism which combines some of the worst ingredients of socialist and capitalist arrangements.

contending that a pro-foreign investment tax credit has allowed the MNC to acquire an overly large share of American capital activities, and that new regulatory approaches are needed to restore balance. In effect, foreign antagonists of American economic penetration by means of the MNC, and domestic critics of the Gilpin variety, arrive at the same conclusion—namely, that the loss of government control over domestic economic well-being has harmful effects and risks.

A related uncertainty involves how the Third World will react to the challenge of the international economy: by bargaining for marginal improvements in *terms* of participation, or by seeking a new *structure* that tends toward greater equality of participation and benefits.* Because of their size and stature, the attitudes of China and India on these issues will be critically important. It is likely that marginalists and structuralists will do battle in these countries in the years ahead.

For the United States, the search for viable world order bargains will be determined by the overall relation of social forces within domestic society. In the event that a progressive coalition takes shape, and is not thwarted by a reactionary coup, the United States will be likely to seek world order bargains that move in the direction of $S_{2(WOMP)}$ rather than $S_{2(CONCERT)}$, $S_{2(MNC)}$, or $S_{2(IMP)}$. Early in such a period, it will be difficult to decide whether to treat a particular action as an S_1 reform, or as a transition step toward $S_{2(WOMP)}$. In isolation an act may partake of both tendencies within S_1. By t_2, such ambiguity will largely be eliminated, and S_1 reformers will be aligned against $S_{2(WOMP)}$ planners, as well as against other categories of S_2 advocates.

If a progressive coalition does not acquire power in the United States by the 1970's, either a concert or market outlook, or possibly an amalgam of the two, is likely to become paramount in government thinking. Given the strains of managing a world of severe inequity, intense interdependence, and ecological fragility, the prospects are for more explicit structures of domination within the United States and in the world as a whole. In this sense, the drift toward an S_2 solution will appear as increasingly inevitable, but if t_1 is never completed the United States is likely to become a leading participant in the creation of

---

* There is no reason, of course, to expect a consistent strategy of reform on the part of Third World governments. Their present orientations toward global reform are very diverse, as are their antagonisms toward one another. However, a pattern may emerge as issues involving global management grow more crystallized. The basic choice, then, would become whether to increase their relative position in S_1, or to pursue an S_2 option that seemed to promote their particular interests in global reform, assuming a consensus could be reached on such an option during the course of t_1.

a regressive, coercive variant of S_2 that seeks to sustain America's relative power, control, and wealth, but involves a conformist nightmare at home and abroad.*

SOME DOMESTIC YARDSTICKS OF
GLOBAL REFORM PROSPECTS

Value changes, including shifts in attitudes toward world order and global reform, are likely to be best understood in domestic arenas. In our special framework, an assessment of t_1—its depth and its countertendencies—can be most successfully made by considering the debates, behavioral patterns, and interrelation of social, economic, and political forces within the United States.

One useful focus would be upon the links between discussions of domestic and global dimensions of the war system; this could be done by comparing the treatment of arms control, arms spending and arms use in foreign policy, with such domestic matters as gun control, prison reform, and crime control. Above all, we should acknowledge our reliance on a "war system" to maintain domestic law and order. Our confidence in democratic processes critically depends on whether governmental authority can administer peaceful procedures fast enough to overcome perceived grievances and deprivations, and whether groups with grievances accept the system's legitimacy.† In the United States

---

* We are arguing, in effect, that there is a continuity between domestic and global politics, that it is impossible to pursue a neo-Darwinian global strategy and a humanist domestic strategy, especially in an overall world situation of deepening ecological and social crisis. Why? It will prove impossible to sustain a domestic consensus based on such a discontinuity. One of the consequences of humanism is to reject artificial confines of national boundaries as the proper orbit of empathy. Thus, the very success of a humanistic approach within the nation will lead to a repudiation of neo-Darwinianism as a global strategy. Also, the degree of global awareness arising from technological innovation and economic interdependence will make it increasingly uncomfortable to wallow in wealth while most others languish in misery; the split condition will induce severe spiritual depressions and might provide fertile territory for a religious revival of really potent force. But suppose the scale of world poverty grows so acute that the only apparent choice is between islands of affluent dignity and an ocean of shared misery? This condition was characteristic for all civilizations prior to the industrial revolution and provided an underpinning for institutions of slavery and the like that was indeed supported by a domestic consensus that embraced most ethically sensitive members of society.

† Perhaps even more important in the United States, will mildly advantaged or less disadvantaged groups regard themselves as victimized by the excessive concern dis-

there has been a recent decline in the legitimacy of governing institutions, stemming from a combination of the Indochina War, "the benign neglect" of minority grievances, and the mounting evidence of official lawlessness.* This decline has generated an offsetting series of populist demands for police protection against "those who take the law into their own hands." Is Father Daniel Berrigan, as civil disobedient, a servant of grace and inspiration, or an arrogant and destructive fool? [57] Both interpretations are so ardently held by different portions of the society, that there is virtually no possibility of a social contract between the government and the citizenry. Contradictions between authority and justice induce repression to sustain the ruler's imperative, while stimulating disobedience and resistance by an aggrieved citizenry.

Prevailing ethical attitudes in the United States support domestic reliance on the war system. The failure of Congress to enact effective legislation prohibiting hand gun sales is indicative, as is public support for brutal police responses to unruly anti-war demonstrations during the latter phase of the Indochina War. By an uncomfortably large margin, public opinion felt that the National Guard was justified in using live ammunition against unarmed student demonstrators at Kent State University in the Spring of 1970, even though four students died as a result. Similarly, the public approved Governor Rockefeller's authorization of lethal force to restore order at Attica Prison in 1971, despite the bloodshed that resulted. These instances disclose a public enthusiasm for violence, provided it is directed against those who seem to militantly oppose the established order.† This approval of vio-

---

played by more advantaged groups for those who are, in socioeconomic respects, the most disadvantaged segments of American society? Blue-collar hostility toward welfare programs directed at the ghetto poor is one manifestation of this phenomenon. Middle American responses to the Woodstock ethos is another. In effect, we can see a kind of anti-liberal insistence that the poorest groups get ahead according to the American work and competitive ethic (i.e., the neo-Darwinian obstacle course which only the fittest can complete). This ethical premise makes welfare payments seem both corrupting to the poor, and unfair to those who work hard to avoid being poor. It is easy to grasp the link between neo-Darwinism of this variety, and its global expression. Our main point here is that among those who can become aggrieved when compassionate politics gain widespread support are those who perceive themselves as victims of their own self-reliance.

* The other side of official illegitimacy—that is, ineffectiveness—is also manifested by increasing self-reliance on the part of urban groups threatened by rampant criminality. Since the government is unable or unwilling to enforce the law and provide its citizenry with personal security, the citizens are inclined to arm themselves and pursue strategies of self-help.

† Reliance on disruptive and illegal tactics by white parents to prevent school busing generated quite opposite sentiments in the general public. The unpopularity of busing

lence also embraced the public acceptance year after year of the cruel and senseless bombardment of Indochina. Many Americans evidently believe that a show of force by the rich and privileged will intimidate change-oriented militancy wherever it occurs.*

The emerging national debate on "amnesty" for Indochina draft resisters will also be indicative of public morality in the United States. It is interesting that no one in mainstream politics talks about "amnesty" for the war-makers, but only for those young people who refused—out of moral scruples, or possibly out of concern for their own safety—to participate in a cruel and remote war.† Admittedly, complicated problems are raised by the amnesty issue. Many young soldiers may have contemplated or unsuccessfully sought amnesty, or wished they had, but may have wound up maimed or dead instead after tours of military service which they reluctantly accepted as their duty. This issue of comparative virtue is poignantly embodied in the Mel Tillis song "Ruby, Don't Take Your Love to Town": ‡

> It wasn't me that started that ole crazy Asian war
> But I was proud to go and do my patriotic chore
>
> . . . .
>
> It's hard to love a man whose legs are bent and paralyzed

The maimed veteran's appeal for love is a pathetic reminder of the costs borne by conscripted citizens and their families. Obviously, bitterness will be present, and those who refused to bear such costs—the draft evaders—will, at the very least, be regarded as unpatriotic, as having defaulted, in the song's terms, on their "patriotic chore."

---

designed to achieve racial integration (as contrasted with the acceptance in the South of busing to thwart integration) led to widespread acceptance of parental rights to engage in resistance activities that were viewed by the same citizens with such disfavor, when engaged in by draft-age students during the Indochina War. Thus, the critical feature is not law abidingness, but the acceptability of the social objective sought by protest.

* Moral confusion in America can be discerned also in the efforts to prohibit pornography rather than ultra-violence. Movie ratings are also indicative: an X-rating usually denotes explicit sexuality, not depravity of mind and spirit as exhibited by violent behavior or by the exploitation of those who are weak and helpless.

† Why should young Americans accept orders or laws so risky to life and limb, when no convincing rationale based on national well-being or personal responsibility is provided? Solicitude for one's own safety is a sign of psychic health; a citizenry that allows itself to be led to slaughter by its rulers abandons its own most solemn prerogatives and responsibilities.

‡ Mel Tillis, "Ruby, Don't Take Your Love to Town," © Copyright 1966—Cedarwood Publishing Co., Inc., 815 16th Ave., S., Nashville, Tenn. 37203. Reprinted by permission.

Amnesty claimants are not "victims" or opponents of the system in the same way as the militant blacks. Reconciliation with the blacks is being sought in ways that do not vindicate disrespect for positive law or governmental authority. "Deserters," even if comparably motivated, are unlikely to receive as considerate national treatment, because their constituency is much more likely to encompass reference groups that are already excluded from the dominant consensus. The "boy next door" is not likely to be a deserter, even though in numerical terms the number of deserters surpasses the number of pre-induction draft resisters or evaders.

The amnesty debate is a world order issue because, as we have argued already, the earliest bearers of world order change will be those who pursue domestic goals which enhance individual and group dignity, social and economic justice, peace, and ecological balance.* The application of WOMP values to domestic social, economic, and political exigencies is itself a desirable contribution to global reform. The "law and order" struggle has profound implications for voluntary government—government which sustains its legitimacy primarily by engendering respect and affection. Voluntary government resorts to force only against those whose "deviance" exploits the polity or injures its members, or those who are so "unreasonably" impatient about adjustment and change that they resort to dangerous violence. A "reasonable" definition of deviance is as a complex sociological and philosophical problem. We believe that any such definition should be sensitive to the views of those who are now societal "victims" by reason of poverty, discrimination, or privation. As the old structures of power and control grow less able to satisfy public expectations, the "victimized" sector of society expands, although the perception of "victimhood" may be delayed and even resisted. Indeed, under such conditions of systemic decline, the victim's identity is defined partially by a condition of alienation; this condition characteristically tends, in turn, to blind individuals to their own social situation. The American labor movement—upholding such leaders of its own betrayal as George Meany and James Hoffa, and demonstrating beneath placards proclaiming "God Bless the Establishment"—exemplifies basic alienation from the objective interests of the average worker in the United States.

The government in the United States, aware of its declining capacity

---

* Of course, honest disagreements may exist among adherents of various belief systems. The invocation of value referents does not settle the issue of normative impact. We are here avowing an anti-Darwinian value creed that is fundamentally humanist in character.

to solve human problems in accordance with its own creed, acts to prevent the mass of people from comprehending the true state of affairs. Therefore, the government's reliance upon secrecy and deception vis-à-vis its own citizenry takes on emblematic importance. Hostility toward a free press and the impulse to "manage the news"—properly held up to scorn when they occur in a totalitarian society—are increasingly prevalent here at home. Hence, the furor over the release of the *Pentagon Papers,* and Agnew's pre-Watergate onslaughts against the media, are weather-vane tendencies; the expanded reliance on surveillance and secret inquisitorial grand jury proceedings also demonstrate concerted government efforts to destroy the seeds of an $S_{2(WOMP)}$ ethos among change-oriented domestic groups.*

This authoritarian orientation is also congruent with the search in world affairs for a moderate variant of the regressive structure of S_1, or an equivalent S_2 option. The United States government would like to maintain present relations of privilege and dominance by neutralizing its "victims"——with alienating techniques if possible, by intimidation and force if necessary. The Nixon–Kissinger–Brezhnev pursuit of concert politics represents a clever move to strike a gigantic world order bargain among "the top dogs." This international approach perfectly complements the domestic governing strategy: our leaders are attempting to base international stability on structures of dominance and exploitation, which can then be reinforced by the capacity and willingness of the powerful to deal brutally with challenges from below.

The reality of the mailed fist is thinly veiled by the increasingly questionable assertion that even poor countries can expect steady increases in living standards, provided only that they organize their economies to sustain indefinite growth. Besides being pre-ecological in its reliance on indefinite expansion of GNP, the myth neglects "the systematic underdevelopment" that results from existing world economic and political structures, as well as the degree to which net increases in GNP benefit only the upper stratum of society or are diverted to accommodate a growing population and an expanding defense budget. In essence, part of the government's mystification of mainstream America consists in its assertion that the affluence and power of the United

---

* The Watergate disclosures provide especially blatant evidence of this assertion, although they may spuriously suggest that the repressive tendency is a matter of political pathology confined to members of the original Nixon entourage. In actuality, the Mitchell–Haldeman–Ehrlichman–Dean mentality was merely an extreme case of recently solidifying Presidential attitudes and policies.[58]

States are in no way responsible for the inequity, poverty, and misery which riddle the present world order system.* Although at this point there is not much evidence that the general public would object to a more candid disclosure of the American role in the world, there nevertheless seems to be a tendency for managers of a cruel system to disguise its nature, even if the manipulators themselves wind up enmeshed in the web of their own deception. One has the impression that American policy-makers are themselves largely unaware of these realities. Hence, they are unable to perceive very clearly the latent dangers embedded in a world order design which further fragments the potential community of mankind by superimposing a politico-economic structure of dominance upon the already existing hierarchy of states.

World order dialogue has failed to consider the main options for global reform. This failure results from an interplay between the general public's false comprehension of the objective situation, and the elite's self-interested effort to maintain its own advantages by refusing to confront its apparent role in consigning most of humanity to a life of misery. Such selfishness and complacency is characteristic of a colonial situation, where ignorance takes the place of innocence or willingness to risk change. Given the dynamics of world relations, we believe that false consciousness imperils the future of America as well as the world, and underestimates the prospects and benefits of a global reform movement built around WOMP values. This case for global reform must be made throughout the United States early in t_1, although even its very statement will generate intense hostility, and any evidence of its serious acceptance on the part of the general public is likely to occasion a repressive movement of considerable virulence. An early domestic formulation of the case for global reform along the lines of $S_{2(WOMP/USA)}$ may concentrate upon the quest for a more survival-oriented world order bargain than is provided by the prospect of a five-power world. Such a bargain would have to depend on a minimal acceptance of human solidarity and the oneness of the earth; on this basis, an American understanding of the need to work for equity and ecological equilibrium on a global scale could begin to take effective shape. Such a movement for global reform could also appeal to the positive side of the American past, to its role as beacon on the hill, as innovator and benefactor of mankind; in this spirit, the quest for appropriate global reform

---

* Indeed, American apologists make the opposite point—that the poor would be poorer without the existence of the rich (by losing markets, jobs, capital, goods), whereas the rich do not depend nearly so much on the poor.

might help America reconcile its goals in world society with those it professes for itself.*

THE POSITIVE POTENTIAL OF THE UNITED STATES FOR GLOBAL REFORM

Value changes and favorable shifts in consciousness are occurring at a rapid rate in the United States. Indeed, some cultural commentators have made "future shock" the main focus of their appraisal of the country. Given WOMP criteria, these changes are moving in contradictory directions.

Some positive factors can be identified. The ending in relative failure of the Indochina War has encouraged American leaders to redefine the country's role in the world, and to explore more carefully the possibilities for global reform. This process of redefinition has also been encouraged by the muting of East–West tensions, and the exacerbation of the Sino–Soviet conflict.

By posing world order issues in new contexts, ecological strains have further exposed the inadequacy of S_1 responses and the need for an S_2 approach. The ecological dimension of many global problems can, if aptly interpreted, provide a crucial learning experience relevant to global reform.†

NASA's Apollo Program of moon landings has helped stimulate a visual appreciation of the wholeness and oneness of the planet. Such imagery fosters an understanding of the artificiality of the statist boundaries and loyalties which have divided mankind into warring nationalities. The earth, as seen from the moon, is emblematic for the new world order awareness which will be required by a post-statist phase of global politics. Although this awareness has not yet exerted

---

* Global reform may provide the indispensable context for domestic reforms compatible with goals of peacefulness, dignity, equity, and ecological regard, rather than the other way around. There is, at least, a dialectic between principal arenas wherein issues of social policy are resolved; different constituencies can have beneficial or harmful learning experiences in different arenas, or even contradictory learning experiences in the same arena.

† The ecological dimension encourages a holistic, unified approach to human problems; by encouraging synthetic and integrative procedures of inquiry, it offsets to some extent the analytic, fractionalizing procedures of inquiry associated with empiricism and behavioral methodologies.

any political influence, it has created unprecedented receptivity to globalist thinking. Excessive infatuation with technological progress has given rise to a "counter-culture" which questions the basic commitments of American society. New attitudes toward people, and even toward artifacts that respect human dignity, engender a sensitivity to social and political relations that is necessarily reformist. The ease of communication and travel, the mobility of ideas and people, give many national elite groups an increasingly transnational and cosmopolitan identity. Individuals often feel a closer identification with their counterparts in transnational reference groups than with their fellow-citizens; these wider symbolic networks of respect, affection, and affiliation erode the state system's narrow ideology of national patriotism.* The market imperatives of world business enterprise are responsible for a nonterritorial S_2 world order design and executive life-style which are increasingly at odds with the economic artificiality and distortion caused by persisting national prerogatives of economic regulation and planning (for instance, a national goal of full employment is increasingly incompatible with economic efficiency). The millenarian context of the year 2000 encourages organic interpretations of world history, and arouses reformist hopes that human energies will be both renewed and refocused.

In addition to these broader currents oriented toward positive change, there are several explicit reform movements now underway in the United States which could be easily linked to a global reform movement based on an $S_{2(WOMP/USA)}$ program.

CONSUMER CONSCIOUSNESS

The efforts of Ralph Nader are both symbolically and inherently significant. Nader has taken on issues that affect the lives of all Americans—auto safety, food quality, building codes—and has demonstrated to large segments of the public that corporations are callous and the gov-

---

* In earlier periods the boundaries of the state set the limits of most networks of human interaction. Individual experiences were bounded in the same way as were national societies. The new transnational nature of much human activity now means that leading citizens typically participate in a series of human networks whose boundaries are wider than the limits of their states.

ernment complicit. Nader has dispelled the bland belief that we can trust official institutions to protect our most basic human interests, or that we can expect large corporations to be motivated by goodwill and conscience. The consumer movement encourages a healthy overall skepticism about governmental solutions to human problems; it vividly demonstrates the need for citizen action and personal responsibility.*

Furthermore, Nader's success as a catalyst of relevant awareness suggests the extent to which change can be stimulated, in fact, *must* be stimulated, by private actions. It also suggests that mass adult education is best conducted outside school buildings. Perhaps, like any successful educational program, it involves a combination of thought and action which is virtually impossible to obtain within most formal educational institutions, given their stress on abstract knowledge, value neutrality, "objectivity," and the separation of thought and action.[59]

The experience with consumer consciousness provides some insight into the direction that a humanist movement for global reform must take, namely: the objective situation must be accurately and precisely described; these ideas must be carried into the realm of action at some personal risk (thereby manifesting the seriousness of the reform commitment); the program of reform must concern itself with the underlying structures of wealth and power that caused the problems or dislocations in the first place.

FEMININE CONSCIOUSNESS

It is difficult to interpret the prospects of the women's movement in the United States at the present time. Nevertheless, there are important indications that women's liberation is a positive development, fully compatible with wider goals of equity, dignity, and nonviolence. For one thing, the cutting edge of feminist ideology involves a challenge directed at the world as structured by male dominance. Hence, there is a strong undertow of antiwar, social justice sentiment in the movement's literature, despite some deviation from the humanist mainstream as a result of factionalism, and an over-liberated insistence by some spokeswomen on issuing sexual manifestos that appear

---

* Such a mood sets the tone for a global populist movement in which the needs and aspirations of people, not the interests of governments, are accorded priority.

to transcend the biological identity and existential yearnings of most women.

Women have clearly mounted a formidable challenge on such bread-and-butter issues as job discrimination and access to power. However, "access to power" is interpreted by the movement to mean more than equal opportunity; there is an insistence that female perspectives be given a major influence in realms of power and authority. Therefore, it is not only a matter of allowing women to compete on an equal basis, so that they might become "prime minister" or members of the National Security Council. The main point is that women should be granted participation in the formulation of policy and transformation of power structures, to enable the pursuit of different societal objectives. Movement leaders such as Bella Abzug, Gloria Steinem, and Betty Friedan have adopted a progressive orientation toward American society and politics that could usefully be complemented by a global or world dimension.[60] It is doubtful, though perhaps not important, whether women can become "the new proletariat" impelling revolutionary change, because their socioeconomic interests crosscut the structure of society to a very great degree.[61] At the same time it does seem significant, as Kate Millet emphasizes, that male-dominated liberation and revolutionary movements have been deeply flawed by their unwillingness to end the exploitation of women.*

It seems clear that the women's movement will gain increasing access to mainstream political arenas in the years ahead and, hence, will have various opportunities to advocate a distinctive vision of the future. Indeed, it seems quite possible that there will be a serious woman Vice-Presidential or Presidential candidate by 1976. If such a woman has a WOMP-oriented outlook on human affairs, her candidacy might not only provide the first opportunity to challenge basic domestic and world structures, but would materially improve the chances of creating a significant political base for a humanist movement of global reform.†

---

* That is, in the past men have carried their regressive attitudes toward women right into the new revolutionary situation. These attitudes are a virus that afflicts prospects for renewal. In this sense, a global reform movement that hopes to achieve peace and justice should seek to purify its own attitudes toward human relations during its consciousness-raising phase. Such purification involves additional exploitative attitudes often embedded in self-righteous reform ideologies: for instance, attitudes toward the young and the old, attitudes toward unborn generations, attitudes toward non-human co-tenants of the planet, and possibly attitudes toward co-tenants of the galaxy and universe.

† The explicitness of the ideological discussions of reform that characterizes the women's movement in America increases the possibility that a woman who is a product

LABOR CONSCIOUSNESS

An important possible source of support for humanist global reform is the American labor movement, despite its regressive record on many key issues, especially in the area of foreign policy.* However, the technological progress of American society is likely to provoke a wide-ranging crisis regarding the dignity of work and workers in post-industrial settings. This crisis may deepen if the multinational corporation stimulates a flight of capital from the high labor costs of domestic production. However, we cannot predict whether this crisis will develop soon, and/or whether it will generate a new kind of labor leader who seeks broad sociopolitical value changes in addition to *ad hoc* socioeconomic bargains with big business. In any event, those who represent the dominant concerns of organized labor will undoubtedly be raising new kinds of questions. Of course, ruling groups will rely on their largely successful tactics of producing a sufficient economic surplus to give labor a material stake in system-maintenance, and of rewarding "pacified" labor leaders with elite status within the system.

We anticipate, however, that domestic strains will begin to split the labor movement into genuine and pacified factions. The beginning of this process may be already evident in the failure of the AFL/CIO Executive Board either to support McGovern's candidacy for President in 1972 or to repudiate America's involvement in the Indochina War.† It remains to be seen whether the present labor leadership will be confronted by a value-based challenge that offers a coherent alternative interpretation of exploitation in American society. Such an interpretation would have to be both post-Marxist and anti-Stalinist in character, and

---

of the movement will seek something more than access to high political power. This *something more* would relate to values that have been underplayed as a consequence of the peculiar orientation of male consciousness; it would very likely include heightened sensitivity to the grievances of other groups in the society, as well as a serious questioning of the war system mentality.[62]

* Unfortunately, the labor movement as a whole cannot now be depended upon to consistently support even domestic reformist goals associated with equity, human dignity, and peace. A status quo conservatism has led union leaders and their rank-and-file to oppose liberalization in American society, partly because their stake in the system has increased and partly because they have been the principal victims of ghetto frustrations and criminality.

† Offsetting these positions, to an unclear extent, is the commitment made by the leadership of organized labor to make a substantial effort to unseat Richard Nixon by impeachment proceedings.

it would have to link the self-realization of American workers with U.S. participation in the world system.

Herbert Marcuse writes that

> the working class remains the potentially revolutionary class, although it would be a class of different composition and with a different consciousness. . . . The impulses for radical change would be rooted, not primarily in material privation but in human degradation . . . in the awareness that it can be otherwise, here and now; that technical progress can become human liberation, that the fatal union of growing productivity and growing destruction can be broken. New needs are becoming a material force; the need for self-determination, for a non-repressive organization of work; the need for a life that has not only to be "earned" but is made an end in itself . . . the new radical consensus is still largely repressed, diffuse; it is articulated mainly among the oppressed racial minorities, among students, women. But it is spreading among labor itself, especially among young workers.[63]

With this new spirit in mind, the tendencies of American labor leaders to stabilize their privileged position must be exposed as inconsistent with the longer term well-being of American workers. Instead, a labor commitment to reformism of the sort implied by WOMP values would greatly help to transform consciousness in the American domestic arena during t_1. Indeed, such a shift in outlook by the American labor movement may be an indispensable ingredient for completing t_1 and initiating t_2.

LINKAGE AND DECOUPLING STRATEGIES

America's economic and political role in the world has led it to ally with a series of governments that abuse their own populations. These alliances sometimes require an endorsement of or involvement in brutal policies that are repudiated within our own society. At present, the United States government lends its active support to a whole series of regimes which torture and otherwise abuse their political opponents. Can we, as a society, endorse policies in foreign countries that contradict our most inimal concepts of decency, without incurring serious consequences? Put differently, can geopolitical opportunism altogether neglect foreign abuses of human rights? The issues are often complex.

The search for world peace may lead to a détente which would be jeopardized by U.S. insistence upon Soviet liberalization of its domestic approach to civil liberties. On the other hand, official indifference to torture, genocide, or apartheid indicates a lack of concern about the rights of individuals which will probably—given any pressure— translate itself into abuse of American rights. The Indochina/Watergate revelations have amply shown how lawless violence in a foreign setting sets the tone for domestic politics. Furthermore, the potential realities of human brotherhood, and a shared destiny that joins all men and women together in the struggle to sustain life and achieve human development on this planet, constitute the moral basis for WOMP-oriented global reform. The international protection of human rights as a genuine national priority is of utmost significance in linking our concern with the plight of others, wherever they may be.

The Nixon Administration has sustained its commitments to repressive regimes abroad. Indeed, in the post-Vietnam period it has moved to make these commitments viable by reducing those costs which, if perceived by American citizens, might otherwise have generated opposition. The idea is to pursue counterrevolutionary aims without huge outlays of American resources or lives. Its execution depends on building up foreign counterinsurgency capabilities, and backing these capabilities with American air and naval power if necessary. The main thrust of this Nixonian effort is to decouple foreign policy from domestic concerns, so that policy-makers can pursue the former without real accountability to the American electorate.

Decoupling strategies rest on a house of cards. In particular, they minimize the dangers of ecological and economic interdependence, thereby making it seem as if the United States can remain prosperous and free, while somehow absolved from responsibility toward the poor and deprived two-thirds of the world's population.

Linkage strategies have so far aimed at a foreign policy that sustains American dominance by controlling critical foreign resources, personnel, and policy. These interventionary approaches are being pursued by low-profile (covert, secret, indirect) tactics, to avoid agitating the domestic polity. To the extent that the domestic population is treated as a potentially hostile audience which must be deceived, the results are negative for the United States. The process of deception tends to destroy the democratic ethos, shatters the social contract underlying the consent of the governed, and vindicates deviant behavior that seeks to keep faith with earlier promises and expectations. These dynamics contribute to a vicious cycle of rebellion and repression that threatens to transform the foundation of "law and order" in America from voluntary respect for the rights of others into the efficiency of the police.

One apparent way to break the cycle is for the United States to attempt a kind of isolationist withdrawal from world involvement—in effect, to break the linkage by having no other foreign policy commitments than our own territorial defense. This repudiation of interventionary diplomacy is healthy, but it understates the realities of interdependence and misses the significance of active participation by the United States in this period of inevitable transition to a more unified system of world order. Therefore, as a nation, we need to pursue a foreign policy that takes account of our domestic ideals, and that explicitly associates the linkage between domestic and global arenas with the prospects for $S_1 \rightarrow S_{2(WOMP/USA)}$. It is here that public education must be made a matter of highest priority. At first, such an educational mission can and will be attempted only at the margins of policy-formation, but hopefully the cogency of its interpretation will gain ever-widening influence.

The bicentennial celebration planned for 1976 could provide an initial focus for American recovery of national pride and confidence. This pride and confidence can exist only if our domestic creed of constitutionalism and human rights is convincingly reconciled with our role as a leading actor in the world. This reconciliation cannot be accomplished by marginal, Nixonian adjustments of imperial policies. Nor will it be attained by any kind of neo-isolationist pretension that, in a disintegrating world order system in which we are the richest and most powerful actor, we can somehow devise self-contained solutions to our domestic problems. The first positive step in t_1 may be to frame the American foreign policy debate around this kind of Hobson's choice. Subsequent steps will be influenced by many factors, including the outcome of parallel debates in other principal foreign societies. Only at the end of t_1 will it be plausible to implement a new foreign policy that reflects a serious American commitment to $S_1 \rightarrow S_{2(WOMP/USA)}$.

It should be remembered that t_1 may never end, if elites in the United States and elsewhere succeed in pacifying, neutralizing, and repressing counter-elites who favor S_2 options in the spirit of WOMP. If t_1 doesn't end, the $S_1 \rightarrow S_2$ is likely to be traumatic and demonic in transition and regressive in outcome. We believe that the momentous uncertainty surrounding transition will be gradually removed by political developments in the United States during the 1970's. These developments will in turn be significantly influenced by whether current American adherence to prevailing S_1/S_2 lines of reform can avoid perceived breakdowns in the realms of economic, ecological, and security policy. As a nation we are unlikely to learn basic world order lessons except through experiences of adversity,* and unless we manage to produce a coherent ideology of drastic global reform that embodies humanist values in its transition and design. Our national resistance to this kind of massive world order educational effort reflects in part the absence of any experience with a foreign war in which hardship and bloodshed penetrate the boundaries of the state and the citizenry witness at first-hand the awesome brutality and general suffering of war. World Wars I and II, Korea, and Indochina were all in foreign theaters; there were no foreign conquerors in our land, and the domestic social and political fabric was never torn asunder.†

A CONCLUDING NOTE

The United States represents a critical arena for value change during t_1. If WOMP values can exert a growing influence on American policy and behavior this influence will probably reinforce tendencies toward corresponding value changes elsewhere in the world. The prospects for the growth of an American humanist movement for global reform are not bright, but neither are they gloomy enough to assure the persistence of the present scale of S_1 values, or their replacement by a neo-Darwinian movement for global reform. We need to be clear about the costs, risk, and gains of global reform carried out according to various contending logics of organization: imperial, duopolistic, or humanist. Once we grasp the options we can make choices, and decide on implementing strategies. Vested interest groups are now pondering global reform options; the American public is not. The first priority of a humanist global reform movement within the United States is to open up the debate so that American citizens can participate.

---

* The energy crisis may have important potential as a world order learning experience, because its impact is so directly related to daily life. It seems very important that global reform groups seize this occasion to provide a WOMP-oriented interpretation of the problem and its most beneficial solution.

† Such assertions are not meant to overlook the sufferings of participants and their families that resulted from these wars. We draw a distinction in national experience between going off to fight a war on foreign territory, and fighting a foreign invader on national territory.

REFERENCES

1. Arthur M. Schlesinger, Jr., *The Imperial Presidency*, Boston, Houghton Mifflin, 1973, p. 418.

2. Edward Everett, Phi Beta Kappa Oration of August 26, 1824, in Perry Miller, ed., *The Transcendentalists*, Cambridge, Mass., Harvard University Press, 1950, pp. 19–21.

3. One prominent example is Jean-François Revel, *Without Marx or Jesus: The New American Revolution Has Begun*, New York, Doubleday, 1970.

4. Among the most important analyses see Michael Tanzer, *The Sick Society: An Economic Examination*, New York, Holt, Rinehart, 1972; Michael T. Klare, *War Without End: American Planning for the Next Vietnams*, New York, Knopf, 1972; Marcus G. Raskin, *Being and Doing; An Inquiry into the Colonization, Decolonization, and Reconstruction of American Society and its State*, New York, Random House, 1971.

5. See also more recent Ginsberg poetry collected in *Talk of America*, San Francisco, City Lights, 1972, esp. "Ecologue," pp. 147–161.

6. Daniel Ellsberg, *Papers on the War*, New York, Simon and Schuster, 1972, p. 9.

7. One judicious and generally favorable appraisal is Robert E. Osgood, "Introduction: The Nixon Doctrine and Strategy," in Osgood, ed., *Retreat from Empire? The First Nixon Administration*, Baltimore, Maryland, Johns Hopkins University Press, 1973, pp. 1–27.

8. This distinction is the central basis of my essay "The United Nations: Various Systems of Operation," in Leon Gordenker, ed., *The United Nations and World Politics*, Princeton, Princeton University Press, 1972, pp. 184–230.

9. For a cogent and original analysis of this possibility see Richard E. Rubenstein, *Left Turn: Origins of the Next American Revolution*, Boston, Little, Brown, 1973.

10. Perhaps the most influential and eloquent statement along these lines is by Pierre Teilhard de Chardin, *The Phenomenon of Man*, New York, Harper and Brothers, 1959.

11. Essay by Revel, *New York Times*, July 5, 1973, p. 35.

12. This leads Rubenstein to argue that the American political middle will be squeezed out of existence, as a result of contention between the controllers from the right and the changers from the left. Rubenstein, *Left Turn*.

13. For the dissenters' own view of their plight see " 'Not One Step Further': An Interview with Solzhenitsyn," *New York Review of Books*, Oct. 4, 1973, pp. 11–15.

14. One estimate of this link is as follows: "About six percent of the world's population consumes close to forty percent of the world's processed resources year by year. The imbalances are equally pronounced in the raw materials sphere: thirty percent of the global population lives in industrialized areas and consumes about ninety percent of the total world production of energy and mineral resources." Nazli Choucri, "Population, Resources, and Technology: Political Implications of the Environmental Crisis," *International Organization*, XXVI:175–212 (1972).

15. Osgood, *Retreat from Empire*, p. 20.

16. "National Security Strategy of Realistic Deterrence," Annual Defense Department Report, FY 1973, Feb. 24, 1972, p. 8.

17. Raymond G. O'Connor, *Force and Diplomacy*, Coral Gables, Florida, University of Miami Press, 1972, pp. 1, 3.

18. Nicholas de B. Katzenbach, "Foreign Policy, Public Opinion, and Secrecy," *Foreign Affairs*, 52: 1–19, at 19 (1973).

19. Edward R. Fried and others, *Setting National Priorities: The 1974 Budget*, Washington, D.C., Brookings, 1973, p. VII; for an analysis of proposed cuts in domestic programs see pp. 23–265.

20. See Charles L. Schultze et al., *Setting National Priorities: The 1973 Budget*, Washington, D.C., Brookings, 1972, p. 82.

21. For a somewhat more expanded perception of available options, but one remaining well within S_1 horizons, see Robert S. Benson and Harold Walman, eds., *Counterbudget: A Blueprint for Changing National Priorities 1972–1976*, New York, Praeger, 1971.

22. In the area of arms policy, an influential defense of marginal proposals on the grounds of rationality is found in Robert A. Levine, *The Arms Debate*, Cambridge, Mass., 1963; of course, this stress on the relevance of thought to policy neglects the findings of students of "bureaucratic politics," who place such stress upon the give and take among bureaucratic constituencies in the policy-forming process.

23. I have argued this position in relation to the reform of American foreign policy with regard to counterinsurgency diplomacy. See Falk, "What We Should Learn from Vietnam," in Robert W. Gregg and Charles W. Kegley, Jr., eds., *After Vietnam: The Future of American Foreign Policy*, New York, Anchor Books, 1971, pp. 324–339.

24. See, for example, the revealing study of the relationship between procurement of weapons systems and the corporate needs of major defense suppliers in James R. Kurth, "Why We Buy the Weapons We Do," *Foreign Policy*, 11: 33–56 (1973); see also Richard J. Barnet, *Roots of War*, New York, Atheneum, 1972; Sidney Lens, *The Military–Industrial Complex*, Philadelphia, Pa., Pilgrim Press, 1970; Seymour Melman, *Pentagon Capitalism: The*

Political Economy of War, New York, McGraw-Hill, 1970; Herbert York, *Race to Oblivion: A Participant's View of the Arms Race*, Simon and Schuster, 1970.

25. The U.S. Arms Control and Disarmament Agency (ACDA) issued its *only* major contract for a study of GCD to a team of known skeptics who, quite predictably, questioned whether drastic disarmament would serve the national interest. See the published version of their study: Arnold Wolfers et al., *The United States in a Disarmed World*, Baltimore, Maryland, Johns Hopkins University Press, 1966; see also *Report from Iron Mountain on the Possibility and Desirability of Peace*, New York, Dial Press, 1967, for a satiric depiction of the hostility of military planners and their business associates to any danger of world peace or disarmament.

26. Henry A. Kissinger, "Central Issues of American Foreign Policy," in Kermit Gordon, ed., *Agenda for the Nation*, Washington, D.C., Brookings, 1968, pp. 585–614.

27. The American role in South Vietnam is generally well-depicted in Frances Fitzgerald, *Fire in the Lake: The Vietnamese and the Americans in Vietnam*, Boston, Little, Brown, 1972.

28. W. W. Rostow, "The Great Transition: Tasks of the First and Second Generations," *Department of State Bulletin*, 56: 491–504, at 504 (1967).

29. Robert S. McNamara, *The Essence of Security*, New York, Harper & Row, 1969, p. 152.

30. See Andrei Sakharov, *Progress, Coexistence, and Intellectual Freedom*, New York, Norton, 2nd rev. ed., 1970.

31. See the very important European Common Market Declaration of December 14, 1973, on the existence of "European identity"; for text, see the *New York Times*, Dec. 15, 1973, p. 6; an excellent seminal book on the subject of European unity written from a post-World War II perspective is Ernst B. Haas, *The Uniting of Europe: Political, Social, and Economic Forces, 1950–1957*, Stanford, Calif., Stanford University Press, 1958; for a more skeptical and quite diverse set of views on European cooperation see Johan Galtung, ed., *Cooperation in Europe*, Oslo, Universitetsforlaget, 1970.

32. "U.S. Foreign Policy for the 1970's: Building for Peace," A Report to the Congress by President Richard M. Nixon, February 25, 1971, Vol. II, pp. 10–21.

33. Speech to Midwestern news executives, Kansas City, Mo., July 6, 1971; text in *Vital Speeches*, Aug. 1, 1971, pp. 611–615.

34. For Kissinger's interpretation of this period see Henry A. Kissinger, *A World Restored: Castlereagh, Metternich and the Restoration of Peace, 1815–1822*, New York, Grosset & Dunlap, 1964.

35. For one assessment see Falk, *This Endangered Planet: Prospects and Proposals for Human Survival*, New York, Random House, 1971; for a slightly more optimistic assessment of the resource scarcity dimension see Richard G. Wilkinson, *Poverty and Progress: An Ecological Perspective on Economic Development*, New York, Praeger, 1973, esp. pp. 173–196.

36. Among the Kahn works I have in mind are the following: *On Thermonuclear War*, Princeton, New Jersey, Princeton University Press, 1960; *On Escalation*, New York, Praeger, 1965; (with Anthony J. Wiener) *The Year 2000: A Framework for Speculation on the Next Thirty-Three Years*, New York, Macmillan, 1967; (with others) *Can We Win in Vietnam?* New York, Praeger, 1968.

37. See, e.g., Stanley Hoffmann, "Choices," *Foreign Policy* 12: 3–42 (1973) and Zbigniew Brzezinski, "U.S. Foreign Policy: The Search for Focus," *Foreign Affairs*, 51: 708–727 (1973).

38. One relatively early appreciation of this emphasis is found in Charles W. Yost, *The Insecurity of Nations*, New York, Praeger, 1968.

39. For an even-handed, persuasive inquiry see Richard J. Barnet, *Who Wants Disarmament?* Boston, Beacon, 1960.

40. For some differing assessments of what to do about the obsolescence of the prevailing national security system see McGeorge Bundy, "To Cap the Volcano," *Foreign Affairs*, 48: 1–20 (1969); Fred Charles Iklé, "Can Nuclear Deterrence Last Out the Century?" *Foreign Affairs*, 51: 267–285 (1973); Barnet, *Roots of War*.

41. Iklé's argument, *op. cit.*, supports this preference.

42. See Wolfgang K. H. Panofsky, "The Mutual Hostage Relationship Between America and Russia," *Foreign Affairs*, 52: 109–118 (1973), and sources therein cited for support of existing deterrence posture against various categories of critics.

43. For a movingly perceptive study of challenging the war system from the perspective of anti-war American Vietnam veterans see Robert Jay Lifton, *Home from the War: Vietnam Veterans: Neither Victims nor Executioners*, Simon and Schuster, 1973, esp. pp. 320–378.

44. See N. J. Spykman, *America's Strategy in World Politics*, New York, Harcourt, Brace, 1942; Hans J. Morgenthau, *Politics Among Nations*, New York, Knopf, 5th ed., 1967; Inis L. Claude, Jr., *Power in International Relations*, New York, Random House, 1962.

45. For a range of views on humanitarian intervention see Richard B. Lillich, ed., *Humanitarian Intervention and the United Nations*, Charlottesville, Va., University of Virginia Press, 1973.

46. See Noam Chomsky, *For Reasons of State*, New York, Pantheon, 1973; Klare, *World Without End*, Norman Miller and Roderick Aya, eds., *National Liberation: Revolution in the Third World*, New York, Free Press, 1971.

47. For a discussion of this contention see Flora Lewis' news analysis, the *New York Times*, July 21, 1972, pp. 1, 13; denial, the *New York Times*, July 27, 1972.

48. For an account of the American involvement as a crusade see Chester L. Cooper, *The Lost Crusade: America in Vietnam*, New York, Dodd, Mead, 1970.

49. A useful overview from a mainstream perspective is found in *The United States and the Developing World: Agenda for Action*, Washington, D.C., Overseas Development Council, 1973; for a more critical account of U.S. role see Robert I. Rhodes, ed., *Imperialism and Underdevelopment: A Reader*, New York, Monthly Review Press, 1970.

50. Such an argument is particularly well-sustained by Wilkinson, *Poverty and Progress*.

51. See Rhodes, *Imperialism and Underdevelopment*; Harry Magdoff, *The Age of Imperialism*, New York, Monthly Review Press, 1969; Osvaldo Sunkel, "Big Business and 'Dependencia': A Latin American View," *Foreign Affairs*; 50: 517–529 (1972); Kenneth Boulding and Tapan Mukerjee, eds., *Economic Imperialism*, Ann Arbor, Mich., University of Michigan Press, 1972.

52. The *New York Times*, July 29, 1972, p. 25.

53. For a highly respected study see Alfred W. McCoy, *The Politics of Heroin in Southeast Asia*, New York, Harper & Row, 1972; for confirmation of allegations in text, see note 51 above.

54. For a clear exposition and assessment of treaty see Mason Willrich, *Non-Proliferation Treaty: Framework for Nuclear Arms Control*, Charlottesville, Va., Michie, 1969.

55. For somewhat differing views on this legislative effort cf. Falk, *The Status of Law in International Society*, Princeton, New Jersey, Princeton University Press, 1970, pp. 423–425 with Richard B. Lillich, *The Protection of Foreign Investment: Six Procedural Studies*, Syracuse University Press, 1965.

56. Robert Gilpin, "The Multinational Corporation and the National Interest," Report prepared for U.S. Senate Committee on Labor and Public Welfare, Oct. 1973, p. XV; the discussion of the MNC in these paragraphs draws heavily on Professor Gilpin's analysis.

57. Father Berrigan poses the question in powerful dramatic form in his rendition of the trial resulting from draft board raids in which he took part, together with his brother, Philip, and several other Catholic activists. Daniel Berrigan, *The Catonsville Nine*, Boston, Beacon Press, 1970; a sensi-

tive, sympathetic interpretation of the Berrigan stance is found in Fransine du Plessix Gray, *Divine Disobedience; Profiles in Catholic Radicalism*, New York, Knopf, 1970, pp. 45–228.

58. This argument is central to Schlesinger's interpretation of Presidential excess in the 1960's; see *The Imperial Presidency*.

59. A profound inquiry in this direction underlies Anthony Wilden, *System and Structure: Essays on Communication and Exchange*, London, England, Tavistock, 1972; see also Ivan Illich, *Tools for Conviviality*, New York, Harper & Row, 1973; Raolo Friere, *Pedagogy of the Oppressed*, New York, Herder and Herder, 1970.

60. See exploratory essay by Kathryn Boals, "The Transformation of Male–Female Relations and the Future of the International Legal Order," paper presented at the Conference on the Future of the International Legal Order, June, 1972, Princeton University.

61. Joan Didion, "The Women's Movement," the *New York Times* Book Review, July 30, 1972, pp. 1, 2, 14.

62. A provocative male-oriented account is developed by Paul Shephard, *The Tender Carnivore and the Sacred Game*, New York, Scribner's, 1973.

63. Herbert Marcuse, the *New York Times*, Aug. 7, 1972, p. 27.

Postscript:

APPEAL TO THE READER

The prospects for global reform patterned around the WOMP/USA proposals are bleak at this time. It is true that principal elites and counter-elites are beginning to grasp the obsolescence of S_1, but there is very little indication that this new understanding is coupled with the type of ethical revolution needed to allow a shift toward $S_{2(WOMP/USA)}$. As we have suggested, the multinational corporate and intergovernmental vision of the future, to the extent that it exists as a coherent approach, seems to involve freezing or even accentuating regressive aspects of the socioeconomic status quo. It presupposes that the rich and powerful few will sustain their control over the many weak and poor. This kind of stratified global system will not be able to get rid of the war system.

We believe that to be beneficial over time, an S_2 rearrangement of authority and control in planetary affairs must rest on the voluntary participation of the main actors in international life and embody a new social contract between global policy-makers and the people of the world. A social contract is impossible, given the depth and spread of misery, unless accompanied by a determined program for the rapid elimination of poverty and other forms of acute privation. Such a program requires extensive resources and would seem to presuppose both large capital transfers from the rich sectors and the de-development of what has been called the overdeveloped (really misdeveloped) portion of the world system.* It also seems plain that ecological constraints are

---

* Terms such as *de-development, overdevelopment, misdevelopment* are used in reference to the materialistic calculus of advanced industrial society, where wants are fabricated in a wasteful fashion and where genuine human needs are neglected. It is inherent in the human species to evolve—develop—and if the orientation is positive there is no danger of overdevelopment and no need for de-development.

492

relevant for global reform. Resources are limited, and the earth's capacity to absorb wastes seems already dangerously overburdened in a variety of respects. Therefore, an S_2 solution must be sensitive to ecological considerations as well as those that pertain to human well-being. Such sensitivity precludes the globalization of permanent economic growth as the basis for dealing with the problems of the poor and the weak.

We also believe that a new social contract should respect the spiritual side of human nature and liberate people to facilitate their self-realization. At minimum, human rights should be secure, and governments must no longer have the prerogative of oppressing their own people.

The argument of this book suggests that each one of us has a major opportunity and responsibility to assist in the process of building the public understanding needed to achieve transition to $S_{2(WOMP/USA)}$ by nonviolent means. We are not optimistic, but neither are we defeatist. The cumulative effects of action taken or not taken by individuals throughout the world will tend to be self-fulfilling. World energy and food shortages are finally confronting individuals with *concrete* demonstrations of the frailties of the present world order system. If such demonstrations can be persuasively interpreted as world order storm warnings, there exists an unprecedented opportunity for rapid mass education on the need for global reform. But there is also a danger that anxieties arising from resource scarcities will make the rich and powerful more predatory than ever, inclining the existing powers that be to make one last effort to sustain their privileged positions by deploying arms to implement strategies of domestic and foreign repression. Such a response would be dangerous and shortsighted even for present power-wielders, but it may well prevail, unless the prospect of drastic global reform along WOMP lines becomes attractive and familiar to large numbers of people, including those highly placed in existing political, social, and economic organizations.

The ancient Roman scholar, Pliny, wrote "How many things are considered impossible until they are actually done!" Locked within our present frame of reference, we seem incapable of visualizing plausible escape routes. Perhaps, however, the religious mood that seems to be reintensifying in a variety of guises around the world may fasten onto a vision of peaceful and just solidarity among peoples. The adoption of such an orientation for a world religious movement could undergird the politics of global reform and provide the needed energy, transnational identity, and resources.

In the end we are left as individuals to make a gamble. Do we allow ourselves to believe in the feasibility of beneficial global reform and act accordingly? We can receive no advance assurance that our gamble will succeed. But what if it fails? What have we lost? And if we refuse to try, then we merely make it more likely than ever that we will lose. Pascal's celebrated sixteenth-century wager on the existence of God was premised on comparable reasoning and served to inspire generations of devout religious adherents. From the perspective of human evolution we have the excitement and agony of finding ourselves at a vital crossroads. If we choose the proper path, and summon the energy and wisdom to confront the various challenges now endangering the spiritual and material status of the species, then the outlook for the future is brighter than it has ever been since man initially appeared on the planet. If we take the wrong path and continue as if no challenge had been posed, then we as individuals, as a nature and culture, and as a species, seem doomed to a destiny of decay and acute misfortune.

Some young people who gathered at Ommen, Holland, in 1972 drafted a statement of purpose which they called The Declaration of Ommen. The simplicity and directness of this Declaration provides a suitable signpost to the future:

> The Group of Ommen,
> > Recognizing the oneness of the world and the interdependence of humankind;
> >
> > the need of a systematic analysis of the world's problems;
> >
> > the need to take account of long-term considerations;
>
> Aware of the present conflict of humankind against itself and of humankind against nature;
>
> Resolves to promote values, policies, and actions at all levels to establish a sustainable, just, and equitable global society consistent with the dignity of the human person and the finite resources and capacities of earth.[1]

We end with an appeal to the reader to join with us in this grave but exhilarating struggle to achieve global reform at the eleventh hour of the human race. As Walt Whitman put it so beautifully,

> Even for the treatment of the universal, in politics, metaphysics, or anything, sooner or later we come down to one single, solitary soul.[2]

REFERENCES

1. Text of Declaration and discussion of Ommen meeting contained in *IDOC–North America*, No. 52, April 1973, pp. 29–861 (Declaration printed on p. 73).

2. Walt Whitman, "Democratic Vistas" in Malcolm Cowley, ed., *The Works of Walt Whitman*, New York, Minerva Press, Vol. II, 1969, p. 232.

INDEX

INDEX